The Dark Side
of Relationship Pursuit

From Attraction to Obsession and Stalking

The Dark Side
of Relationship Pursuit

From Attraction to Obsession and Stalking

William R. Cupach
Illinois State University

Brian H. Spitzberg
San Diego State University

LEA

2004

LAWRENCE ERLBAUM ASSOCIATES, PUBLISHERS

Mahwah, New Jersey

London

Copyright © 2004
   All rights reserved. No part of this book may be reproduced in any
form, by photostat, microfilm, retrieval system, or any other
means, without prior written permission of the publisher.

Lawrence Erlbaum Associates, Inc., Publishers
10 Industrial Avenue
Mahwah, NJ 07430

Cover design by Kathryn Houghtaling Lacey

Library of Congress Cataloging-in-Publication Data

Cupach, William R.
   The dark side of relationship pursuit : from attraction to obsession
and stalking / William R. Cupach, Brian H. Spitzberg.
      p. cm.
   Includes bibliographical references and index.
ISBN 0-8058-4449-X (alk. Paper)
ISBN 0-8058-4450-3 (pbk. : alk. Paper)
   1. Interpersonal relations. 2. Relationship addiction. 3. Stalking—
   Psychological aspects.   I. Spitzberg, Brian H.   II. Title.

HM1106.C86 2004
302—dc22
                                                           2003058418
                                                           CIP

Books published by Lawrence Erlbaum Associates are printed
on acid-free paper, and their bindings are chosen for strength
and durability.

Printed in the United States of America
10 9 8 7 6 5 4 3 2 1

To students

Contents

Preface

The individual desire for connection with others is profound, universal, and endemic to the human condition (Baumeister & Leary, 1995). Yet individuals simultaneously want freedom from interference and imposition from others (Brown & Levenson, 1987). Indeed, partners in all interpersonal relationships, even in the most compatible of relationships, must manage the dialectical tension between competing needs for autonomy and connection (Baxter & Montgomery, 1996). When one person persistently pursues relational connection with another that the other expressly eschews, then the individuals become enmeshed in a fundamentally disjunctive and dysfunctional relationship. Such relationships are reified in patterns of behavior called *obsessive relational intrusion* (ORI) and *stalking*. Although it may seem counterintuitive, stalking and relational intrusion constitute relationships between perpetrators and victims because they involve consequential symbolic interactions with serial continuity. Our book endeavors to shed light on these paradigmatic forms of disjunctive relating.

Although stalking and unwanted intrusion can occur for reasons other than pursuing a relationship, by far the most common impetus is the desire for relational connection—that is, the drive to cultivate or retain companionship, romance, or closeness with a particular other. And much of the stalking that derives from a motive for revenge occurs in response to relational rejection when the stalker finally realizes that the relationship goal is illusory. In these cases, the underlying motivation for stalking transforms from seeking a relationship to salving the wounds of humiliation. Such transformations may be gradual or sudden, and it is not uncommon for desperate relationship pursuers to intersperse messages of both affinity and vengefulness as manifestations of their own dialectical struggle with the competing motives of rage and romance.

The phenomena of unwanted relationship pursuit and stalking receive attention from a number of scholarly and professional fields, including social, clinical, and forensic psychology, psychiatry, counseling, communication, criminal justice, law enforcement, sociology, social work, threat assessment and management, and family studies. In a relatively short time span, research efforts have ballooned exponentially and relevant findings have accumulated rapidly. Because this knowledge flows from several different disciplines, its accumulation grows increasingly fragmented. Our aim is to synthesize the expanding multidisciplinary base of knowledge about unwanted relationship pursuit and stalking. We hope to provide a clearer picture of the current state of knowledge and, in so doing, to identify productive paths for scholarly inquiry, and ultimately bolster the effectiveness of prevention and intervention efforts. It is also our hope to promote and publicize the multidisciplinary nature of stalking research such that cross-fertilization of interested fields might yield new and better insights.

This volume represents our continued interest in the "dark side" of interpersonal interactions and relationships (see Cupach & Spitzberg, 1994; Spitzberg & Cupach, 1998). Because we conceptualize obsessive relationship pursuit as emerging out of estranged relationships and normal everyday practices associated with the negotiation of relationship development, maintenance, and dissolution, we draw on the multidisciplinary scholarship on social and personal relationships. We believe that knowledge about the challenges of everyday mundane relating can offer insights into disjunctive relationships such as stalking. We concur with Duck (1994), who argued that the dark aspects of relationships must be studied alongside the more positive features of relationships, as these are two sides of a single coin. He stated, "Like the dark side of the moon, the dark side of relationships can be found to co-exist in the same entity as the light side. We need to explore and understand it not in itself but in its relation to everything else that has ever been learned about relationships" (p. 20).

Our text consists of five chapters. In chapter 1 we provide historical and definitional frames for studying unwanted relationship pursuit. After conceptualizing stalking and ORI as disjunctive relationship forms, we trace the evolution of the rhetorical construction of the concept of stalking. We consider the role of such sources as the media, law, and social science research in shaping the contemporary multifaceted and multifarious conceptualizations of stalking. We demonstrate that there is considerable variation in perceptions among members of society regarding what counts as stalking, due to such complicating factors as gender.

Chapter 2 elaborates our assumption that much unwanted relationship pursuit owes to complications inherent in the processes of constructing and dismantling relationships. We indicate that a number of factors conspire to create slippage between two persons' conceptions of their "shared" relationship. These include mismatched goals for a relationship, the use of ambiguous labels to describe a relationship, the fuzzy definitional boundaries of relationship prototypes that guide expectations for relationships, individual variations in the criterial attributes that people ascribe to different relationship types, and the indirect manner in which relationship definitions are communicated and co-constructed. In addition, cultural practices associated with relationship dissolution tend to reinforce persistence in unwanted pursuit. The expectation that dissolved relationships are sometimes repaired and reconciled, perhaps numerous times within a particular relationship history, reinforces a rejected partner's belief that persistent reconciliation effort will pay off. Moreover, in attempting to mitigate the face-threatening nature of rejection for the rejected partner, disengaging partners tend to communicate in ways that undermine efficient termination and foster the rejected partner's persistence in trying to reestablish the relationship.

Chapter 3 charts the topography of unwanted pursuit. After compiling the available literature, various findings were subjected to descriptive meta-analyses and interpretive coding. The results offer a unique and comprehensive synthesis of relevant research bearing on several issues. First, we summarize evidence regarding estimates of the prevalence of stalking. Then we present detailed synthetic typologies of pursuer motives, types of pursuers, and tactical manifestations of unwanted pursuit. We conclude this chapter with a review of the temporal stages and characteristics of stalking.

We consider promising theories and variables for explaining the occurrence of unwanted pursuit in chapter 4. Two complementary theoretical frameworks are reviewed. First, we present attachment theory, which locates unwanted pursuit in childhood experiences of disrupted relationships with primary caregivers. This approach has received the most attention and empirical support in the literature thus far. Next, we propose our own explanation for ORI and stalking, relational goal pursuit theory. This approach grounds obsessive pursuit in the proximal challenges and dynamics that attend everyday relationship management. Given the relative dearth of theory being applied to stalking and ORI at this point in time, we also summarize the host of individual and contextual variables that have been linked to unwanted pursuit.

Chapter 5 turns to the issues pertinent to managing unwanted pursuit. Again we present original findings based on comprehensive coding and descriptive meta-analyses of relevant research. We begin by offering a comprehensive typology of victim consequences of pursuit. Next we review the evidence regarding the incidence of and connection between more severe forms of stalking (i.e., threats and violence). We also elaborate a systematic and detailed typology of victim coping tactics. Next we review information regarding law enforcement intervention, with particular emphasis on the evidence concerning the relative efficacy of restraining orders. Finally, we conclude the book with some thoughts about "correcting courtship." Drawing on the interpersonal competence literature, we speculate on ways that enhancing relationship management skills could help diminish the incidence and debilitating consequences of ORI and stalking.

Acknowledgments

No effort of this size and complexity is ever accomplished alone, and this project is no exception. Substantively, an intellectual debt is owed to the members and meetings of the San Diego Stalking Strike Force and the San Diego chapter of the Association of Threat Assessment Professionals, whose collegial insights and activities have provided an invaluable grounding in the trenches of crime and law enforcement. In particular, Wayne Maxey, Robert Jones, Joe Davis, Glen Lipson, and many others among these groups have graciously assisted, and accepted, the bridging of the "intellectual" with the "applied." We also want to express appreciation to the many scholars and colleagues who have forwarded prepublication drafts, unpublished sources of data, and obscure sources of information on our request. We fear we often were quite the pest, and hope our product justifies our persistence. Furthermore, thanks to Damon Chapman and his colleagues, and to Yuki Hamada for assisting with the translation of two foreign language studies. Without such selfless help, the role of stalking in foreign cultures would remain even more mysterious than it does now. We are very grateful for the support we receive from the folks at Lawrence Erlbaum Associates. Linda Bathgate, as always, indulged us with her patience, good cheer, and confidence in our efforts. We also extend our thanks to our many students, who continually provide a crucible of everyday relevance for our concepts and conjectures, and assistance with our work. In particular, Mary Alice Ladwig, Maria Jose Zeledon, and Bryan Nickerson were instrumental in coding the stalking tactics and refining the final coding scheme, and their tireless efforts to make deadlines are much appreciated. We also wish to extend gratitude to Mary Alice Ladwig for assisting with the author index and Bonnie Lucks for additional proof-reading assistance. On a more personal level, we extend our gratitude to our loved ones, family, friends, and furry quadrupeds, who put up with our late nights, missed appointments, surly attitudes, and our many moments of singular focus that no doubt made us seem as obsessed as those who are the subject of our investigations.

CHAPTER ONE

The Evolution
of Relationship Intimacy
and Intrusion

We are supposed to pursue the things we love. It is something bred deeply into our consciousness, half memories of 5 million years of primate evolution and 5 millennia of interactions in communal endeavors creeping toward civilization. Both individual survival and the promotion of progeny require coupling, communicating, and mating. Love is more than a mere selfish symptom of nature, which Tennyson described as "red in tooth and claw." Love is the dream as well as the drive, our saving state of grace and the shadow of our despair. In love is the seed of pursuit of such dreams, and the shadows in the nightmares that dreams may become.

Love has been socially constructed throughout history as an entity unto itself (e.g., Buss, 1994; Fisher, 1992; Giddens, 1992; Hunt, 1959; Kern, 1992; Murstein, 1974; Roussel, 1986). Many people across many cultures of the world still form their primary mateships and marriages based on parental prerogative rather than romantic rapture. The cultural concept of romantic love is itself a relatively contemporary construction, and has undergone considerable contemporary social revision (e.g., Bailey, 1989; Holland & Eisenhart, 1990; Phillips, 2000; Radway, 1991; Rothman, 1984). But what a concept it is. The manifestations of love display the mundane and the deviant, the beautiful and the bizarre, the affectionate and the aggressive. "Wherever there is the possibility for romantic interaction and attachment, there is also the possibility for obsessive attraction, and stalking tendencies" (Lee, 1998, p. 414). "If there is a heart of darkness in the desire to bond with another, it is stalking" (Meloy, 1999b, p. 85). Such ironies of love have fascinated poets and scientists alike, and are very much the spine of the story of stalking and unwanted pursuit.

1

Pursuit is a goal-oriented activity. To pursue is to seek actively, to exert effort toward an object, outcome, or destination. In its earliest uses (circa 1400–1600s), the *Compact Oxford English Dictionary* (Oxford University Press, 1971, p. 2368) noted "pursue" meant "to follow with hostility or enmity, to seek to injure, (a person); to persecute; to harass, worry, torment." Its later meanings were more in line with contemporary usage, such as to follow or to proceed continuously toward one's objective(s). Pursuit is often associated with desire, want, need, or preference, of which the concepts of love and attraction are subsets. However, pursuit can be avoidant, in the sense that the path of least resistance or the lesser of two evils may be pursued.

Any journey into the dark side of relationship pursuit needs to chart a preliminary course, despite the scarcity of compass and maps. The journey begins with a consideration of the nature of disjunctive relationships. This is followed by a backward glance to see what textual traces have been left behind in the historical, literary, and dramatic accounts of stalking and unwanted pursuit. This retrospection meanders to the present day, and thus a need to define the basic terms that will serve as landmarks along the way to come. Finally, these definitions may or may not be shared by the public at large, and thus, consideration is given to how stalking and stalking legislation are perceived by the public.

RELATIONSHIPS: CONJUNCTIVE AND DISJUNCTIVE

Historically, many of the theories of why people form relationships, mateships, and couplings with others have focused on the motivation of desire. Implicit in most such theories is the underlying assumption of mutuality. From theories of propinquity (e.g., Newcomb, 1956), to seeking balance (e.g., Pepitone, 1964), to exchange reciprocity (e.g., Huston & Burgess, 1979), to similarity (of interests, attitudes, personality, communication skills; see Burleson & Denton, 1992; Murstein, 1971; Sunnafrank, 1991), the general presumption is that romantic relationships emerge from shared mutuality in the desire to develop the relationship. Most models of "ideal" relationships envision an ongoing dialogue in which common understanding, common ground, and mutual respect are pursued in ways that maintain the relationship over time (e.g., McNamee & Gergen, 1999). "Dialogical" relationships, relationships characterized by dialogue rather than monologue, are defined by the characteristics of coordination (or cooperation), coherence, reciprocity, and mutuality (Linell, 1998). Generally speaking, relationships are envisioned as interpersonal states pursued to the extent that the participants in the relationship possess and establish similar understandings and seek similar interests, commitments, and futures.

Because of this interest in relationships of mutuality, there is a relative paucity of theory and research to account for nonmutual relationships. When individuals pursue mutual activities and states, their shared relationship may be considered conjunctive in structure. Conversely, when relationships are nonmutual, they may be considered disjunctive in structure. Stalking and unwanted pursuit represent disjunctive relationship structures (Cupach & Spitzberg, 1998, 2000; Spitzberg & Cupach, 2001a, 2002a). There are examples of such disjunctive forms of interaction and relationship (e.g., privacy invasion, unwanted relationships, sexual harassment, sexual coercion, domestic violence, etc.), but few seem so prototypical of disjunction as stalking and obsessive relational intrusion. There is something fundamentally coercive in the disjunctive nature of stalking. "Stalking ... is always a desperate endeavor to force a relationship on another party" (Kamir, 2001, p. 15). "The process of stalking forces a relationship upon the victims whether they want it or not" (Babcock, 2000, p. 3). Fundamental notions of privacy, which include perceived rights to personal space, ownership of personal information, and social distance boundaries (Burgoon, 1982; Pedersen, 1999; Petronio, 2000), are disjunctively violated by stalking and unwanted pursuit.

Obsessive relational intrusion (ORI) is the repeated pursuit of intimacy with someone who does not want such attentions (see Cupach & Spitzberg, 1998; Cupach, Spitzberg, & Carson, 2000; Spitzberg, Nicastro, & Cousins, 1998). *Stalking*, broadly defined, "is a situation in which one individual imposes on another unwanted and fear-inducing intrusions in the form of communications or approaches" (Mullen, Pathé, & Purcell, 2000a, p. 3). Both types of relationship, to be defined more extensively later, are the primary topics of analyses to follow.

What is a relationship? A relationship is any reciprocally contingent pattern of interaction over time. The closer the relationship, the greater is the interdependence or contingency of the interaction over time (Kelley et al., 1983). Although various affective and cognitive features are often associated with "closeness" of relationships, these are not necessary defining characteristics. Relationships exist in the behavioral contingency of participants' actions; all else is the décor of the relationship, rather than the structure on which such decoration is hung.

Indeed, as reviewed by Spitzberg and Cupach (2002a), by any number of standards, stalking and unwanted pursuit may meet the criteria of a close relationship. First, a majority of stalking and ORI relationships emerge from the vestiges of a previous relationship. That is, unwanted pursuit is often an extension or transformation of an existing relationship. Second, stalking and ORI commonly last for an extended time period, often for years. Third, stalking and ORI often involve frequent interaction, or pursuer action and object reaction. Indeed, stalkers and unwanted pursuers may call, write, and make contact far more frequently than people in a typical dating relationship. Fourth, research shows the objects of pursuit are strongly affected by the process of pursuit. The pursuit often becomes the pursuers' primary raison d'etre for a broad range of their daily activities. For the persons who are the objects of such pursuit, their quality of life and patterns of action are often significantly disrupted. Finally, stalking and ORI tend to take place in a diversity of contexts, employing a diversity of types of contact and interaction. Thus, stalking and ORI typically involve two or more people interacting over an extended period of time, using a wide variety of forms of interaction across a variety of contexts, in ways that significantly affect their lives. Many people cannot make these claims of their typical valued and mutual relationships. Despite its disjunctive structure, stalking represents a *relationship*, and unfortunately, often a *close relationship*.

THE STORY OF STALKING

There is an intriguing race afoot; the contestants have yet to name it, and may not even be fully aware of their competitors in the race. The race is to stalk the historical origins of stalking. The deepest historical analysis to date is provided by Kamir (2001), who traced the pattern of consuming surveillance and (usually sexual) threat of others to the myth of Lilit in 1000 b.c.e. Mesopotamia. Dan and Kornreich (2000) traced stalking themes to the Hebrew myth of Joseph and Zuleika in Genesis. They further claimed that the "archetype of stalking has many derivations in Jewish, Arabic, Syriac, Persian, Indian, and medieval European lore" (p. 282). Specific literary descriptions of stalking have been interpreted in Ovid's *Art of Love* (1 b.c.e.; Lee, 1998, p. 389), Lamb's *Glenarvon* (1816), Shelley's *Frankenstein: or The Modern Prometheus*, Varney's serialized vampire stories (Kamir, 2001, p. 99), Louisa May Alcott's *A Long Fatal Love Chase* (1866; Meloy, 1997c, p. 177), and Shakespeare's sonnets (Skoler, 1998), as well as Dante and Petrarch's descriptions of their own actual pursuit of women (Mullen et al., 2000c, p. 9). As late as 1985, even an adolescents' book entitled *The Stalker* (Nixon, 1985, p. 73) was published in which the antagonist voiced to himself: "Careful, careful, little girl. I'm keeping track of you."

> Most such stories conform to one or more of the following structures: (1) a strong, sexually initiating, dangerous Lilit woman stalks a man, threatening him and his family; (2) a "Jack the Ripper"/serial-killer "shadow" male character stalks a sexual, evil woman because she "asked for it," "had it coming," and "brought it on herself"; or (3) a monstrous male stalks a weak, domestic,

Eve-woman, who is saved only if she is revealed to be a Virgin Mary character. (Kamir, 2001, p. 17)

In addition to literary tradition, Finch (2001, p. 30) traced exemplars of stalking-type activities in British case law as far back as *Dennis v Lane* (1704), and *R v Dunn* (1840). Apparently, the notion of unwanted pursuit dates as far back in antiquity as oral traditions and written history record. However, for reasons no one has yet suggested, this theme apparently never received its own distinctive name until very recent times. This leads to the question of the more recent history through which society would import a term for other purposes to the phenomenon currently recognized as stalking.

The media are a widely acknowledged influence on the naming of stalking. The *Compact Oxford English Dictionary* (Oxford University Press, 1971) traced the origins of the word stalking to the activity of hunting game (circa 1400s). This theme of hunting game was a relatively natural generalization to the narratives of hunting people. "The obsessive pursuit of another is a standard theme in American popular culture; many movies, novels, and popular songs center around obsessive love" (Lowney & Best, 1995, p. 50). The craft of filmmaking and the film industry clearly found the theme of fear-inducing and unwanted pursuit a popular narrative structure. Kamir (2001) identified stalking themes in an extensive list of films, including *The Student of Prague* (1913), *The Cabinet of Dr. Caligari* (1919), *The Golem* (circa 1920), *Pandora's Box* (1928), *Dr. Jekyll and Mr. Hyde* (1931), *Dracula* (1931), *The Mummy* (1932), and several of Hitchcock's films such as *The Lodger* (1926), *Rebecca* (1940), *Shadow of a Doubt* (1943), *Rear Window* (1954), and *To Catch a Thief* (1955). In 1971 *Play Misty for Me* constructed the contemporary stereotypical motif for the crazed celebrity stalker, and in 1979, a made-for-TV movie was aired called *The Night Stalker* that preyed on the vampire motif (Kamir, 2001). Later films would make the stalking motif more explicit, including *Taxi Driver* and *Fatal Attraction* (Kamir, 2001), as well as subsequent films such as *Copycat, Pacific Heights, Unlawful Entry, The Seduction, Stalked,* and *Stalker* (Finch, 2001).

That the cultural vernacular permitted the naming of stalking at this time is not surprising. In 1975, a rapist self-attributed the label: "It became an exciting thing to do, not just the act itself, but the stalking, the creeping, the buildup" (Footlick, Howard, Camper, Sciolino, & Smith, 1975, p. 70). As Kamir (2001) traced, news reports had begun to refer to the serial killer Son of Sam in 1976 as having "stalked" his victims, and independently referred to a celebrity photographer as "stalking" Jackie Kennedy for photographs. Thus, by 1985, all the pieces were in place for a serial killer in Los Angeles to be dubbed "the night stalker." "Following Son of Sam, *stalker* and *stalking* quickly became common terms in newspaper reports of serial killing, rapes, and celebrity assassinations. The perpetrators of these acts were now labeled *stalkers"* (Kamir, 2001, p. 148).

Media can play a very active role in the social construction of crimes (e.g., Brownstein, 1996; Chermak, 1995; Kappeler, Blumberg, & Potter, 1996; Lipschultz & Hilt, 2002; Meyers, 1997; Spitzberg & Cadiz, 2002; Surrette, 1998; Voumvakis & Ericson, 1984). In general,

> the news media present a carefully selected microcosm of the cases available which emphasize the sensational aspects of the stories. Stalking cases that are bizarre, extreme, dramatic or involve celebrities are presented to the public with little or no indication that these are anything other than standard stalking cases. (Finch, 2001, p. 114)

The media unsurprisingly tend to be drawn to the more deviant types of crime stories (Angermeyer & Schulze, 2001; Pritchard & Hughes, 1997), of which stalking among serial killers and celebrities make good candidates. "Predatory stalkers constitute a small but salient subset of stalkers, who have been disproportionately represented, in their most ostentatious and dramatic forms, in fictional portrayals of stalking" (Mullen et al., 2000a, p. 98). Similarly, celebrity stalking "cases attract media attention, [and] thus may reasonably be perceived as more prevalent than cases involving 'ordinary' victims" (Finch, 2001, p. 96). Interestingly, "for at least the previous decade, there had been complaints about the very behaviors that would later constitute the crime of stalking, although those claims neither evoked great public concern nor led to antistalking laws" (Lowney & Best, 1995, p. 35). It is also relevant that media reports from the late 1980s to the late 1990s displayed an increasing public intolerance of domestic violence (Johnson & Sigler, 2000). It may be that public apprehension of stalking had to undergo a gestation period, during which media cultivated the image of stalking in the public psyche.

An analysis of 169 print media articles about stalking in Victoria, Australia between 1993 and 1998 (Dussuyer, 2000, p. 94), during which time antistalking legislation was passed, showed "representation of the sex of stalking victims and offenders is similar to the profiles derived from police and court figures." The stalking activities most often reported mirror typical stalking behaviors such as following, telephoning, loitering near residence, and leaving or sending offensive materials, rather than potentially more bizarre or spectacular types of behavior such as kidnapping, assault, or showing up in a celebrity's bedroom. However, the media reports tended to focus more on the stalker than the victim, and were biased toward stranger stalking. For example, the representation of spousal or "de facto spousal" stalking was revealed in a minority of articles (14%) and actually decreased over time (Dussuyer, 2000). In short, the print media appear to provide a variegated picture of stalking, some of which is likely to be biased and some of which is likely to be reasonably representative. The impact of such biases is not always easy to anticipate.

Research strongly supports the tendency for media to affect public attitudes and beliefs about crime. For example, people who consume high levels of media tend to have significantly biased views of their personal risk of violent crime (e.g., Lowry, Nio, & Leitner, 2003; Romer, Jamieson, & Aday, 2003). When a few particularly violent cases that fit the media and public prototypes of stalkers occurred in the late 1980s, society may have been well primed for legislative action.

The evolution of the term "stalking" was systematically analyzed by Lowney and Best (1995; see also Best, 1999). They analyzed stalking and stalking-like reportage in "24 U.S. popular magazine articles and 47 nationally televised news and information broadcasts between 1980 and June 1994" (p. 36). Between 1980 and 1988, Lowney and Best claimed, stalking-like behavior was referred to as sexual harassment, obsession, and psychological rape. These activities were exclusively perpetrated by males on female victims. From 1989 to 1991, 69% of the articles and broadcasts concerning stalking-like activities referred to celebrity victims. This period corresponds with the highly publicized murder of Rebecca Schaeffer by Robert Bardo, whereupon parallels were drawn with Arthur Jackson's stalking of Theresa Saldana in 1982 and John Hinckley's stalking of Jody Foster (and peripherally, President Reagan) in 1991. In the period between 1992 and 1994, there was a vast increase in stories about stalking, in which unfounded estimates of prevalence were rampant (and often irresponsibly repeated; see Spitzberg & Cadiz, 2002). It was in this period that stalking became more closely and rhetorically connected to domestic violence. Lowney and Best (1995) summarized the convoluted construction of stalking in media typifications:

> After 1992, the press portrayed stalking as a violent crime against women, typically committed by former husbands or lovers. This construction built upon earlier (1989–1991) concern about star-stalking by men and women suffering from erotomania. And the issue of celebrity stalking had precursors in still earlier claims about harassment, obsession, and psychological rape, claims that, in retrospect, resemble the later claims about stalking. (p. 47)

Of course, claiming that stalking has experienced an evolution of rhetorical construction in the media is far from the same thing as claiming *the media constructed* the concept of stalking for society. The evolutionary pathways of societal constructs such as stalking are almost always manifold. In the case of stalking, the media influences interacted with legislative and public agendas in important ways.

Perhaps the earliest case-based research on stalking-related phenomena consisted of descriptions by de Clérambault and Kraepelin and others (Lloyd-Goldstein, 1998) of patients diagnosed with disorders of passion, typically associated with delusions of another of higher status being in love with the patient. This disorder came to be known as erotomania, and has been closely associated with stalking ever since (see also Brüne, 2001, 2003; Dunlop, 1988; Evans, Jeckel, & Slott, 1982; Fitzgerald & Seeman, 2002; Gillett, Eminson, & Hassanyeh, 1990; Harmon, Rosner, & Owens, 1995; Leong, 1993; Lipson & Mills, 1998; Meloy, 1989, 1999a; Menzies, Fedoroff, Green, & Isaacson, 1995; Meyers, 1998; Mullen, 2000; Noone & Cockhill, 1987; Raskin & Sullivan, 1974; Rudden, Sweeney, & Frances, 1990; Segal, 1989; Signer, 1989; Taylor, Mahendra, & Gunn, 1983; Zona, Sharma, & Lane, 1993). A largely separate and relatively unnoticed line of research later emerged in the study of psychotic visitors to the White House or other government agencies. Most of these cases were remanded to a particular hospital for psychiatric evaluation and could be studied as a set of cases over time. They have been referred to as "White House cases," and many of them display patterns similar to stalking (Hoffman, 1943; Shore et al., 1989). It seems "many of the patients announced their arrival by letter or telegram and returned again and again although they had been turned away from the White House gates several times" (Sebastiani & Foy, 1965, p. 684). Most of these cases were clearly "issue-based" stalkers, although some revealed a sense of personal relationship with the government official they were seeking to meet.

The first criminalization of stalking occurred in California in 1990. By most accounts, this legislation was motivated significantly by two sets of events: Several women in Orange County, California, were murdered by their domestic partners despite the protective orders in place, and the television actress Rebecca Schaeffer was murdered by an obsessed fan (Kamir, 2001; Keenahan & Barlow, 1997). The murder of Rebecca Schaeffer in particular "became the typifying example of what the media termed 'star stalking'" (Finch, 2001, p. 104). In contrast, Baldry (2002) attributed the parameters of the law itself more to domestic violence policy (see also Lowney & Best, 1995). Others attributed the yoking of stalking legislation to domestic violence concerns to post hoc political strategies of those affiliated with women's interests (Mullen et al., 2000a). Indeed, Kamir (2001, pp. 182–183) pointed out the California statute would not have been particularly applicable to either Schaeffer's case or the spate of domestic murders because the law required willful, malicious harassment, threat, and placing the victims in fear of their safety, which were not indicative of these cases.

Between 1990 and 2000, all 50 United States, the federal government, Canada, Australia, Great Britain, Ireland, and several other European countries passed legislation referring to stalking or criminal harassment (Smartt, 2001). "The speed with which these laws were enacted is noteworthy" (Mullen et al., 2000a, p. 267). This reflects an extraordinary pace of legislative reform, suggesting both that (a) stalking struck a responsive chord in the public's psyche, and (b) existing legislation (e.g., harassment, terroristic threats, etc.) was insufficient to manage stalking phenomena. Nevertheless, from a legal standpoint stalking "is still largely confined not just to the developed world, but to the English-speaking world" (Mullen et al., 2000c, p. 12). Most countries other than the United States have preferred the term "criminal harassment," whereas some European cultures have preferred the term "mobbing." However, in most European societies "the fact remains that 'stalking' as a new social phenomenon is difficult to define culturally, ethically or within codified socio-legal boundaries" (Smartt, 2001, p. 217).

CONCEPTUALIZING STALKING AND OBSESSIVE RELATIONAL INTRUSION

Manifold are the avenues of interpersonal aggression. Several attempts have been made to formulate a typology of aggression, whereas others have endeavored to view all forms of aggression on a continuum of severity (e.g., Christopher, 1988; Kelly, 1987; Spitzberg, 1998a; Sugarman, Aldarondo, & Boney-McCoy, 1996). For example, Leidig (1992) argued for a continuum of violence against women consisting of the following, ranging from less severe to more severe destructiveness: street hassling, grabbing, obscene telephone calls, voyeurism, indecent exposure, lesbian baiting, prostitution, pornography, medical violence, sexual harassment, abuse by professionals, rape, battering, and incest. There are three significant problems with such a continuum. First, as displayed by this continuum, it ignores certain types of aggression, such as prowling, mobbing and bullying, and stalking. In some cases, such as mobbing and stalking, these crimes had not really been recognized socially or legally, suggesting the incompleteness of any such continuum relative to the potential evolution of types of abusive behavior. Second, such a static continuum suggests that, for example, sexual harassment is more destructive than prostitution. While this may be accurate in some instances, it seems improbable that it is consistently true. Regardless, it is an empirical question and not a conceptual question as to the severity of such experiences. Third, this is clearly as much an ideological continuum as it is a conceptual continuum. For example, to view prostitution as a form of "violence against women" presupposes that it is a nonvoluntary activity under the strategic control of men. Although this may be true in many or most instances, such assumptions are not intrinsic to the definition or conceptualization of prostitution. They are interpretations that emerge from a particular theoretical and value-based view of the nature of society, and not inherent to the nature of the lived experience of those involved in the process of prostitution. Despite these limitations, the efforts at formulating continua help clarify the existence of multiple forms or types of aggression. Stalking is a member of this domain of aggression (e.g., Belknap, Fisher, & Cullen, 1999).

According to some, there currently "is a glaring lack of agreement in the literature on what is meant by *stalking*" (Westrup & Fremouw, 1998, p. 256). For these observers, stalking behavior "ranges from the outwardly innocuous to the seriously criminal, rendering it virtually impossible to find any common denominator to the conduct upon which to base a definition" (Finch, 2001, p. 11). In contrast, we are considerably more sanguine about the definitional status of stalking. Under the various ways of defining stalking lie fairly consistent themes. These themes can be examined in several different contexts of usage.

As a cultural concept, stalking has evolved along narrative, media, legal, and social dimensions. Consequently, there is the "actual" process of stalking, and then there are the many cultural constructions of this process. Furthermore, such a variegated and complex process tends to accommodate a diversity of cultural constructions. "It is not easy to encapsulate the characteristics of stalking in a comprehensive yet concise definition. The need for both breadth and specificity is a particularly tortuous combination to encompass within a simple definition" (Finch, 2001, p. 27). One of the approaches to managing these problems is to provide definitions of stalking for relatively specific purposes. There are general conceptual definitions, behavioral operational definitions, and legalistic definitions, each of which tends to serve somewhat different purposes. General conceptual definitions are common in the narrative explanations of stalking, and are sometimes employed operationally in surveys. Behavioral operational definitions tend to constitute the lists of actions in a survey or coding form that provide the empirical data of stalking research. Legalistic definitions describe categories of conduct and jurisprudential criteria (e.g., stalker intent to cause fear) required for determination of guilt.

"Stalking refers to a harmful course of conduct involving unwanted communications and intrusions repeatedly inflicted by one individual on another" (Pathé, Mullen, & Purcell, 2000, p. 191). It is possible from such a general conceptual definition to extract several of the common themes of stalking. Stalking is harmful to some degree to the victim, if in no other way but that it is unwanted. As such, stalking can be considered a "victim-defined" crime. "It is not the intentions of the putative stalker that are the defining element but the reactions of the recipients of the unwanted attentions who, in the act of experiencing themselves as victimized, create a stalking event" (Mullen et al., 2000a, p. 9). This feature is important because much of the behavior of relational stalking is indistinct from culturally sanctioned courtship behavior. "It is clear that the early stages of relational interaction create a range of potential situations in which normal dating behaviour and stalking may overlap" (Finch, 2001, p. 66). These conceptions of stalking point "to the possibility that stalking may not arise from individual differences, but from deeply embedded notions of romance found in Western culture" (Lee, 1998, p. 388).

Stalking is also a "course of conduct," engaged in "repeatedly," which means there is more than a single event involved. "The defining characteristic of stalking is its relentless and persistent nature" (Finch, 2001, p. 171). Communications and intrusions are the products and means of such pursuit. The process of following is often considered prototypical of stalking, but if no attempts are made to contact or be noticed by the object of pursuit, following alone is unlikely to be recognized as unwanted by the victim.

By these general definitions, there are "three central characteristics of stalking—repeated conduct that is unwanted and which provokes an adverse reaction in the recipient" (Finch, 2001, p. 80). "It is proposed then, that *stalking behavior* be defined as one or more of a constellation of behaviors that (a) are repeatedly directed toward a specific individual (the 'target'), (b) are unwelcome and intrusive, and (c) induce fear or concern in the target" (Westrup & Fremouw, 1998, p. 258). "As used by the general public, media, and law enforcement communities, however, *stalking* loosely refers to a broader range of repeated behaviors (e.g., telephoning, letter writing, conducting surveillance) whose overall effect is to threaten and/or harass another individual" (Westrup & Fremouw, 1998, p. 256).

The fact that following, intrusions, and various forms of symbolic contact are attempted in stalking relationships places stalking in the domain of communication. This does not diminish the significance of personality, perceptions, developmental histories, or cultural norms. It merely acknowledges that at a fundamental level, a "relationship" only exists in the behavior exchanged between the participants. We know what we think (most of the time), and we know what we think others are thinking (some of the time), but all we can really *know* about another is the way she or he behaves toward us. Thus, the *relationship* between the stalker or pursuer and the object of pursuit consists of a process of interaction or communication.

Behavioral operational definitions tend to be used by researchers. Like rape victims (Koss, 1989, 1992b), stalking victims may have experienced the behaviors of stalking but not perceptually *label* what they experienced as stalking (Tjaden, Thoennes, & Allison, 2000). There may be a variety of reasons why people do not label themselves as stalking victims, and even more reasons why stalkers may not perceive themselves as stalkers. Stalking victims may acquire a stigmatized identity. It may be more stigmatizing for male victims than female victims. Given that stalking is still a relatively new legal phenomenon, people may simply be ignorant of what constitutes stalking. Conversely, stalkers tend to view their actions as justified, and therefore are unlikely to self-attribute such a deviant label to themselves.

Behavioral operational definitions tend to list a series of behavioral criteria or events. Anyone who fulfills a certain number of these criteria is classified as a stalking victim or perpetrator. There are two typical ways in which these behavioral definitions operate. First, there is a list of stalking and stalking-like behaviors. Behaviors such as "followed," "called constantly," "left notes or letters on my car," and "threatened me" are listed and a respondent is asked whether or not she or he has experienced (if assessing victims) or engaged in (if assessing perpetrators) the behaviors. Second, some type of contextualizing or framing device is used to characterize such behaviors as "unwanted," fear-inducing, and/or repetitive. The repetitive character of these behaviors is often established through a rating scale referencing frequency (e.g., 0 = never, 1 = at least once, 2 = two to three times, 4 = more than three times), either over a specified period of time (e.g., the past year) or during one's lifetime. Various criteria may be used, but typically some collective set of behaviors experienced on more than one occasion would be required to qualify someone as a stalking victim or perpetrator. Such operational "list" definitions in many ways do not actually establish a single definition (Finch, 2001). That is, one victim is someone who received unwanted calls and notes, and another is someone who received unwanted threats and following.

Legalistic definitions attempt to establish conditions of pursuit that would qualify as a prosecutable offense according to a specific or typical statute. It is a tall order to create legislation and case law to "distinguish between robust wooing and intimidation" (Sheridan & Davies, 2001a, p. 138). One early attempt to identify characteristics of stalking statutes delineated the following requirements (McAnaney, Gurliss, & Abeyta-Price, 1993, pp. 892–897; see also Koedam, 2000, p. 133):

1. *Stalking*: that is, following without legitimate purpose or harassing another.
2. *Repeatedly following*: that is, following or pursuing contact on more than one occasion.
3. *Harassing*: that is, the behavior is threatening in nature.

4. *Course of conduct*: that is, a pattern of behavior is established over time.
5. *Harm*: that is, a reasonable person would experience distress due to the course of conduct.
6. *Credible threat*: that is, the pursuer appears to have the ability to carry out a threat and thereby produces reasonable fear in the object of pursuit.

A more contemporary distillation of statutes was offered by Schell and Lantaigne (2000, p. 17): "The three key features of most anti-stalking codes drafted in the United States and in other jurisdictions include: (1) the existence of threatening behavior, (2) criminal intent by the offender, and (3) repetition of the activity." Miller (2001b, p. 8) suggested a slightly different set of prosecutorial elements: "The defendant's multiple acts were willful or intentional. Threats were expressed by those acts. Victim fear resulted."

There is some concern that statutes and case law are too crude an instrument to carve up the domain of stalking. "Finding appropriate definitions or legal strategies to separating the 'harassing' ex-husband from the 'classic' stalker is probably an impossible task" (Infield & Platford, 2002, p. 231). Although general conceptual definitions view stalking as a victim-defined crime, most legislation does not rely on victim reaction to define the crime. Indeed, "the largest hindrance to enforcement of anti-stalking statutes may be that stalking is a specific intent crime. Under almost every statute, the state must prove that the defendant had the intent to harass or threaten the victim or to put the victim in fear of death or bodily injury" (Sohn, 1994, p. 220). Furthermore, many statutes define fear or threat in terms of a "reasonable person" standard. That is, a victim need not evidence fear if the pursuer's conduct would make a typical reasonable person fearful.

A close relative of stalking is unwanted relational pursuit. Cupach and Spitzberg (1998, pp. 234–235) defined obsessive relational intrusion (ORI) as a pattern of "repeated and unwanted pursuit and invasion of one's sense of physical or symbolic privacy by another person, either stranger or acquaintance, who desires and/or presumes an intimate relationship." That is, obsessive relational intrusion is a process of pursuing intimacy in ways unwanted by the object of that pursuit. ORI and stalking overlap substantially but are not isomorphic. ORI may be annoying, pestering, or frustrating, but not necessarily threatening. Stalking has to be threatening or reasonably fear-inducing. Stalking may be conducted for completely nonrelational reasons. An assassin or "issue" stalker (e.g., a pro-life advocate stalks a doctor who performs abortions) is not seeking a relationship with the victim. Despite these differences, research shows that the large majority of stalkers either already had prior relationships with their objects of pursuit, or are seeking one (Spitzberg, 2002b). Furthermore, even relatively "mild" forms of unwanted pursuit and intrusion are often perceived as threatening by the recipients of such harassment (Cupach & Spitzberg, 2000). Thus, most stalking is a form of ORI, and most ORI constitutes stalking, but neither entirely encompasses the other.

In the remainder of this book, we generally refer to these phenomena as roughly equivalent, except in instances where their differences merit particular attention. Both constructs share at least two essential features:

1. Both ORI and stalking constitute structurally disjunctive relationships, in which the participants have fundamentally incompatible relationship objectives and definitions. "Perceiving the other as intrusive and harassing, and oneself as stalked, is a measure of the experienced disjunction between the intentions and perceptions of the protagonist of the relationship and that of the unwilling object of those aspirations" (Mullen et al., 2000a, p. 14).
2. Both ORI and stalking consist primarily of an interaction pattern of communication over time.

To economize rhetorically, we view both constructs as subsets of a process of unwanted pursuit.

These two essential features, disjunction and a pattern of interaction, are shared by other phenomena. Such constructs include sexual harassment (Infield & Platford, 2002; Kamir, 2001; Koedam, 2000; Schell & Lanteigne, 2000), bullying (McCann, 2002), prowling (Babcock, 2002), sexual coercion and rape (Finch, 2001; Infield & Platford, 2002), and even aspects of domestic violence (Kurt, 1995; Lee, 1998; Logan, Nigoff, Walker, & Jordan, 2002; Melton, 2000; Pearce & Easteal, 1999; Sinwelski & Vinton, 2001). Sexual harassment, in particular, shares some overlap with stalking. Examination of the behavioral indicators of sexual harassment often reveals actions indistinguishable from ORI and stalking actions (e.g., see Larkin & Popaleni, 1994; Leonard et al., 1993; Roscoe, Strouse, & Goodwin, 1994). Eventually, both the conceptual and empirical distinctions among these phenomena will need to be investigated. For our purposes, however, we intend to focus on stalking and ORI as forms of unwanted pursuit.

PERCEPTIONS OF PURSUIT

Given the extent to which stalking has appeared in important cultural narratives throughout history, "it is likely that prototypes exist in the minds of community members as to what stalking is, what types of people engage in stalking, and what types of people are victims" (Dennison & Thomson, 2002, p. 546). It is in this cultural matrix that people's conception of stalking is likely to interact with their conception of other cultural prototypes, such as gender. Indeed, research indicates females and males tend to differ in their perception of stalking. Females appear significantly more afraid of (Bjerregaard, 2000; Davis, Coker, & Sanderson, 2002) and threatened by (Cupach & Spitzberg, 2000) stalking behaviors than males (cf. McFarlane, Willson, Malecha, & Lemmey, 2000). Females are more likely than males to identify stalking-like behaviors as stalking in hypothetical scenarios (Dennison & Thomson, 2002). Males appear to associate such behaviors as more embedded in the process of courtship than women. In a scenario study, Hills and Taplin (1998) found females were more worried than males by a stalking scenario, whereas males were more likely than females to feel flattered or indifferent. Females were also more likely to experience a variety of negative states (e.g., worry, concern, fright, etc.) and were more likely to engage in a variety of coping responses.

These gender differences suggest a rather specific difference between general, behavioral, and legalistic definitions of stalking. Legal definitions tend to require a "reasonable person" standard; that is, stalking has occurred when "a reasonable person" perceives a course of harassing conduct as threatening. The research on gender, however, suggests that males and females are differentially "reasonable" in their judgments of threat (see also Spitzberg & Cadiz, 2002; Stanko, 1985, 1990). For example, although both men and women tend to perceive themselves at greater risk of assault from strangers than from friends or relatives, women perceive even greater risk from strangers than men, and are generally more fearful in potentially threatening interpersonal encounters than men (Harris & Miller, 2000). Women also appear more sensitive to privacy invasions than men (Buslig & Burgoon, 2000).

These types of gender differences are sensitive to other factors, such as the degree of romanticization of the behavior. Lee (1998, p. 419) hypothesized that "college students may not easily discern between stalking and flattery, if the interest is laced with romance, until flattery transforms into blatant obsession." Scenario-based studies by Dunn (1999, 2002) manipulated symbols of courtship in otherwise stalking-like actions. For example, upon breaking off a relationship after a first date (or after a long-term relationship), the jilted paramour is encountered sitting on the jilter's doorstep with a bouquet of flowers. Women were more annoyed and frightened and less flattered and romanced when these actions were undertaken by a former first date than by a former long-term partner (see also Hills & Taplin, 1998). Furthermore, the use of "romantic imagery appears to counter increasing levels of 'invasiveness'" (Dunn, 1999, p. 446).

That is, it appears that stalking behaviors are less likely to be perceived as threatening, frightening, or as stalking if they are produced by ex-partners or if they "look like" courtship behavior. It stands to reason that stalkers often are either dimly or acutely aware of this, and exploit the trappings of courtship in their activities (Dunn, 2002). It follows further that men may often misperceive their own victimization. In one study, "Men who met the legal definition of a stalking victim were significantly less likely to define themselves as stalking victims than their female counterparts" (Tjaden et al., 2000, p. 15).

Conversely, when stalkers are male, they are perceived as more likely than female stalkers to engage in violence and police intervention is viewed as more essential (Sheridan, Gillett, Davies, Blaauw, & Patel, 2003). In a small impressionistic study, DuPont-Morales (1999, p. 369) reported that "male and female students were adamant that a male being stalked by a female is more of a nuisance than a crime." Similarly, Sinclair and Frieze's (2000, p. 33) research suggests "that fear may be associated with even mild forms of male 'stalking,' but that female 'stalkers' may not generate fear, even for more extreme behaviors." These gender differences collectively suggest male victims of stalking may be significantly underrepresented in surveys. Males are less likely to perceive themselves as victims of stalking, especially when stalked by a female. If society at large possesses the same prototypical notions, then an added disincentive is provided for any given male to perceive his own victimization: others, from friends to police, are unlikely to take his victimization seriously. DuPont-Morales (1999, p. 373) claimed that "male victims of this abuse report finding victim support difficult, and law enforcement callous when taking reports or conducting investigations." Although males may be underreported as stalking victims, and the threat implied by female stalkers may be underestimated, most research nevertheless indicates women are more likely to be harmed by stalking than men (see chap. 3 and chap. 5).

Other factors influence the perception of stalking. Dennison and Thomson (2002) found that evidence of intent to stalk is powerfully related to the attribution of stalking, but even in the absence of evidence of intent, relatively low persistence and intrusiveness still appear sufficient for people to attribute the label stalking to behavior. When presented with scenario descriptions of stalking and the key features of legislation defining stalking, laypersons appear capable of making sensitive discriminations among different stalking depictions (Sheridan & Davies, 2001c). Given such legalistic features, it might be expected that law-enforcement representatives would fare even better in applying statutory criteria to stalking cases. Unfortunately, the evidence is not particularly encouraging. Dussuyer (2000) presented four scenarios to police and judges (i.e., magistrates) in Australia. There was more agreement than disagreement across the scenarios as to what constituted stalking and what did not. However, in one scenario 34.5% of the judges, compared to 18.8% of the police, thought "the offender should *definitely be charged with stalking*." Just as importantly, 10% of the magistrates, compared to 54.3% of the police, thought "the offender *should not be charged* with stalking" (p. 59). A survey of police officers in the United States revealed 48% "did not know whether the police department had a written policy on stalking" and "18 percent of police officers defined stalking in a manner consistent with the state statute" (Farrell, Weisburd, & Wyckoff, 2000, p. 164). When presented with two scenarios with stalking features, only about half of the officers (56% in the ex-partner scenario, 53% in the stranger scenario) thought the events should be recorded as stalking. Similarly, when police in Australia were presented with several stalking scenarios, "it was found that most would not elect to use the stalking legislation when confronted with stalking behaviour within the domestic violence context" (Pearce & Easteal, 1999, p. 167). A study of 1,785 police domestic violence reports in Colorado identified narrative elements of stalking in 285 (16.5%). Of these, "only 1 resulted in the police officer charging the suspect with stalking" (Tjaden & Thoennes, 2000d, p. 432). It appears those who should be most informed about stalking legislation are still largely ignorant of its relevance, or influenced by cultural biases in recognizing the seriousness of stalking. In short, even when stalking is clearly defined in law, it may not be clearly recognized in actual behavior.

CONCLUSION

Stalking, obsessive relational intrusion, and other forms of unwanted relationship pursuit present unique challenges to law enforcement, society in general, and the individuals struggling to extricate themselves from such relationships. These disjunctive relationships also pose challenges to scholars, theorists, and researchers whose task it is to understand such relationships and to eventually comprehend how to better prevent their darker manifestations. In our previous two volumes (Cupach & Spitzberg, 1994; Spitzberg & Cupach, 1998) and in other contributions to the study of the disjunctive and dark sides of human relations (Baumeister & Wotman, 1992; Kowalski, 1997, 2001; Leary, 2001), advances have been made in the understanding of coercive and calamitous relationships. Much more yet needs to be understood. This text is intended as a further step in this direction.

CHAPTER TWO

The Pursuit
of Ordinary Relationships

Relationship construction is tricky business. In courtship and friendship alike, the mutuality of goals, intentions, and interpretations is relative, not absolute. When initiating relationships, "we travel across a complex social and interpersonal minefield. Traversing the pitfalls that lie between encountering and relating is rarely straightforward. The opportunities are many, not just for failure but for producing unsolicited responses of anger or fear" (Mullen et al., 2000a, p. 14). Even the most successful relationships emerge from interactions that necessarily involve equivocal messages, ambiguous meanings, and second-guessing. The day-to-day navigation of relationships presents much opportunity for miscommunication, misinterpretation, and mismatching of interpersonal agendas. Such complexities undoubtedly contribute to interpersonal problems and relational conflict (Canary, Cupach, & Messman, 1995). Indeed, the intricacies and difficulties that attend the negotiation of interpersonal relationships engender many instances of ORI and stalking. We agree with Emerson, Ferris, and Gardner (1998, p. 290), who argued much unwanted relational pursuit grows

> out of glitches and discontinuities in two very common and normal relationship processes—coming together and forming new relationships on one hand, and dissolving and getting out of existing relationships on the other. In this way the processes and experience of being stalked are intricately linked to normal, everyday practices for establishing, advancing, and ending relationships.

In this chapter we elaborate on some of the challenges of ordinary relationship pursuit that can help explain the occurrence of ORI and stalking. We contend the seeds of much unwanted pursuit are sewn in the complications surrounding the processes of relationship definition, initiation, escalation, and disengagement.

THE MISMATCHING OF RELATIONAL GOALS

Relationships emerge from the interactions that people share and the cumulative conceptions of those interactions derived by each respective partner. The fact that two people "share" a relationship does not require their goals and intentions to be mutual. People sometimes maintain undesired relationships with disliked others (Hess, 2000, 2003). These relationships are seen as "involuntary" in the sense that one or more barrier forces keep individuals from dissolving them. Individuals tolerate difficult coworkers for the sake of continued employment, stay in unhappy marriages for the sake of the children, and associate with annoying others because of mutual ties to friends and family (e.g., see Attridge, 1994; Cupach & Metts, 1986).

The flip side of maintaining a dispreferred relationship with someone is wanting a relationship but not being able to have it. This is reflected in the common experiences of unrequited love (Baumeister & Wotman, 1992; Bratslavsky, Baumeister, & Sommer, 1998), unrequited lust (Cupach & Spitzberg, in press), limerance (Tennov, 1979, 1998), and the like. In Aron, Aron, and Allen's (1998) sample of 907 undergraduate students, 82 percent "reported having at least one experience of unreciprocated love" (p. 787). Baumeister, Wotman, and Stillwell (1993) studied experiences of both rejecting a love interest and being rejected by a love interest. Nearly everyone in their student sample was able to recount an unrequited love experience, and approximately 93% reported at least one such experience of "moderate" or "powerful" intensity over the last 5 years. Sinclair and Frieze (2000) sampled individuals who "had at least one experience of loving someone who did not reciprocate those feelings. The large majority of women and men in the sample reported more than one instance of unrequited love. Thirty-four percent said this had happened twice and 44% reported this happening 3 or more times" (p. 29). Notably, many instances of unrequited love occur in the context of otherwise ordinary dating relationships and platonic friendships (Baumeister et al., 1993).

On the surface a relationship can appear mutual even though partner goals for the relationship may be at odds. One partner may be satisfied with the ongoing platonic friendship, for example, unaware that the other partner possesses a strong motivation to make the relationship romantic/sexual. Individuals sometimes settle for a relationship other than what they desire with a particular partner, harboring the expectation that they eventually will be able to alter the partner's relational goal.

The dynamic nature of relational goals, intentions, and meanings also militates against complete mutuality in defining a relationship. Relationships are emergent and developmental—their form and meaning undergo constant revision and refinement as partners continue to interact, and as partners continue to make sense of the relationship in between episodes of interaction (Miell, 1987; Planalp, 1987). Each partner's goals for a shared relationship may change over time, and the partners may not change in the same direction or at the same pace. Furthermore, individuals can experience ambivalence about what type of relationship they desire, and what expectations and activities they want to incorporate into the relationship (e.g., O'Sullivan & Gaines, 1998). Ambivalence manifests itself in fluctuating relational goals, inconsistent expectations, and conflicting portrayals to the partner of one's own relationship definition.

Most relationships are conjunctive efforts—that is, both partners share goals and meanings for the relationship, even though their respective orientations to the relationship are not identical. Nevertheless, virtually all relationships demonstrate some elements of disjunction. Virtually all relational partners must balance the conflicting dialectical tensions of closeness and distance, candor and restraint, novelty and predictability (Baxter & Montgomery, 1996; Rawlins, 1992). Conflict is inevitable in close relationships (Canary et al., 1995), and it commonly stems from incompatible goals. In relationships that are considered normal and ordinary, partners sometimes do things that communicate disjunction—they create problematic events (Samp & Solomon, 1998), violate expectations (Afifi & Metts, 1998), criticize one another (Cupach & Carson, 2002; Trees & Manusov, 1998), spy on one another (Patterson & Kim, 1991), demonstrate undue possessiveness (Pinto & Hollandsworth, 1984) and jealousy (Guerrero & Andersen, 1998), commit relational transgressions (Metts, 1994) and acts of betrayal (Jones & Burdette, 1994; Jones, Moore, Schratter, & Negel, 2001), and say and do hurtful things that convey devaluation of the relationship (Leary, Springer, Negel, Ansell, & Evans, 1998; Vangelisti, 1994; Vangelisti & Young, 2000). Ironically, the opportunities to perform aversive interpersonal behaviors are greatest in relationships that are relatively more intimate (Miller, 1997). Partners regularly manage such disjunctive elements in the course of their relationships, and seemingly negative events and behaviors often produce positive consequences as well (see Kowalski, 2001; Spitzberg & Cupach, 1998).

The presence of disjunctive elements in otherwise mutual and desired partnerships suggests that relationships represent unfinished business (Duck, 1990), and that each partner's relationship definition undergoes frequent challenge, testing, and modification. People expect their relationships to require routine and strategic efforts at maintenance (Canary &

Stafford, 1994) and rejuvenation (Wilmot, 1994). When one faces relational trouble or threat to a desired relationship, the natural tendency is to attempt to repair it rather than abandon it (Duck, 1984; Emmers-Sommer, 2003; Roloff & Cloven, 1994). Individuals can remain committed to having a relationship with a particular partner, but nevertheless dislike aspects of the relationship. In this sense, partners' relationship goals and definitions overlap, but not entirely. Partners' conceptions of the relationship exhibit both conjunctive and disjunctive elements.

Discerning the mutuality of relationship goals and intentions is complicated by the fact that the details of relationship definition are neither explicitly negotiated nor precisely codified in verifiable text. Overt discussion of relationship definition can be awkward, and it typically is considered to be a taboo topic (e.g., Baxter & Wilmot, 1985). As Baxter (1987, p. 194) suggested, the process of defining a relationship "is not dominated by open, direct relationship communication, but rather involves the construction of a web of ambiguity by which partners signal their relationship indirectly." As relationships develop, partners tacitly negotiate the intricacies of shared relationship definition via implicature. Indirectness permits both parties to save face while testing the relational waters, and "may 'buy time' for the relationship parties in perpetuating the illusion of agreement until the relationship bond is on firmer ground to withstand difference and conflict" (Baxter, 1987, p. 209).

THE FUZZY NATURE OF RELATIONSHIP DEFINITIONS

Based on direct and vicarious experience, people possess mental frameworks called *relational schemas* (Baldwin, 1992; Planalp, 1985, 1987), which depict "regularities in patterns of interpersonal relatedness" (Baldwin, 1992, p. 461). Relational schemas provide a basis for interpreting the meanings of interpersonal behavior, and they shape expectations for what behaviors are expected within different kinds of relationships. Individuals also rely on relational schemas to guide the implementation of relational goals and intentions. If one desires a certain kind of relationship with another, then one draws on the features contained in the corresponding schema and enacts the behaviors consistent with the features of the schema. If one wishes to create a romantic relationship, then one makes bids for such a relationship by performing behaviors consistent with the schema for a prototypical romantic relationship.

One type of relational schema provides mental representations of relationship prototypes by stipulating the ideal criterial attributes that characterize intimacy (Waring, Tillman, Frelick, Russell, & Weisz, 1980) and various types of relationships (Wilmot, 1995). Relationship prototypes are summarized by ordinary language labels associated with different kinds of relationships, such as friend, best friend, acquaintance, lover, casual dating partner, and so on (e.g., Knapp, Ellis, & Williams, 1980). Each relationship prototype consists of expectations regarding the essential qualities that define a relationship type, as well as the behaviors that are obligated or prohibited within that relationship type (Gudykunst & Nishida, 1987; Hecht, 1984; Hornstein, 1985). For example, friendship might include expectations that friends (a) repay debts and favors, (b) trust and confide in one another, (c) respect each other's privacy, and (d) do not express romantic or sexual interest (e.g., Argyle & Henderson, 1984). One infers the type of relationship shared with another by observing the presence of the pertinent features during interactions with the other. For example, if the observed features tend to characterize the prototype for casual friendship, then that is the relationship type inferred. Observations of how relational partners behave toward one another during interaction evidences the type of relationship shared.

In addition to schemas about types of relationships, people possess schemas that depict the processes by which relationships progress and evolve (Baxter, 1987; Wilmot & Baxter, 1983). These process schemas consist of knowledge structures that indicate such things as (a) the rate at which relationships escalate and intensify, (b) the behaviors that typify different developmental stages of relationships, (c) the behaviors that are necessary to achieve a relationship stage or function, and (d) the sequential and contingent patterning of behaviors characterizing relationship development (and decline) (e.g., Battaglia, Richard, Datteri, & Lord, 1998; Baxter, 1987; Honeycutt, 1993; Honeycutt, Cantrill, & Greene, 1989; Honeycutt, Cantrill, Kelly, & Lambkin, 1998).

There are several potential sources of mismatch in two partners' definitions for a shared relationship. First, relationship prototypes exhibit fuzzy, overlapping boundaries. Although each relationship type may contain some unique distinguishing features, common features may characterize different relationship types (Wilmot, 1995). For example, trust and openness may be expected features of friendship, but they usually attend romantic relationships as well. Sexual intimacy is often characteristic of romance, but some individuals incorporate this feature into non-romantic friendships (e.g., Afifi & Faulkner, 2000). If different relationship types possess similar characteristics, then the presence of those characteristics may be interpreted by one partner (e.g., friendship) differently than the other partner (e.g., romance).

Second, although they are likely to overlap, any two individuals' schemas for a particular relationship type are not likely to be isomorphic. One person may, for instance, believe that companionate love is an essential characteristic of close friendship; another may not see love per se as particularly relevant to the definition of close friendship. Moreover, the meanings attached to the criteria for defining a relationship type vary considerably. To one person the attribute of love may mean showing respect, but another person may instantiate love as being available in times of need. One person may view trust as keeping confidences whereas the partner may see trust as keeping the relationship exclusive. In short, what counts as satisfying the criterial attributes characterizing relationship prototypes varies from person to person. Similarly, people's conceptions regarding how relationships normally progress are somewhat idiosyncratic, even though they derive from cultural schemas and scripts. Each individual's lived and vicarious relationship experiences—the source of relational schemas—will differ more or less. It is these differences in relationship definition that lie at the heart of relationship breakdowns (Morton, Alexander, & Altman, 1976) and often underlie the dissolution of relationships (e.g., Argyle & Henderson, 1984; Baxter, 1986).

Although partners share their episodes of interaction, the ultimate sense-making that determines a relationship definition occurs within the individual. Partner mismatch on relational goals, the ambiguous nature of relationship labels (Knapp et al., 1980), the fuzzy definitional boundaries of relationship prototypes, individual variations in the criterial attributes that are assigned to relationship prototypes, idiosyncratic expectations regarding how relationships should progress over time, and the indirect manner in which relationship definitions are communicated, all contribute to the potential for slippage between two person's conceptions of their "shared" relationship. When such slippery conceptions are caught within the matrix of a context that promotes potentially discrepant relational motives and criteria, such as courtship, problems of relationship definition increase. In the sections that follow, we attempt to illustrate that the processes of relationship initiation and dissolution also entail ambiguities that challenge the coordination of relationship mutuality.

THE TOPOGRAPHY OF RELATIONSHIP INITIATION AND ESCALATION

When initiating a relationship, one must convey interest in the potential partner, and convince the partner that one is worthy of reciprocation (Baxter & Philpott, 1982). To accomplish these interrelated goals, Baxter and Philpott (1982) identified five relationship initiation strategies. Other enhancement (i.e., giving compliments) and inclusion (i.e., bringing the other into one's interaction proximity) demonstrate one's interest in initiating a relationship, whereas displays of similarity and presentations of one's unique and favorable image evidence one's worthiness as a relational partner. Rendering favors and rewards to the object of interest show both "that one is interested and that one is appealing" (Baxter, 1987, p. 204).

One way in which people endeavor to create relationships of various types with one another is by seeking affinity, which is the "social-communicative process by which individuals attempt to get others to like and to feel positive toward them" (Bell & Daly, 1984, p. 91; Daly & Kreiser, 1994). Bell and Daly (1984) developed a typology of 25 distinct affinity-seeking strategies. Some strategies involve the affinity-seeker actively presenting a positive self-image, such as appearing trustworthy, enthusiastic, sensitive, interesting, attractive, and attentive. Other techniques are geared toward involving the target in interaction, such as eliciting the target's self-disclosure. Another set of strategies is designed to influence the level of intimacy in interaction. This would include such moves as signaling interest through nonverbal immediacy, disclosing personal information, and engaging in behaviors that lead the target to perceive the relationship as closer than it has actually been (Bell & Daly, 1984). Some affinity seeking simply works to create opportunities for interaction between the affinity-seeker and the target. This involves activities such as manipulating the environment to engineer frequent contact with the target and altruistically attempting to assist the target whenever possible.

Clark, Shaver, and Abrahams (1999) investigated the techniques individuals use to initiate romantic relationships, and Tolhuizen (1989) studied people's strategies for intensifying a dating relationship from casual to serious. Both studies identified strategies consistent with Bell and Daly's (1984) affinity-seeking techniques. In addition to direct verbal relational bids, individuals escalated relationships by increasing contact with the partner, escalating verbal and nonverbal expressions of affection for the target, self-disclosing to the target, and enlisting the aid of social network members. Honeycutt et al. (1998) similarly found that ingratiation, explanation, and direct requests were the most common means reported for escalating intimacy in a romantic relationship.

A number of studies document the subtle, microscopic behaviors that characterize episodes of flirtation (e.g., Grammar, 1990; McCormick & Jones, 1989). Observing women in a variety of natural settings, Moore (1985, 1995) catalogued 52 different nonverbal "solicitation cues" including facial and head patterns (e.g., head toss, hair flip, neck presentation), gestures (e.g., gesticulation, primp, object caress), and posture patterns (e.g., lean, parade, knee touch). Moore (1985, p. 238) argued that "these nonverbal displays are courtship signals; they serve as attractants and elicit the approach of males and ensure the continued attraction of males." Her claim is supported by the observed context and consequence of the behavioral displays. Specifically, Moore (1985, 1995) observed that women exhibited a higher frequency of solicitation behaviors in "mate relevant" contexts (e.g., a bar versus a library), and men approached women who displayed cues more often, regardless of context. Moreover, Moore and Butler (1989) demonstrated that the frequency of women's solicitation cues overrode their physical attractiveness in predicting approaches by men.

Muehlenhard and colleagues (Muehlenhard, Koralewski, Andrews, & Burdick, 1986) also identified a number of behaviors women might employ to indicate to men an interest in dating. The nonverbal cues conveying interest, such as eye contact, touching, smiling, and leaning forward, were similar to those observed by Moore (1985) and others. Muehlenhard et al. identified verbal cues for displaying interest that included such things as making efforts to sustain the conversation, asking the man questions, and complimenting the man. These cues are consistent with the strategies identified by Baxter and Philpott (1982) and Bell and Daly (1984).

In addition to seeking affinity and conveying interest, people are motivated to reduce uncertainty about liked others (Berger, 1987). Strategies for gathering information fall into three general categories: passive, active, and interactive (Berger, 1979; Berger & Bradac, 1982). Passive strategies involve unobtrusively observing the target (e.g., Berger & Douglas, 1981; Berger & Perkins, 1978), whereas active strategies refer to manipulating the environment to see how the target responds, as well as acquiring information about the target through third parties (e.g., Hewes, Graham, Doelger, & Pavitt, 1985). Interactive techniques for acquiring information include asking the target questions, self-disclosing to the target in hopes of reciprocation, and relaxing the target (e.g., Berger & Kellermann, 1983).

Attempts to reduce uncertainty extend beyond obtaining information about a target person per se. Individuals also employ strategies to reduce uncertainty about their relationship (e.g., Knobloch & Solomon, 1999, 2002). In initial interactions, affinity-seekers attempt to discern whether or not their liking of the other is reciprocated. Douglas (1987) identified various strategies designed to test another's affinity, including behaviors that served to sustain interaction, increase immediacy, and create conditions favorable to being approached by the other. Beyond initial interaction, in more developed relationships, individuals perform "secret tests" to gauge the state of the relationship (Baxter & Wilmot, 1984; Bell & Buerkel-Rothfuss, 1990). Such tests include asking social network members what they think, testing the partner's interest in other relationship partners, testing the limits of the relationship, hinting or joking about the nature of the relationship, separating from the partner, and spying on the partner.

Several observations regarding affinity seeking, information seeking and affinity testing strategies are noteworthy. First, many of the behaviors that seek affinity simultaneously can work to reduce uncertainty. Dindia and Timmerman (2003, p. 701) remarked, for example, "An individual can joke or hint about a more serious relationship or flirt and see how the partner responds as a means to test how the partner feels about the relationship and to escalate the relationship. Similarly, increasing verbal and nonverbal intimacy behaviors (e.g., touch, self-disclosure) and then observing the partner's reaction is used as a strategy to escalate a relationship and to assess the state of the relationship."

Second, affinity testing techniques are largely indirect (Baxter & Wilmot, 1985; Douglas, 1987). One does not normally ask a casual conversational partner, "Do you like me?" Similarly, flirtation behavior is intentionally ambiguous (Sabini & Silver, 1982). This "provides participants with several advantages, including (a) infusing sexuality into interaction without violating norms against explicit sex talk among relative strangers, (b) the option of deniability of intent, and (c) safe 'testing' of receivers' intentions" (Metts & Spitzberg, 1996, p. 54).

Although indirect communication is less risky in terms of experiencing embarrassment and spoiled self-image, it is also less reliable. Individuals may bias their processing of relational information such that ambiguous cues are interpreted in a favorable way, and negative cues are ignored or discounted. As Bell and Buerkel-Rothfuss (1990) suggested, individuals may employ secret tests "that their partners cannot fail" (p. 79). Individuals who rely on ambiguous cues to confirm their relationship expectations may be particularly susceptible to overestimating the degree of mutuality in their relationship intentions. The ambiguity inherent in flirtation episodes contributes to miscommunication and misperception (Abbey, 1987; for reviews, see Cupach & Metts, 1991; Metts & Spitzberg, 1996). These misperceptions are exacerbated by the fact that compared to women, men tend to overattribute sexual interest and seductive connotations to women's friendly behavior (Abbey, 1982, 1991; Abbey & Melby, 1986; Saal, Johnson, & Weber, 1989; Shotland & Craig, 1988).

As we describe in the next chapter, many of the behaviors that attempt to seek affinity and reduce uncertainty in normal interactions are mirrored in circumstances that involve ORI and stalking. Relationship pursuit inherently involves activities that function to establish and sustain contact with the partner, increase immediacy and intimacy, and reduce relational uncertainty.

THE FUZZY BOUNDARIES OF PERSISTENCE

The point at which relationship pursuit becomes excessively persistent is not always clear, for a number of reasons. First, some degree of persistence in relationship pursuit is expected and seen as normal by both pursuers and pursued. "One tenet of courtly love is that the value of the love depends upon how difficult it is to achieve it" (Lee, 1998, p. 392). "The stereotype of the ardent pursuer eventually winning over the object given sufficient effort is a familiar one, reinforced by the occasional experience of persistence paying off, as well as fictional portrayals in popular media" (Spitzberg & Cupach, 2001a, p. 122). Second, some of a pursuer's degree of persistence is masked from the pursued, at least for a time, as some of the pursuer's information gathering and surveillance activity is covert. The pursued individual can be unaware of the full extent of the pursuer's efforts. Third, the threshold for perceiving persistence as undue and inappropriate varies not only from person to person, but also from relationship to relationship, and culture to culture. That is, a pursued individual probably exhibits more or less tolerance for persistence in different relationships and with different pursuers. Finally, the full meaning of relationship pursuit behaviors requires an appreciation of the cumulative impact of affinity seeking activity (e.g., see Babcock, 2000, p. 2; Melton, 1994, p. 156).

> The core activities of "pre-stalking," activities such as writing, calling, following, visiting, and gathering information about the other, also mark familiar, everyday courtship and uncoupling practices. Those who become the focus of such attention may initially frame these activities as romantic pursuit or friendship-building, only later reinterpreting them as stalking. (Emerson et al., 1998, p. 292)

Thus, "it is the cumulative impact of a series of incidents, which may be totally harmless when considered individually, that is at the heart of the nature of the harm in stalking cases" (Finch, 2001, p. 40).

Given all the potential ambiguities of relationship escalation, especially romantic relationship escalation, the partner pursued may well be inclined to rationalize or normatively reinterpret pursuers' actions in ways that disregard inappropriate attempts to escalate the relationship. As Dunn (1999, p. 455) argues, "symbols of love and romance such as cards, gifts, and flowers are powerful, emotion-laden images that cloud women's sense of invasion by triggering ambivalence and confusion and thus masking the intrusive, instrumental character of interaction that follows the expressed desire that such interaction cease." Thus, the cultural script for courtship fosters the framing of persistent pursuit as normative.

Stalking represents the extreme boundary of pursuit persistence that easily qualifies as excessive. Less extreme forms of ORI often appear on the surface to be normal and regulated attempts at relationship building. Indeed, the obsessive nature of persistent pursuit can emerge subtly and incrementally as ordinary bids for intimacy gradually appear more desperate and unregulated. The exact point of passage from normal to excessive persistence is often gray and indefinite.

Nevertheless, relationships marked by ORI appear as caricatures of normal relationships. We illustrate the similarities and differences between a normal relationship and an obsessive one in Table 2.1 (see Spitzberg & Cupach, 2002a). We identified some of the common dimensions of intimacy in the relationships literature (Floyd, 1998; Roscoe, Kennedy, & Pope, 1987; Waring et al., 1980), and used these to construct prototypical relationship profiles for each type of relationship (i.e., normal relationships vs. relationships marked by ORI). In normal relationship pursuit, for example, self-disclosure is cautious, incremental, more positive than negative, and commensurate with the intimacy level of disclosure reciprocated by the partner. Expressions of affection and attempts to escalate closeness occur in progressive but measured increments, and relationship commitment is mutually negotiated. In relationships characterized by ORI, self-disclosure and expressions of affection tend to be premature, excessive, and inconsistent with the level of intimacy achieved in the relationship. Closeness is accomplished through possessiveness and imposition; relationship commitment is demanded and sought prematurely. In short, compared to "normal" relationships, "ORI relationships are characterized by forms of intimacy that are distorted, exaggerated, accelerated, more intense, and more desperate" (Spitzberg & Cupach, 2002a, p. 206).

THE NATURE OF RELATIONSHIP DISSOLUTION

Conventional wisdom might suggest, "It takes two to make a relationship, but only one to break it." The occurrence of ORI and stalking, however, suggests that relationship disengagement is a negotiated accomplishment (Cupach & Spitzberg, 1998; Emerson et al., 1998; Spitzberg & Cupach, 2002a). One person usually wants to dissolve the relationship more than the other; hence dissolution is most commonly initiated unilaterally (e.g., Hill, Rubin, & Peplau, 1976; Sprecher, Felmlee, Metts, Fehr, & Vanni, 1998). In the end, however, the rejected partner must acquiesce, even if reluctantly so, in order for termination to be successfully achieved.

Relationship dissolution represents one of the most distressing and identity-threatening events people experience (e.g., Frazier & Cook, 1993; Simpson, 1987; Sprecher et al., 1998; Stephen, 1984; Vaughan, 1986; Weber, 1998). Although both the disengager and the rejected partner experience distress, it is particularly acute for the rejected partner, perhaps because the disengager has had some time to contemplate the termination and has a head start on reconfiguring a personal identity that does not include the partner (Vaughan, 1986). The disengager may experience a combination of guilt and relief when ending an unwanted relationship, whereas the rejected partner is likely to experience sadness, anger, and anxiety (e.g., Hill

TABLE 2.1

Comparison of Prototypical "Normal" and Obsessive Relational Intrusion (ORI) Relationships Along Dimensions of Intimacy

Intimacy Dimension	"Normal" Relations Prototype	ORI Relations Prototype
Self-disclosure	Disclose cautiously/progressively; significantly higher ratio of positive to negative disclosures.	A spillway of relatively unregulated disclosure.
Emotional expression	Steady progression of sharing of personal feelings and direct expression of affection.	Attempts to elicit disclosures from O re: feelings toward P through P's own incessant disclosures of feelings for O.
Closeness	Seek progressive but punctuated increase in time together and "familiarity" with other.	Hyperactive possessiveness and immediate sense of total familiarity illustrated through privacy invasions.
Liking/loving	Displays of affection, caring, empathy, but consistent with stage of progression for the relationship.	Showering of O with gifts, tokens, notes, calls, etc., generally all oriented to expressing affection for O.
Commitment	Measured negotiation of acceptable or desired level of relational exclusivity.	Instantaneous and frequent insistence on relational exclusivity and fidelity.
Trust and loyalty	Slow but steady progression of faith that partners will "be there" for each other, through "thick and thin."	Intense ambivalence of P due to O's avoidance/rejection, leading to P's frequent conflicts with O regarding O's faithfulness.
Interests and activities	Individual interests are shared and nurtured to develop common spheres of mutual interest.	P "takes up" O's interests as a way "into" O's life, and to fabricate coincidental meetings.
Compatibility	Gradual interpenetration of activities and negotiation of mutually consistent values and/or agreements to disagree.	Frequent assertions of how "fate" made P and O "perfect" for each other.
Physical interaction	Escalation of frequency, comfort, intimacy, sexuality, and publicness of bodily contact.	P expresses desire for physical contact O denies to P; P provides graphic descriptions of past or imagined physical trysts.

(*continued on next page*)

TABLE 2.1 (*continued*)

Intimacy Dimension	"Normal" Relations Prototype	ORI Relations Prototype
Interaction comfort	Development of conversational rapport, interaction rituals, and behavioral synchrony.	Ongoing "strain" of P attempting to develop rapport, made difficult by O's avoidance and/or rejection.
Autonomy	Each person brings out the "best" in the other, and helps other fulfill individual objectives unrelated to the relationship.	P feels complete only if O joins P; P behaves unilaterally or coercively to fulfill own autonomy and self.
Lack of conflict	Conflict is generally limited in intensity and frequency, and when it does occur, it serves to advance the relationship.	Conflict is unpleasant, but P views it as a necessary evil to make O realize P's correctness.

Note. From Spitzberg and Cupach (2002a).
P = pursuer, O = object of pursuit.

et al., 1976; Sprecher, 1994). Distress over losing a desired relationship motivates some rejected partners to attempt to repair the relationship and to reconcile with the disengager. Moreover, rejecting partners can experience ambivalence in their desire to terminate the relationship, and it is not uncommon for the rejecting and rejected parties to reverse roles during the course of a protracted disengagement (Vaughan, 1986). The breakups of more serious relationships often involve multiple, intermittent attempts at relationship repair before the termination is finalized (Battaglia et al., 1998; Baxter, 1985; Cupach & Metts, 1986).

Even after relationship termination is seemingly finalized, it is not uncommon for a rejected partner to attempt reconciliation with the disengaging partner, and such efforts can be quite aggressive (e.g., Clark & Labeff, 1986; Dunn, 1999; Jason, Reichler, Easton, Neal, & Wilson, 1984). Attempts to recover a terminated relationship should not be surprising given that rejected partners value the lost relationship, and reconciliation attempts sometimes meet with success.

Jason et al. (1984) reported one of the earliest investigations of post-breakup harassment. In a survey of 48 undergraduate women, the researchers found that 56% of respondents said a former partner had harassed them "for at least a month after indicating a desire not to date" (p. 265). In a separate purposive sample of 50 women who were harassed for at least 1 month after breaking off a relationship, Jason et al. (1994) discovered that harassment continued on average for 13 months, and ranged from 1 month to 10 years. The harassing behaviors that women experienced included phone calls (92%), visits at home or work (48%), verbal or physical threats or assaults (30%), being followed or watched (26%), and being sent flowers, letters, or notes (6%).

More recent studies confirm both the range of behaviors rejected partners employ in an effort to reconcile, and the degree of effort they exert. Davis, Ace, and Andra (2000), for example, reported two studies on self-reported courtship persistence following the breakup of a romantic relationship. Their composite measure of relationship pursuit included behaviors ranging from mild harassment (such as "Wrote, called or e-mailed after s/he told me not to" and "Made a point of talking with friends or co-workers") to threats and vandalism. In Study 1 they found that 61.5% of their respondents did not engage in post-breakup harassment. However, 30.1% engaged in 1 to 5 harassing behaviors and 10.7% engaged in 6 to 23 harassing behaviors. In Study 2, 55.4% of respondents did not harass, whereas 36.4% reported engaging in 1 to 5 harassing acts and 7.6% engaged in 6 to 33 harassing behaviors. Across the two studies, 1.9% and 4.6% of respondents admitted to engaging in high levels of threat and vandalism, respectively.

Langhinrichsen-Rohling, Palarea, Cohen, and Rohling (2000) also studied disengagers and rejected partners who had experienced the termination of an important intimate relationship. The authors assessed the post-breakup occurrence of a wide range of unwanted pursuit behaviors. Mild acts included unwanted phone messages, gifts, visits, and family contact. Severe behaviors included threats, property damage, and injury. Nearly all rejected partners (99.2%) admitted to engaging in at least one unwanted pursuit behavior. The most frequently reported activities were unwanted phone calls (77.5%) and unsolicited in-person conversations (73.3%). Five percent "reported perpetrating at least one unwanted pursuit act that included following, threatening, and/or injuring their ex-partner and/or ex-partner's friends, pets, or family members" (pp. 80–81). Among disengagers, 88.9% reported that their former partner engaged in at least one unwanted pursuit behavior. The most common behaviors "were having your ex-partner show up at places unexpectedly (39.6%), receiving an unwanted phone call (36.3%) and having an ex-partner ask friends about you (56.3%)" (p. 81).

Inevitably some couples reconcile their relationship after its apparent demise. In their study of terminated romantic relationships, for example, Langhinrichsen-Rohling et al. (2000) found more than 40% of their "sample had broken up at least once previous to the breakup they were describing" (p. 77). Similarly, Cupach and Metts (2002) reported that among their respondents who sought to reconcile a terminated relationship, 39% indicated they and their former partner had broken up and reconciled at least once prior to the most recent breakup. Some couples display a pattern of repeatedly breaking up and getting back together. In her study of stalking victims, Dunn (2002) discovered that 30% "had left their partners repeatedly prior to prosecution for stalking, and 7.6 percent of victims resumed a relationship with the defendant during prosecution—leading to the dismissal of charges for 'insufficient evidence'" (p. 77). In our own primary and secondary data gathering we have seen anecdotal evidence of individuals occasionally marrying partners who previously stalked them.

When former partners share a history of breaking up and getting back together again, the rejected partner is more likely to persist in seeking reconciliation. Prior reconciliations reinforce the perceived chance of success in the current reconciliation attempt. Given a history of second chances, relational rejection is seen as temporary and the short-term face loss that the rejected party experiences is outweighed by the perceived face support he or she anticipates obtaining when the partner is finally persuaded to reconcile. Consistent with this interpretation, Davis and colleagues (2000) found the number of prior breakups pursuers reported with a particular partner was associated with greater frequency of harassing-like behaviors following the most recent breakup. In a similar study, Cupach and Metts (2002) found the frequency of prior reconciliations reported by rejecting partners was positively associated with the frequency of the rejected partner's reconciliation attempts and the perceived degree of reconciliation persistence.

Individuals often rely on indirect techniques to accomplish relationship dissolution, particularly for relatively casual relationships (Baxter, 1982, 1985). Reducing contact, diminishing the breadth and depth of self-disclosure, and being unresponsive to a partner can be enacted to communicate loss of interest in a partner. These methods of "distance cueing" (Baxter, 1985) permit the disengager to avoid confrontation with the rejected partner, and thereby accomplish termination with a minimum of effort. Of course, indirectness can be ineffective insofar as the rejected party fails to take the hint. If the relationship holds importance for the rejected person, that person might continue to pursue the relationship until a more explicit declaration of dissolution by the disengager is forthcoming. At a minimum, the rejected party may call for an accounting of the reasons for termination.

As a relationship achieves a greater degree of closeness, the disengager is less likely to employ indirect disengagement strategies, and more likely to display directness and other-orientation when breaking up (Banks, Altendorf, Greene, & Cody, 1987; Baxter, 1982; Cody, 1982). There are several reasons for this. First, greater closeness magnifies the degree of face loss that the breakup creates for the rejected partner. Consequently, the disengager incurs greater obligation to redress the rejected partner's face loss (Baxter, 1985, 1987; Metts, 1992, 2000). At a minimum, the disengager "owes" the rejected party a face-to-face declaration of the desire to disengage (Baxter, 1985). Second, disengagers realize that termination is hurtful to the rejected partner who is emotionally invested in the relationship. The guilt rejectors experience (Bratslavsky et al., 1998; Baumeister et al., 1993; Dunn, 1999, 2002) may motivate more sensitive disengagement. Third, rejectors want to avoid the risk of being branded by social network members as heartless, cruel, and insensitive. Fourth, failing to provide an accounting for the termination adds insult to injury of the rejected partner—thereby inviting possible retaliation against the rejector. Former partners usually know secrets about one another that could be broadcast to get revenge. Thus it is in the rejector's interest to part on amicable terms, if possible. Fifth, rejectors sometimes wish to redefine a relationship rather than completely terminate it—such as when romantic partners scale back to a friendship (e.g., Lannutti & Cameron, 2002; Metts, Cupach, & Bejlovec, 1989; Schneider & Kenny, 2000), or when divorced partners continue to relate as co-parents (Metts & Cupach, 1995). Finally, as Baxter (1987, p. 207), noted, "directness may be employed in close relationships simply because the web of interdependence is so complex that indirectness is inadequate to the dissolution task (e.g., determining who gets which household goods)."

Disengagers can be maximally polite and sensitive when they are apologetic, provide a face-saving account for the failure of the relationship, and show regard for the rejected partner's esteem. However, such positively toned messages also entail the risk of being inefficient or ineffective in accomplishing disengagement. The rejected partner could incorrectly interpret the politeness as a sign of hope that the romantic relationship could be restored at some point. Those who are inclined to cling to a doomed relationship may be particularly susceptible to such rationalizing (Spitzberg & Cupach, 2001a, 2002a). Thus, direct but only moderately polite disengagement strategies may be more effective in terminating close relationships, in the sense of discouraging reconciliation attempts by the rejected partner (Cupach & Metts, 2002). Such disengagement involves bilateral discussion in which both partners have the opportunity to assign blame and/or negotiate the dissolution (Baxter, 1985; Metts, 1992). Unfortunately, no disengagement strategy guarantees successful uncoupling when one person is determined to continue a relationship.

CONCLUSION

Getting into and out of ordinary relationships is as tricky as it is ubiquitous. Relationships are negotiated accomplishments whereby individuals seek to establish mutuality. Mutuality is an ideal state; hence, its achievement is relative rather than absolute. All relationships contain disjunctive elements, yet they can provide immense satisfaction when partners converge on some personally important expectations and meanings. First and foremost, partners must agree that they will relate to one another. Disjunction on this fundamental point represents an inherent relationship crisis, and a miserable situation for each person. And yet even when individuals agree to have "a relationship," they frequently have very different conceptions of how that relationship is to be conceptually and operationally defined. Indeed, the enactment of a relationship is an ongoing, mostly tacit endeavor to cultivate overlapping conceptions. Such enactments are particularly challenging given that each individual's conception is dynamic. When relationship conceptions fail to sufficiently converge, the relationship loses its value and meaning. Ironically, people can disagree on the extent to which they perceive that their conceptions converge. When they have such disagreement, the relationship does not merely possess disjunctive elements, rather, the relationship itself is disjunctive.

We have seen that many of the ordinary behaviors that serve to initiate, escalate, or maintain everyday relationships are exhibited in disjunctive relationships by obsessive relationship pursuers and stalkers. This does not merely reflect similarity in the surface features of ordinary and obsessive relationships. Rather, the subtle complexities entailed in creating and modifying relationships create the opportunities for ORI and stalking. As becomes evident in the next chapter, it turns out most stalkers know their victims and, paradoxically, the most common motive for stalking is the pursuit of a friendly or romantic relationship.

CHAPTER THREE

The Topography
of Unwanted Pursuit

The research on stalking and unwanted pursuit is still in its infancy. Psychiatrists described cases of delusional lovesickness as early as the 1920s (de Clérambault, 1942; Goldstein, 1987; Leong, 1993). Starting in the 1940s, and continuing in the 1960s and 1980s, a few studies reported on cases of psychotic individuals visiting the White House, often with great persistence and in the face of frequent prior rejection (Hoffman, 1943; Sebastiani & Foy, 1965; Shore et al., 1985, 1989). Research in the early 1990s examined threats made on public officials (Dietz, Mathews, Martell, Stewart, Hrouda, & Warren, 1991) and celebrities (Dietz, Mathews, Van Duyne, Martell, Parry, Stewart, Warren, & Crowder, 1991). By the late 1970s, research on sexual harassment began exploring patterns of behavior that would later be interpretable as stalking and obsessive relational intrusion (e.g., Herold, Mantle, & Zemitis, 1979). However, research explicitly investigating the phenomenon of stalking did not begin until the mid-1990s.

In the span of less than a decade, over 100 studies have been conducted in which statistics on stalking or obsessive relational intrusion have been reported by victims or about perpetrators (Spitzberg, 2002b). Several other studies have examined people's reactions to scenarios of stalking to explore normative views of legislation or the prototypical nature of stalking (e.g., Dennison & Thomson, 2000a, 2000b; Dussuyer, 2000; Farrell et al., 2000; Hills & Taplin, 1998; Lee, 1998; Pearce & Easteal, 1999; Sheridan & Davies, 2001c; Sheridan et al., 2003). During this rapid escalation of research, different investigators and research teams, clinics, and jurisdictions have attempted to map the terrain of stalking. Unfortunately, due to the infancy of research, different researchers employ different assessments and criteria, and pursue different questions. The result is a veritable Babel of findings and claims, only occasionally comparable across studies. This problem is far from unique to stalking—most social scientific research domains can claim similar problems. It is particularly notable in the case of stalking because there is an opportunity in the early stages of this research to develop some agreed-on common distinctions and understandings that can significantly enhance the cumulative potential of future research.

Currently, it is difficult to see the forest for the trees in the research on stalking. Few scholars pursue similar research agendas, and even fewer employ comparable measures. Only three measures of stalking tactics appear to have been used with any consistency across studies. Coleman's (1997) Stalking Behavior Checklist (SBC) has been employed in several studies (e.g., Del Ben, 2000; Del Ben & Fremouw, 2002; Logan, Leukefeld, & Walker, 2000; Mechanic, Uhlmansiek, Weaver, & Resick, 2000; Mechanic, Weaver, & Resick, 2000; Melton, 2001), presumably because it was one of the first published in a journal recognized by criminal justice and psychology disciplines. A second stalking victimization survey (SVS) is a hybrid of Tjaden and Thoennes's (1998b) stalking tactic list and a measure of harassing behaviors developed by Sheridan (in her unpublished dissertation research) (e.g., Gist et al., 2001; Lemmey, 1999; McFarlane, Campbell, & Watson, 2002; McFarlane, Willson, Lemmey, & Malecha, 2000; McFarlane, Willson, Malecha, & Lemmey, 2000; Willson et al., 2000). Finally, we have used both long- and short-version measures of obsessive relational intrusion tactics, cyberintrusion tactics, coping tactics, and symptoms (Cupach & Spitzberg, 2000; Dutton-Greene & Winstead, 2001; Montero, 2003; Spitzberg, 2000a; Spitzberg & Cupach, 1999, 2001b; Spitzberg & Hoobler, 2002; Spitzberg, Marshall, & Cupach, 2001; Spitzberg et al., 1998; Spitzberg & Rhea, 1999).

Although the SBC and SVS are straightforward lists of behavioral items, we have evolved a different tact with "cluster items" (see Appendix 1). Under the assumption that there is no reasonable hope of producing a comprehensive list of potential stalking behaviors, we instead decided to employ behavioral prototypes in the item lists. For example, a traditional measure would list an item such as "left threatening messages on the phone." Our item, in contrast, reads:

Has anyone ever undesirably & obsessively pursued you by ...

15. LEAVING UNWANTED THREATENING MESSAGES (e.g., hang-up calls, notes, cards, letters, voice-mail, e-mail, messages with friends, implying harm or potential harm, etc.)

Such items permit greater breadth of coverage with relatively little loss of the diagnostic behavioral profile of the pursuit and coping.

Despite some consistency of measurement within and across research teams, there is still considerable inconsistency across the entire domain of stalking and unwanted pursuit research. Although there are many examples that could illustrate the problem, one relatively simple one should suffice. Persistent harassment and intrusion through the telephone are often considered prototypical of victimization. On the face of it, this might seem a relatively simple experience to reference through survey or interview. Thus, there should be a way to summarize across studies approximately what percentage of stalking victims were harassed through the telephone as a medium of pursuit. To do so, however, requires smoothing over potentially important distinctions, as illustrated by the following items culled from a selection of studies that have provided estimates of the percentage of victims experiencing calls from stalkers or unwanted pursuers:

- Telephone calls (86%; Blaauw, Winkel, Arensman, Sheridan, & Freeve, 2002).
- Unsolicited phone calls (61%; Davis, Coker, & Sanderson, 2002; Tjaden & Thoennes's 1998 NVAW data).
- Telephoned (15%; Dussuyer, 2000).
- Phone calls/letters (11.5%; Gill & Brockman, 1996).
- Threatening/harassing phone call (12%; Hackett, 2000).
- Threatening phone calls/letters/gifts (49%; Harris, 2000).
- Silent phone calls (13%; Harris, 2000).
- Obscene phone calls (3%; Harris, 2000).
- Phone calls (89%; Kamphuis & Emmelkamp, 2001).
- Threatening or harassing phone calls (10%; Kong, 1996).
- Phone message (25%; Langhinrichsen-Rohling et al., 2000).
- Repeated phone calls (71%; LeBlanc, Levesque, & Berka, 2001).
- Unwanted phone calls (45%; McFarlane et al., 1999).
- Threatening messages on phone (22%; McFarlane et al., 1999).
- Telephoned/sent mail (1.5%; McLennon, 1995/1996).
- Phone calls at home (66%; Mechanic, Weaver, & Resick, 2000).
- Phones and/or leaves messages (83%; Meloy & Boyd, 2003).
- Repeated phone/email (67%; Morrison, 2001).
- Letters, telephone calls, or material of a sexual nature (18%; Morgan & Porter, 1999).
- Oral/written threats or telephone calls without physical approach (59%; Sandberg, McNiel, & Binder, 1998).
- Repeated, excessive, unwanted telephone calls (29%; Sheridan, Gillett, & Davies, 2000).
- Hung around/telephoned workplace (7%; Sheridan et al., 2000).

- Excessive unwanted telephone calls regardless of content (25%; Sheridan, Davies, & Boon, 2001b).
- Obscene, threatening, or mysterious phone calls (9.5%; Sheridan, Gillett, & Davies, 2002).
- Calling pager/phone at home/workplace (55%; Suzuki, 1999).
- Harassing phone calls or other verbal harassment (77%; Tucker, 1993).
- Anonymous phone calls (47%; Westrup, Fremouw, Thompson, & Lewis, 1999).
- Calls, amorous (48%; Brewster, 1998, 2000).
- Calls, threatening (67%; Brewster, 1998, 2000).
- Calls, angry (38%; Brewster, 1998, 2000).
- Calls, delusional accusation (13%; Brewster, 1998, 2000).
- Calls, friendly (4%; Brewster, 1998, 2000).
- Calls, apologetic (3%; Brewster, 1998, 2000).
- Calls, hang-ups (32%; Brewster, 1998, 2000).
- Calls, checkup (7%; Brewster, 1998, 2000).

Many of these items are "double-barreled," in the sense that they reference more than one possible response (e.g., calls or e-mail; telephone calls or materials of a sexual nature). Many include features of content or function (e.g., apologetic, checkup, threatening, etc.) and others include multiple types of media (telephone, pager, e-mail, etc.). Many specify psychological or physical features regarding the call (e.g., "unwanted," "persistent," "without physical approach," etc.). So, what summary could be made about how often the telephone is part of the process of unwanted pursuit? Summarizing across such diverse items seems inappropriate on the one hand, given that there are so many subtle and not-so-subtle differences among the items. On the other hand, these items clearly share more in common with one another than they do with items about the use of physical violence, or following behavior, or breaking and entering one's home.

One potential solution is to rely on those studies that are large scale (i.e., over 1,000 respondents) or employ representative sampling methods (e.g., Budd & Mattinson, 2000; Elliott & Brantley, 1997; Fisher, Cullen, & Turner, 2000; Hackett, 2000; Kohn, Flood, Chase, & McMahon, 2000; Kong, 1996; McLennon, 1995/1996, 1996; Purcell, Pathé, & Mullen, 2002; Tjaden & Thoennes, 1998b). Certainly, such studies serve as important benchmarks. However, every such study noted employed different operational definitions from the rest. Several were explicitly studies of specific populations, such as criminal justice or college populations. Others were framed as "crime" or "violence" surveys, and such framing devices have been debatable for their potential biasing impact on responses (Straus, 1999). Any single study exhibits a unique set of choices that limit its internal and external validity (e.g., see in Miller, 2001b, for discussion of Tjaden & Thoennes, 1998b, study). Further, to date, most large-scale studies are unique within their national population—that is, there have been almost no large-scale replications within any given country. Thus, as vital as these studies are, it is important to find other touchstones of integration and generalization within the stalking research.

If research is to become cumulative in the social science of stalking, it is imperative that common vocabularies of scholarship be established. This chapter offers a series of topographic maps of stalking motives and tactics. These typologies are extracted directly from examination of the existing studies with quantifiable estimates of motives and behaviors. These typologies of motive and behavior are examined in light of existing typologies of stalkers. In the process of examining these typologies, a picture of a forest that is dark, deep, and expansive will begin to emerge. The sheer variety and creativity of stalkers will be unveiled, and it will become relatively obvious how victims become lost in such encompassing tangles of interpersonal terrorism.

A DESCRIPTIVE META-ANALYSIS AND INTERPRETIVE CODING OF STALKING RESEARCH

Meta-analysis is a technique for the aggregation of statistical estimates across disparate studies. Study A and study B may have been undertaken by entirely different researchers, employing different conceptualizations, and for very different purposes. But both studies may have asked a question about whether or not the study respondents had ever been stalked. Despite different wording for their questions, responses to both items can be treated as "estimates of stalking." Furthermore, differences between these items can be coded into groups (e.g., "lifetime" vs. "within the past year"), and differences in responses within these groups can be averaged to examine whether such coded features make a difference across studies. The added advantage of such aggregations is that they vastly increase the number of persons or cases examined relative to any single study. Thus, as a way of reviewing the literature, meta-analysis offers a way to achieve more generalizable findings than any individual study because it generalizes estimates across a larger, more diverse set of studies.

At this relatively nascent stage of stalking research, there have not been enough studies investigating the connection of stalking, threat, or violence to other variables to summarize relationships among variables, as meta-analyses often permit. However, it is possible to average descriptive estimates across studies. As the number of studies aggregated increases, and as the number of subjects or cases entailed in such aggregations increase, the resulting estimates are likely to become more and more valid representations of the actual level of occurrence of those phenomena. As the number of studies increases over time, sources of variation within these estimates can be further accounted for by locating features on which such differences depend.

Another approach to reviewing the literature is interpretive reductive coding. In the context of this study, interpretive reductive coding is an attempt to extract the most essential information from lists of items in various studies, reduce them to their verbal elements (e.g., verb–subject clauses), and then identify interpretive themes within those lists that permit a higher order organizational typology. The process is largely inductive, in the sense that themes emerge from large lists of items. As themes emerge, isolated categories (i.e., categories with very few items comprising the category) often reveal subordinate membership with other larger categories. Once higher order categories are identified and labeled, even higher order categories often emerge to further organize the categories. For example, the list of "telephone" tactics given earlier emerged as a category because so many studies listed telephone-related themes. However, once all the tactics were categorized, "telephones" emerged as only one of several themes later categorized under a "Mediated Contacts" theme of stalking behavior.

There are several limitations of such methods. First, they presuppose a relatively comprehensive coverage of the topic in prior assessment approaches. If there are "blind spots" in a paradigm of research (i.e., types of stalking that researchers have not thought to study), then the resulting typology is likely to suffer the same blind spot. Second, interpretive themes are likely to reflect the interpreter's ideological or conceptual biases. A feminist scholar might identify different themes than a traditional clinical psychologist, who in turn might identify different themes than a traditional criminal justice scholar. However, without such reductive coding, there is nothing but trees, and the forest remains elusive because studies are noncomparable and noncumulative. Therefore, in an effort to construct a more useful map of the stalking terrain, this chapter reports several typologies derived from this reductive coding process. We have made similar efforts previously (Spitzberg, 2002b; Spitzberg & Cupach, 2001a, 2003), but the typologies reported in this chapter represent an entirely new process of reductive coding, based on a larger sample of studies.

For the purpose of this chapter, the primary database is a collection of 143 studies, representing 149 separate samples or sample groups, of stalking, criminal harassment, or unwanted relational pursuit, and 7 studies that reanalyzed existing study data sets already represented in the meta-analysis (see Appendix 2). These studies have been collected through a variety of means, including locating all studies of stalking, criminal harassment, and obsessive relational intrusion through *PsycInfo*, *NCJRS* reference list, *Criminal Justice Abstracts*, and *Communication Abstracts*. In addition, all available reviews and studies were examined for reference to additional studies that could be located. Further, data presentations at stalking conferences, as well as sources of published and unpublished data made available through personal contact with stalking researchers, were included. Most of these studies have been the source of previous analysis (Spitzberg, 2002b), but those data have been further refined (i.e., double-checked, new variables coded) and the study sample expanded as new studies have been located.

A few studies reported their results only as separate groups, and these samples were treated separately, but counted as part of a single study. Furthermore, there have been several reanalyses of the NIJ/CDC National Violence Against Women Survey data (Tjaden & Thoennes, 1998b) and one femicide-related database (McFarlane, Campbell, & Watson, 2002). To avoid duplication, these reanalysis studies are listed in Appendix 2 but their data are not part of the analysis. There are some studies that either were not available through standard means despite repeated efforts to obtain further information (e.g., Hargreaves, n.d.) or were simply too abbreviated in their reporting to permit analysis (e.g., DuPont-Morales, 1999; Hargreaves, 2000; NOP, 1997). Finally, studies assessing lay perceptions of stalking scenarios or legislation (e.g., Dennison & Thomson, 2002; Dunn, 1999; Dussuyer, 2000; Farrell, Weisburd, & Wyckoff, 2000; Hills & Taplin, 1998; Pearce & Easteal, 1999; Sheridan & Davies, 2001c; Sheridan et al., 2003) were not included unless they also asked questions about respondents' actual experiences of stalking or unwanted pursuit.

Before summarizing the results of this meta-analysis, several limitations and qualifications need to be considered. First, despite the relatively objective nature of some of the coding involved, there are nevertheless points of subjectivity. For example, although many samples are classified as "clinical," many of these could also be considered "forensic" in the sense that the patients were remanded by law enforcement or the judicial process for clinical evaluation. Domestic violence samples are "victim" samples, but not samples selected because they specifically are "stalking victims." Second, the sample sizes often are deceiving because they reflect all people surveyed, even though only a minority represented stalking victims. Third, some estimates clearly serve as biasing outliers. For example, studies of domestic violence victims will likely inflate estimates of victimization prevalence, and law enforcement samples of persons required to undergo clinical evaluation are likely to inflate estimates of prevalence of perpetration. Some of these biases can be controlled by parceling the data by type of sample. Finally, some of the studies investigated stalkers, some studies investigated stalking victims, and others studied both (from the attributed perspective of whomever was the primary source of information). By its nature, stalking is often designed to maintain a degree of surprise and stealth, and therefore victims are reporting on who they *think* their stalkers were and what they *think* their stalkers were doing. For example, hang-up calls may or may not be the pursuer, but such experiences are likely to be attributed by victims as originated by their pursuer.

Despite these limitations, this data set reflects the most comprehensive and systematic attempt at review of the research on stalking and unwanted pursuit yet available. Mullen et al. (2000a, p. 219) proclaimed that "meta-analysis of a number of existing studies is tempting, but in our view the populations studied, and the methods of data-gathering, are still too disparate to justify combining results in this manner." However, these types of variations in populations and methods can be coded, and data compared across such differences to see if such differences make a difference. Although the data to be reviewed have not been coded in such a way as to delineate all the potential variables of interest, they are available for such coding in the future, and available for a wide variety of analyses at present.

Collectively, the data are comprised of 19 clinical (12.8%), 38 forensic (25.5%), 11 general population (7.4%), 47 college (31.5%), 1 adolescent (0.7%), 11 victim only (7.4%), 9 domestic violence (6.0%), 2 homicide (1.3%), 8 organizational or professional (5.4%), and 3 multiple sample or unclassifiable (2.0%) studies. These types of samples can be collapsed into three macro categories: clinical/forensic (clinical, forensic, domestic violence, homicide), general population (adolescent, victim, organizational or professional, other) and college. With this grouping scheme, there are 69 clinical/forensic (46.3%), 34 general population (22.8%), and 46 college (30.93%) studies.

In terms of the gender of the sample studied directly, 37 (24.8%) studies investigated females only, 6 (4.0%) studied males exclusively, and 104 (69.8%) studied both males and females, with 2 (1.3%) studies classified as indeterminate. Fully 94 percent of the sample ($n = 140$) employed some form of convenience sampling or routine reporting method, with only 9 studies (6.0%) employing some form of random or representative sampling technique. There is a very strong "Anglo" bias in the research, with 104 studies in the United States (69.8%), 14 (9.4%) Australian studies, 11 (7.4%) British studies, 8 (5.4%) Canadian studies, 2 (1.3%) European studies, 2 Asian studies (1.3%), and 8 (5.4%) studies with mixed nationality samples or samples from other cultural areas (e.g., Caribbean). In total,

85,036 persons or cases have been queried, observed, or analyzed in regard to stalking and unwanted pursuit. This is a conservative estimate given that (a) some scenario studies ask no questions about "actual" stalking experiences (and therefore were not included in this data base), and (b) some forensic data bases contain data from years that were not included due to lack of completeness or non-comparability of variables across years. The summary profile of the studies is arrayed in Table 3.1.

THE EXTENT OF STALKING AND UNWANTED PURSUIT

Stalking is not an isolated occurrence experienced by a narrow group of people. Neither, however, is stalking a universal experience. According to Finch (2001, p. 9), "It is probable that no accurate measurement of the prevalence of stalking is possible." This conclusion seems unduly pessimistic. If only large-scale studies (i.e., samples greater than 1,000) are examined, prevalence estimates for the general population tend to range between 10% and 23%. Estimates of prevalence for men range between 2% and 13% for men, and from 8% to 32% for women (see Table 3.2). It is possible the differences among such diverse estimates could be due to differences in operational definition, sample type, country or culture, or other factors not obvious from surface features of the studies or data sets.

For example, at this point, both prevalence and incidence estimates are grouped together. Prevalence tends to refer to the percentage of the sample currently experiencing a phenomenon, whereas incidence is the cumulative percentage of the sample that have experienced a phenomenon over the time frame of the study (e.g., over the past year, or over the respondent's lifetime). However, at this point, there is little basis for ascertaining structural sources of variance among such estimates. For example, Tjaden et al. (2000) found that prevalence estimates vary significantly according to the type of operational definition (e.g., legalistic behavioral definitions vs. victim self-perceived). What other factors might serve to account for differences in estimates across studies requires substantially more research, analogous to the research investigating various methodological factors in the assessment of rape victimization (e.g., Craig, 1990; Gilbert, 1993; Gylys & McNamara, 1996; Koss, 1992a, 1992b, 1993; Muehlenhard, Sympson, Phelps & Higby, 1994; Porter & Critelli, 1992; Ross & Allgeier, 1996). Despite differences in prevalence estimates, there is surprising similarity across studies of the proportion of women versus men who experience stalking victimization. Between 75% and 80% of victims of stalking are women, according to these large-scale studies.

An alternative approach to estimating the prevalence and gender ratios of stalking victimization is to summarize these estimates across all avail-

TABLE 3.1
Summary Profile of Studies of Stalking and Unwanted Pursuit

	Study N	Minimum	Maximum	Mean	SE	SD	Skewness	SE	Kurtosis	SE
Sample size	149*	13.00	16,000.00	570.71	147.12	1795.80	6.19	.20	43.58	.40
Mean duration (months)	26	3.69	85.00	22.22	4.06	20.68	1.64	.46	2.37	.89
Female victim prevalence (%)	36	1.00	92.00	26.29	3.98	23.88	1.69	.39	2.39	.77
Female perpertrator prevalence (%)	8	.00	33.00	8.94	3.73	10.56	2.02	.75	4.69	1.48
Male victim prevalence (%)	16	.00	29.00	10.22	2.21	8.82	.80	.56	-.26	1.09
Male perpetrator prevalence (%)	8	1.00	53.00	14.75	6.35	17.95	1.75	.75	2.60	1.48
Overall victim prevalence (%)	47	.00	100.00	21.91	3.31	22.70	2.23	.35	4.95	.68
Overall perpetrator prevalence (%)	7	3.50	90.00	34.79	10.79	28.54	1.31	.79	1.98	1.59
Female victim proportion stalked (%)	51	13.00	100.00	75.00	2.79	19.95	-1.22	.33	1.04	.66
Male victim proportion stalked (%)	50	.00	87.00	24.72	2.76	19.54	1.32	.34	1.29	.66
Female perpetrator proportion stalker (%)	60	.00	92.00	21.73	2.69	20.82	1.70	.31	2.60	.61
Male perpetrator proportion stalker (%)	59	8.00	100.00	77.25	2.77	21.241	-1.64	.31	2.21	.61
Relationship: general—intimate (%)	54	32.00	100.00	77.32	2.22	16.35	-.84	.33	.52	.64
Relationship: general—stranger (%)	50	.00	68.00	21.39	2.13	15.09	.96	.34	.89	.66

Relationship										
Relationship: specific—miscellaneous (%)	11	2.50	36.00	12.36	3.24	10.74	1.52	.66	1.47	1.28
Relationship: specific—stranger (%)	32	.00	48.00	18.09	2.00	11.34	1.03	.42	1.02	.82
Relationship: specific—neighbor (%)	2	5.00	16.00	10.50	5.50	7.78	.....			
Relationship: specific—colleague (%)	23	1.00	30.00	12.07	1.78	8.53	.60	.48	-.77	.94
Relationship: specific—service-related (%)	11	1.00	100.00	26.36	7.86	26.07	2.54	.66	7.81	1.28
Relationship: specific—acquaintance (%)	35	8.00	64.00	23.34	2.10	12.41	1.46	.40	2.75	.79
Relationship: specific—intimate nonromantic (%)	21	2.00	78.00	15.24	4.04	18.50	2.29	.50	5.94	.97
Relationship: specific—intimate romantic (%)	47	13.00	100.00	48.02	3.35	22.93	.61	.35	-.10	.68

Note. There were six studies that were counted more than once due to split or separate samples, but their data are not duplicative in the remainder of the table.

TABLE 3.2
Summary Profile of Large-Scale (i.e., > 1,000 subjects) Studies

Authors (year)	Type	Sample Country	Size	Overall prevalence[a]	Female prevalence (%)	Male prevalence (%)	Abridged operational definition notes
Budd and Mattinson (2000)	General population	Great Britain	9,988	12%			"Persistent and unwanted attention" since age of 16
Elliott and Brantley (1997)	College	United States	1,752		45%	25%	"Have you ever been stalked or harassed with obscene phone calls?"
Fisher et al. (2000)	College	United States	4,446		13%		"Since school began in the fall ... has anyone ... repeatedly followed you, watched you, phoned, written, e-mailed, or communicated with you in other ways that seemed obsessive and made you afraid or concerned for your safety?"
Hackett (2000)	Police reports	Canada	5,910		(77%)	(23%)	"Criminal harassment:" "following ... repeatedly communicating ... besetting or watching ... engaging in threatening conduct directed at the other person or any member of their family"
Kohn et al. (2000)	General population	United States	1,171		15%		"Have you ever been stalked, harassed, or threatened with violence for more than one month by someone who would not leave you alone?"
Kong (1996)	Police reports	Canada	7,472		(80%)	(20%)	"Criminal harassment:" "following ... repeatedly communicating ... besetting or watching ... engaging in threatening conduct directed at the other person or any member of their family"

Study	Setting	Country	N	Prevalence	Female	Male	Definition
McLennan (1995/1996)	Court reports	Australia	1,397		(59%)	(41%)	Repeated behaviour which includes ... :following ...; contacting ... by telephone or fax; entering or loitering ...; interfering with anyone's property; giving someone offensive material; ... surveillance; ... acting in a way which may make someone scared for their own safety or someone else's safety[b]
McLennan (1996)	General population	Australia	6,300	15%			More than one of the following behaviors: "telephoned/sent mail, watched, followed, loitered outside home or workplace or place of leisure, gave/left offensive material, interfered with/damaged property" more than once in lifetime
Purcell et al. (2002)	General population	Australia	3,700	23%	32% (75%)	13% (25%)	"Any person ... ever: (a) followed ... (b) spied ... (c)loitered ... (d) made unwanted approaches ... (e) made unwanted telephone calls ... (f) sent you unwanted letters, faxes, or e-mails (g) sent you offensive materials (h) ordered things ... (i) interfered with your property"
Tjaden and Thoennes (1998b, 2000a, 2000b)	General population	United States	16,000		8/12%[c] (79%)	2/6% (21%)	"Anyone ... ever ... followed or spied ..., sent you unsolicited letters ..., made unsolicited phone calls ..., stood outside your home, school, or workplace, showed up at places ..., left unwanted items ..., tried to communicate ... against your will ... vandalized your property ..."

Note. Parenthetical percentages in the female and male prevalence columns represent the proportion of the victims who were female and male, respectively.
[a]Percentages are rounded.
[b]Legislative definition abstracted from *No to Violence* website: http://www.ntv.net.au/ntv_eight2.htm (retrieved 6 March 2003).
[c]The lower figures reflect strict legal criteria, and the higher figures reflect self-reported, more liberal criteria.

able studies, large and small. Table 3.1 indicates that across 47 studies, an average of almost 22% ($SD = 22.70$) of people are at risk of stalking victimization. Because many studies included in this estimate are of exclusively female samples, and only a few are exclusively male, this overall estimate may reflect certain sample biases. Indeed, several differences emerge when gender-based estimates of victimization are examined. Female victimization prevalence across 36 studies is about 26% ($SD = 23.88$), and male victimization prevalence across 16 studies is 10.22% ($SD = 8.82$). Fewer studies offer estimates of perpetration prevalence. According to 8 studies of each gender group, almost 9% of females ($SD = 10.56$) and almost 15% of males ($SD = 17.95$) have engaged in stalking behavior.

Some of these estimates are lifetime, and some represent shorter time frames. Further, the large standard deviations suggest that there may be systematic sources of variance within these estimates. One such source would be the type of sample. When the prevalence estimates are divided according to the three broad categories of sample type, none of the prevalence differences reached statistical significance, although the cell sizes are generally too small to provide sufficient power. Female victimization appears higher in clinical/forensic samples ($M = 34.33$, $SD = 40.10$, $n = 6$) than in either general population ($M = 28.50$, $SD = 25.14$, $n = 15$) or college ($M = 21.84$, $SD = 12.28$, $n = 14$) samples, but the difference is not statistically significant. Furthermore, the prevalence of overall stalking victimization appears higher in clinical/forensic samples ($M = 31.17$, $SD = 31.17$, $n = 12$) than in general population ($M = 19.41$, $SD = 18.53$, $n = 18$) and college ($M = 18.71$, $SD = 9.66$, $n = 16$) samples, although the difference was not statistically significant.

Another avenue of exploring the role of gender in stalking victimization is to examine the ratio or proportion of female-to-male victims and perpetrators. Across 51 studies, an average of 75% of victims are female ($SD = 19.95$), and across 59 studies the average proportion of perpetrators who are male is 77% ($SD = 21.24$). In a virtual, and unsurprising, mirror image, about 25% of stalking victims are males ($SD = 19.54$, $n = 50$) and almost 22% of stalking perpetrators are female ($SD = 20.82$, $n = 60$). Again, the large standard deviations suggest the possibility that certain features of these studies might influence the variation. When gender proportions are divided by sample type, two differences did emerge as significant. The proportion of female victimization varied significantly ($F = 5.00$; $df = 2,48$; $p < .011$; $\eta^2 = .17$) across general population ($M = 60.90$, $SD = 29.30$; $n = 10$), clinical/forensic ($M = 80.82$, $SD = 14.28$, $n = 33$), and college ($M = 68.63$, $SD = 17.76$, $n = 8$) samples. Correspondingly, male victimization proportion ($F = 5.14$; $df = 2,47$; $p < .010$; $\eta^2 = .18$) varied across sample type: general population ($M = 38.40$, $SD = 28.83$, $n = 10$), clinical/forensic ($M =$

18.78, SD = 13.52, n = 32), and college (M = 31.38, SD = 17.76, n = 8). In general, the trends suggest that clinical/forensic samples produce estimates in which females are much more likely to be the victim and males much less likely to be victims.

These results are suggestive of at least two interpretations. First, males may be reluctant to present themselves as victims of stalking in the public, formal, male-dominated or "macho" context of law enforcement. Such a victim identity may seem incompatible with self-concept, and men may anticipate their complaints would not be regarded with much seriousness by law enforcement personnel. Second, and not inconsistent, the law enforcement system may in fact not let male victimization cases into the law enforcement system as readily as female victimization cases (DuPont-Morales, 1999). Much has been written about the various barriers to women's access to and respect from the law enforcement and judicial process in cases of intimate violence (e.g., Avakame & Fyfe, 2001; Chaudhuri & Daly, 1992; Fischer & Rose, 1995; Fyfe, Klinger, & Flavin, 1997; Grau, Fagan & Wexler, 1985; Hart, 1996; Rigakos, 1995; Stephens & Sinden, 2000; Zoellner et al., 2000). However, relatively little has been written about male reluctance to use the law enforcement and judicial process, and the reluctance of that same system to be amenable to their situation. These speculations are compounded by a probable tendency of males not to define themselves as victims of stalking as readily as females, despite identical experiences on which such a self-attribution could be made (Tjaden et al., 2000). Despite the differences between samples in the proportion of male and female victimization, it is clear that the sizable majority of victims of stalking are female regardless of type of sample.

The data are relatively consistent across studies that females are more likely to be the victim, and males more likely to be the perpetrator, of stalking and unwanted pursuit. This, however, is far from the entire picture. One of the less understood facets of gender and stalking dynamics is the *dyadic* gender composition. For example, Bjerregaard (2000) found 32% of stalking cases were males pursuing males, and 4% females pursuing females. Boon and Sheridan (2001) found in their British sample that half of their male victims were pursued by males. Pathé, Mullen, and Purcell (1999) found 11% of their cases involved females pursuing females, and 7% males pursuing males (see also Mullen, Pathé, Purcell, & Stuart, 1999; Pathé & Mullen, 1997). One clinical study has thus far focused on same-gender stalking (Pathé et al., 2000), and two have focused on women stalkers (Meloy & Boyd, 2003; Purcell, Pathé, & Mullen, 2001). Collectively these studies are notable for the relative lack of systematic differences based on the gender composition of the stalking relationship. Police statistics of almost 800 cases in Australia showed 86% of male stalkers stalked females, with only 14% of males stalking other males. Women, in contrast, were somewhat more likely to stalk women (57%) than men (43%). "Women stalking women made up 7 per cent of all stalking incidents, while women stalking men comprised 5.3 percent" (Dussuyer, 2000, p. 40).

Of course, forensic and clinical samples may be biased in ways that make male victims, especially male victims of female stalking, less prone to be represented. In their large-scale representative sample, Purcell et al. (2001, p. 2058) found "the rate of same-gender stalking was significantly higher among female stalkers, with 48% ($n = 19$) pursuing other women, whereas 9% ($n = 13$) of the men stalked other men." However, a later analysis by this Australian team (Purcell et al., 2002, p. 117) showed a rate of 24% same-gender stalking, "with males significantly more likely to experience such harassment than females" (76% vs. 8% ...). A large-scale study in the United States by Tjaden and Thoennes (1998b) found 60% of male victims were pursued by males and only 6% of females were pursued by females.

The meaning of these findings is difficult to ascertain, especially given their inconsistency across samples. One possibility is that the proportion of such same-gender stalking incidents reflects same-sex preference relationships. This explanation lacks parsimony unless and until a reasonable gender role explanation can be integrated with sexual preference to account for disparities across same-gender dyads. A second possibility is that many of these same-gender stalking relationships reflect qualitatively distinct motivations. Perhaps males are stalking other males because these peripheral targets of their pursuits are perceived as rivals for their affections for a primary female target of affection. Such cases may be represented in higher proportions among stalking cases arising from neighbors and work-based relationships, in which sexual preference is less relevant to the motivation. Differences may also reflect in some studies the possibility that female–female stalking may be underreported because female pursuers do not appear to evoke fear as prominently as male pursuers (Sinclair & Frieze, 2000) or, conversely, that males tend not to perceive male pursuers as a type of "stalking" (Tjaden et al., 2000). Clearly, more research is needed before such speculations can be disentangled.

One of the more important variables by which stalking relationships are categorized is the type of relationship from which they emerged. Although the type of prior relationship seems imminently important to understanding the dynamics of stalking, it is a deceptively complicated variable to operationalize. For example, across 53 studies in which stalking prevalence was contrasted by prior relationship, there were at least 75 unique relationship labels used to specify type of prior relationship. Obviously, it would be virtually impossible to summarize data across such a proliferation of relationship types. Consequently, these labels were categorized into a more usable typology (see Table 3.3). The more common categories were then employed in the meta-analysis in Table 3.1 to summarize stalking prevalence by relationship type.

In terms of the relational origins of stalking, across 54 studies (see Table 3.1), approximately 77% of victims know their pursuer from some form of previous relationship, and across 50 studies about 21% are complete strangers or unknown pursuers. When the specific types of relationship origins are elaborated, almost half ($M = 48.02\%$, $n = 47$) emerged from a current or previously romantic relationship. As dominant as both the stranger and romantic themes are in the stalking literature, it is important to note that stalking can emerge from a wide variety of relational origins. Previous relationships include neighbors ($M = 10.50\%$, $n = 2$), colleagues, fellow students and coworkers ($M = 12.07\%$, $n = 23$), service-related persons such as car repair workers, counselors, teachers, bank tellers, and such ($M = 26.36\%$, $n = 11$), acquaintances ($M = 23.34\%$, $n = 35$), and nonromantic relationships such as good friends, best friends, family members, and relatives ($M = 15.24\%$, $n = 21$). Clearly these percentages add up to more than 100% because (a) different studies employ different relationship terms in their response options, and (b) some studies only offered a subset of possible response options. Nevertheless, it is clear that (a) the single most common origin of stalking and unwanted pursuit is a romantic relationship, (b) there are various other relational origins to stalking that have yet to be studied very extensively, and (c) about a fifth of all stalking is perpetrated by complete strangers.

Finally, the question arises whether or not stalking is increasing in prevalence among the population. Even with periodic sources of systematic data collection, such questions are always problematic. Increases in prevalence can be attributed to actual increases or to increased awareness of and sensitivity to the crime. However, there are no systematic sources of data collection on stalking that report it in comparable ways over time. Consequently, the question of whether or not stalking is increasing in society is difficult to answer. There are, however, two indirect sources of information pertinent to this question that to date have been overlooked in the stalking literature. For most years of the 1990s to 2002, Gallagher and colleagues (Gallagher, 1997; Gallagher, Bruner, & Lingenfelter, 1993; Gallagher, Christofidis, Gill, & Weaver-Graham, 1996; Gallagher, Gill, & Goldstrohm, 1997, 1998; Gallagher, Gill, Goldstrohm, & Sysko, 1999; Gallagher et al., 2000; Gallagher, Sysko, & Zhang, 2001; Gallagher & Zhang, 2002) conducted a survey of college counseling centers across the United States. A question on these surveys, responded to by an average of 311.5 center directors, asked whether the center encountered any cases of "obsessive pursuit" in the previous year. Those centers that affirmed encountering any cases reported the number of

TABLE 3.3

Relationship Labels Employed to Characterize the Former Relationship Status of Stalking Victims and Stalkers

1. **Unknown**

2. **Stranger**
   - none
   - no previous contact/no prior relationship
   - not known to victim

3. **Public**
   - celebrities
   - media [personage]
   - public/public figures
   - seen from distance—fan, etc.

4. **Acquaintance**
   - acquaintance, casual
   - acquaintances, former/prior
   - knew but no prior relationship
   - knew slightly
   - known but not intimate: acquaintance
   - "slight social" or "brief relationship"
   - social encounter

5. **Neighbor**
   - Neighbor, casual

6. **Colleague/Professional/Service**
   - service-incidental
     - former patient
   - colleague: work-related
     - business relationship
     - business/work acquaintance
     - coworker
     - employee
     - employer
     - employment
     - professional
     - supervisor
     - work-related interaction
     - work-related, other
   - school–related
     - classmate
     - graduate teaching assistant

- professor
- students/trainees
- knew from school or office or club

7. **Know/known**
   - knew
   - knew well
   - known but not intimate: other

8. **Friend**
   - ex-friend
   - family friend
   - friend of a friend
   - friends, estranged
   - known but not intimate: friend

9. **Intimate: general**
   - intimate, former
   - intimate, general
   - intimate, prior

10. **Intimate: romantic**
    - romantic
      - intimate romantic
      - relationship, former
      - romantic, nonmarital
      - romantic, prior
      - sexual intimate, prior
    - date
      - date, casual
      - date, serious
      - dated/dated previously
      - dating casually
      - dating seriously or casually
      - dating/engaged, seriously
      - intimate or former intimate: date
    - boy/girlfriend
      - boyfriend/date
      - ex-boyfriend/ex-girlfriend
      - intimate or former intimate: boyfriend/girlfriend
    - partner
      - intimate
      - ex-partner
      - intimate or former intimate: partner

TABLE 3.3 (*continued*)

- intimate partner, present
- relationship, current
■ spouse
  - (Ex)spouse/former spouse/ex-husband
  - husband/ex-husband
  - intimate: spouse
  - married
  - married/living together
■ cohabiting/cohabitee
■ separated
  - divorced
  - divorced/separated
  - separated/divorced/widowed

11. **Intimate nonromantic: relative**

  ■ family
  ■ co-parent
  ■ family member
  ■ family, other
  ■ parent
  ■ household member
  ■ known but not intimate: relative
  ■ relative/related

12. **Miscellaneous**

  ■ e-mail correspondent
  ■ non-cohabitee
  ■ other
  ■ personal
  ■ relationship, some prior
  ■ widowed

Note. Across 49 studies, there are 12 macro categories, representing at least 75 distinct subcategory labels (Blaauw, Winkel, Arensman, et al., 2002; Bjerregaard, 2000; Blackburn, 1999; Boon & Sheridan, 2001; Brewster, 1998, 2000, 2003; Budd & Mattinson, 2000; Burgess et al., 1997; Feldman, Holt, & Hellard, 1997; Fisher et al., 1999; Fremouw, Westrup, & Pennypacker, 1997; Gill & Brockman, 1996; Hargreaves, 2000; Harmon et al., 1995, 1998; Hills & Taplin, 1998; Huffhines, 2001; Kamphuis & Emmelkamp, 2001; Kienlen et al., 1997; Kileen & Dunn, 1998; Kohn et al., 2000; Kong, 1996; Lemmey, 1999; Lyon, 1997; Marshall & Castle, 1998; McCreedy & Dennis, 1996; McFarlane et al., 2002; McLennan, 1996; Meloy & Boyd, 2003; Mullen & Pathé, 1994a; Mullen et al., 1999; New Jersey State Police, 1997; Nicastro et al., 1999; Pathé & Mullen, 1997; Pathé et al., 2000; Purcell et al., 2002; Rosenfeld & Harmon, 2002; Sandberg et al., 1998; Schwartz-Watts et al., 1997; Sheridan, 2001; Sheridan & Davies, 2001b; Sinclair & Frieze, 2000; Spencer, 1998; Spitzberg & Rhea, 1999; Suzuki, 1999; Tjaden & Thoennes, 1998b; Tucker, 1993; Working to Halt Online Abuse, 2001).

cases ($M = 310.29, SD = 101.66, n = 7$), the number in which the victim was injured, and the number of cases in which a victim was killed (see chap. 5 for discussion). The available data points are displayed in Fig. 3.1. There do not appear to be any systematic trends suggesting that the percentage of collegiate counseling centers reporting obsessive pursuit has been increasing or decreasing. The second source of indirect data is based on two of the Gallagher et al. surveys, in which counseling center directors were asked whether they perceived obsessive pursuit cases to be increasing based on their encounters with their clinics. Gallagher, Harmon, and Lingenfelter (1994) reported data from their 1992 survey that 26% of directors reported an increase, compared to 74% perceiving no change, in obsessive pursuit cases. Gallagher et al. (1993) reported in the 1993 survey that 31% of directors reported increases, with 47% reporting such cases "staying about the same." Given the limitations of these data, there is little evidence of clear trends of stalking and obsessive pursuit over time.

In summary, stalking is a relatively common experience. It certainly is not comprised almost entirely by the prototypical "crazed celebrity stalker" who always ends up on the news in a jail jumpsuit and shackles. Most stalkers are people considered normal enough to establish relationships with, and who later become persons who cannot let go for one reason or another. Women appear at much greater risk of stalking than men, although this is evidenced substantially more in clinical and forensic populations than in studies of more ordinary populations.

MOTIVES: THE RAISON D'ÊTRE OF RELATIONAL PURSUIT

W. H. Auden (in *Death's Echo*, 1937) once suggested that "the desires of the heart are as crooked as corkscrews." Such seems to describe the paradoxical features of obsessive relational intrusion and stalking. "Stalking is ... usually embedded in such paradoxical, confusing, and contradictory passions as love and hate, jealousy and self-interest, attraction and repulsion, intimacy and fear, desire for acceptance and retaliatory hostility" (Kamir, 2001, p. 16). Motivation clearly overlaps with causation, and it is important to frame both within a comprehensive consideration of why pursuers pursue those who do not wish to be pursued. However, it is important to understand that what is known of stalker motivations is necessarily based on flawed information. Victims cannot always know why their pursuer is harassing them. Counselors often have access to much case information, but diagnoses are not entirely the same thing as motive. Indeed, "Stalkers do not always know themselves why they are pursuing their actions in the way that they do" (Badcock, 2002, p. 127). Any attribution of motive, therefore, is a highly interpretive and potentially error-prone affair.

As a preface to considering the motivational structure of stalking and unwanted pursuit, it seems necessary to consider the themes of power and control. Since the relatively early days of societal and legislative interest in stalking, there has been a powerful influence of the women's movement and feminism in aligning agendas (Best, 1999; Lowney & Best, 1995). The alignment of these agendas, for example, has constructed a rationale in which domestic violence and stalking are closely linked (e.g., Albrecht, 2001; Baldry, 2002; Bernstein, 1993; Burgess et al., 1997; Coleman, 1997; Currie, 2000; D'Arcy, 2000; Douglas & Dutton, 2001; Gouda, 2000; Jordan, 1995; Keilitz, 1997; Kurt, 1995; Melton, 2001; National Institute of Justice, 1996; Pearce & Easteal, 1999; Salame, 1993; U.S. Department of Justice, 1998, 2001; Walker & Meloy, 1998; Whitford & Howells, 2000).

Male dominance, control, power, and patriarchy are common themes in the domestic violence literature, and they have inevitably found their way

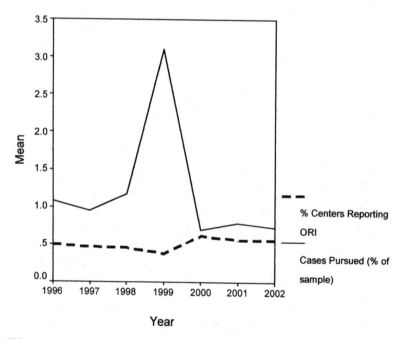

FIG. 3.1.   Trends of percentage of college counseling centers reporting obsessive pursuit cases and percentage of obsessive pursuit cases relative to sample size, by year (based on data reported by Gallagher et al., 1996, 1997, 1998, 1999, 2000, 2001; Gallagher & Zhang, 2002).

into the stalking literature (e.g., Larkin & Popaleni, 1994), although clearly it is possible to view most interpersonal aggression as instrumental without overlaying patriarchal implications (e.g., Felson, 2002). Finch (2001, p. 47) asserted that "stalkers, either deliberately or unconsciously, seek control over their victims." Kamir (2001, p. 68) claimed the male and patriarchal motivational motif dates back to the transformation from female deities to the all-powerful, overseeing, manipulative male deities, who were depicted as motivated by: "total control, objectification, spying, and stalking." Badcock (2002, p. 130) described the appeal of stalking thusly: "Controllingness and both a desire to control the relationship and satisfaction from the experience of having control of a relationship can arise naturally from obsessing thoughts, since a desire to possess is part of the obsession and control is a form of possession."

A few studies that have focused on domestic violence samples have found a prevalence of stalking, but far from a one-to-one correspondence. Tjaden and Thoennes (2000c) found 16.5% of the domestic violence police reports they examined had narrative elements of stalking in them. Mechanic, Weaver, and Resick (2000) found a prevalence of 29% of their domestic violence sample who had separated from their abuser who labeled themselves as having been stalked within the past month. Perhaps the most blatant exemplar is Lee's (1998, p. 379) claim that "Stalking, like street harassment, is part of the spectrum of ways in which men may try to restrict women's citizenship, while forcing them to acknowledge man's presence and perceived power." Ironically, such claims are rhetorical efforts at control and manipulation: efforts to frame the public agenda and perception of a phenomenon absent evidence for such claims. We view stalker motivations as an empirical question rather than a rhetorical question.

Historically speaking, the social sciences for over half a century have understood the conceptual rationale for viewing affect (i.e., love, affiliation, communion, intimacy, etc.) and power (i.e., status, control, dominance, etc.) as (a) the primary axes of social life, and (b) potentially ortho- gonal, that is, unrelated (e.g., Birtchnell, 1993; Leary, 1957; McAdams, 1988; Schutz, 1966; Spitzberg, 1989). Extended to stalking and unwanted pursuit, this means that it is theoretically possible for pursuit to be motivated by love but not power, power but not love, or love and power (whether or not unwanted pursuit could be motivated by neither is an interesting issue, but a possibility most such theories would consider implausible). Indeed, many if not most of the typologies of stalkers implicitly or explicitly incorporate both motives as potential primary axes of causation. Meloy (2002) points out a variety of distinctions between "predatory" and "affective" violence that reflect similar motive structures.

The evidence directly examining the control motive in stalking is relatively sparse but enlightening. First, it is interesting to note that stalkers are often described by victims as acting in "uncontrolled" ways (e.g., Sheridan et al., 2000, 2001b, 2002). Davis et al. (2000) found that "need for control" was a significant predictor of stalking, although its multivariate path coefficient revealed only a moderate effect (.30 to .32), similar in size to the multivariate effects of the more affective motives of anger/jealousy (.26 to .28). Dye and Davis (2003) found a .33 relationship between need for control and obsessive relational intrusion. Similarly, Del Ben (2000) found that stalking victims reported their partners as significantly more "controlling," but also more "hostile" and "jealous" compared to nonstalked partners. Melton (2001, p. 144) found that "Women who reported more severe control at Time 1, experienced less severe stalking at Time 3." Such findings suggest that there is an association of power and control motives with stalking, but they also indicate that these are empirically insufficient motivational motifs within which to subsume stalking and unwanted pursuit research. In short, based on the research to date, stalking is inevitably a *form* of power, but it is not all necessarily *about* power. It follows therefore that there is a need to examine the research on stalking motivations in the hope of developing a more comprehensive and workable motivational schema for unwanted pursuit.

Perhaps the simplest typology of motives is suggested by Meloy (1997a, p. 181), that "Stalking is bad (antisocial) behavior done by mad (angry or psychotic, or both) people." Finch (2001) expanded this typology by implying stalker motivations can be classified as bad (e.g., revenge), mad (e.g., delusional), or sad (e.g., lonely). Under the assumption there might be more variegations than this tripartite distinction suggests, a systematic approach was employed to identify the motives of stalking. A reductive interpretive coding process was undertaken with 23 studies in which either victims reported on motives they attributed to their pursuer, or pursuers' motives were gleaned by examination of case files or interviews with pursuers. These were studies that provided percentage estimates of how common various motives were, typically based on checklists or brief sets of categories (Bjerregaard, 2000; Blackburn, 1999; Brewster, 1998; Budd & Mattinson, 2000; Burgess, Harner, Baker, Hartman, & Lole, 2001; Coleman, 1999; Corder & Whiteside, 1996; Dussuyer, 2000; D. M. Hall, 1997, 1998; Harmon et al., 1995; Harris, 2000; Kienlen, Birmingham, Solberg, O'Regan, & Meloy, 1997; McCann, 2000; Meloy & Boyd, 2003; Melton, 2001; Morrison, 2001; Mullen & Pathé, 1994b; Nicastro, Cousins, & Spitzberg, 2000; Sheridan, Davies, & Boon, 2001a; Sinclair & Frieze, 2000; Tjaden & Thoennes, 1998b; Wright et al., 1996). These are far from the only sources of information on stalker motives. However, given their quantification, they seemed a reasonable place to begin to develop a typology of stalker motives.

After stripping unnecessary terms from the phrases, items were examined for unifying themes. Once lower-order categories began to emerge, higher-order categories were interpretively constructed. Once the preliminary categories emerged, other research was examined for any overlooked categories. The resulting items are listed in Appendix 3. The categories with entries in which percentage of occurrence estimates are noted originated from the sample of 23 studies. Those categories without items with percentage estimates were identified in related literatures.

The typology that emerged has considerable a priori sensibility. There are four major categories of motives: expressive, instrumental, personalogical, and contextual. Expressive motives are oriented toward giving voice to internal desires, emotions, or relational preferences. Instrumental motives are oriented toward power qua power, or the desire to control or influence another. Personalogical causes tend to reflect incapacities, dependencies, or defects in character, whereas contextual causes represent situational exigencies, stressors, and circumstances that elicit pursuit. To a large extent, the first two categories could be considered teleological, or goal-directed and volitional. Consequently, in attribution theory terms, these would be considered largely controllable. The latter two categories reflect what attribution theory would classify as uncontrollable causes, but for very distinct reasons. The personalogical category reflects mainly trait-like characteristics that suggest people stalk because of something having to do with "the way they are." These internal causes tend to be conceptualized as relatively intrinsic and stable. In contrast, contextual causes represent more ephemeral factors that arise due to the particular circumstances in which people find themselves. People are likely to view themselves as reacting to compelling external environmental factors, stressors or "triggers." The abbreviated version of this typology is displayed in Table 3.4. There is no assumption implied by this typology that a person cannot experience multiple motives or causes. Indeed, it seems likely that the typical pursuer does experience ambivalent and manifold motivations, especially given the context of pursuit in the face of rejection.

Obsessive pursuers and stalkers are often emotional beings. They may be drawn by motives of infatuation and love. "Manic," erotic (Sinclair & Frieze, 2000; Spitzberg, 2000a), "dependent," and even companionate (Brewster, 2002; Langhinrichsen-Rohling et al., 2000) love styles have been implicated as a risk factor for stalking (Sinclair & Frieze, 2000). Furthermore, such love is often unrequited. "It appears that, by the early 20s, nearly everyone has had at least one experience on each side of unrequited love" (Baumeister & Wotman, 1992, p. 11; see also Bratslavsky et al., 1998;

Sinclair & Frieze, 2000). When love goes unreciprocated, anger, rage, and grief may well result. To the extent rejected paramours experience anger or grief, they are likely to look for someone to blame, and the object of affection is often the most obvious locus of perceived responsibility.

Obsessive pursuers often seek a relationship in much the same way most people seek relationships, through a process of relationship evolution. This evolution progresses through stages of development, from contact and initial attempts at sparking a relationship. The relationship may begin with romance in mind, but if friendship develops, one of the relational partners may make a move toward courtship and romance. As the relationship continues, one of the partners may make bids to escalate the level of closeness or intimacy. If these bids, or even the relationship itself, are rejected, processes of reconciliation may be attempted to maintain the connection. Finally, some people simply find that they cannot let go of the relationship once the other person has attempted to end it, or moved on.

The cultural models of romance and courtship are far from the only relational trajectories (Bachen & Illouz, 1996; Tucker, Marvin, & Vivian, 1991). However, extensive research reveals a commonly held cultural script of romantic relationships evolving along stages from initial contact to romantic intimacy (e.g., Alksnis, Desmarais, & Wood, 1996; Honeycutt, 1993; Honeycutt & Cantrill, 1991; Honeycutt, Cantrill, & Allen, 1992; Laner & Ventrone, 2000; Pryor & Merluzzi, 1985; Rose & Frieze, 1993). A notable feature of such scripts is that males are generally perceived as the initiators of the early stages of relationship escalation, especially bids for romantic escalation (Metts & Spitzberg, 1996; Vanwesenbeeck, Bekker, & Lenning, 1998).

For a variety of reasons, men are more inclined than women to be more sexually motivated and more willing to engage in casual sex (Clark, 1990; Regan & Dreyer, 1999; Symons & Ellis, 1989). Men also are more likely to perceive greater sexual interest in women's behavior than women intend, whereas women perceive more friendship intent in men's behavior than men intend (e.g., Kowalski, 1993; Metts & Spitzberg, 1996; Saal et al., 1989; cf. Abrahams, 1994). Add to these gender differences such relatively new "romantic" prototypes such as the "hookup" date (Paul & Hayes, 2002; Paul, McManus, & Hayes, 2000) and "friends with benefits" (Mongeau, Ramirez, & Vorell, 2003), as well as cultural redefinitions of what constitutes "sex" (Bogart, Cecil, Wagstaff, Pinkerton, & Abramson, 2000), and it is clear that the nature of courtship and romantic relationships is inherently ambiguous. Even friendship is a frequently problematic process of negotiation. Cross-sex friendships are imbued with ambivalent motives and sexual tensions (Egland, Spitzberg, & Zormeier, 1996; Floyd & Voloudakis, 1999; Kaplan & Keys, 1997; Messman, Canary, & Hause, 2000). Collectively, therefore, there are many cultural, social, interactional, and

TABLE 3.4

**A Typology of Motives and Causes of Stalking
and Obsessive Unwanted Intrusion**

1. EXPRESSIVE:
    A. Affective: emotionally expressive: positive (love, amorous, etc.), negative (anger, rage, etc.), ambivalent (jealousy, envy, grief):
        i. Infatuation/love
        ii. Jealousy/envy
        iii. Betrayal/blame
        iv. Anger/rage
        v. Grief
    B. Relational bid: definition, desire for contact (to talk, loneliness), courtship (for a date), concern for other:
        i. Contact
        ii. Initiation
        iii. Friendship
        iv. Courtship
        v. Escalation bid
        vi. Reconciliation
        vii. Can't let go
        viii. Sexual: sexual attraction, desire for sexual interaction.
2. INSTRUMENTAL:
    A. Agenda: attitude based (see also "contextual" categories, e.g., conflict with neighbors):
        i. Dispute
        ii. Issue retaliation
        iii. Prejudice
    B. Control: intimidation, isolation, self-protection:
        i. Self-protection
        ii. Need for power
        iii. Control
        iv. Intimidation
        v. Possession
        vi. Isolation
    C. Instrumental affect: (Note: "intimidation" implies a clear contingent outcome, whereas "instrumental affect" implies such emotionally oriented processes as "revenge" where the object is to give vent to one's rage or to get back at or scare the person for the sake of doing so):
        i. Attention/status-seeking
        ii. Harass
        iii. Humiliate
        iv. Jealous possessiveness
        v. Revenge/retaliation
        vi. To scare/frighten

(continued on next page)

TABLE 3.4 (*continued*)

3. PERSONALOGICAL:

   A. Dependency: drugs, alcohol

   B. Mental/personality disorder: emotional problems, mood disorder, Axis I or II, psychological problems, delusional disorder, erotomania, paranoia, schizophrenia, personality disorder, borderline disorder, antisocial personality, narcissism, obsessional disorder, or other pathology

   C. Incompetence: social skills deficit, problems with establishing or maintaining relationships

   D. Childhood/family of origin: childhood abuse, parental abuse or neglect

   E. Attachment disorder: insecure attachment style, manic love style

   F. Criminality (violence): criminal record or history of offenses, arrests, misdemeanors, felonies, convictions, violence, etc.

4. CONTEXTUAL:

   A. Breakup/separation: reaction to relationship termination or change

   B. Incidental: chance encounters, stalking that extends to persons peripherally or indirectly involved in the pursuit of another

   C. Interactional: pursuit that emerges from the norms and "rules" of interaction (e.g., returning a call or e-mail)

   D. Interdependencies: common activities, relatives, children, activity spaces, employment, etc., that require ongoing or continued interaction

   E. Nostalgia: marking special occasions (e.g., birthdays, anniversaries, "special places" or events)

   F. Rival: reaction to the appearance, possibility, or actions of a rival, real or imagined

   G. Incidental life stressor(s): unemployment, employment or economic stress, loss of significant other

psychological tendencies at work to create misunderstandings and mismatched motives in development of romantic relationships. As we contended in chapter 2, such sites of ambiguity and disjunctive motive represent a potent potential nexus for unwanted, even obsessive pursuit.

Stalkers and obsessive pursuers may be motivated by specific issues or by the desire to manipulate, dominate, and isolate the object of their pursuit. Specific issues represent particular agendas, problems, decisions, policies, practices, or situations that pursuers want to see changed. Most of these types of stalkers are not likely to be pursuing a relationship, and instead are seeking a change in the status quo. A neighbor may engage in a campaign of harassment that mimics stalking in an attempt to alter some decision or practice of another neighbor. Another may stalk a celebrity for a personal meeting or for a perceived slight of bypassing a city in a concert schedule. A citizen may stalk a local politician for a vote on a city ordinance. When played out over an extended time span, such ongoing intersections of pursuer and pursued may take on many of the characteristics of a "relationship," but seldom reflect the kinds of relational motives ordinarily associated with pursuing a relationship such as friendship or romance.

Love and power have been recognized as inextricably intertwined motives since antiquity. Given the common role of intimidation and threat in campaigns of pursuit, it is hardly surprising that many stalkers and obsessive pursuers are motivated by a desire to control and manipulate their object of pursuit. This motive structure has been reinforced by the interpretive paradigms common to the women's and feminist movements that in the early days of stalking legislation constructed political affiliations between stalking and domestic violence victimization (Lowney & Best, 1995). Often overlooked in the discussion of this motive structure is the notion that power and possession are viewed as ends in and of themselves. This suggests that the fundamental motive (i.e., drive, desire, arousal, catharsis, relief, or intent) of a pursuer is the reinforcement provided by the control over another, and that the prospect of establishing a particular relationship end state per se is secondary. In other words, is the relationship the means to power, or is power the means to a relationship? The easy answer is that the relationship is integral to the wielding of power, but this answer suggests that the power motive is a mixed motive, because it would be intrinsically tied to relational motives (e.g., idealized love) as well. Need for control has been shown to predict stalking (Davis et al., 2000; Dye & Davis, 2003; Eke, 1999; Melton, 2001), and stalkers are often perceived as "controlling" (Del Ben, 2000). However, it should be noted that stalkers are also sometimes referred to as acting in an "uncontrolled, aggressive or insulting manner" (Sheridan et al., 2000, 2001b). In short, power is clearly implicated in stalking and obsessive pursuit, but it can play both an instrumental and terminal motivational role or either one.

A particular hybrid of motives emerged from the research that illustrates the ambivalent nature of power as a motive. The instrumental affect category of motives reflects a range of cognition–emotion blends in which the particular reinforcement of stalking arises from the desire or need to draw attention to oneself, to possess another, or to harm another through intimidation, humiliation, terrorism, or revenge. Jealousy and possessiveness, in particular, have been shown to correlate with stalking and obsessive relational intrusion behaviors (Brewster, 2000; Davis et al., 2000; Del Ben, 2000; D. M. Hall, 1997, 1998; Langhinrichsen-Rohling et al., 2000; Roberts, 2002; Spitzberg & Cupach, 1999; Tjaden & Thoennes, 1998b). These motives appear to have some form of emotional need underlying them, but also reveal a terminal motive of influencing the other person into a particular state of emotion, thought, or action. As such, they are explicitly influence-based motives, seeking a particular outcome in the other person.

Personalogical causes generally represent disabilities, incapacities, or background traits of the individual that predispose deviant, aggressive or stalking types of behaviors. A common finding is a high percentage of drug or alcohol use among stalkers, or an association between drug use and dependency with stalking activities (e.g., Burgess et al., 1997; D. M. Hall, 1997, 1998; Harmon, Rosner, & Owens, 1998; Huffhines, 2001; Melton, 2001; Roberts, 2002; Sandberg et al., 1998; Willson et al., 2000; Zona et al., 1993), although some research finds relatively small percentages of use (e.g., Blackburn, 1999; Gill & Brockman, 1996; Kienlen et al., 1997; Meloy, 2001; Meloy & Boyd, 2003; Meloy et al., 2000; Morrison, 2001) or no such association (e.g., Brewster, 1998, 2000; Meloy et al., 2000; Schwartz-Watts, Morgan, & Barnes, 1997). In particular, it is important to consider whether drug use is comparable between stalkers and other populations. For example, Lyon (1997) found drug use among stalkers did not differ from a comparison group of nonstalking criminals. Drug use may be a better predictor of violence in stalking relationships than a predictor of stalking itself (Mullen et al., 1999; Rosenfeld & Harman, 2002). It is also interesting to note that victim involvement with licit (Fisher, Cullen, & Turner, 1999, 2000) and illicit drugs appears to be a risk factor for stalking victimization (Mustaine & Tewksbury, 1999). Thus, drugs may be implicated in stalking activities, but it seems most likely that they play a primarily peripheral role relative to other risk factors.

The most inclusive category of personalogical causes of stalking is clearly mental and personality disorder. This is admittedly a broad category. Many of the personal defects or disorders in this category reflect the vocabulary of the *Diagnostic and Statistical Manual of Mental Disorders* (American Psychiatric Association, 1987). This manual sets forth the diagnostic criteria of various disorders, typically based on two primary axes. Axis I disorders include anxiety, childhood, cognitive, dissociative, eating, factitious, impulse control, mood, psychotic, sexual and gender identity, sleep, somatoform, substance-related, and adjustment disorders. Axis II disorders consist mainly of mental retardation and personality disorders. However, the disorders are diagnosed in a polythetic system, in which criteria are established for a given diagnosis, only some of which have to be satisfied to justify a particular diagnosis of disorder. Thus, for example, there are "93 different ways to meet the DSM III-R criteria for BPD [borderline personality disorder] and 149,495,616 different ways to meet the DSM III-R criteria for APD [Antisocial Personality Disorder]" (Widiger & Trull, 1994, p. 218). Nevertheless, the *DSM* has been useful in identifying risk factors for a wide variety of mental, emotional, and social problems. Meloy (2001) suggested that the most common Axis I diagnoses among stalkers are substance abuse, mood disorders, or schizophrenia, and the most common Axis II diagnoses are narcissism, borderline, and antisocial disorders. Other studies employ less specific labels, such as "emotional problems" (Blackburn, 1999; Morrison, 2001), "psychological problems" (Gill & Brockman, 1996), or "mental health problems" (Huffhines, 2001; Roberts, 2002).

Axis I disorders have been implicated as a risk factor for stalking in a number of studies (Gentile, 2001; Harmon et al., 1995, 1998; Morrison, 2001; Mullen et al., 1999; Rosenfeld & Harmon, 2002; Schwartz-Watts et al., 1997). Indeed, Kienlen et al. (1997) recommend dichotomizing stalkers as either psychotic or nonpsychotic. In their study, 78% of psychotic stalkers had Axis I disorders, but none of the nonpsychotic stalkers had Axis I disorders. In other studies, Axis II disorders, especially borderline disorder, have been implicated (Lewis, Fremouw, Del Ben, & Farr, 2001; Romans, Hays, & White, 1996). In still other studies, both Axis I and Axis II disorders have been implicated in stalking (Harmon et al., 1998; Meloy & Boyd, 2003; Meloy et al., 2000; Meloy & Gothard, 1995; Mullen et al., 1999; Sandberg et al., 1998). According to Meloy (1998, p. 87), "Most stalkers have both Axis I and Axis II diagnoses ... Only one in five stalkers, however, is psychotic at the time of the pursuit." Diagnoses of Axis I disorders have been found to increase the likelihood of violence in some studies of stalking (e.g., Harmon et al., 1998), and to decrease the likelihood of violence in at least one other study (Meloy, Davis, & Lovette, 2001). Similarly, Axis II diagnoses showed a relationship to violence in one study (Harmon et al., 1998) and no relationship to violence in another (Meloy et al., 2001). Other studies find no relationship between psychiatric diagnosis and violence among stalkers (Palarea, Zona, Lane, & Langhinrichsen-Rohling, 1999).

Incompetence represents mental, behavioral or social deficit in basic adaptive skills. A lack of social skills or competence is often identified as a root cause of stalking and obsessive relational pursuit. Several studies indicate that stalkers tend to be socially incompetent (Meloy & Boyd, 2003; Mullen & Pathé, 1994a) or have a history of failed relationships (Lyon, 1997; Meloy, 2001; Mullen et al., 1999; Roberts, 2002). However, social incompetence is unlikely to be the only distinguishing factor. As Meloy (1996b, p. 159) argued, "The psychopathology of obsessional following appears to be, in part, a maladaptive response to social incompetence, social isolation, and loneliness. What differentiates these individuals from others, however, appears to be their aggression and pathological narcissism."

Another form of incompetence would be general mental deficit. Stalkers have been characterized as being higher in IQ than comparable nonstalking criminal populations (Meloy, 1998). However, the data are not very extensive to implicate basic intelligence in any specific role in regard to stalking. For example, IQ has been found to be negatively related to violence in one study of stalking cases (Rosenfeld & Harmon, 2002), but unrelated in another (Meloy et al., 2000).

A few studies suggest that stalkers are more likely to have had traumatic, abusive, or neglectful childhoods (Blackburn, 1999; Gentile, 2001; D. M. Hall, 1997, 1998; Kienlen et al., 1997), although at least one study found no such relationship (Langhinrichsen-Rohling & Rohling, 2000). If violent or abusive trauma is not consistently implicated in stalking, perhaps generally inconsistent nurturing or parental neglect accounts for obsessive pursuit of intimacy. One approach to this question is to examine the relationship between attachment style and aggressive pursuit behavior. Attachment theory proposes that infants develop primary attachments with caregivers, and that this relationship develops a set of mental schema by which future relationship information is organized. People who develop in contexts of consistent, nurturing parental care and peer relations are likely to develop a secure attachment style in relating to others, characterized by confidence, affability, and generally satisfying relationships. People who have parents and peers who are inconsistently available, neglectful, or inconsistently rewarding tend to develop an insecure attachment style. Depending on the particular style a person develops, insecurely attached persons can become obsessed with intimacy, anxiously needing connection with others but not really trusting its potential for satisfaction. Several studies have found insecure attachment styles related to stalking and obsessive relational intrusion (Brewster, 2000; Davis et al., 2000; Del Ben, 2000; Dutton-Greene & Winstead, 2001; Eke, 1999; Langhinrichsen-Rohling et al., 2000; Lewis et al., 2001; Spitzberg, 2000a). In this sense, much stalking can be viewed as a form of attachment disorder (Meloy, 1992).

Finally, stalkers may stalk because they are generally aggressive persons, and this aggressiveness extends to their relationships as well. Such an attribution would be reinforced by evidence that stalkers are more likely to have criminal histories, arrests, prior misdemeanors and felonies, prior convictions, and a history of violence. There is extensive evidence supporting such an attribution. Numerous samples of stalking perpetrators (or victim attributions of perpetrators) have found sizable percentages of criminal history (31%: Blackburn, 1999; 62%: Brewster, 1998; 53%: Gill & Brockman, 1996; 61%: Huffhines, 2001; 63%: Kienlen et al., 1997; 53%: Logan et al., 2002; 56%: Lyon, 1997; 37%: Meloy

& Boyd, 2003; 39%: Mullen et al., 1999; 46%: Roberts, 2002; 62%: Rosenfeld & Harmon, 2002).

Criminal history has been implicated in the likelihood of violence in stalking cases as well (Harmon et al., 1998). Interestingly, Farnham and James (2000) found that violence among stalkers was predicted by a *lack* of criminal history. They interpreted this as suggesting stalking violence is largely a manifestation of expressive motives rather than the extension of a basically aggressive predisposition. Similarly, Meloy et al. (2001) found that prior criminal history was unrelated to violence among stalkers. It seems more likely that a history of violence, rather than a history of law enforcement or judicial encounters, will provide better prediction of violence in stalking cases (e.g., Burgess et al., 1997; Kienlen et al., 1997; Nicastro et al., 2000; Palarea et al., 1999; cf. Brewster, 1998).

An important caveat about this category of causes is that the research supporting personalogical causes is heavily weighted by studies of clinical and forensic samples. It seems likely such samples create biases that are "a product of the skewed nature of clinic and court samples that over-represents the more persistent and outrageous forms of stalking" (Mullen et al., 2000a, p. 117). There is little doubt that such motives exist and account for a fair proportion of stalking activities in society. However, the spectrum of stalking extends across a wide swath of the population, and it is likely that stalking and obsessive relational intrusion are also often extensions of relatively normal courtship behavior enacted by otherwise relatively normal persons.

The final category of motives and causes entails contextual and situational triggers of stalking. Consideration of contextual causes leads to the possibility of implying that stalkers are not responsible for their actions. However, external, situational factors such as life stressors are ubiquitous in people's lives, and yet most people do not stalk others. Contextual causes are best viewed as "triggers" or stimuli that start a progressive slide of actions. Thus, stalking is not an inexorable result of such causes, but may be initially stimulated by them.

The most common contextual cause is the breakup or termination of an existing relationship. This is as much a "marker" of the beginning of pursuit as it is a cause. Although stalking can occur during a relationship (Mechanic, Weaver, & Resick, 2000; Nicastro et al., 1999; Tjaden & Thoennes, 1998b), stalking and obsessive relational pursuit are obviously more likely when the partner is relationally unavailable. It is interesting to speculate, however, about how much stalking emerges from relationships that subtly diverge in the process of development, and how many emerge from already full-fledged mutual intimate relationships that terminate. Although the former seem more prone to issues of ambiguous definition and aspiration, the latter seem more prone to the emotional shock of unilateral relationship termination. How these alternative trajectories play out in the process of stalking is a subject in much need of further investigation.

Some stalking arises from relatively incidental processes. For example, although stalkers try in a variety of ways to run into their object of pursuit, such encounters can also occur accidentally. Stalkers sometimes end up pursuing associates of the object of pursuit because those associates may lead the pursuer to their object. Such pursuit of associates can take on more strategic purposes, but may also be relatively opportunistic and situational.

When relationships break up, there are often vestiges of the relationship that still remain. These vestiges reflect common property, children, employment, group affiliations, resources, or other connections that involve ongoing interaction and negotiation. In the literature on the violation of restraining orders, for example, women often note that their partner violated the orders in the process of trying to see their children (Harrell & Smith, 1996). Corder and Whiteside's (1996) sample of psychologists reported an association between stalking and child custody and divorce issues with clients.

Stalkers often focus on significant moments or events in attempting to connect with their objects of pursuit. For example, stalkers may obsessively attempt contact or send symbols of affection or threat (e.g., cards, flowers, gifts) during anniversary dates, birthdays, holidays, or other important dates that were "marked" as significant in one or both of their lives.

Given that jealousy, possessiveness, and suspicion are implicated as motives of stalking (Roberts, 2002), it is little surprise that rivals often serve as stimuli to obsessive pursuit and surveillance. Sometimes stalking is designed to ward off potential rivals, and at other times stalking comes to encompass the rival, real or imagined, in the net of pursuing activities.

Finally, stalking may be set off by the experience of incidental life stressors. Unemployment, career instability, economic stress, the loss of a family member, friend or pet, an illness in the family, and other such major life stressors may trigger an acute sense of need for intimacy with or support from another. Coleman (1999) found that 7% of stalkers had experienced a death of a friend or family member, and another 7% had moved over the previous year. Gentile (2001) found 18.5% of stalkers had recently experienced the loss of a family member, 41% had experienced a divorce or relationship breakup recently, and 22% experience "some other" important loss or stressor. Morrison (2001) found that 2% of stalkers had experienced a death or serious illness in their family prior to stalking, 23% had legal problems with someone other than the victim, and 3% reported relationship problems with someone other than the victim. Kienlen et al. (1997) concluded that 80% of their sample of stalkers had experienced a stressor within 7 months of stalking onset.

When the findings regarding employment are examined across studies, it emerges as one of the most surprisingly consistent indicators of the stalker profile. Numerous studies have found high percentages of unemployment among stalkers (31%: Brewster, 1998; 16%: Brewster, 2002; 37%: Coleman, 1999; 50%: Gill & Brockman, 1996; 60%: Kienlen et al., 1997; 20%: Lyon, 1997; 44%: Mullen et al., 1999; 53%: Spencer, 1998). Other studies found that substantial percentages of stalkers had "lost" or been fired from their jobs (15%: Coleman, 1999; 18.5%: Gentile, 2001; 10%: Melton, 1994; 10%: Morrison, 2001). Meloy and Gothard (1995) reported that a "majority" of their cases revealed unemployment or an unstable work history. Of course, it is no accident that unemployment not only serves as a general life stressor, it also permits a person more time, and time is integral to any obsessive pattern of activity.

TYPES OF STALKERS AND PURSUERS

One of the implications of identifying a complex domain of motives and causes for stalking is that stalkers and pursuers constitute a heterogeneous population (Kropp, Hart, & Lyon, 2002; Meloy, 1997a). Stalkers are not all cut of the same fabric. The most common approach to representing this complexity is to identify distinct types of stalkers. There have been many typologies proposed, and only a few that have been investigated empirically. "No generally accepted approach to classifying stalkers has yet emerged" (Mullen et al., 2000a, p. 78). Virtually all of these typologies have relied on one or more of three dimensions of differentiation (Del Ben & Fremouw, 2002): type of original relationship (e.g., stranger vs. intimate), motive (e.g., amorous vs. persecutory), and underlying psychological disorder (e.g., delusional vs. nondelusional).

A number of relatively unsubordinated or simple typologies have been offered, based typically on relatively intuitive or "experience-based" conjectures. For example, Palarea et al. (1999) offered one of the simplest relational typologies, dichotomizing stalkers into nonintimate and intimate types. Hall (1997) expanded this typology by one category, trichotomizing postintimate, prior-acquaintance, and stranger relationships. In contrast to a relationship-based distinction, Schell and Lanteigne (2000) recommended a motive-based typology consisting of revenge and relational stalkers. Bates (1999) hypothesized a mixture of these typologies, suggesting three types of stalkers: intimate partner, delusional, and vengeful. Dziegielewski and Roberts (1995; Roberts & Dziegielewski, 1996) identified three stalker types: domestic violence, erotomania or delusional, and nuisance. Kropp et al. (2002) refer to the grudge stalker, the love obsessional stalker, and the delusional stalker.

Asymmetrically blending relationship and motive dimensions, Emerson et al. (1998) articulated five types of stalker: unacquainted, pseudo-acquainted (e.g., celebrity), semi-acquainted (e.g., coworkers), revenge, and relational stalkers. Cupach and Spitzberg (1998), summarizing prior typologies (e.g., McCann, 1998b; Zona et al., 1993; Zona, Palarea, & Lane, 1998), suggested four types of relational pursuers: erotomanic, borderline erotomanic, obsessional acquaintance, and obsessional estranged lovers. Erotomanics delusionally believe their object of affection is in love with them. They therefore frequently suffer from an underlying disorder, often schizophrenia or other psychosis. Borderline erotomanics are generally relative strangers who have an unstable personality structure or attachment disorder, but are not delusional about the love of their object of affection. Obsessional acquaintances are former or present friends, colleagues, or other acquaintances who fixate and pursue another, whereas obsessional estranged lovers fixate on those with whom they had a previously romantic relationship.

Other typologies have offered multi-axial category schemes in which multiple dimensions are crossed to create types of stalkers. For example, Batza and Taylor (1999) indicated there would be two basic types, public figure stalkers and interpersonal stalkers, within which there would be various subtypes: attachment seekers, identity seekers, rejection-based and delusion-based stalkers. Harmon et al. (1998) crossed amorous and persecutory motives with prior relationship (i.e., stranger, acquaintance, intimate), but did not label the possible intersections. Similarly, Davis and Chipman (1997a) selectively used the level of disorder (i.e., erotomanic vs. love-obsessional vs. simple-obsessional) by degree of relationship (i.e., target known vs. target unknown) to identify seven subtypes: erotomanic target-unknown (random-targeting, celebrity-targeting, and single-issue targeting), love-obsessional target known (intimate partner-targeting, coworker-targeting), simple-obsessional target former intimate (intimate partner-targeting, domestic violence-targeting).

Spitzberg and Cupach (2001a, 2002a) proposed a conceptual 2 (motive: love vs. hate) × 2 (mode: instrumental vs. expressive) typology, which produced four styles of obsessive pursuit. The annoying pursuer is seeking affection and intimacy, and gives voice to these motives in the expression of affection. The intrusive pursuer also seeks intimacy, but through the use of more instrumental, manipulative, and exploitive tactics. The organized stalker seeks retribution or harm, and strategically plans modes of approach and intrusion. The disorganized stalker, in contrast, tends to be enraged and vengeful in spontaneous and unplanned ways.

Rosenfeld (2000) constructed a dimensional typology relying primarily on motive (love vs. revenge), relationship (real vs. fantasy), and level or type of disorder. These dimensions were unfolded into six types of stalker: dependent/borderline personality, psychotic mood disorder (love motive/real relationship), paranoid/antisocial/borderline (love motive/fantasy relationship), delusional disorder, erotomanic psychotic/mood disorder (love motive/fantasy relationship), and delusional disorder, persecutory psychotic disorder (revenge motive/fantasy relationship).

Holmes (1993, 1998b) constructed a complex typology in which celebrity (e.g., attention-seeking or erotomanic), "hit" (e.g., assassin), political (i.e., issue-based), lust, scorned, and domestic stalkers are distinguished by their unique combinations of the following features: victim type (i.e., stranger vs. nonstranger), target selection (i.e., random vs. planned), motivation (i.e., intrinsic vs. extrinsic), anticipated gain (i.e., psychological vs. material), intended fatal violence (no intent vs. intent), and sexual motivation (sexual vs. nonsexual). Melton (2000) attempted to integrate the more important elements of the Holmes (1993, 1998), Roberts and Dziegielewski (1996), and Zona et al. (1993, 1998) typologies. The resulting typology crossed level of disorder by level of relationship: delusional/unknown (i.e., erotomanic or delusional vs. love obsessional vs. celebrity), nondelusional/unknown (i.e., domestic or simple obsessional vs. nuisance).

These conceptual typologies are useful for pointing out the most intuitive elements differentiating stalkers. Motive has significant legal precedent as a relevant diagnostic category, and seems obviously relevant to questions of risk. Type of prior relationship certainly seems relevant to questions of the degree of interdependence or prior knowledge. However, it is also clear that type of prior relationship is almost always going to be correlated with issues of underlying disorder. Despite obvious occasional exceptions, as a general tendency people avoid establishing ongoing friendships, much less romantic relationships, with people who are overtly delusional, antisocial, or pathologically controlling. In other words, erotomanics, schizophrenics, and other psychotic individuals are far less likely to be represented in certain categories of prior relationships (e.g., domestic, romantic, intimate, etc.) among stalking victims. If these dimensions are correlated (see Rosenfeld & Harmon, 2002), then it makes them poor candidates for the construction of orthogonal typologies. In addition, issues such as motive are easily confounded with behavior. It may be difficult to establish that a pursuer has a motive of revenge if there is no behavioral evidence of threat or attempted injury. As such, the behavior may be sufficient to determine motive, but may offer unique additional information as well. One way of formulating a typology that is not necessarily dependent on these three dimensions is to extract them empirically from case or subject-based data.

Several data based typologies have begun to emerge. One of the first empirical typologies to emerge is technically not a typology of stalkers, but it has implications for interpreting risk factors that may be involved in stalking cases. Calhoun (1998) examined 3,096 "inappropriate communications and assaults" made toward federal judicial officials reported to the U.S. Marshals Service between 1980 and 1993. He identified two types of communicator, which he labeled howlers and hunters. Howlers tended to make threats but not enact them. Hunters, in contrast, tended to be more determined to enact their violent intention without providing prior notice of their threatening intentions.

Hargreaves (2000, n.d.) employed a multivariate statistical technique (i.e., smallest space analysis on 3,636 stalking acts) on a small number of stalking cases ($n = 26$) to develop a 4 (i.e., prior relationship: stranger, acquaintance, non-cohabitee, cohabitee) × 2 (i.e., interpersonal distance: detached, attached) × 2 (i.e., role of information: exploring vs. exploiting) scheme. The result is four styles of stalker. The hunter (i.e., stranger: detached and exploring) is a stranger seeking to track or monitor the object of pursuit from a distance. The manipulator (i.e., acquaintance: detached and exploiting) experiences contacts of "detached familiarity" to maneuver or influence the object of pursuit to more intimate relationship objectives. Oppressors (i.e., noncohabitee: attached and exploiting) tend to exploit their prior knowledge of and relationship to the victim to coerce the victim into reestablishing a relationship. Finally, the invader (cohabitee: attached and exploring) manifests close contact, possessiveness, and control over the victim.

Boon and Sheridan (2001) used stalker case ($n = 124$) characteristics to develop an empirical typology, which they hoped would specifically be useful for law enforcement. It is one of the few typologies that has been assessed to assure independent intercoder reliability in classification, and to which specific risk and management characteristics are attached. Their research resulted in four types: ex-partner harassment/stalking (e.g., long-term duration, hate/resentment motive, victim risk contingent on proximity and closeness), infatuation harassment (e.g., short duration, love motive, victim risk low), delusional fixation stalking (e.g., long-term duration, fixation motive, high victim risk), and sadistic stalking (e.g., long duration, control motive, high victim risk).

In a typology that has served to classify forensic and counseling cases for an Australian team of psychologists specializing in stalking cases, Mullen, Pathé and Purcell (Mullen et al., 1999, 2000a, 2000b; Pathé et al., 2000) identified five basic types of stalker. Each stalker type is constructed from distinct combinations of motive, relationship background, and level of disorder. Rejected stalkers are driven by ambivalent motives of rage and reconciliation. Intimacy-seeking stalkers are essentially motivated by infatuation. Incompetent stalkers are attracted to their object of affection, but have no illusions about the likelihood of developing a relationship. Incompetent stalkers simply "want a date." Resentful stalkers intend to intimidate and instill fear in others. Finally, predatory stalkers strategically plan sexual attack or coercion.

Del Ben and Fremouw (2002; Del Ben, 2000) developed an empirical typology using factor and cluster analysis of 396 college females' reports of pursuer behaviors and motives. The resulting four types of stalker were labeled harmless, low threat, violent/criminal, and high threat. Harmless stalkers appeared rather casual and emotionally detached in their pursuit. Low-threat stalkers were least likely to engage in violent or criminal activity. Violent/criminal stalkers, in contrast, were most likely to engage in violent or illegal behavior. In general, both harmless and low-threat stalkers tended to be less hostile or aggressive in their behavior. High-threat stalkers tended to display particularly high levels of control and possessiveness in their initial meetings with the victims, and were more likely to emerge from more serious prior relationships.

This broad array of typologies leads to several conclusions. First, by their nature, typologies oversimplify. "Typologies exaggerate the differences between different types of behavior" (Felson, 2002, p. 98). As theoretical and practical tools, they assist interpretation by providing abstract maps to unknown or mysterious territories. However, by exaggerating differences, assigning a stalker to a type risks various oversights of potentially important individual case characteristics (Zorza, 2001). As the general semanticists remind, the map is not the territory. Consequently, typologies require empirical validation and refinement. Unfortunately,

> builders of typologies rarely translate them into testable propositions, with the result that the typology becomes a finished product rather than a prerequisite for theorizing .... In the end, they do not generate abstract propositions; rather, they typically describe empirical events with a new vocabulary. (Turner, 1990, p. 25)

Therefore, future work with typologies needs to develop prospective predictions rather than inductive description.

A second conclusion regarding typologies is that there are currently several different maps to the same territory of stalking. These typologies are typically presented as objective sets of dimensions, but they generally reflect implicit theoretical assumptions. The most common yet submerged assumption is that there are indeed types of stalkers. That is, it is assumed that individuals can be usefully distinguished in terms of their stalking characteristics. As intuitive as this assumption may be, it is not a necessary assumption.

For example, typologies of people are overly static and nondynamic. They imply that individuals can be characterized by a set of predispositions or characteristics across time, relationships, and contexts. In contrast, were a typology established on the basis of patterns of stalking behaviors rather than patterns of individual motives or disorder, then it could open up the possibility of truly interpersonal or process-based typologies, in which patterns of interaction between people classify stalking *relationships*. Nonrelational typologies tend to exclude the victim. Yet, "The victim is central to stalking .... The reaction of the victim becomes central to the definition of the crime rather than, as is customary, the criminal intentions of the offender. Thus, stalking becomes a victim-defined crime" (Pathé & Mullen, 2002, p. 1).

A third, and related, conclusion regarding stalking typologies is that they tend to rely on a limited number of dimensions. The underlying assumption of most of these typologies is that the optimal distinctions among stalkers are (a) level of psychological functioning, (b) former relationship, and (c) motivation. The interest in psychological functioning is a direct legacy of the origins of stalking research in counseling, psychiatric, and forensic evaluation disciplines. This does not invalidate such distinctions, but it does suggest that sociologists, communication scholars, neurologists, or other disciplinary scholars might develop quite different typologies. To date, such alternative disciplinary models have not been very unique (e.g., Emerson et al., 1998; Spitzberg & Cupach, 2001a). However, new dimensions may yet emerge as alternative disciplinary perspectives and tools are brought to the investigative and theoretical task of classifying stalking processes. For example, there might be a number of potentially productive features along which typologies could be constructed. Stalking might be classified by stage of stalking, or the profile of stalking tactics employed, or a contingency matrix of prior stalking tactics with victim coping strategies, or the linguistic structure of threats, or a profile of critical events (e.g., types of relationship definition conversations experienced). Until typologies successfully predict socially important outcomes such as violence or duration or victim trauma, they will remain little more than interesting theoretical exercises. Their main value to date is that they have provided a more parsimonious set of dimensions or categories by which to make sense of a vast array of information about stalkers. However, as evident in earlier discussion, the growth of distinct typological trees is beginning to obscure the forest of stalkers through sheer proliferation.

TACTICAL MANIFESTATIONS OF STALKING AND UNWANTED PURSUIT

When a pursuer's focus, fixation, obsession, and persistence meet rejection and disinterest from the object of pursuit, it follows that the purser is likely to value creativity in tactics. Creativity is very much in evidence when examining case files, narratives, and research on stalking and obsessive relational pursuit. "One of the most notable features of stalking is the immense range of conduct that it encompasses" (Finch, 2001, p. 35). Stalkers pursue a goal while the victim is attempting to deny the stalker that goal. In the face of such rejection and avoidance, stalkers employ both repetition and innovation in the pursuit of their goal.

A typical approach to articles and books about stalking is to provide illustrative case studies that reveal the creativity and breadth of stalker behavior. The typical study of stalking provides a list of 5 to 25 stalker tactics. Consequently, to date the research has yet to sample the actual breadth of stalking behavior. "The immense variability of the conduct concerned makes any generalisation as to the nature of stalking difficult. It is, however, possible to identify several broad categories of conduct" (Finch, 2001, p. 119). The review offered next provides a systematic synthesis of 73 studies of strategies, tactics, and behaviors, representing a far more extensive review than previously available. More importantly, rather than simply listing tactics, a hierarchical typology is provided as a basis for organizing these tactics.

Every study was examined from the sample of 125 studies that provided percentage estimates of the prevalence in the sample of any stalker pursuit or harassment behaviors. The tactics were extracted from the studies, and thematically grouped until categories could be interpretively labeled. Once these categories were identified, higher order categories were sought. The result was over 1,000 tactics categorized within an eight-category typology (see Table 3.5). After these categories were organized, conceptual definitions were developed to facilitate future efforts at typology refinement and elaboration. The coded items are listed in Appendix 4.

Several important caveats need to be considered in interpreting the tactic typology. First, any data-based typology is only as valid as the data from which it is constructed. If there are blind spots in the tactic lists employed in previous research, then those blind spots are likely to remain in the typology. However, sometimes the development of higher order categories is heuristic in generating additional subcategories that logically fulfill the possibilities of that higher-order category. For example, when a category of "indirect interactional pursuit" emerged, even though most illustrative tactics were of "proxy pursuit" (e.g., monitoring another person through intermediary persons), several distinctions seemed possible: pursuing another with or without the knowledge of intermediaries, pursuing the intermediaries themselves, or pursuing through lay or professional intermediaries. These possibilities may not have all emerged

TABLE 3.5
A Typology of Stalking and Obsessive Relational Intrusion Tactics

1. Hyper-Intimacy: (a pattern of face-to-face excessive or inappropriate expressions of desire for relational enhancement or escalation):

    A. Affection expression: verbal or nonverbal messages of desire

    B. Ingratiation: unsolicited offers of assistance (with or without the victim knowledge), compliments, and positive regard

    C. Relational repair/escalation bids: specific suggestions of preferred relationship states

    D. Hypersexuality: verbal or nonverbal messages with nonviolent but strong sexual content (e.g., pornography, hypothetical scenarios of sexual tryst, etc.)

2. Mediated contacts (the frequency or duration of attempted or actual contact through various communication modes):

    A. Telephonic: telephone, cellular telephone, pagers, text messaging

    B. Mail/notes: standard mail, notes on windshields or doorsteps, etc.

    C. Tokens (gifts, photos, objects, etc.): artifacts with no overt threatening content

    D. CMC/e-mail/electronica: computer-mediated messaging (e.g., personal digital assistant devices [PDAs], e-mail, etc.)

3. Interactional contacts (the frequency or duration of attempted or actual communication through face-to-face interaction):

    A. Direct interactional: actual or attempted interaction through proximity-enhancing moves in public spaces

        i. Contact (general): conversational or interactional contact of a general nature with victim or others (includes arguing, complaining, and bragging about relationship)

        ii. Approaches: movement from a "public" distance toward a more intimate distance

        iii. Appearances: "showing up" at work, school, door, gym, etc., or "lying in wait" at locations frequented by V

        iv. Interactional intrusions: interruption of V's ongoing interactions with others (includes episodes of "forcing to interact" or "cornering" through nonassaultive physical constraint)

        v. Personal space invasion: including touching or nonthreatening grabbing

        vi. Involvement in activities: unilateral attempt to involve V in activities P can be involved with

    B. Indirect interactional: actual or attempted intermediated interactional pursuit through proxy or of third-parties affiliated with V in order to communicate with V

        i. Coopting victim affiliates: actual or attempted involvement of V's network of friends, family, colleagues, etc., without their knowledge to obtain information, proximity, or contact with V

    ii.   Harassing/pursuing victim affiliates: actual or attempted intrusion or intimidation of V's network of friends, family, colleagues, etc., into providing opportunity for contact with V

    iii.   Coopting pursuer associates: actual or attempted involvement of P's network of friends, family, colleagues, etc., without their knowledge to obtain information, proximity, or contact with V

    iv.   Coordinating pursuer associates: actual or attempted involvement of P's network of friends, family, colleagues, etc., with their knowledge to obtain information, proximity, or contact with V

    v.   Professionalized pursuit: actual or attempted involvement of private investigative services, law enforcement, or proxies to contact V for P

4. Surveillance (covert efforts at monitoring V and/or obtaining information about V):

    A.   Synchronizing activities: the process of P altering schedule, hobbies, classes, job, etc., so as to be more correspondent with V's life activity patterns

    B.   Loitering: P situates in locations common to V's activities (distinct from "approaches" or "appearances" by virtue of its primarily "at a distance" and noninteractional nature)

    C.   Surveillance/watching: covert efforts to observe V (including voyeurism, telescopic and photographic observations, and systematic "at a distance" monitoring, including watching from parked car)

    D.   Following: "on foot" or vehicular pursuit of V's course of movement and activity

    E.   Drive-bys: vehicular following or proximal vehicular-based observations of V

5. Invasion (violation of formal/legal or informal/social privacy boundaries extending to property not directly damaging to the property):

    A.   Information theft: attempted or actual acquisition of private information about V (e.g., diaries, agenda, unlisted address or contact information, employee records, medical records, etc.)

    B.   Property theft: attempted or actual acquisition of physical objects belonging to V (e.g., underwear, photographs, symbolic tokens, jewelry, etc.)

    C.   Property invasion: trespass or breaking and entering of V's home, office, or property (including property of relatives, friends, etc.)

    D.   Exotic surveillance: actual or attempted bugging, CMC viruses or other technological efforts at obtaining information about V or others

6. Harassment and intimidation (attempted or actual efforts to introduce challenges into V's life; these challenges may be implicitly or explicitly tied to P's contingent preferences for V to change behavior, or they may be merely intended to decrease V's quality of life):

    A.   Nonverbal intimidation: implicitly threatening actions, including photos, objects, standing and staring with malevolent facial expressions, gestures (e.g., giving the finger, etc.)

(continued on next page)

TABLE 3.5 *(continued)*

B. Verbal/written harassment: notes, e-mails, graffiti, oral or other statements of derogatory content

C. Reputational harassment: notes, e-mails, graffiti, oral or other statements of derogatory content to affiliates of V, or of V in public, academic, or professional settings

D. Network harassment: notes, e-mails, graffiti, oral or other statements of derogatory content, economic or regulatory hassling of people affiliated with V

E. Regulatory harassment: use of technological, bureaucratic, legal, or administrative means of complicating V's life (e.g., signing V up for unwanted subscriptions, taking out restraining order on V, contempt of protective order, calling police on V, identity theft, forgery, electronic proxy stalking, etc.)

F. Economic harassment: increasing the burden on V's economic vitality (e.g., filing nuisance lawsuits against V, tying V's assets up in court, etc.)

G   Unrelenting persistence: systematic saturation of V's time with attempts to contact (e.g., a war of attrition through incessant calls, appearances, etc.—differs from other subcategories by the sheer quantity and unresponsiveness of the tactic) and/or refusing to accept attempts to close off discussion (e.g., refusing to take "no" for an answer)

H. Bizarre behavior or leavings: exposing V to odd, deviant, or otherwise distressing actions or objects (e.g., leaving a baggie of semen on V's doorstep, P exposes self to V, mischief, offensive material, etc.)

I. Isolation and network alienation: disenfranchising V from V's social network, or otherwise making it difficult for V to socialize

7. Coercion and threat (implicit or explicit messages in any medium [letter, telephone, computer, verbal or nonverbal, etc.] of harms to occur contingent on V's behavior):

A. General/vague threats: statements or actions implying "something bad" will happen (includes "warnings," which are noncontingent forebodings of some harm)

B. Threaten reputation: statements or actions implying V's status or preferred face or image will be harmed

C. Threaten property: statements or actions implying V's valued possessions will be harmed

D. Threaten economic livelihood: statements or actions implying V's economic health will be harmed (including extortion)

E. Threaten victim affiliates (family, friends, pets): statements or actions implying V's valued social, professional, or familial network will be harmed

F. Threaten unaffiliated other(s): statements or actions implying other unknown to V will suffer harm

G. Threaten self (suicide): statements or actions implying P will harm or kill self

H. Coercive communication: P forces (nontelephonic) communication event upon V

I.   Sexual coercion: attempting to or actually obtaining sexual interaction with V through implicit or explicit threat

J.   Threaten physical violence without weapon: statements of actions implying harm to V or others

K.   Threaten violence with weapon: statements of actions (may include suggesting ownership or potential use of weapons) implying extreme physical harm to V

L.   Threaten victim's life: statements or actions directly implying V's life is in danger from P's behavior

8.   Aggression and violence (actions intended to harm V or other(s) contextually relevant to P's relationship with V):

A.   Vandalism: P damages property of V or V's social network

B.   Assault (general): nonverbal actions intended to unilaterally harm V or other(s) contextually relevant to P's "relationship" with V (e.g., fights, assault without weapon, etc.)

C.   Endangerment: unsuccessful nonverbal attempt intended to harm V or other(s) contextually relevant to P's "relationship" with V (e.g., driving dangerously toward V or V's partner)

D.   Kidnapping: actual or attempted containment, transport or constraint of V or other(s) contextually relevant to P's "relationship" with V

E.   Sexual assault/rape (including attempted): nonverbal actions intended to unilaterally engage in sexual interaction with V or other(s) contextually relevant to P's "relationship" with V, including rape, attempted rape, and sexual assault

F.   Assault with weapon: use of weapon intended to harm V or other(s) contextually relevant to P's "relationship" with V

G.   Harmed or injured: physical trauma intentionally caused directly or indirectly by P or P's actions to V or other(s) contextually relevant to P's "relationship" with V

H.   Attempted suicide: P unsuccessfully attempts suicide in manner contextually, implicitly, or explicitly contingent on V's behavior toward P

I.   Suicide: P successfully and intentionally commits suicide in manner contextually, implicitly, or explicitly contingent on V's behavior toward P

J.   Killed victim: P successfully and intentionally kills V through action or inaction

Note. P = pursuer; V = victim.

from previous lists of tactics, but they seem logical extensions of the category of indirect pursuit.

An example of a category that may be underrepresented in the current typology is cyberstalking. Stalking and unwanted pursuit, like most crimes and forms of interaction before them, adapt rapidly to new media and con-

texts. Computer-mediated communication (CMC) is an increasingly common means of initiating, maintaining, and deescalating relationships (Knox,
Daniels, Sturdivant, & Zusman, 2001; McKenna, Green, & Gleason, 2002;
Parks & Floyd, 1996; Parks & Roberts, 1998; Pew Internet, 2001, 2002;
Rumbough, 2001; Scharlott & Christ, 1995). CMC sometimes substitutes for
face-to-face (FTF) interaction and at other times supplements or comple-
ments it. In the context of unwanted pursuit, *cyberstalking* is "the use of the
internet, email, or other electronic communications devices to stalk another
person" (U.S. Attorney General, 1999, p. 2). Although cyberstalking may
seem less threatening than real-space stalking, the former often is used in
conjunction with, or subsequently leads to, the latter (Lee, 1998). Estimates
as to the prevalence of cyberstalking to date tend to be highly speculative
(e.g., Cyberangels, 2000; U.S. Attorney General, 1999). The few studies that
have included items on email suggest rates from below 5% (e.g., Meloy et al.,
2000; Sinclair & Frieze, 2000) to as much as 25% (Fisher et al., 1999). The risk
appears both more prominent and potentially hazardous for children
(Finkelhor, Mitchell, & Wolak, 2000). In one of the few studies explicitly
about cyberstalking, Spitzberg and Hoobler (2002) identified 24 potential
types, and found incidence rates in a college sample ranging 1 to 31%. The
prognosis generally is that cyberstalking is sufficiently distinct to treat as a
separate type of tactic, and that it is likely to increase as the technologies become more accessible, facile, and powerful (see Burgess & Baker, 2002;
Deirmenjian, 1999; Lucks, 2001; McGrath & Casey, 2002; Miceli, Santana, &
Fisher, 2001; Ogilvie, 2001; U.S. Department of Justice, 1999; Working to Halt
Online Abuse, 2001).

A second caveat of the typology is that the categories are not mutually
exclusive. For example, some of the categories refer to *mode* of contact (e.g.,
mediated vs. interactional or face-to-face), whereas other categories refer
to function (e.g., surveillance, coercion). Obviously, a pursuer can engage
in surveillance or send coercive messages both through media and
interactional means. Indeed, there is reason to suspect that most stalkers
will engage in multiple types of pursuit. Consequently, the typology
should be viewed as an interpretive scheme that helps simplify and unify
the vocabulary of unwanted pursuit, rather than a formal typology. As
such, the typology can, and should, be expanded, refined, and elaborated
through future research.

The first category of stalker behavior is *hyperintimacy*. Hyperintimacy
plays off of cultural prototypes of courtship, flirtation, and romance. However, such expressions appear inappropriate or excessive relative to the
norms of these prototypes. For example, potential paramours are expected
to send messages of affection or interest to the object of their interest. So
flowers, gifts, and even suggestions of sex may be common. However,

there is a difference between a rose left on a doorstep and five dozen roses sent at different times of the same day. There is a difference between saying "You are beautiful" and saying "You are the most beautiful person in the world." There is a difference between offering to help the person do their gardening, and actually doing their gardening without permission. There is a difference between saying "I love you" after a year of dating and after one date. Hyperintimacy typically is revealed in five types of behaviors. *Affection expressions* are statements or gestures indicating desire or attraction. *Flirtation* involves culturally prototypical gestures exploring and suggesting interest in pursuing romance. *Ingratiation* involves the unsolicited offer or performance of compliments, statements of positive regard, favors, and support. *Relational bids* are specific attempts to negotiate a more preferred level of relational intimacy. *Hypersexuality* refers to behaviors, texts, or symbols that are explicitly suggestive of sexual activity (e.g., pornography, underwear, etc.).

The next two categories of pursuer activity reflect the mode of actual or attempted contact. Specifically, contact can be mediated or interactional in nature. *Mediated contacts* represent actual or attempted communications through the uses of *telephonic means, mail or notes* (e.g., letters, cards, graffiti, written artifacts, etc.), *tokens and artifacts* (e.g., gifts, photographs, symbolic objects), and *computer-mediated communication* (CMC) or other electronic technological contacts (e.g., e-mail, pagers, personal data assistants, etc.). The stealth, relative anonymity, and "detached attachment" reflected in some of the stalker typologies are suggestive of the value of mediated contact. Media permit stalking from a distance in ways that are time-efficient and relatively protective for the pursuer.

Interactional contacts represent the most subordinated category of pursuit tactics. Interactional contacts are forms of pursuit involving proximal face-to-face interaction, typically but not necessarily consisting of conversation or dialogue. There are two subtypes of unwanted interactional pursuit and intrusion: direct and indirect. *Direct interactional* pursuits involve general contacts, approaches, appearances and interactional intrusions, personal space intrusions, and involvements in activities. *General contacts* represent the strategy of attempted contact, without specific reference to the means through which such contact is (to be) achieved. *Approaches* are attempts to shift from a more anonymous or distant proximity to a more intimate or personal proximity. Approaches are attempts to get physically near to the object of pursuit, typically with the intent of initiating interaction or conversation. *Appearances* are successful attempts at approach, but typically manufactured through strategic location or navigation. The most common tactics noted in the research are "showing up" at one's work, home, school, place of worship, gym, parking spot, and so forth, such that contact is made verbally or nonverbally. *Interactional intrusions* involve the maneuvering of action space so as to enter the interactional space of a victim. Specifically, most of the items in the research discussed "forcing to interact" or "cornering" a victim, or "entering into" an ongoing conversation the victim was having with someone else. *Personal space intrusions* are violations of "private" bodily proximity boundaries. Finally, *involvement in activities* represents a broad spectrum of manipulating events or spaces so as to permit interaction with the victim.

Indirect interactional contacts use third parties or intermediaries to contact, pursue, monitor, or otherwise harass the victim. For purposes of this typology, *affiliates* are defined as members of the victim's social network, and *associates* are members of the stalker's social network. Stalkers sometimes engage in *coopting victim affiliates* by deceptively inveigling themselves into the network of the victim's affiliates (i.e., friends, coworkers, or family of the victim) to elicit information about the victim. For example, when victims try to avoid their pursuers by unlisting their telephone number, stalkers will commonly present themselves as a friend of the victim to other friends of the victim, and at an appropriate time or with a seemingly legitimate excuse (e.g., "She gave me her new unlisted number but I misplaced it ... "), solicit information about the victim. Some stalkers simply solicit the help of associates. A stalker might convince such associates that the object of pursuit has treated him or her unfairly, or owes things, or simply "deserves what's coming." Pursuers also sometimes generalize their *harassment and pursuit of victim affiliates* by extending the scope of their campaign to those surrounding the primary object of pursuit. Stalkers and pursuers may also engage in *coopting pursuer affiliates* by convincing their own friends or family to assist in the campaign of pursuit. Finally, stalkers *professionalize* the process by hiring private investigators, maneuvering bureaucratic resources, or soliciting systematic pursuit or harassment regarding the object of pursuit.

These first three categories of unwanted pursuit represent the most "culturally sanctioned" aspects of relating. It is in these categories of hyperintimacy and contact that images of courtship are most intertwined. In the context of these types of behavior, "stalking is not predominately socially-deviant behavior, but in fact, to a certain extent, socially-sanctioned behavior, instituted and encouraged by Western courtship mores and ideas of romance" (Lee, 1998, pp. 373–374). In the larger context of relating, "Stalking behaviours merge with a multitude of social interactions that, however irritating and unwelcome, form part of many people's everyday experience" (Mullen et al., 2000b, p. 455). Stalking, however, extends much more deeply into the darker realms of human relations.

A fourth category of unwanted pursuit and intrusion tactics is perhaps the most prototypical of stalking: surveillance. *Surveillance* consists of covert (or attempted covert) efforts to monitor or obtain information about the victim. Several intriguing patterns of surveillance emerged from the data. First, many stalkers appear to keep tabs on their victims by *synchronizing activities* with the object of pursuit. By joining or participating in similar groups, classes, hobbies, religious activities, some stalkers simply obtain more opportunity to observe their victim. Other stalkers simply engage in *loitering* around locations the victim is known to frequent or encounter. This is distinct from "appearances" or "approaches" in the sense that loitering is designed to observe rather than interact. *Surveillance* or watching involves a more strategic type of loitering, in which tactical positions, often intended as covert, are taken up to observe the victim. *Following* involves a pattern of distant proximity, in which a victim's movements are mirrored in proximal time and space. Finally, *drive-bys* emerged as a distinct category of surveillance in which pursuers drive by, typically a residence, to check up on the victim's location or activity.

A fifth category of stalking tactics is labeled invasion. *Invasion* involves the violation of property privacy boundaries. At least four types of invasion emerged in the data. The first form of invasion is *information theft*, in which information belonging to the victim, or maintained in presumably secure form, is stolen by the stalker. This information theft often occurs in the form of information extracted from formal bureaucratic records (e.g., getting a student's schedule from a registrar's office, a person's address from a driver's license bureau, or an employee's social security number from a secretary), or through more direct means such as going through the victim's schedule left on a table while the victim goes to the restroom. The second form of invasion is *property theft*, in which victim's property is stolen, even if momentarily. A third type of invasion is *property invasion*, referring to territorial notions of property, such as a car, home or office space. This "B & E" (i.e., breaking and entering) is likely to occur in the victim's absence, but may even be performed with the risk of physical encounter. Finally, there are means for *"exotic" surveillance*, such as an entire range of computer-mediated invasion. "Spy" technologies are increasingly available to the average person. Sophisticated hackers can extract enormous amounts of information about a person either from that person's own computer or through computers to which the victim is networked. Much of this category would therefore include what is broadly referred to as cyberstalking, although some of the other functional categories to follow can be achieved through computerized media as well.

The sixth form of unwanted pursuit is *harassment and intimidation*. Harassment can be similar to annoyance, but can also include a systematic campaign to wear a person down, complicate his or her life, or otherwise hassle the person. Intimidation, in contrast, implies a contingency. That is, the harassment is intended to influence the victim's behavior in some way. A person intimidates another to get that person to do something or react in a certain way. A variety of harassment and intimidation techniques emerged from the data. *Nonverbal intimidation* typically involved objects or artifacts that implicitly connote threat. The narratives and cases of stalkers are replete with examples of creative alterations of photographs or objects (e.g., a photo of the victim and an affiliate with a rifle-scope crosshairs drawn around the affiliate's head). Nonverbal intimidation would also include staring at the victim with malevolent facial expressions or otherwise implying a threatening demeanor or intention. *Verbal or written harassment* entails the construction of written or verbal messages in the form of notes, e-mails, graffiti, or oral utterances intended to challenge or hassle the victim. Such messages are often harassing or intimidating less by their content than by their persistence and ubiquity. *Reputational harassment* involves efforts to spoil the victim's identity in a larger sphere of status and recognition, such as with friends, family, coworkers, or the public at large. For example, a rejected paramour might post photographs of the lost object of affection around a campus, falsely referring to the victim as a slut or drug addict. *Network harassment* involves any of these other forms of harassment and intimidation, only targeting the affiliates of the victim. Such network harassment is often a way of forcing the victim's hand in reestablishing contact with the pursuer. *Regulatory harassment* refers to a category of creative techniques of intruding in a person's life through bureaucratic means. For example, signing a person up unknowingly for subscription to pornographic magazines, giving anonymous but false tips to law enforcement about the victim's abuse of children, taking out a restraining order on one's victim as if the victim were the pursuer, and other techniques represent efforts at entangling the victim in challenging regulatory encounters. Such regulatory harassment sometimes blends in with economic harassment, in which efforts are made to deplete the victim's financial resources. Filing lawsuits, for example, might be intended not to entangle the victim so much as simply cost the victim money for legal expenses. *Economic harassment* represents activities through which a pursuer attempts to deplete the economic resources and health of a victim. One of the easily overlooked facets of harassment and intimidation is the *unrelenting persistence* involved in pursuit. When contact of any sort is unilaterally attempted in constant, unremitting manner, it is likely to function in harassing and intimidating ways. Harassment, and especially intimidation, are often achieved through the symbolic placement of *bizarre objects* or through bizarre or extremely deviant behavior. Leaving pubic hairs in an envelope in the victim's mailbox, or spray painting the victim's pet, overtly masturbating outside the victim's bedroom, or sending a book about a famous celebrity stalking to the victim, represent bizarre but not explicitly threatening activities designed to obtain certain reactions from the victim. Finally, harassment may involve *isolation and network alienation*, in which the object of pursuit is prevented or inhibited from social interaction. A pursuer may make it too much hassle for the victim to engage in social activities, thereby eliciting social withdrawal by the victim.

Intimidation is a slippery slope to *coercion and threat*, the next category of stalking behavior. Tedeschi and Felson (1994, p. 168) defined a coercive action as "an action taken with the intention of imposing harm on another person or forcing compliance. Actors engaged in coercive actions expect that their behavior will either harm the target or lead to compliance, and they value one of these proximate outcomes." In the context of this typology, the intent to inflict actual harm is reserved for the final category, and here it is the contingency of explicit threatening actions or messages to intended compliance that is of interest. Specifically, coercive and threatening actions are those in which a contingency is implied such that noncompliance by the target will result in some harm to the target, most typically harm under the control of, induced by, or enforced by the stalker.

The topography of threat that emerged from the data illustrates a pastiche of potential harms. The first category of coercion is *general or vague* threats. This category represented items in the data that literally referred to "vague" or "general" threats without specifying what form those threats might take. The subsequent series of threat types progress along a normatively escalating seriousness of harm. Threats to *reputation, property*, and *economic livelihood* represent possible losses of objects of value. In contrast, threats to *victim affiliates* (i.e., victim's social and family network) and *unaffiliated other(s)* (i.e., persons not directly affiliated with the victim), or to *self* (i.e., the pursuer) represent potential losses of life or quality of life among those for whom the victim may feel responsibility. Sometimes a message or pattern of interaction may be characterized as *coercive communication* if it seems threatening and manipulative in intent or nature. A stalker might specifically engage in *sexual coercion* in an effort to solicit sex from the victim. A person can also threaten various forms of *violence*, both through the use or display of weapons or without such weapons, or explicitly threaten the victim's *life*.

The final category of stalking behavior is *aggression and violence*. Rather than contingent threats of impending harm, this category concerns actions taken with the intent of causing actual harm. Whether such actions are instrumental of further coercive ends is irrelevant to the more important criterion of whether proximal physical harm or injury are intended by the action. Once more, a broad array of aggressive actions emerged from the data, which are more or less ordinally extreme. *Vandalism* consists of property destruction or damage. *General assault* typically involves slapping, hitting, shoving, and physical fights. *Endangerment* involves those actions that place a person in potential harm—they are unsuccessful attempts at harm. *Kidnapping* and attempted kidnapping represent any coercive efforts to restrain a person or transport them against their will. *Sexual assault and rape*, whether actual or attempted, represent efforts to force sexual contact or intercourse. *Assault with a weapon* involves attempts to harm with objects that could injure the victim, such as bats, pepper spray, knives, or guns. For the purposes of this typology, the covert use of "date-rape" drugs to incapacitate the victim would be considered assault with a weapon, chemical in nature. The next category is *harming or injuring* the person. This is a general category that simply represents any form of harm actually achieved, regardless of method. *Attempted suicide* and *actual suicide* are forms of potential or actual self-harm that may be used as a form of revenge or coercion against the victim. Finally, in a very small minority of all stalking cases the stalker may *kill* the victim.

Several conclusions emerge from this typology of unwanted pursuit tactics. First, at this stage in the evolution of stalking research, there seems relatively little need for further purely descriptive research unless it extends this typology in significant ways, for example, through new categories of behavior or new organizational schema for the typology. Second, any attempt to conduct empirical research on stalking needs to employ assessment instruments that are representative of all the major categories of this typology. To date, relatively few studies have been even remotely comprehensive in their representation of stalking activities. Third, this typology offers a significant opportunity for unification of assessment approaches. There is relatively little hope of unifying different approaches to the underlying psychology, sociology, and anthropology of stalking. Scholars can take a number of theoretical approaches to conceptualizing stalking. However, there is considerable potential for consensus on the behavioral topography of stalking. Behavior is far more objective than underlying motives or societal forces, despite the subjectivity of interpretive categorical and hierarchical schemes. Fourth, given that prior behavior is often considered the best predictor of future behavior, and given that behaviors are observable (in contrast to motives or intentions), developing a reliable and valid map of stalker behavior seems a more urgent priority in the research agenda. This typology offers a first effort toward such ends.

STAGES AND TEMPORAL CHARACTERISTICS

A typology of stalking tactics is analogous to a cross section of a tree. The internal structure of the tree is made apparent, but the longitudinal progress of the tree is difficult to ascertain from the cross section. In other words, typologies are rather static depictions of the stalking process. Yet stalking is defined in part by the characteristic of persistence over time. To understand stalking requires a longitudinal perspective of how stalking and pursuit evolve over time (Lemmey, 1999; Melton, 2000). Unfortunately, almost no research has actually studied stalking over time. Instead, a number of cross-sectional studies have asked victims to make judgments regarding the time elements of their ordeal. Although this is an imperfect picture, at least a few observations emerge regarding the evolutionary features of stalking and obsessive relational intrusion.

The most studied chronological feature of stalking is its duration. "The duration of stalking increases with the stalker's emotional investment in the relationship" (Pathé & Mullen, 2002, p. 5). Several studies have offered estimates of duration in forms that do not translate to overall averages. Interestingly, one study of police data suggested 40% of stalking "incidents were reported to occur within a day" (Dussuyer, 2000, p. 44). Coleman (1999) reported a mean duration of 7.5 months for "intimate" stalking victims and 12.25 months for "non-intimate" stalking victims. Dussuyer (2000) broke duration down into hours (6%), 1–2 weeks (13%), 3–4 weeks (26%), 1–5 months (29%), 6–12 months (9%), 1–2 years (8%), and 3 or more years (3%). Gill and Brockman (1996) similarly found percentages of their sample experiencing the following durations of stalking: less than 1 month (30%), 1–3 months (28%), 3–12 months (23%), and a year or more (18%). Hall's (1997) stalking victims reported the following durations: 1–6 months (17%), 6–12 months (23%), 1–3 years (29%), 3–5 years (18%), and more than 5 years (13%). Oddie (2000) reported 71% of victims stalked for less than a year, and 28% stalked for more than a year. Similarly, Suzuki (1999) found half of victims were stalked for less than a year, and half more than a year. Such numerical breakdowns are difficult to summarize in any meaningful statistic because their mode of assessment is varied and crude. When the 143 studies are examined, 26 studies offered an average statistic (i.e., mean, median, mode) that could be converted to months. When multiple estimates were provided, the mean was preferred most, and if the mean was not available, the median was preferred. Treating all these statistics as measures of central tendency, the average number of months for stalking duration across these 26 studies is 22.22 months ($SD = 20.68$, range = 3.69–85), or close to 2 years.

This measure of 22 months, as striking as it is, still is difficult to comprehend. One way of framing the meaning of this statistic is to contextualize it not only in reference to the myriad forms of stalking invasion, intrusion, harassment, and violence, but also in the frequency of such activities. Relatively few studies have bothered to examine frequencies of behaviors in any form that is easily summarized. Blaauw, Winkel, Arensman, Sheridan, and Freeve (2002) and Meloy et al. (2000) reported a median of about six stalking behaviors per relationship. Jason et al. (1984) found an average of 6.5 times per week being harassed by someone wanting to reestablish the relationship. The Mechanic, Weaver, and Resick (2000) study of battered women found an average of 11 different stalking and harassing behaviors experienced by their sample. Fisher et al. (1999, 2000), in their study of college stalking victims, reported a mean of 2–6 activities a week, with 10% experiencing stalking activities more than once a day, 13% at least once daily, 41% 2–6 times a week, 16% at least once a week, 14% 2–3 times a month, and 4% less than twice a month. Gill and Brockman (1996) report that 28% of their sample experienced less than 10 contacts, 18% between 10 and 20 contacts, and over half (54%) experienced over 20 contacts by their pursuer. Kienlen et al. (1997), using a similar scale, found 15% were contacted less than 10 times, 32% contacted 10–19 times, 32% contacted 20–49 times, and 20% contacted more than 80 times. Meloy and Boyd (2003) estimated 48% of their stalkers made daily contact, 32% made weekly contact, and 12% made only yearly contact. Sheridan and colleagues (Sheridan & Davies, 2001b; Sheridan et al., 2001a) found average experiences with stalking contacts of more than once a day (20%), once per day (17%), 2–3 times a week (31%), several times per month (23%), and some less frequently (10%). Such estimates of frequency are diverse, but collectively suggest stalking is at least a weekly experience on average.

Despite their ominous implications, neither frequency nor duration per se seems to capture the potential impact of stalking. Instead, it is frequency × duration, or the cumulativeness of stalking behaviors, that seems most traumatizing. "Individual actions by the stalker can seem almost unimportant when looked at in isolation, but the effect of cumulative actions over a period of time is to produce states of utmost intimidation, control and fear" (Babcock, 2000, p. 2). The studies on frequency and duration do not offer a very consistent picture, with some suggesting the average stalking relationship involving only a half dozen total contacts, and others indicating an almost constant weekly barrage. However, when even the conservative estimates of frequency are considered in light of the average duration of almost 2 years, the full impact of stalking can begin to be understood.

Another temporal feature of stalking concerns its progression over time. Some observers have suggested stalking simply tends to escalate in severity. Jordan (1995, p. 376), for example, speculated, "Most stalkings of former partners occur in the context of an increasingly violent relationship." Several other conceptual conjectures have suggested the possibility that stalking evolves over stages. The fact that stalking often emerges from existing relationships suggests that if nothing else, there is likely a distinction between the "normal" and the "abnormal" fabric of interaction. "Attempts by a stranger or acquaintance to initiate a relationship are not likely to be interpreted as stalking from the outset. The similarities and overlap between activities involved in this type of relational stalking and normal pre-dating behaviour and the societal rules of dating behaviour create scope for a variety of interpretations to be placed on the same events" (Finch, 2001, p. 62). Such a dichotomous distinction implies a perceptual or behavioral separation between stalking and acceptable behavior. Unfortunately, "a clear dividing line between stalking and acceptable behavior has never been established" (Dennison & Thomson, 2002, p. 543). This dichotomous temporal feature provides little insight into the progression of stalking or unwanted pursuit activities over time.

The possibility exists that stalking either tends to follow certain paths or trajectories, or that stalking prototypically progresses through stages. Several studies have provided tantalizing evidence that stalking tends to progress through stages. Sheridan (2001) asked victims to divide their stalking relationships into three stages (initial, middle, and most recent or final approach). In all, 90% of victims perceived the course of stalking to have changed over these periods, with 83% claiming it intensified, and only 7% claiming it became less intense. "Over time, stalkers decreased the amount of time in which they were proximal to the victim, but they also became more violent" (p. 69). Blaauw, Winkel, Arensman, Sheridan, and Freeve (2002) found a somewhat bimodal evolution. Although stalking that occurred on a daily basis was more common (68%) in the beginning than in the end (34%) periods of stalking, almost half (47%) showed this frequency decreased whereas 48% remained fairly stable in frequency of daily contact. Boon and Sheridan (2001) found stalkers decreased the amount of time spent stalking over time, but displayed a tendency to become more violent over time as well. Sheridan et al. (2001a) found 72% of their stalking victims perceived the stalking behavior to have "worsened" over time. Del Ben (2000) found that the average frequency of stalking behaviors tended to increase as the relationship became more intimate. Meloy and Boyd (2003) found two-thirds of their sample of stalkers escalated their pursuit throughout the course of stalking.

A few scholars have suggested actual functional or behavioral stages in the evolution of stalking. Burgess et al. (1997), for example, conceptualized the following stages: calling, harassing, discrediting, contact at home/work, love turning to hate, contacts in public, contacting others, following, and sending gifts. In contrast, Emerson et al. (1998), based on

interviews with "relational" stalking victims, hypothesized the following stages: being followed, access information and being pursued, initial proposals and initial rejections, persistence and recognition of
stalking, and turning toward revenge. Employing a more psychological
motif, Meloy (1996b, 1999b) suggested a six-stage model, in which (a) a
narcissistic linking fantasy is attributed to the target, (b) rejection is perceived from the target, (c) shame and humiliation are experienced, (d)
rage is experienced in compensation of the shame and humiliation, (e)
which in turn is compensated for through controlling activities, and
subsequently retaliation activities, (f) followed by the rebuilding of
linking fantasies with the victim, often in the form of violence.

Other temporal speculations about stalking have viewed it as part of a
cyclical process. "Stalking can be considered a core ingredient of the cycle
of violence, that takes place after the relationship has ended, becoming a
further stage of the cycle, or even before" (Baldry, 2002, p. 91). A cyclical
approach to stalking may better reflect the sense of stalking being episodic
rather than continuous. Current approaches to studying stalking mitigate
against such cyclical or episodic understandings of the process.

Finally, related to an episodic view of stalking, some studies suggest
stalking activities represent reactions to critical incidents. A critical incidents approach suggests that stalking does not progress along a linear set
of stages or a continuous trajectory of escalation, but instead is triggered
by particular significant events or manifest by singular important moments or actions. According to one small-scale study, for example, 80% of
the stalkers had experienced some significant psychosocial stressor (e.g.,
loss of a loved one) in the previous 7 months (Kienlen et al., 1997). Stalking
may evolve along discontinuous trajectories, shifting on the basis of such
precipitating or dramatic events.

> *Dramatic moments* in stalking cases are events which humiliate or shame the
> perpetrator, stoke his fury, and increase his risk of violence. Such events in-
> clude, but are not limited to, first actual approach and rejection; unacknowl-
> edged letters, notes, and gifts; contact by a third party warning to stop the
> behavior; issuance and service of a protection order; court appearances; visi-
> tations by the police at the subject's home; first arrest; first incarceration; de-
> nial of bail; trial appearances of the victim; conviction; and sentencing.
> (Meloy, 1997a, p. 183)

For example, Mullen et al. (2000a, 2000b) recommended a 2-week rule,
such that if a pursuer continues past 2 weeks, the attention is likely to continue and be a basis for concern. Melton (2001), echoing a theme consistent
with extensive data on violence risks in domestic violence literature, found
that stalking often began while the relationship was still intact, but in-

creased in intensity upon relationship termination in 48% of the cases. This type of finding helps account for the differences found in stalking victimization between those who break up with another and those who are the rejected party (e.g., Brewster, 2000; Del Ben, 2000; Langhinrichsen-Rohling et al., 2000; Sinclair & Frieze, 2000). Such a critical incident perspective is also consistent with the research on motives, triggers, and stressors, which suggests that stalking progresses in discontinuous stages throughout the typical course of unwanted pursuit.

CONCLUSION

Myriad and manifold are the reasons and forms of pursuit and intrusion. Like the process of predation from which the term *stalking* is etymologically derived, stalkers may be driven by many ends, and employ an extraordinary variety of moves, maneuvers, and machinations in pursuit of the prey. Given that stalking is a process that occurs over time, there is time to envision, consider, plan, and react to the changing circumstances, including the protective responses of the target. This chapter has offered the most comprehensive and systematic typology of stalking behavior yet developed. Not only does such a typology offer the possibility of unifying the assessment vocabulary of various researchers, it also provides the basic elements necessary for mapping stalkers' actions. Furthermore, any attempt at assessment of stalking and unwanted pursuit that ignores categories of behavior identified by this typology risks misrepresenting the process by overlooking behaviors that may be predictive of relevant outcomes.

Among the behaviors of most interest are threats, physical violence, sexual violence, and homicide. We review the evidence regarding these behaviors in chapter 5. The research is still in its nascent stages, but does offer glimpses into the darker recesses of unwanted pursuit. Threats occur in about half, physical violence in about one-third, and sexual violence in about one-tenth of all stalking cases. Stalking-related homicide appears to be rare, but stalking appears to be a clear risk factor for homicide in domestic violence relationships.

The average duration of stalking is approximately 22 months, within which time stalking behavior may vary widely both in its qualitative forms and its frequencies. Although some stalking appears to escalate over time, for others it goes through distinct phases of occurrence. Considering that as much as 27% of all women and 10% of all men can expect to be stalked, and that most of such stalking emerges from relationships otherwise considered close or romantic, it is clear that stalking merits both concern from the average person, and attention from the scholarly and law enforcement disciplines.

CHAPTER FOUR

Explaining Unwanted Pursuit

In a relatively short time span, researchers and practitioners have generated a wealth of important knowledge about relational intrusion. The lion's share of this information is descriptive in nature, providing important insights regarding the prevalence of stalking and ORI, the different types of perpetrators, the manner of perpetration, and the consequences of victimization. There has been a paucity of well-developed theory, however, to explain why unwanted pursuit occurs. The development of such theories will be important if the knowledge base is to expand. Theories are needed to provide a coherent sense of understanding about the phenomena, to assist in organizing research findings, and to focus research efforts by indicating what variables deserve empirical attention. Ideally, theories eventually will permit prediction and control that enable assessments of the likelihood that unwanted pursuit will occur, the projected intensity, severity, and dangerousness of impending pursuit, as well as the relative efficacy of various victim responses.

In this chapter we sketch two theoretical frameworks that offer partial and complementary explanations for unwanted pursuit. We begin by summarizing attachment theory, which offers a distal explanation for the perpetration of unwanted pursuit by rooting it in childhood experiences of disrupted relationships with primary caregivers. Attachment theory resonates well with clinical approaches to unwanted pursuit (see Kienlan, 1998; Kienlan et al., 1997; Meloy, 1992, 1996a, 1996b) and has already received a modicum of empirical support in the context of stalking. Attachment theory and its cousins in the clinical arsenal such as object relations theory "focus more on psychopathology and peculiar cases; they focus less on processes that are manifested in more common instances of otherwise normal individuals engaged in relational pursuit that has run amok" (Cupach et al., 2000, p. 137). Thus, we also describe our own alternative perspective, relational goal pursuit theory. This approach offers an account of ORI and stalking grounded in the proximal dynamics that occur during serial episodes of pursuit. The development of relational goal pursuit theory and its application to ORI and stalking are recent, but preliminary empirical support shows promise for this explanation. Because the study of ORI and stalking is still mostly pretheoretical, we conclude the chapter with a summary of variables that have been shown to predict unwanted pursuit. A coherent framework does not tie these variables together, but collectively they offer useful clues about unwanted pursuit. More theoretical and empirical work is needed to determine the relative importance of these factors.

ATTACHMENT THEORY

Conceptualization of Attachment

Attachment theory has emerged as a coherent and useful explanatory framework for understanding unwanted relationship pursuit. The early work by Bowlby (1969, 1973, 1980) and Ainsworth, Blehar, Waters, and Wall (1978) explicated the importance of infant bonding with primary caregivers. An accessible and responsive caregiver provides a sense of security and assurance, which allows the child to successfully explore the environment. Disruption of the attachment bond is distressing to the child and leads to attachment behavior that attempts to reestablish proximity with the caregiver or obtain the caregiver's attention. Bowlby (1980, p. 42), explained that

> since the goal of attachment behaviour is to maintain the affectional bond, any situation that seems to be endangering the bond elicits action designed to preserve it; and the greater the danger of loss appears to be the more intense and varied are the actions elicited to prevent it.

When the caregiver abandons the child or repeatedly demonstrates rejection or indifference, then the child is likely to develop an insecure attachment.

Research indicates that infants exhibit three distinct styles or patterns of attachment (Ainsworth et al., 1978). *Secure* infants, when distressed, successfully rely on the caregiver as a base of security. *Avoidant* infants show signs of detachment and avoidance of the caregiver when distressed, whereas *anxious/ambivalent* infants show both approach and avoidance behaviors.

An individual's attachment pattern becomes internalized as a "working model" that guides the orientation to attachment figures throughout the life course (e.g., Collins & Read, 1990; Hazan & Shaver, 1987). Characteristics of the infant–caregiver bond manifest themselves in adult romantic relationships (e.g., Ainsworth, 1989; Weiss, 1991). Hazan and Shaver (1987; Shaver & Hazan, 1988) conceptualized romantic love in terms of attachment processes, and demonstrated that the nature and frequency of occurrence of the three attachment styles among adults were roughly equivalent to those observed among infants. They also demonstrated that adult relationship experiences differed among those possessing different attachment styles. Those with a secure style reported love experiences characterized as happy, friendly, and trusting, whereas individuals with an avoidant style expressed a fear of intimacy, and those who were classified as anxious/ambivalent "experienced love as involving obsession, desire for reciprocation and union, emotional highs and lows, and extreme sexual attraction and jealousy" (Hazan & Shaver, 1987, p. 515). It seems obvious that the obsessive and possessive tendencies of anxious ambivalent individuals could contribute to their risk of perpetrating ORI and stalking.

Bartholomew and Horowitz (1991; Bartholomew, 1990) conceptualized four categories of adult attachment style by crossing two dimensions. Individuals possess either a positive (i.e., self is worthy of love and support) or negative (i.e., self is unworthy of love and support) working model of self, and a positive (i.e., others are trustworthy and available) or negative (i.e., others are unreliable and rejecting) working model of others. Crossing these two dimensions yields the four categories of attachment. Individuals with *secure* attachment possess positive views of both self and others and demonstrate comfort with intimacy and autonomy. *Preoccupied* individuals have a negative view of self, but a positive view of others. "This combination of characteristics would lead the person to strive for self-acceptance by gaining the acceptance of valued others" (Bartholomew & Horowitz, 1991, p. 227). This group corresponds to Hazan and Shaver's anxious/ambivalent group. Individuals with negative views of both self and others are labeled *fearful-avoidant*, corresponding to the avoidant category in Hazan and Shaver's (1987) scheme. "By avoiding close involvement with others, this style enables people to protect themselves against anticipated rejection by others" (Bartholomew & Horowitz, 1991, p. 227). Finally, those who possess a positive image of self but a negative image of others are considered *dismissive-avoidant*. "Such people protect themselves against disappointment by avoiding close relationships and maintaining a sense of independence and invulnerability" (Bartholomew & Horowitz, 1991, p. 227).

Several studies have confirmed that two fundamental dimensions underlie and distinguish the different styles of attachment (e.g., Brennen, Clark, & Shaver, 1998; Feeney, Noller, & Callan, 1994; Simpson, Rholes, & Phillips, 1996). Individuals who exhibit an *avoidance* attachment orientation feel uncomfortable with relationship closeness and tend to withdraw from intimacy in relationships. Those who possess an *anxiety* orientation display ambivalent attachment, obsessively worrying about abandonment and loss yet needing extreme closeness. The avoidance dimension pertains to working models of others, whereas anxiety pertains to working models of self (Feeney, 1999). Thus, "the dismissing and fearful groups report less comfort with closeness than the secure and preoccupied groups ... [whereas] preoccupied and fearful groups report greater anxiety over relationships than secure and dismissing groups" (Feeney, 1999, p. 362).

Insecure Attachment and Stalking

Individuals who are insecurely attached, particularly those who exhibit anxiety about relationships, tend to possess characteristics that would logically put them at risk for obsessively pursuing relationships. Studies indicate that ambivalently attached individuals tend to possess manic possessive, dependent (Levy & Davis, 1988; Shaver & Hazan, 1988) and desperate (Sperling & Berman, 1991) love styles. Feeney and Noller (1990) found, for example, that ambivalent attachment was associated with a scale measuring "neurotic" love, which entailed obsessive preoccupation, emotional dependence, and idealization of partner. Consistent with these findings, anxious attachment is associated with feelings of jealousy and anger toward a romantic partner (Brennen & Shaver, 1995) or ex-partner (Davis et al., 2000). Such emotional reactions, in turn, associate with surveillance of partner and the commission of other stalking-like behaviors (e.g., Carson & Cupach, 2000; Davis et al., 2000; Guerrero, 1998).

Anxiously attached persons tend to frame relationship-distressing events in dysfunctional ways. This is illustrated in the manner in which they manage relational conflict. Simpson et al. (1996) observed that after discussing a relational problem, individuals with an anxious attachment orientation perceived their partner and their relationship less positively. Other studies have shown that those with anxious attachment have difficulty regulating emotions and behaviors during interpersonal conflict (e.g., Creasey, 2002; Creasey & Hesson-McInnis, 2001). An ambivalent attachment style has been associated with dominating (Levy & Davis, 1988) and obliging (Pistole, 1989) conflict styles, rather than problem solving or compromising. Feeney et al. (1994) found anxious attachment was associated with reports of marital conflict being coercive and distressing. After reviewing the attachment literature, Feeney (1999, p. 374) concluded that individuals with an anxious orientation to relationships

> report more relationship conflict, suggesting that much of this conflict is driven by basic insecurities over issues of love, loss, and abandonment. Those who are anxious about their relationships also engage in coercive and dis-

trusting ways of dealing with conflict, which are likely to bring about the very outcomes they fear most.

It is reasonable to assume "that those who lack the skills to successfully meet their relationship needs while they are dating, may also lack the skills to endure relationship termination successfully" (Langhinrichsen-Rohling et al., 2000, p. 87). Indeed, research indicates that insecurely attached individuals have more difficulty in coping with the breakup of desired relationships. Barbara and Dion (2002) studied participants' reactions to their recently terminated romantic relationships, and the connection of such reactions to attachment styles. They discovered preoccupied attachment was positively associated with (a) feeling that the breakup was a tough experience; (b) continued rumination about the past relationship (and not yet being involved in a new relationship); (c) believing the breakup was a mistake that should be rectified; and (d) experiencing more frequent negative emotions regarding the breakup. Preoccupied attachment was also negatively associated with experiencing more frequent positive emotions associated with the breakup. These findings are consistent with those obtained by Feeney and Noller (1992), who found ambivalent attachment was positively associated with breakup reactions of surprise and upset, and negatively associated with relief. Simpson (1990), however, failed to find an association between anxious attachment and post-breakup emotional distress.

Several studies have directly shown that anxious, insecure, preoccupied, or ambivalent attachment styles reveal small to moderate relationships with stalking (Davis et al., 2000; Dutton-Green & Winstead, 2001; Dye & Davis, 2003; Langhinrichsen-Rohling & Rohling, 2000; Lewis et al., 2001; Montero, 2003; Spitzberg, 2000a) whereas securely attached persons are less likely to engage in stalking (Lewis et al., 2001). As an example, Langhinrichsen-Rohling et al. (2000) investigated unwanted pursuit behaviors following the dissolution of romantic relationships from the perspectives of both disengagers ("relationship dissolvers") and rejected partners ("breakup sufferers"). Rejected partners who self-reported higher levers of attachment anxiety and emotional dependence (i.e., need for partner nurturance and support) also reported engaging more frequently in severe unwanted pursuit behaviors. Severe behaviors were those that participants judged had a negative impact on the recipient. In parallel fashion, the researchers found that disengagers "who described their ex-partner as insecurely and anxiously attached in the relationship" experienced a greater number of pursuit behaviors (Langhinrichsen-Rohling et al., 2000, p. 83). In a similar study, Dutton-Greene and Winstead (2001) found a positive association between rejected partners' attachment anxiety and their degree of obsessive pursuit following relationship termination. The authors explained that

> anxious attachment is characterized by fear of abandonment, a strong need for reassurance, resentment when the partner spends time away, and chronic worry about the status of the relationship. Anxiously attached individuals would be likely to try to reestablish a terminated relationship by pursuing the partner because much of their self-worth and sense of security is tied to the relationship. (p. 20)

Summary

An insecure attachment style seems to increase one's propensity to obsessively pursue a relationship. In particular, those with an ambivalent attachment style or an anxious orientation, especially preoccupied individuals, possess a number of tendencies that collectively promote ORI and stalking. They crave closeness and intimacy, demonstrate a manic and desperate orientation to close relationships, worry obsessively about rejection and abandonment, experience jealousy and anger in response to relationship threats, feel distressed about relationship conflict, and exhibit negative behavior patterns in managing relational conflict. Moreover, several investigations have shown small to moderate associations between preoccupied attachment and perpetration of unwanted pursuit behaviors. Kienlen (1998, p. 60) argued, "While individuals with preoccupied attachments may most clearly resemble stalkers due to their active pursuit of the attachment figure's approval, stalkers are a diverse group and may exhibit a variety or combination of pathological attachment patterns, including preoccupied, fearful, and dismissing." However, avoidant attachment style does not appear consistently related to stalking (Lewis et al., 2001; Montero, 2003). "Dismissing individuals emphasize achievement and self-reliance, maintaining a sense of self-worth at the expense of intimacy. Fearful individuals desire intimacy but distrust others; they avoid close involvements, which may lead to loss or rejection" (Feeney, 1999, p. 361). It may be that fearful attachment is not related to the likelihood of engaging in unwanted pursuit per se, as much as it predicts the use of violence in the face of rejection (e.g., Dutton, Saunders, Starzomski, & Bartholomew, 1994).

RELATIONAL GOAL PURSUIT THEORY

Consistent with our assumption that ORI and stalking typically evolve from activities that attend the ordinary navigation of relationship development and dissolution, we propose relational goal pursuit as a theoretical lens for explaining how everyday relationship striving becomes excessive and obsessive. We argue that all relationship pursuit is motivated by the pursuer's goal of having a relationship with a specific target person. Obsessive relational pursuers exaggerate the importance of the relationship goal, feeling their self-worth is contingent on attainment of the desired relationship. Consequently, when the relational goal is blocked, obsessive pursuers redouble their efforts to attain the desired relationship rather than abandon the relationship goal. The combination of the elevated importance of the relationship goal and the frustration in goal achievement fosters processes of rumination, rationalization, and emotional flooding (Cupach, Spitzberg, & Carson, 2000; Spitzberg & Cupach, 2001a, 2002a). These processes, in turn, disinhibit the pursuer's conception of appropriate affinity-seeking behavior and thereby promote irrational persistence of relationship pursuit. In the following sections we elaborate this framework, drawing on several lines of prior scholarship, including the work of McIntosh, Martin, and colleagues on the concepts of goal linking and rumination (Martin & Tesser, 1989, 1996a, 1996b; McIntosh, 1996; McIntosh, Harlow, & Martin, 1995; McIntosh & Martin, 1992), and Bagozzi and colleagues' work regarding goal setting and goal striving in consumer behavior (Bagozzi, Baumgartner, & Pieters, 1998; Bagozzi & Dholakia, 1999; Bagozzi & Edwards, 2000; Bagozzi & Warshaw, 1990; Perugini & Bagozzi, 2001). Table 4.1 summarizes some of the key propositions of our theory.

The Pursuer's Formation of a Relational Goal

Goals represent outcomes that people desire to achieve or maintain (e.g., Dillard, 1997). A very common goal is to acquire, sustain, or change a personal relationship with a particular person (Cody, Canary, & Smith, 1994; Dillard, 1989; Rule, Bisanz, & Kohn, 1985). Such a desired end state may be referred to as a *relational goal*. People select goals they perceive to be both desirable and feasible (Heckhausen, 1991; Locke & Latham, 1990). Hence, a relational goal represents one person's desire for interdependence with another person, and that interdependence is viewed as possible as well as beneficial.

In this context we consider the relational goal to be a primary goal. Primary goals motivate action and frame what an interaction between people is about, whereas secondary goals shape and constrain the manner in which primary goals are pursued (Dillard, Segrin, & Harden, 1989). When pursuit of a relationship is a primary goal, secondary goals would include such considerations as the desire to avoid imposing on others and the desire to appear socially appropriate. Importantly, the terms *primary* and *secondary* are not intended to indicate the relative importance of goals per se.

TABLE 4.1

Propositions From Relational Goal Pursuit Theory

1. Obsessive pursuers link the relationship goal to higher order goals (e.g., life happiness or self-worth).

2. Linking results in exaggerated positive attitude regarding the consequences of relational goal success.

3. Exaggerated positive attitude regarding relational goal success is associated with heightened anticipatory positive emotions (e.g., imagined happiness).

4. Linking produces exaggerated negative attitude regarding the consequences of relational goal failure (i.e., pursuers predict dire consequences of relational goal failure).

5. Exaggerated negative attitude regarding relational goal failure is associated with heightened anticipatory negative emotions (e.g., imagined sadness or frustration).

6. Linking renders goal abandonment less likely in the face of failure.

7. The exaggerated attitudes regarding the consequences of relational goal success and failure, and the corresponding anticipatory emotions, reinforce the importance of the relational goal.

8. Strength of attitudes regarding relational goal success and failure predict persistence of relational goal pursuit.

9. Intensity of anticipatory emotions associated with relational goal success and failure predict persistence of relational goal pursuit.

10. Relational goal frustration produces rumination.

11. Linking exacerbates rumination.

12. Negative attitudes and negative anticipatory emotions regarding relational goal failure exacerbate rumination.

13. Rumination intensifies over time.

14. Rumination fosters persistence in relational goal pursuit.

15. Relational goal frustration produces emotional flooding.

16. Rumination exacerbates emotional flooding.

17. Negative attitudes and negative anticipatory emotions regarding relational goal failure exacerbate emotional flooding.

18. Emotional flooding exacerbates rumination.

19. Emotional flooding predicts persistence in relational goal pursuit.

20. Obsessive pursuers rationalize interpretations of their own and their objects' behaviors in ways that justify persistence of relational goal pursuit.

21. Self-efficacy in enacting goal pursuit behaviors predicts the persistence of relational goal pursuit.

22. Action-outcome expectancies regarding goal pursuit behaviors predict the persistence of relational goal pursuit.

A primary goal may or may not be more important than any secondary goal in a given interaction (Wilson, 2002).

The formation of a relational goal emerges when one becomes aware of a desirable potential relational partner. Most commonly this occurs after individuals have interacted with one another and have had the opportunity to develop impressions. Such impressions comprise the raw materials for judging that a target possesses the features that would satisfy the type of relationship that is sought (e.g., companion, lover, friend, etc.). Of course, one can develop impressions about a complete stranger and set a relational goal accordingly, but normally some contact between parties acts as the stimulus for relational goal formation. A relational goal may become salient when one feels an existing desired relationship is threatened (i.e., experiences jealousy or relationship breakdown), or when a desired relationship is unilaterally terminated (e.g., divorce) or redefined (e.g., scaling back from romance to friendship) by a partner.

Strategic activity designed to achieve a relational goal is called *relational pursuit*. As we indicated in chapter 2, relationship pursuit involves a number of actions including attempts to seek the affinity of the target (Bell & Daly, 1984; Clark et al., 1999; Daly & Kreiser, 1994), acquire information about the target (Berger, 1987), manipulate the level of intimacy with the target (Honeycutt et al., 1998; Tolhuizen, 1989), and discern the mutuality of feelings and relationship intentions (Baxter & Wilmot, 1984; Bell & Buerkel-Rothfuss, 1990; Douglas, 1987). When such efforts intensify over time, particularly in response to or in the face of nonreciprocation, resistance, or rejection, then relational goal pursuit is considered persistent. According to the *American Heritage Dictionary*, to persist is "to be obstinately repetitious, insistent, or tenacious in some activity" and "to hold firmly and steadfastly to some purpose, state, or undertaking, despite obstacles, warnings, or setbacks" (Morris, 1979, p. 978).

When pursuit of a goal meets with initial difficulty or resistance, the natural impulse is to escalate goal-directed effort (e.g., Di Paula & Campbell, 2002). Numerous studies, for example, demonstrate support for the so-called rebuff phenomenon (see Hample & Dallinger, 1998); when an initial attempt to gain compliance meets with resistance, subsequent compliance-seeking messages are more aggressive (e.g., deTurck, 1985, 1987; Hample & Dallinger, 1998; Rule & Bisanz, 1987; Wilson, Whipple, & Grau, 1996). The degree of goal pursuit persistence depends on the perceived attainability and desirability of the goal. When obstacles to goal attainment seem insurmountable, an individual normally abandons the goal and redirects effort to pursue an alternative goal. When a goal seems attainable, then the effort expended to attain the goal is commensurate with its difficulty if potential motivation is sufficiently high (i.e., if the goal is sufficiently desirable; Brehm & Self, 1989; Wright, 1996). Oettingen and Gollwitzer (2001, p. 342) explained:

> If potential motivation is low, people do not find it worthwhile to expend more effort when an easy task becomes more difficult. The upper limit of effort expenditure is low and quickly reached. If potential motivation is high, however, an increase in difficulty is matched by investment of effort up to high levels of difficulty. The upper limit of effort expenditure is high and is reached only after much effort expenditure has occurred.

Thus, thwarted goals are abandoned when they are substitutable, when they lack importance (i.e., potential motivation is low), or when they are perceived to be unattainable. Goals are persistently pursued when they are seen as attainable, highly desirable, and not substitutable. The pursuer's commitment to the relational goal contributes to persistence of its pursuit. Persistent cognitive and affective processes that elevate the importance of the relational goal, thereby intensifying efforts to reach the goal, foster persistence of relational pursuit. We explicate these processes in the following sections.

Linking and Relational Goal Pursuit

An individual's goals are organized hierarchically (e.g., Berger, 2002; Martin & Tesser, 1989). Goals higher in the hierarchy tend to be more global, abstract, and important compared to goals lower in the hierarchy. Moreover, achievement of lower order goals is usually instrumental in accomplishing higher order goals. For example, the lower order goal of expressing a compliment may service the higher order goal of communicating affection. Compared to higher order goals, lower order goals are substituted more easily and more easily abandoned. The goal of giving a compliment might be replaced with the goal of performing a favor, which also could service the higher order goal of communicating affection.

Goal *linking* occurs when a person believes the attainment of particular lower order goals is *essential* to the attainment of a higher order goal (McIntosh & Martin, 1992). When the fulfillment of a higher order goal is *contingent* on the achievement of certain lower order goals, the goals are said to be linked within the goal hierarchy. We propose that obsessive relational pursuers link their lower order relational goal to higher order goals such as happiness (McIntosh & Martin, 1992; McIntosh et al., 1995) and self-worth (Pomerantz et al., 2000; Pyszczynski & Greenberg, 1987). In other words, they regard success in attaining the desired relationship as necessary for achieving happiness and they feel their self-worth is predicated on attaining the desired relationship. Hence, the lower order relational goal takes on the enduring quality of the higher order goal to which it is linked.

When it is linked to a higher order goal, the relationship goal takes on an exaggerated urgency and importance. Commitment to the relational goal fosters persistence of its pursuit, even in the face of failure (Brunstein & Gollwitzer, 1996; McIntosh & Martin, 1992). As McIntosh (1996, p. 62) argued, some "people may be unwilling or unable to give up a goal, even if the discrepancy is large and attaining the goal is difficult or impossible." Specifically, "people may not be able to disengage from a goal when it is seen as necessary in facilitating the attainment of an enduring, higher order goal." Consistent with a goal-linking interpretation, Dutton-Greene and Winstead (2001) found that perceiving a lack of alternatives to a desired relationship was associated with a greater degree of obsessive relational intrusion. Anecdotally, stalkers often make statements such as "we are fated to be together," and "there is no one else for me but you." In stalking narratives, typically "at least one person, usually the stalker, believes that an extraordinary, fundamental (potential or materialized) bond exists between two people, usually the stalker and the target" (Kamir, 2001, p. 15).

Anticipated Consequences of Relational Goal Success/Failure

The desirability of a relational goal is determined by the pursuer's assessment of the consequences of attaining or not attaining the goal. Bagozzi and Warshaw (1990) extended the theory of reasoned action (Fishbein & Ajzen, 1975) to explain goal pursuit. Trying to attain a goal (i.e., goal striving or goal pursuit behavior) is predicted from intentions to try, which in turn are predicted from attitude toward success in achieving the goal (weighted by the expectation of success) and attitude toward failure to achieve the goal (weighted by the expectation of failure). Because obsessive relational pursuers are heavily invested in the relational goal, they exaggerate both the benefits of attaining the desired relationship and the detriments of failing to attain the relationship. The pursuer's appraisal of these consequences, in turn, elicits positive and negative anticipatory emotions (Bagozzi et al., 1998). For example, the pursuer imagines the joy and happiness that will result from relational goal accomplishment. At the same time, the pursuer anticipates the sadness, distress, and fear that would attend goal failure. Because obsessional pursuers are so committed to their relational goal, they are likely to experience intense anticipatory emotions. Pomerantz et al. (2000) found, for example, that individuals who were highly invested in their goals were particularly susceptible to making predictions that goal nonattainment would be devastating. "Because people may feel that failure to meet the goals to which they are devoted will threaten their self-worth, they may make dire predictions about the emotional impact of such failure" (Pomerantz et al., 2000, p. 618). Bagozzi et al. (1998) argued that it is the intensity of anticipatory emotions that motivates goal-related volitions (i.e., intentions, plans, and decision to expend energy) and goal-directed behaviors.

Self-Efficacy and Outcome Expectancies

In addition to expectations regarding consequences, persistence of goal pursuit is driven by a consideration of feasibility. In particular, goal pursuers develop expectations about their ability to perform behaviors instrumental to goal achievement. Persistent pursuers have high self-efficacy (Bandura, 1997), which means they are confident they can enact the goal-directed behaviors. Self-efficacy is positively associated with the persistence of goal pursuit (Bagozzi, 1992; Bagozzi & Edwards, 2000; Bandura, 1997; Locke & Latham, 1990).

Goal pursuers also possess outcome expectancies—that is, "assessments of the likelihood that the initiation of goal-directed behaviors as means to an end will lead to goal achievement" (Bagozzi & Dholakia, 1999, p. 28). Persistent pursuers believe their goal-directed actions will result in successful goal achievement (Bagozzi, 1992). In combination, self-efficacy and positive outcome expectancies bolster the pursuer's belief that persistence in goal striving will pay off.

Rumination

When an important goal is frustrated, it leads to rumination (Brunstein & Gollwitzer, 1996; Martin & Tesser, 1989, 1996b; Martin, Tesser, & McIntosh, 1993; Millar, Tesser, & Millar, 1988). Rumination consists of repeated, intrusive, aversive thoughts associated with the inability to achieve a goal (Martin & Tesser, 1996b). Although the experience of intrusive thoughts is common, ruminative thoughts are relatively persistent, intense, and adhesive (Rachman, 1997). Attempts to control unwanted, intrusive thoughts by simply suppressing them does not work. Thought suppression provides a temporary distraction, but it paradoxically exacerbates the subsequent resurgence of the intrusive thoughts (Salkovskis & Campbell, 1994; Wegner, 1992; Wegner & Erber, 1992; Wegner, Schneider, Carter, & White, 1987; Wegner & Zanakos, 1994).

Stalkers are generally prone to ruminative thought (Eke, 1999), and persistent relationship pursuers obsessively worry about their insufficient progress in attaining the relational goal (Carson & Cupach, 2000). They mull over the unfinished business of relationship pursuit and become preoccupied and prepossessed with the object of pursuit. Among other things, "rumination involves attempts to find alternate means to reach important unattained goals or reconciling oneself to not reaching those goals" (Martin & Tesser, 1989, p. 311). Given the importance of the relation-ship goal (due to linking), the latter option of reconciling oneself to not reaching the goal is the less likely path for the obsessive pursuer.

Evidence suggests that rumination fuels persistence of relationship pursuit. In a study of intact romantic relationships, Carson and Cupach (2000) observed that relationship-specific rumination stimulated by ro-mantic jealousy was associated with a number of behavioral responses re-sembling profiles of ORI and stalking, such as heightened efforts to bolster relationship closeness, possessiveness and restriction of partner's move-ments, surveillance of partner, and threats and violence against partner. Ironically, the clandestine nature of some pursuer activity may enhance the attractiveness of the target and contribute to the pursuer's obsessive preoccupation (e.g., Lane & Wegner, 1994; Wegner, Lane, & Dimitri, 1994). Dutton-Greene (2003) conducted a pilot study ($n > 500$) of individuals who "had difficulty letting go of a partner of the same or other sex after the breakup of a romantic relationship." She asked participants to report expe-riences of rumination about the relationship at the time they had difficulty letting go of an ex-partner. Rumination was positively associated with the frequency of engaging in unwanted pursuit behaviors. In a similar study, Davis et al. (2000) employed five items to assess emotional reactions to a terminated relationship, which they labeled the "anger-jealousy cluster." Notably, two of the five emotional response items assessed rumination (i.e., "Couldn't get s/he off my mind" and "Thought about him/her a lot"). This measure was associated with perpetration of post-breakup ha-rassment and stalking.

Linking lower order goals to higher order goals contributes to rumina-tion. McIntosh and colleagues (McIntosh & Martin, 1992; McIntosh et al., 1995) observed that linkers (i.e., individuals who demonstrate a general tendency to link lower order goals to life happiness) were more likely to ru-minate than nonlinkers. McIntosh and Martin (1992) also provided evi-dence that this tendency occurred specifically among individuals who possessed an unmet relational goal. In a similar vein, Pomerantz et al. (2000) found that "goal investment was strongly associated with the fore-cast that failure would be upsetting. In fact, such forecasts accounted for the relation between goal investment and worrying, predicting increased worrying over time" (p. 627). To the extent that the obsessive pursuer's commitment to the relational goal leads to the tendency to predict that the consequences of goal failure would be dire, worrying about goal failure be-comes chronic (Pomerantz et al., 2000).

Rumination intensifies over time and persists until the unmet goal is ei-ther achieved or abandoned. Because obsessive pursuers are so devoted to the relational goal by virtue of linking it to happiness and self-worth, they are unlikely to abandon the goal. Individuals are "very reluctant to give up a goal that promises long-term happiness. They may cling to such goals even in the face of much negative affect" (McIntosh & Martin, 1992, p. 243). Insofar as pursuers retain the relational goal, rumination motivates intensified goal striving (Carson & Cupach, 2000; Cupach et al., 2000). As Pomerantz and colleagues (2000, p. 618) contended, "the worrying fostered by high goal investment may be one strategy people use to motivate themselves to reach the goals in which they are invested."

Emotional Flooding

Concomitant with the experience of negative thoughts associated with a thwarted goal, pursuers experience negative affect. Being denied something that one wants so desperately is emotionally distressing (Carver & Scheier, 1990; Millar et al., 1988). Hurt feelings derive from the pursuer's realization that the relational goal is not mutual (Leary & Springer, 2001; Leary et al., 1998). In addition, interpersonal rejection tends to elicit a complex blend of emotions such as fear, anger, guilt, shame, jealousy, and sadness (Leary, Koch, & Hechenbleikner, 2001). Research indicates that the persistence of attempts to reconcile a terminated relationship is positively associated with the degree of experiencing negative emotional reactions to the breakup, including general distress (Dutton-Greene, 2003; Dutton-Greene & Winstead, 2001), jealousy, anger (Davis et al., 2000; Dutton-Greene, 2003), and shame/guilt (Dutton-Greene, 2003). Similarly, Sinclair and Frieze (2000) found that reactions of frustration, hurt, anger, and depression associated with an experience of unrequited love were positively correlated with enacting stalking-like courtship behaviors.

Rumination contributes to the persistence of negative affect (McIntosh & Martin, 1992). Negative reactions polarize over time (Tesser, 1978; Tesser & Conlee, 1975), becoming more extreme and intense. States of unhappiness (McIntosh & Martin, 1992) and depression (McIntosh et al., 1995; Pyszczynski & Greenberg, 1987) are perpetuated by ruminative thought. The more pursuers dwell on the unmet relational goal, the more overwhelmed they feel. Emotional flooding occurs to the extent that the pursuer's negative thoughts and feelings are absorbing and consuming. Dutton-Greene (2003) found rumination due to the breakup of a desired relationship was positively associated with feelings of anger, jealousy, shame/guilt, and a global measure of absorbing negative affect (e.g., "I felt overwhelmed with bad feelings about the situation with my ex-partner.").

The emotional distress of thwarted goal achievement is self-perpetuating. The experience of negative feelings serves as a nagging reminder that an important goal remains unmet (Martin & Tesser, 1996a, 1996b). Bodily sensations confirm the miscalculated importance of obsessive thoughts (e.g., Rachman, 1998). In this way, negative affect exacerbates rumination. "The pursuer gets trapped in a vicious cycle of absorbing and aversive rumination and affect. Increasing rumination leads to greater negative affect, which in turn increases rumination, and so on, thereby perpetuating persistence in the recovery or development of the desired relationship" (Cupach et al., 2000, p. 141).

Rationalization and Disinhibition

Obsessive relationship pursuers are relatively ineffective in regulating their relational goal-directed behavior. In the face of mounting rumination and negative affect, rationalizations become necessary to enable continued goal pursuit. Pursuers systematically distort interpretations of the object's intentions and behaviors, adopt kind attributions regarding their own pursuit behavior, and acquire an attitude that legitimizes persistent and aggressive pursuit. These rationalizations disinhibit the pursuer's sense of appropriate goal-directed behavior.

The tendency to idealize a desired relational partner characterizes ordinary relationship development. To a degree, the possession of positive illusions contributes to relationship satisfaction and maintenance (Murray, Holmes, & Griffin, 1996). When a relationship is not reciprocated, however, the obsessive pursuer's persistent positive illusions about the object motivate unwanted pursuit. In Tennov's (1979) study of limerance, a type of obsessive and unreciprocated love, individuals in a state of limerance demonstrated "a remarkable ability to emphasize what is truly admirable in [the object of affection] and to avoid dwelling on the negative, even to respond to a compassion for the negative and render it, emotionally if not perceptually, into another positive attribute" (p. 24). Such idealization of a desired partner greatly magnifies the perceived attractiveness of the object, thereby strengthening the importance of the relational goal. The pursuer imagines an unrealistic vision of the desired relationship and greatly exaggerates its ostensible merits.

Obsessive pursuers' misconstruals extend to the meaning of the object's behavior. Avoidance of the pursuer is taken as encouragement. Even minimal doses of civility or attention from the object are construed as reciprocation of interest. Tennov (1998) recognized this feature in limerant lovers. She explained that they possess "an extraordinary ability to devise or invent 'reasonable' explanations for why the neutrality or even rejection that the disinterested observer might see in LO's [the limerant object's] behavior is in fact a sign of hidden passion" (p. 78). The fact that social rejection tends to be communicated in indirect and face-preserving ways (e.g., Folkes, 1982;

Metts, Cupach, & Imahori, 1992; Snow, Robinson, & McCall, 1991) makes it easier for the pursuer to entertain self-serving attributions. Obsessive pursuers bias their interpretations of ambiguous rejection to service their relational goal. They regard polite rejection as a sign of encouragement (Bratslavsky et al., 1998; de Becker, 1997a; Emerson et al., 1998). Blunt rejection is perceived to be token as "the determined stalker will ignore, deny or rationalise even the clearest of rejections" (Finch, 2001, p. 65). In their study of unwanted pursuit following the breakup of a romantic relationship, Langhinrichsen-Rohling and colleagues (2000, p. 86) discovered

> a surprising number of both relationship dissolvers and breakup sufferers indicated a positive response to the unwanted pursuit behavior. If unwanted pursuit behaviors occur frequently at the end of intimate relationships and if these behaviors sometimes have positive consequences for the pursuer (e.g., they are received positively or they restart the relationship), then it is likely to be more difficult to prevent many types of unwanted pursuit and to determine when unwanted pursuit clearly warrants intervention.

Obsessive pursuers may justify their persistence by over-reliance on cultural scripts for goal pursuit in general, and relational goal pursuit in particular. Persistence despite repeated rejection may be fostered by conventional beliefs such as, "If at first you don't succeed, try, try again," and "Quitters never win, and winners never quit." "The 'no means yes' ideology central to courtly persistence is rooted in Western romantic tradition, as love and courtship texts unmistakenly invoke this belief" (Lee, 1998, p. 389). Ubiquitous images in popular culture offer copious evidence for the obsessive relational pursuer that persistence ultimately succeeds. "Movies, books, and songs often portray the would-be lover's persistence as paying off when the rejector comes to his or her senses and recognizes the would-be lover for the wonderful person he or she is" (Bratslavsky et al., 1998, p. 251).

Overly persistent pursuers miscalculate the consequences of their persistence. To defend against the devastating consequences of relational goal failure, they rationalize their ability to achieve success (Gollwitzer, Wicklund, & Hilton, 1982). They are so overly invested in the relational goal, they become entrapped in its pursuit. Self-efficacy and outcome expectancies pertinent to the relational goal are unrealistically high. Obsessive pursuers steadfastly believe they can control the ultimate outcome of pursuit. They envision that success is inevitable, indeed necessary, and that they have the ability to stay in the game long enough to perform the behaviors that will produce success.

Obsessive pursuers are so preoccupied with pursuing the relational goal, they fail to grasp the consequences of their persistence for the object—"there is simply no sense that anything wrong or untoward is being done" (Babcock, 2000, p. 5). Perpetrators of relational transgressions in general tend to downplay the inimical consequences of their actions for victims (e.g., Baumeister, Stillwell, & Wotman, 1990; Mikula, 1994), and this tendency is especially acute among obsessive relationship pursuers. The pursuer over-looks the anxiety and inconvenience experienced by the object. Pursuit be-haviors that are aggravating and even fear-inducing for the object are merely seen as pathways to a necessary end state. The pursuer, moreover, may come to believe that increasingly aggressive actions are justified by honorable, even noble, intentions. Burgess et al. (2001, p. 320), for example, described the rationalizations of abusive partners who stalk:

> There are two positions taken by batterers who stalk: (1) their behaviors of stalking and terrorizing are legitimate actions and not worthy of interfer-ence by others; and (2) there are stalkers who admit, make excuses for the be-havior, see the behavior as wrong, but view their actions as defensible. In neither group do the stalkers assume responsibility for their behavior and its consequences. In one there is nothing wrong with the behavior in the mind of the predator and in the second, although the behavior might be wrong, the perpetrator is not responsible. What is operative in both of these aforementioned situations is that each is preoccupied with thoughts and fantasies regarding the victim.

As the obsessive pursuer becomes more desperate to compensate for the lack of success in achieving the relational goal, the pursuer's primary and secondary goal structure changes. The primary goal of having the desired relationship drowns out the secondary goals that would normally calibrate the appropriate degree of persistence. Secondary goals, such as the desire to present a positive self-image and the desire to appear socially appropriate, normally would prevent relational pursuit from becoming excessive. In the face of repeated rejection, normal pursuers realize that further persistence would engender negative attributions about them. Obsessive pursuers ei-ther fail to realize that the object and others perceive them to be desperate, weak, mentally unstable, or socially incompetent, or they do not care.

Summary

Relational goal pursuit theory identifies processes that conspire to transform otherwise normal relationship pursuit into obsessive relational intrusion and stalking. All relationship pursuit begins with a relational goal. For obses-sive pursuers, the relational goal is linked to higher order goals such as life happiness and self-worth. Given the extreme importance of these higher or-der goals, the pursuer invests undue importance in the relationship goal, making the relationship goal very difficult to abandon. In the face of resistance, the pursuer steps up efforts to achieve the thwarted relational goal. The pursuer's persistence in relational goal striving is fostered by several inter-related dynamics. The pursuer: (a) exaggerates the perceived conse- quences of relational goal success and failure consistent with persistent goal striving; (b) experiences anticipatory emotions associated with relational goal success and failure that motivate persistence; (c) believes relational goal pursuit will eventually be successful; (d) obsessively worries about not at- taining the desired relational goal; (e) feels increasingly emotionally dis- tressed and overwhelmed over time by the failure to attain the relational goal; and (f) rationalizes in a variety of ways that disinhibit pursuit behaviors that otherwise would be perceived as excessive and inappropriate. In short, obsessive pursuers become hypermotivated to pursue a relational goal be- cause of its perceived degree of desirability (necessity) and feasibility. Cognitions and emotions that escalate over time as the object of pursuit shows resistance serve to further motivate persistence and undermine more rational assessments of striving for an unrealistic goal.

PREDICTORS OF PURSUIT

Embedded in the development of most stalker typologies is the assumption that individual characteristics "typify" stalkers (or, conversely, stalking victims, although to date there are no stalking victim typologies per se). A natural extension of such reasoning is that stalkers (or stalking victims) can be differentiated from nonstalkers by some set of features or characteristics. Numerous studies have explored such characteristics in the hope of pre- dicting stalking or, at least, developing a profile of stalkers that could assist law enforcement, counselors, and prospective victims in risk management. Here we summarize contextual as well as individual factors that have been implicated in stalking research.

Individual Factors

One of the most common characteristics or predictors identified among stalkers is a history of previous criminality, conviction, and involvement in the criminal justice system (e.g., Harmon et al., 1995, 1998; Meloy, 1996a; Mullen & Pathé, 1994b; Roberts, 2002). Part of this pattern may reflect a sampling bias of the studies reporting these findings. That is, studies of col- lege students tend not to ask such questions, and therefore null findings are not reported. Furthermore, it stands to reason that the perpetrators of more severe cases that are likely to emerge in clinical and forensic samples are those with more enduring aggressive tendencies, and thus, those who are more likely to have experienced previous legal entanglements. Nevertheless, numerous studies show small to large percentages of stalkers with criminal records, convictions, or arrests (see Table 4.2). Indeed, in one sample, the stalkers on average had been arrested over 20 times (Scocas et al., 1996). At least one study, however, has shown that violence in stalking relationships is predicted by *lack* of criminality (Farnham & James, 2000), which suggests that violence is expressive rather than instrumental. This is consistent with research indicating violence is more likely when there has been a prior sexual relationship (Meloy et al., 2000), which is more characteristic of "normal" relationships than uniquely criminal populations.

A popular and oft-evidenced assumption in the prediction of violence is that past behavior is the best predictor of future behavior. If stalking is viewed as a subgroup of the domain of interpersonal aggression, it would follow that a history of violence would be predictive of stalking. Working deductively, one would also assume that stalkers would disproportionately reveal histories of physical and sexual violence in their past (Fisher et al., 1999, 2000; Nicastro et al., 2000; Roberts, 2002). Kienlen et al. (1997) found 32% and Burgess et al. (1997) found 53% of their stalking samples had histories of violence. Other studies have found that stalking victims are likely to report prior relational violence at the hands of stalkers (70%: Blackburn, 1999; 65%: Brewster, 1998, 2000; 12%: Sandberg et al., 1998). Sandberg et al. (1998) also found 82% of their sample had a "history of suicidal behavior or self harm." Related, several studies have found small to moderate relationships between stalking and psychological abuse and verbal aggression tactics (Burgess et al., 2001; Davis et al., 2000; Logan et al., 2000), or that substantial percentages of stalkers engage in behaviors such as "fear-inducing behavior" (e.g., 53%: Sandberg et al., 1998).

Stalking suggests, among other things, a pattern of deviant behavior that is relatively inattentive to social prescriptions and proscriptions. As such, it may reflect a general pattern of risk-taking behavior. One indication of such a risk-taking proclivity would be drug use or abuse. Many of the studies that have examined this have separated alcohol from drug use and abuse, whereas others have operationalized these collectively as an either/or item. The proportions of stalker samples with diagnosed or attributed drug abuse problems range from a relatively small minority to a majority (11%: Blackburn, 1999; 72%: Brewster, 1998; 50%: Burgess et al., 1997; 10%: Gill & Brockman, 1996; 52%: Harmon et al., 1995; 21%: Harmon et al., 1998; 64%: Kienlen et al., 1997; 32%: Lyon, 1997; 27%: Meloy & Boyd, 2003; 48%: Meloy et al., 2000, 15%: Morrison, 2001; 19%: Mullen & Pathé, 1994a; 76%: Sandberg et al., 1998; 43%: Zona et al., 1993). Several studies identified drug use or abuse as a risk factor for stalking in their samples (e.g., Roberts, 2002; Willson et al., 2000), and others identified substance abuse as a sub-diagnosis of Axis I disorders (e.g., Meloy et al., 2000).

TABLE 4.2
Studies Reporting Percentage of Stalkers With Criminal Records, Convictions, or Arrests

Percent With Criminal History	Source
12% had prior prison records	Blackburn (1999)
31% were attributed with criminal histories	Blackburn (1999)
62% had prior criminal record	Brewster (1998)
53% had prior criminal record	Hacket (2000)
63% had prior criminal history	Kienlen et al. (1997)
56% had criminal history of one or more convictions	Lyon (1997)
53% had prior misdemeanor or felony conviction	Logan et al. (2002)
66% had prior criminal history	Meloy et al. (2001)
37% had an adult criminal history	Meloy & Boyd (2003)
39% had prior criminal convictions	Mullen et al. (1999)
91% had prior arrests	Nicastro et al. (2000)
30% had prior arrests	Rosenfeld & Harmon (2002)
62% had some form of criminal history	Rosenfeld & Harmon (2002)

Before drug use and abuse are unequivocally associated with stalking risk, however, two important caveats need to be considered. First, the extent to which drug use is a risk factor should always be viewed as a relative factor. The question is not how many stalkers abuse drugs, but how much *more* likely are they to abuse drugs than (a) other criminal populations and (b) more normal populations. If the risk is not relatively greater than comparable populations, then drug use is not a demonstrable risk factor for stalking (see Lyon, 1997; Meloy et al., 2000; Schwartz-Watts et al., 1997). Second, drug use and abuse may be a mutual or reciprocal risk factor. That is, victim drug abuse may reflect a pattern of risk-taking behavior that entangles the victim with the prospective stalker. At least three studies have found victim drug use is associated with risk or level of stalking victimization (Burgess et al., 1997; Melton, 2001; Mustaine & Tewksbury, 1999).

As discussed earlier under motives, stalking is often assumed to be a product of mental disturbance, emotional problems, or general psychological disorder (Roberts, 2002). Across a variety of samples of stalkers (or victims' attributions about their stalkers), the percentages of general psychiatric or mental health problems have been estimated (13%: Blackburn,

1999; 14%: Hacket, 2000; 30%: Harmon et al., 1995; 22%: Huffhines, 2001; 80%: Kienlen et al., 1997; ~66%: Meloy & Gothard, 1995; 39%: Morrison, 2001; 38%: Pathé et al., 2000). Axis I characteristics, including mood disorders (e.g., 56% mood disorder: Gentile, 2001; 21% adjustment or mood disorder: Harmon et al., 1998; 10% mood disorder: Morrison, 2001), psychotic or schizophrenic disorders (e.g., 24%: Harmon et al., 1998; 35%: Kienlen et al., 1997; 49%: Meloy & Boyd, 2003; 9%: Morrison, 2001; 41%: Mullen et al., 1999; 40%: Rosenfeld & Harmon, 2002) with delusional symptoms (e.g., 29%: Harmon et al., 1995; 15%: Harmon et al., 1998; 36% Meloy & Boyd, 2003) or erotomanic subtype (e.g., 3%: Meloy et al., 2000; 12%: Sandberg et al., 1988; see also Sandberg et al., 1998; Zona et al., 1993). Collectively, several studies, especially those of clinical and forensic samples, find sizable percentages of stalking samples reflect Axis I disorders (e.g., 89%: Gentile, 2001; 78%: Kienlen et al., 1997; 60%: Meloy & Gothard, 1995; 86%: Meloy et al., 2000; 42%: Mullen et al., 1999; 34%: Rosenfeld & Harmon, 2000; 78%: Schwartz-Watts et al., 1997). Axis II disorders (74%: Gentile, 2001; 0%: Kienlen et al., 1997; 85%: Meloy & Gothard, 1995; 62%: Meloy et al., 2000; 60%: Romans et al., 1996), typically personality disorders (e.g., 32%: Harmon et al., 1998; 26%: Morrison, 2001; 51%: Mullen et al., 1999; 47%: Sandberg et al., 1998) such as borderline (e.g., 63%: Gentile, 2001; see also Lewis et al., 2001) or antisocial (see Meloy et al., 2000), or obsessive (e.g., 69%: Morrison, 2001) disorders are also implicated in stalking. Most of these studies were conducted with clinical and forensic samples, and therefore almost certainly overestimate the population prevalence of such disorders among all stalkers.

Erotomania (also referred to as de Clérambault's syndrome) represents a specific psychiatric disorder that is commonly associated with stalking (e.g., Harmon et al., 1995; Mullen & Pathé, 1994b). In some classification schemes, erotomanics constitute a specific category of obsessive pursuers (e.g., Cupach & Spitzberg, 1998; Zona et al., 1993). Pathé et al. (2000, p. 191) estimate that "Erotomania … is diagnosed in about 10 percent of stalker populations." According to Rosenfeld (2000, p. 533), "estimates of the frequency of erotomania among samples of individuals charged with or convicted of obsessional harassment ranges 10–30%." Interestingly, erotomanics are among the least dangerous stalkers (Menzies et al., 1995). Meloy (1992, p. 38) contended that "the best estimate is that less than 5% of individuals with the erotomanic subtype of Delusional (Paranoid) Disorder will be violent."

In its pure form, erotomania consists of the following features: (a) the erotomanic person possesses the delusional belief that another person (the object) passionately loves the erotomanic; (b) the object usually possesses higher social and financial status than the erotomanic; (c) the onset of erotomania is sudden; (d) its course is chronic, and fixed on a single object; (e) the erotomanic repeatedly attempts to approach or contact the object; and (f) the erotomanic exhibits paradoxical conduct, rationalizing that express denials of love by the object are actually secret affirmations of the object's love. Segal (1989, p. 1261) elaborated:

> Although the [erotomanic] patient insists that the object was the first one to declare his love, and can describe in elaborate detail the evidence for her belief (meaningful glances, messages passed through newspapers or the gestures of passersby, or telepathic communication, for example), in reality patient and object have had at most very casual contact and, in some cases, have never even met.

Individuals classified as having primary (or pure) erotomania generally are not diagnosed with other mental disorders, and they exhibit rationality on issues that do not pertain to the object. However, individuals diagnosed as erotomanic frequently present other symptoms, such as schizophrenia, schizoaffective disorders, bipolar disorder, and a host of organic factors ranging from dementia to the use of birth control pills (Carrier, 1990; Doust & Christie, 1978; Drevets & Rubin, 1987; El Gaddal, 1989; Gillett et al., 1990; Menzies et al., 1995; Mullen & Pathé, 1994a; Raskin & Sullivan, 1974; Rudden et al., 1990; Signer & Cummings, 1987). Such individuals are classified as showing secondary (or symptomatic) erotomania. Mullen et al. (2000a, p. 143) explicated the features characterizing secondary erotomania:

1. The erotomania owes its genesis and evolution to an underlying mental disorder that emerges prior to or contemporaneously with the erotomanic beliefs.
2. The clinical features of the underlying disorder are present alongside the erotomanic features.
3. The erotomania usually resolves as the underlying disorder resolves.

A common finding in stalker populations is a high proportion of unemployment or unstable work histories (Meloy & Gothard, 1995). Across studies, the rates vary, but suggest much higher than normal population unemployment (16%: Brewster, 2002; 18.5%: Gentile, 2001; 20%: Lyon, 1997; 31%: Brewster, 1998; 44%: Mullen et al., 1999; 50%: Hacket, 2000; 53%: Spencer, 1998; 60%: Kienlen et al., 1997). Employment status of both the stalker and the victim appears to be a predictor of stalking (Tjaden & Thoennes, 2000d). From a personality and attachment perspective, unemployment is a shock and stressor to the person's life that may stimulate aggressive pursuit of relational attachments as ways of compensating for the disorientation brought on by unemployment. From a routine activities perspective, not having a job provides much more time for stalking and the rumination and planning of such stalking. Interestingly, however, victims may be more at risk of stalking when they are employed (Mustaine & Tewksbury, 1999; Nicastro et al., 2000). Employment creates a predictable location and routine for victims that provides a greater range of opportunities for stalker pursuit and contact.

A wide variety of personality variables have been investigated as possible correlates of stalking behavior. The effect sizes have typically been relatively small. Stalking and persistent unwanted pursuit activities have been correlated with abusiveness (Burgess et al., 2001; Langhinrichsen-Rohling et al., 2000), anger (Burgess et al., 2001), controllingness or need for control (Davis et al., 2000; Dye & Davis, 2003; Del Ben, 2000; Melton, 2001; Montero, 2003; Spitzberg & Cupach, 2001b), hostility (Montero, 2003), and exploitativeness (Montero, 2003). In contrast, empathy was negatively related to stalking in one study (Spitzberg & Cupach, 2001b) and unrelated in another (Lewis et al., 2001). Macho-ism (Montero, 2003), hyperfemininity (Blackburn, 1999), and sex role identity (Turell, 2000; cf. Spitzberg & Cupach, 2001b) have revealed nonsignificant relationships with stalking and unwanted pursuit.

Love styles refer to the types of love people experience in their relationships, and can also be conceptualized as dispositional orientations to loving (Hatfield & Rapson, 1993; Hendrick & Hendrick, 1986). Lee (1976) developed a typology of six styles, with three primary (*eros*, *ludus*, and *storge*) and three secondary blends (*mania*, *pragma*, and *agape*). *Eros* is the prototypical passionate romantic type of love. *Ludus* is a game-playing and exploitative style of love. *Storge* is commonly known as platonic love, or companionate love. *Mania* is a possessive, dependent, and addictive style of love, blending *eros* and *ludus* (Nelson, Hill-Barlow, & Benedict, 1994; Speziale, 1994; Timmreck, 1990). *Pragma* is a calculated and rational approach to love, blending *storge* and *ludus*. *Agape* is a selfless, idealistic love, blending *eros* and *storge*. It seems likely that *agape* and *storge* would be negatively related to stalking, and *mania* would be positively related to stalking. Indeed, *mania* has revealed a small positive relationship (Brewster, 1998; Langhinrichsen-Rohling & Rohling, 2000; Sinclair & Frieze, 2000; Spitzberg, 2000a) and *storge* has shown a small negative relationship (Spitzberg, 2000a) to stalking. Unexpectedly, *eros* (Dye & Davis, 2003; Sinclair & Frieze, 2000) and even *storge* (Brewster, 1998) have revealed small isolated relationships with obsessive relational intrusion, but not consistently.

Insecurely attached or manic lovers are likely to be jealous and possessive. Most people who experience jealousy are not violent, but a high proportion of intimate violence is motivated by jealousy (Guerrero, Spitzberg

& Yoshimura, in press). Certainly morbid or pathological jealousy would seem a strong candidate for promoting stalking activity. Several studies have identified jealousy or suspicion as a risk factor (Del Ben, 2000; Harmon et al., 1995), although the effect sizes tend to be small (Brewster, 1998; Davis et al., 2000; Langhinrichsen-Rohling et al., 2000; Montero, 2003; Roberts, 2002; Spitzberg & Cupach, 1999; Tjaden & Thoennes, 1998b).

A key developmental feature that could affect attachment and love styles is the experience of abuse in one's family of origin. Family-of-origin factors have been suggested as risk factors in several studies. Kienlen et al. (1997) found 55% and Gentile (2001) found 67% of stalkers reported abuse as a child. Blackburn (1999) found stalking victims were more likely than nonstalking subjects to have been physically or sexually abused both as children and as adults. Harmon et al. (1995) found 31% of stalkers had a family background of violence. In contrast, Langhinrichsen-Rohling and Rohling (2000) found amount of unresolved family conflict was associated with amount of unwanted pursuit victimization, yet having witnessed family-of-origin violence was not associated with unwanted pursuit (Langhinrichsen-Rohling & Rohling, 2000).

Closely related to the attachment loss hypothesis is the social incompetence hypothesis. Specifically, as a population, stalkers are expected to display disproportionately lower social skills than normal populations. Mullen, Pathé, and Purcell (2001, p. 340) asserted that "it is unusual to encounter a stalker with adequate, let alone good, interpersonal and social skills. Most are drawn from the awkward, oversensitive and isolated of the world." Likewise, Meloy (1996b, p. 159) claimed, "The psychopathology of obsessional following appears to be, in part, a maladaptive response to social incompetence, social isolation, and loneliness. What differentiates these individuals from others, however, appears to be their aggression and pathological narcissism." "Many stalkers are unable to sustain normal social and personal relationships and prefer an 'arms length' relationship which is pseudointimate and which they can control" (Babcock, 2000, p. 3). The hypothesis suggests that, among other things, "stalking behavior is one manifestation of a maladaptive social behavior repertoire" (Westrup & Fremouw, 1998, p. 272). Stalkers are often characterized as displaying inappropriate emotion and as having difficulty forming relationships (Roberts, 2002). Stalkers appear less likely to be married (Meloy & Gothard, 1995; Schwartz-Watts et al., 1997) or to be in a long-term relationship (Mullen et al., 1999). In one small sample study, over half of the sample of stalkers was characterized as socially incompetent or having poor social functioning (Mullen & Pathé, 1994a). In contrast, in Lyon's (1997) sample of stalkers only 12% rated their social/interpersonal functioning as "poor" and 65% felt they were "outgoing" and had good social networks. When these rates were compared with the nonstalking criminal population, there was no difference. Again, the question of effect needs to be weighed in terms of not only prevalence of a characteristic among stalkers, but its prevalence *relative* to nonstalking populations.

Contextual Factors

One of the contextual features of relational stalking that may influence its course is locus of relationship breakup. Research on domestic violence has indicated that attempted or actual separation may be the most dangerous time for women (e.g.,Wilson & Daly, 1993). Part of this effect is likely the face threat created for the relational partner who is rejected. Several studies have provided evidence that the person "dumped" is more prone to engaging in stalking and unwanted pursuit than those who do the "dumping" (e.g., Brewster, 1998; Davis et al., 2000; Dye & Davis, 2003). However, the nationally representative study by Tjaden and Thoennes (1998b) found that 21% of victims were stalked before breakup, 36% were stalked before and after, and 43% were stalked only after the breakup. Similarly, Hacket (2000) found one-third of couples were living together during the stalking. However, consistent with homicide research (Wilson & Daly, 1993), evidence indicates risks of stalking are elevated when the relationship is "former" rather than "current" (e.g., Burgess et al., 2001). In one study, "those who were not involved with the abuser in the prior 6 months prior to Time 1 were more than twice as likely (53.5%) to report the highest levels of stalking than those who were involved with the abuser (24.9%)" (Melton, 2001, p. 121). A factor reinforcing such influences may be the attachment loss per se in such breakups. That is, any proximal significant loss or disruption of one's close relationship network is likely to create an attachment vacuum. It is not surprising therefore that high proportions of stalkers appear to have experienced recent attachment loss (e.g., Gentile, 2001; Kienlen et al., 1997) and are currently without an intimate partner (e.g., Meloy & Gothard, 1995; Mullen et al., 1999).

The routine activities perspective anticipates stalking victimization is more probable because of various opportunity and risk factors. People who engage in activities that increase their (a) actual or apparent vulnerability, (b) public profile or exposure, or (c) social and relational risk-taking, are likely to be at higher risk of drawing the attentions of an unwanted pursuer. Various routine-based factors have been shown to increase the risk of stalking, or to be more prominent among stalking victims. For example, frequenting places with alcohol (Fisher et al., 1999, 2000), living in privately rented housing (Budd & Mattinson, 2000), living alone (Burgess et al., 1997; Fisher et al., 1999, 2000), engaging in various computer activities (LeBlanc et al., 2001), and having student status (Budd & Mattinson, 2000) have shown relationships to stalking victimization. It seems reasonable to expect that dozens of other such factors may be predictive of both stalker behaviors and risk of victimization. A likely reason for such factors remaining elusive is a general psychocentric bias of research, in which the cause of stalking is presumed to exist in the individual and the individual's history and psychological makeup, rather than in the relationship or the contexts in which people find themselves. Ultimately, a complete theory of stalking and unwanted pursuit will need to accommodate all of these factors.

Summary

The breadth and diversity of factors that display association with stalking are clearly difficult to summarize. Meloy (1996b, 2001) attempted to summarize the most prominent factors associated with stalkers: They are more likely to be more educated, unemployed or underemployed, have a history of failed heterosexual relationships, have prior criminal histories, and the more extensive the criminal history, the more likely an antisocial personality disorder, Axis I (most commonly substance abuse and/or mood disorder and/or schizophrenia) and Axis II (cluster B: narcissism, borderline, antisocial) disorders; antisocial disorder probably affects 10% of stalkers (Meloy, 2001). Westrup and Fremouw (1998) identified a somewhat similar profile of the typical stalker:

1. Stalkers are likely to have either an Axis I or an Axis II mental disorder (or both) and/or a prior history of mental illness ….
2. Although many women engage in stalking behavior, most stalkers are men ….
3. Most stalkers are single, and many have never been married ….
4. Stalkers in offender populations are typically older than other offenders ….
5. Stalkers are better educated … and more intelligent … than other offenders. (Westrup & Fremouw, 1998, p. 268)

However, the breadth of studies on individual factors associated with stalking and the dearth of studies on temporal and contextual factors associated with stalking illustrate an important disciplinary bias of stalking research. There is extensive research on *who* stalks *whom* and *how* they stalk, but there is minimal research on the *where* and *when* of stalking. Much more research, specifically sequential, act-based, longitudinal and relational (i.e., dyadic) research, is needed to address such biases and provide a sufficiently comprehensive and complex predictive model of the stalking process.

CONCLUSION

Although knowledge about ORI and stalking is rapidly accumulating, the state of development can be regarded as mostly pretheoretical. The construction and application of theory to the dynamics of unwanted pursuit hold the promise of elevating the value of current information and enhancing the abilities to explain and predict. Because the profiles of unwanted pursuit are quite varied, multiple and complementary theoretical maps are needed to chart the complex territory of victimization and perpetration. A complete understanding of unwanted pursuit requires attention to multiple levels of analysis, with variables ranging from the individual, to the relational, to the social and cultural levels (White, Kowalski, Lyndon, & Valentine, 2000).

In this chapter we summarized two theoretical frameworks for understanding some aspects of unwanted pursuit. Attachment theory offers a distal explanation tied to disruptions in an individual's childhood bonding with primary caregivers. Relational goal pursuit theory represents an attempt to identify the proximal dynamics that transform otherwise ordinary relationship pursuit into an obsessive and excessive endeavor. Both frameworks exhibit heuristic value. More research is needed to identify the complex associations attachment style might have with stalking. Davis et al. (2000), for example, found that the influence of insecure attachment on stalking behaviors was mediated by the emotional reactions to a breakup of jealousy and anger. It could be useful in future research to explore what factors might moderate, that is, augment or attenuate, the effects of insecure attachment on stalking tendencies. Relational goal striving is in the early stages of development. Most of its empirical support is indirect at this stage, thus work on measurement and testing is needed. In the meantime, additional theories should emerge as contenders for explaining ORI and stalking. Theory development is necessary to move beyond a veritable shopping list of predictor variables.

CHAPTER FIVE

Managing Unwanted Pursuit

Any attempt to understand the nature of stalking and unwanted pursuit requires an understanding of the victim of such harassment. Stalkers and obsessive pursuers may be the primary actors in structuring their dramas, and victims may primarily behave in a reactive mode to the unwanted attention, but both patterns of activity are an integral part of the equation of unwanted pursuit. No chess game can be fully understood without considering the countermoves in reaction to the moves.

This chapter examines these moves and countermoves by first examining the various effects that stalking and unwanted pursuit and intrusion can have on the objects of such harassment. In order to explicate these effects, a new typology of stalking symptoms is developed. After reviewing the typology, we examine in greater detail the particularly severe consequences of stalking—threats and violence. The chapter next articulates a systematic typology of coping tactics available to victims of unwanted pursuit. Next, the role of law enforcement and institutional resources is examined, with special emphasis on the efficacy of restraining orders as one of the primary preventative tactics employed by victims. Finally, some speculations are offered on relational skills that may facilitate more competent management of courtship and relationship development.

Several important points of departure deserve mention before presenting the symptom typology. Specifically, the research on the symptomology of stalking has revealed several gaping blind spots. Some of these blind spots reflect ideological and political biases of those investigating the phenomenon. Others reflect general inattention to the broader scholarly literatures relevant to understanding stalking. One blind spot is the exclusion of potential neutral and positive outcomes of stalking victimization. Indeed, "whether a situation can be correctly termed 'stalking' if the recipient does not have an adverse reaction to the experience is open to debate" (Finch, 2001, p. 51). It may be that "those who are stalked do not invariably mani-

119

fest psychological disturbance or other ill-effects as a consequence" (Mullen et al., 2000a, p. 221).

We do not intend to suggest stalking victimization tends to or, on balance, produces positive effects on those affected by its activities. However, the possibility exists that some portion of stalking victims either experience relatively minor or insubstantial reactions, and still others may construct positive outcomes *in addition to* any deleterious effects of victimization. "There are a range of possible reactions to stalking ranging from amusement, indifference and tolerance to the more unfavourable reactions such as anger, distress and anxiety" (Finch, 2001, p. 48). There are those who are likely to be too politically correct or too intellectually timid to pursue this line of investigation. The fear may be that to admit such possibilities is to either (a) undercut the seriousness of antistalking enforcement in the societal agenda or (b) imply victim complicity or responsibility for their outcomes, thereby absolving correspondingly the culpability of the stalker.

We have two responses to such reservations. First, they are contrary to the search for empirical reality. We believe social problems are best managed when the most accurate information is available. Second, and more importantly, if certain victims turn out to be more resilient than others, it becomes vital to understand what characteristics enable such resilience. Such factors may guide future therapeutic intervention efforts, diagnostic approaches, and better prioritization of public resources. For example, a few studies have found that in addition to their negative outcomes, victims of intimate violence sometimes find silver linings or catharsis effects in their experience (e.g., Greenberg, Wortman, & Stone, 1996; McMillen, Zuravin, & Rideout, 1995). To date, with the exception of one study (Spitzberg & Rhea, 1999), research on stalking has presupposed that stalking victimization inevitably produces only destructive, undesirable consequences for the victim. We do not make this assumption, and believe future research and assessment efforts must at least account for the possibility of positive or neutral outcomes in addition to negative outcomes to stalking. Such commitments are reflected by a symptoms measure adapted from the Spitzberg and Rhea (1999) study, which is displayed in Appendix 5, in which several potential items are included reflecting victim resilience.

A second oversight of most stalking research is an excessive focus on the individual who is the primary target of the unwanted pursuit. Although research occasionally recognizes third parties may be intentionally or incidentally involved in the stalker's campaign of pursuit, there has been relatively little systematic attention to these possibilities (cf. Sheridan et al., 2001a). The possibility of others being involved in victimization beyond the primary target of pursuit has been discussed as the "radiating impact" of intimate violence (Riger, Raja, & Camacho, 2002). A distinction is made among first-order, second-order, and third-order effects. First-order effects are symptoms as typically conceptualized—harms to the individual who is the direct target of abuse or violence. Stalking victims may experience a fear or paranoia about the prospect of being confronted by a stalker in some future encounter. Second-order effects are impacts on that victim's relationships with others, such as family, friends, coworkers, romantic partners, or relatives. A stalking victim's fear may lead a victim to respond with relative isolation and curtailment of social activities, which leads to the deterioration of that victim's relationships with others. "Stalking characteristically produces in the victim hypervigilance and suspicion. This, though entirely appropriate, tends to alienate victims from many of the usual sources of support, thus adding to their sense of isolation and vulnerability" (Mullen et al., 2000b, p. 456). Third-order effects are the direct, unique effects on those third parties. "Those close to the stalking victim may experience profound misery and upheaval regardless of any direct intimidation from the stalker" (Pathé & Mullen, 2002, p. 9). If a victim's marriage breaks up because of the stress caused by stalking victimization, this divorce or separation has unique effects on the victim's spouse. If a stalker attacks a perceived rival to his or her affections, then these are unique direct effects on third parties who otherwise would not be victims to the stalking. We presume that any typology of symptoms needs to include all three orders of effects at a minimum to claim comprehensiveness.

A third oversight of symptoms research, one that only emerged once the typological work was completed for this project, is that "macro" symptoms have been completely ignored by current research on stalking. Given the psychological and counseling bias of much stalking research, the emphasis of research has been on what can be measured psychologically in the individual victim. However, no research has examined the *societal* or *institutional* symptoms of stalking. Research has examined *cultivation effects* of crime in general, and violent crime in particular. When the media display violence in their content in frequencies or levels of severity that are massively disproportionate relative to societal levels of actual occurrence, it tends to create a societal sense of fear and apprehension about the chances of personal victimization. Thus, people who watch more television tend to have significantly inflated perceptions of their actual risk of violent victimization (e.g., Lowry et al., 2003; Romer et al., 2003). It is possible that the prevalence of stalking, the ways in which news of such stalking is represented in the media, and the fictionalization of stalking all have cultivation effects on society's collective sense of personal safety, its trust and faith in various institutions (e.g., law enforcement), and its reactions to political and social agendas regarding stalking. The fact that all 50 states in the United States, the federal government, and at least four other countries passed antistalking legislation in the narrow time span of 1990 to 1998 evidences the societal perception of an imminent threat from stalking. Whether or not that perceived threat is proportional to actual risks is a question yet to be addressed, but such macro-level effects of stalking need to be considered in any comprehensive survey of its impact on others.

CONSEQUENCES OF VICTIMIZATION

Research has extensively evidenced the traumatizing effects of criminal and violent victimization (e.g., Norris & Kaniasty, 1994; Ruch, Gartrell, Amedeo, & Coyne, 1991; Senn & Dzinas, 1996). In light of other lines of research on the assessment of symptoms (e.g., Attansasio, Andrasik, Blanchard, & Arena, 1984; Brewin et al., 2002; Briere & Runtz, 1990; Derogatis, Lipman, Rickels, Uhlenhuth, & Covi, 1974; Derogatis, Rickels, & Rock, 1976), there is already a solid foundation for organizing the typical types of symptoms to expect among stalking victims. Research on activities bearing a resemblance to features of stalking, such as sexual harassment (Lees-Haley, Lees-Haley, Price, & Williams, 1994), sexual coercion (e.g., Arata & Burkhart, 1996; Zweig, Barber, & Eccles, 1997), and obsessive relational intrusion (Cupach & Spitzberg, 2000), reveals a relatively consistent tendency toward adverse emotional and psychological effects.

Stalking victims in particular are generally presumed to be "living in hell" (Draucker, 1999). However, to date most research has haphazardly listed a series of possible symptoms or effects with little or no effort to sample systematically from the universe of potential effects of interest. Others focused on more severe forms of trauma, such as posttraumatic stress syndrome (PTSD; see de Girolamo & McFarlane, 1996; Friedman & Marsella, 1996; Wallace & Silverman, 1996), a particularly severe and diffuse form of negative effect (Mechanic, Uhlmansiek, Weaver, & Resick, 2000; Pathé & Mullen, 1997; Westrup et al., 1999). The potential severity of stalking victimization is dramatically revealed in a study of Dutch stalking victims, 59% of whom "reported a clinically significant level of psycho-medical symptoms ... comparable to those reported in samples of victims of generally recognized traumata ... very similar to the proportion recently reported among victims of the Boeing 737-2D6C crash in Coventry" (Kamphuis & Emmelkamp, 2001, pp. 796–797). Davis et al. (2002), in a reanalysis of Tjaden and Thoennes's (1998b) nationally representative data found stalking victims who were afraid of their stalker revealed elevated risks of poor current health, likelihood of developing a chronic disease, and injury. However, at least one study found that (a) stalking behavior accounted for relatively minor proportions of variance in victim trauma, and (b) this may be due to variations in victim resilience, (c) which is suggested by the finding in this sample that "previous psychological difficulties were reported by approximately half the victims" (Blaaw, Winkel, Sheridan, Malsch, & Arensman, 2002, p. 31). In other words, part of some victims' trauma is a symptom of preexisting vulnerabilities that may correlate but not be causally connected to their stalking victimization. Such findings do not deny victims are traumatized, but do imply caution in making causal attributions of symptoms to stalking victimization that rely merely on ambiguous correlational data.

If such subtleties are to be disentangled, a clear vocabulary of symptomology is necessary. Nevertheless, to date surveys of stalking symptomology have yet to construct a typological vocabulary for summarizing the impact of stalking. In order to rectify this, an effort was undertaken to develop such a typology. The first step was to survey the general symptomology literature already noted for the suggestion of relevant categories and types. The second step was to review the stalking literature generally for suggestions of effects. Finally, the 143 studies on stalking were examined. Those studies reporting percentage prevalence estimates for symptoms were identified. Those estimates were extracted and itemized and then coding procedures similar to those reported in chapter 3 were conducted. Excess verbiage was stripped and core terms were placed in primary sentence locations, whereupon semantic and conceptual groupings were sought. As these groupings emerged, isolated symptoms were examined to see if they could be bootstrapped into other categories. Once most symptoms had a category label, higher order categories were constructed. The result is the typology in Table 5.1, the specific items of which appear in Appendix 6. The typology identifies 11 categories of effects. Most categories are capable of including either positive or negative effects.

Two types of rather vague or broad-based life disruption emerged from the data. General effects describe those items that identified diffuse or collective injury to one's quality of life, including PTSD. This category included generic items such as "general stress," "psychologically or emotionally injured," and "quality of life costs." Percentage prevalence in this category ranged from 11 to 100% of stalking victims. The second broad-based disruption category is behavioral disruption. Behavioral effects refer to wide-ranging changes to everyday activity patterns. Most of the exemplars in this category reflect unwanted disruptions, such as forcing one to change work or school activities, transit patterns, or day-to-day behavior. Some victims perceived themselves changing their interpersonal behavior patterns, such as becoming more aggressive. The prevalence of these deleterious behavioral effects indicated a range of 27 to 53% of stalking victims. In contrast, in one study, 51% of victims also reported developing "better coping skills" as a consequence of being stalked.

TABLE 5.1
Stalking Symptom Typology

1. General effects (i.e., vague or diverse deleterious effects on quality of life; e.g., PTSD, general disturbance of well-being, etc.)

2. Behavioral effects (i.e., interference in patterns of behavior; e.g., changing one's routes to work)

3. Affective health effects (i.e., changes in emotional quality of life; e.g., depression, anxiety, sadness, grief, etc.)

4. Cognitive health effects (i.e., changes in volitional/rational quality of life; e.g., distrust, suspicion, lack of concentration, etc.)

5. Physical/physiological health effects (i.e., changes in physical quality of life; e.g., sleep disorders, loss of appetite, illness, etc.)

6. Social health effects (i.e., changes in relational quality of life; e.g., losing or gaining friends, straining or strengthening family relationships, etc.)

7. Resource health effects (i.e., changes in property or economic quality of life; e.g., changing careers, investing in home security, etc.)

8. Spiritual effects (i.e., changes in quality of faith-based belief systems; e.g., loss of faith in god, spiritual malaise, etc.)

9. Societal effects (i.e., cultivation effects, collective changes in cultural belief systems; e.g., societal suspicion, fear of crime, distorted stereotypes of stalkers, etc.)

10. Ambivalent effects (i.e., coexisting mixed effects, particularly of both positive and negative effects; e.g., feeling relief at knowing "where" one's pursuer is, feeling angry and empowered, etc.)

11. Minimal effects (i.e., experiencing few, minor, or no appreciable effects)

The next seven categories of symptoms contain relatively specific content groupings. The category labels represent rather standard conceptual *topoi* for organizing social life. No pretense is made that these are either exhaustive or entirely mutually exclusive. For example, paranoia clearly has cognitive, affective, behavioral, and social health effects. However, in the interest of interpretability, an effort was made to identify the primary thrust of each classified item.

Affective health effects primarily refer to the influence of stalking victimization on the emotional life of the victim. Among the negative affective experiences, the most common were: anger ($M = 31.78\%$, $n = 9$), annoyance ($M = 39.67\%$, $n = 3$), anxiety ($M = 59.00\%$, $n = 5$), depression ($M = 26.00\%$, $n = 5$), fear/terror/frightened ($M = 38.67\%$, $n = 24$), and stress/distress/frustration ($M = 37.88\%$, $n = 8$). There were miscellaneous other affective outcomes, such as disgust, guilt, embarrassment, jealousy, sadness, and surprise, that were isolated effects. Four items were interpreted as possible positive affective effects of stalking victimization, which were collectively labeled attractiveness, including feeling admired, loved, cared for, and flattered. These are consistent with findings from Dunn's (1999, 2002) research on the ambivalent experiences women report in stalking-like romantic scenarios.

Cognitive effects refer to primarily mental, analytical, contemplative types of effects. Among the negative cognitive symptoms, the most typical were: general loss of faith ($M = 7\%$, $n = 3$), loss of faith in or regard for self ($M = 20.09\%$, $n = 11$), loss of faith in others ($M = 43.00\%$, $n = 3$), loss of faith in institutions ($M = 6.25\%$, $n = 4$), a sense of isolation or alienation ($M = 25.29\%$, $n = 7$), aggressive thoughts ($M = 36.67\%$, $n = 3$), a sense of apprehension and cautiousness ($M = 37.14\%$, $n = 14$), and distraction or confusion ($M = 26.71\%$, $n = 7$). There were nine items indicating potentially positive cognitive effects of stalking victimizations. These were collectively labeled compensation–resilience, and included better safety awareness, sense of direction and purpose, and strengthened self-concept.

There was a broad range of somatic symptoms displayed in the literature. The negative effects included sleep disruption ($M = 26.33\%$, $n = 9$), physical injury ($M = 21.67\%$, $n = 15$), self-injury ($M = 7\%$, $n = 2$), illness or loss of vitality ($M = 7.5\%$, $n = 2$), eating or digestive effects ($M = 19.00\%$, $n = 6$), addiction ($M = 11.50\%$, $n = 2$), and headache ($M = 13.33\%$, $n = 3$). There were no positive behavioral effects examined in these studies—that is to say, no researchers included positive behavioral effects among their research items. It is possible to conceive of patterns of greater responsibility over one's job, family, or hobbies, an enhanced level of caution in one's behavior, heightened attention to the safety of one's social network, and even such outcomes as improved health due to exercise or enrollment in self-defense classes. Some of these results occurred, but were classified in the typology of coping responses (to be reviewed later), and therefore are underrepresented in this symptom typology.

Social effects, or largely what would be considered second-order or third-order effects, consisted of both positive and negative outcomes. The negative social effects included symptoms such as avoiding people and places, curtailing social activity, deterioration of relationships, loneliness, and loss of valued relationships ($M = 36.80\%$, $n = 10$). Three positive social effects emerged, all referring to strengthened relationships ($M = 48.83\%$, $n = 3$). These effects could come about through increased interdependence or proximity with certain people, and may also reflect the possibility of "finding out" who "one's real friends are."

Resource effects consisted of uniformly negative outcomes, including such experiences as reduced work, financial costs, and loss of job ($M =$

32.25%, $n = 8$). Although the literature is replete with anecdotal reports of victims having to invest in home security, changing telephone numbers, purchasing different telephones or answering machines, obtaining a post office box, and so forth, these types of responses are typically not viewed as resource costs. Many of these responses do indeed cost money and time, although they are categorized in the coping response typology rather than as symptoms.

There was one isolated item suggesting that at least one symptom of being stalked might be spiritual in nature. This could have been classified as a cognitive effect, but spiritual effects such as a loss of faith in God seem more far-reaching in nature. Furthermore, it seems reasonable to conjecture that it is possible for some victims to develop a stronger spiritual system of belief or "relationship" with their god(s) due to the crisis of stalking victimization.

Although no examples emerged, once the typology began to form, it seemed logically possible for stalking victimization, taken broadly, to have effects at a more macro level of society. Specifically, given that enculturation research demonstrates effects of violent crime, and especially the effects of reporting violent crime in the various media, it seems reasonable to expect stalking victimization to have such effects as well. Future research needs to include items that refer to general attitudes toward the possibility of personal victimization as well as the relative importance of stalking to other types of crimes or societal priorities. Thus far, research indicates stalking does not increase fear of crime or decrease sense of general safety among stalking victims (McCreedy & Dennis, 1996; Romans et al., 1996), so such enculturation effects may not be substantial, but they should at least be included in the assessment. However, it appears that no research to date has examined cultivation effects of stalking media consumption and perceptions of personal or societal risks.

Two somewhat unexpected categories emerged from the data. Ambivalent effects represent simultaneously mixed or opposing feelings, such as "relief mixed with extreme nervousness." This is reminiscent of Dunn's (1999, p. 449) study in which she found that more than "one quarter of the women are both moderately or extremely romanced *and* at least moderately frightened, and almost half the sample are both moderately or extremely flattered *and* at least moderately annoyed" by intrusive courtship activities. The other unexpected category of effects was little or no effects. Minimal effects were found in items from two studies. However, the possibility of minimal effects is probably significantly underestimated because (a) few studies have included items explicitly referring to ambivalent or minimal effects, and (b) these studies have yet to analyze their data to examine what percentage of victims reported *none* of the symptoms listed in the checklists.

Our typology provides a more comprehensive set of symptoms than previously recognized in the stalking literature. However, there are limitations to any such typology. One important flaw is that, like stalking, symptoms are temporal in nature (see chap. 3). For example, symptoms may get progressively worse over time. Indeed, some conjecture that the cumulative temporal nature of stalking is what makes it uniquely traumatizing: "Stalking is a cumulative crime, the effects of which increase, almost exponentially, with each new manifestation— … the one-hundreth occasion is incomparably worse than the first precisely because there have been ninety-nine previous occasions" (Infield & Platford, 2002, p. 233). Perhaps it is not the cumulative linear effect per se but its cyclical nature that is most harmful. Kamir (2001, p. 17) speculated, "Stalking tends to replace a linear feeling of passing time with a cyclical one." In contrast, Finch (2001, p. 40) suggested such cycles may have unanticipated effects, in which victims experience "paradoxical feelings of relief when the stalking recommenced after a period of inactivity, especially if there had been previous periods of dormancy." Finally, there is yet almost no sense of the duration of symptoms over time relative to case characteristics. "Hardly anything is known about the relationship between the frequency, duration, intensity and intrusiveness of stalking behaviour on the one hand and the seriousness of victims' symptoms on the other" (Blaaw, Winkel, Sheridan, Malsch, & Arensman, 2002, p. 30). Although the vast majority of research indicates that the typical stalking victim experiences a wide range of moderate to severe negative symptoms, to date there is almost no research connecting particular features of victimization to the nature of the symptoms.

In examining the consequences of stalking and unwanted pursuit, there are three categories that take on notable social significance. Although technically "threat," "physical violence," and "sexual violence" can be considered "tactics" of stalking, they also by definition represent consequences to the victim. Therefore, these tactics are examined here as a separate domain of victim consequences.

THE SEVERITY OF STALKING: THREAT AND PHYSICAL AND SEXUAL VIOLENCE

Threat and violence are of special concern to policymakers, law enforcement, threat management professionals, scholars, and especially victims. Stalking is in large part defined by the perception and imminence of threat, and threat is intimately related to harm, injury, and violence. Although other forms of pursuit and intrusion may produce substantial decrements in quality of life, it is the imminence of physical harm (i.e., threats) and actual physical harm (i.e., physical violence) and violation (i.e., sexual violence) that tend to strike the most acute fear in most people's minds. The presumption of most stalking experts is that "all stalking victims are at risk for personal safety" (Wright et al., 1996, p. 500). Indeed, threats were the focus of some of the earliest stalking-related research (Dietz, et al., 1991; Dietz, et al., 1991) and have been a central concern to the prevention of violence (Calhoun, 1998; Fein & Vossekuil, 1999; McGee & Debernardo, 1999). Collectively, however, relatively little is known about the relationship between specific features of threats and subsequent violence.

Threats, when explicit, are messages of prospective harm contingent on target compliance (MacDonald, 1968). That is, a threat implies or explicitly claims that a punishment under the control of the communicator will befall the target if the target does not engage in some course of action (or inaction) specified by the communicator. Threats are distinct from "warnings." Warnings indicate that harm is likely to occur, but such harm is not under the control of the messenger. This distinction is not always clear. A stalker who says "Bad things are going to happen to you" may easily be perceived as making an implicit threat rather than a generic warning.

Mullen et al. (2000a, p. 218) claimed, "Threats should be regarded as promises." This is a counterproductive analogy. Promises are messages of prospective reward (not harm) contingent on target compliance. If promises and threats are viewed as equivalent, there is no space within which more productive forms of communication can be constructed. Mullen et al. (2000a, p. 218) also claimed that "threats are, in and of themselves, acts of violence." This too is a counterproductive perspective. Symbolic interaction may bruise the psyche, but (a) jurisprudential law would have to be significantly rewritten to accommodate an equivalence between symbolic aggression and physical violence, and (b) again, there needs to be space within which to differentiate purely symbolic forms of behavior from forms of aggressive physical contact. Threats are purely symbolic; symbols are not the things to which they refer. As such, threats are often used in everyday life as a form of negotiating influence with others. Labor unions threaten to strike, businesspersons threaten to walk out on a deal, and parents threaten to withhold dessert from their children. Violence is an action intended to inflict harm; threats sometimes are explicitly intended to avoid harm through subsequent compliance. It becomes vital, therefore, to ascertain how and in what way threats are related to violence in the context of stalking.

As integral as threats are to the arsenal of stalking, relatively little is known about the specific contingencies between the utterance of threats, their particular idiom or content, and outcomes in the stalking case. In addition, it is important to recognize that threats are often implicit or contextual in nature, and therefore not always explicitly verbalized. "Feeling threatened is an extremely common response to being stalked, but this is frequently due to the situation itself rather than any explicit threat" (Finch, 2001, p. 130). Such a sense of threat is assumed common among stalking victims. For example, Pathé and Mullen (2002, p. 11) conjectured that "victims of stalking live in a state of persistent threat, regardless of any explicit threat or actual physical violence."

Threats are often categorized as instrumental or expressive (Meloy, 2001, 2002). Instrumental threats are realistically contingent—that is, they are intended to manipulate and control the behavior of the target toward a particular end. Expressive threats, in contrast, are uttered as manifestations of rage, jealousy, or other affective state, but not particularly intended as directed toward a particular persuasive outcome. Meloy (2002) speculated that stalkers of public figures (i.e., strangers) tend to employ instrumental threats, whereas private figure stalkers (i.e., estranged or would-be lovers) tend to employ affective threats. Another distinction can be made between implicit threats and explicit threats. Implicit threats, typically nonverbal in nature, suggest the possibility or likelihood of contingent harm rather than offering specific propositional reference to a contingent harm. A photograph of the target of pursuit with the eyes cut out implies ominous possibilities, but is not a specific proposition of intended action. Explicit threats, in contrast, tend to specify intended and contingent harmful action. At least one study found that stalkers making explicit threats (66%) were more likely than those making implicit threats (24%) to enact violence (Brewster, 2002).

The studies that have provided some estimate of the prevalence of these three forms of stalking activity are summarized in Table 5.2. Across 74 studies with some estimate of any one of these three key statistics, an average of over 48% of unwanted pursuit relationships involve threats of some form, 29% involve physical violence, and almost 11% involve sexual aggression of some form. The percentage of threats varied significantly ($F = 11.87$; $df = 2,43$; $p < .001$; $\eta^2 = .36$) across clinical/forensic ($M = 61.48$, $SD = 16.54$, $n = 24$), general population ($M = 40.67$, $SD = 23.18$, $n = 12$), and college ($M = 26.95$, $SD = 23.27$, $n = 10$) samples, with Scheffé post hoc contrasts revealing clinical/forensic samples significantly higher ($p < .05$) than college and general population samples, which did not differ significantly from each other. It should be noted that a disproportionate number of entries in the estimates of violence come from the Gallagher et al. studies (Gallagher, 1997; Gallagher et al., 1993, 1996, 1997, 1998, 1999, 2000, 2001; Gallagher & Zhang, 2002). These were surveys of university counseling centers, in which the question asked was whether the center

TABLE 5.2
Studies Providing Prevalence Estimates of Threat and Violence

	Study	Percent Threat	Percent Physical Violence	Percent Sexual Violence
1	Bjerregaard, 2000	32	23	
2	Blaauw, Winkel, Arensman, Sheridan, & Freeve, 2002		56	
3	Blackburn, 1999	47	23	7
4	Brewster, 1998, 2000, 2003	53	46	
5	Budd & Mattinson, 2000		23	6
6	Burgess et al., 1997		56	19
7	Burgess et al., 2001		6	
8	Cupach & Spitzberg, 2000	33	33	18
9	Cupach & Spitzberg, 2000	36	37	20
10	Cupach & Spitzberg, 2000	22	25	11
11	Davis & Gonzales, in press	56	31	
12	Dinkelmeyer & Johnson, 2002			
13	Eke, 1999	77	47	23
14	Farnham et al., 2000		37	
15	Fisher et al., 2000	15	30	10
16	Gallagher et al., 1996		7	
17	Gallagher et al., 1997		7	
18	Gallagher et al., 1998		7	
19	Gallagher et al., 1999		13	
20	Gallagher et al., 2000		21	
21	Gallagher et al., 2001		14	
22	Gallagher & Zhang, 2002		35	
23	Gentile, 2001; Gentile et al., 2002			
24	Gill & Brockman, 1996		14	
25	Hackett, 2000	52	11	2
26	Hall, 1997	41	38	22
27	Ammell, Hoyt, & Lipson, 1996	71	28	
28	Harmon et al., 1998	66	46	1
29	Harris, 2000	60	15	
30	Holloway, 1994	18	14	
31	Huffhines, 2001		38	
32	Jason et al., 1984		30	
33	Kamphuis & Emmelkamp, 2001		55	
34	Kienlen et al., 1997		24	4
35	Kileen & Dunn, 1998	75	52	10

TABLE 5.2 (continued)

	Study	Percent Threat	Percent Physical Violence	Percent Sexual Violence
36	Kohn et al., 2000	75	24	
37	Kong, 1996	24	5	3
38	Langhinrichsen-Rohling et al., 2000	1	1	
39	Logan et al., 2000	5	6	
40	McCann, 2000a	62	31	
41	McCann, 2001	65	38	
42	Mechanic, Weaver, & Resick, 2000	94	89	6
43	Meloy & Boyd, in press	65	25	
44	Meloy et al., 2001	68	0.50	60
45	Meloy & Gothard, 1995	70	25	
46	Meloy et al., 2000	75	52	3
47	Morewitz, 2001b, 2003	60	70	7
48	Morrison, 2001	68	28	7
49	Mullen & Pathé, 1994a		50	32
50	Mullen & Pathé, 1994b		36	29
51	Mullen et al., 1999	58	36	10
52	Nicastro et al., 2000	67	38	13
53	Oddie, 2000	35	25	
54	Palarea et al., 1999	65	19	
55	Pathé & Mullen, 1997	58	31	7
56	Pathé et al., 2000	72	38	7
57	Purcell et al., 2001	57	34	
58	Purcell et al., 2002	29	18	2
59	Roberts, 2002		86	
60	Romans et al., 1996		4	
61	Rosenfeld & Harmon, 2002	62	34	
62	Sandberg et al., 1998		38	7
63	Schwartz-Watts et al., 1997		39	
64	Sheridan & Davies, 2001b	53	32	3
65	Sheridan, Gillett, & Davies, 2000	7		
66	Sheridan, Gillett, & Davies, 2002		3	
67	Sinclair & Frieze, 2000	2.50	0.50	4
68	Spitzberg & Cupach, 2001b		9	10
69	Tjaden & Thoennes, 1998b			
69	Tjaden & Thoennes, 1998b	44	81	31

(continued on next page)

TABLE 5.2 (*continued*)

Study	Percent Threat	Percent Physical Violence	Percent Sexual Violence
70 Tjaden & Thoennes, 2000d		31	
71 Tucker, 1993		8	
72 Westrup et al., 1999	76	36	
73 Yokoi, 1998	13	4	6
74 Zona et al., 1993	45	3	
N of studies	46	73	31
Mean	48.54	29.32	10.90
Standard deviation	24.27	20.00	8.91
Range	1–94	0–89	1–32

had experienced any cases involving obsessively pursued students that year. If the answer was "yes," the center director was asked to estimate the number of cases, the number of those cases who were injured, and the number killed. In the event that these estimates might bias the data, they were removed and the estimates calculated again. The differences were very small, never varying by more than 2% from the estimates with the Gallagher studies included.

Threats are sometimes followed by violence (true positives), and sometimes not (false positives). Violence sometimes occurs without threats (false negatives), and sometimes there are neither threats nor violence (true negatives). These are complementary statistics, in the sense that true positives are the converse of false positives, and true negatives are the converse of false negatives. True positive rates of violence directed against the victim have varied somewhat across studies, as have false negative rates (see Table 5.3). Across studies, the average false positive rate is 62% ($SD = 12.35$, $n = 12$), indicating that on average, 38% of the time a threat of violence is uttered, it is associated with some act(s) of violence. The false negative rate averaged almost 16% ($M = 15.70$, $SD = 7.70$, $n = 10$), indicating that violence occurs in about 16% of stalking relationships in which there is no explicit threat. In other words, threats may have little actual relationship with violence or enactment of such threats (e.g., Kaci, 1992; cf. Fleury, Sullivan, & Bybee, 2000). Summarizing this literature, Meloy (1999b, p. 90) concluded that "threatening communications occur in most cases of stalking, usually at a rate of 50% to 75%; most individuals do not act on their threatening communications, generating false-positive rates of approxi-

TABLE 5.3

**Summary of Studies Providing False Positive and False Negative Rates
of Association Between Threats and Violence**

		Percent False Positive[a]	Percent False Negative
1.	Bjerregard, 2000	61	—
2.	Brewster, 1998	54	—
3.	Eke, 1999	—	0
4.	Harmon et al., 1995	68	13
5.	Harmon et al., 1998	41	19
6.	Kienlen et al., 1997	68	—
7.	Meloy & Gothard, 1995	73	22
8.	Meloy & Boyd, 2003	70	15
9.	Meloy et al., 2000	72	15
10.	Mullen et al., 1999	52	23
11.	Oddie, 2000	48	9
12.	Palarea et al., 1999	84	14
13.	Purcell et al., 2002	56	27
	Mean	62.25	15.70
	SD	12.35	7.70

[a]Some figures derived from Meloy (2002, Table 7.3).

mately 75%; … a few individuals are violent but do not threaten, generating false-negative rates of 10% to 15%."

In order to establish a more representative estimate, the prevalence of threats was examined as a separate tactic in the sample of 143 studies. Because many studies included multiple items on threats, typically the threat item closest to threats of physical harm to the victim was identified as the best estimate. Consequently, these estimates are likely to be very conservative relative to all the possible types of threats (e.g., threats against victim's friends, family, pets, or property) that could be uttered (see Appendix 3). Across 46 studies that had prevalence estimates for threats, the range was 1% to 94%, with an average of over 48% (SD = 24.27). That is, on average, about half of all stalking and obsessive relational pursuit relationships involved threat or threats against the victim.

Another way of summarizing the relationship between threats and violence is to examine their correlation. Eke (1999) found a strong association ($V(29) = .49$). Jaynes-Andrews (2001) found a small relationship ($b = .175$), and similarly Sheridan and Davies (2001b) found threats correlated at .24 with actual assaults. In Morrison's (2001) study, threats correlated with violence at .54, indicating a large relationship. There were 44 studies among the 143 that had estimates of both threat prevalence and physical violence. Threat prevalence correlated at .60 with physical violence prevalence ($p < .001$). That is, the occurrence of threats accounts for 36% of the variance in the occurrence of physical violence. In practice, this is probably a conservative estimate of the true positive rate of threats to physical violence. Interestingly, similar to Sheridan and Davies (2001b), threat prevalence did not correlate significantly with sexual violence prevalence ($r = .004$, $n = 24$, ns).

An important limitation on interpretations of the threat–violence relationship is that very little of this research is truly time-sensitive. That is, most of the research to date is correlational, and therefore cannot determine whether threats even preceded the violence, much less whether they were temporally, proximally, or causally related to the violent behavior implied by the threat. For example, it is entirely possible that violent behavior in a relationship lowers the threshold for the acceptability of using threats as an influence tactic in relationships.

Physical violence is perhaps the most feared aspect of stalking. The role of violence in stalking is a point of contention among scholars. Meloy (2002, p. 105) claimed, "Stalking per se does not include any violent behavior." In contrast, Mullen et al. (2000a, p. 220) claimed, "Stalking is in and of itself a form of violence perpetrated by one individual against another." We view violence as one among many of the forms or means of stalking. Violence is an expressive manifestation of raging emotions within the pursuer, and/or an attempt to influence the target of the violence. The fear of violence, however, seems to underlie much of the public concern about stalking. This fear is probably in part a lingering echo of years of typifying stalkers in the media as serial killers and crazed celebrity stalkers. There is also likely to be an effect of uncertainty due to the deviance of the obsessive pursuit itself. The fact that a person is engaging in deviant behavior is itself an indicator that the person might be capable of any number of other deviant behaviors.

Violence is a relatively rare phenomenon relative to the baseline of everyday behavior, and even among stalkers, only a minority engage in violence, and even fewer of these produce injuries in their victims (Meloy, 1999b, 2001). "The most valid and reliable finding in the research is that most stalkers are not violent, and, when they are, the physical injury to the victim is not severe" (Meloy, 1999b, p. 91). The relative rarity of violent behavior makes it particularly difficult to study, given that very large samples need to be obtained to achieve even a moderately large sample of stalkers, much less violent stalkers. It is not surprising, therefore, that there is still a paucity of valid research identifying reliable predictors of violence in stalking relationships.

Given this caveat, a few studies have identified correlational predictors of violence in stalking relationships. The most studied and most reliable predictor is prior intimacy, particularly romantic or sexual intimacy, which has been referred to as "sexual precedence" in the sexual coercion literature (e.g., Shotland & Goodstein, 1992). Prior intimacy, especially sexual intimacy, has been found to significantly increase the likelihood of violence relative to unwanted pursuit relationships in which there was little or no prior intimacy (Farnham, James, & Cantrell, 2000; D. M. Hall, 1997, 1998; Kohn et al., 2000; Meloy et al., 2000; Meloy et al., 2001; Meloy & Boyd, 2003; Morrison, 2001; Oddie, 2000; Palarea et al., 1999; Purcell et al., 2002; Rosenfeld & Harmon, 2002; Sheridan & Davies, 2001b; cf. Eke, 1999). "The studies reviewed almost unanimously indicate that those being stalked by an ex-intimate are at a higher risk of being attacked than are those pursued by acquaintances or strangers" (Mullen et al., 2000a, p. 217). Although being stalked by a stranger may be more stereotypically threatening, it appears that being stalked by a former intimate is more prototypically dangerous. The irony is that the former intimate is the one who seemed normal, attractive, and promising. Strangers, it seems, more often do not know us well enough to want to harm us.

Other variables have revealed significant relationships to violent behavior, although most of the effects have been small and isolated to only one or two studies. Both McFarlane, Campbell, and Watson (2002) and Mechanic, Uhlmansiek, Weaver, and Resick (2000; see also Mechanic, Weaver, & Resick, 2000) independently found an association between whether children in the relationship are threatened and amount of violence. Prior history of violence (Morrison, 2001) or criminal behavior (Mullen et al., 1999), as well as the existence of a prior restraining order (Oddie, 2000), appear to be significantly related to violence (cf., Brewster, 1998, 2000), although in one study, prior arrests, prior violence and personality disorder failed to predict violence (Rosenfeld & Harmon, 2002).

Violence has also been predicted by negative affect (Morrison, 2001), verbal abuse, theft of items, unwanted approaches (Eke, 1999), manic love style (Sinclair & Frieze, 2000), male gender (e.g., Huffhines, 2000), recent relationship breakup (Moracco, Runyan, & Butts, 1998; Morton, Runyan, Moracco, & Butts, 1998), drug use (Rosenfeld & Harmon, 2002), and the relentless nature of the stalking (Mechanic, Uhlmansiek, Weaver, & Resick, 2000), but weakly related, unrelated, or negatively related to Axis I and

Axis II diagnoses (Meloy et al., 2001; cf. Rosenfeld & Harmon, 2002). Particular reactions to being the rejected person in a relationship breakup also correlated with mild aggression and violence, including feeling hurt, angry, depressed, vengeful, and feeling deceived (Sinclair & Frieze, 2000). Interestingly, across studies in our data the percentage of threat or of physical or sexual violence did not correlate significantly to either the proportion of the sample that was known or the proportion of the sample that consisted of female victims. However, the percentage of physical violence did correlate with the proportion of the sample that was previously *romantically involved* ($r = .37, p < .04, n = 31$). Meloy (2002, p. 119) summarized the current state of violence prediction: "The very limited predictive research to date has ferreted out three variables which significantly and strongly predict personal and/or property violence among stalkers: prior criminal convictions, substance abuse and prior sexual intimacy with the victim."

These miscellaneous findings suggest at least three things. First, there is a wide variety of potential variables that might facilitate prediction of violence in stalking relationships. Second, clearly more research is needed to both replicate prior findings and identify new, more powerful constructs in predicting violence in stalking cases. One possibility is the differentiation of the dependent variable. Meloy (2002) pointed out a variety of qualitative differences between affective and predatory violence. Predatory violence is planned, emotionally "cold," and strategic. In contrast, affective violence is more arousal based (i.e., emotionally "hot") and reactionary. Meloy (2002) predicted that different types of stalkers are likely to employ predatory violence (i.e., stranger stalkers) than affective violence (i.e., estranged or would-be lovers). There might be a host of distinct predictors of these distinct types of violence.

A third conclusion that is not as obvious is that future research clearly needs to be multivariate in nature. For example, Rosenfeld and Harmon (2002) found that relationship status was strongly correlated with psychoticism. Had only one of these variables been included in each study, it would be difficult to know how to interpret findings across studies. In other words, several of the correlates of violence just identified may in fact be manifestations of other, more causally relevant variables that simply have not yet been included in the studies to date. Finally, an almost completely unexamined facet of stalking is the reciprocity of violence. The tactic typology indicates that victims sometimes resort to aggression and violence in retaliation, self-defense, or deterrence of the pursuer. For example, in the study reported by Blaaw, Winkel, Sheridan, Malsch, and Arensman (2002, p. 29), 19% of victims "assaulted the stalker or had the stalker assaulted by friends or acquaintances (although a few of these assaults were acts of self-defense)." It is often assumed that the greatest risk is posed by the stalker, and the data to date support this conclusion. However, stalkers may elicit the very violence peremptorily in ways and in circumstances not yet investigated.

The most severe form of violence commonly associated with stalking is homicide or murder. The media association of stalking with serial killing probably fuels the cultural connection of stalking and homicide. Indeed, "the typical 'professional profile' of the serial killer closely resembled both Bundy and Son of Sam; stalking was one of its fundamental elements" (Kamir, 2001, p. 149). However, the fear of homicide in stalking cases has been rhetorically exaggerated by the frequent repetition of an unfounded statistic: "it is estimated that ... between 29 percent and 54 percent of all female murder victims were battered women and that stalking preceded the murder in 90 percent of the cases" (Melton, 2000, p. 253). Spitzberg and Cadiz (2002) located this statistic in 18 separate publications on stalking, and there are undoubtedly more. In examining the empirical foundations for such an appealing quote, Spitzberg and Cadiz (2002) found four studies directly relevant to this statistic. Moracco et al. (1998) found that 23% of femicides (i.e., women killed by their domestic partner) had been stalked prior to the event. The McFarlane et al. (1999, p. 308) study found 76% of femicides and 85% of attempted femicides were preceded by "at least one episode of stalking" in the previous year. The Morton et al. (1998, p. 96) study of partner murder-suicides indicated approximately one-third of their sample had "harassed, followed, or otherwise monitored the activities of the victim in the weeks or days preceding the homicide-suicide event." A study by McFarlane, Campbell, and Watson (2002; see also McFarlane, Campbell, Sharps, & Watson, 2002) of attempted and actual femicide cases across 10 cities identified a 68% rate of stalking. Thus, within the context of physically violent intimate relationships, stalking is associated with homicide. However, across the population of all stalking cases, the risk of homicide in stalking cases is very low.

Early, rather speculative, estimates suggested homicide rates around 2% in stalking cases (Meloy, 1996b, 1998, 1999b). Such estimates were later qualified: "the highest estimation is that one in four hundred individuals who are stalked by prior sexual intimates will be intentionally killed by them" (Meloy, 2002, p. 112). In some forensic samples of stalkers, the rate can be as high as 8% (e.g., Kienlen et al., 1997). In a sample of serial killers, 12% showed evidence of stalking, defined as "stalked for a period of one day (24 hours) or longer by their killer. This includes any evidence of break-ins at the victim's home when the victim was absent" (Godwin, 2000, p. 86).

The relevance of such estimates for the general population has been criticized, not on direct evidence but through a form of reverse deduction. Mullen et al. (2000a) argued that given a very conservative societal prevalence of stalking over 1%, a 2% prevalence of homicide would "produce a homicide rate of 1 in 5000 per annum," which exceeds any reasonable estimates of actual homicide risks in the population. They concluded that "homicide rates in stalking cannot conceivably approach rates of 2% or even 0.2%" (Mullen et al., 2000a, p. 216). Unfortunately, such a conclusion is still unacceptable. There are many reasons to expect that victims underreport stalking victimization. Many police are still not trained in managing, much less recognizing, stalking. Thus, "police may not even have been aware that stalking preceded a homicide if the victim had never reported it" (Kong, 1996, p. 4). Stalking is not one of the traditional categories of crimes that national victim surveys and government databases necessarily require to be catalogued or reported. More importantly, stalking may be a correlative crime of homicide that is overlooked because it does not appear to be a proximal cause. Unfortunately, there is relatively little direct evidence bearing on the relationship between homicide and stalking. Studies vary widely in the prevalence of stalkers threatening to kill their victim (e.g., 1.2%: Burgess et al., 2001; 75%: Kileen & Dunn, 1998; 25%: Sheridan & Davies, 2001b).

Tucker's (1993) survey of police departments in Florida revealed that 8% of departments reporting stalking arrests had at least one case in which "murder of the victim" was one of the stalking acts reported. A table of the most serious charge in the files of those charged with stalking in Delaware in 1994 reveals that only 1 person (0.4%) out of 242 charged with stalking also had a charge of homicide (Scocas, O'Connell, Huenke, Nold, & Zoeckler, 1996). Obviously, this is suggestive but not sufficient for associating homicide with the process of stalking. Kong's (1996) review of Canadian criminal harassment data indicated "less than 1% of related offences involved a homicide or attempted murder" (p. 4). Hackett's (2000) summary of Canadian data identified 9 homicides over a 3-year period associated with criminal harassment, out of 15,894 reported victims during those 3 years. This produces a rate of 0.000566, or 6 stalking-related homicides per 10,000.

Moracco et al. (1998) conducted a population study in North Carolina. From 1991 to 1993, they identified 586 femicides, half ($n = 293$) of which were femicides involving current or former partners. About two-thirds of these ($n = 196, 66.9\%$) involved some form of domestic violence. Of those with a history of domestic violence, 23.4% ($n = 46$) involved stalking. The percentage of stalking associated with the nondomestic violence cases is not reported, so assuming conservatively that it is zero, the rate of stalking-associated femicides in North Carolina would be approximately 0.078259, or almost 8 per 100 femicides.

Morton et al. (1998) examined 119 homicide-suicide events involving female homicide victims in North Carolina occurring between 1988 and

1992. The investigators did not make specific attributions to stalking, but they did note that in a subclassification of the sample, among those female victims who had separated from their partner (n = 39, 45%), more than one-third had previously sought protection through protection order or arrest. "In nearly 70% of cases in which the victim and perpetrator were separated the perpetrator had harassed, followed, or otherwise monitored the activities of the victim in the weeks or days preceding the homi-cide-suicide event" (p. 96). Again, by conservative extrapolation, assuming zero stalking-associated suicide-femicides in the remainder of the original sample of 119, the rate of stalking-associated suicide-femicide among such events is approximately 0.2294117, or almost 23% of sui-cide-femicides.

McFarlane et al. (1999) investigated 141 femicide and 65 attempted femicide cases from 10 cities. "The prevalence of stalking was 76% for femicide victims and 85% for attempted femicide victims" (p. 300). In an expanded sample, McFarlane, Campbell, and Watson (2002) examined 263 femicides, 174 attempted femicides, and a comparison group of 384 female domestic violence victims in files across 10 U.S. cities. There were no apparent sample differences between the femicide and attempted femicide victims, so these samples were combined for analysis. Stalking was significantly more common among the femicide group (68%) than among the domestic violence comparison group (51%, χ^2 = 24.75, $p \le$ .001). Abuse was significantly related to stalking, with "79% of abused attempted/actual femicides also reporting stalking, as compared with 49% of the nonabused attempted/actual femicides who reported stalking" (p. 61). Importantly, logistic regression indicated that stalking was a significant risk factor for attempted/actual femicide, increasing the odds of attempted or actual femicide by 2.4 times (CI = 1.55, 2.96).

Finally, across at least 10 years (1991–2002), a research team headed by Gallagher (Gallagher, 1997; Gallagher et al., 1993, 1996, 1997, 1998, 1999, 2000, 2001, Gallagher & Zhang, 2002) surveyed a broad national cross section of directors of college counseling centers. One of the questions, whether any student clients had been obsessively pursued, resulted in an estimate of the number of such cases in the previous year. Further, the numbers injured and killed in these cases were estimated. Data are only available to us from the years 1993 and 1996 to 2002. The average number of centers responding to the survey during each of these years was 311, collectively reporting an average of 310 cases of "obsessive pursuit" each year across centers. Trends for estimates of injuries and deaths are illustrated in Fig. 5.1. The lines represent the percentage of "obsessive pursuit" cases presenting to college counseling centers involving injury or homicide. There is no obvious trend in the homicide pattern over time, but there is an

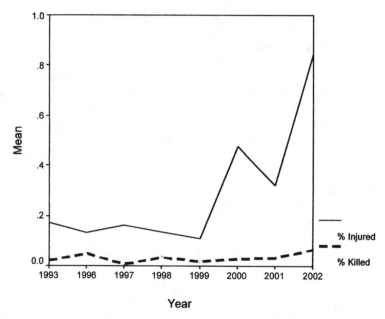

FIG. 5.1. Trends of percentage of college counseling centers reporting percentage of obsessive pursuit cases injured, and percentage of obsessive pursuit cases killed, by year (based on data reported by Gallagher, 1997; Gallagher et al., 1993, 1996, 1997, 1998, 1999, 2000, 2001; Gallagher & Zhang, 2002).

apparent trend toward obsessive pursuit becoming more injurious among college students in recent years. During these 8 years, the percentage of presenting obsessive pursuit cases recalled by directors of college counseling centers across the nation who were injured averaged 29.45%, and the percentage killed averaged 3.14%. This latter estimate is close to Meloy's original estimate of 2% of stalking cases resulting in homicide. It is also, however, an estimate that is likely biased in a variety of ways. First, the students who present to a counseling center are likely to be the more severe types of cases, and therefore not representative of all cases of obsessive pursuit. Second, homicides are almost certainly more likely to be remembered by directors of such centers, whereas everyday cases of obsessive pursuit may be easily underestimated in recall of such caseloads. Third, these are college populations, and may therefore be distinct in a variety of ways from the general population. Nevertheless, these data are among the most persuasive that homicide is clearly a risk, even if small, in cases of "obsessive pursuit."

These fragmentary findings are suggestive, but far from definitive. Collectively, they indicate that the *population* risk of stalking-associated homicide is very low. The findings also suggest that when stalking is part of a larger precedent pattern of relational violence, especially among female victims, it apparently significantly increases the risk of homicide. There is also some resonance between the concepts of stalking and homicide, and proprietariness activity, which reveals itself in jealousy and possessiveness activities associated with intimate homicide (Wilson & Daly, 1998). However, it is important to recognize that other factors could account for much of the relationship between stalking and homicide. First, to say that stalking occurred in homicide cases is much different from saying the stalking is causally related to the homicide. Stalking may be one of many means employed in a campaign of terrorizing another person, but it may be incidental to the actual homicide. Second, many of these studies provide little evidence of the proximity of stalking to the crime. Stalking could have occurred subsequent to attempted femicides, and it could have occurred much earlier in some of the cases in which homicide later occurred. Third, stalking and violence risk are both correlated to other phenomena that may be the root causes of homicide, such as relationship and sexual intimacy, jealousy, and proximity of relationship breakup or rejection. Disentangling the role of stalking in homicide will require time-sensitive multivariate techniques combined with qualitative data collection, and even then, causality will be difficult to demonstrate. Despite these potential difficulties, there is ample evidence to indicate that stalking is a risk factor for lethal violence when it is part of a broader pattern of violent behavior in close and formerly close relationships.

MAPPING RISK MANAGEMENT

Many popular press books have provided practical and typical tactics for victims seeking to avoid unwanted pursuit (e.g., Banks, 1997; de Becker, 1997a; Gedatus, 2000; Goddnough, 2000; Gross, 2000; Hitchcock, 2002; Landau, 1996; LaRue, 2000; Spence-Diehl, 1999; Wright, 2000). There are also rich literatures untapped by stalking researchers that identify a panoply of strategies for restoring privacy (e.g., Burgoon et al., 1989; Buslig & Burgoon, 2000; Hosman & Siltanen, 1995), rejecting unwanted attentions (e.g., Snow et al., 1991) or relationships (e.g., Rowatt, Cunningham, & O'Hara, 1999), and managing undesired relationships (Hess, 2002, 2003) and potentially threatening encounters (e.g., Harris & Miller, 2000). In addition, more than 30 studies have provided prevalence estimates indicating the normative frequency with which stalking victims respond with various coping strategies. However, the stalking research to date has merely provided brief lists of coping strategies. These lists have not been grounded in the rich yet diverse literature on coping strategies in other research domains. These other domains often reflect processes of coping with stressful contexts or with disjunctive unwanted relationships.

Like stalking behavior, the breadth of coping choices represents a forest obscured by the trees. "Stalkers do not go away, and victims must continue to cope with them over time. This necessitates the use of varied situation- and context-specific strategies" (Dunn, 2001, p. 297). When the coping tactics investigated in other contexts are considered along with the coping options of stalking victims, the choices overwhelm the senses. The only way to bring order to such a vast array of coping resources is to construct a typology of coping strategies and tactics. The development of the typology presented here proceeded in a manner similar to the formation of the previously introduced typologies. There are two important differences. First, unlike the previous typologies, this one was heavily influenced by a previous typology developed by Spitzberg and Cupach (2001a, 2003; Cupach & Spitzberg, in press). Second, as an informal test of the utility of this typology, many investigations of coping strategies and tactics from literatures other than stalking were included as a way of assuring appropriate breadth and depth of representation.

The typology is unabashedly eclectic in its sources. In addition to studies on stalking, it derives from investigations of general coping skills (e.g., Bouchard, Sabourin, Lussier, Wright, & Richer, 1997; Harnish, Aseltine, & Gore, 2000; Hobfoll & Schröder, 2001; Valentiner, Foa, Riggs, & Gershuny, 1996), relationship coping (Levitt, Silver, & Franco, 1996; Pollina & Snell, 1999), distance regulation (e.g., Hess, 2002, 2003), privacy management (Buslig & Burgoon, 2000; Hosman & Siltanen, 1995; Pedersen, 1999), hypothetical coping advice (e.g., Harris & Miller, 2000), sexual assaults (Meyer & Taylor, 1986; Schneider, 1991), sexual harassment (Bingham & Burleson, 1989; Gruber, 1989), physical assaults (Thompson, Simon, Saltzman, & Mercy, 1999), courtship violence (Coffey, Leitenberg, Henning, Bennett, & Jankowski, 1996; Stith, Jester, & Bird, 1992), survivors of abuse (Fry & Barker, 2002; Proulx, Koverola, Fedorowicz, & Kral, 1995; Yoshihama, 2002), threat management (Maier, 1996), courtship regulation tactics (e.g., Snow et al., 1991), conflict management (e.g., Roloff & Ifert, 2000), relationship redefinition (Rowatt et al., 1999), and undercover police tactics (Jacobs, 1994), as well as a meta-analytic attempt at a comprehensive coding system for coping strategies (i.e., Tamres, Janicki, & Helgeson, 2002). These are literatures that stalking research to date has generally ignored.

One of the advantages of such an inclusive approach is that both macro and micro tactics can be represented. Macro tactics tend to represent a relatively generic action or action category (e.g., "confront the pursuer"). In contrast, micro tactics specify particular types of behavior or examples (e.g., "either redefine the harasser's behavior as something other than harassment—e.g., teasing—or re-describe the situation so that the harassment is implied to be problematic, but also include denigration of the harasser, complaints, threats, or fail to make situational goals clear"). The latter example is a specific instance of the larger category of "confronting" the pursuer, but it obviously describes a different way of confronting the pursuer than, for example, "yelling and screaming at the pursuer." The proposed typology accommodates both levels of abstraction in describing responses. Because most existing research on stalking has derived from psychology and law enforcement disciplines, relatively little such research has conceptualized coping at a micro or interactional level.

The typology of coping strategies and tactics is displayed in Table 5.4, and the complete list of tactics is provided in Appendix 7. The broad architecture of the typology is an extension of Horney's (1945) belief that humans relate to one another in any of three fundamental ways. People can move with (or toward) others, in ways that reflect a cooperative or collaborative manner. People can move against others, in ways intended to harm others. People can also (attempt to) move away from others through avoidance. There are at least two additional modes of interaction unanticipated by Horney's tripartite system: moving inward and moving outward. Moving inward implies an attempt to cope with a situation by focusing on oneself or one's own responsibility, through such moves as denial, therapy, or distraction. Moving outward is an attempt to elicit support or assistance of others.

Clearly, some tactics cross over these broad functions. For example, victims can seek others to protect them (moving outward) or to harm the pursuer (moving against). Victims can seek protection orders, which require the assistance of others in law enforcement or the judiciary (moving outward) but also attempt to put the pursuer at risk of prosecution (moving against). Threats are clearly negatively valenced attempts to suggest possible harm to the pursuer (moving against), yet they involve discursive interaction with the pursuer and assume a degree of rationality in the process (moving with). Nevertheless, it is possible to interpret a predominant proximal function for most of the tactics examined in previous research. Furthermore, with a general functional category system, it is possible to provide a consistent interpretive vocabulary for what is otherwise an extremely diverse literature. In Table 5.4, when a percentage is noted, it represents a study specifically of the prevalence in that sample of stalking victims who engaged in that tactic as a way of coping with their unwanted pursuit.

Moving with (or toward) tactics are discursive efforts or actions that involve interaction with the unwanted pursuer. Many such efforts involve very negative forms of interaction (e.g., threats, criticism, etc.) but collec-

TABLE 5.4
A Typology of Stalking Coping Strategies and Tactics
(N = 58 studies, 491 tactics)

MW: Moving With (or Toward): Any discursive effort(s) or act(s) to interact with and influence the pursuer discursively, rationally, or even through threat. Negative forms of MW are distinct from Mag because they still treat the problem as one resolvable through interaction. Exemplars include arguing, yelling, criticizing, reconciling, or otherwise interacting with the pursuer in an effort to negotiate an "understanding" of boundaries or type of relationship.

- MW (general): e.g., face-to-face
- MW (acceptance/reconciliation): compliance: recanting
- MW (deception): disengagement: hiding information about self—deception
- MW (excuses: attachments): escape (e.g., say you're already in a relationship etc.)
- MW (excuses—misc.): distancing techniques: parental-recrimination excuses
- MW (interaction management): disengagement: hiding information about self
- MW (interactional: derogate): active resistance: using sarcasm
- MW (interactional: disconfirmation): nonempathetic cooling-out tactics
- MW (negotiation: boundary setting): demanded to be left alone
- MW (negotiation: conflict): active resistance: yelling/swearing
- MW (negotiation: confrontation): confront the pursuer on their own
- MW (negotiation: deflection): rhetorical minimal message (e.g., teasing)
- MW (negotiation: emotional): expressive minimal message (i.e., react emotionally)
- MW (negotiation: rationality): communicated that attention was unwanted
- MW (negotiation: relational definition): ended or tried to end relationship
- MW (negotiation: threat): active resistance: threatening to call 911
- MW (seek pursuer reform): suggested that he get help
- MW (seek sympathy): cried in front of perpetrator
- MW (seek sympathy): pleading with stalker
- MW (threat management): talking up "cold"

MAg: Moving Against: Any intentional effort(s) or act(s) to cause material harm, injury or damage to the quality of life of the pursuer. The proximal intent is to harm the pursuer, not to engage in interaction, even though the distal intent may be to deter or otherwise incapacitate the pursuer's ability or inclination to continue the harassment. Exemplars include physically attacking or obtaining the assistance of others in attacking the pursuer, filing charges or legally prosecuting the pursuer, attempting to damage the career or livelihood of the pursuer. Note: Discursive efforts such as threats, criticism, sarcasm, yelling, etc. are classified as "moving with."

TABLE 5.4 (continued)

- Mag (abuse, general): abused offender/family
- Mag (physical): assaulted stalker
- Mag (legal): charged/legal action
- Mag (physical): harmed stalker not in self-defense
- Mag (legal): help-seeking: asking for a jail term
- Mag (physical): physically fight if attacked

MAw: Moving Away: Any effort(s) or act(s) to avoid contact with the pursuer, including: not being where the pursuer is or is likely to be, hardening the target to the pursuer's access or deterring the pursuer's inclination to engage in further harassment. Exemplars include enhancing home security, screening calls or changing the telephone number, moving, changing careers, and changing everyday routines.

- Maw (proximity access—general): avoidance: leaving scene
- Maw (communicative access): avoidance tactics (tie signs)
- Maw (communicative access—phone): caller ID
- Maw (information control): anonymity
- Maw (interactional: exclusion): avoided discussing issue with person
- Maw (interactional: exclusion): don't argue with attacker
- Maw (proximity access—escape): left the partner permanently
- Maw (proximity access—escape): left the partner temporarily
- Maw (proximity access—isolation): avoidance: hiding
- Maw (proximity access—job/school): avoidance: changing jobs
- Maw (proximity access—location): changed address
- Maw (proximity access—routine): altered daily routines
- Maw (target hardening): avoidance: taking security measures

MI: Moving Inward: Any effort(s) or act(s) to repair, empower, enrich, or merely focus on self as the source of managing the disruption of unwanted pursuit, independent of others' role (i.e., the pursuer, third parties) in the episode. Exemplars include therapy, keeping active, taking drugs, contemplating the situation, and various means of "preparing" for potential encounter(s) with the pursuer, such as taking self-defense classes, buying a gun, carrying pepper spray, etc.

- MI (acceptance): accept responsibility
- MI (immobility): no action
- MI (catharsis): mobilizing support (e.g., let your feelings out somehow)
- MI (chemical): used alcohol or drugs
- MI (cognitive control): did things to calm down or relax
- MI (contemplation): reasoning

(continued on next page)

TABLE 5.4 (*continued*)

- MI (denial): avoidance: ignoring
- MI (distraction): self-control, escape
- MI (immobility): no action
- MI (monitoring): sought information
- MI (positivity): focused on positive aspects of partner or relationship
- MI (preparation): carry a cellular phone
- MI (preparation—aggressive): active resistance: getting a weapon
- MI (regret): self-criticism (e.g., I kick myself for letting this happen)
- MI (self-destructive): attempted suicide
- MI (spiritual): religious coping (e.g., I seek God's help)
- MI (therapy): obtained psychotherapy

MO: Moving Outward: Any effort(s) or act(s) to obtain assistance of others for guidance, information, or intermediary contact with the pursuer with the intent of deterring or avoiding further victim contact. Exemplars include seeking advice or consultation with counselors, religious advisers, law enforcement, victims' advocates, friends or family, or threat management professionals. Note: Direct efforts to obtain the assistance of third parties to harm or imprison the pursuer are classified as "moving against." Furthermore, seeking therapy, rather than merely consultation, is categorized as "moving inward."

- MO (general): sought assistance
- MO (counsel): seek clergy
- MO (counsel—legal): contacted legal professionals
- MO (disclosure): defusion: social support (e.g., told peers or coworkers)
- MO (intermediary): ask someone to confront the person
- MO (intermediary): had family/friends talk to stalker
- MO (partner—existing): sought help from partner
- MO (partner—new attachment): became involved with new people
- MO (police): approached police for assistance
- MO (professional protection): hiring security guard
- MO (protective order): apply for RO
- MO (safety in numbers): arranged escort
- MO (service agency): sought professional help
- MO (social network): seeking social support—turning to others
- MO (social network—safety planning): discussing safety issues with loved ones

Unclassifiable: problem solving

tively represent interactional approaches to managing harassment and the harasser. Such discursive approaches tend to presume a degree of rationality in the pursuer, subject to persuasion and intellective or empathic forms of influence. Victims can, and with surprisingly frequency do, attempt to comply or reconcile with or otherwise accept ongoing relations with their pursuer. For example, in domestic or romantic dating relationships in which a spouse or ex-partner is stalking the other spouse or partner in the context of separation, it is entirely possible for the relationship to stop, start, stop, and restart. Victims can also deceive their pursuers in a variety of ways that deflect or divert the pursuer. The victim may provide excuses as to why a relationship or encounter is not possible. Victims may manage the delicate maneuvers of conversation so as to minimize their disclosures and provision of information that might be used against them. In contrast, victims can also disclose or express their emotions in ways to seek sympathy or deter the pursuer. Victims can also employ a variety of tactics to derogate the pursuer, or treat the pursuer as a nonentity in the process of interaction, presumably to escalate the costs of interaction and thereby decrease one's attractiveness as a target of pursuit. Other tactics available to victims include direct attempts to define the relationship or the boundaries of the pursuer's actions, or to construct rational reasons for the pursuer to stop. Such interactional processes often involve conflict and confrontation. Victims can engage in a variety of threats or can engage in discursive threat management as a way of regulating the pursuer's activities.

When rationality and discourse fail, it is not surprising that victims resort to aggression. Moving-against tactics attempt material harm against the pursuer. There are two common approaches to aggressive retaliation against unwanted pursuers: prosecution of legal rights in ways that threaten the pursuer with penalty or imprisonment, or physically through forms of assault, either directly or indirectly achieved. There is little evidence in the stalking literature, but research on domestic and intimate violence shows violence tends to be highly reciprocal (Spitzberg, 1997; Stets, 1990, 1992). Ironically, victims may take up the very tactics that make them victims in an effort to manage their pursuit. The difference is in the punctuation of events—victims tend to engage in such aggression as a means of defense or deterrence rather than possession. However, such behaviors can also be employed in retaliatory ways, which begins to blur the lines between the pursuer and the pursued.

The largest category of coping responses to unwanted pursuit is moving away. The most natural response to unwanted approach is compensation or escape. As stalkers have become very creative in their means of pursuit, so victims display surprising creativity in their pursuit of avoidance. Interactionally, victims can establish "tie signs" with others. Tie signs are behaviors that show or suggest intimate connections with others (e.g., holding hands, rings, kissing, etc.), which ordinarily deter rivals from intrusion. Given that the telephone is one of the most prominent media through which pursuers stalk their prey, it stands to reason victims will employ all available telephonic means to avoid communicating with their pursuer. Such means of information control also extend to the information victims disclose to the pursuer or others. Efforts to unlist addresses, restrict personal disclosure, and change one's name reflect attempts to close oneself off from the pursuer's access. There are a variety of interactional techniques through which people try to exclude others through the communication of avoidance (e.g., Beatty, Valencic, Rudd, & Dobos, 1999), disinterest (e.g., Wagner, 1980), disrespect (e.g., Gaines, 1994), rejection (e.g., Asher, Rose, & Gabriel, 2001; Folkes, 1982), criticism (e.g., Cupach & Carson, 2002), ostracism (e.g., Williams, 1997), aggression (e.g., Richardson & Green, 1997), or to make others feel hurt (e.g., Vangelisti, 1994), embarrassed (e.g., Sharkey, 1997), or guilty (Vangelisti, Daly, & Rudnick, 1991). The rhetoric of disengagement, disconfirmation, and disrespect illustrates a few among many forms of "dissing" (Kellermann & Lee, 2001) through which disaffiliation is communicated.

Various insidious forms of moving away include isolation, through which a victim withdraws from social activity and hides from the pursuer. Such activities lead to restrictions in one's social network, which may reduce peripheral risks to that network, but also reduces the social resources and support available to the victim when the victim is most in need of support. Victims may also engage in a variety of asynchrony maneuvers, through which the victim attempts to not be wherever the pursuer is. Such moves involve changing activity routines, work, school, hobbies, home address, transportation routes, and even lifestyle patterns.

Finally, victims can harden the target in a variety of ways. Hardening the target involves enhancing the security of residences, autos, place of employment, and other physical locations. Such enhancements are primarily avoidance tactics because they attempt to keep the pursuer from gaining access to the victim, rather than to harm or trap the pursuer.

The next two coping strategies are moving inward and moving outward. One tends to exclude others while focusing on the self. The other actively solicits the role of others in assisting one's management of the stressful situation. There has been extensive research on the importance of social support for the well-being and personal management of stressful relational experiences such as sexual assault and domestic abuse (e.g., Fry & Barker, 2002; Golding, Wilsnack, & Cooper, 2002). However, social support is not univocally positive or functional. When support is delivered incompetently, or when it is sought excessively, it can be an added source of stress (e.g., LaGaipa, 1990; Ray, 1993; Rook & Pietromonaco, 1987). Social support is also time-consuming and often leads to increased exposure both in terms of public appearances as well as the exposure of one's social support network to the pursuer. There are more options to moving outward than just social support. First, there are various types of roles and relationships people can seek with others, including seeking disclosure or consultation with police, clergy, human resources, personnel managers, coworkers, counselors, psychologists, victim services agencies, friends, family, and relational partners. Furthermore, such support can be instrumental (i.e., tangible, problem-solving in orientation) or emotional (i.e., comforting, cathartic, bonding in orientation). A seldom-studied form of moving outward is that victims can seek others to serve as intermediaries in a more professional vein (e.g., hiring a bodyguard or a threat management consultant) or with a more malicious purpose (e.g., getting someone to talk to, threaten, harm, or otherwise deter the pursuer).

Finally, victims can move inward by focusing on their own efficacy, responsibility, or role in the scheme of the unwanted relationship, or even in the grander scheme of life. Traumatizing events often move people to contemplate their lives, and sometimes this contemplation is productive and instrumental (e.g., planning, monitoring, etc.). At other times such contemplation becomes tangentially beneficial (e.g., exercising, meditating, finding spiritual growth, etc.). At still other times, however, such inward movement becomes self-destructive (e.g., taking drugs, abusing alcohol, considering or attempting suicide, etc.). Most moving-inward tactics are ultimately not focused on resolving the relational facets of the unwanted pursuit, and therefore probably have less potential for productively ending the unwanted pursuit than the other coping strategies.

TO ORDER OR DISORDER?

A person's coping behavior is likely to function primarily in one of five possible ways: to move with (e.g., negotiation), against (e.g., attack), away (e.g., avoid), inward (e.g., meditation), or outward (e.g., police). One of the primary tactics of the moving away strategy is to contact police or law enforcement. A major study reported by the Centers for Disease Control and Prevention found that 39% of women victimized by an intimate partner in the previous 5 years received police assistance (Hathaway, Silverman, Aynalem, Mucci, & Brooks, 2000). Tjaden and Thoennes's (1998b) large-scale study found that 55% of women and 48% of men victimized by stalking reported it to the police. The potential importance of the role of police intervention is suggested by a study of women stalking victims who were killed by their intimate partners. The study found that 30% of the victims contacted the police in the year prior to their deaths (Sharps et al., 2001).

Despite the fact that many victims of stalking contact the police, clearly many do not. There is reason to believe many victims of unwanted pursuit and stalking either never contact the police, or do so only as something akin to a last resort (Spitzberg, 2002a). Women in particular often report they are, or are interpreted by researchers as, victimized by both their harasser and the insensitive or gender-biased treatment by the police (e.g., Harris, Dean, Holden, & Carlson, 2001; Rigakos, 1995; Stephens & Sinden, 2000). Structurally, studies have found male-on-female violence does not seem to merit the same severity of punishment by police (e.g., arrest) as other forms of assault (e.g., Avakame & Fyfe, 2001; Fyfe et al., 1997).

We identified 23 studies that assessed the prevalence of cases or victims in which police were contacted. Averaging across these studies, approximately 50% of all stalking victims contact police (Bjerregaard, 2000, 22%; Blaauw, Winkel, Arensman, Sheridan, & Freeve, 2002, 89%; Blackburn, 1999, 35%; Budd & Mattinson, 2000, 33%; Dussuyer, 2000, 3%; Eke, 1999, 97%; Fisher et al., 1999, 17%; Gentile, 2001, 41%; Gill & Brockman, 1996, 32%; Kileen & Dunn, 1998, 92%; Kohn et al., 2000, 89%; Mechanic, Uhlmansiek, Weaver, & Resick, 2000, 83.5%; Morewitz, 2003, 31%; Morrison, 2001, 56%; Nicastro et al., 2000, 96%; Pathé & Mullen, 1997, 69%; Pathé et al., 2000, 60%; Purcell et al., 2002, 35%; Romans et al., 1996, 9%; Sheridan et al., 2001a, 92%; Suzuki, 1999, 11%; Tjaden & Thoennes, 1998b, 53%). If nothing else, this suggests the enormous potential the police possess in stalking intervention. Unfortunately, this potential is often not successfully actualized.

There are several reasons why police or law enforcement intervention is problematic in stalking cases (Miller, 2001a; Spitzberg, 2002a). Stalking can be highly erratic as a pattern of behavior, starting and stopping, and restarting again over a period of weeks, months, years, or even decades. Pursuit tactics can vary considerably, and when one tactic fails, another new tactic may be attempted. The burden of evidence collection is placed disproportionately on the victim, who typically is not prepared to document such probative evidence. Furthermore, because stealth is often a feature of stalking, stalkers are often cognizant of law enforcement methods and the gray boundaries between what is legal and what is not. Relational stalking often mimics acceptable forms of courtship, such that the line between legal and illegal is often fuzzy at best (Cupach & Spitzberg, 1998; Dunn, 2002; Spitzberg & Cupach, 2001a, 2002a). In stalking crimes, there is often no crime scene in the traditional sense of the term. "Stalking is an on-going, usually long-term crime without a traditional crime scene" (Wright et al., 1995, p. 39). There is often "no *there* there" because the crime is often intended to instill fear rather than physical injury. Related to the issue of the crime scene, stalking often crosses over law enforcement jurisdictions, complicating the coordination of law enforcement efforts. Many police have not received in-depth training on stalking (Farrell et al., 2000), have never formally investigated a stalking case, and often find it easier to throw stalking cases into "domestic violence," "threat," or "harassment" prosecutorial pigeonholes rather than treating them as the nature of case they are (Tjaden & Thoennes, 2000d). Finally, Sheridan's (2001) qualitative study of 29 stalking victims found one-fifth of the victims noted "legal intervention" as a factor that "worsened the stalker's behavior" (p. 69). Legal intervention represents a potentially significant escalation of the seriousness with which everyone involved may interpret the situation, and, as such, can provoke the pursuer into more extreme endeavors.

Stalking presents rather unique problems for police and law enforcement intervention. There are success stories and successful approaches (e.g., Boles, 2001; Wells & Maxey, 2001; White & Cawood, 1998), reflecting jurisdictions and communities that prioritize stalking. However, such concerted efforts are still the minority of all law enforcement departments and efforts. Given all these limitations, however, it is probably advisable to contact police in cases in which there is a perceived threat. According to one speculation, for example, "confrontation by the police is the most effective known measure. Up to half of stalkers will desist, from pursuing their current victim at least, as a result" (Babcock, 2000, p. 7). This claim is not yet evidenced sufficiently to evoke such confidence, but its sentiment is probably justified nonetheless.

Often the most convenient and popular law enforcement response to victims of stalking is to recommend a restraining order (RO), also referred to as protective order (PO) or temporary restraining order (TRO). One large-scale study found almost 34% of women who had experienced intimate partner violence in the preceding 5 years had obtained a restraining order (Hathaway et al., 2000). Tjaden and Thoennes's (1998a) study found almost 24% of stalking victims reported obtaining a restraining order. Logan et al. (2002) found 64.7% of the stalkers studied had a restraining order against them at some time during the study. Restraining orders are granted by a judge on request of a plaintiff, although such orders can also be requested mutually by the parties involved (Meloy, Cowett, Parker, Hofland, & Friedland, 1997; Topliffe, 1992). Such orders can specify a wide variety of conditions (Wallace & Kelly, 1995), including a physical distance the potential pursuer must keep away from the plaintiff, cessation of contact through all means of communication, and rights to common spaces (e.g., school, employment, etc.).

There are several other advantages to the restraining order. It has an intuitive appeal, because it is a legal order that, if effective, achieves precisely what most victims most desire: to get the pursuer to stay away (Carlson, Harris, & Holden, 1999; Kaci, 1994; Meloy et al., 1997). "Protective orders ... offer the benefit of being flexible enough to incorporate the specific behavior the victim is being forced to suffer. This flexibility provides a distinct advantage over both traditional criminal statutes and the new antistalking statutes" (Sohn, 1994, p. 218). Such orders also often offer the victim a sense of legal confirmation. Victims sometimes feel others view them as "crazy" or "overly sensitive" because stalking often leaves relatively little evidence of tangible harm. A restraining order provides validation of the victim's plight from a formal source (Fischer & Rose, 1995). Independent of their practical efficacy, many victims feel better or more satisfied on receipt of an order (Horton, Simonidis, & Simonidis, 1987; Keilitz, 1997; Keilitz, Davis, Efkeman, Flango, & Hannaford, 1998). Finally, in the event that prosecution is eventually called for, protection orders provide a useful prosecutorial resource because once a protection order is in place, demonstrated violation of that order often (but not inevitably) kicks the crime from a misdemeanor to a felony.

Despite the many advantages of restraining orders, they also have several potential drawbacks. First, they provide an opportunity for the pursuer to (a) know she or he has "gotten" to the victim, and (b) be in the presence of the victim at least one more time (i.e., in court). Sometimes, these are precisely the types of reinforcements that can motivate the stalker.

Second, stalkers may simply reconstruct their stalking activities "around" the court order, effectively circumventing it. As Sohn (1994, p. 217) indicated, "restraining orders are easy to avoid on technicalities." Case studies indicate that often "some stalkers do go to great lengths to ensure that their conduct does not contravene the law and ... they derive additional satisfaction from the knowledge that the police are powerless to intervene" (Finch, 2001, p. 15). In such cases, the order may provide the pursuer a new challenge to overcome and thereby evidence their devotion to their cause.

Third, restraining orders must be granted and enforced. Qualifying for a restraining order is not guaranteed. Indeed, Gist et al. (2001) found women who qualified for a restraining order did not differ in stalking victimization from those who did not qualify. Even if granted, police may not deem it feasible to make an on-site call every time a pursuer steps 10 feet within a 50-foot boundary or leaves an unsigned note on a windshield, even though these may technically violate the order. A study by Kane (2000, p. 576) found that "even at their strongest predictive level, RO violations led to arrest in less than half of all cases." A study in British Columbia concluded, "Civil restraining orders, in cases of violence against women, are less likely to be enforced than criminal court orders.

Both orders, however, rarely result in an arrest when breached" (Rigakos, 1997, p. 210). Police appear most motivated to manage the risk to the victim in such instances (Kane, 1999), so cases of violation that appear to present low levels of victim risk are unlikely to result in arrest (Coulter, Kuehnle, Byers, & Alfonso, 1999).

Fourth, and perhaps most importantly, restraining orders clearly "ratchet up" the stakes of stalking. "Expert opinion and anecdotal evidence suggest that restraining orders may be counterproductive for many stalking victims" (Mullen et al., 2000a, p. 234). By seeking a PO, the victim has taken what the stalker may have considered a private relational affair into the public realm and, further, made the stalker out to be the "bad guy" in a very public way. Conversely, some pursuers engage in stalking because they are seeking attention. Such stalkers may be distinctly energized by such attention. There is therefore often concern that the issuance of restraining orders risks an escalation of the frequency, severity, or violence of stalking (Harrell & Smith, 1996). "Realizing that waving a piece of paper in front of an obsessed stalker is probably of little value, many victims are reluctant to risk his wrath" (Sohn, 1994, p. 209). "Data do indicate that protection orders, on rare occasions, escalate stalking and violence" (Meloy, 1997a, p. 179). However, for some victims, such threat steels their resolve to persist in completing the restraining order process (Zoellner et al., 2000). This is consistent with the finding that the most seriously abused or stalked victims are also those most inclined to seek restraining orders (e.g., Nicastro et al., 1999; Wolf, Holt, Kernic, & Rivara, 2000). Ironically, however, protective orders may be most effective in preventing abuse in relationships involving milder levels of abuse; physically abusive partners may be more inclined to ignore such restraints (Grau et al., 1985).

Most research to date on restraining orders has been in domestic violence contexts. Domestic violence relationships often involve stalking, but as demonstrated in chapter 1, these are far from identical processes. Nevertheless, if all studies that have provided some estimate of the efficacy of restraining orders are viewed as cut from the same cloth, then some estimate of their efficacy can be gleaned. Table 5.5 lists the studies that could be located for this purpose. Across 41 studies total, 40 studies provided an estimate of 40% noncompliance ($M = 40.29\%$, $SD = 23.97$) and 10 studies indicated approximately 22% of restraining orders were perceived to be followed by an escalation or exacerbation of the situation ($M = 22.00$, $SD = 15.43$). In other words, understanding the limits of generalizing across very different samples and, just as importantly, different ways of estimating noncompliance, there is evidence that about 4 out of 10 restraining orders are violated, and there is some evidence that

TABLE 5.5

Studies Providing Estimates of Protective Order Efficacy and Exacerbation

	Study	Sample (Type of Order)	Percent Non-compliance	Percent Escalation
1.	Adhikari, Reinhard, & Johnson (1993)	41 domestic violence victims (PO)	56.0	17.0
2.	Blackburn (1999)	83 F stalking victims (RO)	48.5	18.5
3.	Brewster (1998)	19 F stalking victims (TRO)	63.0	21.0
		96 F stalking victims	62.0	16.0
4.	Buzawa, Hotaling, & Klein (1998a)	356 F DV victims (RO)	26.0	
5.	Carlson et al. (1999)	210 F (Civil PO) applicants	23.0	
6.	Chaudhuri & Daly (1992)	30 F (TRO) applicants	37.0	10.0
7.	Fischer & Rose (1995)	287 F DV victims (PO)	60.0	60.0
8.	Gill & Brockman (1996)	601 criminal harassment cases (RO)	18.0	
9.	Grau et al. (1985)	270 DV (RO) cases	56.0	
10.	Hall (1997)	145 F stalking victims	52.0	21.0
11.	Hammell et al. (1996)	178 mental health workers	NA	32.0
12.	Harmon et al. (1995)	78 stalking cases	51.0	
13.	Harmon et al. (1998)	175 stalking cases	66.0	
14.	Harrell & Smith (1996)	355 F DV victims (TRO) applicants	75.0	
15.	Harris (2000)	167 stalking cases (RO: England)	1.0	
16.	Horton et al. (1987)	820 DV victims & (TRO) applicants	46.0	
17.	Huffhines (2001)	40 stalking cases (RO)	28.0	
18.	Kaci (1992)	224 DV victims (TRO) court records	18.0	22.0
19.	Kaci (1994)	42 DV (TRO, Permanent ROs)	21.0	2.5
20.	Kane (2000)	818 DV incidents	17.0	
21.	Keilitz (1997)	177 F (PO) applicants	16.0	
22.	Kienlen et al. (1997)	25 stalkers	36.0	
23.	Kileen & Dunn (1998)	128 felony stalking cases	78.0	
24.	Langford & Isaac (2000)	121 intimate homicide cases (RO)	40.0	
25.	Logan et al. (2000)	130 college stalking victims	3.0	
26.	Lyon (1997)	54 stalker case breaches (Canada)	24.0	
27.	Marshall & Castle (1998)	1855 DV & (RO) applicants (Australia)	15.5	
28.	Mechanic, Uhlmansiek, Weaver, & Resick (2000)	114 DV F victims (RO)	36.0	
29.	Meloy et al. (1997)	200 domestic civil (PO) defendants	18.0	
30.	Melton (2001)	6 DV victims (RO)	67.0	

(continued on next page)

TABLE 5.5   (continued)

31. Moracco et al. (1998)	196 (att. or actual) femicide cases	9.0
32. Morrison (2001)	100 stalkers (PO: Canada)	93.0
33. Morton et al. (1998)	86 femicide cases	~33.0
34. Mullen & Pathé (1994b)	14 erotomanic cases	33.0
35. Nicastro et al. (2000)	55 stalking (PO) cases	67.0
36. Sheridan et al. (2000)	19 stalking victims (CI: England)	79.0
37. Sheridan et al. (2001a)	95 stalking victims (CI: England)	12.0
38. Tjaden & Thoennes (1998a)	182 stalking (PO) victims	70.0
39. Tjaden & Thoennes (2000d)	485 DV (RO) cases	35.0
40. Tucker (1993)	90 police agencies (Florida)	57.0
41. Westrup et al. (1999)	79 stalked or harassed colleges	6.0

Note. PO = protective order, RO = restraining order, TRO = temporary restraining order, CI = court injunction, F = female, M = male, DV = domestic violence, Ss = subjects.

about a fifth of such orders are perceived as making the situation worse. Furthermore, despite the fact that 60% are not overtly violated, the question remains whether the protective order was the causal factor in the cessation of stalking. In the Tjaden and Thoennes (1998b) study, "less than 1 percent [of victims] said the stalking stopped because they obtained a restraining order against their stalker" (pp. 12–13). Thus, although protective orders may temporarily salve the psychological wounds of the stalking victim, the evidence on their efficacy is decidedly mixed. In a small but notable percentage of cases, such orders appear to make matters worse.

In a very well-designed and time-sensitive study, over a 12-month period of time, *temporary* restraining orders were found to predict a slight but statistically nonsignificant increase in subsequent physical violence, and a significant quadruple-increased risk of psychological violence, which included stalking as part of its index (Holt, Kernic, Lumley, Wolf, & Rivara, 2002). However, *permanent* restraining orders were predictive of a substantial (80%) decrease in the likelihood of physical violence. There was little effect of permanent restraining orders on reducing subsequent psychological violence, and homicide rates did not differ by restraining order status. It appears "that the time shortly after the index incident, when most temporary protection orders are issued, may be one of exceptional volatility" (p. 593). Consequently, pursuit of protective orders to quell the unwanted pursuit of another is an option that should be weighed carefully by the victim as well as those who provide counsel to victims.

CORRECTING COURTSHIP

If stalking and unwanted pursuit are generally a product of distorted or deviant forms of relationship development, it follows that people skilled in managing relationships, courtship, and intimacy should be less likely to pursue others in unwanted ways, and less likely to fall victim to such pursuit. The simplistic principle underlying this reasoning is that stalkers and their victims are likely to be relationally incompetent relative to nonstalkers and nonvictims. Such a hypothesis, of course, begs the question: What constitutes relational competence? Skill in managing interaction in relationships is referred to as *interpersonal* or *relational competence* (Carpenter, Hansson, Rountree, & Jones, 1983; Davis & Oathout, 1987; Hansson, 1986; Hansson, Jones, & Carpenter, 1984; Spitzberg & Hecht, 1984) and is analogous to what was referred to in less politically correct times as heterosocial competence or skills (see, e.g., Covey & Dengerink, 1984; Martinez-Diaz & Edelstein, 1980).

Scholarly interest in communication skills is millennia old (Harper, 1979). The systematic study of skills in interpersonal communication and relationship management is considerably more contemporary. Despite hundreds of studies across a variety of disciplines, the study of interpersonal skills and competence has been hampered by a lack of cohesive integrating theory and measurement (Spitzberg & Cupach, 1984). More than 130 distinct constructs are associated with interpersonal competence, not including dozens of peripheral constructs and well over 100 competence measures reflecting a wide diversity of factors interpreted as interpersonal skills (Spitzberg & Cupach, 1989). These "skill" lists were later expanded and synthesized by Spitzberg and Cupach (2002b), who identified common themes across many prior efforts. Among these common themes of interpersonal competence were the following: empathy, concern, comfort/support, disclosure, narrative skill, referential skill, arousal/excitement, conversational skill, persuasive skill, regulative skill, assertion, ego support, and relaxation. Many of these are also implicit in various efforts to conceptualize and operationalize the construct of relational competence (Carpenter et al., 1983; Davis & Oathout, 1987; Hansson et al., 1984; Spitzberg & Hecht, 1984).

Many of the skills commonly associated with relational competence imply an inclination to sustain and promote dialogue among interactants. It is no surprise that for many scholars, "dialogue" has become a prototype of ideal interaction. Dialogic communication tends to require "the following characteristics: (1) genuineness, (2) accurate empathic understanding, (3) unconditional positive regard, (4) presentness, and (5) spirit of mutual equality" (Johannesen, 1971, pp. 375–376). These characteristics seem closely aligned with other attributes of dialogue, such as "coordination (or cooperation), coherence, reciprocity and mutuality (e.g., with regard to moral commitments)" (Linell, 1998, p. 14). Echoing the skills traditionally associated with interpersonal competence, the interactional abilities thought to enable such dialogic characteristics include empathy, confirmation, relaxed readiness, perspective reflection, meta-communication, congruence, and shared humor (Kristiansen & Bloch-Poulson, 2000, p. 184). Pearce and Pearce (2000, p. 172) explicitly envisioned dialogue as analogous to a social skill that is "learnable, teachable, and contagious." This skill involves "remaining in the tension between holding your own perspective, being profoundly open to others who are unlike you, and enabling others to act similarly" (p. 172).

What is peculiar about most of the research and speculation on interpersonal and relational competence is its surprising apparent inapplicability to the predicaments of stalking and unwanted pursuit. Most existing theory and research on relational and interpersonal competence propose skills such as message management, coorientation, and adaptability *for the purpose of engendering mutual respect and sustenance of ongoing dialogue.* Yet mutual respect and sustenance of dialogue are often precisely the objectives the unwanted pursuer seeks to impose on the victim, and precisely what the victim seeks to deny the stalker.

Herein is a central interactional dilemma in unwanted relational pursuit. More relationally competent persons tend to be rewarding to talk to in large part precisely because they make interaction easy almost regardless of the skill level of the interactional partner. That is, relationally competent interactants often compensate through adaptation for the skill deficits of their partners. This may well be uniquely seductive to potential stalkers, who may have difficulty initiating or maintaining relationships due to their own interactional awkwardness. Furthermore, relationally competent persons may be particularly reluctant to extricate themselves from relationships with persistent paramours. Ending relationships creates a variety of potential face threats to the rejected party (Metts, 1992). The rejecting person in an unrequited love relationship often feels guilt about, and concern for, the rejected suitor (Bratslavsky et al., 1998). Despite the efficiency of assertive, even aggressive, disaffiliation (Kellermann & Lee, 2000), relationally competent individuals especially may endeavor to avoid such normatively inappropriate behavior to their own peril. "The harshness of an outright rejection is not an option for many people, who prefer to mitigate the rejection by offering an excuse or using avoiding tactics" (Finch, 2001, p.

64). One study found only 16% of respondents reported using assertive or aggressive interpersonal strategies to restore privacy when they perceived they had less privacy than preferred (Buslig & Burgoon, 2000). Although some people may be comfortable with employing aggressive means of distancing themselves from unwanted relationships (Hess, 2003), it appears most people are aware that aggressive tactics are "more likely to lead to conflict and explosive responses" from the distanced person (Buslig & Burgoon, 2000, p. 193).

Relationally competent individuals may be disinclined to even believe others can be relationally exploitative because it runs counter to their perceived norms or ideals of interaction and relationships. People may be inclined to disregard or rationalize away the creeping inappropriateness of their suitor. "Stalking typically commences with unwanted telephone calls or physical approaches ... but may initially be perceived by the victim as only peculiar or inappropriate" (Meloy, 1999b, p. 90). Inappropriate behavior "is often minimized by the victim as a random act or harmless behavior" (Meloy, 1997a, p. 177). In one study, almost a fifth of victims reported "the stalking was occurring throughout the relationship ... [but] at the time they did not see it as stalking behavior" (Melton, 2001, p. 156). Such disregard and rationalization, combined with the sense of incompetence associated with outright and abrupt rejection of another's ingratiating pursuit, may lead to a preference for gentle deescalation. "Verbal limit-setting, however, is ineffective" (Meloy, 1999b, p. 90). If the pursuer's behavior is easily disregarded, it is even easier for the "determined stalker" to "ignore, deny or rationalise even the clearest of rejections" (Finch, 2001, p. 65).

"Perhaps the most common mistake that stalking victims make is to initiate personal contact with the stalker" (Meloy, 1999b, p. 94) to try to negotiate an end to the relationship, or to set boundaries on the pursuer's behavior. It seems that "contact, however intermittent, will only reinforce the unwanted behaviour" (Mullen et al., 2000b, p. 458). A well-known principle of behavioral reinforcement is invoked by such contact: "*each victim contact with the perpetrator is an intermittent positive reinforcement and predicts an increase in frequency of subsequent approach behavior*" (Meloy, 1997a, p. 177). As de Becker (1997a) so aptly cautioned, if a victim screens 99 calls by the pursuer and finally breaks down and picks up on the 100th call, it rewards the pursuer's efforts and teaches that it takes 100 calls to obtain such a reward. "The more the victim seeks to end the correspondence, the more desperate, bizarre and dangerous the stalker's behavior becomes. As the stalker is increasingly rebuffed, the obsession escalates, and the stalker will vacillate between deep hate for his subject and profound love and attachment" (Jordan, 1995, pp. 366–367).

If traditional conceptions of relational competence put victims at risk both by presenting a rewarding object for affection and by making bold rejection of the suitor less likely, what corrections to courtship are needed to facilitate both the avoidance of stalkers and extrication from such relationships once begun? At least two stages of concern are prevention and management, or what Buslig and Burgoon (2000) referred to as privacy protection and privacy restoration. *Prevention* requires that potential unwanted pursuers are "recognized" through their behavior before relational involvements or entanglements occur or that the "target is hardened" in ways that deter or foil prospective pursuers. *Management* refers to the way in which unwanted pursuit is handled once it has already begun.

Prevention conceivably ranges from making oneself unattractive to unavailable, from hardening the target to making prospective pursuers the target of perpetual distancing. The extreme forms of such strategies carry unacceptable personal, social, and economic costs for the typical individual. People can become hermits, alienate their entire social network, and effectively impose imprisonment on themselves before others might impose it on them. However, most people need less draconian strategies for protecting their privacy from the attentions of unwanted pursuers. Aside from the relatively obvious forms of target hardening recommended by a host of available practical guides (e.g., security systems, proximity-sensitive home lights, shredding of disposable personal documents, variations of routine, etc.), individuals are likely to need a more sensitively attuned personal warning system for prospective obsessive pursuers. One of the most articulate proponents of such a warning system is de Becker (1997a), who referred to the "gift of fear." The gift is that people are innately fearful of things that seem inappropriate and potentially threatening. He claimed that politeness norms have largely suppressed such apprehensions in everyday interaction episodes, and consequently, many people do not trust their fears when either suitors or strangers intrude in subtle ways suggestive of potential obsession.

Such fear, in fact, is part of a larger continuum of physiological arousal, and various theories of arousal are suggestive of the mechanisms by which such arousal may serve the purposes of self-protection. Privacy management theories (Burgoon et al., 1989; Petronio, 2000) suggest people internalize rules of appropriate psychological, informational, and social privacy. These rules represent internal models of one's boundaries, which are more or less permeable to intrusion based on factors such as type of relationship, context, individual differences, and so forth. When people make moves toward intimacy, and especially when privacy boundaries are violated in the process, such moves initially evoke physiological arousal and subsequent cognitive appraisals of the meaning of these intrusions.

Andersen's (1998) cognitive valence theory claims extreme arousal is automatically treated as threatening, resulting in compensatory (e.g., distancing, or privacy restoration) reactions. For example, a pursuer who suddenly grabs the other by the throat may automatically elicit reactions of self-defense and escape. Extremely mild intrusions (e.g., passing by on a crowded sidewalk) are too unobtrusive to be noticed. In contrast, arousal due to moderate intimacy moves and intrusions are likely to be evaluated in terms of appropriateness standards. If the behavior is appraised as inappropriate to one's sense of cultural, relational, contextual, or individual boundary rules, then the evaluator is likely to compensate (i.e., move away) rather than reciprocate (i.e., move toward). However, societal rules also tend to militate against explicit rejection as a form of distancing, as such moves are viewed as face-threatening to both the user and receiver. de Becker (1997a) recommended that people learn to trust such initial instincts and engage in more direct and definitive rejections of unwanted pursuits and intrusions. Such "early warning signs" and immediate compensatory responses could go a long way toward preventing unwanted pursuit before it ever gets started.

Unfortunately, given that approximately three-quarters of stalking cases emerge from prior established relationships, prevention is only part of the solution. In other words, most stalking and unwanted pursuit gets in under the early warning system because in the early stages the pursuit is not unwanted; in the early stages it is conjunctive rather than disjunctive. Therefore, unwanted pursuit requires extrication from an already existing relationship of some sort. This requires that the person manage the unwanted pursuit.

Competent coping with unwanted pursuit has been studied extensively in descriptive ways, but there is relatively little prescriptive research. Prescriptive research will require sequential, longitudinal, and possibly dyadic research, each of which is extremely challenging with deviant populations. There is, however, extensive speculative and expert advice on competent coping with stalking. At the risk of oversimplification, in the framework of the typology presented herein, moving toward or with, moving against (with the exception of legal prosecution), and moving inward are all likely to be ineffective or counterproductive, whereas moving outward and especially moving away are most likely to be productive ways of coping with unwanted pursuit. Moving toward or with simply provides the pursuer with opportunities for contact, which, regardless of their content, are viewed as positive reinforcements by the pursuer who craves contact. Moving against lets the pursuer know she or he is having an impact on the victim's life, another likely reinforcement.

Moving inward not only is unlikely to deter the pursuer, but is likely to isolate the victim and make the victim more accessible as a target. In contrast, moving outward mobilizes a social network that can make it difficult for the pursuer to enact a campaign of pursuit. There is often actual safety in numbers, and others can serve as an additional network of insulation and warning if properly notified of the risks. Moving away, although often costly in terms of time, effort, and potentially money, is generally considered the most likely to erode the pursuer's interest. Moving away includes hardening the target (e.g., heightened security measures) as well as changing routes, routines, and general accessibility. By being where the pursuer is not, such techniques increase the possibility of diminishing rewards for the pursuer until such time as the pursuer may simply give up and move on, or amass a trail sufficient for legal intervention to take effect.

Competent management of unwanted pursuit, once it has begun, serves any of several primary functions, including (a) redefining the relationship with the pursuer, (b) avoiding immediate contacts with the pursuer, (c) deterring the pursuer from continued pursuit, and (d) establishing formal and informal social networks in the event such resources need to be mobilized (e.g., police, coworkers, friends, etc.). All of these functions involve relationship negotiation processes, which in turn require relational competence. Spitzberg and Cupach (1984, 2002b; see also Spitzberg, 2000b; Spitzberg & Hecht, 1984) proposed that relational competence is a function of three primary components: motivation, knowledge, and skills.

How does a person enact competent behavior in any given context? First, the person needs to be motivated to behave competently. Motivation can fail for at least two reasons. Some people are impaired because of their anxiety or apprehension (i.e., negative motivation), or by their perception of insufficient reward or personal goal relevance. A person may be motivated to behave competently, yet lack the knowledge of what to say and do in the context. Knowledge can fail for many reasons, including lack of familiarity with or experience in a context, misreading the relevant scripts that apply to the context, distraction that interferes with knowledge processing, and insufficient knowledge search into one's repertoire of available knowledge. A person who is both motivated and knowledgeable still needs the skills of enacting this motivation and knowledge. An actor may desire to give a great performance and know the "script" with great acuity, yet lack the depth and facility of acting skills to perform competently.

Motivation in the context of unwanted pursuit is virtually axiomatic. People being pursued in *unwanted* ways by definition are motivated to avoid such pursuit. Given the propositions of privacy and cognitive valence theories, the more severe is the violation of one's boundaries, the more motivated the person should be. Knowledge in this context represents a cognitive understanding of the types of issues raised in this and other texts on stalking and unwanted pursuit (e.g., Boon & Sheridan, 2002; Davis & Chipman, 2001; Davis, Frieze, & Maiuro, 2002; de Becker, 1997a; Finch, 2001; Gross, 2000; Hitchcock, 2002; McCann, 2000b; Meloy, 1998; Morewitz, 2003; Mullen et al., 2000a; Schell & Lantaigne, 2000; Snow, 1998). Skills in the context of unwanted pursuit represent internalizing the repertoire of coping strategies identified here and elsewhere (e.g., Spitzberg, 2002b; Spitzberg & Cupach, 2001a, 2002a, 2003), and demonstrating proficiency in performing the various coping tactics that instantiate such strategies. To date, there is surprisingly little research, but much anecdotal speculation, on the efficacy of specific coping tactics. The most consistent recommendations are to end all contact with the pursuer, to be unresponsive to pursuer contact attempts, and to maintain records in case legal intervention may be required. The empirical efficacy of this last tactic, no matter how well advised, still awaits sequentially sensitive research confirmation.

Another conceptual element of the model of relational competence, however, proposes an important potential diagnostic for the early warning system of courtship. A person who is motivated, knowledgeable, and skilled will enact a sequence of behaviors. These behaviors will be evaluated by both the interactant and those with whom she or he interacts. This evaluation process is guided by two relatively fundamental dimensions of evaluation: appropriateness and effectiveness. Appropriateness is a judgment of legitimacy, fit, and acceptability. Behavior that violates valued expectations or rules of social conduct is judged as inappropriate, and thereby incompetent. Effectiveness is a judgment of the extent to which valued objectives or outcomes are achieved through one's actions. These outcomes are evaluated in relative terms, such that sometimes the most effective course of action is one that minimizes negative outcomes rather than that maximizes positive outcomes. Behavior that fails to achieve relatively valued outcomes is judged ineffective, and thereby incompetent. Although these evaluative criteria can be, and are, applied by interactants both to their own behavior and the behavior of others, there is a certain asymmetry to their relevance. Appropriateness tends to be a judgment most appropriately made by others, whereas effectiveness is a judgment best made by oneself. Only the self can validly evaluate the achievement and relative value of personal goals, and only the other person can know if she or he has been offended by another's behavior. The myriad implications of these criteria have been discussed at length elsewhere (Spitzberg, 1993, 1994, 2000b; Spitzberg & Cupach, 1984, 2002b).

The relevance of these evaluative criteria for unwanted pursuit lies in their suggestion of decision rules for relational compensation. That is, there are two potentially important reasons to consider monitoring, guarding, and potentially departing from a relationship. If the relationship is fundamentally contrary to one's own effectiveness, one's autonomy in pursuing one's own goals, then the value of the relationship is suspect. In addition, if the behavior of the other person violates one's own sense of boundaries or propriety, the relationship justifies reevaluation. All relationships with others are likely to violate these criteria in various short-term incidents, and most people accommodate such losses by evaluating the past rewards and propriety relative to the costs and improprieties, and projecting such experiences into the future. Of course, various rationalization processes and biases can distort such evaluations, especially in the courtship process (e.g., Metts & Spitzberg, 1996). Nevertheless, to the extent that a pursuer's or partner's behavior violates one's boundaries and sense of appropriateness, it should serve as a vital indicator of potential violations to come. In these situations, one's own effectiveness is threatened by the other's inappropriate behavior. Such violations clearly indicate a pursuer's potential for attending only to his or her own agenda (i.e., effectiveness) rather than the pursued's sense of acceptable boundaries (i.e., appropriateness). Relational competence represents an optimal balancing of appropriateness and effectiveness across the span of a relationship, however long the relationship lasts. Repeated, or significant singular, violations indicate a condition of risk in the relationship, and should stimulate what de Becker (1997a) referred to as the "gift of fear."

This is the essential competence problematic for victims of unwanted pursuit. Victims seek autonomy in the pursuit of their own personal goals, but find such pursuits blocked by the unwanted pursuit of a suitor. This problem is exacerbated by a general reluctance to *appear* inappropriate to the suitor by being blunt in distancing and rejecting the suitor's advances. The victim's need to be competent sacrifices personal effectiveness for the sake of appropriateness until it is too late for blunt rejection to be effective. The pursuer has already rationalized the appropriateness of his or her behavior, and therefore is relatively immune to concerns about competence. We suggest that people incorporate a stricter attention to their own relational goals while simultaneously attending more strictly to the appropriateness of any given suitor's behavior. Such attention to the mutual achievement of competent interaction in relationships would be greatly assisted with cultural changes that would reinforce a more mutually responsible model of competence in personal relationships. Until such standards of relational competence are incorporated in the larger cultural venue, they will have to be the responsibility of the individual.

Until such time as a more thorough theory of both unwanted pursuit and coping efficacy is formulated, it is vital to note that these speculations are relatively irrelevant to nonrelational pursuers. Issue-based stalkers, delusional stalkers, and antisocial stalkers may present a far more problematic set of risks, and require more formal forms of third-party and professional intervention. For such pursuers, professional consultation (e.g., police, psychologist or psychiatrist, victim advocacy and services) is always recommended.

CONCLUSION

In a world of six billion people, increasingly enabled with means of mobility and communication across increasingly permeable boundaries, unwanted pursuit seems an increasing risk of modern life. Such a world may engender increasing alienation and shallow relationships that motivate certain people to pursue affection through persistent efforts relatively unimpeded by traditional notions of relational restraint and courtly constraint. It may be that there are fewer places to hide, and more opportunities to become the object of someone else's unwanted attentions.

In traditional conceptions of what constitutes a "relationship," there is an emphasis on mutuality of objectives, coordination of activities, and pursuit of increasingly common futures. Such relationships reveal a predominately conjunctive structure of interaction. However, in instances of stalking and unwanted pursuit, interaction becomes fundamentally disjunctive. One person seeks relational fusion, the other relational fission. These opposing pursuits create a disturbed dance in which neither participant is responding to the same music, but both respond to the other's lead. Neither person is likely to be pleased with the progress of the relationship, but neither seems capable of insulating her- or himself from its effects.

The study of the dark side of human interaction and relationships leads to a fascination with such paradoxical dualities. The behavior of stalking and unwanted pursuit is millennia old, even if the "crime" is of relatively contemporary construction. Research has rapidly provided a useful descriptive profile of the process of unwanted pursuit. However, the more vexing questions of the unfolding contingencies of courtship, the discourses of romance, and the disjunctions of desire have been neither investigated nor theorized thoroughly in the context of unwanted pursuit. These are ultimately far more intriguing and important questions. As this book has displayed, there is extensive knowledge about the who, what, and why of stalking and unwanted pursuit. There is as yet precious little known about when, where, and how. That is, how unwanted pursuit "begins," how it unfolds over time, and the contexts that facilitate such disjunctions are to date still largely a mystery. As mystery is one of the driving forces of the dark side, we anticipate a vibrant scholarly pursuit of answers to such questions. It is in this ironic sense, therefore, that we encourage the wanton and persistent pursuit of such elusive prey.

Appendix 1
Short-Form Measures of Obsessive Relational Intrusion and Coping

---

OBSESSIVE RELATIONAL INTRUSION
(© Spitzberg & Cupach, 1997)

People often pursue intimate relationships without realizing that the person being pursued does not want such a relationship. These pursuers may want friendship, or romantic intimacy, or perhaps just recognition. In addition, they often do things that do not appear in normal circumstances to be intimate, such as invading your privacy, intruding into your life, and/or making threats (e.g., "if you don't go out with me, I'll kill myself"), or refusing to let go. We are interested in finding out if you have ever experienced such a "relationship," and what kinds of actions this pursuer displayed.

In your lifetime, how often, if at all, has anyone ever obsessively pursued you over a period of time for the purpose of establishing an intimate relationship that you <u>did NOT</u> want? That is, ...

	NEVER	ONLY ONCE	2 to 3 TIMES	4 to 5 TIMES	OVER 5 TIMES

Circle the best Answer

Has anyone ever undesirably & obsessively pursued you by...
1. LEAVING UNWANTED GIFTS
   (e.g., flowers, stuffed animals, photographs, jewelry, etc.)
       0   1   2   3   4

Has anyone ever undesirably & obsessively pursued you by...
2. LEAVING UNWANTED MESSAGES OF AFFECTION
   (e.g., romantically-oriented notes, cards, letters, voice-mail, e-mail, messages with friends, etc.)
       0   1   2   3   4

Has anyone ever undesirably & obsessively pursued you by...
3. MAKING EXAGGERATED EXPRESSIONS OF AFFECTION
   (e.g., saying "I love you" after limited interaction, doing large and unsolicited favors for you, etc.)
       0   1   2   3   4

Has anyone ever undesirably & obsessively pursued you by...
4. FOLLOWING YOU AROUND
   (e.g., following you to or from work, school, home, gym, daily activities, etc.)
       0   1   2   3   4

Has anyone ever undesirably & obsessively pursued you by...
5. WATCHING YOU
   (e.g., driving by home or work, watching you from a distance, gazing at you in public places, etc.)
       0   1   2   3   4

Has anyone ever undesirably & obsessively pursued you by...
6. INTRUDING UNINVITED INTO YOUR INTERACTIONS
   (e.g., "hovers" around your conversations, offers unsolicited advice, initiates conversations when you are clearly busy, etc.)
       0   1   2   3   4

Has anyone ever undesirably & obsessively pursued you by...
7. INVADING YOUR PERSONAL SPACE
   (e.g., getting too close to you in conversation, touching you, etc.)
       0   1   2   3   4

Has anyone ever undesirably & obsessively pursued you by...
8. INVOLVING YOU IN ACTIVITIES IN UNWANTED WAYS
   (e.g., enrolling you in programs, putting you on mailing lists, using your name as a reference, etc.)
       0   1   2   3   4

Has anyone ever undesirably & obsessively pursued you by...
9. INVADING YOUR PERSONAL PROPERTY
   (e.g., handling your possessions, breaking and entering into your home, showing up at your door or car, etc.)
       0   1   2   3   4

165

In your lifetime, how often, if at all, has anyone ever obsessively pursued you over a period of time for the purpose of establishing an intimate relationship that you <u>did NOT</u> want? That is . . .

	NEVER	ONLY ONCE	2 to 3 TIMES	4 to 5 TIMES	OVER 5 TIMES

Circle the best Answer

Has anyone ever undesirably & obsessively pursued you by...
10. INTRUDING UPON YOUR FRIENDS, FAMILY OR COWORKERS   0   1   2   3   4
(e.g., trying to befriend your friends, family or coworkers; seeking to
be invited to social events, seeking employment at your work, etc.)

Has anyone ever undesirably & obsessively pursued you by...
11. MONITORING YOU AND/OR YOUR BEHAVIOR   0   1   2   3   4
(e.g., calling at all hours to check on your whereabouts,
checking up on you through mutual friends, etc.)

Has anyone ever undesirably & obsessively pursued you by...
12. APPROACHING OR SURPRISING YOU IN PUBLIC PLACES   0   1   2   3   4
(e.g., showing up at places such as stores, work, gym;
lying in wait around corners, etc.)

Has anyone ever undesirably & obsessively pursued you by...
13. COVERTLY OBTAINING PRIVATE INFORMATION   0   1   2   3   4
(e.g., listening to your message machine, taking photos of you
without your knowledge, stealing your mail or e-mail, etc.)

Has anyone ever undesirably & obsessively pursued you by...
14. INVADING YOUR PROPERTY   0   1   2   3   4
(e.g., breaking and entering your home, car, desk, backpack or
briefcase, etc.)

Has anyone ever undesirably & obsessively pursued you by...
15. LEAVING UNWANTED THREATENING MESSAGES   0   1   2   3   4
(e.g., hang-up calls; notes, cards, letters, voice-mail, e-mail,
messages with friends, implying harm or potential harm, etc.)

Has anyone ever undesirably & obsessively pursued you by...
16. PHYSICALLY RESTRAINING YOU   0   1   2   3   4
(e.g., grabbing your arm, blocking your progress, holding
your car door while you're in the car, etc.)

Has anyone ever undesirably & obsessively pursued you by...
17. ENGAGING IN REGULATORY HARASSMENT   0   1   2   3   4
(e.g., filing official complaints, spreading false rumors to officials--
boss, instructor, etc., obtaining a restraining order on you, etc.)

Has anyone ever undesirably & obsessively pursued you by...
18. STEALING OR DAMAGING VALUED POSSESSIONS   0   1   2   3   4
(e.g., you found property vandalized; things missing, damaged or hurt
that only this person had access to, such as prior gifts, pets, etc.)

Has anyone ever undesirably & obsessively pursued you by...
19. THREATENING TO HURT HIM- OR HERSELF   0   1   2   3   4
(e.g., vague threats that something bad will happen to
him- or herself, threatening to commit suicide, etc.)

In your lifetime, how often, if at all, has anyone ever obsessively pursued you over a period of time for the purpose of establishing an intimate relationship that you did NOT want? That is . . .

	Circle the best Answer				
	NEVER	**ONLY ONCE**	**2 to 3 TIMES**	**4 to 5 TIMES**	**OVER 5 TIMES**

Has anyone ever undesirably & obsessively pursued you by...
20. THREATENING OTHERS YOU CARE ABOUT   0   1   2   3   4
(e.g., threatening harm to or making vague warnings
about romantic partners, friends, family, pets, etc.)

Has anyone ever undesirably & obsessively pursued you by...
21. VERBALLY THREATENING YOU PERSONALLY   0   1   2   3   4
(e.g., threats or vague warnings that something bad will
happen to you, threatening personally to hurt you, etc.)

Has anyone ever undesirably & obsessively pursued you by...
22. LEAVING OR SENDING YOU THREATENING OBJECTS   0   1   2   3   4
(e.g., marked up photographs, photographs taken of you
without your knowledge, pornography, weapons, etc.)

Has anyone ever undesirably & obsessively pursued you by...
23. SHOWING UP AT PLACES IN THREATENING WAYS   0   1   2   3   4
(e.g., showing up at class, office or work, from behind a corner,
staring from across a street, being inside your home, etc.)

Has anyone ever undesirably & obsessively pursued you by...
24. SEXUALLY COERCING YOU   0   1   2   3   4
(e.g., forcefully attempted/succeeded in kissing, feeling, or
disrobing you, exposed him/herself, forced sexual behavior, etc.)

Has anyone ever undesirably & obsessively pursued you by...
25. PHYSICALLY THREATENING YOU   0   1   2   3   4
(e.g., throwing something at you, acting as if s/he will hit you,
running finger across neck implying throat slitting, etc.)

Has anyone ever undesirably & obsessively pursued you by...
26. PHYSICALLY HURTING YOU   0   1   2   3   4
(e.g., pushing or shoving you, slapping you, hitting you
with fist, hitting you with an object, etc.)

Has anyone ever undesirably & obsessively pursued you by...
27. KIDNAPPING OR PHYSICALLY CONSTRAINING YOU   0   1   2   3   4
(e.g., by force or threat of force, trapped you in a car or room;
bound you; took you places against your will; etc.)

Has anyone ever undesirably & obsessively pursued you by...
28. PHYSICALLY ENDANGERING YOUR LIFE   0   1   2   3   4
(e.g., trying to run you off the road, displaying a weapon
in front of you, using a weapon to subdue you, etc.)

The next items ask that you indicate whether you have experienced a certain type of relationship pursuit at some point in your life. If at any point your answer is "NO," or the item does not apply to you, skip to the next item of the survey.

29. If you answered any of the previous 28 items with anything other than "0", what is the sex of the person who was the most persistent unwanted pursuer?   ___ MALE   ___ FEMALE

30. During some period of my life I have experienced being followed and/or harassed and/or obsessively pursued by someone.   ___ YES   ___ NO

31. If "yes," approximately how long did it occur, in approximately   ___ Years   ___ Months

32. If "yes," did it occur in a manner that you personally felt was threatening, or placed you in fear of your own safety, or the safety and security of your family, friends, or possessions . . .   ___ YES   ___ NO

33. If "yes," would you consider what you experienced as a form of "stalking." That is, **have you ever been "stalked"?**   ___ YES   ___ NO

34. If "yes" to #33 above, on average how many times a month did this person do something to intrude in your life in unwanted ways?   ___ Number?

35. If "yes" to 33 above, how many different people have you been stalked by?   ___ Number?

36. If "yes" to 33 above, what was the sex of the person pursuing you?   ___ MALE   ___ FEMALE

37. What is your sex?   ___ MALE   ___ FEMALE

38. If "yes" to 33 above, what type of relationship did you have, if any, prior to the time that the pursuit became unwanted?
    ___ STRANGER
    ___ ACQUAINTANCE RELATIONSHIP
    ___ COLLEAGUE, OR SERVICE RELATIONSHIP
    ___ FRIENDSHIP
    ___ FAMILY MEMBER OR RELATIVE
    ___ CASUALLY DATING RELATIONSHIP
    ___ SERIOUS DATING RELATIONSHIP
    ___ SPOUSE, EX-SPOUSE
    ___ OTHER (Please specify:_____)

39. How long did the relationship in #34 last before it became unwanted?   ___ Years   ___ Months

40. How long ago did the relationship in #34 begin?   ___ Years   ___ Months

41. If "yes" to 33 above, do you have reason to believe that this person has stalked others before or after you?   ___ YES   ___ NO

42. Do you believe that YOU have ever engaged in romantic pursuit in ways that the person you were pursuing might consider your behavior to be stalking?   ___ YES   ___ NO

CYBER-PURSUIT
(Spitzberg & Cupach, 2000)

People often pursue intimate relationships without realizing that the person being pursued does not want such a relationship. People sometimes also pursue others through "electronic" means such as the computer, chat rooms, voice-mail or e-mail. These pursuers may want friendship, romantic intimacy, or perhaps just recognition. In addition, they often do things that do not appear in normal circumstances to be intimate, such as invading your privacy, intruding into your life, and/or making threats (e.g., "if you don't go out with me, I'll kill myself"), or refusing to let go. We are interested in finding out if you have ever experienced such an electronic "relationship," and what kinds of actions this pursuer displayed.

In your lifetime, how often, if at all, has anyone ever obsessively pursued you through electronic means (computer, e-mail, chat room, etc.) over a period of time for the purpose of establishing an intimate relationship that you <u>did NOT</u> want? That is, . . .

| | | Circle the best Answer | | | |
	NEVER	ONLY ONCE	2 to 3 TIMES	4 to 5 TIMES	OVER 5 TIMES
Has anyone ever undesirably & obsessively communicated with or pursued you through computer or other electronic means, by... 1. SENDING TOKENS OF AFFECTION (e.g., poetry, songs, electronic greeting cards, praise, etc.)	0	1	2	3	4
Has anyone ever undesirably & obsessively communicated with or pursued you through computer or other electronic means, by... 2. SENDING EXAGGERATED MESSAGES OF AFFECTION (e.g., expressions of affections implying a more intimate relationship than you actually have, etc.)	0	1	2	3	4
Has anyone ever undesirably & obsessively communicated with or pursued you through computer or other electronic means, by... 3. SENDING EXCESSIVELY DISCLOSIVE MESSAGES (e.g., inappropriately giving private information about his/her life, body, family, hobbies, sexual experiences, etc.)	0	1	2	3	4
Has anyone ever undesirably & obsessively communicated with or pursued you through computer or other electronic means, by... 4. SENDING EXCESSIVELY "NEEDY" OR DEMANDING MESSAGES (e.g., pressuring to see you, assertively requesting you go out on date, arguing with you to give him/her "another chance", etc.)	0	1	2	3	4
Has anyone ever undesirably & obsessively communicated with or pursued you through computer or other electronic means, by... 5. SENDING PORNOGRAPHIC/OBSCENE IMAGES OR MESSAGES (e.g., photographs or cartoons of nude people, or people or animals engaging in sexual acts, etc.)	0	1	2	3	4
Has anyone ever undesirably & obsessively communicated with or pursued you through computer or other electronic means, by... 6. SENDING THREATENING WRITTEN MESSAGES (e.g., suggesting harming you, your property, family, friends, etc.)	0	1	2	3	4

* * * **Please continue on next page** * * *

In your lifetime, how often, if at all, has anyone ever obsessively pursued you through electronic means (computer, e-mail, chat room, etc.) over a period of time for the purpose of establishing an intimate relationship that you did NOT want? That is, . . .

	NEVER	ONLY ONCE	2 to 3 TIMES	4 to 5 TIMES	OVER 5 TIMES

Circle the best Answer

Has anyone ever undesirably & obsessively communicated with or pursued you through computer or other electronic means, by...
7. SENDING SEXUALLY HARASSING MESSAGES
   (e.g., describing hypothetical sexual acts between you, making sexually demeaning remarks, etc.)

0   1   2   3   4

Has anyone ever undesirably & obsessively communicated with or pursued you through computer or other electronic means, by...
8. SENDING THREATENING PICTURES OR IMAGES
   (e.g., images of actual or implied mutilation, blood, dismemberment, property destruction, weapons, etc.)

0   1   2   3   4

Has anyone ever undesirably & obsessively communicated with or pursued you through computer or other electronic means, by...
9. EXPOSING PRIVATE INFORMATION ABOUT YOU TO OTHERS
   (e.g., sending mail out to others regarding your secrets, embarrassing information, unlisted numbers, etc.)

0   1   2   3   4

Has anyone ever undesirably & obsessively communicated with or pursued you through computer or other electronic means, by...
10. PRETENDING TO BE SOMEONE SHE OR HE WASN'T
   (e.g., falsely representing him- or herself as a different person or gender, claiming a false identity, status or position, pretending to be you, etc.)

0   1   2   3   4

Has anyone ever undesirably & obsessively communicated with or pursued you through computer or other electronic means, by...
11. 'SABOTAGING' YOUR PRIVATE OR SOCIAL REPUTATION
   (e.g., spreading rumors about you, your relationships or activities to friends, family, partner, etc.)

0   1   2   3   4

Has anyone ever undesirably & obsessively communicated with or pursued you through computer or other electronic means, by...
12. 'SABOTAGING' YOUR WORK/SCHOOL REPUTATION
   (e.g., spreading rumors about you, your relationships or activities in organizational networks, electronic bulletin boards, etc.)

0   1   2   3   4

Has anyone ever undesirably & obsessively communicated with or pursued you through computer or other electronic means, by...
13. ATTEMPTING TO DISABLE YOUR COMPUTER
   (e.g., downloading a virus, sending too many messages for your system to handle, etc.)

0   1   2   3   4

Has anyone ever undesirably & obsessively communicated with or pursued you through computer or other electronic means, by...
14. OBTAINING PRIVATE INFORMATION WITHOUT PERMISSION
   (e.g., covertly entering your computer files, voicemail, or the files of co-worker, friend or family member, etc.)

0   1   2   3   4

Has anyone ever undesirably & obsessively communicated with or pursued you through computer or other electronic means, by...
15. USING YOUR COMPUTER TO GET INFORMATION ON OTHERS
   (e.g., stealing information about your friends, family, co-workers, etc.)

0   1   2   3   4

* * * Please continue on next page * * *

In your lifetime, how often, if at all, has anyone ever obsessively pursued you through electronic means (computer, e-mail, chat room, etc.) over a period of time for the purpose of establishing an intimate relationship that you <u>did NOT</u> want? That is, . . .

	Circle the best Answer				
	NEVER	ONLY ONCE	2 to 3 TIMES	4 to 5 TIMES	OVER 5 TIMES

Has anyone ever undesirably & obsessively communicated with or
pursued you through computer or other electronic means, by...
16. 'BUGGING' YOUR CAR, HOME, OR OFFICE   0   1   2   3   4
   (e.g., planting a hidden listening or recording device, etc.)

Has anyone ever undesirably & obsessively communicated with or
pursued you through computer or other electronic means, by...
17. ALTERING YOUR ELECTRONIC IDENTITY OR PERSONA   0   1   2   3   4
   (e.g., breaking into your system and changing your signature,
   personal information, or how you portray yourself electronically, etc.)

Has anyone ever undesirably & obsessively communicated with or
pursued you through computer or other electronic means, by...
18. TAKING OVER YOUR ELECTRONIC IDENTITY OR PERSONA   0   1   2   3   4
   (e.g., representing him or herself to others as you in chatrooms,
   bulletin boards, pornography or singles sites, etc.)

Has anyone ever undesirably & obsessively communicated with or
pursued you through computer or other electronic means, by...
19. DIRECTING OTHERS TO YOU IN THREATENING WAYS   0   1   2   3   4
   (e.g., pretending to be you on chat lines and requesting risky
   sex acts, kidnapping fantasies, etc.)

Has anyone ever undesirably & obsessively communicated with or
pursued you through computer or other electronic means, by...
20. MEETING FIRST ON-LINE AND THEN FOLLOWING YOU   0   1   2   3   4
   (e.g., following you while driving, around campus or work, to or
   from the gym or social activities, etc.)

Has anyone ever undesirably & obsessively communicated with or
pursued you through computer or other electronic means, by...
21. MEETING FIRST ON-LINE AND THEN INTRUDING IN YOUR LIFE   0   1   2   3   4
   (e.g., showing up unexpectedly at work, front door, in parking lot,
   intruding in your conversations,)

Has anyone ever undesirably & obsessively communicated with or
pursued you through computer or other electronic means, by...
22. MEETING FIRST ON-LINE AND THEN THREATENING YOU   0   1   2   3   4
   (e.g., threatening to engage in sexual coercion, rape, physical restraint,
   or to harm him or herself, your possessions, pets, family, or friends)

Has anyone ever undesirably & obsessively communicated with or
pursued you through computer or other electronic means, by...
23. MEETING FIRST ON-LINE AND THEN HARMING YOU   0   1   2   3   4
   (e.g., corresponding with you through an on-line dating service
   and then following, harassing, or otherwise stalking you)

Has anyone ever undesirably & obsessively communicated with or
pursued you through computer or other electronic means, by...
24. FIRST MEETING YOU ON-LINE AND THEN STALKING YOU   0   1   2   3   4
   (e.g., corresponding through an on-line dating service or as acquaintances
   and then following, harassing, or otherwise stalking you)

* * * **Please continue on next page** * * *

In your lifetime, how often, if at all, has anyone ever obsessively pursued you through electronic means (computer, e-mail, chat room, etc.) over a period of time for the purpose of establishing an intimate relationship that you did NOT want? That is, . . .

		Circle the best Answer			
	NEVER	**ONLY ONCE**	**2 to 3 TIMES**	**4 to 5 TIMES**	**OVER 5 TIMES**

Has anyone ever undesirably & obsessively communicated with or pursued you through computer or other electronic means, by...
25. OTHER MEANS NOT MENTIONED ABOVE (please describe: 0   1   2   3   4
    (e.g., _____

_____)

COPING

(Spitzberg & Brundige, 2001 ©)

If you have ever in your adult life experienced someone who has obsessively intruded upon, pursued, harassed, or stalked you in an unwanted way, please respond to the items below. The items represent several types of responses that you may or may not have used in an effort to cope with this unwanted pursuit. For each behavior, please indicate the extent to which you used it, if at all, according to the response scale provided. Please circle only one answer per item. If you have not been obsessively pursued, please skip to the last page.

Circle the best Answer

	NEVER	OCCAS IONALLY	OFTEN	VERY OFTEN	CONST- ANTLY

MOVING INWARD:

While this person was pursuing you, did you ever...
1. IGNORE THE PROBLEM (e.g., wait, assume problem will go away on its own, etc.)

| 0 | 1 | 2 | 3 | 4 |

While this person was pursuing you, did you ever...
2. MINIMIZE THE PROBLEM IN YOUR OWN MIND (e.g., rationalize that the problem is less significant or serious than it actually is, etc.)

| 0 | 1 | 2 | 3 | 4 |

While this person was pursuing you, did you ever...
3. DENY THE PROBLEM (e. g., refuse to acknowledge the problem at all; rationalize alternative explanations for experiences, etc.)

| 0 | 1 | 2 | 3 | 4 |

While this person was pursuing you, did you ever...
4. BLAME YOURSELF (e.g., attribute responsibility for problems to self actions or perceptions, etc.)

| 0 | 1 | 2 | 3 | 4 |

While this person was pursuing you, did you ever...
5. SEEK THERAPIES (e.g., invest time and effort into hobbies, drugs, exercise, medicine, therapeutic activities such as massage, meditation, exercise, watch television, internet, etc.).

| 0 | 1 | 2 | 3 | 4 |

While this person was pursuing you, did you ever...
6. SEEK MEANING IN GENERAL (e.g., invest time and effort into making sense of your situation, trying to find a reason, etc.)

| 0 | 1 | 2 | 3 | 4 |

While this person was pursuing you, did you ever...
7. SEEK MEANING IN CONTEXT (e.g., invest time and effort into religion, philosophy, education, literature, etc.)

| 0 | 1 | 2 | 3 | 4 |

While this person was pursuing you, did you ever...
8. ENGAGE IN SELF-DESTRUCTIVE ESCAPISM (e.g., using drugs or alcohol, doing addictive things, attempting suicide, etc.)

| 0 | 1 | 2 | 3 | 4 |

MOVING OUTWARD:

While this person was pursuing you, did you ever...
9. SEEK SYMPATHY FROM OTHERS (e.g., cry, explain personal problems caused by the pursuer, etc.)

| 0 | 1 | 2 | 3 | 4 |

While this person was pursuing you, did you ever...
9. ENGAGE SOCIAL SUPPORT (e.g., seek or obtain emotional and/or instrumental support from friends, family, counselor, etc.)

| 0 | 1 | 2 | 3 | 4 |

	Circle the best Answer				
	NEVER	OCCAS IONALLY	OFTEN	VERY OFTEN	CONST- ANTLY

While this person was pursuing you, did you ever...
11. ENGAGE DIRECT INVOLVEMENT OF OTHERS (e.g., seek
or obtain protection or deterrence through signals of
relationships with or by friends, family, colleagues, etc.)   0   1   2   3   4

While this person was pursuing you, did you ever...
12. ENGAGE LEGAL/LAW ENFORCEMENT INPUT (e.g., seek or
obtain input from victims advocate, report to public attorney,
police, domestic violence unit, social worker, etc.)   0   1   2   3   4

While this person was pursuing you, did you ever...
13. ENGAGE INDEPENDENT/PRIVATE ASSISTANCE (e.g.,
private investigator, bodyguard, protection service, etc.)   0   1   2   3   4

MOVING AWAY:

While this person was pursuing you, did you ever...
14. BEHAVE CAUTIOUSLY (e.g., make plans of action and escape,
become more aware of environment, become more conservative
or careful in daily routine, etc.)   0   1   2   3   4

While this person was pursuing you, did you ever...
15. IGNORE THE PERSON'S BEHAVIOR (e.g., avoid eye contact,
be non-responsive to pursuer's talk and behaviors)   0   1   2   3   4

While this person was pursuing you, did you ever...
16. CONTROL THE INTERACTION (e.g., avoid asking questions,
use closed body orientation, stand/sit closer with others during
conversation, etc.)   0   1   2   3   4

While this person was pursuing you, did you ever...
17. DISTANCE YOURSELF (e.g., maintain or increase physical
distance, lean away during conversation, walk away, etc.)   0   1   2   3   4

While this person was pursuing you, did you ever...
18. DETATCH OR DEPERSONALIZE (e.g., act impersonal,
unemotional, uninvolved, avoid jokes or intimate communication,
behave ritualistically, act strictly polite, etc.)   0   1   2   3   4

While this person was pursuing you, did you ever...
19. REDIRECT OR DIVERT ATTENTION OF PURSUER (e.g., get
pursuer interested in other activities, hobbies, or another person
with whom she or he might be more compatible, etc.)   0   1   2   3   4

While this person was pursuing you, did you ever...
20. USE VERBAL "ESCAPE" TACTICS (e.g., make excuses, claim
prior commitments, existing relationship, role restrictions, etc.)   0   1   2   3   4

While this persona was pursuing you, did you ever...
21. RESTRICT YOUR ACCESSABILITY (e.g., change schedule, arrive
or leave earlier, shift activities to more public venues, etc.)   0   1   2   3   4

While this person was pursuing you, did you ever...
22. BLOCK YOUR PHYSICAL ACCESSABILITY (e.g., arrange
environment to avoid contact: close office doors, harden home
security, caller ID, *69, hang up when called, change locks, etc.)   0   1   2   3   4

	Circle the best Answer				
	NEVER	OCCAS IONALLY	OFTEN	VERY OFTEN	CONST- ANTLY

While this person was pursuing you, did you ever...
23. **BLOCK YOUR ELECTRONIC OR MEDIA ACCESSABILITY (e.g., get caller ID, *69, change e-mail address, contact ISP or internet provider to block certain contact sources, etc.)**

| 0 | 1 | 2 | 3 | 4 |

While this person was pursuing you, did you ever...
24. **RELOCATE (e.g., change jobs, change address, change classes, change hobby/recreational locations, etc.)**

| 0 | 1 | 2 | 3 | 4 |

While this person was pursuing you, did you ever...
25. **ATTEMPT TO END THE RELATIONSHIP (e.g., claim relationship is over, provide relationship ultimatum or define boundaries, etc.)**

| 0 | 1 | 2 | 3 | 4 |

MOVING TOWARD/WITH:

While this person was pursuing you, did you ever...
26. **DIMINISH THE SERIOUSNESS OF THE SITUATION (e.g., tease or joke with the pursuer, make light of the pursuer's actions, etc.)**

| 0 | 1 | 2 | 3 | 4 |

While this person was pursuing you, did you ever...
27. **DECIEVE THEM (e.g., flirt or hint at interest to get out of immediate situation, arrange or suggest future meetings with no intent to keep date, etc.)**

| 0 | 1 | 2 | 3 | 4 |

While this person was pursuing you, did you ever...
28. **USE PROBLEM SOLVING NEGOTIATION (i.e., confront pursuer with responsibility for actions and alternative approaches to achieve objectives, etc.)**

| 0 | 1 | 2 | 3 | 4 |

While this person was pursuing you, did you ever...
29. **NEGOTIATE RELATIONSHIP DEFINITION (i.e., discuss pursuer's own preferred relationship objectives to arrive at a mutual definition; e.g., just be friends, just be colleagues, reconciliation of previous relationship, etc.)**

| 0 | 1 | 2 | 3 | 4 |

While this person was pursuing you, did you ever...
30. **BARGAIN (e.g., offer compromises, promises, or other rewards to get pursuer to alter behavior, etc.)**

| 0 | 1 | 2 | 3 | 4 |

While this person was pursuing you, did you ever...
31. **ACCEPT PROMISES (e.g., believe or hope that discussions that pursuer will behave more appropriately will work, etc.)**

| 0 | 1 | 2 | 3 | 4 |

While this person was pursuing you, did you ever...
32. **USE NONVERBAL AGGRESSION (e.g., yell at, criticize, insult, make fun of, show anger, annoyance, frustration, use harsh or hostile voice, write a strongly worded e-mail, etc.)**

| 0 | 1 | 2 | 3 | 4 |

MOVING AGAINST:

While this person was pursuing you, did you ever...
33. **ATTEMPT TO DETER FUTURE BEHAVIOR (e.g., carry air horn or mace, show weapon, get self-defense training, put security stickers on car and home windows, etc.)**

| 0 | 1 | 2 | 3 | 4 |

		Circle the best Answer			
	NEVER	OCCAS IONALLY	OFTEN	VERY OFTEN	CONST- ANTLY

While this person was pursuing you, did you ever...
34. USING ELECTRONIC RETALIATORY RESPONSES
   (e.g., sabotaging pursuer's website, "spamming" pursuer's
   e-mail, sending viruses to pursuer's e-mail, etc.)   0   1   2   3   4

While this person was pursuing you, did you ever...
35. USE PROTECTIVE RESPONSES TO CURRENT BEHAVIOR
   (e.g., call police, seek restraining order, press charges, sue, etc.)   0   1   2   3   4

While this person was pursuing you, did you ever...
36. USE ELECTRONIC PROTECTIVE RESPONSES
   (e.g., contact on-line service to block or investigate e-mail access,
   enhance firewalls in computer, sabotaging pursuer's website, etc.)   0   1   2   3   4

While this person was pursuing you, did you ever...
37. ISSUE VERBAL WARNINGS/THREATS (e.g., articulate
   punishments or sanctions that the pursuer will experience if
   pursuit continues, threaten the police, violence, etc.)   0   1   2   3   4

While this person was pursuing you, did you ever...
38. USE PHYSICAL VIOLENCE (e.g., hit, shove, use a weapon,
   throw an object, blackmail, restrain, beat up, etc.)   0   1   2   3   4

While this person was pursuing you, did you ever...
39. BUILD A LEGAL CASE (e.g., save voice mail/e-mail, save
   gifts/notes, keep log of phone calls, try to entrap them)   0   1   2   3   4

While this person was pursuing you, did you ever...
40. PURSUE A LEGAL CASE (e.g., sue, swear out a complaint, hire a
   lawyer, pursue indictment on harassment or stalking laws, etc.)   0   1   2   3   4

Appendix 2
Primary Studies Included in Research Summary

Primary Studies Included in Research Summary

Study No.	Reference	Sample Size	Sample Type	Country
1	Adams, Pitre, & Smith, 2001	106	Clinical	Canadian
2	Bjerregaard, 2000	788	College	USA
3	Blaauw, Winkel, et al., 2002	246	Victim	European
4	Blackburn, 1999	257	College	US
5	Boon & Sheridan, 2001	124	Forensic	Great Britain
6	Brewster, 1998, 2000, 2003	187	Victim	USA
7	Brüne, 2001, 2003	246	Clinical	Other
8	Budd & Mattinson, 2000	9,988	General Population	Great Britain
9	Burgess et al., 1997	120	Victim	USA
10	Burgess et al., 2001	165	DV	USA
11	Buzawa et al., 1998a	356	DV	USA
12	Coleman, 1997	141	College	USA
13	Coleman, 1999	130	Clinical	USA
14	Corder & Whiteside, 1996	60	Organizational	USA
15.1	Cupach & Spitzberg, 2000	300	College	USA
15.2	Cupach & Spitzberg, 2000	366	College	USA
15.3	Cupach & Spitzberg, 2000	209	College	USA
16	Davis & Gonzales, 2003	16	Clinical	USA
17.1	Davis et al., 2000	169	College	USA
17.2	Davis et al., 2000	203	College	USA
18	Del Ben, 2000	396	College	USA
19	Dinkelmeyer & Johnson, 2002	17	Clinical	USA
20	Dunn, 1999	267	College	USA
21	Dunn, 2001	128	Forensic	USA
22.1	Dussuyer, 2000	232	Forensic	Australia
22.2	Dussuyer, 2000	16	Forensic	Australia
23	Dye & Davis, 2003	338	College	USA
24	Eisele, Watkins, & Matthews, 1998	51	Organizational	USA

(continued on next page)

Appendix 2 *(continued)*

Study No.	Reference	Sample Size	Sample Type	Country
25	Eke, 1999	30	Victim	Canadian
26	Elliott & Brantley, 1997	1,752	College	USA
27	Farnham et al., 2000	50	Forensic	Great Britain
28	Feldman et al., 1997	38	Organizational	USA
29	Fisher et al., 2000	4,446	College	USA
30.1	Fremouw et al., 1997	294	College	USA
30.2	Fremouw et al., 1997	299	College	USA
31	Gallagher et al., 1993	355	College	USA
32	Gallagher, 1997 (re: 1994 data)	504	College	USA
33	Gallagher et al., 1996	338	College	USA
34	Gallagher et al., 1997	331	College	USA
35	Gallagher et al., 1998	325	College	USA
36	Gallagher et al., 1999	311	College	USA
37	Gallagher et al., 2000	286	College	USA
38	Gallagher et al., 2001	274	College	USA
39	Gallagher & Zhang, 2002	272	College	USA
40	Gentile, 2001; Gentile et al., 2002	238	Clinical	USA
41	Gill & Brockman, 1996	601	Forensic	Canadian
42	Gist et al., 2001	90	Forensic	USA
43	Hackett, 2000	5,910	Forensic	Canadian
44	Hall, 1997	145	Victim	USA
45	Hammell et al., 1996	499	Clinical	USA
46	Harmon et al., 1995	48	Clinical	USA
47	Harmon et al., 1998	175	Forensic	USA
48	Hargreaves, n.d.	26	Other	Other
49	Harris, 2000	167	Forensic	Canadian
50	Herold et al., 1979	103	College	USA
51	Hills & Taplin, 1998	172	General Population	Australia
52	Holloway, 1994	79	Organizational	USA
53	Huffhines, 2001	40	Forensic	USA
54	Hughes, Marshall, & Sherrill, 2003	564	College	USA
55	Human Rights Watch, 2001	20	DV	Other

56	Jagessar & Sheridan, 2002	354	General Population	Other
57	Jason et al., 1984	50	College	USA
58	Jordan, Logan, Walker, & Nigoff, 2003	390	Forensic	USA
59	Kamphuis & Emmelkamp, 2001	201	Victim	European
60	Kienlen et al., 1997	25	Forensic	USA
61	Kileen & Dunn, 1998	128	Forensic	USA
62	Kohn et al., 2000	1,171	General Population	USA
63	Kong, 1996	7,472	Forensic	Canadian
64	Kordvani, 2000	100	Forensic	Other
65	Krishnan, Hilbert, & VanLeeuwen, 2001	102	Victim	USA
66	Langhinrichsen-Rohling et al., 2000	282	College	USA
67	Langhinrichsen-Rohling & Rohling, 2000	213	College	USA
68	LeBlanc et al., 2001	172	College	USA
69	Lemmey, 1999	83	DV	USA
70	Lewis et al., 2001	240	College	USA
71	Logan et al., 2000	337	College	USA
72	Logan et al., 2002	390	Forensic	USA
73	Lyon, 1997	54	Forensic	Canadian
74	Marshall & Castle, 1998	29	Forensic	Australia
75	McCann, 2000a	13	Clinical	USA
76	McCann, 2001	26	Adolescent	USA
77	McCreedy & Dennis, 1996	760	College	USA
78.1	McFarlane et al., 1999	141	Homicide	USA
78.2	McFarlane et al., 1999	65	Other	USA
79	McFarlane, Willson, Lemmey, & Malecha, 2000	90	DV	USA
80	McFarlane, Campbell, & Watson, 2002	821	DV	USA
81	McLennan, 1996	6,300	General Population	Australia
82	McLennan, 1995/96	1,397	Forensic	Australia
83.1	Mechanic, Weaver, & Resick, 2000	114	DV	USA
83.2	Mechanic, Uhlmansiek, Weaver, & Resick, 2000			

(*continued on next page*)

Appendix 2 (*continued*)

Study No.	Reference	Sample Size	Sample Type	Country
84	Meloy & Boyd, 2003	82	Other	Other
85	Meloy et al., 2001	59	Forensic	USA
86	Meloy & Gothard, 1995	20	Clinical	USA
87	Meloy et al., 2000	65	Forensic	USA
88	Melton, 2001	178	Forensic	USA
89	Montero, 2003	260	College	USA
90	Moracco et al., 1998	586	Homicide	USA
91	Morewitz, 2001b, 2003	145	Forensic	USA
92	Morrison, 2001	100	Forensic	Canadian
93	Mullen & Pathé, 1994a	16	Clinical	Australia
94	Mullen & Pathé, 1994b	14	Clinical	Australia
95	Mullen et al., 1999	145	Forensic	Australia
96	Mustaine & Tewksbury, 1999	861	College	USA
97	New Jersey State Police, 1997	345	Forensic	USA
98	Nicastro et al., 2000	55	Clinical	USA
99	Nishith, Griffin, & Poth, 2002	27	DV	USA
100	Oddie, 2000	148	Victim	USA
101	Omata, 2002	434	College	Japan
102	Palarea et al., 1999	223	Forensic	USA
103	Pathé & Mullen, 1997	100	Clinical	Australia
104	Pathé et al., 2000	163	Clinical	Australia
105	Purcell et al., 2001	190	Clinical	Australia
106	Purcell et al., 2002	1,844	General Population	Australia
107	Roberts, 2002	305	College	Great Britain
108	Romans et al., 1996	178	Organizational	USA
109	Rosenfeld & Harmon, 2002	204	Clinical	USA
110	Sandberg et al., 1998	17	Clinical	USA
111	Sandberg et al., 2002	62	Organizational	USA
112	Schwartz-Watts et al., 1997	18	Forensic	USA
113	Scocas et al., 1994	242	Forensic	USA
114	Seeck, 1998	106	Clinical	USA
115	Sheridan, 2001	29	Victim	Great Britain
116	Sheridan & Davies, 2001b; Sheridan et al., 2001a	95	Victim	Great Britain
117	Sheridan et al., 2001b	348	General Population	Great Britain

118	Sheridan et al., 2000	80	Organizational	Great Britain
119	Sheridan et al., 2002	210	General Population	Great Britain
120	Sheridan et al., 2003	168	College	Great Britain
121	Sinclair & Frieze, 2000	241	College	USA
122	Spencer, 1998	240	Forensic	USA
123	Spitzberg, 2000a	166	College	USA
124	Spitzberg et al., 2001	367	College	USA
125	Spitzberg & Cupach, 1999	178	College	USA
126	Spitzberg & Cupach, 2001b	163	College	USA
127	Spitzberg et al., 1998	162	College	USA
128	Spitzberg & Hoobler, 2002	223	College	USA
129	Spitzberg & Rhea, 1999	360	College	USA
130	Suzuki, 1999	600	General Population	Japan
131.1	Tjaden & Thoennes, 1998b	16,000	General Population	USA
131.2	Tjaden et al., 2000c			
131.3	Tjaden & Thoennes, 2001			
131.4	Davis, Coker, & Sanderson, 2002			
131.5	Jaynes-Andrews, 2001			
132	Tjaden & Thoennes, 2000d	285	DV	USA
133	Tucker, 1993	90	Organizational	USA
134	Turell, 2000	501	General Population	USA
135	Department of Justice, Victoria, 1995	170	Forensic	Australia
136	Wallis, 1996	151	Forensic	Great Britain
137	Westrup et al., 1999	232	College	USA
138	WHOA, 2001	408	Victim	Other
139	Willson et al., 2000	180	Forensic	USA
140	Wisconsin Department of Justice, 1996	135	Forensic	USA
141	Wright et al., 1996	30	Forensic	USA
142	Yokoi, 1998	34	Forensic	Japan
143	Zona et al., 1993	74	Forensic	USA

Note. Where the study number shows decimal entries, it indicates either the sample was divided for analysis (e.g., attempted femicides vs. actual femicides), or that multiple studies have analyzed the same primary data set. In the latter case, the data are not repeated in the data set we analyzed so as to avoid informational redundancy.

Appendix 3
Raw Items for the Unwanted Pursuit Motivation Typology

1. EXPRESSIVE:
   A. Affective: emotionally expressive: positive (love, amorous, etc.), negative (anger, rage, etc.), ambivalent (jealousy, envy, grief)
      i. Infatuation/Love:
         - Relational (Concern): concern (e.g., concerned about her and the kids) (5.5% Burgess et al., 2001)
         - Affective (+Infatuation): [psychological] dependency (37% Meloy & Boyd, 2003)
         - Affective (+Infatuation): infatuation (20% Wright et al., 1996) (see also "incompetence" category)
         - Affective (+Infatuation): infatuation/fixation (39% Morrison, 2001) (see also "incompetence" category)
         - Relational (+ Love): affectionate/amorous (62.5% Harmon et al., 1995)
         - Relational (+ Love): amorous: call content (48% Brewster, 1998, 2000)
         - Relational (+ Love): amorous: letter content (77% Brewster, 1998, 2000)
         - Relational (+ Love): express love for you: call (F:64% Bjerregaard, 2000)
         - Relational (+ Love): express love for you: call (M:57% Bjerregaard, 2000)
         - Relational (+ Love): love (24% Sheridan et al., 2001a)
         - Relational (+ Love): love (3% Harris, 2000)
         - Relational (+ Love): love (e.g., because I loved her) (16% Burgess et al., 2001)
         - Relational (+ Love): love for you: encounter (F:60% Bjerregaard, 2000)
         - Relational (+ Love): love for you: encounter (M:60% Bjerregaard, 2000)
         - Relational (+ Love): love for you: mail (F:82% Bjerregaard, 2000)

Relational (+ Love): love for you: mail (M:57% Bjerregaard, 2000)

ii. Jealousy/Envy:
- Affective (-/+Jealousy/Envy): envy (12% Meloy & Boyd, 2003)
- Affective (-/+Jealousy/Envy): jealous (27% Hall, 1997) (see also "instrumental affect" categories)
- Affective (-/+Jealousy/Envy): jealous: demeanor (4% Nicastro et al., 2000) (see also "instrumental affect" categories)
- Affective (-/+Jealousy/Envy): jealousy (14% Brewster, 1998, 2000) (see also "instrumental affect" categories)
- Affective (-/+Jealousy/Envy): jealousy (18% Nicastro et al., 2000) (see also "instrumental affect" categories)
- Affective (-/+Jealousy/Envy): jealousy (24% Kienlen et al., 1997) (see also "instrumental affect" categories)
- Affective (-/+Jealousy/Envy): jealousy (33% Meloy & Boyd, in press) (see also "instrumental affect" categories)
- Affective (-/+Jealousy/Envy): jealousy: trigger (16% Brewster, 1998, 2000) (see also "instrumental affect" categories)
- Affective (-/+Jealousy/Envy): jealousy: violence motive (14% Mullen et al., 1999) (see also "instrumental affect" categories)

iii. Betrayal/Blame
- Affective (-Betrayal/Blame): betrayal (33% Meloy & Boyd, 2003)
- Affective (-Betrayal/Blame): projection of blame (53% Kienlen et al., 1997)

iv. Anger/Rage:
- Affective (-Anger/Rage): abandonment rage (44% Meloy & Boyd, 2003); (see also "Context—break-up")
- Affective (-Anger/Rage): anger (16% Nicastro et al., 2000)
- Affective (-Anger/Rage): anger/hostility (63% Meloy & Boyd, 2003)
- Affective (-Anger/Rage): anger/hostility (65% Kienlen et al., 1997)
- Affective (-Anger/Rage): anger/retaliation (40% Wright et al., 1996) (see also "instrumental affect")
- Affective (-Anger/Rage): angry (24% Melton, 1994)

- Affective (-Anger/Rage): angry: call content (38% Brewster, 1998, 2000)
- Affective (-Anger/Rage): angry: demeanor (60% Nicastro et al., 2000)
- Affective (-Anger/Rage): angry: letter content (12% Brewster, 1998, 2000)
- Affective (-Anger/Rage): rage at rejection: violence motive (14% Mullen et al., 1999)

v.   Grief:
- Affective (-/+Grief): grief (1% Meloy & Boyd, 2003)

B. Relational bid: definition, desire for contact (to talk, loneliness), courtship (for a date), concern for other
   i.   Contact:
- Relational (Contact): communication (e.g., to talk, to resolve misunderstanding) (19% Burgess et al., 2001)
- Relational (Contact): desire for contact: call (F:69% Bjerregaard, 2000)
- Relational (Contact): desire for contact: call (M:33% Bjerregaard, 2000)
- Relational (Contact): desire for contact: mail (F:68% Bjerregaard, 2000)
- Relational (Contact): desire for contact: mail (M:57% Bjerregaard, 2000)
- Relational (Contact): loneliness (37% Meloy & Boyd, 2003)
- Relational (Contact): to talk: motive for using threat (16% Blackburn, 1999)

   ii.   Initiation:
- Relational (Initiation): start a relationship (22% Budd & Mattinson, 2000)
- Relational (Initiation): to initiate intimate relationship (23% Hall, 1997)

   iii.   Friendship:
- Relational (Friendship): friendly but not amorous: letter content (7% Brewster, 1998, 2000)

   iv.   Courtship:
- Relational (Courtship): date (27% Blackburn, 1999)

- Relational (Courtship): date: motive for using threat (8% Blackburn, 1999)

v. Escalation Bid:
  - Relational (Escalation Bid): desire to marry: encounter (F:27% Bjerregaard, 2000)
  - Relational (Escalation Bid): desire to marry: encounter (M:33% Bjerregaard, 2000)
  - Relational (Escalation Bid): desire to marry: mail (F:44% Bjerregaard, 2000)
  - Relational (Escalation Bid): desire to marry: mail (M:57% Bjerregaard, 2000)
  - Relational (Escalation Bid): develop relationship with victim (15% Coleman, 1999)
  - Relational (Escalation Bid): express desire to marry: call (F:35% Bjerregaard, 2000)
  - Relational (Escalation Bid): express desire to marry: call (M:19% Bjerregaard, 2000)

vi. Reconciliation:
  - Relational (Reconciliation): apologetic: call content (3% Brewster, 1998, 2000)
  - Relational (Reconciliation): apologetic: letter content (6% Brewster, 1998, 2000)
  - Relational (Reconciliation): attempted reconciliation (18% Meloy & Boyd, 2003)
  - Relational (Reconciliation): continue a relationship (12% Budd & Mattinson, 2000)
  - Relational (Reconciliation): keep in relationship (25% Blackburn, 1999)
  - Relational (Reconciliation): keep victim in relationship (20% Tjaden & Thoennes, 1998b)
  - Relational (Reconciliation): reconciliation (40% Nicastro et al., 2000)
  - Relational (Reconciliation): reconciliation (75% Brewster, 1998, 2000)
  - Relational (Reconciliation): reconciliation (e.g., to make up with her) (7% Burgess et al., 2001)
  - Relational (Reconciliation): stop from leaving the relationship (25% Blackburn, 1999)
  - Relational (Reconciliation): to get back in relationship: motive for using threat (19% Blackburn, 1999)

- Relational (Reconciliation): win back former partner (55% Coleman, 1999)

vii. Can't Let Go:
- Relational (Can't let go): could not let go after end of relationship (46% Sheridan et al., 2001a)
- Relational (Can't let go): would not accept end of relationship (58% Hall, 1997)

C. Sexual: sexual attraction, desire for sexual interaction
- Sexual: desire for sex: encounter (F:24% Bjerregaard, 2000)
- Sexual: desire for sex: encounter (M:33% Bjerregaard, 2000)
- Sexual: desire for sex: mail (F:38% Bjerregaard, 2000)
- Sexual: desire for sex: mail (M:43% Bjerregaard, 2000)
- Sexual: desire for sexual contact with victim (39% McCann, 2000a)
- Sexual: express desire for sex: call (F:35% Bjerregaard, 2000)
- Sexual: express desire for sex: call (M:33% Bjerregaard, 2000)
- Sexual: for sex: motive for using threat (10% Blackburn, 1999)
- Sexual: sexual (2% Nicastro et al., 2000)
- Sexual: sexual attacks: violence motive (29% Mullen et al., 1999)
- Sexual: sexual attraction/infatuation (32% Dussuyer, 2000)
- Sexual: sexual intent (18% Meloy & Boyd, 2003);
- Sexual: sexual preoccupation (26% Meloy & Boyd, in press)
- Sexual: sexual relations (33% Blackburn, 2003)

2. INSTRUMENTAL:
A. Agenda: attitude based (see also "contextual" categories, e.g., conflict with neighbors):
  i. Dispute:
  - Agenda (Dispute): business dispute (3% Harris, 2000)
  - Agenda (Dispute): disputes over property/money (14% Harris, 2000)
  - Agenda (Dispute): escalation of conflict with a neighbor (7% Sheridan et al., 2001a)
  - Agenda (Dispute): neighborhood disputes (3% Dussuyer, 2000)
  - Agenda (Dispute): personal dispute (25% Harris, 2000)

  ii. Issue Retaliation:

- Agenda (Issue Retaliation): catch victim doing something (1% Tjaden & Thoennes, 1998b)
- Agenda (Issue Retaliation): road rage (2% Dussuyer, 2000) (see also "context" categories)

   iii. Prejudice:
- Agenda (Prejudice): racially motivated (2% Harris, 2000)

B. Control: intimidation, isolation/possession, self-protection:
   i. Self-Protection:
- Control (Self-Protection): to stop legal action: motive for using threat (12% Blackburn, 1999)

   ii. Need for Power:
- Control (Need): need for power and control (12% Kienlen et al., 1997)
- Control (Need): need for power and control (19% Meloy & Boyd, 2003)

   iii. Control:
- Control: control issues (29% Melton, 1994)
- Control: control victim (21% Tjaden & Thoennes, 1998b)

   iv. Intimidation:
- Control (Intimidation): intimidation (29% Blackburn, 1999)
- Control (Intimidation): intimidation (6% Brewster, 1998, 2000)
- Control (Intimidation): scare victim (16% Tjaden & Thoennes, 1998b)
- Control (Intimidation): threatening: call content (67% Brewster, 1998, 2000)
- Control (Intimidation): threatening: letter content (28% Brewster, 1998, 2000)

   v. Possession:
- Control (Possession): possession (30% Wright et al., 1996)
- Control (Possession): possession/control (27% Brewster, 1998, 2000)

   vi. Isolation:
- Control (Isolation): stop victim finding new romance (34% Coleman, 1999)

- Control (Isolation): to stop victim from seeing someone else: motive for using threat (11% Blackburn, 1999)

C. Instrumental Affect: retaliation, revenge, harassment, humiliation:
  i.   Attention/status-seeking: (see discussion of "howlers" in Fein & Vossekuil, 1999)

  ii. Harass:
       - Instrumental Affect (Harass): annoy or upset the victim (16% Budd & Mattinson, 2000)

  iii. Humiliate:
       - Instrumental Affect (Humiliation): humiliation and shame (17% Meloy & Boyd, 2003)

  iv. Jealous Possessiveness:
       - Instrumental Affect (Jealous Possessiveness): jealousy-possessiveness-control of victim (9% Dussuyer, 2000) (see also "affective -/+" categories)
       - Instrumental Affect (Jealous): (49% Roberts, 2002)
       - Suspiciousness/suspicion: (51% Roberts, 2002)

  v.   Revenge:
       - Instrumental Affect (Revenge): hostility/retaliation (41% Morrison, 2001)
       - Instrumental Affect (Revenge): persecutory/angry (31% Harmon et al., 1995)
       - Instrumental Affect (Revenge): retaliation (24% Meloy & Boyd, 2003)
       - Instrumental Affect (Revenge): retaliation (32% Hall, 1997)
       - Instrumental Affect (Revenge): revenge (41% Coleman, 1999)
       - Instrumental Affect (Revenge): revenge (45% Brewster, 1998, 2000)
       - Instrumental Affect (Revenge): revenge or anger (23% McCann, 2000a)

3. PERSONALOGICAL:
  A. Drugs/Dependency:
     - Drugs/Dependency: dependency (47% Kienlen et al., 1997)
     - Drugs/Dependency: drug/alcohol abuse: trigger (27% Brewster, 1998, 2000)

- Drugs/Dependency: influence of drugs/alcohol (6% Meloy & Boyd, 2003)

B. Mental/Personality Disorder: emotional problems, mood disorder, Axis I or II, psychological problems, delusional disorder, erotomania, psychosis, paranoia, schizophrenia, personality disorder, borderline disorder, antisocial personality, narcissism, or other pathology:
  - Mental Disorder: delusional accusations: call content (13% Brewster, 1998, 2000)
  - Mental Disorder: delusional accusations: letter content (6% Brewster, 1998, 2000)
  - Mental Disorder: delusional/erotomanic individual (24% Sheridan et al., 2001a)
  - Mental Disorder: delusional: demeanor (4% Nicastro et al., 2000)
  - Mental Disorder: irrational: demeanor (36% Nicastro et al., 2000)
  - Mental Disorder: mental illness (2% Brewster, 1998, 2000)
  - Mental Disorder: mental imbalance (12% Dussuyer, 2000)
  - Mental Disorder: mentally disordered (7% Harris, 2000)
  - Mental Disorder: mentally ill or abusing drugs or alcohol (7% Tjaden & Thoennes, 1998b)
  - Mental Disorder: unification through death: violence motive (7% Mullen & Pathé, 1994b)
  - Mental Disorder: victim secretly loved stalker (37% Coleman, 1999)
  - Mental Disorder: obsessed (56% Hall, 1997)
  - Mental Disorder: obsession (47% Kienlen et al., 1997)
  - Mental Disorder: obsession (63% Meloy & Boyd, 2003)

C. Incompetence: social incompetence, lack of social skills, inability to establish or maintain relationships
  - Social Incompetence: social incompetence (12% Meloy & Boyd, 2003)
  - Social Incompetence: difficulty forming relationships (73% Roberts, 2002)
  - Low IQ:

D. Childhood/Family of Origin: childhood abuse (see findings by Blackburn, 1999; Harmon, et al., 1995; Keinlen et al., 1997, showing association between family of origin violence and stalking)

   E. Attachment disorder: insecure attachment style, manic love style
       (see, e.g., discussion by Keinlen, 1998)

   F. Criminality: prior convictions, felonies, misdemeanors, arrests,
       history of violence
       • Violent: violent: demeanor (27% Nicastro et al., 2000)

4. CONTEXTUAL:
   A. Break-up/Separation:
       • Break-up/Separation: distress over divorce (6% Meloy &
         Boyd, 2003)
       • Break-up/Separation: ended relationship (43% Harris,
         2000)
       • Break-up/Separation: failed relationship (6% Nicastro et
         al., 2000)
       • Break-up/Separation: inability to handle rejection/
         break-up (33% Dussuyer, 2000)
       • Break-up/Separation: recent loss (9% Meloy & Boyd,
         2003)
       • Break-up/Separation):break-up: trigger (33% Brewster,
         1998, 2000); (see also "affective—abandonment rage")

   B. Incidental: by-product of stalking: violence motive (7% Mullen et
       al., 1999)

   C. Interactional: returning a call (4% Burgess et al., 2001)

   D. Interdependencies:
       • Interdependencies: issues regarding children (2% Harris,
         2000)
       • Interdependencies: distress over custody (2% Meloy &
         Boyd, 2003)
       • Interdependencies: child custody concerns (14% Morri-
         son, 2001)

   E. Nostalgia: special occasion (e.g., it was her birthday) (2% Burgess
       et al., 2001)

   F. Rival:
       • Rival: new boyfriend: trigger (11% Budd & Mattinson, 2000)
       • Rival: stalked by the new partner of an ex-partner (2%
         Sheridan et al., 2001a)

G. Significant Events: victim had baby (4% Brewster 2002)

H. Incidental Life Stressors: unemployment, employment or economic stress, loss of significant other (e.g., court proceedings upcoming) (9% Brewster, 2002)

UNCODABLE/MISCELLANEOUS:

- Uncodable: calm: demeanor (18% Nicastro et al., 2000)
- Uncodable: wanted or liked the attention (5% Tjaden & Thoennes, 1998b)
- Uncodable: no apparent reason (2% Harris, 2000)
- Uncodable: no reason (15% Sheridan et al., 2001a)
- Uncodable: other (7% Wright et al., 1996)
- Uncodable: unsure of stalker motive (12% Tjaden & Thoennes, 1998b)

Note: M = Male; F = Female.

Appendix 4
Coded Stalking and Unwanted Pursuit Tactics

1. HYPERINTIMACY:
   A. Affection Expression:
   - 1A ask out as friends (F: 58%, M: 77% Sinclair & Frieze, 2000)
   - 1A called radio station and devoted songs to you (17%, 15%, 14% Cupach & Spitzberg, 2000)
   - 1A comments of spending eternity or spiritual union with victim (53% Eke, 1999)
   - 1A exaggerated affection (22.5% Spitzberg & Cupach, 1999)
   - 1A exaggerated affection (26.5% Spitzberg, 2000a)
   - 1A exaggerated affection (21% Spitzberg & Cupach, 2001b)
   - 1A exaggerated messages of affection (25% Nicastro et al., 2000)
   - 1A expressed affection (48% Meloy & Boyd, 2003)
   - 1A professing love (36% Kileen & Dunn, 1998)
   - 1A wolf-whistling in street (22% Sheridan et al., 2002)

   B. Flirtation:
   - 1B agreeing with everything target says (23% Sheridan et al., 2002)
   - 1B favors (F: 72%, M: 74% Sinclair & Frieze, 2000)
   - 1B making arrangements including target without consulting (9% Sheridan et al., 2002)
   - 1B offers of help (9% Sheridan et al., 2002)
   - 1B performed large favors without your permission (58%, 60%, 38% Cupach & Spitzberg, 2000)
   - 1B stranger offering to buy drink (25% Sheridan et al., 2002)

   C. Ingratiation:
   - 1C apologized for past wrongs or transgressions (58%, 62%, 50% Cupach & Spitzberg, 2000)
   - 1C ask out on date (F: 39%, M: 72% Sinclair & Frieze, 2000)
   - 1C asked for another chance (63%, 70%, 58% Cupach & Spitzberg, 2000)
   - 1C asked if you were seeing someone (74%, 45%, 67% Cupach & Spitzberg, 2000)
   - 1C begging to return (35% Kileen & Dunn, 1998)

- 1C exaggerated claims about affection (65%, 54%, 54% Cupach & Spitzberg, 2000)
- 1C excessive self-disclosure (49%, 70%, 44% Cupach & Spitzberg, 2000)
- 1C pressure for dates (36% Morgan & Porter, 1999)

D. Relational Repair/Escalation Bids:
  - 1D described acts of sex (41%, 43%, 25% Cupach & Spitzberg, 2000)
  - 1D engaging in inappropriate personal/intimate discussions (11% Sheridan et al., 2002)
  - 1D obscene suggestions from a stranger (10% Sheridan et al., 2002)
  - 1D person met at bar asks if interested in sexual intercourse (27% Sheridan et al., 2002)
  - 1D sexual act (e.g., masturbating, sending porno, etc.) (18% Huffhines, 2001)
  - 1D sexual comments from stranger on the street (15% Sheridan et al., 2002)
  - 1D sexual proposition (16% Kienlen et al., 1997)
  - 1D sexual teasing, jokes, remarks, questions, looks or gestures (81% Morgan & Porter, 1999)

E. Hyper-sexuality(see, e.g., discussion of voyeurism, fetishism, etc., by Davis, in press)

2. MEDIATED CONTACTS:
  A. Telephonic:
    - 2A anonymous phone calls (47% Westrup et al., 1999)
    - 2A call and hang up without answering (73%, 75%, 63% Cupach & Spitzberg, 2000)
    - 2A called (70% Huffhines, 2001)
    - 2A called and argued (73%, 78%, 68% Cupach & Spitzberg, 2000)
    - 2A called and hung up (55% Lemmey, 1999)
    - 2A called at all times of the day to check up (50%, 58%, 41% Cupach & Spitzberg, 2000)
    - 2A called on phone (77% Holloway, 1994)
    - 2A called while working (44%, 47%, 33% Cupach & Spitzberg, 2000)
    - 2A calling (71% Meloy et al., 2000)

- 2A calling pager/phone at home/workplace (55% Suzuki, 1999)
- 2A calls (63% Lemmey, 1999)
- 2A calls (71% Nicastro et al., 2000)
- 2A calls (83% Eke, 1999)
- 2A calls (84% Blackburn, 1999)
- 2A calls (92% Jason et al., 1984)
- 2A calls to home (36% Guy et al., 1992)
- 2A calls to office (40% Guy et al., 1992)
- 2A calls, abusive (44% Sheridan et al., 2001a)
- 2A calls, amorous (48% Brewster, 1998, 2000)
- 2A calls, angry (38% Brewster, 1998, 2000)
- 2A calls, apologetic (3% Brewster, 1998, 2000)
- 2A calls, check-up (7% Brewster, 1998, 2000)
- 2A calls, conversational (58% Sheridan et al., 2001a)
- 2A calls, delusional accusation (13% Brewster, 1998, 2000)
- 2A calls, friendly (4% Brewster, 1998, 2000)
- 2A calls, hang-up (4% Burgess et al., 2001)
- 2A calls, hang-ups (32% Brewster, 1998, 2000)
- 2A calls, obscene (F: 25%, M: 14% Budd & Mattinson, 2000)
- 2A calls, obscene (31%, 28%, 30% Cupach & Spitzberg, 2000)
- 2A calls, rings then hangs up (60% Sheridan et al., 2001a)
- 2A calls, silent (F: 45%, M: 44% Budd & Mattinson, 2000)
- 2A calls, silent (57% Sheridan et al., 2001a)
- 2A calls, threatening (67% Brewster, 1998, 2000)
- 2A hang-up calls (58% Mechanic, Weaver, et al., 2000)
- 2A hang-ups: call content (32% Brewster, 1998, 2000)
- 2A harassed by phone (86% Westrup et al., 1999)
- 2A harassing phone calls or other verbal harassment (77% Tucker, 1993)
- 2A messages (56% Mechanic, Weaver, et al., 2000)
- 2A messages on your answering machine (52%, 50%, 32% Cupach & Spitzberg, 2000)
- 2A obscene phone calls (3% Harris, 2000)
- 2A obscene, threatening, or mysterious calls from an unknown caller (39% Sheridan et al., 2000)
- 2A phone (57% Zona et al., 1993)
- 2A phone (78% Mullen et al., 1999)
- 2A phone calls (31% Romans et al., 1996)
- 2A phone calls (36%, 78% Langhinrichsen-Rohling et al., 2000)

- 2A phone calls (45%, 43% McFarlane et al., 1999)
- 2A phone calls (89% Kamphuis & Emmelkamp, 2001)
- 2A phone calls at home (66% Mechanic, Weaver, et al., 2000)
- 2A phone calls to victim (29% 48% McFarlane, Campbell & Watson, 2002)
- 2A phone calls/letters (11.5% Gill & Brockman, 1996)
- 2A phone message (25%, 55% Langhinrichsen-Rohling et al., 2000)
- 2A phones and/or leaves messages (83% Meloy & Boyd, 2003)
- 2A repeated telephoning (77% Kileen & Dunn, 1998)
- 2A silent phone calls (13% Harris, 2000)
- 2A telephone (40% Meloy & Gothard, 1995)
- 2A telephone (84% Oddie, 2000)
- 2A telephone calls (15% McCann, 2000a)
- 2A telephone calls (56% Purcell et al., 2002)
- 2A telephone calls (61% Rosenfeld & Harmon, 2002)
- 2A telephone calls (78% Purcell et al., 2001)
- 2A telephone calls (86% Blaauw, Winkel, Arensman, et al., 2000)
- 2A telephone calls (87% Hall, 1997)
- 2A telephone calls (90% Brewster, 1998, 2000)
- 2A telephoned (15% Dussuyer, 2000)
- 2A telephoned (40% Meloy & Gothard, 1995)
- 2A telephoned (68% Kienlen et al., 1997)
- 2A telephoned (78% Fisher et al., 1999; 2000)
- 2A telephoned/sent mail (1.5% McLennon, 1996)
- 2A telephones (57% Mullen & Pathé, 1994b)
- 2A threatening messages on phone (22%, 12% McFarlane et al., 1999)
- 2A threatening or harassing phone calls (10% Kong, 1996)
- 2A threatening or mysterious phone calls (10% Sheridan et al., 2002)
- 2A threatening/harassing phone call (12% Hackett, 2000)
- 2A unsolicited phone calls (F: 61% M: 47% Davis et al., 2002; Tjaden-NVAW data)
- 2A unwanted calls (61% Melton, 2001)

B. Mail/Notes:
- 2B cards or letters (44%, 46%, 35% Cupach & Spitzberg, 2000)
- 2B correspondence (60% Eke, 1999)
- 2B excessive notes or letters (13% Sheridan et al., 2001b)

- 2B excessive, unwanted notes or letters (14% Sheridan et al., 2000)
- 2B gifts (38% Brewster, 1998, 2000)
- 2B harassed by mail (22% Westrup et al., 1999)
- 2B inappropriate sexually explicit letters (2% Sheridan et al., 2001b)
- 2B leaving written messages (36% Kileen & Dunn, 1998)
- 2B left anonymous notes (28% Westrup et al., 1999)
- 2B left notes (42% LeBlanc et al., 2001)
- 2B left notes on car (12% Lemmey, 1999)
- 2B left written messages in or at residence (43%, 47%, 25% Cupach & Spitzberg, 2000)
- 2B letter writing (15% McCann, 2000a)
- 2B letter writing and slandering (14% Meloy et al., 2000)
- 2B letters (10%, 15% McFarlane et al., 1999)
- 2B letters (11% Burgess et al., 2001)
- 2B letters (15% Lemmey, 1999)
- 2B letters (25% Meloy & Gothard, 1995)
- 2B letters (27% Mechanic, Weaver, et al., 2000)
- 2B letters (31% Fisher et al., 1999, 2000)
- 2B letters (41% Blaauw, Winkel, Arensman, et al., 2000)
- 2B letters (41% Oddie, 2000)
- 2B letters (55% Blackburn, 1999)
- 2B letters (57% Mullen & Pathé, 1994b)
- 2B letters (59% Brewster, 1998, 2000)
- 2B letters (61% Zona et al., 1993)
- 2B letters (65% Mullen et al., 1999)
- 2B letters (8%, 12% McFarlane, Campbell, & Watson, 2002)
- 2B letters and unwanted gifts (78% Meloy & Boyd, 2003)
- 2B letters, amorous (77% Brewster, 1998, 2000)
- 2B letters, angry (12% Brewster, 1998, 2000)
- 2B letters, apologetic (6% Brewster, 1998, 2000)
- 2B letters, delusional accusation (6% Brewster, 1998, 2000)
- 2B letters, friendly but not amorous (7% Brewster, 1998, 2000)
- 2B letters, telephone calls or material of a sexual nature (18% Morgan & Porter, 1999) (see 2A)
- 2B letters/cards (F: 27%, M: 27% Budd & Mattinson, 2000)
- 2B letters/cards/notes (38% Morrison, 2001)
- 2B letters/faxes/e-mail (65% Purcell et al., 2001)
- 2B letters/gifts (19%, 44% Langhinrichsen-Rohling et al., 2000)

- 2B mail (10% Dussuyer, 2000)
- 2B mail (70% Kamphuis & Emmelkamp, 2001)
- 2B mail, abusive/offensive (25% Sheridan et al., 2001a)
- 2B mail, conversational (20% Sheridan et al., 2001a)
- 2B mail, mixture of mail-related intrusions (27% Sheridan et al., 2001a)
- 2B mail, pleading/begging (43% Sheridan et al., 2001a)
- 2B mailing letters/faxing (12% Suzuki, 1999)
- 2B messages (33% Spitzberg, 2000a)
- 2B messages (32% Spitzberg & Cupach, 2001b)
- 2B messages (34% Spitzberg & Cupach, 1999)
- 2B messages (53% Melton, 2001)
- 2B messages/letters/notes (27% Nicastro et al., 2000)
- 2B 'nice' letters/gifts (16% Harris, 2000)
- 2B notes on car windshield (42%, 59%, 35% Cupach & Spitzberg, 2000)
- 2B notes or letters (56% Holloway, 1994)
- 2B notes, letters, e-mail or other written communication (F: 71%, M: 79% Sinclair & Frieze, 2000)
- 2B notes/letters (14% Sheridan et al., 2002)
- 2B postal mail (25% LeBlanc et al., 2001)
- 2B sent flowers/letters/notes (24% Jason et al., 1984)
- 2B sent letters (50% Hall, 1997)
- 2B sent letters (52% Kienlen et al., 1997)
- 2B sexually explicit letters (3% Sheridan et al., 2002)
- 2B threatening notes on victim's car (10%, 11% McFarlane et al., 1999)
- 2B unsolicited letters or other written correspondence (F: 25%, M: 20% Davis et al., 2002; Tjaden-NVAW data)

C. Tokens:
   - 2C flowers (30% Blackburn, 1999)
   - 2C flowers or gifts (40% Burgess et al., 2001)
   - 2C gifts (10% Meloy & Gothard, 1995)
   - 2C gifts (10% Meloy & Gothard, 1995)
   - 2C gifts (11% Sheridan et al., 2001b)
   - 2C gifts (12% Spitzberg & Cupach, 1999)
   - 2C gifts (15% Huffhines, 2001)
   - 2C gifts (17% Sheridan et al., 2000)
   - 2C gifts (24% Blackburn, 1999)
   - 2C gifts (29% Mechanic, Weaver, et al., 2000)
   - 2C gifts (3% Sheridan et al., 2002)

- 2C gifts (8% Spitzberg & Cupach, 2001b)
- 2C gifts (34%, 37%, 31% Cupach & Spitzberg, 2000)
- 2C gifts (37% Oddie, 2000)
- 2C gifts (39% Hall, 1997)
- 2C gifts (17.5% Spitzberg, 2000a)
- 2C gifts (48% Mullen et al., 1999)
- 2C gifts (F: 51%, M: 67% Sinclair & Frieze, 2000)
- 2C gifts, malicious (7% Sheridan et al., 2001a)
- 2C gifts, mixture of (10% Sheridan et al., 2001a)
- 2C gifts, non-malicious (34% Sheridan et al., 2001a)
- 2C gifts/objects (24% Kienlen et al., 1997)
- 2C gifts/photos/tapes (4% Nicastro et al., 2000)
- 2C in person gifts (13%, 30% Langhinrichsen-Rohling et al., 2000)
- 2C items/gifts (F: 19%, M: 16% Budd & Mattinson, 2000)
- 2C jewelry (8% Blackburn, 1999)
- 2C leaving gifts (16.5% Kileen & Dunn, 1998)
- 2C mailed or left gifts you previously gave (19%, 17%, 13% Cupach & Spitzberg, 2000)
- 2C materials (43% Eke, 1999)
- 2C photos, tapes (16.5% Kileen & Dunn, 1998)
- 2C sending gifts (3% Meloy et al., 2000)
- 2C sending gifts (7% Suzuki, 1999)
- 2C sending unsolicited material (48% Purcell et al., 2001)
- 2C sent gifts (3% Fisher et al., 1999, 2000)
- 2C sent gifts/flowers (18% Morrison, 2001)
- 2C sent offensive photographs (6%, 7%, 3% Cupach & Spitzberg, 2000)
- 2C sent unwanted gifts, photos, letters (28% Melton, 2001)
- 2C unsolicited goods (5% Purcell et al., 2002)

D. CMC/Email/Electronica:
- 2D computer (6% Oddie, 2000)
- 2D counter-allegations of stalking (39% Sheridan et al., 2001a)
- 2D cyber-attempting to disable your computer (3% Spitzberg & Hoobler, 2002)
- 2D cyber-exposing private information to others (17% Spitzberg & Hoobler, 2002)
- 2D cyber-pretending to be someone she or he wasn't (20% Spitzberg & Hoobler, 2002)
- 2D cyber-sabotaging reputation (12% Spitzberg & Hoobler, 2002)

- 2D cyber-sending exaggerated messages of affection (31% Spitzberg & Hoobler, 2002)
- 2D cyber-sending excessively 'needy' or demanding messages (25% Spitzberg & Hoobler, 2002)
- 2D cyber-sending excessively disclosive messages (26% Spitzberg & Hoobler, 2002)
- 2D cyber-sending pornographic/obscene messages (19% Spitzberg & Hoobler, 2002)
- 2D cyber-sending sexually harassing messages (18% Spitzberg & Hoobler, 2002)
- 2D cyber-sending threatening pictures/images (5% Spitzberg & Hoobler, 2002)
- 2D cyber-sending threatening written messages (9% Spitzberg & Hoobler, 2002)
- 2D cyber-sending tokens of affection (31% Spitzberg & Hoobler, 2002)
- 2D fax (2% Oddie, 2000)
- 2D first meeting online and then stalking you (1% Spitzberg & Hoobler, 2002)
- 2D internet (1% Meloy et al., 2000)
- 2D meeting first online and then following (1% Spitzberg & Hoobler, 2002)
- 2D meeting first online and then harming you (1% Spitzberg & Hoobler, 2002)
- 2D meeting first online and then intruding in life (3% Spitzberg & Hoobler, 2002)
- 2D meeting first online and then threatening (3% Spitzberg & Hoobler, 2002)
- 2D stalked by means of the internet (2% Kamphuis & Emmelkamp, 2001)
- 2D telephoned/sent mail (1.6% McLennan, 1996)
- 2D tried other communications (58% Lemmey, 1999)
- 2D unwanted faxes, letters, or e-mails (19% Purcell et al., 2002)
- 2D web pages (0% LeBlanc et al., 2001)

3. INTERACTIONAL CONTACTS:
   A. Direct Interactional:
      i. Contact (General)
         - 3Ai argued about your relationships with others (55%, 58%, 53% Cupach & Spitzberg, 2000)

- 3Ai complained how you ruined his/her life (45%, 48%, 32% Cupach & Spitzberg, 2000)
- 3Ai contacted at home (48.5% Burgess et al., 2001)
- 3Ai contacted at work (27% Burgess et al., 2001)
- 3Ai contacted friends/family (16% Burgess et al., 2001)
- 3Ai contacted in public places (15% Burgess et al., 2001)
- 3Ai gossiped or bragged about your relationship to others (63%, 67%, 53% Cupach & Spitzberg, 2000)
- 3Ai in person conversation (31%, 73% Langhinrichsen-Rohling et al., 2000)
- 3Ai repeated approaches in public (86% Mullen et al., 1999)
- 3Ai stranger engages in unsolicited conversation (31% Sheridan et al., 2002)
- 3Ai talked about target to friends after only one meeting (27% Sheridan et al., 2002)
- 3Ai tried to argue in public places (48%, 56%, 45% Cupach & Spitzberg, 2000)

ii. Approaches
- 3Aii approach (63% Rosenfeld & Harmon, 2002)
- 3Aii approach, direct unwanted (92% Blaauw, Winkel, Arensman, et al., 2000)
- 3Aii approached (93% Mullen & Pathé, 1994b)
- 3Aii approached victim (31% Morrison, 2001)
- 3Aii approaches and tries to speak (66% Sheridan et al., 2001a)
- 3Aii direct contact (84% Kienlen et al., 1997)
- 3Aii direct contacts (79% Pathé & Mullen, 1997)
- 3Aii home visits (23%, 29% Langhinrichsen-Rohling et al., 2000)
- 3Aii home visits (60% Oddie, 2000)
- 3Aii intrusive approaches (56% Purcell et al., 2002)
- 3Aii intrusive approaches (84% Purcell et al., 2001)
- 3Aii knocked on window unexpectedly (31%, 28%, 16% Cupach & Spitzberg, 2000)
- 3Aii location (32% Zona et al., 1993)
- 3Aii personal approaches (21% Sheridan et al., 2000)
- 3Aii physical approaches (54% McCann, 2000a)
- 3Aii repeated personal approaches by stranger (12% Sheridan et al., 2002)

- 3Aii show up at places (39%, 33% Langhinrichsen-Rohling et al., 2000)
- 3Aii unwanted approaches (67% Eke, 1999)
- 3Aii waited around near your conversation with another person (43%, 46%, 30% Cupach & Spitzberg, 2000)

iii. Appearances
- 3Aiii appearances (63% Blackburn, 1999)
- 3Aiii appearing at workplace (54% Hall, 1997)
- 3Aiii came unwanted (58% Melton, 2001)
- 3Aiii comes round to visit uninvited (13% Sheridan et al., 2002)
- 3Aiii coming around to visit, uninvited, on a regular basis (21% Sheridan et al., 2001b)
- 3Aiii home (32% Zona et al., 1993)
- 3Aiii personal contact at home/work (34% Gill & Brockman, 1996)
- 3Aiii pestered at work or home (79% Kamphuis & Emmelkamp, 2001)
- 3Aiii school/work visits (13%, 21% Langhinrichsen-Rohling et al., 2000)
- 3Aiii show up at events (F: 85%, M: 79% Sinclair & Frieze, 2000)
- 3Aiii showed up at places inappropriately (F: 1%, M: 1% Davis et al., 2002; Tjaden-NVAW data)
- 3Aiii showed up before or after classes (38%, 40%, 23% Cupach & Spitzberg, 2000)
- 3Aiii showed up before or after work (50%, 52%, 38% Cupach & Spitzberg, 2000)
- 3Aiii showed up uninvited (5% Fisher et al., 1999; 2000)
- 3Aiii showed up where you were (54% Lemmey, 1999)
- 3Aiii showed up without warning (71% Lemmey, 1999)
- 3Aiii showing up at home (85% Kileen & Dunn, 1998)
- 3Aiii showing up at places (2% Spitzberg & Cupach, 1999)
- 3Aiii showing up at places (4% Spitzberg, 2000a)
- 3Aiii showing up at places (2.5% Spitzberg & Cupach, 2001b)
- 3Aiii showing up at victim's work (38% Kileen & Dunn, 1998)
- 3Aiii unwanted visits at home (62% Mechanic, Weaver, et al., 2000)
- 3Aiii unwelcome visits to home/work (55% Morrison, 2001)

- 3Aiii visited at work (50%, 51%, 42% Cupach & Spitzberg, 2000)
- 3Aiii visited home (60% Meloy & Gothard, 1995)
- 3Aiii visited home (64% Kienlen et al., 1997)
- 3Aiii visited home or work (43% Jason et al., 1984)
- 3Aiii visited victim at work (39% Westrup et al., 1999)
- 3Aiii visited work/school (50% Kienlen et al., 1997)
- 3Aiii visited workplace (10% Meloy & Gothard, 1995)
- 3Aiii visiting home (66% Meloy et al., 2000)
- 3Aiii visiting home/working place (28% Suzuki, 1999)
- 3Aiii visiting places known to frequent (13% Sheridan et al., 2002)
- 3Aiii visiting places the target frequents (22% Sheridan et al., 2001b)
- 3Aiii visiting workplace (23% Meloy et al., 2000)
- 3Aiii visits (74% Kamphuis & Emmelkamp, 2001)
- 3Aiii visits at work (42% Mechanic, Weaver, et al., 2000)
- 3Aiii went to victim's home (60% Meloy & Gothard, 1995)
- 3Aiii went to victim's workplace (10% Meloy & Gothard, 1995)
- 3Aiii work visits (42% Oddie, 2000)

iv. Interactional Intrusions
- 3Aiv followed in a walking conversation (36%, 35%, 19% Cupach & Spitzberg, 2000)
- 3Aiv forced to talk (F: 52%, M: 39% Budd & Mattinson, 2000)
- 3Aiv intruding in interactions (12% Spitzberg & Cupach, 1999)
- 3Aiv intruding in interactions (10% Spitzberg & Cupach, 2001b)
- 3Aiv intruding on interactions (19% Spitzberg, 2000a)
- 3Aiv joined uninvited while conversing with others (44%, 48%, 33% Cupach & Spitzberg, 2000)

v. Personal Space Invasions
- 3Av inappropriately touched you in an intimate way (37%, 42%, 27% Cupach & Spitzberg, 2000)
- 3Av invading personal space (13% Spitzberg & Cupach, 2001b)
- 3Av invading personal space (12% Spitzberg, 2000a)
- 3Av invading personal space (16% Spitzberg & Cupach, 1999)

- 3Av physical contact (67% LeBlanc et al., 2001)
- 3Av physical touching (8% McCann, 2000a)
- 3Av touched or grabbed victim (F: 34%, M: 30% Budd & Mattinson, 2000)
- 3Av touching, leaning over or cornering (47% Morgan & Porter, 1999)

vi. Involvement in Activities
  - 3Avi checked up on you through mutual acquaintances (60%, 63%, 50% Cupach & Spitzberg, 2000)
  - 3Avi involving in activities (18% Spitzberg, 2000a)
  - 3Avi involving in activities (5% Spitzberg & Cupach, 1999)
  - 3Avi involving in activities (3% Spitzberg & Cupach, 2001b)
  - 3Avi tried to move into victim's social circle (22% Sheridan et al., 2001a)

B. Indirect Interactional:
  i. Co-opting Victim Affiliates
   - 3Bi ask friends about him/her (F: 92%, M: 86% Sinclair & Frieze, 2000)
   - 3Bi ask friends about you (54%, 56% Langhinrichsen-Rohling et al., 2000)
   - 3Bi called friends or relatives to check (37% Holloway, 1994)
   - 3Bi checked up (76% Melton, 2001)
   - 3Bi contacted third party (68% Kienlen et al., 1997)
   - 3Bi contacting victim's family (36% Kileen & Dunn, 1998)
   - 3Bi enlisted help of others to stalk their victim (40% Boon & Sheridan, 2001)
   - 3Bi enlisted others (stalking by proxy) (72% Sheridan, 2001)
   - 3Bi falsely gained information (65% Kamphuis & Emmelkamp, 2001)
   - 3Bi increased contact with family members to stay involved (41%, 44%, 27% Cupach & Spitzberg, 2000)
   - 3Bi information obtained via friends and acquaintances (14% LeBlanc et al., 2001)
   - 3Bi inquiry through friends (75% LeBlanc et al., 2001)
   - 3Bi intruded upon friends/coworkers/family (27% Nicastro et al., 2000)
   - 3Bi involved others (82% Kamphuis & Emmelkamp, 2001)
   - 3Bi involving other victim's family members (57% Brewster, 1998, 2000)

- 3Bi involving victim's friends (58% Brewster, 1998, 2000)
- 3Bi proxy stalking through victims family members and/or friends (40% Eke, 1999)
- 3Bi tried to obtain information from victim's friends/family/coworkers (76% Sheridan, 2001)
- 3Bi tries to gain information from victim's family, friends, etc. (77% Sheridan et al., 2001a)
- 3Bi trying to become acquainted with target's friends (19% Sheridan et al., 2002)
- 3Bi used third parties to "spy" or keep tabs on you (60%, 59%, 46% Cupach & Spitzberg, 2000)

  ii. Harassing/Pursuing Victim Affiliates
- 3Bii intruding on friends/family (15% Spitzberg & Cupach, 1999)
- 3Bii intruding on friends/family (7% Spitzberg & Cupach, 2001b)
- 3Bii intruding on friends/family (12% Spitzberg, 2000a)

  iii. Co-opting Pursuer Associates
- 3Biii friends and/or family of the stalker involved in the harassment (40% Sheridan & Davies, 2001b)
  iv. Coordinating Pursuer Associates
- 3Biv stalker had others talk to them" as "proxy stalkers" (52% Melton, 2001)
  v. Professionalized Pursuit

4. SURVEILLANCE:
   A. Synchronizing Activities:
- 4A alter class/office/activity to be near (F: 23%, M: 26% Sinclair & Frieze, 2000)
- 4A efforts to run into you (20%, 25% Langhinrichsen-Rohling et al., 2000)
- 4A moves closer to home (1% Sheridan et al., 2002)
- 4A moving (house) closer to home or places frequented (.6% Sheridan et al., 2001b)
- 4A same individual seen at roughly same time each day (12% Sheridan et al., 2002)
- 4A stalked (45% Meloy & Gothard, 1995)
- 4A visiting places known to frequent (13% Sheridan et al., 2002)

B. Loitering:
- 4B hanging around/telephoning target's workplace (11% Sheridan et al., 2001b) (see 2B)
- 4B hanging around/telephoning workplace (4% Sheridan et al., 2002)
- 4B hung around/telephoned workplace (7% Sheridan et al., 2000)
- 4B loitered (93% Mullen & Pathé, 1994b)
- 4B loitered at place of pleasure (3% Dussuyer, 2000)
- 4B loitered home (12% Dussuyer, 2000)
- 4B loitered outside home (1% McLennon, 1996)
- 4B loitered outside place of leisure (.5% McLennon, 1996)
- 4B loitered outside workplace (.5% McLennon, 1996)
- 4B loitered work (8% Dussuyer, 2000)
- 4B loitering in neighborhood (13% Sheridan et al., 2000)
- 4B loitering in neighborhood (9% Sheridan et al., 2002)
- 4B loitering in the target's neighborhood (15% Sheridan et al., 2001b)
- 4B loitering nearby (35% Purcell et al., 2002)
- 4B standing and staring regularly at home and/or workplace (8% Sheridan et al., 2001b)
- 4B standing and staring regularly at home/workplace (4% Sheridan et al., 2002)
- 4B standing/parked outside (49% Harris, 2000)
- 4B stood and stared regularly at your home and/or workplace (19% Sheridan et al., 2000)
- 4B stood or sat in car outside house/school/workplace (28%, 46.5% McFarlane, Campbell, & Watson, 2002)
- 4B stood outside home/school/workplace (M: 41% Davis et al., 2002; Tjaden-NVAW data)
- 4B stood outside home/school/workplace (F: 53% Davis et al., 2002; Tjaden-NVAW data)
- 4B stood outside home/work (48% Lemmey, 1999)
- 4B wait/stand outside place (F: 60%, M: 58% Sinclair & Frieze, 2000)
- 4B waited at places (52% Fisher et al., 1999; 2000)
- 4B waited in a nearby car (37%, 43%, 26% Cupach & Spitzberg, 2000)
- 4B waited outside house/school/work (46%, 47% McFarlane et al., 1999)
- 4B waited outside place (38%, 45%, 26% Cupach & Spitzberg, 2000)

- 4B waited outside victim's place of work (F: 28%, M: 22% Budd & Mattinson, 2000)
- 4B waiting on way home (40% Suzuki, 1999)

C. Surveilance/Watching/Monitoring:
- 4C constantly watched or "spied on" (16% Sheridan et al., 2000)
- 4C constantly watching victim, loitering, and prowling (4% Tucker, 1993)
- 4C constantly watching/spying (13% Sheridan et al., 2001b)
- 4C followed from place to place (31%, 36%, 15% Cupach & Spitzberg, 2000)
- 4C followed or kept under surveillance (71% Pathé & Mullen, 1997)
- 4C following/watching (65% Blackburn, 1999)
- 4C maintaining surveillance (31% Purcell et al., 2002)
- 4C monitoring behavior (19% Spitzberg, 2000a)
- 4C monitoring behavior (21% Spitzberg & Cupach, 2001b)
- 4C monitoring behavior (22% Spitzberg & Cupach, 1999)
- 4C observing from a distance (12% Suzuki, 1999)
- 4C recorded conversations without knowledge (10%, 9%, 4% Cupach & Spitzberg, 2000)
- 4C sat in car by home/work (45% Lemmey, 1999)
- 4C shadowing/watching (30% Suzuki, 1999)
- 4C spied on you (M: 35% Davis et al., 2002; Tjaden-NVAW data)
- 4C spied on you (F: 46% Davis et al., 2002; Tjaden-NVAW data)
- 4C spied on you (47%, 54%, 36% Cupach & Spitzberg, 2000)
- 4C spy (F: 23%, M: 12% Sinclair & Frieze, 2000)
- 4C spying or watching (26% Kileen & Dunn, 1998)
- 4C surveillance (25% Westrup et al., 1999)
- 4C surveillance (watching) (20% Nicastro et al., 2000)
- 4C surveillance at home/work/other (40% Morrison, 2001)
- 4C surveillance of home (74% Blaauw, Winkel, Arensman, et al., 2000)
- 4C surveillance of home (84% Hall, 1997)
- 4C taking photographs without knowledge (2% Sheridan et al., 2001b)
- 4C taking photographs without knowledge (2% Sheridan et al., 2002)
- 4C took photos you without knowledge or consent (15%, 13%, 6% Cupach & Spitzberg, 2000)

- 4C waited in a nearby car (37%, 43%, 26% Cupach & Spitzberg, 2000)
- 4C watched (1.2% McLennon, 1996)
- 4C watched (15% Dussuyer, 2000)
- 4C watched (71% Mechanic, Weaver, et al., 2000)
- 4C watched from afar (44% Fisher et al., 1999; 2000)
- 4C watched or stared from a distance (63%, 68%, 55% Cupach & Spitzberg, 2000)
- 4C watched without knowledge (7% Burgess et al., 2001)
- 4C watched/observed (48% Kienlen et al., 1997)
- 4C watches (91% Sheridan et al., 2001a)
- 4C watching (78% Brewster, 1998, 2000)
- 4C watching (93% Eke, 1999)
- 4C watching/spying (6% Sheridan et al., 2002)

D. Following:
- 4D behavioral following (48% Meloy et al., 2000)
- 4D follow (36% Morrison, 2001)
- 4D follow (F: 24%, M: 26% Sinclair & Frieze, 2000)
- 4D follow or spy (29%, 56% McFarlane, Campbell, & Watson, 2002)
- 4D followed (1% McLennon, 1996)
- 4D followed (15% Dussuyer, 2000)
- 4D followed (18% Romans et al., 1996)
- 4D followed (F: 43%, M: 30% Budd & Mattinson, 2000)
- 4D followed (42% Fisher et al., 1999; 2000)
- 4D followed (49% Meloy & Boyd, 2003)
- 4D followed (M: 50% Davis et al., 2002; Tjaden-NVAW data)
- 4D followed (F: 62% Davis et al., 2002; Tjaden-NVAW data)
- 4D followed (63% Mechanic, Weaver, et al., 2000)
- 4D followed (75% LeBlanc et al., 2001)
- 4D followed (79% Mullen & Pathé, 1994b)
- 4D followed (80% Hall, 1997)
- 4D followed around (28% Holloway, 1994)
- 4D followed in the street (43% Sheridan et al., 2000)
- 4D followed on street (75% Kamphuis & Emmelkamp, 2001)
- 4D followed or spied (53%, 60% McFarlane et al., 1999)
- 4D followed or stalked (21% Rosenfeld & Harmon, 2002)
- 4D followed or watched (26% Jason et al., 1984)
- 4D followed to car (4% Burgess et al., 1997)

- 4D followed victim (81% Westrup et al., 1999)
- 4D followed/spied (58% Lemmey, 1999)
- 4D followed/watched (59% Melton, 2001)
- 4D following (13% Sheridan et al., 2002)
- 4D following (15% Harris, 2000)
- 4D following (28% Kienlen et al., 1997)
- 4D following (29% Sheridan et al., 2001b)
- 4D following (3%, 7% Langhinrichsen-Rohling et al., 2000)
- 4D following (32% Suzuki, 1999)
- 4D following (49% Purcell et al., 2002)
- 4D following (53% Kileen & Dunn, 1998)
- 4D following (66% Oddie, 2000)
- 4D following (68% Brewster, 1998, 2000)
- 4D following (70% Eke, 1999)
- 4D following (72% Purcell et al., 2001)
- 4D following (74% Blaauw, Winkel, Arensman, et al., 2000)
- 4D following around (12% Spitzberg & Cupach, 2001b)
- 4D following around (51% Nicastro et al., 2000)
- 4D following around (15% Spitzberg & Cupach, 1999)
- 4D following around (14% Spitzberg, 2000a)
- 4D following/watching (83% Huffhines, 2001)
- 4D follows (82% Sheridan et al., 2001a)
- 4D repeatedly following (81% Tucker, 1993)
- 4D repeatedly following-watching (20% Gill & Brockman, 1996)
- 4D surveillance and persistent following (73% Mullen et al., 1999)

E. Drive-bys:
- 4E drive by home (77% Hall, 1997)
- 4E drive/ride/walk bys (F: 75%, M: 63% Sinclair & Frieze, 2000)
- 4E drive-bys (14% Sheridan et al., 2000)
- 4E drive-bys (6% Sheridan et al., 2002)
- 4E drives by home or office or school (73% Meloy & Boyd, 2003)
- 4E driving by work/home/school (36% Nicastro et al., 2000)
- 4E driving past the target, house, workplace, etc. ("drive-bys") (12% Sheridan et al., 2001b)
- 4E driving/walking by house (54% Brewster, 1998, 2000)
- 4E drove by house or work (57%, 64%, 51% Cupach & Spitzberg, 2000)

5. INVASION:
  A. Information Theft:
- 5A covertly obtaining information (6% Spitzberg & Cupach, 2001b)
- 5A covertly obtaining information (11% Spitzberg & Cupach, 1999)
- 5A covertly obtaining information (10% Spitzberg, 2000a)
- 5A find out information (F: 74%, M: 70% Sinclair & Frieze, 2000)
- 5A had mail stolen/read (61% Mechanic, Weaver, et al., 2000)
- 5A information obtained via phone book (21% LeBlanc et al., 2001)
- 5A intercepting mail deliveries (3% Sheridan et al., 2002)
- 5A intercepting mail/deliveries (2% Sheridan et al., 2001b)
- 5A obtaining private information (7% Nicastro et al., 2000)
- 5A stole/read mail (43% Melton, 2001)
- 5A stole/read mail (F: 0%, M: 9% McCann, 2000a)
- 5A went through private things in your room (35%, 39%, 28% Cupach & Spitzberg, 2000)

  B. Property Theft:
- 5B burglarized (25% Huffhines, 2001)
- 5B items taken (53% Eke, 1999)
- 5B possessions taken (4% Romans et al., 1996)
- 5B secretly take belongings (F: 8%, M: 7% Sinclair & Frieze, 2000)
- 5B steal items (0%, 3% Langhinrichsen-Rohling et al., 2000)
- 5B steal/damage possessions (5% Spitzberg & Cupach, 1999)
- 5B steal/damage possessions (3% Spitzberg & Cupach, 2001b)
- 5B steal/damage possessions (4% Spitzberg, 2000a)
- 5B stealing property (31% Kileen & Dunn, 1998)
- 5B stealing victim's property (25% Brewster, 1998, 2000)
- 5B stealing/damaging valued possessions (25% Nicastro et al., 2000)
- 5B stole from victim (30% Sheridan et al., 2001a)
- 5B stole personal property (8% Westrup et al., 1999)
- 5B stole victim's property (8% Huffhines, 2001)

- 5B taking garbage away/stealing (0% Suzuki, 1999)
- 5B taking things away/stealing (4% Suzuki, 1999)
- 5B theft (2% Kong, 1996)
- 5B trespassed (38% Huffhines, 2001)

C. Property Invasion:
- 5C actual home break-in (30% Mechanic, Weaver, et al., 2000)
- 5C attempted breaking and entering (31% Nicastro et al., 2000)
- 5C attempted home break-in (31% Mechanic, Weaver, et al., 2000)
- 5C attempted to break into car (F: 4%, M: 9% McCann, 2000a)
- 5C attempted to break into house (F: 4%, M: 0% McCann, 2000a)
- 5C break and enter (17% Morrison, 2001)
- 5C breaking and entering (5.5% Kong, 1996)
- 5C breaking and entering (6% Hackett, 2000)
- 5C breaking into house or car (36% Brewster, 1998, 2000)
- 5C broke into car (F: 0%, M: 0% McCann, 2000a)
- 5C broke into home (14% Westrup et al., 1999)
- 5C broke into home (39% Hall, 1997)
- 5C broke into home (F: 0%, M: 0% McCann, 2000a)
- 5C broke into home or apartment (10%, 11%, 4% Cupach & Spitzberg, 2000)
- 5C broke into/damaged inside of victim's home (32% Sheridan et al., 2001a)
- 5C broke/attempted to break into home/car (35% Melton, 2001)
- 5C entered home with no permission (5% Burgess et al., 2001)
- 5C entering without permission (66% Kileen & Dunn, 1998)
- 5C invading personal property (14% Nicastro et al., 2000)
- 5C invading property (7% Spitzberg & Cupach, 1999)
- 5C invading property (2% Spitzberg, 2000a)
- 5C invading property (5% Spitzberg & Cupach, 2001b)
- 5C smeared home (19% Kamphuis & Emmelkamp, 2001)
- 5C trespass (F: 6%, M: 2% Sinclair & Frieze, 2000)
- 5C trespass on property (72% Tucker, 1993)
- 5C trespassed on property (69% Meloy & Boyd, 2003)

- 5C trespasses on victim's property (68% Sheridan et al., 2001a)
- 5C trespassing (53% Brewster, 1998, 2000)
- 5C trespassing (54% Nicastro et al., 2000)
- 5C unlawful entry into home (41% Blaauw, Winkel, Arensman, et al., 2000)

D. Exotic Surveillance:
  - 5D bugged victim's home (13% Sheridan et al., 2001a)
  - 5D bugging your car, home, or office (7% Spitzberg & Hoobler, 2002)
  - 5D cyber-obtaining private information without permission (10% Spitzberg & Hoobler, 2002)
  - 5D information obtained via web utilities, including e-mail (13% LeBlanc et al., 2001)
  - 5D tapping phones/listening in (7% Kileen & Dunn, 1998)
  - 5D using your computer to get information on others (7% Spitzberg & Hoobler, 2002)

6. HARASSMENT AND INTIMIDATION:
  A. Nonverbal Intimidation:
    - 6A approached in threatening or harassing manner (24% Sandberg et al., 1998)
    - 6A harassed in person (17% Westrup et al., 1999) (see 6B)
    - 6A nonviolent physical harassment (14% Harris, 2000)
    - 6A physically intimidated (F: 45%, M: 33% Budd & Mattinson, 2000)
    - 6A scare (F: 10%, M: 9% Sinclair & Frieze, 2000)

  B. Verbal/Written Harassment:
    - 6B attempt verbal abuse (F: 15%, M: 7% Sinclair & Frieze, 2000)
    - 6B displayed rage/anger (36% Nicastro et al., 2000)
    - 6B face-to-face verbal harassment (60% Harris, 2000)
    - 6B harass (F: 10%, M: 5% Sinclair & Frieze, 2000)
    - 6B harassment (62% Nicastro et al., 2000)
    - 6B insults target (13% Sheridan et al., 2002)
    - 6B offensive language (51% Nicastro et al., 2000)
    - 6B shouts abuse/obscenities (51% Sheridan et al., 2001a)
    - 6B stalked (45% Meloy & Gothard, 1995)
    - 6B uncontrolled, aggressive or insulting upon seeing with other(s) (25% Sheridan et al., 2000)

- 6B uncontrolled, aggressive or insulting upon seeing with other(s) (14% Sheridan et al., 2002)
- 6B uncontrolled, aggressive, or insulting upon seeing out with others (15% Sheridan et al., 2001b)
- 6B verbal abuse (56% Kileen & Dunn, 1998)
- 6B verbal abuse/left messages intended to fear (49% Morrison, 2001)
- 6B verbal assault (34% Romans et al., 1996)
- 6B verbally abuse (F: 13%, M: 14% Sinclair & Frieze, 2000)
- 6B verbally abused you (F: .4%, M: 0% Davis et al., 2002; Tjaden-NVAW data)
- 6B written harassment (signs, letters, etc.) (61% Tucker, 1993)
- 6B written threats (49% Meloy & Boyd, 2003)

C. Reputational Harassment:
- 6C accused you of being unfaithful (55%, 54%, 50% Cupach & Spitzberg, 2000)
- 6C accused you of sleeping around (49%, 46%, 38% Cupach & Spitzberg, 2000)
- 6C emotional harassment (telling lies to victim's network; canceling credit cards, etc.) (5% Tucker, 1993)
- 6C made up things about past relationship (46%, 48%, 34% Cupach & Spitzberg, 2000)
- 6C offenses against person and reputation (6% Hackett, 2000)
- 6C offensive materials (5% Purcell et al., 2002)
- 6C release harmful information (1%, 2% Langhinrichsen-Rohling et al., 2000)
- 6C sabotaging employment (34% Brewster, 1998, 2000)
- 6C slanders/defames character (60% Sheridan et al., 2001a)
- 6C spread false rumors to your friends (51%, 47%, 49% Cupach & Spitzberg, 2000)
- 6C spread gossip (48% Hall, 1997)
- 6C spread rumors and lies (82% Kamphuis & Emmelkamp, 2001)
- 6C told others more intimate than you currently were (52%, 61%, 40% Cupach & Spitzberg, 2000)
- 6C tried to get victim fired from job (16%, 19% McFarlane et al., 1999)
- 6C used profanity and/or obscenities in reference to you (46%, 49%, 45% Cupach & Spitzberg, 2000)

D. Network Harassment:
- 6D harass other 3rd parties (23% Morrison, 2001)
- 6D harassment of family (37% Harris, 2000)

E. Regulatory Harassment:
- 6E altering your electronic identity or persona (1% Spitzberg & Hoobler, 2002)
- 6E criminal contempt for violation of court order (57% Tucker, 1993)
- 6E cyber-directing others to you in threatening ways (2% Spitzberg & Hoobler, 2002)
- 6E made false charges (45% Kamphuis & Emmelkamp, 2001)
- 6E regulatory harassment (3% Spitzberg & Cupach, 1999)
- 6E regulatory harassment (2.5% Spitzberg & Cupach, 2001b)
- 6E regulatory harassment (1% Spitzberg, 2000a)
- 6E signatures (23% Oddie, 2000)
- 6E spurious legal actions (8% Mullen et al., 1999)
- 6E taking over your electronic identity or persona (3% Spitzberg & Hoobler, 2002)
- 6E violated restraining order (11% Westrup et al., 1999)
- 6E violated restraining order (F: 0%, M: 9% McCann, 2000a)

F. Economic Harassment:
- 6F ordered items and charged them to victim's account (23% Kamphuis & Emmelkamp, 2001)

G. Unrelenting Persistence:
- 6G asking for date after being refused (26% Sheridan et al., 2002)
- 6G claimed to still be in a relationship with you (39%, 42%, 22% Cupach & Spitzberg, 2000)
- 6G cluttered e-mail with messages (13%, 13%, 5% Cupach & Spitzberg, 2000)
- 6G excessive unwanted telephone calls regardless of content (25% Sheridan et al., 2001b)
- 6G outstaying welcome in home (23% Sheridan et al., 2002)
- 6G refused to take hints he or she wasn't welcome (61%, 67%, 54% Cupach & Spitzberg, 2000)

- 6G refused to take no for an answer (F: 36%, M: 22% Budd & Mattinson, 2000)
- 6G refusing to accept prior relationship is over (22% Sheridan et al., 2001b)
- 6G refusing to accept relationship is over (21% Sheridan et al., 2002)
- 6G repeated e-mails (58% LeBlanc et al., 2001)
- 6G repeated excessive calls regardless of content (17% Sheridan et al., 2002)
- 6G repeated phone calls (71% LeBlanc et al., 2001)
- 6G repeated phone/email (67% Morrison, 2001)
- 6G repeated, excessive, unwanted telephone calls (29% Sheridan et al., 2000)
- 6G repeatedly approaching target, remaining a stranger (16% Sheridan et al., 2001b)
- 6G repetitive, unwanted mail (75.5% Rosenfeld & Harmon, 2002)

H. Bizarre Behavior or Artifacts:
- 6H bizarre or sinister items at your home or workplace (5% Sheridan et al., 2000)
- 6H bizarre or sinister items to home or workplace (4% Sheridan et al., 2001b)
- 6H bizarre or sinister, obscene items (7% Sheridan et al., 2002)
- 6H exposed him/herself (30%, 34%, 14% Cupach & Spitzberg, 2000)
- 6H exposing self (3% Meloy et al., 2000)
- 6H gave/left offensive material (.3% McLennon, 1996)
- 6H leave unwanted items (F: 9%, M: 9% Sinclair & Frieze, 2000)
- 6H left things on property (43% Hall, 1997)
- 6H left unwanted items for you (20% Lemmey, 1999)
- 6H left unwanted items to find (F: 18%, M: 16% Davis et al., 2002; Tjaden-NVAW data)
- 6H mischief (11% Hackett, 2000)
- 6H odd items (2% Morrison, 2001)
- 6H offensive material (5% Dussuyer, 2000)
- 6H offensive materials (5% Purcell et al., 2002)
- 6H packages (e.g., semen, blood, locks of hair, etc.) (3% Hall, 1997)

- 6H unusual parcels (F: 6%, M: 5% Sinclair & Frieze, 2000)

I. Isolation and Network Alienation: (see "Isolation—Alienation" category under "Cognitive Effects" in Appendix 5.1)

7. COERCION AND THREATS:
A. General/Vague Threats:
- 7A "other threats" (13% Meloy & Boyd, 2003)
- 7A direct or explicit threat (62% McCann, 2000a)
- 7A explicit threats (29% Purcell et al., 2002)
- 7A mail, threatening (30% Sheridan et al., 2001a)
- 7A making vague threats (1%, 9% Langhinrichsen-Rohling et al., 2000)
- 7A manipulate/coerce into dating (F: 17%, M: 28% Sinclair & Frieze, 2000)
- 7A obscene and/or threatening inappropriate language (20% Sheridan et al., 2001b)
- 7A obscene or threatening language (15% Sheridan et al., 2002)
- 7A obscene, threatening, or mysterious calls from an unknown caller (39% Sheridan et al., 2000)
- 7A oral threats (87% Meloy & Boyd, 2003)
- 7A oral/written threats or telephone calls without physical approach (59% Sandberg et al., 1998)
- 7A overt threats (57% Mullen & Pathé, 1994b)
- 7A overt threats (58% Pathé & Mullen, 1997)
- 7A threaten emotionally (F: 5%, M: 5% Sinclair & Frieze, 2000)
- 7A threaten verbally (3% Spitzberg & Cupach, 1999)
- 7A threaten verbally (4% Spitzberg & Cupach, 2001b)
- 7A threaten verbally (3% Spitzberg, 2000a)
- 7A threaten victims (75% Meloy et al., 2000)
- 7A threatened (47% Blackburn, 1999)
- 7A threatened (65% Meloy & Boyd, 2003)
- 7A threatened both person and property (10% Meloy & Gothard, 1995)
- 7A threatened to harm you (F: 8%, M: 0% McCann, 2000a)
- 7A threatened to harm/kill (68% Kienlen et al., 1997)
- 7A threatened to leave victim (15%, 14% McFarlane et al., 1999)
- 7A threatened with harm (94% Mechanic, Weaver, et al., 2000)

- 7A threatened with physical assault (53% Sheridan & Davies, 2001b)
- 7A threatened you or family (M: .4% Davis et al., 2002; Tjaden-NVAW data)
- 7A threatened you or family (F: 6% Davis et al., 2002; Tjaden-NVAW data)
- 7A threatening (28% Brewster, 1998, 2000)
- 7A threatening notes/letters/ messages (18%, 19%, 12% Cupach & Spitzberg, 2000)
- 7A threatening or harassing message or letter (15% Romans et al., 1996)
- 7A threatening phone calls/letters/gifts (49% Harris, 2000)
- 7A threatening to hurt victim (46% Kileen & Dunn, 1998)
- 7A threats (57% Purcell et al., 2001)
- 7A threats (58% Mullen et al., 1999)
- 7A threats (65% McCann, 2001)
- 7A threats (65% Palarea et al., 1999)
- 7A threats (72% Sandberg et al., 1998)
- 7A threats against victim (65% Palarea et al., 1999)
- 7A threats or attempts to harm (15% Fisher et al., 1999; 2000)
- 7A threats to victim (47% Morrison, 2001)
- 7A uttering threats (20% Hackett, 2000)
- 7A vague warnings that bad things will happen to you (36%, 41%, 26% Cupach & Spitzberg, 2000)
- 7A verbal threats (67% Nicastro et al., 2000)
- 7A verbal threats (76% Westrup et al., 1999)
- 7A verbal threats (77% Eke, 1999)
- 7A verbal threats against personal safety (28% Guy et al., 1992)
- 7A verbal/written threats (78% Huffhines, 2001)
- 7A warned bad things would or might happen to you (29%, 34%, 25% Cupach & Spitzberg, 2000)
- 7A written threats (19% Westrup et al., 1999)

B. Threaten Reputation:
- 7B assaulted (36% Mullen & Pathé, 1994b)
- 7B threaten information release (2%, 3% Langhinrichsen-Rohling et al., 2000)
- 7B threatened to report drug use (4%, 3% McFarlane et al., 1999)

- 7B threatened to report to authorities (4%, 8% McFarlane et al., 1999)

C. Threaten Property:
   - 7C threatened property (23% Holloway, 1994)
   - 7C threatened property damage (15% Meloy & Gothard, 1995)
   - 7C threatened to harm property (2% Kienlen et al., 1997)
   - 7C threatening objects (1% Spitzberg & Cupach, 1999)
   - 7C threatening objects (1% Spitzberg, 2000a)
   - 7C threatening objects (1% Spitzberg & Cupach, 2001b)

D. Threaten Economic Livelihood:
   - 7D extortion or threat of extortion (14% Morrison, 2001)

E. Threaten Victim Affiliates (e.g., family, friends, pets, etc.):
   - 7E behaving threateningly toward family and/or friends (6% Sheridan et al., 2001b)
   - 7E frightened victim's family (24%, 31% McFarlane et al., 1999)
   - 7E stalked another person(s) (30% Hall, 1997)
   - 7E stalked members of victim's family (59% Sheridan et al., 2001a)
   - 7E threaten others (3% Spitzberg & Cupach, 1999)
   - 7E threaten others (2% Spitzberg & Cupach, 2001b)
   - 7E threaten others (2% Spitzberg, 2000a)
   - 7E threaten others (F: 3%, M: 6%, McCann, 2000a)
   - 7E threaten pets/family (1%, 2% Langhinrichsen-Rohling et al., 2000)
   - 7E threaten to harm Ex (1%, 0% Langhinrichsen-Rohling et al., 2000)
   - 7E threaten to harm kids (11%, 13% McFarlane et al., 1999)
   - 7E threatened family (34% Lemmey, 1999)
   - 7E threatened family/friends/partner(s) of victim (39% Sheridan et al., 2001a)
   - 7E threatened others (33% Nicastro et al., 2000)
   - 7E threatened third party (20% Kienlen et al., 1997)
   - 7E threatened to harm kids (16% Lemmey, 1999)
   - 7E threatened to hurt third parties (16% Purcell et al., 2002)
   - 7E threatened to kill pets (M: 1% Davis et al., 2002; Tjaden-NVAW data)
   - 7E threatened to kill pets (F: 2% Davis et al., 2002; Tjaden-NVAW data)

- 7E threatened/contacted family (7% Dussuyer, 2000)
- 7E threatened/harmed new partner (14% Melton, 2001)
- 7E threatening behavior towards family/friends (6% Sheridan et al., 2002)
- 7E threatening to hurt children (4% Kileen & Dunn, 1998)
- 7E threatening to kidnap children (15% Kileen & Dunn, 1998)
- 7E threatening to kill children (8% Kileen & Dunn, 1998)
- 7E threatening victim's family (39% Kileen & Dunn, 1998)
- 7E threats against others (36% Purcell et al., 2001)
- 7E threats to harm third party (18% Morrison, 2001)
- 7E threats to new partner (18% Mechanic, Weaver, et al., 2000)
- 7E threats to new partner (F: 4%, M: 9% McCann, 2000a)
- 7E threats to third parties (39% Mullen et al., 1999)
- 7E threats to third party (20% Huffhines, 2001)
- 7E threats toward family, friends, coworkers, or affiliates (37% Brewster, 1998, 2000)
- 7E verbal threats about loved ones (14% Guy et al., 1992)

F. Threaten Unaffiliated Other(s):
- 7F stalked others unconnected with victim (39% Boon & Sheridan, 2001)
- 7F stalked others unrelated to victim (48% Sheridan, 2001)
- 7F threatened other (18% Holloway, 1994)
- 7F threatened to harm others (41% Hall, 1997)

G. Threaten Self:
- 7G threaten self-harm/attempt suicide (7% Nicastro et al., 2000)
- 7G threaten suicide (10% Sheridan et al., 2002)
- 7G threaten to hurt self (4% Spitzberg, 2000a)
- 7G threaten to hurt self (5% Spitzberg & Cupach, 1999)
- 7G threaten to hurt self (4% Spitzberg & Cupach, 2001b)
- 7G threaten to hurt self (F: 8%, M: 2% Sinclair & Frieze, 2000)
- 7G threatened self (25% Holloway, 1994)
- 7G threatened self-harm (F: 13%, M: 9% McCann, 2000a)
- 7G threatened suicide (14% Sheridan et al., 2000)
- 7G threatened to harm themselves (30% Lemmey, 1999)
- 7G threatened to kill self (19%, 34% McFarlane et al., 1999)
- 7G threatening suicide (14% Sheridan et al., 2001b)
- 7G threatening suicide (30% Kileen & Dunn, 1998)
- 7G threats of self-harm (33% Mechanic, Weaver, et al., 2000)

H. Coercive Communication:
- 7H communicated in other ways against will (F: .4% Davis et al., 2002; Tjaden-NVAW data)
- 7H communicated in other ways against will (M: 1% Davis et al., 2002; Tjaden-NVAW data)
- 7H communicated in other ways against will (33%, 39% McFarlane et al., 1999)
- 7H told you to stop doing certain things (58%, 59%, 51% Cupach & Spitzberg, 2000)
- 7H tried to communicate against will (15%, 38% McFarlane, Campbell, & Watson, 2002)
- 7H unwanted messages (49% Spitzberg & Cupach, 2001b)

I. Sexual Coercion:
- 7I sexually coercing (10% Spitzberg & Cupach, 2001b)
- 7I sexually coercing (13% Nicastro et al., 2000)
- 7I sexually coercing (2% Spitzberg & Cupach, 1999)
- 7I sexually coercing (4% Spitzberg, 2000a)
- 7I sexually coercing; threaten physically (1% Spitzberg & Cupach, 2001b)

J. Threaten Physical Violence Without Weapon:
- 7J implied physical threat (27% Nicastro et al., 2000)
- 7J physically threaten (2% Spitzberg, 2000a)
- 7J physically threaten (2% Spitzberg & Cupach, 1999)
- 7J physically threaten (5% Spitzberg & Cupach, 2001b)
- 7J threatened with physical injury (45% Meloy & Gothard, 1995)
- 7J verbally or physically threatened or hit (30% Jason et al., 1984)

K. Threaten Violence with weapon:
- 7K brought weapon (17% Romans et al., 1996)
- 7K frightened with a weapon (39%, 40% McFarlane et al., 1999)
- 7K threaten with a weapon (0%, 0% Langhinrichsen-Rohling et al., 2000)
- 7K threaten with weapon (20% Nicastro et al., 2000)
- 7K threatened to cause harm (3% Burgess et al., 2001)
- 7K threatened to use violence (F: 27%, M: 32% Budd & Mattinson, 2000)

- 7K threatened violence (74% Kamphuis & Emmelkamp, 2001)
- 7K threatened with physical harm (33%, 36%, 22% Cupach & Spitzberg, 2000)
- 7K threatening with a weapon (30% Kileen & Dunn, 1998)
- 7K threatens victim with physical assault (53% Sheridan et al., 2001a)
- 7K threats of violence (16.5% Gill & Brockman, 1996)
- 7K threats of violence (62% Rosenfeld & Harmon, 2002)
- 7K threats of violence (73% Brewster, 1998, 2000)
- 7K threats with firearm in person (.2% Gill & Brockman, 1996)
- 7K threats with weapon in person (2% Gill & Brockman, 1996)

L. Threaten Victim's Life:
- 7L attempting to kill victim (3% Kileen & Dunn, 1998)
- 7L death threats (3% Sheridan et al., 2002)
- 7L death threats (3.5% Sheridan et al., 2001b)
- 7L death threats toward you (7% Sheridan et al., 2000)
- 7L homicidal threat (49% Meloy & Boyd, 2003)
- 7L solicitation to commit murder, attempted murder (3% Tucker, 1993)
- 7L threatened to kill (1% Burgess et al., 2001)
- 7L threatening to kill victim (75% Kileen & Dunn, 1998)
- 7L threats of death or bodily injury and assault (76% Tucker, 1993)
- 7L threats to harm or kill victim (45% Blaauw, Winkel, Arensman, et al., 2000)

8. AGGESSION AND VIOLENCE:
A. Vandalism:
- 8A arson (1% Hall, 1997)
- 8A arson/attempted arson (3% Morrison, 2001)
- 8A broke something important (66% Melton, 2001)
- 8A criminal damage to or vandalism of property (12% Sheridan et al., 2000)
- 8A criminal damage/vandalism to property (10% Sheridan et al., 2002)
- 8A criminal damage/vandalism to property (6% Sheridan et al., 2001b)

- 8A damage property (1%, 3% Langhinrichsen-Rohling et al., 2000)
- 8A damage property (40% Mullen et al., 1999)
- 8A damage to property (38% Harris, 2000)
- 8A damage to property or pets (45% Sandberg et al., 1998)
- 8A damaged outside of home/garden (38% Sheridan et al., 2001a)
- 8A damaged personal property (31% Westrup et al., 1999)
- 8A damaged property (64% Kamphuis & Emmelkamp, 2001)
- 8A damaged property of new partner (F: 0%, M: 20% McCann, 2000a)
- 8A damaged property or possessions (30%, 29%, 19% Cupach & Spitzberg, 2000)
- 8A damaged victim's car (50% Sheridan et al., 2001a)
- 8A destroyed or vandalized property or destroyed something loved (27%, 41% McFarlane, Campbell, & Watson, 2002)
- 8A destroyed property (48% Lemmey, 1999)
- 8A destroyed/vandalized property (34%, 49% McFarlane et al., 1999)
- 8A destruction of home (14% Guy et al., 1992)
- 8A destruction of office contents (26% Guy et al., 1992)
- 8A disabling vehicle (28% Kileen & Dunn, 1998)
- 8A had property damaged intentionally by stalker (27% Blackburn, 1999)
- 8A interfered with/damaged property (.2% McLennon, 1996)
- 8A interfered/damaged property (8% Dussuyer, 2000)
- 8A property damage (21% Morrison, 2001)
- 8A property damage (36% Mullen & Pathé, 1994b)
- 8A property damage (36% Pathé & Mullen, 1997)
- 8A property damage (38% Purcell et al., 2001)
- 8A property damage (43% Hall, 1997)
- 8A property damage (44% Brewster, 1998, 2000)
- 8A property damage (47% Eke, 1999)
- 8A property destruction (65% Blaauw, Winkel, Arensman, et al., 2000)
- 8A property violence (24% Meloy & Boyd, 2003)
- 8A vandalism (20% Kienlen et al., 1997)
- 8A vandalism (23% Oddie, 2000)
- 8A vandalism (4% Tucker, 1993)
- 8A vandalism (47% Nicastro et al., 2000)

- 8A vandalism on victim's property (35% Huffhines, 2001)
- 8A vandalized (4% Romans et al., 1996)
- 8A vandalized personal property (F: 24% Davis et al., 2002; Tjaden-NVAW data)
- 8A vandalized personal property (M: 27% Davis et al., 2002; Tjaden-NVAW data)
- 8A vandalized property (61% Lemmey, 1999)
- 8A vandalizing others' property (8% Kileen & Dunn, 1998)
- 8A vandalizing property (62% Kileen & Dunn, 1998)
- 8A violence against property (33% Palarea et al., 1999)
- 8A violent to victim's property only (7% Meloy et al., 2001)

B. Assault (General):
- 8B actual physical assault(s) (32% Sheridan et al., 2001a)
- 8B assaulted (18% Purcell et al., 2000)
- 8B assaulted (50% Mullen & Pathé, 1994a)
- 8B assaulted family/friends/partner(s) of victim (17% Sheridan et al., 2001a)
- 8B assaulted someone else (31% Westrup et al., 1999)
- 8B assaulted victim (36% Westrup et al., 1999)
- 8B assaulted/abused others (47% Eke, 1999)
- 8B assaults (34% Purcell et al., 2001)
- 8B attack victim (36% Mullen et al., 1999)
- 8B attacks (38% Sandberg et al., 1998)
- 8B attempted to kill victim (25% Sheridan et al., 2001a)
- 8B committed act of violence toward victim (31% McCann, 2000a)
- 8B common assault (11% Hackett, 2000)
- 8B harm family/pet (0%, 0% Langhinrichsen-Rohling et al., 2000)
- 8B hit or beat (38% Hall, 1997)
- 8B personal violence (3% Zona et al., 1993)
- 8B physical acts of violence (14% Holloway, 1994)
- 8B physical assault (16% Sheridan & Davies, 2001b)
- 8B physical assault (52% Kileen & Dunn, 1998)
- 8B physical assault (56% Blaauw, Winkel, Arensman, et al., 2000)
- 8B physical assault without weapon (28% Morrison, 2001)
- 8B physical assaults (47% Eke, 1999)
- 8B physical attacks on loved ones (17% Guy et al., 1992)
- 8B physical force (F: 19%, M: 24% Budd & Mattinson, 2000)
- 8B physical violence (14% Gill & Brockman, 1996)

- 8B physical violence with victim (38% Huffhines, 2001)
- 8B physically assault (25% Meloy & Gothard, 1995)
- 8B physically assaulted (24% Kienlen et al., 1997)
- 8B physically assaulted (31% Pathé & Mullen, 1997)
- 8B physically assaulted (32% Sheridan & Davies, 2001b)
- 8B physically assaulted (4% Romans et al., 1996)
- 8B physically assaulted and had attempt made on life (14% Sheridan & Davies, 2001b)
- 8B physically injuring others (7% Kileen & Dunn, 1998)
- 8B physically shoved, slapped, or hit (33%, 37%, 25% Cupach & Spitzberg, 2000)
- 8B physically violent (0% Sandberg et al., 1998)
- 8B physically violent (52% Meloy et al., 2000)
- 8B post-separation physical assault (22%, 4% Mechanic, Uhlmansiek, et al., 2000)
- 8B threats followed by actual violence against person or property (36% Palarea et al., 1999)
- 8B tried to kill them (10%, 25% Sheridan & Davies, 2001b)
- 8B used violence (55% Kamphuis & Emmelkamp, 2001)
- 8B violence (25% Meloy & Boyd, 2003)
- 8B violence (37% Farnham et al., 2000)
- 8B violence (38% McCann, 2001)
- 8B violence (46% Brewster, 1998, 2000)
- 8B violence against person (19% Palarea et al., 1999)
- 8B violence or physical abuse (49% Hall, 1997)
- 8B violence, prior (70% Blackburn, 1999)
- 8B violent (34% Rosenfeld & Harmon, 2002)
- 8B violent act (62% Hall, 1997)
- 8B violent behavior (15% Harris, 2000)
- 8B violent to victim and victim's property (25% Meloy et al., 2001)
- 8B violent to victim only (25% Meloy et al., 2001)

C. Endangerment:
- 8C attempt physical harm (F: 16%, M: 2% Sinclair & Frieze, 2000)
- 8C attempted harm (88% Mechanic, Weaver, et al., 2000)
- 8C attempted to harm you (F: 4%, M: 9% McCann, 2000a)
- 8C inappropriately touched you in an intimate way (37%, 42%, 27% Cupach & Spitzberg, 2000)
- 8C physically endanger (1% Spitzberg & Cupach, 1999)
- 8C physically endanger (1% Spitzberg & Cupach, 2001b)

- 8C physically endanger (1% Spitzberg, 2000a)

D. Kidnapping:
- 8D confining the target against will (10% Sheridan et al., 2001b)
- 8D kidnap/hold against will (0%, 1% Langhinrichsen-Rohling et al., 2000)
- 8D kidnap/restrain (1% Spitzberg & Cupach, 1999)
- 8D kidnap/restrain (3% Spitzberg & Cupach, 2001b)
- 8D kidnap/restraint (1% Spitzberg, 2000a)
- 8D kidnapped (12% Kienlen et al., 1997)
- 8D kidnapped/restrained (0% Spitzberg & Cupach, 2001b)
- 8D kidnapping (1% Kong, 1996)
- 8D kidnapping (4% Nicastro et al., 2000)
- 8D kidnapping (8% Hall, 1997)
- 8D kidnapping (8% Kileen & Dunn, 1998)
- 8D kidnapping children (6% Kileen & Dunn, 1998)
- 8D physically restraining (6% Spitzberg & Cupach, 1999)
- 8D physically restraining (5% Spitzberg & Cupach, 2001b)
- 8D physically restraining (5% Spitzberg, 2000a)
- 8D physically restraining/endangering (38% Nicastro et al., 2000)
- 8D preventing from leaving (32% Kileen & Dunn, 1998)
- 8D preventing victim from calling for help (25% Kileen & Dunn, 1998)

E. Sexual Assault/Rape or Attempted Rape
- 8E actual sexual assault (3% Sheridan et al., 2001a)
- 8E attempted rape (4% Blackburn, 1999)
- 8E force sex after break-up (0%, 2% Langhinrichsen-Rohling et al., 2000)
- 8E forced or attempted sexual contact" (10% Fisher et al., 1999, 2000)
- 8E forced sexual act (F: 9%, M: 3% Budd & Mattinson, 2000)
- 8E forced sexual behavior (18%, 20%, 11% Cupach & Spitzberg, 2000)
- 8E raped (4% Blackburn, 1999)
- 8E sexual assault (14% Morrison, 2001)
- 8E sexual assault (19% Burgess et al., 1997)
- 8E sexual assault (2% Purcell et al., 2001)
- 8E sexual assault (2% Purcell et al., 2002)

- 8E sexual assault (22% Hall, 1997)
- 8E sexual assault (28.5% Mullen & Pathé, 1994b)
- 8E sexual assault (3% Hackett, 2000)
- 8E sexual assault (3% Meloy et al., 2000)
- 8E sexual assault (4% Kienlen et al., 1997)
- 8E sexual assaults (23% Eke, 1999)
- 8E sexual assaults (7% Sandberg et al., 1998)
- 8E sexually assaulted (3% Sheridan & Davies, 2001b)
- 8E sexually assaulted (32% Mullen & Pathé, 1994a)
- 8E sexually assaulted (7% Pathé & Mullen, 1997)
- 8E sexually assaulting victim (10% Kileen & Dunn, 1998)
- 8E unwanted sexual advances (39% McCann, 2000a)

F. Assault with Weapon:
- 8F assault with a weapon or cause bodily harm (4% Hackett, 2000)
- 8F assault with weapon (7% Morrison, 2001)
- 8F harm with weapon (9% Nicastro et al., 2000)
- 8F physical violence with weapon (1% Gill & Brockman, 1996)
- 8F used weapon (3% Huffhines, 2001)

G. Harmed or Injured:
- 8G assaulted/injured (39% Schwartz-Watts et al., 1997)
- 8G battery of victim (64% Tucker, 1993)
- 8G beat face (56% Burgess et al., 1997)
- 8G harmed your new partner (F: 0%, M:0% Logan et al., 2000)
- 8G hurt a pet on purpose (11%, 11% McFarlane et al., 1999)
- 8G injure (0%, 3% Langhinrichsen-Rohling et al., 2000)
- 8G injured (9% Gallagher et al., 1994)
- 8G injuring or killing animals (6% Kileen & Dunn, 1998)
- 8G injuring victim with a weapon (5% Kileen & Dunn, 1998)
- 8G injury requiring medical care (9% Meloy & Boyd, 2003)
- 8G involved some injury (30% Fisher et al., 1999, 2000)
- 8G killed (F: 2% Davis et al., 2002; Tjaden-NVAW data)
- 8G killed or injured family pet (13% Hall, 1997)
- 8G killed pet (1% Lemmey, 1999)
- 8G killed pets (F: 2% Davis et al., 2002; Tjaden-NVAW data)

- 8G killed pets (M: 1% Davis et al., 2002; Tjaden-NVAW data)
- 8G killing of victim's pets (3% Tucker, 1993)
- 8G physical injury (5% Kong, 1996)
- 8G physically harm slightly (F: 9%, M: 2% Sinclair & Frieze, 2000)
- 8G physically harmed (89% Mechanic, Weaver, et al., 2000)
- 8G physically harmed partner (6% Burgess et al., 2001)
- 8G physically hurt (4% Spitzberg & Cupach, 1999)
- 8G physically hurt (5.5% Spitzberg & Cupach, 2001b)
- 8G physically hurt (6% Spitzberg, 2000a)
- 8G physically hurting (45% Nicastro et al., 2000)
- 8G strangle by hands (42% Burgess et al., 1997)

H. Attempted Suicide:
- 8H attempt to hurt self (F: 8%, M: 9% Sinclair & Frieze, 2000)
- 8H injuring themselves (4% Kileen & Dunn, 1998)
- 8H physical attacks on self (22% Guy et al., 1992)
- 8H physically harmed self (F: 4%, M:9% McCann, 2000a)
- 8H physically hurt self (F: 4%, M: 7% Sinclair & Frieze, 2000)
- 8H violence against self and property (35% Meloy & Boyd, 2003)

I. Suicide:

J. Killed Victim:
- 8J homicide or attempted murder (1% Kong, 1996)
- 8J murder of victim (8% Tucker, 1993)
- 8J murdered (8% Kienlen et al., 1997)

Note: Some items show multiple percentage estimates. These occur because the study reported percentages by sub-sample categories (e.g., abused, nonabused). When the sub-sample estimates are divided by sex, the designations are reported as "F" for females and "M" for males.

Appendix 5
Measure of Symptoms Due to ORI and Stalking

	Never	Occa-sionally	Often	Very Often	Con-stantly
1. Frustration	1	2	3	4	5
2. Depression	1	2	3	4	5
3. Frightened	1	2	3	4	5
4. Feeling watched or followed at all times	1	2	3	4	5
5. Anxiety	1	2	3	4	5
6. Sense of personal power	1	2	3	4	5
7. Paranoia	1	2	3	4	5
8. Nightmares	1	2	3	4	5
10. Thoughts of ending your life	1	2	3	4	5
10. Loss of appetite	1	2	3	4	5
11. Healthier level of cautiousness	1	2	3	4	5
12. General stress	1	2	3	4	5
13. Loss of faith in law enforcement	1	2	3	4	5
14. Physical illness	1	2	3	4	5
15. Greater awareness of myself and others	1	2	3	4	5
16. Anger	1	2	3	4	5
17. Distrust of others	1	2	3	4	5
18. More realistic view of relationships	1	2	3	4	5
19. Loss of faith in the justice system	1	2	3	4	5
20. Terror anticipating next encounter	1	2	3	4	5
21. Stronger relationships with significant others	1	2	3	4	5
22. A sense of helplessness	1	2	3	4	5
23. Sense of imprisonment	1	2	3	4	5
24. Feeling empowered	1	2	3	4	5
25. Headaches	1	2	3	4	5
26. Sleeplessness	1	2	3	4	5

27. Deeper empathy for others	1	2	3	4	5
28. Loss of concentration	1	2	3	4	5
29. Renewed determination to take control of your life	1	2	3	4	5
30. Other_____	1	2	3	4	5

Appendix 6

Prevalence of Symptoms Across 35 Studies of Stalking and ORI Victimization

GENERAL EFFECTS:
- General (-): "All" of the above (41% Sheridan et al., 2001a)
- General (-): clinically significant psycho-medical symptoms (59% Kamphuis & Emmelkamp, 2001)
- General (-): general stress (11% Pathé & Mullen, 1997)
- General (-): general stress (66% Spitzberg & Rhea, 1999)
- General (-): injured emotionally or psychologically (30% Fisher et al., 1999, 2000)
- General (-): personalities changed (83% Hall, 1997)
- General (-): psychological injury (100% Romans et al., 1996)
- General (-): PTSD (37% Pathé & Mullen, 1997)
- General (-): quality of life costs of some sort (99% Brewster, 1998, 2000)
- General (-): somewhat negatively affected (36% Blackburn, 1999)
- General (-): stalking experience worse than other crimes experienced (85% Brewster, 1998, 2000)
- General (-): very negatively affected (30% Blackburn, 1999)

BEHAVIORAL EFFECTS:
- Behavioral (+): coping skills (51% Spitzberg & Rhea, 1999)
- Behavioral (-): work/school, disruption of (44% Mullen & Pathé, 1994a)
- Behavioral (-): day-to-day activities, change in (40% McLennan, 1996)
- Behavioral (-): aggressive, more (27% Hall, 1997)
- Behavioral (-): workplace-school-career, change in (37% Pathé & Mullen, 1997)
- Behavioral (-): school/work disruption (53% Pathé & Mullen, 1997)
- Behavioral (-): more frequently late for or absent from school (3% Omata, 2002)
- Behavioral (-): your academic grades had dropped (3% Omata, 2002)
- Behavioral (-): avoid talking to or seeing others (8% Omata, 2002)
- Behavioral (-): scene (avoid place where victimized) (33% Omata, 2002)

AFFECTIVE EFFECTS:
   A. ANGER:
   - Affective (-): anger (24% Brewster, 1998, 2000)
   - Affective (-): anger (29% Pathé & Mullen, 1997)
   - Affective (-): anger (3% Sheridan et al., 2001a)
   - Affective (-): anger toward the stalker (47% Suzuki, 1999)
   - Affective (-): anger/rage (50% Spitzberg & Rhea, 1999)
   - Affective (-): angry (14% Sheridan, 2001)
   - Affective (-): angry (39% Boon & Sheridan, 2001)
   - Affective (-): angry (70% Gentile, 2001)
   - Affective (-): angry or hateful (10% Melton, 1994)

   B. ANNOYANCE:
   - Affective (-): annoyed (20% Pathé & Mullen, 1997)
   - Affective (-): annoyed (7% Sheridan, 2001)
   - Affective (-): annoyed or irritated (92% Budd & Mattinson, 2000)

   C. ANXIETY:
   - Affective (-): anxiety (63% Spitzberg & Rhea, 1999)
   - Affective (-): anxiety attacks (2% Pathé & Mullen, 1997)
   - Affective (-): anxiety symptoms (73% Pathé et al., 2000)
   - Affective (-): anxiety, heightened (83% Pathé & Mullen, 1997)
   - Affective (-): anxious (74% Gentile, 2001)

   D. DEPRESSION:
   - Affective (-): depressed (10% Melton, 1994)
   - Affective (-): depression (21% Brewster, 1998, 2000)
   - Affective (-): depression (46% Spitzberg & Rhea, 1999)
   - Affective (-): depression (9% Pathé & Mullen, 1997)
   - Affective (-): depression, heavy (44% Suzuki, 1999)

   E. FEAR:
   - Affective (-): fear & distress (69% Mullen & Pathé, 1994a)
   - Affective (-): fear (18% Sheridan et al., 2001a)
   - Affective (-): fear and anxiety (45% Suzuki, 1999)
   - Affective (-): fear for personal safety (32% McLennan, 1996)
   - Affective (-): fear level "high," (80% Brewster, 1998, 2000)
   - Affective (-): fear/terror (57% Brewster, 1998, 2000)
   - Affective (-): fearful (54% Boon & Sheridan, 2001)
   - Affective (-): fearful (80% Pathé & Mullen, 1997)
   - Affective (-): frightened (44% Gentile, 2001)

- Affective (-): frightened, now easily (52% Hall, 1997)
- Affective (-): intimidated (38% Boon & Sheridan, 2001)
- Affective (-): intimidated (7% Sheridan et al., 2001a)
- Affective (-): nervous (33% Pathé & Mullen, 1997)
- Affective (-): nervous/jumpy (31% Brewster, 1998, 2000)
- Affective (-): nervousness (21% Suzuki, 1999)
- Affective (-): nervousness/anxiousness (10% Brewster, 1998, 2000)
- Affective (-): panic attacks (0% Gentile, 2001)
- Affective (-): scared (71% Melton, 1994)
- Affective (-): terrified (52% Sheridan, 2001)
- Affective (-): terror anticipating next encounter (5% Pathé & Mullen, 1997)
- Affective (-): terror at prospect of next meeting with pursuer (23% Spitzberg & Rhea, 1999)
- Affective (-): terrorized (15% Sheridan et al., 2001a)
- Affective (-): terrorized (48% Boon & Sheridan, 2001)
- Affective (-): threatened (43% Pathé & Mullen, 1997)

F. STRESS, DISTRESS, & FRUSTRATION:
- Affective (-): distressing or upsetting (74% Budd & Mattinson, 2000)
- Affective (-): frustration (12% Brewster, 1998, 2000)
- Affective (-): frustration (82% Spitzberg & Rhea, 1999)
- Affective (-): frustration (9% Pathé & Mullen, 1997)
- Affective (-): irritability (34% Spitzberg & Rhea, 1999)
- Affective (-): stress (53% who perceived as dangerous, Kohn et al., 2000)
- Affective (-): upset (35% Boon & Sheridan, 2001)
- Affective (-): upset (4% Sheridan et al., 2001a)

G. ATTRACTIVENESS:
- Affective (+): admired (3% Blackburn, 1999)
- Affective (+): cared for (2% Blackburn, 1999)
- Affective (+): flattered (3% Blackburn, 1999)
- Affective (+): loved (2% Blackburn, 1999)

H. MISCELLANEOUS EMOTIONAL EFFECTS:
- Affective (-): disgusted (15% Gentile, 2001)
- Affective (-): embarrassment (4% Pathé & Mullen, 1997)
- Affective (-): guilty (7% Gentile, 2001)
- Affective (-): jealousy (8% Pathé & Mullen, 1997)

- Affective (-): comfort, loss of sense of… (44% Spitzberg & Rhea, 1999)
- Affective (-): emotions, restricted ranges of… (24% Spitzberg & Rhea, 1999)
- Affective (-): sad (11% Gentile, 2001)
- Affective (-): surprised (26% Gentile, 2001)
- Affective (-): less motivated to do anything (8% Omata, 2002)
- Affective (-): less motivated to study (8% Omata, 2002)

COGNITIVE EFFECTS:
A. LOSS OF FAITH, GENERAL:
- Cognitive (-): hopeless (0% Gentile, 2001)
- Cognitive (-): less trustful or more cynical (6% Fisher et al., 1999, 2000)
- Cognitive (-): sense of shortened future (15% Spitzberg & Rhea, 1999)

B. LOSS OF FAITH IN SELF:
- Cognitive (-): felt suicidal in direct response to the stalking (18% Blackburn, 1999)
- Cognitive (-): helplessness (36% Spitzberg & Rhea, 1999)
- Cognitive (-): loss of self-esteem (2% Sheridan et al., 2001a)
- Cognitive (-): loss of self-esteem (33% Boon & Sheridan, 2001)
- Cognitive (-): powerless (37% Boon & Sheridan, 2001)
- Cognitive (-): powerlessness (4% Sheridan et al., 2001a)
- Cognitive (-): sense of helplessness (7% Pathé & Mullen, 1997)
- Cognitive (-): humiliated (24% Melton, 1994)
- Cognitive (-): seriously considered or attempted suicide (24% Pathé & Mullen, 1997)
- Cognitive (-): suicidal thoughts (5% Pathé & Mullen, 1997)
- Cognitive (-): weaker self-concept (31% Spitzberg & Rhea, 1999)
- Cognitive (-): more self-hatred (11% Omata, 2002)
- Cognitive (-): less self-confident (11% Omata, 2002)

C. LOSS OF FAITH IN OTHERS:
- Cognitive (-): distrustful/suspicious (44% Brewster, 1998, 2000)
- Cognitive (-): loss of trust in others (52% Spitzberg & Rhea, 1999)

- Cognitive (-): more distrustful of others (33% Melton, 1994)
- Cognitive (-): more distrustful of man (32% Omata, 2002)
- Cognitive (-): more distrustful of teacher (10% Omata, 2002)

D. LOSS OF FAITH IN INSTITUTIONS:
- Cognitive (-): loss of faith in justice system (4% Pathé & Mullen, 1997)
- Cognitive (-): loss of faith in justice system (6% Spitzberg & Rhea, 1999)
- Cognitive (-): loss of faith in mental health system (6% Spitzberg & Rhea, 1999)
- Cognitive (-): loss of faith in police (9% Spitzberg & Rhea, 1999)

E. ISOLATION—ALIENATION:
- Cognitive (-): alienation (46% Spitzberg & Rhea, 1999)
- Cognitive (-): imprisoned (36% Boon & Sheridan, 2001)
- Cognitive (-): imprisoned (5% Sheridan et al., 2001a)
- Cognitive (-): loss of interest in relationships (41% Spitzberg & Rhea, 1999)
- Cognitive (-): sense of imprisonment (24% Spitzberg & Rhea, 1999)
- Cognitive (-): sense of imprisonment (5% Pathé & Mullen, 1997)
- Cognitive (-): sense of isolation (20% Spitzberg & Rhea, 1999)
- Cognitive (-): abandonment (feel self-abandoned more often) (1% Omata, 2002)

F. AGGRESSION—AGGRESSIVENESS:
- Cognitive (-): aggressive thoughts toward stalker (65% Pathé & Mullen, 1997)
- Cognitive (-): thought about harming stalker (34% Blackburn, 1999)
- Cognitive (-): thought about killing stalker (11% Blackburn, 1999)

G. APPREHENSION:
- Cognitive (-): constantly looking over shoulder (94% Brewster, 1998, 2000)
- Cognitive (-): feeling being watched (9% Pathé & Mullen, 1997)
- Cognitive (-): feeling followed (28% Spitzberg & Rhea, 1999)
- Cognitive (-): hypervigilence (8% Spitzberg & Rhea, 1999)

- Cognitive (-): lowered sense of safety (0% Romans et al., 1996)
- Cognitive (-): more cautious (88% Hall, 1997)
- Cognitive (-): overreactive (31% Spitzberg & Rhea, 1999)
- Cognitive (-): paranoia (36% Brewster, 1998, 2000)
- Cognitive (-): paranoia (38% Spitzberg & Rhea, 1999)
- Cognitive (-): paranoia (7% Pathé & Mullen, 1997)
- Cognitive (-): paranoid (41% Hall, 1997)
- Cognitive (-): very concerned about being stalked (30% Tjaden & Thoennes, 1998b)
- Cognitive (-): very concerned about personal safety (42% Tjaden & Thoennes, 1998b)
- Cognitive (-): think personal safety has gotten worse (68% Tjaden & Thoennes, 1998b)

H. DISTRACTION—CONFUSION:
- Cognitive (-): confused (28% Sheridan, 2001)
- Cognitive (-): could not focus on study/work (8% Suzuki, 1999)
- Cognitive (-): loss of concentration (43% Spitzberg & Rhea, 1999)
- Cognitive (-): loss of concentration (5% Pathé & Mullen, 1997)
- Cognitive (-): questioning choice in men (11% Brewster, 1998, 2000)
- Cognitive (-): distressing recollections/memories (37% Spitzberg & Rhea, 1999)
- Cognitive (-): intrusive recollections/flashbacks (55% Pathé & Mullen, 1997)
- Cognitive (-): flashback of memory of victimization (29% Omata, 2002)

I. COGNITIVE COMPENSATION—RESILIENCE:
- Cognitive (+): better safety awareness (42% Spitzberg & Rhea, 1999)
- Cognitive (+): did not want to hurt the pursuer's feelings (16% Blackburn, 1999)
- Cognitive (+): sense of direction or purpose (38% Spitzberg & Rhea, 1999)
- Cognitive (+): sense of personal strength (55% Spitzberg & Rhea, 1999)
- Cognitive (+): stronger self-concept (48% Spitzberg & Rhea, 1999)

PHYSICAL EFFECTS:
  A. SLEEP:
- Physical (-): insomnia (13% Brewster, 1998, 2000)
- Physical (-): nightmares (22% Spitzberg & Rhea, 1999)
- Physical (-): nightmares (4% Pathé & Mullen, 1997)
- Physical (-): major physical harm (5% Pathé & Mullen, 1997)
- Physical (-): minor physical harm (38% Pathé & Mullen, 1997)
- Physical (-): sleep disturbance (41% Gentile, 2001)
- Physical (-): sleep disturbance (74% Pathé & Mullen, 1997)
- Physical (-): sleeplessness (35% Spitzberg & Rhea, 1999)
- Physical (-): sleeplessness (5% Pathé & Mullen, 1997)
- Physical (-): insomnia (more frequently unable to sleep) (1% Omata, 2002)

  B. INJURY:
- Physical (-): assaulted/injured (39% Schwartz-Watts et al., 1997)
- Physical (-): bleeding (14% Pathé & Mullen, 1997)
- Physical (-): somewhat dangerous or life threatening (75% Kohn et al., 2000)
- Physical (-): injured (9% Gallagher et al., 1994)
- Physical (-): injury (15% Gill & Brockman, 1996)
- Physical (-): injury (9% Purcell et al., 2000)
- Physical (-): physical illness (11% Pathé & Mullen, 1997)
- Physical (-): physical illness (12.5% Spitzberg & Rhea, 1999)
- Physical (-): physical injuries (37% Brewster, 1998, 2000)
- Physical (-): physical injuries (31.5% perceiving as dangerous, Kohn et al., 2000)
- Physical (-): physical injury (5% Kong, 1996)
- Physical (-): physical injury (6% Spitzberg & Rhea, 1999)
- Physical (-): physically hurt—not severely (13% Blackburn, 1999)
- Physical (-): physically hurt—severely (4% Blackburn, 1999)
- Physical (-): serious woundings (44% Farnham et al., 2000)

  C. SELF-INJURY:
- Physical (-): attempted suicide in response to stalking (14% Blackburn, 1999)

- Physical (-): committed suicide (0% Nicastro et al., 2000)

D. ILLNESS/VITALITY:
- Physical (-): fatigue (11% Gentile, 2001)
- Physical (-): blackouts/fainting spells (4% Spitzberg & Rhea, 1999)

E. EATING/DIGESTIVE:
- Physical (-): appetite disturbance (48% Pathé & Mullen, 1997)
- Physical (-): eating disturbance (0% Gentile, 2001)
- Physical (-): loss of appetite (28% Spitzberg & Rhea, 1999)
- Physical (-): loss of appetite (4% Pathé & Mullen, 1997)
- Physical (-): persistent nausea (30% Pathé & Mullen, 1997)
- Physical (-): stomachaches (4% Gentile, 2001)
- Physical (-): appetite decreased (1% Omata, 2002)
- Physical (-): stomach etc. out of order (4% Omata, 2002)

F. ADDICTION:
- Physical (-): alcohol problems (10% Purcell et al., 2000)
- Physical (-): cigarette smoking (13% Purcell et al., 2000)

G. HEADACHE:
- Physical (-): headaches (32% Spitzberg & Rhea, 1999)
- Physical (-): headaches (4% Gentile, 2001)
- Physical (-): headaches (4% Pathé & Mullen, 1997)

SOCIAL EFFECTS:
- Social (-): avoided certain places/people (59% Budd & Mattinson, 2000)
- Social (-): curtailed social outings (59% Pathé et al., 2000)
- Social (-): curtailed social outings (70% Pathé & Mullen, 1997)
- Social (-): deterioration in intimate partner relationships (14% Purcell et al., 2000)
- Social (-): loneliness (39.5% Spitzberg & Rhea, 1999)
- Social (-): loss of family relationships (17.5% Spitzberg & Rhea, 1999)
- Social (-): loss of friends (25% Spitzberg & Rhea, 1999)
- Social (-): loss of romantic partner (37% Spitzberg & Rhea, 1999)
- Social (-): went out less than before (35% Budd & Mattinson, 2000)
- Social (-): worsening of family relations (12% Purcell et al., 2000)
- Social (+): stronger family relationships (46% Spitzberg & Rhea, 1999)
- Social (+): stronger relationships (46% Spitzberg & Rhea, 1999)

- Social (+): stronger romantic relationships (39.5% Spitzberg & Rhea, 1999)

RESOURCE EFFECTS:
- Resource (-): experienced diminished work productivity (45% Pathé et al., 2000)
- Resource (-): experienced lifestyle changes (90% Boon & Sheridan, 2001)
- Resource (-): financial costs (80% Brewster, 1998, 2000)
- Resource (-): loss of income/property (5% Spitzberg & Rhea, 1999)
- Resource (-): loss of job (4% Spitzberg & Rhea, 1999)
- Resource (-): lost jobs (10% Melton, 1994)
- Resource (-): mentioned how "expensive" ordeal was (14% Melton, 1994)
- Resource (-): took time off work (10% McLennan, 1996)

SPIRITUAL EFFECTS:
- Spiritual (-): loss of faith in god (10% Spitzberg & Rhea, 1999)

SOCIETAL EFFECTS: (no exemplars located)
- e.g., cultivation effects, such as society developing exaggerated or biased views of risk of stalking victimization
- e.g., cultivation effects, such as society expending disproportionate resources on security, law enforcement, etc., on stalking protection and prosecution
- e.g., legislative agenda effects, such as excessive application of felony penalties or charges in stalking cases

AMBIVALENT EFFECTS:
- Ambivalent (+/-): "mixed feelings about the attention" (10% Blackburn, 1999)
- Ambivalent (+/-): relief mixed with extreme nervousness after stalking ended (67% Sheridan, 2001)

MINIMAL EFFECTS:
- Minimal Effect (0): no emotional reaction (0% Gentile, 2001)
- Minimal Effect (0): no general reaction (22% Gentile, 2001)
- Minimal effect (0): not negatively affected or only affected "a little bit;" (25% Blackburn, 1999)

Appendix 7
Typology of Stalking and Unwanted Pursuit Coping Strategies and Tactics

MW: Moving With (or Toward): Any discursive effort(s) or act(s) to interact with and influence the pursuer discursively, rationally, or even through threat. Negative forms of MW are distinct from MAg because they still treat the problem as one resolvable through interaction. Exemplars include: arguing, yelling, criticizing, reconciling, or otherwise interacting with the pursuer in an effort to negotiate an "understanding" of boundaries or type of relationship.

- MW (general): face-to-face (58% Blackburn, 1999)
- MW (general): talked to troublesome partner (Levitt et al., 1996)
- MW (general): verbally resisted (Schneider, 1991),
- MW (general): writing (10% Blackburn, 1999)
- MW (acceptance/reconciliation): actively cutting off communications with others (e.g., retracted charges, refused to respond to phone calls, refused to talk with police, advisors, counselors, etc.) (Fry & Barker, 2001)
- MW (acceptance/reconciliation): avoidance tactics: withholding complaints (Roloff & Ifert, 2000)
- MW (acceptance/reconciliation): compliance: accepting phone calls (61% Kileen & Dunn, 1998)
- MW (acceptance/reconciliation): compliance: continuing to have sex (4% Kileen & Dunn, 1998)
- MW (acceptance/reconciliation): compliance: going somewhere with defendant (7% Kileen & Dunn, 1998)
- MW (acceptance/reconciliation): compliance: initiating contact with defendant (10% Kileen & Dunn, 1998)
- MW (acceptance/reconciliation): compliance: letting defendant in residence (18% Kileen & Dunn, 1998)
- MW (acceptance/reconciliation): compliance: meeting defendant somewhere (9% Kileen & Dunn, 1998)
- MW (acceptance/reconciliation): compliance: not reporting (27% Kileen & Dunn, 1998)
- MW (acceptance/reconciliation): compliance: not returning investigator calls (11% Kileen & Dunn, 1998)

- MW (acceptance/reconciliation): compliance: opening the door to talk (27% Kileen & Dunn, 1998)
- MW (acceptance/reconciliation): compliance: recanting (8% Kileen & Dunn, 1998)
- MW (acceptance/reconciliation): compliance: requesting case dismissal (16% Kileen & Dunn, 1998)
- MW (acceptance/reconciliation): compliance: requesting no jail or lesser term (1% Kileen & Dunn, 1998)
- MW (acceptance/reconciliation): compliance: requesting report only (14% Kileen & Dunn, 1998)
- MW (acceptance/reconciliation): compliance: returning prior to case (28% Kileen & Dunn, 1998)
- MW (acceptance/reconciliation): compliance: trying to reason/interact (38% Kileen & Dunn, 1998)
- MW (acceptance/reconciliation): compliance: visiting defendant in jail (3% Kileen & Dunn, 1998)
- MW (acceptance/reconciliation): compliance: writing to defendant (3% Kileen & Dunn, 1998)
- MW (acceptance/reconciliation): cooperate with attacker (Harris & Miller, 2000)
- MW (acceptance/reconciliation): current contact occurring (Langhinrichsen-Rohling et al., 2000)
- MW (acceptance/reconciliation): defusion: masking (e.g., went along with, stalled, made a joke, tried to defuse) (Gruber, 1989)
- MW (acceptance/reconciliation): more love and affection toward partner (e.g., I express greater affection to my partner) (Pollina & Snell, 1999)
- MW (acceptance/reconciliation): returning during case (7% Kileen & Dunn, 1998)
- MW (acceptance/reconciliation): went along with request (Schneider, 1991)
- MW (deception): disengagement: hiding information about self—deception ("Lying to or misleading the other person on information about oneself") (Hess, 2003; see also Hess, 2002)
- MW (deception): tease (e.g., flirt, say you'll call, say yes but don't show up, say maybe some other time, etc.) (Rowatt et al., 1999)
- MW (excuses: attachments): distancing techniques: claims of existing interpersonal attachment (Jacobs, 1994)
- MW (excuses: attachments): escape (e.g., say you already have plans, make up an excuse, say you're already in a relationship, etc.) (Rowatt et al., 1999)

- MW (excuses: misc.): distancing techniques: extracurricular-role-obligation excuses (Jacobs, 1994)
- MW (excuses—misc.): distancing techniques: parental-recrimination excuses (Jacobs, 1994)
- MW (excuses—misc.): feigned interest followed by unforeseen-circumstance excuses or appeals to defeasibility (Jacobs, 1994)
- MW (excuses—misc.): initial cooling out tactics (polite refusal, excuses, joking) (Snow et al., 1991)
- MW (interaction management): disengagement: hiding information about self—restrict topics ("Limiting conversation to topics that are not intimate") (Hess, 2003; see also Hess, 2002)
- MW (interactional: derogate): active resistance: using sarcasm (3% Kileen & Dunn, 1998)
- MW (interactional: derogate): cognitive dissociation: derogating other person—degrade ("Perceiving the other person as less than human, such as by ignoring her/his feelings, or seeing the other person as incompetent") (Hess, 2003; see also Hess, 2002)
- MW (interactional: derogate): confrontation: assertive personal responses (e.g., attacked verbally, attacked physically, demanded harasser stop, confronted) (Gruber, 1989)
- MW (interactional: derogate): cursed at suspect (7% Nicastro et al., 2000)
- MW (interactional: derogate): expressive unifunctional message (i.e., "Criticize and condemn the harasser and his behavior") (Bingham & Burleson, 1989)
- MW (interactional: derogate): used hostile voice (5% Nicastro et al., 2000)
- MW (interactional: derogate): yelled at stalker (58% Blackburn, 1999)
- MW (interactional: derogate): yelled at suspect (9% Nicastro et al., 2000)
- MW (interactional: disconfirmation): cognitive dissociation: disregarding—discount message ("Disregarding or minimizing what the other person says") (Hess, 2003; see also Hess, 2002)
- MW (interactional: disconfirmation): disengagement: interact less personally—humoring ("Considering the other person to be eccentric and someone just to be tolerated, but not taken seriously") (Hess, 2003; see also Hess, 2002)
- MW (interactional: disconfirmation): disengagement: interact less personally—impersonal ("Treating the other person like a stranger; that is, interacting with her/him as a role rather than as a unique individual") (Hess, 2003; see also Hess, 2002)
- MW (interactional: disconfirmation): nonempathetic cooling-out tactics (studied seriousness, defensive incivility, self-evident justification) (Snow et al., 1991)

- MW (negotiation: boundary setting): active resistance: stating boundary (70% Kileen & Dunn, 1998)
- MW (negotiation: boundary setting): demanded to be left alone (Schneider, 1991)
- MW (negotiation: boundary setting): indicated they didn't want to see person (e.g., not accept calls) (26% Jason et al., 1984)
- MW (negotiation: boundary setting): initial cooling out tactics (polite refusal, excuses, joking) (Snow et al., 1991)
- MW (negotiation: boundary setting): negotiation: direct request (e.g., mildly responded directly, asked harasser to stop, threatened to tell others, tried to reason with) (Gruber, 1989)
- MW (negotiation: boundary setting): specifically requested person stop (female victims 78% Bjerregaard, 2000)
- MW (negotiation: boundary setting): specifically requested person stop behavior (male victims 55% Bjerregaard, 2000)
- MW (negotiation: boundary setting): told offenders to go away or leave them alone (6% Morewitz, 2003)
- MW (negotiation: boundary setting): told suspect what he/she was doing was wrong (13% Nicastro et al., 2000)
- MW (negotiation: boundary-setting): declaring topics taboo (Roloff & Ifert, 2000)
- MW (negotiation: conflict): active resistance: arguing with defendant (19% Kileen & Dunn, 1998)
- MW (negotiation: conflict): active resistance: yelling/swearing (19% Kileen & Dunn, 1998)
- MW (negotiation: conflict): angry letters to stalker (5% Blackburn, 1999)
- MW (negotiation: conflict): angry phone calls (18% Blackburn, 1999)
- MW (negotiation: conflict): argued with stalker (2% Brewster, 1998, 2000)
- MW (negotiation: conflict): defensive (Snow et al., 1991)
- MW (negotiation: confrontation): confront the pursuer on their own (Hills & Taplin, 1998)
- MW (negotiation: confrontation): confronted (16% Fisher et al., 1999, 2000)
- MW (negotiation: confrontation): confronted other in public (respondent, partner, both, neither: 3%, 13%, 3%, 82%) (Holloway, 1994)
- MW (negotiation: confrontation): confronted partner (Yoshihama, 2002)
- MW (negotiation: confrontation): confronted stalker (Fremouw et al., 1997)
- MW (negotiation: confrontation): confronted/talked to stalker (38% Morrison, 2001)

- MW (negotiation: confrontation): physically confronted suspect (18% Nicastro et al., 2000)
- MW (negotiation: deflection): rhetorical minimal message (i.e., "Either redefine the harasser's behavior as something other than harassment—e.g., teasing—, or redescribe the situation so that the harassment is implied to be problematic, but also include denigration of the harasser, complaints, threats, or fail to make situational goals clear") (Bingham & Burleson, 1989)
- MW (negotiation: emotional): expressive minimal message (i.e., "React emotionally toward the harasser") (Bingham & Burleson, 1989)
- MW (negotiation: emotional): negative arousal (e.g., expressing negative arousal, confrontation) (see Burgoon et al., 1989; Hosman & Siltanen, 1995)
- MW (negotiation: rationality): communicated that attention was unwanted (85.5% Blackburn, 1999)
- MW (negotiation: rationality): conventional minimal message (i.e., "Deflect the harasser's threat and/or issue a directive for the harasser to stop and change this behavior") (Bingham & Burleson, 1989)
- MW (negotiation: rationality): conventional multifunctional message (i.e., "Deflect the harasser's threat and/or issue a directive for the harasser to stop or change his behavior, but do so while attempting to show consideration for the harasser") (Bingham & Burleson, 1989)
- MW (negotiation: rationality): conventional unifunctional message (i.e., "Deflect the harasser's threat and/or issue a directive for the harasser to stop or change his behavior") (Bingham & Burleson, 1989)
- MW (negotiation: rationality): expressive multifunctional message (i.e., "Express vague or confused thoughts and feelings toward the harassment predicament and the need to deal with it, without including overtly negative affect toward the harasser") (Bingham & Burleson, 1989)
- MW (negotiation: rationality): rhetorical multifunctional message (i.e., "Redefine the situation. Persuade the harasser to retract his threat and/or to discontinue or change his behavior, while also deflecting the implication that the harasser has a negative identity or that his behavior has harmed the personal or working relationship") (Bingham & Burleson, 1989)
- MW (negotiation: rationality): rhetorical unifunctional message (i.e., "Redefine the situation. Persuade the harasser to retract his threat and/or to discontinue or change his behavior") (Bingham & Burleson, 1989)
- MW (negotiation: rationality): tried to be nice (politely talk, tried to reason) (20% Jason et al., 1984)

- MW (negotiation: relational definition): ended or tried to end relationship (Levitt et al., 1996)
- MW (negotiation: relational definition): friendly negotiation (e.g., say you value them as friend, say you just want to be friends, etc.) (Rowatt et al., 1999)
- MW (negotiation: relational definition): wanted to remain friends or were unclear in the message communicated (20% Jason et al., 1984)
- MW (negotiation: threat): active resistance: threatening to call 911 (27% Kileen & Dunn, 1998)
- MW (negotiation: threat): negotiation: direct request (e.g., mildly responded directly, asked harasser to stop, threatened to tell others, tried to reason with) (Gruber, 1989)
- MW (negotiation: threat): threaten to harm perpetrator (4% Nicastro et al., 2000)
- MW (negotiation: threat): threatened to call police (14% Nicastro et al., 2000)
- MW (negotiation: threat): threatened to get stalker in trouble at work (4% Brewster, 1998, 2000)
- MW (negotiation: threat): threatened to tell others at work (Schneider, 1991)
- MW (negotiation: threat): threatening to call police (13% Brewster, 1998, 2000)
- MW (negotiation: threat): verbal threats (28% Blackburn, 1999)
- MW (seek pursuer reform): suggested that he get help (Yoshihama, 2002)
- MW (seek sympathy): cried in front of perpetrator (5% Nicastro et al., 2000)
- MW (seek sympathy): emotional expression and reaction (e.g., I start feeling depressed and blue) (Pollina & Snell, 1999)
- MW (seek sympathy): pleading with stalker (19% Brewster, 1998, 2000)
- MW (threat management): talking down "hot" (axis I: intense, escalating) threats (i.e., overdose with agreement, divide attention with choices, limit setting and agreement to disagree, debriefing) (Maier, 1996)
- MW (threat management): talking up "cold" (axis II: controlling) threats (i.e., record-monitor-evaluate-confront threatener; identify threat—calm down—disclose—respond to specific nature of threat) (Maier, 1996)

MAg: Moving Against: Any intentional effort(s) or act(s) to cause material harm, injury or damage to the quality of life of the pursuer. The proximal intent is to harm the pursuer, not to engage in interaction, even though the distal intent may be to deter or otherwise incapacitate the pursuer's ability or inclination to continue the harassment. Exemplars include: physically attacking or obtaining the assistance of others in attacking the pursuer, filing charges or legally prosecuting the pursuer, attempting to damage the career or livelihood of the pursuer. Note: discursive efforts such as threats, criticism, sarcasm, yelling, etc., are classified as "moving with."

- MAg (abuse, general): abused offender/family (5% Dussuyer, 2000)
- MAg (legal): charged/legal action (1% Dussuyer, 2000)
- MAg (legal): filed civil charges (1% Fisher et al., 1999, 2000)
- MAg (legal): filed criminal charges (2% Fisher et al., 1999, 2000)
- MAg (legal): filed grievance with University (3% Fisher et al., 1999, 2000)
- MAg (legal): filed police report (94% Nicastro et al., 2000)
- MAg (legal): gone to court (female victims 9% Bjerregaard, 2000)
- MAg (legal): help-seeking: asking for a jail term (19% Kileen & Dunn, 1998)
- MAg (legal): help-seeking: insisting on arrest (30% Kileen & Dunn, 1998)
- MAg (legal): help-seeking: insisting on prosecution (37% Kileen & Dunn, 1998)
- MAg (legal): initiated lawsuit (45% Blaauw, Winkel, Arensman, et al., 2000)
- MAg (legal): pressed charges (69% Nicastro et al., 2000)
- MAg (legal): took action (harassment charges, had 3rd party talk to harasser) (34% Jason et al., 1984)
- MAg (physical): active resistance: fighting/struggling (25% Kileen & Dunn, 1998)
- MAg (physical): asked someone else to hurt/threaten perpetrator (4% Nicastro et al., 2000)
- MAg (physical): assaulted stalker (19% Blaauw, Winkel, Arensman, et al., 2000)
- MAg (physical): fought off assailant (24% Omata, 2002)
- MAg (physical): confrontation: assertive personal responses (e.g., attacked verbally, attacked physically, demanded harasser stop, confronted) (Gruber, 1989)
- MAg (physical): harmed stalker in self defense (12% Blackburn, 1999)
- MAg (physical): harmed stalker not in self-defense (4% Blackburn, 1999)
- MAg (physical): hostility (e.g., look of disgust, walk away, ignore, keep conversation short, slap him/her, etc.) (Rowatt et al., 1999)

- MAg (physical): physically fled if attacked (Harris & Miller, 2000)
- MAg (physical): physically resisted (Schneider, 1991)

MAw: Moving Away: Any effort(s) or act(s) to avoid contact with the pursuer, including: not being where the pursuer is or is likely to be, hardening the target to the pursuer's access or deterring the pursuer's inclination to engage in further harassment. Exemplars include: enhancing home security, screening calls or changing the telephone number, moving, changing careers, and changing everyday routines.

- MAw (proximity access—general): avoidance: leaving scene (40% Kileen & Dunn, 1998)
- MAw (proximity access—general) avoidance ("Trying not to be in the presence of the other person") (Hess, 2003; see also Hess, 2002)
- MAw (proximity access—general): avoidance: obstruction (e.g., avoided) (Gruber, 1989)
- MAw (proximity access—general): avoided (11% Nicastro et al., 2000)
- MAw (proximity access—general): avoided (27% Morrison, 2001)
- MAw (proximity access—general): avoided or attempted to avoid (43% Fisher et al., 1999, 2000)
- MAw (proximity access—general): avoided person (Levitt et al., 1996)
- MAw (proximity access—general): emotion-focused behavior: avoidance ("efforts to distract from or avoid the stressor") (Tamres et al., 2002)
- MAw (proximity access—general): emotion-focused: distancing/avoidance (Bouchard et al., 1997)
- MAw (communicative access): avoidance tactics (tie signs, nonverbal cues of disinterest, flight) (Snow et al., 1991)
- MAw (communicative access—phone): active resistance: hanging up (23% Kileen & Dunn, 1998)
- MAw (communicative access—phone): avoidance: changing phone number (24% Kileen & Dunn, 1998)
- MAw (communicative access—phone): avoidance: screening phone calls (40% Kileen & Dunn, 1998)
- MAw (communicative access—phone): caller ID (5% Fisher et al., 1999, 2000)
- MAw (communicative access—phone): changed phone # (Fremouw et al., 1997)
- MAw (communicative access—phone): changed phone # or screened (18% Dussuyer, 2000)
- MAw (communicative access—phone): changed phone line (6% Morrison, 2001)

- MAw (communicative access—phone): changed phone number (14% Brewster, 1998, 2000)
- MAw (communicative access—phone): changed phone number (24% Meloy & Boyd, 2003)
- MAw (communicative access—phone): changed phone number (62% Kamphuis & Emmelkamp, 2001)
- MAw (communicative access—phone): changed phone number (9% Nicastro et al., 2000)
- MAw (communicative access—phone): changed phone number (female victims 22% Bjerregaard, 2000)
- MAw (communicative access—phone): changed phone number (male victims 17% Bjerregaard, 2000)
- MAw (communicative access—phone): changed telephone number (14% Purcell et al., 2002)
- MAw (communicative access—phone): changed to unlisted telephone number (25% Romans et al., 1996)
- MAw (communicative access—phone): changing phone # or call-blocking (32% Brewster, 1998, 2000)
- MAw (communicative access—phone): hung up when called (16% Nicastro et al., 2000)
- MAw (communicative access—phone): not returning phone calls (29% Blackburn, 1999)
- MAw (communicative access—phone): obtained answering service (11% Gentile, 2001)
- MAw (communicative access—phone): obtained caller ID (13% Brewster, 1998, 2000)
- MAw (communicative access—phone): obtained caller ID/*69 (11% Nicastro et al., 2000)
- MAw (communicative access: phone): phone (53% Blackburn, 1999)
- MAw (communicative access—phone): screened phone calls (14% Nicastro et al., 2000)
- MAw (communicative access—phone): tried to protect self (e.g., changed phone number, moved) (18% Jason et al., 1984)
- MAw (communicative access—phone): unlisted phone (81% Blaauw, Winkel, Arensman, et al., 2000)
- MAw (communicative access—phone): unlisted telephone number (15% Gentile, 2001)
- MAw (communicative access—phone): withdraw (e.g., *don't answer doorbell, don't answer phone*, more than two drinks a day, glad to be alive) (Meyer & Taylor, 1986)
- MAw (information control): anonymity (Pedersen, 1999)
- MAw (information control): changed name (1% Dussuyer, 2000)

- MAw (information control): changed name/identity (2% Morrison, 2001)
- MAw (information control): no listing of home address in phone directory (30% Guy et al., 1992)
- MAw (information control): refusing to disclose personal data to patients (41% Guy et al., 1992)
- MAw (information control): unlisted home address (22% Gentile, 2001)
- MAw (information control): used maiden name at work (2% Romans et al., 1996)
- MAw (interactional: exclusion): avoidance tactics (tie signs, nonverbal cues of disinterest, flight) (Snow et al., 1991)
- MAw (interactional: exclusion): avoidance: avoiding—ignoring ("Acting as if the other person is not there") (Hess, 2003; see also Hess, 2002)
- MAw (interactional: exclusion): avoidance: reducing interaction during encounter—reserve ("Being unusually quiet and uncommunicative when with the other person") (Hess, 2003; see also Hess, 2002)
- MAw (interactional: exclusion): avoidance: reducing interaction during encounter—shorten interaction ("Doing what it takes to end the interaction as quickly as possible") (Hess, 2003; see also Hess, 2002)
- MAw (interactional: exclusion): avoided discussing issue with person (Levitt et al., 1996)
- MAw (interactional: exclusion): did not acknowledge messages (9% Fisher et al., 1999, 2000)
- MAw (interactional: exclusion): disengagement: disengaged communication style—inattention ("Giving as little attention as possible to the other person") (Hess, 2003; see also Hess, 2002)
- MAw (interactional: exclusion): disengagement: disengaged communication style—nonimmediacy ("Displaying verbal or nonverbal cues that minimize closeness or availability") (Hess, 2003; see also Hess, 2002)
- MAw (interactional: exclusion): distancing (e.g., increase distance interactionally) (see Burgoon et al., 1989; Hosman & Siltanen, 1995)
- MAw (interactional: exclusion): don't argue with attacker (Harris & Miller, 2000)
- MAw (interactional: exclusion): hostility (e.g., look of disgust, walk away, ignore, keep conversation short, slap him/her, etc.) (Rowatt et al., 1999)
- MAw (interactional: exclusion): interaction control (e.g., topic change, postpone interaction) (see Burgoon et al., 1989; Hosman & Siltanen, 1995)

- MAw (interactional exclusion): avoidance: reducing interaction during encounter—group interaction ("Avoiding one-on-one interactions with the person") (Hess, 2003; see also Hess, 2002)
- MAw (proximity access—escape): left the partner permanently (Yoshihama, 2002)
- MAw (proximity access—escape): left the partner temporarily (Yoshihama, 2002)
- MAw (proximity access—isolation): avoidance: hiding (32% Kileen & Dunn, 1998)
- MAw (proximity access—isolation): avoided going out of their houses (55% Kamphuis & Emmelkamp, 2001)
- MAw (proximity access—isolation): avoided social outings (63% Blaauw, Winkel, Arensman, et al., 2000)
- MAw (proximity access—isolation): became reclusive/high security (1% Dussuyer, 2000)
- MAw (proximity access—isolation): changed clinical population (7% Gentile, 2001)
- MAw (proximity access—isolation): curtailed social outings (59% Pathé et al., 2000)
- MAw (proximity access—isolation): disengagement: interact less personally—restraint ("Curtailing social behaviors that one would normally do, which (if done) would have led to greater relational closeness) (Hess, 2003; see also Hess, 2002)
- MAw (proximity access—isolation): emotion-focused behavior: isolation ("removal of oneself from social activities") (Tamres et al., 2002)
- MAw (proximity access—isolation): help-seeking: making a victim information screening (9% Kileen & Dunn, 1998)
- MAw (proximity access—isolation): isolation (Pedersen, 1999)
- MAw (proximity access—isolation): restricted social outings (16% Purcell et al., 2002)
- MAw (proximity access—isolation): screened new patients for potentially dangerous behavior (33% Gentile, 2001)
- MAw (proximity access—isolation): social withdrawal (e.g., I avoid being with people) (Pollina & Snell, 1999)
- MAw (proximity access—isolation): stay home (e.g., rarely leave home, dress moderately, etc.) (Meyer & Taylor, 1986)
- MAw (proximity access—isolation): went "underground" (40% Blaauw, Winkel, Arensman, et al., 2000)
- MAw (proximity access—job/school): avoidance: changing jobs (2% Kileen & Dunn, 1998)

- MAw (proximity access—job/school): avoidance: removal of self (e.g., quit or transferred) (Gruber, 1989)
- MAw (proximity access—job/school): changed careers (27% Pathé et al., 2000)
- MAw (proximity access—job/school): changed employment (Meloy & Boyd, 2003)
- MAw (proximity access—job/school): changed job (male victims 7% Bjerregaard, 2000)
- MAw (proximity access—job/school): changed jobs (21% Blaauw, Winkel, Arensman, et al., 2000)
- MAw (proximity access—job/school): changed jobs (female victims 8% Bjerregaard, 2000)
- MAw (proximity access—job/school): changed work and/or school (4% Nicastro et al., 2000)
- MAw (proximity access—job/school): quit job or worked less (39% Blaauw, Winkel, Arensman, et al., 2000)
- MAw (proximity access—job/school): reported absenteeism (15% Purcell et al., 2002)
- MAw (proximity access—job/school): stopped work or school (23% Kamphuis & Emmelkamp, 2001)
- MAw (proximity access—location): avoidance: moving within the area (22% Kileen & Dunn, 1998)
- MAw (proximity access—location): avoidance: staying with family/friends (37% Kileen & Dunn, 1998)
- MAw (proximity access—location): changed address (15% Dussuyer, 2000)
- MAw (proximity access—location): changed address (Fremouw et al., 1997)
- MAw (proximity access—location): changed address (15% Meloy & Boyd, 2003)
- MAw (proximity access—location): changed addresses within or moved to another city (30% Kamphuis & Emmelkamp, 2001)
- MAw (proximity access—location): changed clinical setting (0% Gentile, 2001)
- MAw (proximity access—location): changed residence (2% Romans et al., 1996)
- MAw (proximity access—location): changed residence (female victims 22% Bjerregaard, 2000)
- MAw (proximity access—location): changed residence (male victims 7% Bjerregaard, 2000)
- MAw (proximity access—location): changed schedule (Fremouw et al., 1997)

- MAw (proximity access—location): left their residence to escape pursuer (10% Morewitz, 2003)
- MAw (proximity access—location): moved (3% Fisher et al., 1999, 2000)
- MAw (proximity access—location): moved (38% Melton, 1994)
- MAw (proximity access—location): moved (48% Kohn et al., 2000)
- MAw (proximity access—location): moved elsewhere (16% Nicastro et al., 2000)
- MAw (proximity access—location): moved residence (23% Pathé et al., 2000)
- MAw (proximity access—location): moved to avoid contact (respondent, partner, both, neither: 42%, 10%, 5%, 43%) (Holloway, 1994)
- MAw (proximity access—location): moved to different house/school/area (13% Morrison, 2001)
- MAw (proximity access—location): moved to new community (1% Romans et al., 1996)
- MAw (proximity access—location): moving (33% Brewster, 1998, 2000)
- MAw (proximity access—location): moving out of the area (6% Kileen & Dunn, 1998)
- MAw (proximity access—location): obtained temporary shelter (7% Morewitz, 2003)
- MAw (proximity access—location): relocated (44% Blaauw, Winkel, Arensman, et al., 2000)
- MAw (proximity access—location): relocated (7% Purcell et al., 2002)
- MAw (proximity access—location): relocated home (4% Gentile, 2001)
- MAw (proximity access—location): seek shelter (71/52% relentless vs. infrequently, Mechanic, Uhlmansiek, et al., 2000)
- MAw (proximity access—location): sought help from shelter (6% Brewster, 1998, 2000)
- MAw (proximity access—location): stayed with friends or family (5% Nicastro et al., 2000)
- MAw (proximity access—routine): active resistance: not letting defendant in (40% Kileen & Dunn, 1998)
- MAw (proximity access—routine): altered daily routines (31% Purcell et al., 2002)
- MAw (proximity access—routine): altered lifestyle (63% Purcell et al., 2002)
- MAw (proximity access—routine): changed daily travel routes (62% Kamphuis & Emmelkamp, 2001)
- MAw (proximity access—routine): changed habit patterns (55% Meloy & Boyd, 2003)
- MAw (proximity access—routine): changed lifestyle/routines/habits (5% Dussuyer, 2000)

- MAw (proximity access—routine): changed routine (93% Kohn et al., 2000)
- MAw (proximity access—routine): changed routine to avoid contact (respondent, partner, both, neither: 47%, 4%, 3%, 47%) (Holloway, 1994)
- MAw (proximity access—routine): changing activity patterns (64% Brewster, 1998, 2000)
- MAw (proximity access—routine): modified usual activities (77% Pathé et al., 2000)
- MAw (target hardening): avoidance: taking security measures (15% Kileen & Dunn, 1998)
- MAw (target hardening): enhanced security (7% Nicastro et al., 2000)
- MAw (target hardening): home security (51% Kamphuis & Emmelkamp, 2001)
- MAw (target hardening): improved security (4% Fisher et al., 1999, 2000)
- MAw (target hardening): increased home security (29% Purcell et al., 2002)
- MAw (target hardening): increased home/work security (43% Meloy & Boyd, 2003)
- MAw (target hardening): increased work security (16% Purcell et al., 2002)
- MAw (target hardening): installed home alarm system (11% Gentile, 2001)
- MAw (target hardening): installed office alarm system (0% Gentile, 2001)
- MAw (target hardening): installed security system (female victims 7% Bjerregaard, 2000)
- MAw (target hardening): installing office alarm system (8% Guy et al., 1992)
- MAw (target hardening): leaving lights on (59% Brewster, 1998, 2000)
- MAw (target hardening): locking doors/windows (72% Brewster, 1998, 2000)
- MAw (target hardening): sought additional security (64% Pathé et al., 2000)
- MAw (target hardening): took additional security measures (65% Blaauw, Winkel, Arensman, et al., 2000)
- MAw (target hardening): used home security devices (7% Romans et al., 1996)

MI:　　Moving Inward: Any effort(s) or act(s) to repair, empower, enrich, or merely focus on self as the source of managing the disruption of unwanted pursuit, independent of others' role (i.e., the pursuer, third parties) in the episode. Exemplars include: therapy, keeping active, taking drugs, contemplating the situation, and various means of "preparing" for potential encounter(s) with the pursuer, such as taking self-defense classes, buying a gun, carrying pepper spray, etc.

- MI (acceptance): accept responsibility (Stith et al., 1992)
- MI (acceptance): acceptance coping (e.g., I get used to the idea that it happened) (Pollina & Snell, 1999)
- MI (acceptance): behavioral disengagement (e.g., I just give up trying to reach a desirable solution) (Pollina & Snell, 1999)
- MI (acceptance): emotion-focused behavior: self-blame ("focuses on his or her own responsibility") (Tamres et al., 2002)
- MI (catharsis): emotion-focused behavior: venting ("outward, sometimes public, release of emotion") (Tamres et al., 2002)
- MI (catharsis): focus on and venting of emotions (e.g., I get upset and let my emotions out) (Pollina & Snell, 1999)
- MI (catharsis): mobilizing support (e.g., let your feelings out somehow) (Valentiner et al., 1996)
- MI (chemical): alcohol and drug use (e.g., I use alcohol or drugs to help me get through it) (Pollina & Snell, 1999)
- MI (chemical): obtained medication (0% Gentile, 2001)
- MI (chemical): took medication (2% Nicastro et al., 2000)
- MI (chemical): used alcohol or drugs (Levitt et al., 1996)
- MI (chemical): used alcohol or drugs (Yoshihama, 2002)
- MI (chemical): withdraw (e.g., don't answer doorbell, don't answer phone, *more than two drinks a day*, glad to be alive) (Meyer & Taylor, 1986)
- MI (cognitive control): cognitive dissociation: cognitive/emotional detachment ("Perceiving or feeling a lack of attachment with the other") (Hess, 2003; see also Hess, 2002)
- MI (cognitive control): did things to calm down or relax (Yoshihama, 2002)
- MI (cognitive control): don't worry about being attacked (Harris & Miller, 2000)
- MI (cognitive control): problem avoidance (e.g., I refuse to spend much time thinking about it) (Pollina & Snell, 1999)
- MI (cognitive control): restraint coping (e.g., I make sure not to make matters worse by acting too soon) (Pollina & Snell, 1999)
- MI (cognitive control): stress reduction (e.g., think positive thoughts, use techniques to reduce stress) (Meyer & Taylor, 1986)

- MI (cognitive control): suppressing arguments (Roloff & Ifert, 2000)
- MI (contemplation): active cognitive (e.g., "how much did you think about strategies for dealing with the situation") (Harnish et al., 2000)
- MI (contemplation): cautious action—approach problem cautiously but not passively, such as looking at options (Hobfoll & Schröder, 2001)
- MI (contemplation): emotion-focused behavior: rumination (dwelling on or "focusing on one's problems and their implications") (Tamres et al., 2002)
- MI (contemplation): planning (e.g., I think about how I might best handle the problem) (Pollina & Snell, 1999)
- MI (contemplation): problem analysis (e.g., I think about the circumstances and learn from my mistake) (Pollina & Snell, 1999)
- MI (contemplation): problem-focused behavior: planning ("gathering information, reviewing possible solutions to a problem") (Tamres et al., 2002)
- MI (contemplation): reasoning (70% Brewster, 1998, 2000)
- MI (contemplation): solitude (Pedersen, 1999)
- MI (contemplation): suppression of competing activities (e.g., I focus on dealing with this problem, and if necessary let other things slide a little) (Pollina & Snell, 1999)
- MI (contemplation): thought about moving (14% Melton, 1994)
- MI (denial): avoidance: ignoring (21% Kileen & Dunn, 1998)
- MI (denial): avoidance: non-recognition (e.g., ignored, did nothing) (Gruber, 1989)
- MI (denial): denial (e.g., I refuse to believe that it has happened) (Pollina & Snell, 1999)
- MI (denial): denial (Stith et al., 1992)
- MI (denial): emotion-focused behavior: denial ("denying the stressor exists, distancing oneself cognitively from the stressor and minimizing the importance of the stressor") (Tamres et al., 2002)
- MI (denial): emotion-focused: denial (Bouchard et al., 1997)
- MI (denial): ignored legal action (7% Nicastro et al., 2000)
- MI (denial): ignored offender (1% Dussuyer, 2000)
- MI (denial): ignored problem (Levitt et al., 1996)
- MI (denial): ignored stalker (38% Morrison, 2001)
- MI (denial): ignored suspect (9% Nicastro et al., 2000)
- MI (denial): ignored/hung up (Fremouw et al., 1997)
- MI (denial): ignoring (43% Brewster, 1998, 2000)
- MI (denial): did nothing (29% Omata, 2002)
- MI (denial): minimization (e.g., can't imagine worse, worst experience ever) (Meyer & Taylor, 1986)

- MI (denial): minimized the seriousness of situation (Yoshihama, 2002)
- MI (denial): suppression (e.g., put rape behind me, no reason to think about it) (Meyer & Taylor, 1986)
- MI (distraction): active (e.g., keep exceptionally busy, keep busy with work) (Meyer & Taylor, 1986)
- MI (distraction): avoidance (e.g., "how much did you do things to take your mind off the situation") (Harnish et al., 2000)
- MI (distraction): avoidance: tendency to withdraw or focus on something else (Hobfoll & Schröder, 2001)
- MI (distraction): emotion-focused behavior: avoidance ("efforts to distract from or avoid the stressor") (Tamres et al., 2002)
- MI (distraction): emotion-focused behavior: exercise ("a physical outlet for distress or as a way to distract") (Tamres et al., 2002)
- MI (distraction): mental disengagement (e.g., I daydream about things other than this) (Pollina & Snell, 1999)
- MI (distraction): self-control, escape (Stith et al., 1992)
- MI (immobility): no action (30% Gentile, 2001)
- MI (immobility): reserve (Pedersen, 1999)
- MI (monitoring): active resistance: logging behaviors (19% Kileen & Dunn, 1998)
- MI (monitoring): documented/collected evidence against stalker (18% Morrison, 2001)
- MI (monitoring): sought information (Yoshihama, 2002)
- MI (positivity): emotion-focused behavior: positive reappraisal ("trying to find the good in the situation") (Tamres et al., 2002)
- MI (positivity): emotion-focused behavior: positive self-talk ("making self-statements that encourage oneself to feel better") (Tamres et al., 2002)
- MI (positivity): emotion-focused behavior: wishful thinking ("wishing that the stressor were not there or imagining that the stressor will disappear on its own") (Tamres et al., 2002)
- MI (positivity): focused on positive aspects of partner or relationship (Yoshihama, 2002)
- MI (positivity): humor coping (e.g., I kid around about the circumstances) (Pollina & Snell, 1999)
- MI (positivity): positive distancing (e.g., accepted the next best thing to what you wanted) (Valentiner et al., 1996)
- MI (positivity): positive reappraisal (e.g., "how much did you try to see things in a positive way") (Harnish et al., 2000)
- MI (positivity): positive reinterpretation and growth (e.g., I look for something good in what is happening) (Pollina & Snell, 1999)
- MI (positivity): self-bolstering (e.g., I provide myself with reassurance that I can cope with the situation) (Pollina & Snell, 1999)

- MI (positivity): stress reduction (e.g., think positive thoughts, use techniques to reduce stress) (Meyer & Taylor, 1986)
- MI (positivity): wishful thinking (e.g., I wish that the situation would go away or somehow be over with) (Pollina & Snell, 1999)
- MI (positivity): wishful thinking (e.g., wished that you could change the way you felt) (Valentiner et al., 1996)
- MI (positivity): withdraw (e.g., don't answer doorbell, don't answer phone, more than two drinks a day, *glad to be alive*) (Meyer & Taylor, 1986)
- MI (preparation): carry a cellular phone (Harris & Miller, 2000)
- MI (preparation): precaution (e.g., always lock door, walk with keys ready, etc.) (Meyer & Taylor, 1986)
- MI (preparation—aggressive): active resistance: getting a weapon (2% Kileen & Dunn, 1998)
- MI (preparation—aggressive): be prepared to shoot an attacker (Harris & Miller, 2000)
- MI (preparation—aggressive): bought gun (female victims 3% Bjerregaard, 2000)
- MI (preparation—aggressive): bought gun (male victims 3% Bjerregaard, 2000)
- MI (preparation—aggressive): carried mace or pepper spray (4% Gentile, 2001)
- MI (preparation—aggressive): carried repellant spray (Fremouw et al., 1997)
- MI (preparation—aggressive): carried weapon (Fremouw et al., 1997)
- MI (preparation—aggressive): carried weapon (8% Meloy & Boyd, 2003)
- MI (preparation—aggressive): carry a loaded firearm (Harris & Miller, 2000)
- MI (preparation—aggressive): carry an unloaded firearm (Harris & Miller, 2000)
- MI (preparation—aggressive): carry mace or pepper spray (Harris & Miller, 2000)
- MI (preparation—aggressive): keeping a weapon at home (5% Guy et al., 1992)
- MI (preparation—aggressive): keeping weapon at the office (2% Guy et al., 1992)
- MI (preparation—aggressive): learned self-defense techniques (3% Romans et al., 1996)
- MI (preparation—aggressive): obtained self-defense training (7% Gentile, 2001)

- MI (preparation—aggressive): obtained weapon (2% Fisher et al., 1999, 2000)
- MI (preparation—aggressive): obtaining self-defense training (4% Guy et al., 1992)
- MI (preparation—aggressive): possessed weapon (0% Gentile, 2001)
- MI (preparation—aggressive): purchased a gun (15% Kohn et al., 2000)
- MI (preparation—aggressive): purchased and carried personal defense devices (4% Romans et al., 1996)
- MI (preparation—aggressive): scream if attacked (Harris & Miller, 2000)
- MI (preparation—aggressive): self-defense class (.4% Fisher et al., 1999, 2000)
- MI (preparation—aggressive): self-defense training for loved ones (2% Guy et al., 1992)
- MI (preparation—aggressive): sought physical protection (Langhinrichsen-Rohling et al., 2000)
- MI (preparation—aggressive): study martial arts (Harris & Miller, 2000)
- MI (preparation—aggressive): take up body building (Harris & Miller, 2000)
- MI (preparation—aggressive): thoughts of harming stalker (41% Blackburn, 1999)
- MI (preparation—aggressive): thoughts of killing stalker (13% Blackburn, 1999)
- MI (preparation—aggressive): took up self-defense (5% Nicastro et al., 2000)
- MI (preparation—aggressive): training in management of assaultive behaviors (15% Guy et al., 1992)
- MI (regret): regrets about behaviors combining action and inaction (e.g., passive acceptance of blame or criticism, passive acceptance of interference from family members, knowingly ignored one's physical health, etc.) (Fry & Barker, 2001)
- MI (regret): regrets about isolating oneself (e.g., becoming homebound, isolating self from friends, etc.) (Fry & Barker, 2001)
- MI (regret): regrets about not seeking complete change of venue after (e.g., did not move, did not change work setting, did not change identity, etc.) (Fry & Barker, 2001)
- MI (regret): regrets about not seeking new avenues of knowledge and information (e.g., should have read more about abuse, should have gotten more assertive about demanding action, should have gone more public about experiences to others, should have gone to the media, etc.) (Fry & Barker, 2001)

- MI (regret): regrets about self-care and self-development after (e.g., did not develop network, supportive relationships, self-defense, counseling and therapy, etc.) (Fry & Barker, 2001)
- MI (regret): regrets about self-protection after (e.g., did not arm myself, did not seek police protection, did not hire body guard, did not take legal action, missed opportunity to shoot and kill aggressor, etc.) (Fry & Barker, 2001)
- MI (regret): self-criticism (e.g., I kick myself for letting this happen) (Pollina & Snell, 1999)
- MI (self-destructive): attempted suicide (Nicastro et al., 2000)
- MI (spiritual): religion (e.g., "how much did you rely on your religious beliefs or your faith to help you cope") (Harnish et al., 2000)
- MI (spiritual): religious coping (e.g., I seek God's help) (Pollina & Snell, 1999)
- MI (spiritual): seek social support—nonspecific, religion ("praying, involvement in religious activities,"…) (Tamres et al., 2002)
- MI (spiritual): spiritual belief or fantasy (Stith et al., 1992)
- MI (therapy): obtained psychotherapy (7% Gentile, 2001)
- MI (therapy): psychologist/psychiatrist/counselor (47% Eke, 1999)
- MI (therapy): saw a counselor (Yoshihama, 2002)
- MI (therapy): seek medical attention (77/55% relentless vs. infrequently, Mechanic, Uhlmansiek, et al., 2000)
- MI (therapy): seek mental health care (77/81% relentless vs. infrequently, Mechanic, Uhlmansiek, et al., 2000)
- MI (therapy): sought counseling (3% Fisher et al., 1999, 2000)
- MI (therapy): sought counseling (female victims 9% Bjerregaard, 2000)
- MI (therapy): sought counseling (Levitt et al., 1996)
- MI (therapy): sought counseling (male victims 3% Bjerregaard, 2000)
- MI (therapy): sought counseling (3% Morewitz, 2003)
- MI (therapy): sought counseling (respondent, partner, both, neither: 52%, 1%, 22%, 25%) (Holloway, 1994)
- MI (therapy): sought help from therapist (28% Brewster, 1998, 2000)

MO: Moving Outward: Any effort(s) or act(s) to obtain assistance of others for guidance, information, or intermediary contact with the pursuer with the intent of deterring or avoiding further victim contact. Exemplars include: seeking advice or consultation with counselors, religious advisers, law enforcement, victims' advocates, friends or family, or threat management professionals. Note: Direct efforts to obtain the assistance of third parties to harm or imprison the pursuer are classified as "moving against." Furthermore, seeking therapy, rather than merely consultation, is categorized as "moving inward."

- MO (general): sought assistance (69% Purcell et al., 2002)
- MO (counsel): seek clergy (43/39% relentless vs. infrequently, Mechanic, Uhlmansiek, et al., 2000)
- MO (counsel): seeking social support for instrumental reasons (e.g., I talk to someone to try to find out more about the situation) (Pollina & Snell, 1999)
- MO (counsel): sought someone's advice (47% Omata, 2002)
- MO (counsel—legal): confrontation: organizational power structure (e.g., told a superior, reported to committee or union, filed a formal complaint, disciplined a person) (Gruber, 1989)
- MO (counsel—legal): contacted legal professionals (12% Purcell et al., 2002)
- MO (counsel—legal): lawyers (45% Pathé et al., 2000)
- MO (counsel—legal): legal counsel (69% Kamphuis & Emmelkamp, 2001)
- MO (counsel—legal): sought help from lawyer (60% Eke, 1999)
- MO (counsel—legal): sought help from legal aid (14% Brewster, 1998, 2000)
- MO (disclosure): defusion: social support (e.g., told peers or coworkers) (Gruber, 1989)
- MO (disclosure): seeking social support for emotional reasons (e.g., I talk to someone about how I feel) (Pollina & Snell, 1999)
- MO (disclosure): social support (e.g., "how much did you talk to someone about how you felt?") (Harnish et al., 2000)
- MO (disclosure): talk to a friend/family/neighbor (Hills & Taplin, 1998)
- MO (disclosure): talked to friends/relatives (Levitt et al., 1996)
- MO (disclosure): told a friend, relative or neighbor (72% Budd & Mattinson, 2000)
- MO (disclosure): told a partner or boy/girlfriend (55% Budd & Mattinson, 2000)
- MO (disclosure): told someone about their stalking at an early stage (86% Sheridan, 2001)
- MO (intermediary): ask someone to confront the person (Hills & Taplin, 1998)
- MO (intermediary): had family/friends talk to stalker (4% Brewster, 1998, 2000)
- MO (intermediary): had someone warn stalker (Fremouw et al., 1997)

- MO (intermediary): mediation/issue resolved (1% Dussuyer, 2000)
- MO (intermediary): negotiation: professional mediation (e.g., sought outside help) (Gruber, 1989)
- MO (intermediary): took action (harassment charges, had 3rd party talk to harasser) (34% Jason et al., 1984)
- MO (partner—existing): devote more time to [wanted] relationship (e.g., I do more things with my partner that s/he enjoys) (Pollina & Snell, 1999)
- MO (partner—existing): dyadic intimacy [with wanted partner] (e.g., move closer, disclosure) (see Burgoon et al., 1989; Hosman & Siltanen, 1995)
- MO (partner—existing): sought help from partner (16% Brewster, 1998, 2000)
- MO (partner—new attachment): became involved with new people (Levitt et al., 1996)
- MO (police): approached police for assistance (35% Blackburn, 1999)
- MO (police): call police/security (56% Morrison, 2001)
- MO (police): called police (96% Nicastro et al., 2000)
- MO (police): called police (Fremouw et al., 1997)
- MO (police): called police (female victims 35% Bjerregaard, 2000)
- MO (police): called police (male victims 10% Bjerregaard, 2000)
- MO (police): contact police (86/81% relentless vs. infrequently, Mechanic, Uhlmansiek, et al., 2000)
- MO (police): contacted police (31% Morewitz, 2003)
- MO (police): contacted police (35% Purcell et al., 2002)
- MO (police): contacted police (41% Gentile, 2001)
- MO (police): contacted police (89% Blaauw, Winkel, Arensman, et al., 2000)
- MO (police): contacted police again (3% Dussuyer, 2000)
- MO (police): help-seeking: calling police (92% Kileen & Dunn, 1998)
- MO (police): help-seeking: writing letters to law enforcement (7% Kileen & Dunn, 1998)
- MO (police): police (60% Pathé et al., 2000)
- MO (police): police were made aware of attention (33% Budd & Mattinson, 2000)
- MO (police): reported stalking to police (89% Kohn et al., 2000)
- MO (police): reported suspicious activity to police (9% Romans et al., 1996)
- MO (police): sought help from police (Langhinrichsen-Rohling et al., 2000)
- MO (police): sought support/help from police (97% Eke, 1999)
- MO (professional protection): hiring security guard (1% Guy et al., 1992)

- MO (protective order): apply for RO (Hills & Taplin, 1998)
- MO (protective order): obtain order of protection (74/45% relentless vs. infrequently, Mechanic, Uhlmansiek, et al., 2000)
- MO (protective order): obtained a restraining order (14% Kohn et al., 2000)
- MO (protective order): obtained intervention order (14% Dussuyer, 2000)
- MO (protective order): obtained restraining order (50% Morrison, 2001)
- MO (protective order): obtained RO (female victims 1% Bjerregaard, 2000)
- MO (protective order): obtained TRO (66% Meloy & Boyd, 2003)
- MO (protective order): restraining order (Fremouw et al., 1997)
- MO (protective order): sought a court order (Gallagher et al., 1994)
- MO (protective order): sought PO (4% Fisher et al., 1999, 2000)
- MO (protective order): sought restraining order (56% Nicastro et al., 2000)
- MO (protective order): took out restraining order (33% Blackburn, 1999)
- MO (safety in numbers): arranged escort (Fremouw et al., 1997)
- MO (safety in numbers): avoiding working alone in the office (22% Guy et al., 1992)
- MO (safety in numbers): get escorted to the car (Harris & Miller, 2000)
- MO (safety in numbers): help-seeking: getting escort (19% Kileen & Dunn, 1998)
- MO (safety in numbers): never alone (7% Dussuyer, 2000)
- MO (safety in numbers): socialize more (e.g., I socialize more than usual, other than with my partner) (Pollina & Snell, 1999)
- MO (safety in numbers): traveled with companion (4% Fisher et al., 1999, 2000)
- MO (service agency): contact community support agency (Hills & Taplin, 1998)
- MO (service agency): contacted health professionals (13% Purcell et al., 2002)
- MO (service agency): crisis center/social services (43% Eke, 1999)
- MO (service agency): medical profession (41% Pathé et al., 2000)
- MO (service agency): medical/general doctor (53% Eke, 1999)
- MO (service agency): sought help from victim service agency (38% Brewster, 1998, 2000)
- MO (service agency): sought help from victim services (70% Eke, 1999)
- MO (service agency): sought help from victim support group (9% Brewster, 1998, 2000)

- MO (service agency): sought help with mental health care agency or professional (93% Blaauw, Winkel, Arensman, et al., 2000)
- MO (service agency): sought professional help (4% Nicastro et al., 2000)
- MO (service agency): told a doctor-social worker (8% Budd & Mattinson, 2000)
- MO (social network): asked friends/family for protection (14% Nicastro et al., 2000)
- MO (social network): called/used friend/family/relative (19% Morrison, 2001)
- MO (social network): confront, social support (Stith et al., 1992)
- MO (social network): consulted family/friends (51% Purcell et al., 2002)
- MO (social network): contacted friends/family/council (2% Dussuyer, 2000)
- MO (social network): emotion-focused behavior: seek social support—emotional ("seeking out comfort or emotional support from others") (Tamres et al., 2002)
- MO (social network): help-seeking: asking employer/coworkers (11% Kileen & Dunn, 1998)
- MO (social network): intimacy with family (Pedersen, 1999)
- MO (social network): intimacy with friends (Pedersen, 1999)
- MO (social network): problem-focused behavior: seek social support—instrumental ("seeking specific, generally concrete help from friends and family…directed toward solving problems") (Tamres et al., 2002)
- MO (social network): problem-focused, confrontation/seeking social support (Bouchard et al., 1997)
- MO (social network): seeking social support—turning to others (Hobfoll & Schröder, 2001)
- MO (social network): social joining: join with others to deal with the situation or coalition building (Hobfoll & Schröder, 2001)
- MO (social network): sought help from coworker (9% Brewster, 1998, 2000)
- MO (social network): sought help from family (54% Brewster, 1998, 2000)
- MO (social network): sought help from family (80% Eke, 1999)
- MO (social network): sought help from friends (Yoshihama, 2002)
- MO (social network): sought help from friends/family (73% Pathé et al., 2000)
- MO (social network): sought help from neighbors (6% Brewster, 1998, 2000)

- MO (social network): sought help from: friends (68% Brewster, 1998, 2000)
- MO (social network): sought support/help from friends (93% Eke, 1999)
- MO (social network—safety planning): contingency plan for family members if client appears (12% Guy et al., 1992)
- MO (social network—safety planning): discussing safety issues with loved ones (30% Guy et al., 1992)
- Unclassifiable: active coping (e.g., I take additional action to try and get rid of the problem) (Pollina & Snell, 1999)

- Unclassifiable: problem solving (Stith et al., 1992)
- Unclassifiable: problem-focused behavior: active coping ("efforts to change or remove the stressor") (Tamres et al., 2002)
- Unclassifiable: active behavioral (e.g., "how much did you do things to improve the situation") (Harnish et al., 2000)
- Unclassifiable: problem-focused behavior: problem-focused coping—general (Tamres et al., 2002)

Notes:

1. Several categories presented problems with mutual exclusivity. For example, screaming during an encounter with the pursuer could be viewed as moving against (i.e., trying to get the pursuer arrested for assault), moving away (i.e., by motivating the person to leave), moving with (i.e., interacting with the pursuer), or moving outward (i.e., by seeking the assistance of passers by). In all cases, an effort was made to consider the proximal function of the action.

2. Some items were double (or triple, or quadruple) barreled. In such instances, these items were duplicated and the element of the item relevant to its classification is italicized.

3. When percentages are provided, they represent the prevalence in that sample that respondents employed that coping tactic in response to stalking or unwanted pursuit. Items without percentages are from investigations of coping in contexts other than, or in addition to, stalking.

BIBLIOGRAPHY

Abbey, A. (1982). Sex differences in attributions for friendly behavior: Do males misperceive females' friendliness? *Journal of Personality and Social Psychology, 42*, 830–838.

Abbey, A. (1987). Misperceptions of friendly behavior as sexual interest: A survey of naturally occurring incidents. *Psychology of Women Quarterly, 11*, 173–194.

Abbey, A. (1991). Misperceptions as an antecedent of acquaintance rape: A consequence of ambiguity in communication between men and women. In A. Parrot & L. Bechhofer (Eds.), *Acquaintance rape: The hidden crime* (pp. 96–112). New York: John Wiley.

Abbey, A., & Melby, C. (1986). The effects of nonverbal cues on gender differences in perceptions of sexual intent. *Sex Roles, 15*, 283–298.

Abrahams, M. F. (1994). Perceiving flirtatious communication: An exploration of the perceptual dimensions underlying judgments of flirtatiousness. *Journal of Sex Research, 31*, 283–292.

Abrams, K. M., & Robinson, G. E. (1998a). Stalking Part I: An overview of the problem. *Canadian Journal of Psychiatry, 43*, 473–476.

Abrams, K. M., & Robinson, G. E. (1998b). Stalking Part II: Victims' problems with the legal system and therapeutic considerations. *Canadian Journal of Psychiatry, 43*, 477–481.

Abrams, K. M., & Robinson, G. E. (2002). Occupational effects of stalking. *Canadian Journal of Psychiatry, 47*, 468–472.

Adams, S. (1999, December 13). Serial batterers (Domestic Violence Special Report). *Probation Research Bulletin*. Office of the Commissioner of Probation, Massachusetts Trial Court, Boston, MA.

Adams, S. J., Pitre, N. L., & Smith, A. (2001). Criminal harassment by patients with mental disorders. *Canadian Journal of Psychiatry, 46*, 173–176.

Adhikari, R. P., Reinhard, D., & Johnson, J. M. (1993). The myth of protection orders. In N. K. Denzin (Ed.), *Studies in symbolic interaction* (Vol. 15, pp. 259–270). Stamford, CT: JAI Press.

Afifi, W. A., & Faulkner, S. L. (2000). On being "just friends": The frequency and impact of sexual activity in cross-sex friendships. *Journal of Social and Personal Relationships, 17*, 205–222.

Afifi, W. A., & Metts, S. (1998). Characteristics and consequences of expectation violations in close relationships. *Journal of Social and Personal Relationships, 15*, 365–393.

Ainsworth, M. D. S. (1989). Attachments beyond infancy. *American Psychologist, 44*, 709–716.

Ainsworth, M. D. S., Blehar, M. C., Waters, E., & Wall, S. (1978). *Patterns of attachment: A psychological study of the strange situation*. Hillsdale, NJ: Lawrence Erlbaum Associates.

Albrecht, S. F. (2001). Stalking, stalkers, and domestic violence: Relentless fear and obsessive intimacy. In J. A. Davis (Ed.), *Stalking crimes and victim protection: Prevention, intervention, threat assessment, and case management* (pp. 69–80). Boca Raton, FL: CRC Press.

Aldwin, C. M., & Revenson, T. A. (1987). Does coping help? A reexamination of the relation between coping and mental health. *Journal of Personality and Social Psychology, 53*, 337–348.

Alksnis, C., Desmarais, S., & Wood, E. (1996). Gender differences in scripts for different types of dates. *Sex Roles, 34*, 321–336.

Altheide, D. L., & Michalowski, R. S. (1999). Fear in the news: A discourse of control. *Sociological Quarterly, 40*, 475–503.

Altman, I. (1977). Privacy regulation: Culturally universal or culturally specific? *Journal of Social Issues, 33*, 66–84.

American Association of University Women Educational Foundation. (1993). *Hostile hallways: The AAUW survey on sexual harassment in America's schools* (Harris/Scholastic Research, Study 923012). Washington, DC: AAUW.

American Prosecutors Research Institute. (1997). *Stalking: Prosecutors convict and restrict.* Alexandria, VA: American Prosecutors Research Institute.

American Psychiatric Association. (1987). *Diagnostic and statistical manual of mental disorders* (3rd ed., rev., *DSM III–R*). Washington, DC: American Psychiatric Association.

Andersen, P. A. (1998). The cognitive valence theory of intimate communication. In M. T. Palmer & G. A. Barnett (Eds.), *Progress in communication science* (Vol. 14, pp. 39–72). Stamford, CT: Ablex.

Anderson, S. C. (1993). Anti-stalking laws: Will they curb the erotomanic's obsessive pursuit? *Law and Psychology Review, 17*, 171–191.

Angermeyer, M. C., & Schulze, B. (2001). Reinforcing stereotypes: How the focus on forensic cases in news reporting may influence public attitudes towards the mentally ill. *International Journal of Law and Psychiatry, 24*, 469–486.

Arata, C. M., & Burkhart, B. R. (1996). Post-traumatic stress disorder among college student victims of acquaintance assault. In E. S. Byers & L. F. O'Sullivan (Eds.), *Sexual coercion in dating relationships* (pp. 79–92). Binghamton, NY: Haworth Press.

Argyle, M., & Henderson, M. (1984). The rules of friendship. *Journal of Social and Personal Relationships, 1*, 211–237.

Aron, A., Aron, E. N., & Allen, J. (1998). Motivations for unreciprocated love. *Personality and Social Psychology Bulletin, 24*, 787–796.

Asher, S. R., Rose, A. J., & Gabriel, S. W. (2001). Peer rejection in everyday life. In M. R. Leary (Ed.), *Interpersonal rejection* (pp. 105–142). New York: Oxford University Press.

Attanasio, V., Andrasik, F., Blanchard, E. B., & Arena, J. G. (1984). Psychometric properties of the SUNYA revision of the psychosomatic symptom checklist. *Journal of Behavioral Medicine, 7*, 247–258.

Attridge, M. (1994). Barriers to dissolution of romantic relationships. In D. J. Canary & L. Stafford (Eds.), *Communication and relational maintenance* (pp. 141–164). San Diego, CA: Academic Press.

Avakame, E. F., & Fyfe, J. J. (2001). Differential police treatment of male-on-female spousal violence. *Violence Against Women, 7*, 22–45.

Babcock, R. J. H. (2000). Psychology of stalking. In P. Infield & G. Platford (Eds.), *The law of harassment and stalking* (pp. 1–8). London: Butterworths.

Bachen, C. M., & Illouz, E. (1996). Imagining romance: Young people's cultural models of romance and love. *Critical Studies in Mass Communication, 13*, 279–308.

Badcock, R. (2002). Psychopathology and treatment of stalking. In J. Boon & L. Sheridan (Eds.), *Stalking and psychosexual obsession: Psychological perspectives for prevention, policing and treatment* (pp. 125–140). West Sussex, England: John Wiley & Sons.

Bagozzi, R. P. (1992). The self-regulation of attitudes, intentions, and behaviour. *Social Psychology Quarterly, 55*, 178–204.

Bagozzi, R. P., Baumgartner, H., & Pieters, R. (1998). Goal-directed emotions. *Cognition and Emotion, 12*, 1–26.

Bagozzi, R. P., & Dholakia, U. (1999). Goal setting and goal striving in consumer behavior. *Journal of Marketing, 63* (Special Issue), 19–32.

Bagozzi, R. P., & Edwards, E. A. (2000). Goal-striving and the implementation of goal intentions in the regulation of body weight. *Psychology and Health, 15*, 255–270.

Bagozzi, R. P., & Warshaw, P. R. (1990). Trying to consume. *Journal of Consumer Research, 17*, 127–140.

Bailey, B. L. (1989). *From front porch to back seat: Courtship in twentieth-century America.* Baltimore, MD: Johns Hopkins University Press.

Baker, D. (1999, December). When cyber stalkers walk. *ABA Journal*, 50–54.

Baker, P. L. (1997). And I went back: Battered women's negotiation of choice. *Journal of Contemporary Ethnography, 26*, 55–74.

Baldry, A. C. (2002). From domestic violence to stalking: The infinite cycle of violence. In J. Boon & L. Sheridan (Eds.), *Stalking and psychosexual obsession: Psychological perspectives for prevention, policing and treatment* (pp. 83–104). West Sussex, England: John Wiley & Sons.

Baldwin, M. W. (1992). Relational schemas and the processing of social information. *Psychological Bulletin, 112*, 461–484.

Bandura, A. (1997). *Self-efficacy: The exercise of control.* New York: Freeman.

Banks, M. A. (1997). *Web psychos, stalkers, and pranksters.* Albany, NY: Coriolis Group Books.

Banks, S. P., Altendorf, D. M., Greene, J. O., & Cody, M. J. (1987). An examination of relationship disengagement: Perceptions, breakup strategies and outcomes. *Western Journal of Speech Communication, 51*, 19–41.

Barbara, A. M., & Dion, K. L. (2000). Breaking up is hard to do, especially for "preoccupied" lovers. *Journal of Personal and Interpersonal Loss, 5*, 315–342.

Barnes, M. T., Gordon, W. C., & Hudson, S. M. (2001). The crime of threatening to kill. *Journal of Interpersonal Violence, 16*, 312–319.

Bartholomew, K. (1990). Avoidance of intimacy: An attachment perspective. *Journal of Social and Personal Relationships, 7*, 147–178.

Bartholomew, K., & Horowitz, L. M. (1991). Attachment styles among young adults: A test of a four-category model. *Journal of Personality and Social Psychology, 61*, 226–244.

Bates, A. (1999). An overview of stalking. *British Journal of Forensic Practice, 1*(4), 33–36.

Battaglia, D. M., Richard, F. D., Datteri, D. L., & Lord, C. G. (1998). Breaking up is (relatively) easy to do: A script for the dissolution of close relationships. *Journal of Social and Personal Relationships, 15*, 829–845.

Batza, D. M., & Taylor, M. (1999). Stalking in the community and workplace. In E. K. Carll (Ed.), *Violence in our lives: Impact on workplace, home, and community* (pp. 66–96). Boston: Allyn and Bacon.

Baumeister, R. F., & Leary, M. R. (1995). The need to belong: Desire for interpersonal attachments as a fundamental human motivation. *Psychological Bulletin, 117*, 497–529.

Baumeister, R. F., Stillwell, A., & Wotman, S. R. (1990). Victim and perpetrator accounts of interpersonal conflict: Autobiographical narratives about anger. *Journal of Personality and Social Psychology, 59*, 994–1005.

Baumeister, R. F., & Wotman, S. R. (1992). *Breaking hearts: The two sides of unrequited love.* New York: Guilford.

Baumeister, R. F., Wotman, S. R., & Stillwell, A. M. (1993). Unrequited love: On heartbreak, anger, guilt, scriptlessness, and humiliation. *Journal of Personality and Social Psychology, 64*, 377–394.

Baxter, L. A. (1982). Strategies for ending relationships: Two studies. *Western Journal of Speech Communication, 46*, 223–241.

Baxter, L. A. (1985). Accomplishing relationship disengagement. In S. Duck & D. Perlman (Eds.), *Understanding personal relationships: An interdisciplinary approach* (pp. 243–265). London: Sage.

Baxter, L. A. (1986). Gender differences in the heterosexual relationship rules embedded in break-up accounts. *Journal of Social and Personal Relationships, 3*, 289–306.

Baxter, L. A. (1987). Cognition and communication in the relationship process. In R. Burnett, P. McGhee, & D. D. Clarke (Eds.), *Accounting for relationships* (pp. 192–212). London: Methuen.

Baxter, L. A., & Montgomery, B. M. (1996). *Relating: Dialogues and dialectics.* New York: Guilford.

Baxter, L. A., & Philpott, J. (1982). Attribution-based strategies for initiating and terminating relationships. *Communication Quarterly, 30*, 217–224.

Baxter, L. A., & Wilmot, W. W. (1984). "Secret tests": Strategies for acquiring information about the state of the relationship. *Human Communication Research, 11*, 171–201.

Baxter, L. A., & Wilmot, W. W. (1985). Taboo topics in close relationships. *Journal of Social and Personal Relationships, 2*, 253–269.

Beatty, M. J., Valencic, K. M., Rudd, J. E., & Dobos, J. A. (1999). A "dark side" of communication avoidance: Indirect interpersonal aggressiveness. *Communication Research Reports, 16*, 103–109.

Beck, M., Rosenberg, D., Chideya, F., Miller, S., Foote, D., Manly, H., & Katel, P. (1992, July 13). Murderous obsession. *Newsweek*, 60–62.

Belknap, J., Fisher, B. S., & Cullen, F. T. (1999). The development of a comprehensive measure of the sexual victimization of college women. *Violence Against Women, 5*, 185–214.

Bell, R. A., & Buerkel-Rothfuss, N. L. (1990). S(he) loves me, s(he) loves me not: Predictors of relational information-seeking in courtship and beyond. *Communication Quarterly, 38*, 64–82.

Bell, R. A., & Daly, J. A. (1984). The affinity-seeking function of communication. *Communication Monographs, 51*, 91–115.

Bennett, J. B. (1988). Power and influence as distinct personality traits: Development and validation of a psychometric measure. *Journal of Research in Personality, 22*, 361–394.

Berger, C. R. (1979). Beyond initial interaction: Uncertainty, understanding, and the development of interpersonal relationships. In H. Giles & R. St. Clair (Eds.), *Language and social psychology* (pp. 122–144). Oxford: Blackwell.

Berger, C. R. (1987). Communicating under uncertainty. In M. E. Roloff & G. R. Miller (Eds.), *Interpersonal processes: New directions in communication research* (pp. 39–62). Newbury Park, CA: Sage.

Berger, C. A. (2002). Goals and knowledge structures in social interaction. In M. L. Knapp & J. A. Daly (Eds.), *Handbook of interpersonal communication* (3rd ed., pp. 181–212). Thousand Oaks, CA: Sage.

Berger, C. R., & Bradac, J. J. (1982). *Language and social knowledge: Uncertainty in interpersonal relations.* London: Edward Arnold.

Berger, C. R., & Douglas, W. (1981). Studies in interpersonal epistemology III: Anticipated interaction, self-monitoring and observational context selection. *Communication Monographs, 48*, 183–196.

Berger, C. R., & Kellermann, K. A. (1983). To ask or not to ask: Is that a question? In R. N. Bostrom (Ed.), *Communication yearbook 7* (pp. 342–368). Newbury Park, CA: Sage.

Berger, C. R., & Perkins, J. (1978). Studies in interpersonal epistemology I: Situational attributes in observational context selection. In B. Ruben (Ed.), *Communication yearbook 2* (pp. 171–184). New Brunswick, NJ: Transaction Books.

Berk, R. A., Berk, S. F., Loseke, D. R., & Rauma, D. (1983). Mutual combat and other family violence myths. In D. Finkelhor, R. J. Gelles, G. T. Hotaling, & M. A. Straus (Eds.), *The dark side of families: Current family violence research* (pp. 197–212). Newbury Park, CA: Sage.

Berns, N. (1999). "My problem and how I solved it": Domestic violence in women's magazines. *Sociological Quarterly, 50*, 85–108.

Berns, S. B., Jacobson, N. S., & Gottman, J. M. (1999). Demand/withdraw interaction patterns between different types of batterers and their spouses. *Journal of Marital and Family Therapy, 25*, 337–348.

Bernstein, H. A. (1981). Survey of threats and assaults directed toward psychotherapists. *American Journal of Psychotherapy, 35*, 542–549.

Bernstein, S. E. (1993). Living under siege: Do stalking laws protect domestic violence victims? *Cardozo Law Review, 15*, 525–567.

Best, J. (1999). *Random violence: How we talk about new crimes and new victims.* Berkeley, CA: University of California Press.

Biden, J. R. (1993). *Antistalking proposals.* Hearing before the Committee on the Judiciary, United States Senate (J-103-5). Washington, DC: U.S. Government Printing Office.

Bingham, J. E., & Piotrowski, C. (1996). On-line sexual addiction: A contemporary enigma. *Psychological Reports, 79*, 257–258.

Bingham, S. G., & Burleson, B. R. (1989). Multiple effects of messages with multiple goals: Some perceived outcomes of responses to sexual harassment. *Human Communication Research, 16*, 184–216.

Birtchnell, J. (1993). *How humans relate: A new interpersonal theory.* Westport, CT: Praeger.

Bjerregaard, B. (2000). An empirical study of stalking victimization. *Violence and Victims, 15*, 389–406.

Blaauw, E., Sheridan, L., & Winkel, F. W. (2002). Designing anti-stalking legislation on the basis of victims' experiences and psychopathology. *Psychiatry, Psychology & Law, 9*, 136–145.

Blaauw, E., Winkel, F. W., Arensman, E., Sheridan, L., & Freeve, A. (2002). The toll of stalking: The relationship between features of stalking and psychopathology of victims. *Journal of Interpersonal Violence, 17*, 50–63.

Blaauw, E., Winkel, F. W., Sheridan, L., Malsch, M., & Arensman, E. (2002). The psychological consequences of stalking victimization. In J. Boon & L. Sheridan (Eds.), *Stalking and psychosexual obsession: Psychological perspectives for prevention, policing and treatment* (pp. 23–34). West Sussex, England: John Wiley & Sons.

Blackburn, E. J. (1999). *"Forever yours": Rates of stalking victimization, risk factors and traumatic responses among college women.* Unpublished doctoral dissertation, University of Massachusetts, Boston.

Bogart, L. M., Cecil, H., Wagstaff, D. A., Pinkerton, S. D., & Abramson, P. R. (2000). Is it "sex"?: College students' interpretations of sexual behavior terminology. *Journal of Sex Research, 37*, 108–116.

Boles, G. S. (2001). Developing a model approach to confronting the problem of stalking: Establishing a threat management unit. In J. A. Davis (Ed.), *Stalking crimes and victim protection: Prevention, intervention, threat assessment, and case management* (pp. 337–350). Boca Raton, FL: CRC Press.

Boon, J., & Sheridan, L. (Eds.) (2002). *Stalking and psychosexual obsession: Psychological perspectives for prevention, policing and treatment.* West Sussex, England: John Wiley & Sons.

Boon, J. C. W., & Sheridan, L. (2001). Stalker typologies: A law enforcement perspective. *Journal of Threat Assessment, 1*, 75–97.

Boon, S. D., & Lomore, C. D. (2001). Admirer-celebrity relationships among young adults: Explaining perceptions of celebrity influence on identity. *Human Communication Research, 27*, 432–465.

Bornstein, R. F. (1996). Sex differences in dependent personality disorder prevalence rates. *Clinical Psychology: Science and Practice, 3*, 1–12.

Bouchard, G., Sabourin, S., Lussier, Y., Wright, J., & Richer, C. (1997). Testing the theoretical models underlying the ways of coping questionnaire. *Journal of Marriage and the Family, 59*, 409–418.

Bowlby, J. (1969). *Attachment and loss: Volume 1. Attachment.* New York: Basic Books.

Bowlby, J. (1973). *Attachment and loss: Volume 2. Separation: Anxiety and anger.* New York: Basic Books.

Bowlby, J. (1980). *Attachment and loss: Volume 3. Loss: Sadness and depression.* New York: Basic Books.

Bozenhard, L. (1998). A comparative examination of stalking laws and related methods of victim protection. In L. J. Moriarty & R. A. Jerin (Eds.), *Current issues in victimology research* (pp. 209–221). Durham, NC: Carolina Academic Press.

Bradburn, W. E., Jr. (1992). Stalking statutes. *Ohio Northern University Law Review, 19*, 271–288.

Brainerd, E. G., Jr., Hunter, P. A., Moore, D., & Thompson, T. R. (1996). Jealousy induction as a predictor of power and the use of other control methods in heterosexual relationships. *Psychological Reports, 79*, 1319–1325.

Bratslavsky, E., Baumeister, R. F., & Sommer, K. L. (1998). To love or be loved in vain: The trials and tribulations of unrequited love. In B. H. Spitzberg & W. R. Cupach (Eds.), *The dark side of close relationships* (pp. 307–326). Mahwah, NJ: Lawrence Erlbaum Associates.

Brehm, J. W., & Self, E. A. (1989). The intensity of motivation. *Annual Review of Psychology, 45*, 560–570.

Brennen, K. A., Clark, C. L., & Shaver, P. R. (1998). Self-report measurement of adult attachment: An integrative overview. In J. A. Simpson & W. S. Rholes (Eds.), *Attachment theory and close relationships* (pp. 46–76). New York: Guilford.

Brennen, K. A., & Shaver, P. R. (1995). Dimensions of adult attachment, affect regulation, and romantic relationship functioning. *Personality and Social Psychology Bulletin, 21*, 267–283.

Brewin, C. R., Roe, S., Andrews, B., Green, J., Tata, P., McEvedy, C., Turner, S., & Foa, E. B. (2002). Brief screening instrument for post-traumatic stress disorder. *British Journal of Psychiatry, 181*, 158–162.

Brewster, M. P. (1998). *An exploration of the experiences and needs of former intimate stalking victims.* Final report submitted to the National Institute of Justice (NCJ 175475). Washington, DC: U.S. Department of Justice.

Brewster, M. P. (2000). Stalking by former intimates: Verbal threats and other predictors of physical violence. *Violence and Victims, 15*, 41–54.

Brewster, M. P. (2001). Legal help-seeking experiences of former intimate-stalking victims. *Criminal Justice Policy Review, 12*, 91–112.

Brewster, M. P. (2002). Trauma symptoms of former intimate stalking victims. *Women & Criminal Justice, 13*, 141–161.

Brewster, M. P. (2003). Power and control dynamics in prestalking and stalking situations. *Journal of Family Violence, 18*, 207–217.

Briere, J., & Runtz, M. (1990). Augmenting Hopkins SCL scales to measure dissociative symptoms: Data from two nonclinical samples. *Journal of Personality Assessment, 55*, 376–379.

Brown, G. P., Dubin, W. R., Lion, J. R., & Garry, L. J. (1996). Threats against clinicians: A preliminary descriptive classification. *Bulletin of the American Academy of Psychiatry and the Law, 24*, 367–376.

Brown, H. (2000). *Stalking and other forms of harassment: An investigator's guide.* London: Metropolitan Police Service, Home Office.

Brown, M. (1992, November 29). State anti-stalking law shadows lovers who won't let go. *Sacramento Bee*, pp. A1, 17.

Brown, P., & Levinson, S. (1987). *Politeness: Some universals in language usage.* Cambridge: Cambridge University Press.

Brownstein, H. H. (1996). *The rise and fall of a violent crime wave: Crack cocaine and the social construction of a crime problem.* Guilderland, NY: Harrow and Heston.

Brüne, M. (2001). De Clérambault's syndrome (erotomania) in an evolutionary perspective. *Evolution and Human Behavior, 22*, 409–415.

Brüne, M. (2003). Erotomanic stalking in evolutionary perspective. *Behavioral Sciences and the Law, 21*, 83–88.

Brunstein, J. C., & Gollwitzer, P. M. (1996). Effects of failure on subsequent performance: The importance of self-defining goals. *Journal of Personality and Social Psychology, 70*, 395–407.

Budd, T., & Mattinson, J. (2000). *Stalking: Findings from the 1998 British crime survey* (Home Office Research, Research Findings No. 129). London: Research Development and Statistics Directorate.

Bufkin, J., & Eschholz, S. (2000). Images of sex and rape: A content analysis of popular film. *Violence Against Women, 6*, 1317–1344.

Bullock, C. F., & Cubert, J. (2002). Coverage of domestic violence fatalities by newspapers in Washington state. *Journal of Interpersonal Violence, 17*, 475–499.

Bureau of Justice Assistance. (1996). *Regional seminar series on developing and implementing antistalking codes* (Monograph, NCJ 156836). Washington, DC: U.S. Department of Justice.

Burgess, A. W., & Baker, T. (2002). Cyberstalking. In J. Boon & L. Sheridan (Eds.), *Stalking and psychosexual obsession: Psychological perspectives for prevention, policing and treatment* (pp. 201–220). West Sussex, England: John Wiley & Sons.

Burgess, A. W., Baker, T., Greening, D., Hartman, C. R., Burgess, A. G., Douglas, J. E., & Halloran, R. (1997). Stalking behaviors within domestic violence. *Journal of Family Violence, 12*, 389–403.

Burgess, A. W., Harner, H., Baker, T., Hartman, C. R., & Lole, C. (2001). Batterers stalking patterns. *Journal of Family Violence, 16*, 309–321.

Burgoon, J. K. (1982). Privacy and communication. In M. Burgoon (Ed.), *Communication yearbook 6* (pp. 206–249). Beverly Hills, CA: Sage.

Burgoon, J. K., Parrott, R., Le Poire, B. A., Kelley, D. L., Walther, J. B., & Perry, D. (1989). Maintaining and restoring privacy through communication in different types of relationships. *Journal of Social and Personal Relationships, 6*, 131–158.

Burleson, B. R., & Denton, W. H. (1992). A new look at similarity and attraction in marriage: Similarities in social-cognitive and communication skills as predictors of attraction and satisfaction. *Communication Monographs, 59*, 268–287.

Buslig, A. L. S., & Burgoon, J. K. (2000). Aggressiveness in privacy-seeking behavior. In S. Petronio (Ed.), *Balancing the secrets of private disclosures* (pp. 181–196). Mahwah, NJ: Lawrence Erlbaum Associates.

Buss, D. M. (1994). *The evolution of desire: Strategies of human mating*. New York: Basic Books.

Buzawa, E., Hotaling, G., & Klein, A. (1998a). The response to domestic violence in a model court: Some initial findings and implications. *Behavioral Sciences and the Law, 16*, 185–206.

Buzawa, E., Hotaling, G., & Klein, A. (1998b). What happens when a reform works? The need to study unanticipated consequences of mandatory processing of domestic violence. *Journal of Police and Criminal Psychology, 13*, 43–54.

Calhoun, F. S. (1998). *Hunters and howlers: Threats and violence against federal judicial officials in the United States, 1789–1993* (USMS No. 80). Washington, DC: U.S. Department of Justice, U.S. Marshals Service.

Canary, D. J., & Cupach, W. R. (1988). Relational and episodic characteristics associated with conflict tactics. *Journal of Social and Personal Relationships, 5*, 305–325.

Canary, D. J., Cupach, W. R., & Messman, S. J. (1995). *Relationship conflict: Conflict in parent-child, friendship, and romantic relationships*. Thousand Oaks, CA: Sage.

Canary, D. J., & Spitzberg, B. H. (1987). Appropriateness and effectiveness in the perception of conflict strategies. *Human Communication Research, 14*, 93–118.

Canary, D. J., & Spitzberg, B. H. (1989). A model of competence perceptions of conflict strategies. *Human Communication Research, 15*, 630–649.

Canary, D. J., & Spitzberg, B. H. (1990). Attribution biases and associations between conflict strategies and competence outcomes. *Communication Monographs, 57*, 139–151.

Canary, D. J., & Stafford, L. (1994). Maintaining relationships through strategic and routine interaction. In D. J. Canary & L. Stafford (Eds.), *Communication and relational maintenance* (pp. 3–22). San Diego, CA: Academic Press.

Carlisle, A. C. (1998). The divided self: Toward understanding of the dark side of the serial killer. In R. M. Holmes & S. T. Holmes (Eds.), *Contemporary perspectives on serial murder* (pp. 85–100). Thousand Oaks, CA: Sage.

Carlson, M. J., Harris, S. D., & Holden, G. W. (1999). Protective orders and domestic violence: Risk factors for re-abuse. *Journal of Family Violence, 14*, 205–226.

Carmody, C. (1994). Deadly mistakes. *ABA Journal, 80*, 68–71.

Carpenter, B. N., Hansson, R. O., Rountree, R., & Jones, W. H. (1983). Relational competence and adjustment in diabetic patients. *Journal of Social and Clinical Psychology, 1*, 359–369.

Carrier, L. (1990). Erotomania and senile dementia. *American Journal of Psychiatry, 147*, 1092.

Carson, C. L., & Cupach, W. R. (2000). Fueling the flames of the green-eyed monster: The role of ruminative thought in reaction to romantic jealousy. *Western Journal of Communication, 64*, 308–329.

Carver, C. S., & Scheier, M. F. (1990). Origins and functions of positive and negative affect: A control-process view. *Psychological Review, 97*, 19–35.

Case, D. O. (2000). Stalking, monitoring and profiling: A typology and case studies of harmful uses of caller ID. *New Media & Society, 2*, 67–84.

Chaudhuri, M., & Daly, K. (1992). Do restraining orders help? Battered women's experience with male violence and legal process. In E. S. Buzawa & C. G. Buzawa (Eds.), *Domestic violence: The changing criminal justice response* (pp. 227–252). Westport, CT: Greenwood.

Chermak, S. M. (1995). *Victims in the news: Crime and the American news media*. Boulder, CO: Westview.

Christopher, F. S. (1988). An initial investigation into a continuum of premarital sexual pressure. *Journal of Sex Research, 25*, 255–266.

Clark, C. L., Shaver, P. R., & Abrahams, M. F. (1999). Strategic behaviors in romantic relationship initiation. *Personality and Social Psychology Bulletin, 25*, 707–720.

Clark, D. A., & Purdon, C. (1993). New perspectives for a cognitive theory of obsessions. *Australian Psychologist, 28*, 161–167.

Clark, J. W., Schneider, H. G., & Cox, R. L. (1998). Initial evidence for reliability and validity of a brief screening inventory for personality traits. *Psychological Reports, 82*, 1115–1120.

Clark, R. D. III. (1990). The impact of AIDS on gender differences in willingness to engage in casual sex. *Journal of Applied Social Psychology, 20*, 771–782.

Clark, R. E., & Labeff, E. E. (1986). Ending intimate relationships: Strategies of breaking off. *Sociological Spectrum, 6*, 245–267.

Cody, M. J. (1982). A typology of disengagement strategies and an examination of the role of intimacy, reactions to inequity and relational problems play in strategy selection. *Communication Monographs, 49*, 148–170.

Cody, M. J., Canary, D. J., & Smith, S. W. (1994). Compliance-gaining goals: An inductive analysis of actors' goal types, strategies, and successes. In J. A. Daly & J. M. Wiemann (Eds.), *Strategic interpersonal communication* (pp. 33–90). Hillsdale, NJ: Lawrence Erlbaum Associates.

Cody, M. J., Kersten, L., Braaten, D. O., & Dickson, R. (1992). Coping with relational dissolutions: Attributions, account credibility, and plans for resolving conflicts. In J. L. Harvey, T. L. Orbuch, & A. L. Weber (Eds.), *Attributions, accounts, and close relationships* (pp. 93–115). New York: Springer-Verlag.

Coffey, P., Leitenberg, H., Henning, K., Bennett, R. T., & Jankowski, M. K. (1996). Dating violence: The association between methods of coping and women's psychological adjustment. *Violence and Victims, 11*, 227–238.

Cohen, W. S. (1993). *Antistalking proposals*. Hearing before the Committee on the Judiciary, United States Senate (J-103-5). Washington, DC: U.S. Government Printing Office.

Coker, A. L., Davis, K. E., Arias, I., Desai, S., Sanderson, M., Brandt, H. M., & Smith, P. H. (2002). Physical and mental health effects of intimate partner violence for men and women. *American Journal of Preventative Medicine, 23*, 260–268.

Coleman, F. L. (1997). Stalking behavior and the cycle of domestic violence. *Journal of Interpersonal Violence, 12*, 420–433.

Coleman, F. L. (1999). *Clinical characteristics of stalkers.* Dissertation (UMI Dissertation Services No. 9949961), University of Memphis, Memphis, TN.

Collins, M. J., & Wilkas, M. B. (2001). Stalking trauma syndrome and the traumatized victim. In J. A. Davis (Ed.), *Stalking crimes and victim protection: Prevention, intervention, threat assessment, and case management* (pp. 317–334). Boca Raton, FL: CRC Press.

Collins, N. L., & Read, S. J. (1990). Adult attachment, working models, and relationship quality in dating couples. *Journal of Personality and Social Psychology, 58,* 644–663.

Committee on Criminal Courts. (1993). *The paper shield: Orders of protection in the New York City Criminal Court.* NY: Association of the Bar of the City of New York.

Copson, G., & Marshall, N. (2002). Police care and support for victims of stalking. In J. Boon & L. Sheridan (Eds.), *Stalking and psychosexual obsession: Psychological perspectives for prevention, policing and treatment* (pp. 49–62). West Sussex, England: John Wiley & Sons.

Corder, B. F., & Whiteside, R. (1996). A survey of psychologists' safety issues and concerns. *American Journal of Forensic Psychology, 14,* 65–72.

Cordes, R. (1993, October). Watching over the watched: Greater protection sought for stalking victims. *Trial, 29,* 12–13.

Coulter, M. L., Kuehnle, K., Byers, R., & Alfonso, M. (1999). Police-reporting behavior and victim-police interactions as described by women in a domestic violence shelter. *Journal of Interpersonal Violence, 14,* 1290–1298.

Cousins, A. V., & Nicastro, A. M. (1997, November). *Voices that have been silenced: A rhetorical analysis of stalking discourse.* Paper presented at the National Communication Association Convention, Chicago.

Covey, M. K., & Dengerink, H. A. (1984). Development and validation of a measure of heterosocial conflict resolution ability (Relational Behaviors Survey). *Behavioral Assessment, 6,* 323–332.

Crabb, P. B. (1999). The use of answering machines and caller ID to regulate home privacy. *Environment and Behavior, 31,* 657–670.

Craig, M. E. (1990). Coercive sexuality in dating relationships: A situational model. *Clinical Psychology Review, 10,* 395–423.

Creasey, G. (2002). Associations between working models of attachment and conflict management behavior in romantic couples. *Journal of Counseling Psychology, 49,* 365–375.

Creasey, G., & Hesson-McInnis, M. (2001). Affective responses, cognitive appraisals, and conflict tactics in late adolescent romantic relationships: Associations with attachment orientations. *Journal of Counseling Psychology, 48,* 85–96.

Cupach, W. R., & Carson, C. L. (2002). Characteristics and consequences of interpersonal complaints associated with perceived face threat. *Journal of Social and Personal Relationships, 19,* 443–462.

Cupach, W. R., & Metts, S. (1986). Accounts of relational dissolution: A comparison of marital and non-marital relationships. *Communication Monographs, 53,* 311–334.

Cupach, W. R., & Metts, S. (1991). Sex and communication in close relationships. In K. McKinney & S. Sprecher (Eds.), *Sexuality in close relationships* (pp. 93–109). Hillsdale, NJ: Lawrence Erlbaum Associates.

Cupach, W. R., & Metts, S. (1994). *Facework.* Thousand Oaks, CA: Sage.

Cupach, W. R., & Metts, S. (2002, July). *The persistence of reconciliation attempts following the dissolution of romantic relationships.* Paper presented at the 11th International Conference on Personal Relationships, Dalhousie University, Halifax, Nova Scotia, Canada.

Cupach, W. R., & Spitzberg, B. H. (Eds.). (1994). *The dark side of interpersonal communication.* Hillsdale, NJ: Lawrence Erlbaum Associates.

Cupach, W. R., & Spitzberg, B. H. (1998). Obsessive relational intrusion and stalking. In B. H. Spitzberg & W. R. Cupach (Eds.), *The dark side of close relationships* (pp. 233–263). Mahwah, NJ: Lawrence Erlbaum Associates.

Cupach, W. R., & Spitzberg, B. H. (2000). Obsessive relational intrusion: Incidence, perceived severity, and coping. *Violence and Victims, 15*, 357–372.

Cupach, W. R., & Spitzberg, B. H. (in press). Unrequited lust. In J. Harvey, A. Wenzel, & S. Sprecher (Eds.) *Handbook of sexuality in close relationships*. Mahwah, NJ: Lawrence Erlbaum Associates.

Cupach, W. R., Spitzberg, B. H., & Carson, C. L. (2000). Toward a theory of obsessive relational intrusion and stalking. In K. Dindia & S. Duck (Eds.), *Communication and personal relationships* (pp. 131–146). New York: John Wiley & Sons.

Currie, S. (2000, December). *Stalking and domestic violence: Views of Queensland Magistrates*. Paper presented to the Criminal Justice Responses Conference, Australian Institute of Criminology, Sydney.

CyberAngels. (2000). *Cyberstalking. Defining the problem*. Retrieved September 25, 2000. http://www.cyberangels.org/stalking/defining.html.

Daly, J. A., & Kreiser, P. O. (1994). Affinity seeking. In J. A. Daly & J. M. Wiemann (Eds.), *Strategic interpersonal communication* (pp. 109–134). Hillsdale, NJ: Lawrence Erlbaum Associates.

Dan, B., & Kornreich, C. (2000, September). Talmudic, Koranic, and other classic reports of stalking. *British Journal of Psychiatry, 177*, 282.

Danto, B. L. (2001). Minimizing potential threats and risks to stalking victims: Case management, security issues, and safety planning. In J. A. Davis (Ed.), *Stalking crimes and victim protection: Prevention, intervention, threat assessment, and case management* (pp. 283–297). Boca Raton, FL: CRC Press.

D'Arcy, M. (2000, December). *Stalking, sexual assault, domestic violence: What's in a name?* Paper presented to the Criminal Justice Responses Conference, Australian Institute of Criminology, Sydney.

Davis, J. A. (2001a). The assessment of potential threat: A second look. *Journal of Police and Criminal Psychology, 16*(1), 1–10.

Davis, J. A. (2001b). Obsession, fantasy, and the falsely alleged stalking victim. In J. A. Davis (Ed.), *Stalking crimes and victim protection: Prevention, intervention, threat assessment, and case management* (pp. 375–384). Boca Raton, FL: CRC Press.

Davis, J. A. (2001c). Staying one step ahead of stalkers and stalking crimes: Personnel development, training, and ongoing education. In J. A. Davis (Ed.), *Stalking crimes and victim protection: Prevention, intervention, threat assessment, and case management* (pp. 489–494). Boca Raton, FL: CRC Press.

Davis, J. A. (in press). Voyeurism: A criminal precursor and diagnostic indicator to a much larger sexual predatory problem in our community. In R. M. Holmes (Ed.), *Sex Crimes* (2nd ed.). Thousand Oaks, CA: Sage.

Davis, J. A., & Chipman, M. A. (1997a). Stalkers and other obsessional types: A review and forensic psychological typology of those who stalk. *Journal of Clinical Forensic Medicine, 4*, 166–172.

Davis, J. A., & Chipman, M. A. (1997b, May). *Stalking: Legal and forensic mental health implications*. Paper presented at the San Diego Stalking Strike Force "Stalking the Stalker" Conference, San Diego, CA.

Davis, J. A., & Chipman, M. A. (2001). Stalkers and other obsessional types: A review and forensic psychological typology of those who stalk. In J. A. Davis (Ed.), *Stalking crimes and victim protection: Prevention, intervention, threat assessment, and case management* (pp. 3–18). Boca Raton, FL: CRC Press.

Davis, J. A., & Gonzales, A. M. (2001). Stalking as a variant of a therapeutic relationship: A meta-analysis of patients who stalk their former treatment providers. *McNair Scholars Journal, 8*, 131–142.

Davis, J. A., Siota, R., & Stewart, L. (1999). Future prediction of dangerous and violent behavior: Psychological indicators and considerations for conducting and assessment of potential threat. *Canadian Journal of Clinical Medicine, 6*(3), 44–57.

Davis, J. A., Stewart, L. M., & Siota, R. (2001). Future prediction of dangerousness and violent behavior: Psychological indicators and considerations for conducting an assessment of potential threat. In J. A. Davis (Ed.), *Stalking crimes and victim protection: Prevention, intervention, threat assessment, and case management* (pp. 261–282). Boca Raton, FL: CRC Press.

Davis, K. E., Ace, A., & Andra, M. (2000). Stalking perpetrators and psychological maltreatment of partners: Anger-jealousy, attachment insecurity, need for control, and break-up context. *Violence and Victims, 15*, 407–425.

Davis, K. E., Coker, A. L., & Sanderson, M. (2002). Physical and mental health effects of being stalked for men and women. *Violence and Victims, 17*, 429–443.

Davis, K. E., & Frieze, I. H. (2000). Research on stalking: What do we know and where do we go? *Violence and Victims, 15*, 473–487.

Davis, K. E., Frieze, I. H., & Maiuro, R. D. (Eds.). (2002) *Stalking: Perspectives on victims and perpetrators*. New York: Springer.

Davis, M. H., & Oathout, H. A. (1987). Maintenance of satisfaction in romantic relationships: Empathy and relational competence. *Journal of Personality and Social Psychology, 53*, 397–410.

Davis, R. C., & Smith, B. (1995). Domestic violence reforms: Empty promises or fulfilled expectations? *Crime and Delinquency, 41*, 541–552.

de Becker, G. (1992). Testimony of Gavin de Becker before Senate Judiciary Committee Hearings on unwanted pursuit. *Antistalking legislation*. Hearing before the Committee on the Judiciary, United States Senate (J-102-86, pp. 87–89). Washington, DC: U.S. Government Printing Office.

de Becker, G. (1997a). *The gift of fear: Survival signals that protect us from violence*. Boston: Little, Brown.

de Becker, G. (1997b, May). *Intervention decisions: The value of flexibility*. Paper presented at the San Diego Stalking Strike Force "Stalking the Stalker" Conference, San Diego.

de Clérambault, C. G. (1942). Les psychoses passionelles. In *Oeuvres psychiatriques* (pp. 315–322). Paris: Presses Universitaires.

de Girolamo, G., & McFarlane, A. C. (1996). The epidemiology of PTSD: A comprehensive review of the international literature. In A. J. Marsella, M. J., Friedman, E. T. Gerrity, & R. M. Scurfield (Eds.), *Ethnocultural aspects of post-traumatic stress disorder: Issues, research, and clinical applications* (pp. 33–86). Washington, DC: American Psychological Association.

Deirmenjian, J. M. (1999). Stalking in cyberspace. *Journal of the American Academy of Psychiatry and the Law, 27*, 407–413.

Del Ben, K. (2000). *Stalking: Developing an empirical typology to classify stalkers*. Unpublished master's thesis, Department of Psychology, West Virginia University, Morgantown.

Del Ben, K., & Fremouw, W. (2002). Stalking: Developing an empirical typology to classify stalkers. *Journal of Forensic Sciences, 47*, 152–158.

Dennison, S., & Thomson, D. M. (2000a). Community perceptions of stalking: What are the fundamental concerns? *Psychiatry, Psychology and Law, 7*, 159–169.

Dennison, S., & Thomson, D. M. (2000b, December). *Is this stalking? A comparison between legal and community definitions of stalking*. Paper presented to the Criminal Justice Responses Conference, Australian Institute of Criminology, Sydney.

Dennison, S. M., & Thomson, D. M. (2002). Identifying stalking: The relevance of intent in commonsense reasoning. *Law and Human Behavior, 26*, 543–561.

Department of Justice, Victoria. (1996). *Crimes family violence act: 1994/95 Monitoring report*. (Caseflow Analysis Section, Courts and Tribunals Services.) Melbourne, Australia: Author.

Derogatis, L. R., Lipman, R. S., Rickels, K., Uhlenhuth, E. H., & Covi, L. (1974). The Hopkins symptom checklist (HSCL): A self-report symptom inventory. *Behavioral Science, 19*, 1–15.

Derogatis, L. R., Rickels, K., & Rock, A. F. (1976). The SCL-90 and the MMPI: A step in the validation of a new self-report scale. *British Journal of Psychiatry, 128*, 280–289.

deTurck, M. A. (1985). A transactional analysis of compliance-gaining behavior: Effects of non-compliance, relational contexts, and actors' gender. *Human Communication Research, 12*, 54–78.

deTurck, M. A. (1987). When communication fails: Physical aggression as a compliance-gaining strategy. *Communication Monographs, 54* 106–112.

Diacovo, N. (1995). California's anti-stalking statute: Deterrent or false sense of security? *Southwestern University Law Review, 24*, 389–421.

Dietz, P. E., Matthews, D. B., Martell, D. A., Stewart, T. M., Hrouda, D. R., & Warren, J. (1991). Threatening and otherwise inappropriate letters to members of the United States Congress. *Journal of Forensic Sciences, 36*, 1445–1468.

Dietz, P. E., Matthews, D. B., Van Duyne, C., Martell, D. A., Parry, C. D. H., Stewart, T., Warren, J., & Crowder, J. D. (1991). Threatening and otherwise inappropriate letters to Hollywood celebrities. *Journal of Forensic Sciences, 36*, 185–209.

Dillard, J. P. (1989). Types of influence goals in personal relationships. *Journal of Social and Personal Relationships, 6*, 293–308.

Dillard, J. P. (1997). Explicating the goal construct: Tools for theorists. In J. O. Greene (Ed.), *Message production: Advances in communication theory* (pp. 47–69). Mahwah, NJ: Lawrence Erlbaum Associates.

Dillard, J. P., Segrin, C., & Harden, J. M. (1989). Primary and secondary goals in the production of interpersonal influence messages. *Communication Monographs, 56*, 19–38.

Dindia, K., & Timmerman, L. (2003). Accomplishing romantic relationships. In J. O. Greene & B. R. Burleson (Eds.), *Handbook of communication and social interaction skills* (pp. 685–721). Mahwah, NJ: Lawrence Erlbaum Associates.

Dinkelmeyer, A., & Johnson, M. B. (2002). Stalking and harassment of psychotherapists. *American Journal of Forensic Psychology, 20*, 5–20.

Di Paula, A., & Campbell, J. D. (2002). Self-esteem and persistence in the face of failure. *Journal of Personality and Social Psychology, 83*, 711–724.

DiVasto, P. V., Kaufman, A., Rosner, L., Jackson, R., Christy, J., Pearson, S., & Burgett, T. (1984). The prevalence of sexually stressful events among females in the general population. *Archives of Sexual Behavior, 13*, 59–67.

Dolan, M., & Doyle, M. (2000). Violence risk prediction: Clinical and actuarial measures and the role of the Psychopathy Checklist. *British Journal of Psychiatry, 177*, 303–311.

Douglas, J., & Olshaker, M. (1998). *Obsession*. New York: Scribner.

Douglas, K. S., & Dutton, D. G. (2001). Assessing the link between stalking and domestic violence. *Aggression and Violent Behavior, 6*, 519–546.

Douglas, W. (1987). Affinity-testing in initial interactions. *Journal of Social and Personal Relationships, 4*, 3–15.

Doust, J. W. L., & Christie, H. (1978). The pathology of love: Some clinical variants of de Clérambault's syndrome. *Social Science Medicine, 12*, 99–106.

Downey, G., & Feldman, S. I. (1996). Implications of rejection sensitivity for intimate relationships. *Journal of Personality and Social Psychology, 70*, 1327–1343.

Downey, G., Feldman, S., & Ayduk, O. (2000). Rejection sensitivity and male violence in romantic relationships. *Personal Relationships, 7*, 45–61.

Draucker, C. B. (1999). "Living in hell": The experience of being stalked. *Issues in Mental Health Nursing, 20*, 473–484.

Dressing, H., Henn, F. A., & Gass, P. (2002). Stalking behavior: An overview of the problem and a case report of male-to-male stalking during delusional disorder. *Psychopathology, 35*, 313–318.

Drevets, W. C., & Rubin, E. H. (1987). Erotomania and senile dementia of Alzheimer type. *British Journal of Psychiatry, 151*, 400–402.

Drucker, S. J., & Gumpert, G. (2000). CyberCrime and punishment. *Critical Studies in Media Communication, 17*, 133–158.

Duck, S. (Ed.). (1984). *Personal relationships 5: Repairing personal relationships*. New York: Academic Press.

Duck, S. (1990). Relationships as unfinished business: Out of the frying pan and into the 1990's. *Journal of Social and Personal Relationships, 7,* 5–28.

Duck, S. (1994). Stratagems, spoils, and a serpent's tooth: On the delights and dilemmas of personal relationships. In W. R. Cupach & B. H. Spitzberg (Eds.), *The dark side of interpersonal communication* (pp. 3–24). Hillsdale, NJ: Lawrence Erlbaum Associates.

Dunlop, J. L. (1988). Does erotomania exist between women? *British Journal of Psychiatry, 153,* 830–833.

Dunn, J. L. (1999). What love has to do with it: The cultural construction of emotion and sorority women's responses to forcible interaction. *Social Problems, 46,* 440–459.

Dunn, J. L. (2001). Innocence lost: Accomplishing victimization in intimate cases. *Symbolic Interaction, 24,* 285–313.

Dunn, J. L. (2002). *Courting disaster: Intimate stalking, culture, and criminal justice*. New York: Aldine de Gruyter.

DuPont-Morales, M. A. (1999). De-gendering predatory violence: The female stalker. *Humanity and Society, 23,* 366–379.

Dupont-Morales, M. A. (1998). The female stalker. In L. J. Moriarty & R. A. Jerin (Eds.), *Current issues in victimology research* (pp. 223–238). Durham, NC: Carolina Academic Press.

Dussuyer, I. (2000, December). *Is stalking legislation effective in protecting victims?* Paper presented to the Criminal Justice Responses Conference, Australian Institute of Criminology, Sydney.

Dutton, D. G. (1995). *The batterer: A psychological profile*. New York: Basic Books.

Dutton, D. G., Saunders, K., Starzomski, A., & Bartholomew, K. (1994). Intimacy anger and insecure attachment as precursors of abuse in intimate relationships. *Journal of Applied Social Psychology, 24,* 1367–1386.

Dutton, D. G., van Ginkel, C., & Landolt, M. A. (1996). Jealousy, intimate abusiveness, and intrusiveness. *Journal of Family Violence, 11,* 411–423.

Dutton-Greene, L. B. (2003). [*Correlates of unwanted pursuit and stalking*]. Unpublished raw data, University of Rhode Island, Kingston.

Dutton-Greene, L. B., & Winstead, B. A. (2001, July). *Factors associated with the occurrence and cessation of obsessive relational intrusion*. Paper presented at the joint conference of the International Network on Personal Relationships and the International Society for the Study of Personal Relationships, Prescott, AZ.

Dye, M. L., & Davis, K. E. (2003). Stalking and psychological abuse: Common factors and relationship-specific characteristics. *Violence & Victims, 18,* 163–180.

Dziegielewski, S. F., & Roberts, A. R. (1995). Stalking victims and survivors: Identification, legal remedies, and crisis treatment. In A. R. Roberts (Ed.), *Crisis intervention and time-limited cognitive treatment* (pp. 73–90). Thousand Oaks, CA: Sage.

Egland, K. L., Spitzberg, B. H., & Zormeier, M. M. (1996). Flirtation and conversational competence in cross-sex platonic and romantic relationships. *Communication Reports, 9,* 105–117.

Eisele, G. R., Watkins, J. P., & Matthews, K. O. (1998). Workplace violence at government sites. *American Journal of Industrial Medicine, 33,* 485–492.

Eke, A. W. (1999). *Stalking offences and victim impact in a forensic sample of Ontario stalking survivors*. Unpublished master's thesis, Graduate Programme in Psychology, York University, Toronto, Ontario, Canada.

El Gaddal, Y. Y. (1989). de Clérambault's Syndrome (erotomania) in organic delusional syndrome. *British Journal of Psychiatry, 154,* 714–716.

Elliott, L., & Brantley, C. (1997). *Sex on campus: The naked truth about the real sex lives of college students*. New York: Random House.

Emer, D. M. (2001). Obsessive behavior and relational violence in juvenile populations: Stalking case analysis and legal implications. In J. A. Davis (Ed.), *Stalking crimes and victim protection: Prevention, intervention, threat assessment, and case management* (pp. 33–68). Boca Raton, FL: CRC Press.

Emerson, R. M., Ferris, K. O., & Gardner, C. B. (1998). On being stalked. *Social Problems, 45,* 289–314.

Emmers-Sommer, T. M. (2003). When partners falter: Repair after a transgression. In D. J. Canary & M. Dainton (Eds.), *Maintaining relationships through communication: Relational, contextual, and cultural variations* (pp. 185–205). Mahwah, NJ: Lawrence Erlbaum Associates.

Erickson, E. V., Cheatham, T. R., & Haggard, C. R. (1976). A survey of police communication training. *Communication Education, 25,* 299–306.

Evans, D. L., Jeckel, L. L., & Slott, N. E. (1982). Erotomania: A variant of pathological mourning. *Bulletin of the Menninger Clinic, 46,* 507–520.

Evans, R. (1994). Every step you take: The strange and subtle crime of stalking. *Law Institute Journal, 68,* 1021–1023.

Evans, T. D., Cullen, F. T., Burton, V. S., Jr., Dunaway, R. G., & Benson, M. L. (1997). The social consequences of self-control: Testing the general theory of crime. *Criminology, 35,* 457–504.

Farnham, F. R., & James, D. (2000, December). *Stalking and serious violence.* Paper presented to the Criminal Justice Responses Conference, Australian Institute of Criminology, Sydney.

Farnham, F. R., James, D. V., & Cantrell, P. (2000). Association between violence, psychosis, and relationship to victim in stalkers. *Lancet, 355,* 199.

Farrell, G., Weisburd, D., & Wyckoff, L. (2000). Survey results suggest need for stalking training. *Police Chief, 67*(10), 162–167.

Fattah, E. A. (1997). Toward a victim policy aimed at healing, not suffering. In R. C. Davis (Ed.), *Victims of crime* (2nd ed., pp. 257–272). Thousand Oaks, CA: Sage.

Feeney, D. J., Jr. (1999). *Entrancing relationships: Exploring the hypnotic framework of addictive relationships.* Westport, CT: Praeger.

Feeney, J. A. (1999). Adult romantic attachment and couple relationships. In J. Cassidy & P. Shaver (Ed.), *Handbook of attachment: Theory, research, and clinical applications* (pp. 355–377). New York: Guilford.

Feeney, J. A., & Noller, P. (1990). Attachment style as a predictor of adult romantic relationships. *Journal of Personality and Social Psychology, 58,* 282–291.

Feeney, J. A., & Noller, P. (1992). Attachment style and romantic love: Relationship dissolution. *Australian Journal of Psychology, 44,* 69–74.

Feeney, J. A., Noller, P., & Callan, V. J. (1994). Attachment style, communication and satisfaction in the early years of marriage. In K. Bartholomew & D. Perlman (Eds.), *Advances in personal relationships: Vol. 5. Attachment processes in adulthood* (pp. 269–308). London: Jessica Kingsley.

Fein, R. A., & Vossekuil, B. (1998). Preventing attacks on public officials and public figures: A secret service perspective. In J. R. Meloy (Ed.), *The psychology of stalking* (pp. 175–191). San Diego, CA: Academic Press.

Fein, R. A., & Vossekuil, B. (1999). Assassination in the United States: An operational study of recent assassins, attackers, and near-lethal approachers. *Journal of Forensic Sciences, 44,* 321–333.

Fein, R. A., Vossekuil, B., & Holden, G. A. (1995, September). *Threat assessment: An approach to prevent targeted violence.* National Institute of Justice Research in Action (NCJ 155000). Washington, DC: U.S. Department of Justice.

Feldmann, T. B., Holt, J., & Hellard, S. (1997). Violence in medical facilities: A review of 40 incidents. *Journal of the Kentucky Medical Association, 95,* 183–189.

Felson, R. B. (2002). *Violence & gender reexamined.* Washington, DC: American Psychological Association.

Fenchel, G. H. (1995). The narcissism of minor differences: Love and hate in intimate relationships. *Issues in Psychoanalytic Psychology, 17,* 84–93.

Fernandez-Esquer, M. E., & McCloskey, L. A. (1999). Coping with partner abuse among Mexican American and Anglo women: Ethnic and socioeconomic influences. *Violence and Victims, 14,* 293–310.

Ferraro, K. J., & Boychuk, T. (1992). The court's response to interpersonal violence: A comparison of intimate and nonintimate assault. In E. S. Buzawa & C. G. Buzawa (Eds.), *Domestic violence: The changing criminal justice response* (pp. 209–226). Westport, CT: Greenwood.

Finch, E. (2001). *The criminalization of stalking: Constructing the problem and evaluating the solution.* London: Cavendish.

Finkelhor, D., Mitchell, K. J., & Wolak, J. (2000). *Online victimization: A report on the nation's youth.* Alexandria, VA: Crimes Against Children Research Center.

Finn, J., & Banach, M. (2000). Victimization online: The down side of seeking human services for women on the internet. *CyberPsychology & Behavior, 3,* 243–254.

Finn, P., & Colson, S. (1990). *Civil protection orders: Legislation, current court practice, and enforcement.* Washington, DC: U.S. Department of Justice, Office of Justice Programs, National Institute of Justice.

Fischer, K., & Rose, M. (1995). When "enough is enough": Battered women's decision making around court orders of protection. *Crime and Delinquency, 41,* 414–429.

Fishbein, M., & Ajzen, I. (1975). *Belief, attitude, intention and behavior: An introduction to theory and research.* Reading, MA: Addison-Wesley.

Fisher, B. S. (2001). Being pursued and pursuing during the college years: Their extent, nature, and impact of stalking on college campuses. In J. A. Davis (Ed.), *Stalking crimes and victim protection: Prevention, intervention, threat assessment, and case management* (pp. 207–238). Boca Raton, FL: CRC Press.

Fisher, B. S., Cullen, F. T., & Turner, M. G. (1999). *The extent and nature of the sexual victimization of college women: A national-level analysis.* Final Report submitted to the National Institute of Justice (NCJ 179977). Washington, DC: U. S. Department of Justice.

Fisher, B. S., Cullen, F. T., & Turner, M. G. (2000). *The sexual victimization of college women.* Washington, DC: National Institute of Justice, Bureau of Justice Statistics, Department of Justice.

Fisher, B. S., Cullen, F. T., & Turner, M. G. (2002). Being pursued: Stalking victimization in a national study of college women. *Criminology and Public Policy, 1,* 257–308.

Fisher, H. E. (1992). *Anatomy of love: The natural history of monogamy, adultery, and divorce.* New York: W. W. Norton.

Fitzgerald, P., & Seeman, M. V. (2002). Erotomania in women. In J. Boon & L. Sheridan (Eds.), *Stalking and psychosexual obsession: Psychological perspectives for prevention, policing and treatment* (pp. 165–180). West Sussex, England: John Wiley & Sons.

Flannery, R. B., Jr., Hanson, M. A., Penk, W. E., & Flannery, G. J. (1994). Violence against women: Psychiatric patient assaults on female staff. *Professional Psychology: Research and Practice, 25,* 182–184.

Fleury, R. E., Sullivan, C. M., & Bybee, D. I. (2000). When ending the relationship does not end the violence: Women's experiences of violence by former partners. *Violence Against Women, 6,* 1363–1383.

Flowers, R. B. (1994). *The victimization and exploitation of women and children: A study of physical, mental and sexual maltreatment in the United States.* Jefferson, NC: McFarland & Co.

Floyd, K. (1998). Intimacy as a research construct: A content-analytic review. *Representative Research in Social Psychology, 22,* 28–32.

Floyd, K., & Voloudakis, M. (1999). Attributions for expectancy violating changes in affectionate behavior in platonic friendships. *Journal of Psychology, 133,* 32–48.

Folkes, V. S. (1982). Communicating the reasons for social rejection. *Journal of Experimental Social Psychology, 18,* 235–252.

Follingstad, D. R., & DeHart, D. D. (1997, June–July). *Defining psychological abuse: Contexts, behaviors, and typologies.* Paper presented at the International Network on Personal Relationships Conference, Oxford, OH.

Footlick, J. K., Howard, L., Camper, D., Sciolino, E., & Smith, S. (1975). Rape alert. *Newseek, 70.* Retrieved April 4, 2003, from http://80-web.lexis-nexis.com.webgate.sdsu.edu:88/universe/document?_m=edc35d667e36606652847ea26702a7ff&_docnum=1&wchp=dGLbVzz-Sl Al&_md5=dd671c59e3407a3719ef7e7ba5d88371.

Frazier, P. A., & Cook, S. W. (1993). Correlates of distress following heterosexual relationship dissolution. *Journal of Social and Personal Relationships, 10,* 55–67.

Freckelton, I. (2001). Stalker sentencing and protection of the public. *Journal of Law and Medicine, 8,* 233–239.

Fremouw, W. J., Westrup, D., & Pennypacker, J. (1997). Stalking on campus: The prevalence and strategies for coping with stalking. *Journal of Forensic Sciences, 42,* 664–667.

Friedman, M. J., & Marsella, A. J. (1996). Posttraumatic stress disorder: An overview of the concept. In A. J. Marsella, M. J., Friedman, E. T. Gerrity, & R. M. Scurfield (Eds.), *Ethnocultural aspects of post-traumatic stress disorder: Issues, research, and clinical applications* (pp. 11–32). Washington, DC: American Psychological Association.

Frieze, I. H. (2000). Violence in close relationships—Development of a research area: Comment on Archer (2000). *Psychological Bulletin, 126,* 681–684.

Fritz, J. M. H. (1997). Responses to unpleasant work relationships. *Communication Research Reports, 14,* 302–311.

Fry, P. S., & Barker, L. A. (2001). Female survivors of violence and abuse: Their regrets of action and inaction in coping. *Journal of Interpersonal Violence, 16,* 320–342.

Fry, P. S., & Barker, L. A. (2002). Quality of relationships and structural properties of social support networks of female survivors of abuse. *Genetic, Social and General Psychology Monographs, 128,* 139–163.·

Fyfe, J. J., Klinger, D. A., & Flavin, J. M. (1997). Differential police treatment of male-on-female spousal violence. *Criminology, 35,* 455–473.

Gaines, S. O., Jr. (1994). Exchange of respect-denying behaviors among male–female friendships. *Journal of Social and Personal Relationships, 11,* 5–24.

Gallagher, R. P. (1997). *Trends in college counseling centers.* Powerpoint document, available from Brian Spitzberg, School of Communication, San Diego State Univeristy.

Gallagher, R. P., Bruner, L. A., & Lingenfelter, C. O. (1993). *National survey of counseling center directors* (Series No. 8-E). Alexandria, VA: International Association of Counseling Services, Inc.

Gallagher, R. P., Christofidis, A., Gill, A. M., & Weaver-Graham, W. (1996). *National survey of counseling center directors* (Series No. 8-F). Alexandria, VA: International Association of Counseling Services, Inc.

Gallagher, R. P., et al. (2000). *National survey of counseling center directors* (Series No. 8-J). Alexandria, VA: International Association of Counseling Services, Inc.

Gallagher, R. P., Gill, A. M., & Goldstrohm, S. (1997). *National survey of counseling center directors* (Series No. 8-G). Alexandria, VA: International Association of Counseling Services, Inc.

Gallagher, R. P., Gill, A. M., & Goldstrohm, S. L. (1998). *National survey of counseling center directors* (Series No. 8-H). Alexandria, VA: International Association of Counseling Services, Inc.

Gallagher, R. P., Gill, A. M., Goldstrohm, S. L., & Sysko, H. B. (1999). *National survey of counseling center directors* (Series No. 8-I). Alexandria, VA: International Association of Counseling Services, Inc.

Gallagher, R. P., Harmon, W. W., & Lingenfelter, C. O. (1994). CSAOs' perceptions of the changing incidence of problematic college student behavior. *NASPA Journal, 32,* 37–45.

Gallagher, R. P., Sysko, H. B., & Zhang, B. (2001). *National survey of counseling center directors* (Series No. 8-K). Alexandria, VA: International Association of Counseling Services, Inc.

Gallagher, R. P., & Zhang, B. (2002). *National survey of counseling center directors* (Series No. 8-L). Alexandria, VA: International Association of Counseling Services, Inc.

Gargan, J. P. (1994, February). Stop stalkers before they strike. *Security Management, 38*, 31–32, 34.

Geberth, V. J. (1992). Stalkers. *Law and Order, 40*, 138–143.

Gedatus, G. (2000). *Stalking* (Perspectives on Violence Series). Mankato, MN: Capstone Press.

Gentile, S. R. (2001). *The stalking of psychologists by their clients: A descriptive study*. Unpublished dissertation, Department of Psychology, Pepperdine University, CA.

Gentile, S. R., Asamen, J. K., Harmell, P. H., & Weathers, R. (2002). The stalking of psychologists by their clients. *Professional Psychology Research & Practice, 33*, 490–494.

Giddens, A. (1992). *The transformation of intimacy: Sexuality, love and eroticism in modern societies*. Stanford, CA: Stanford University Press.

Gilbert, N. (1993). Examining the facts: Advocacy research overstates the incidence of date and acquaintance rape. In R. J. Gelles & D. R. Loseke (Eds.), *Current controversies on family violence* (pp. 120–132). Newbury Park: Sage.

Gill, R., & Brockman, J. (1996). *A review of section 264 (criminal harassment) of the Criminal Code of Canada*. Working document WD 1996-7e. Research, Statistics and Evaluation Directorate. Ottawa, Ontario: Department of Justice, Canada.

Gillett, T., Eminson, S. R., & Hassanyeh, F. (1990). Primary and secondary erotomania: Clinical characteristics and follow-up. *Acta Psychiatrica Scandinavica, 82*, 65–69.

Gist, J. H., McFarlane, J., Malecha, A., Fredland, N., Schultz, P., & Willson, P. (2001). Women in danger: Intimate partner violence experienced by women who qualify and do not qualify for a protective order. *Behavioral Sciences and the Law, 19*, 637–647.

Gmelch, G., & San Antonio, P. M. (1998). Groupies and American baseball. *Journal of Sport & Social Issues, 22*, 32–45.

Godwin, G. M. (2000). *Hunting serial predators: A multivariate classification approach to profiling violent behavior*. Boca Raton, FL: CRC Press.

Golding, J. M., Wilsnack, S. C., & Cooper, M. L. (2002). Sexual assault history and social support: Six general population studies. *Journal of Traumatic Stress, 15*, 187–197.

Goldstein, R. L. (1987). More forensic romances: De Clérambault's syndrome in men. *Bulletin of the American Academy of Psychiatry and Law, 15*, 267–274.

Gollwitzer, P. M., Wicklund, R. A., & Hilton, J. L. (1982). Admission of failure and self-completion: Extending Lewinian theory. *Journal of Personality and Social Psychology, 43*, 358–371.

Gondolf, E. W., McWilliams, J., Hart, B., & Stuehling, J. (1994). Court response to petitions for civil protection orders. *Journal of Interpersonal Violence, 9*, 503–517.

Goodnough, D. (2000). *Stalking* (A Hot Issue Series). Berkeley Heights, NJ: Enslow.

Gouda, N. (2000, December). *Legislative and criminal justice responses to stalking in the context of domestic violence*. Paper presented to the Criminal Justice Responses Conference, Australian Institute of Criminology, Sydney.

Graham, D. L. R. (1994). *Loving to survive: Sexual terror, men's violence, and women's lives*. New York: New York University Press.

Grammar, K. (1990). Strangers meet: Laughter and nonverbal signs of interest in opposite-sex encounters. *Journal of Nonverbal Behavior, 14*, 209–236.

Grau, J., Fagan, J., & Wexler, S. (1985). Restraining orders for battered women: Issues of access and efficacy. In C. Schweber, & C. Feinman (Eds.), *Criminal justice politics and women: The aftermath of legally mandated change* (pp. 13–28). New York: Haworth.

Greenberg, M. A., Wortman, C. B., & Stone, A. A. (1996). Emotional expression and physical health: Revising traumatic memories or fostering self-regulation? *Journal of Personality and Social Psychology, 71*, 588–602.

Gross, L. (1994). *To have or to harm: From infatuation to fatal attraction.* New York: Warner Books.

Gross, L. (2000). *Surviving a stalker: Everything you need to know to keep yourself safe.* (reprint; previous title: *To have or to harm*). New York: Marlowe.

Gruber, J. E. (1989). How women handle sexual harassment: A literature review. *Sociology and Social Research, 74,* 3–9.

Gudykunst, W. B., & Nishida, T. (1987). The influence of cultural variability on perceptions of communication behavior associated with relationship terms. *Human Communication Research, 13,* 147–166.

Guerrero, L. K. (1998). Attachment-style differences in the experience and expression of romantic jealousy. *Personal Relationships, 5,* 273–291.

Guerrero, L. K., & Andersen, P.A. (1998). The dark side of jealousy and envy: Desire, delusion, desperation, and destructive communication. In B. H. Spitzberg & W. R. Cupach (Eds.), *The dark side of close relationships* (pp. 33–70). Mahwah, NJ: Lawrence Erlbaum Associates.

Guerrero, L. K., Andersen, P. A., Jorgensen, P. F., Spitzberg, B. H., & Eloy, S. V. (1995). Coping with the green-eyed monster: Conceptualizing and measuring communicative and behavioral reactions to romantic jealousy. *Western Journal of Communication, 59,* 1–35.

Guerrero, L. K., Spitzberg, B. H., & Yoshimura, S. M. (in press). Sexual and emotional jealousy. In J. Harvey, A. Wenzel, & S. Sprecher (Eds.), *Handbook of sexuality in close relationships.* Mahwah, NJ: Lawrence Erlbaum Associates.

Guy, J. D., Brown, C. K., & Poelstra, P. L. (1992). Safety concerns and protective measures used by psychotherapists. *Professional Psychology: Research and Practice, 23,* 421–423.

Gylys, J. A., & McNamara, J. R. (1996). A further examination of the validity for the Sexual Experiences Survey. *Behavioral Sciences and the Law, 14,* 245–260.

Hackett, K. (2000). Criminal harassment. *Juristat, 20*(11), Catalogue no. 85-002-XIE. Ontario: Statistics Canada/Canadian Centre for Justice Statistics.

Hall, C. (1998, January 8). 1 in 20 GPs is sexually harassed by patient. *Electronic Telegraph* (www.telegraph.co.uk).

Hall, D. (1996). *Outside looking in: Stalkers and their victims.* Paper presented to the Academy of Criminal Justice Sciences Conference, Claremont Graduate School, San Francisco, CA.

Hall, D. M. (1997). *Outside looking in: Stalkers and their victims.* Unpublished doctoral dissertation, Claremont Graduate School, Claremont, CA.

Hall, D. M. (1998). The victims of stalking. In J. R. Meloy (Ed.), *The psychology of stalking* (pp. 113–137). San Diego, CA: Academic Press.

Hammell, B., Hoyt, D., & Lipson, G. (1996, August). *Stalking of mental health professionals.* Powerpoint presentation to the "Stalking the Stalker" Conference, San Diego, CA.

Hample, D., & Dallinger, J. M. (1998). On the etiology of the rebuff phenomenon: Why are persuasive messages less polite after rebuffs? *Communication Studies, 49,* 305–321.

Hansson, R. O. (1986). Relational competence, relationships, and adjustment in old age. *Journal of Personality and Social Psychology, 50,* 1050–1058.

Hansson, R. O., Jones, W. H., & Carpenter, B. N. (1984). Relational competence and social support. *Review of Personality and Social Psychology, 5,* 265–284.

Hargreaves, J. (2000). Stalking. In J. M. Siegel, P. J. Saukko, & G. C. Knupfer (Eds.), *Encyclopedia of forensic sciences* (pp. 1350–1356). San Diego, CA: Academic.

Hargreaves, J. (n.d.). Stalking behaviour. In D. V. Canter & L. Alison (Eds.), *Profiling rape and murder* (Offender Profiling Series V, pp. 1–16). Aldershot, England: Ashgate.

Harmon, R. B., Rosner, R., & Owens, H. (1995). Obsessional harassment and erotomania in a criminal court population. *Journal of Forensic Sciences, 40,* 188–196.

Harmon, R. B., Rosner, R., & Owens, H. (1998). Sex and violence in a forensic population of obsessional harassers. *Psychology, Public Policy, and Law, 4,* 236–249.

Harnish, J. D., Aseltine, R. H., Jr., & Gore, S. (2000). Resolution of stressful experiences as an indicator of coping effectiveness in young adults: An event history analysis. *Journal of Health and Social Behavior, 41*, 121–136.

Harper, N. (1979). *Human communication theory: The history of a paradigm*. Rochelle Park, NJ: Hayden.

Harrell, A., & Smith, B. E. (1996). Effects of restraining orders on domestic violence victims. In E. S. Buzawa & C. G. Buzawa (Eds.), *Do arrests and restraining orders work?* (pp. 214–242). Thousand Oaks, CA: Sage.

Harrell, A., Smith, B., & Newmark, L. (1993). *Court processing and the effects of restraining orders for domestic violence victims* (Executive Summary). Washington, DC: Urban Institute.

Harris, J. (2000). *The Protection From Harassment Act 1997—An evaluation of its use and effectiveness* (Research Findings No. 130). London: Great Britain Home Office Research and Development and Statistics Directorate.

Harris, M. B., & Miller, K. C. (2000). Gender and perceptions of danger. *Sex Roles, 43*, 843–863.

Harris, S. D., Dean, K. R., Holden, G. W., & Carlson, M. J. (2001). Assessing police and protective order reports of violence: What is the relation? *Journal of Interpersonal Violence, 16*, 602–609.

Hart, B. (1996). Battered women and the criminal justice system. In E. S. Buzawa & C. G. Buzawa (Eds.), *Do arrests and restraining orders work?* (pp. 98–114). Thousand Oaks, CA: Sage.

Hatfield, E., & Rapson, R. (1993). Love and attachment processes. In M. Lewis & J. M. Haviland (Eds.), *Handbook of emotions* (pp. 595–604). New York: Guilford.

Hathaway, J., Silverman, J., Aynalem, G., Mucci, L., & Brooks, D. (2000). Use of medical care, police assistance, and restraining orders by women reporting partner violence—Massachusetts, 1996–1997. *Morbidity and Mortality Weekly Report, 49*, 485–488.

Hays, J. R., Romans, J. S. C., & Ritchhart, M. K. (1995). Reducing stalking behaviors for college and university counseling services. *Journal of College Student Psychotherapy, 10*, 57–63.

Hazan, C., & Shaver, P. (1987). Romantic love conceptualized as an attachment process. *Journal of Personality and Social Psychology, 52*, 511–534.

Hecht, M. L. (1984). Satisfying communication and relationship labels: Intimacy and length of relationship as perceptual frames of naturalistic conversations. *Western Journal of Speech Communication, 48*, 201–216.

Heckhausen, H. (1991). *Motivation and action*. Heidelberg: Springer-Verlag.

Hendin, H. M., & Cheek, J. M. (1997). Assessing hypersensitive narcissism: A reexamination of Murray's narcissism scale. *Journal of Research in Personality, 31*, 588–599.

Hendrick, C., & Hendrick, S. (1986). A theory and method of love. *Journal of Persoanlity and Social Psychology, 50*, 392–402.

Herold, E. S., Mantle, D., & Zemitis, O. (1979). A study of sexual offenses against females. *Adolescence, 14*, 65–72.

Hess, J. A. (2000). Maintaining nonvoluntary relationships with disliked partners. *Human Communication Research, 26*, 458–488.

Hess, J. A. (2002). Distance regulation in personal relationships: The development of a conceptual model and a test of representational validity. *Journal of Social and Personal Relationships, 19*, 663–683.

Hess, J. A. (2003). Maintaining undesired relationships. In D. J. Canary & M. Dainton (Eds.), *Maintaining relationships through communication: Relational, contextual, and cultural variations* (pp. 103–122). Mahwah, NJ: Lawrence Erlbaum Associates.

Hewes, D. E., Graham, M. K., Doelger, J., & Pavitt, C. (1985). "Second guessing": Message interpretation in social networks. *Human Communication Research, 11*, 299–334.

Hill, C. T., Rubin, Z., & Peplau, L. A. (1976). Breakups before marriage: The end of 103 affairs. *Journal of Social Issues, 32*, 147–168.

Hills, A. M., & Taplin, J. L. (1998). Anticipated responses to stalking: Effect of threat and target-stalker relationship. *Psychiatry, Psychology and Law, 5,* 139–146.

Hinde, R. A. (1979). *Towards understanding relationships.* London: Academic Press.

Hitchcock, J. A. (2002). *Net crimes & misdemeanors* (L. Page, Ed.). Medford, NJ: Information Today.

Hobfoll, S. E., & Schröder, K. E. E. (2001). Distinguishing between passive and active prosocial coping: Bridging inner-city women's mental health and AIDS risk behavior. *Journal of Social and Personal Relationships, 18,* 201–217.

Hockenberry, S. L. (1995). Dyadic violence, shame, and narcissism. *Contemporary Psychoanalysis, 31,* 301–325.

Hockley, C. (2000, December). *Women stalking women at work: A preliminary study on nurses' experiences.* Paper presented to the Criminal Justice Responses Conference, Australian Institute of Criminology, Sydney.

Hoffman, J. L. (1943). Psychotic visitors to government offices in the national capital. *American Journal of Psychiatry, 99,* 571–575.

Hoffman, S., & Baron, A. (2001). Stalkers, stalking, and violence in the workplace setting. In J. A. Davis (Ed.), *Stalking crimes and victim protection: Prevention, intervention, threat assessment, and case management* (pp. 139–160). Boca Raton, FL: CRC Press.

Holland, D. C., & Eisenhart, M. A. (1990). *Educated in romance: Women, achievement, and college culture.* Chicago: University of Chicago Press.

Holloway, S. L. (1994). *Relationship abuse and the termination process: Female mental health professionals' retrospective reports.* Unpublished doctoral dissertation, Indiana University of Pennsylvania, Indiana, PA.

Holmes, D. A., Taylor, M., & Saeed, A. (2000, January). Stalking and the therapeutic relationship. *Forensic Update, 60,* 31–35.

Holmes, R. M. (1993). Stalking in America: Types and methods of criminal stalkers. *Journal of Contemporary Criminal Justice, 9,* 317–327.

Holmes, R. M. (1998a). Sequential predation: Elements of serial fatal victimization. In R. M. Holmes & S. T. Holmes (Eds.), *Contemporary perspectives on serial murder* (pp. 101–112). Thousand Oaks, CA: Sage.

Holmes, R. M. (1998b). Stalking in America: Types and methods of criminal stalkers. In R. M. Holmes & S. T. Holmes (Eds.), *Contemporary perspectives on serial murder* (pp. 137–148). Thousand Oaks, CA: Sage.

Holmes, R. M. (2001). Criminal stalking: An analysis of the various typologies of stalkers. In J. A. Davis (Ed.), *Stalking crimes and victim protection: Prevention, intervention, threat assessment, and case management* (pp. 19–29). Boca Raton, FL: CRC Press.

Holmstrom, D. (1992, Dec. 22). Efforts to protect women from "stalkers" gain momentum at state, federal levels. *Christian Science Monitor, 1.*

Holt, V. L., Kernic, M. A., Lumley, T., Wolf, M. E., & Rivara, F. P. (2002). Civil protection orders and risk of subsequent police-reported violence. *Journal of American Medical Association, 288,* 589–594.

Honeycutt, J. M. (1993). Memory structures for the rise and fall of personal relationships. In S. Duck (Ed.), *Individuals in relationships* (pp. 60–86). Newbury Park, CA: Sage.

Honeycutt, J. M., & Cantrill, J. G. (1991). Using expectations of relational actions to predict number of intimate relationships: Don Juan and Romeo unmasked. *Communication Reports, 4,* 14–22.

Honeycutt, J. M., Cantrill, J. G., & Allen, T. (1992). Memory structures for relational decay: A cognitive test of sequencing of de-escalating actions and stages. *Human Communication Research, 18,* 528–562.

Honeycutt, J. M., Cantrill, J. G., & Greene, R. W. (1989). Memory structures for relational escalation: A cognitive test of the sequencing of relational actions and stages. *Human Communication Research, 16,* 62–90.

Honeycutt, J. M., Cantrill, J. G., Kelly, P., & Lambkin, D. (1998). How do I love thee? Let me consider my options: Cognition, verbal strategies, and the escalation of intimacy. *Human Communication Research, 25,* 39–63.

Horney, K. (1945). *Our inner conflicts: A constructive theory of neurosis.* New York: Norton.

Hornstein, G. A. (1985). Intimacy in conversational style as a function of the degree of closeness between members of a dyad. *Journal of Personality and Social Psychology, 49,* 671–681.

Horton, A. L., Simonidis, K. M., & Simonidis, L. L. (1987). Legal remedies for spousal abuse: Victim characteristics, expectations, and satisfaction. *Journal of Family Violence, 2,* 265–279.

Hosman, L. A., & Siltanen, S. A. (1995). Relationship intimacy, need for privacy, and privacy restoration behaviors. *Communication Quarterly, 43,* 64–74.

Hueter, J. A. (1997). Lifesaving legislation: But will the Washington stalking law survive constitutional scrutiny? *Washington Law Review, 72,* 213–240.

Huffhines, D. M. (2001). *Recidivism rates of convicted stalkers in San Diego County.* Unpublished master's thesis, Department of Public Administration, San Diego State University, CA.

Hughes, P. P., Marshall, D., & Sherrill, C. (2003). Multidimensional analysis of fear and confidence of university women relating to crimes and dangerous situations. *Journal of Interpersonal Violence, 18,* 33–49.

Human Rights Watch. (2001). Sacrificing women to save the family? Domestic violence in Uzbekistan. *Human Rights Watch, 13,* 3–54. Retrieved June 4, 2002 from http://www.hrw.org/report/2001/Uzbekistan.

Hunt, M. M. (1959). *The natural history of love.* New York: Alfred A. Knopf.

Huston, T. L., & Burgess, R. L. (1979). Social exchange in developing relationships: An overview. In R. L. Burgess & T. L. Huston (Eds.), *Social exchange in developing relationships* (pp. 3–28). New York: Academic.

Hutt, M. J., Iverson, H. I., Bass, H., & Gayton, W. F. (1997). Further validation of the vengeance scale. *Psychological Reports, 80,* 744–746.

Infield, P., & Platford, G. (2000). *The law of harassment and stalking.* London: Butterworths.

Infield, P., & Platford, G. (2002). Stalking and the law. In J. Boon & L. Sheridan (Eds.), *Stalking and psychosexual obsession: Psychological perspectives for prevention, policing and treatment* (pp. 221–236). West Sussex, England: John Wiley & Sons.

Jacobs, B. A. (1992). Undercover deception: Reconsidering presentation of self. *Journal of Contemporary Ethnography, 21,* 200–225.

Jacobs, B. A. (1994). Undercover social-distancing techniques. *Symbolic Interaction, 17,* 395–410.

Jagessar, J. D. H., & Sheridan, L. P. (2002). *A cross-cultural investigation into stalking.* Unpublished manuscript available from the first author, University of Leicester, Leicester, UK.

Jasinski, J. L., & Mustaine, E. E. (2001). Police response to physical assault and stalking victimization: A comparison of influential factors. *American Journal of Criminal Justice, 26,* 23–41.

Jason, L. A., Reichler, A., Easton, J., Neal, A., & Wilson, M. (1984). Female harassment after ending a relationship: A preliminary study. *Alternative Lifestyles, 6,* 259–269.

Jaynes-Andrews, S. (2001). *Explaining the severity of injury to battered women using male partner characteristics and behaviors.* Unpublished doctoral dissertation, School of Social Work, Boston College, Boston.

Johannesen, R. L. (1971). The emerging concept of communication as dialogue. *Quarterly Journal of Speech, 57,* 373–382.

Johnson, I. M., & Sigler, R. T. (2000). Public perceptions: The stability of the public's endorsements of the definition and criminalization of the abuse of women. *Journal of Criminal Justice, 28,* 165–179.

Jones, R. L., & Lipson, G. S. (2001). The dynamics of campus stalkers and stalking: Security and risk management perspectives. In J. A. Davis (Ed.), *Stalking crimes and victim protection: Prevention, intervention, threat assessment, and case management* (pp. 239–258). Boca Raton, FL: CRC Press.

Jones, W. H., & Burdette, M. P. (1994). Betrayal in relationships. In A. L. Weber & J. H. Harvey (Eds.), *Perspectives on close relationships* (pp. 243–262). Boston: Allyn & Bacon.

Jones, W. H., Moore, D. S., Schratter, A., & Negel, L. A. (2001). Interpersonal transgressions and betrayals. In R. M. Kowalski (Ed.), *Behaving badly: Aversive behavior in interpersonal relationships* (pp. 233–255). Washington, DC: American Psychological Association.

Jordan, C. E., Logan, TK, Walker, R., & Nigoff, A. (2003). Stalking: An examination of the criminal justice response. *Journal of Interpersonal Violence, 18*, 148–165.

Jordan, T. (1995). The efficacy of the California Stalking law: Surveying its evolution, extracting insights from domestic violence cases. *Hastings Women's Law Journal, 6*, 363–383.

Kaci, J. H. (1992). A study of protective orders issued under California's domestic violence prevention act. *Criminal Justice Review, 17*, 61–76.

Kaci, J. H. (1994). Aftermath of seeking domestic violence protective orders: The victim's perspective. *Journal of Contemporary Criminal Justice, 10*, 204–219.

Kamir, O. (1995). *Stalking: History, culture and law*. SJD dissertation, University of Michigan Law School, Ann Arbor.

Kamir, O. (2001). *Every breath you take: Stalking narratives and the law*. Ann Arbor, MI: University of Michigan Press.

Kamphuis, J. H., & Emmelkamp, P. M. G. (2000). Stalking—A contemporary challenge for forensic and clinical psychiatry. *British Journal of Psychiatry, 176*, 206–209.

Kamphuis, J. H., & Emmelkamp, P. M., G. (2001). Traumatic distress among support-seeking female victims of stalking. *American Journal of Psychiatry, 158*, 795–798.

Kane, R. J. (1999). Patterns of arrest in domestic violence encounters: Identifying a police decision-making model. *Journal of Criminal Justice, 27*, 65–79.

Kane, R. J. (2000). Police responses to restraining orders in domestic violence incidents: Identifying the custody-threshold thesis. *Criminal Justice and Behavior, 27*, 561–580.

Kaplan, D. L., & Keys, C. B. (1997). Sex and relationship variables as predictors of sexual attraction in cross-sex platonic friendships between young heterosexual adults. *Journal of Social and Personal Relationships, 14*, 191–206.

Kappeler, V. E., Blumberg, M., & Potter, G. W. (1996). *The mythology of crime and criminal justice* (2nd ed.). Prospect Heights, IL: Waveland.

Katz, G. (2001). Adolescents and young adults with developmental disabilities interface the internet: Six case reports of dangerous liaisons. *Mental Health Aspects of Developmental Disabilities, 4*(2), 77–84.

Katz, J. E. (1994). Empirical and theoretical dimensions of obscene phone calls to women in the United States. *Human Communication Research, 21*, 155–182.

Keenahan, D., & Barlow, A. (1997). Stalking: A paradoxical crime of the nineties. *International Journal of Risk, Security and Crime Prevention, 2*, 291–300.

Keilitz, S. L. (1997). Victims' perceptions of effectiveness of protective orders as an intervention in domestic violence and stalking. In *Domestic violence and stalking* (Second Annual Report to Congress under the Violence Against Women Act, pp. 37–44). Washington, DC: Office of Justice Programs, U.S. Department of Justice.

Keilitz, S. L., Davis, C., Efkeman, H. S., Flango, C., & Hannaford, P. L. (1998, January). *Civil protection orders: Victims' views on effectiveness* (National Institute of Justice Research Preview). Washington, DC: U.S. Department of Justice.

Kellermann, K., & Lee, C. M. (2001, November). *Seeking disaffinity: Making others dislike and feel negatively about you*. Paper presented at the National Communication Association Convention, Seattle, WA.

Kelley, H. H., Berscheid, E., Christensen, A., Harvey, J. H., Huston, T. L., Levinger, G., McClintock, E., Peplau, L. A., & Peterson, D. R. (1983). Analyzing close relationships. In H. H. Kelley, E. Berscheid, A. Christensen, J. H. Harvey, T. L. Huston, G. Levinger, E. McClintock, L. A. Peplau, & D. R. Peterson (Eds.), *Close relationships* (pp. 20–67). New York: W. H. Freeman.

Kelly, L. (1987). The continuum of sexual violence. In J. Hanmer & M. Maynard (Eds.), *Women, violence and social control* (pp. 46–60). Atlantic Highlands, NJ: Humanities Press.

Kern, S. (1992). *The culture of love: Victorians to moderns.* Cambridge, MA: Harvard University Press.

Kienlen, K. K. (1998). Developmental and social antecedents of stalking. In J. R. Meloy (Ed.), *The psychology of stalking* (pp. 51–67). San Diego, CA: Academic Press.

Kienlen, K. K., Birmingham, D. L., Solberg, K. B., O'Regan, J. T., & Meloy, J. R. (1997). A comparative study of psychotic and nonpsychotic stalking. *Journal of the American Academy of Psychiatry and Law, 25,* 317–334.

Kileen, K., & Dunn, J. (1998, August). *Victim and law enforcement strategies for managing forceful interaction and coercive pursuit.* Paper presented at the Annual Threat Management Conference, Anaheim, CA.

Kinkelmeyer, A., & Johnson, M. B. (2002). Stalking and harassment of psychotherapists. *American Journal of Forensic Psychology, 20,* 5–19.

Klein, A. R. (1996). Re-abuse in a population of court-restrained male batterers: Why restraining orders don't work. In E. S. Buzawa & C. G. Buzawa (Eds.), *Do arrests and restraining orders work?* (pp. 192–213). Thousand Oaks, CA: Sage.

Knapp, M. L., Ellis, D. G., & Williams, B. A. (1980). Perceptions of communication behavior associated with relationship terms. *Communication Monographs, 47,* 262–278.

Knobloch, L. K., & Solomon, D. H. (1999). Measuring the sources and content of relational uncertainty. *Communication Studies, 50,* 261–278.

Knobloch, L. K., & Solomon, D. H. (2002). Information seeking beyond initial interaction: Negotiating relational uncertainty within close relationships. *Human Communication Research, 28,* 243–257.

Knox, D., Daniels, V., Sturdivant, L., & Zusman, M. E. (2001). College student use of the internet for mate selection. *College Student Journal, 35,* 158–160.

Koedam, W. S. (2000). Sexual harassment and stalking. In F. W. Kaslow (Ed.), *Handbook of couple and family forensics: A sourcebook for mental health and legal professionals* (pp. 120–141). New York: John Wiley & Sons.

Kohn, M., Flood, H., Chase, J., & McMahon, P. M. (2000). Prevalence and health consequences of stalking—Louisiana, 1998–1999. *Morbidity and Mortality Weekly Report, 49*(29), 653–655.

Kong, R. (1996). Criminal harassment. *Juristat, 16* (12, Statistics Canada: Canadian Centre for Justice Statistics), 1–13.

Kordvani, A. H. (2000, December). *Women stalking in Iran.* Paper presented to the Criminal Justice Responses Conference, Australian Institute of Criminology, Sydney.

Koss, M. P. (1989). Hidden rape: Sexual aggression and victimization in a national sample of students in higher education. In M. A. Pirog-Good & J. E. Stets (Eds.), *Violence in dating relationships: Emerging social issues* (pp. 145–168). New York: Praeger.

Koss, M. P. (1992a). Defending date rape. *Journal of Interpersonal Violence, 7,* 122–1126.

Koss, M. P. (1992b). The underdetection of rape: Methodological choices influence incidence estimates. *Journal of Social Issues, 48,* 61–75.

Koss, M. P. (1993). Detecting the scope of rape: A review of prevalence research methods. *Journal of Interpersonal Violence, 8,* 198–222.

Kowalski, R. M. (1993). Inferring sexual interest from behavioral cues: Effects of gender and sexually relevant attitudes. *Sex Roles, 29,* 13–36.

Kowalski, R. M. (1997). The underbelly of social interaction: Aversive interpersonal behaviors. In R. M. Kowalski (Ed.), *Aversive interpersonal behaviors* (pp. 2–9). New York: Plenum Press.

Kowalski, R. M. (2001). The aversive side of social interaction revisited. In R. M. Kowalski (Ed.), *Behaving badly: Aversive behavior in interpersonal relationships* (pp. 297–309). Washington, DC: American Psychological Association.

Krishnan, S. P., Hilbert, J. C., & VanLeeuwen, D. (2001). Domestic violence and help-seeking behaviors among rural women: Results from a shelter-based study. *Family Community Health, 24,* 28–38.

Kristiansen, M., & Bloch-Poulsen, J. (2000). The challenge of the unspoken in organizations: Caring container as a dialogic answer? *Southern Communication Journal, 65,* 176–190.

Kropp, P. R., Hart, S. D., & Lyon, D. R. (2002). Risk assessment of stalkers: Some problems and possible solutions. *Criminal Justice & Behavior, 29,* 590–616.

Kurt, J. L. (1995). Stalking as a variant of domestic violence. *Bulletin of the Academy of Psychiatry and the Law, 23,* 219–230.

LaGaipa, J. J. (1990). The negative effects of informal support systems. In S. Duck (Ed.), *Personal relationships and social support* (pp. 122–139). Newbury Park, CA: Sage.

Lamberg, L. (2001). Stalking disrupts lives, leaves emotional scars: Perpetrators are often mentally ill. *Journal of the American Medical Association, 286,* 519–523.

Landau, E. (1996). *Stalking.* New York: Franklin Watts/Grolier.

Lane, J. (1993). *Antistalking legislation.* Hearing before the Committee on the Judiciary, United States Senate (J-102-86, pp. 69–73). Washington, DC: U.S. Government Printing Office.

Lane, J. D., & Wegner, D. M. (1994). Secret relationships: The back alley to love. In R. Erber & R. Gilmour (Eds.), *Theoretical frameworks for personal relationships* (pp. 67–85). Hillsdale, NJ: Lawrence Erlbaum Associates.

Laner, M. R., & Ventrone, N. A. (2000). Dating scripts revisited. *Journal of Family Issues, 21,* 488–500.

Langford, L., & Isaac, N. (2000). Criminal and restraining order histories of intimate partner-related homicide offenders in Massachusetts, 1991–1995. In P. H. Blackman, V. L. Leggett, B. L. Olson, & J. P. Jarvis (Eds.), *The varieties of homicide and its research: Proceedings of the 1999 Meeting of the Homicide Research Working Group.* Washington, DC: Federal Bureau of Investigation. Retrieved from http://www.fbi.gov/td/academy/bsu/homicide.pdf

Langhinrichsen-Rohling, J., Palarea, R. E., Cohen, J., & Rohling, M. L. (2000). Breaking up is hard to do: Unwanted pursuit behaviors following the dissolution of a romantic relationship. *Violence and Victims, 15,* 73–90.

Langhinrichsen-Rohling, J., & Rohling, M. (2000). Negative family-of-origin experiences: Are they associated with perpetrating unwanted pursuit behaviors? *Violence and Victims, 15,* 459–471.

Lannutti, P. J., & Cameron, K. A. (2002). Beyond the breakup: Heterosexual and homosexual post-dissolutional relationships. *Communication Quarterly, 50,* 153–170.

Lardner, G., Jr. (1995). *The stalking of Kristin.* New York: Atlantic Monthly Press.

Larkin, J., & Popaleni, K. (1994). Heterosexual courtship violence and sexual harassment: The private and public control of young women. *Feminism and Psychology, 4,* 213–227.

LaRue, P. (2000). *Stalking: Surviving the hidden terror.* Sevierville, TN: Insight Publishing.

Lawson-Cruttenden, T. (1996a). The government's proposed stalking law—A discussion paper. *Family Law, 26,* 755–758.

Lawson-Cruttenden, T. (1996b). Is there a law against stalking? *New Law Journal, 146,* 418–420.

Leary, M. R. (1990). Responses to social exclusion: Social anxiety, jealousy, loneliness, depression, and low self-esteem. *Journal of Social and Clinical Psychology, 9,* 221–229.

Leary, M. R. (2001). Toward a conceptualization of interpersonal rejection. In M. R. Leary (Ed.), *Interpersonal rejection* (pp. 3–20). New York: Oxford.

Leary, M., R., Koch, E. J., & Hechenbleikner, N. R. (2001). Emotional responses to interpersonal rejection. In M. R. Leary (Ed.), *Interpersonal rejection* (pp. 145–166). New York: Oxford University Press.

Leary, M. R., & Springer, C. A. (2001). Hurt feelings: The neglected emotion. In R. M. Kowalski (Ed.), *Behaving badly: Aversive behavior in interpersonal relationships* (pp. 151–175). Washington, DC: American Psychological Association.

Leary, M. R., Springer, C., Negel, L., Ansell, E., & Evans, K. (1998). The causes, phenomenology, and consequences of hurt feelings. *Journal of Personality and Social Psychology, 74*, 1225–1237.

Leary, T. (1957). *Interpersonal diagnosis of personality*. New York: Ronald Press.

LeBlanc, J. J., Levesque, G. J., & Berka, L. H. (2001). Survey of stalking at WPI. *Journal of Forensic Sciences, 46*, 367–369.

Lee, J. A. (1976). *The colors of love*. Englewood Cliffs, NJ: Prentice Hall.

Lee, R. K. (1998). Romantic and electronic stalking in a college context. *William & Mary Journal of Women and the Law, 4*, 373–466.

Lees-Haley, P. R., Lees-Haley, C. E., Price, J. R., & Williams, C. W. (1994). A sexual harassment-emotional distress rating scale. *American Journal of Forensic Psychology, 12*, 39–54.

Leets, L., de Becker, G., & Giles, H. (1995). Fans: Exploring expressed motivations for contacting celebrities. *Journal of Language and Social Psychology, 14*, 102–123.

Leidig, M. W. (1992). The continuum of violence against women: Psychological and physical consequences. *Journal of American College Health, 40*, 149–155.

Lemmey, D. (1999). *Stalking of battered women before and after seeking criminal justice help*. Unpublished doctoral dissertation, Nursing Program, Texas Women's University, Denton.

Leonard, R., Ling, L. C., Hankins, G. A., Maidon, C. H., Potorti, P. F., & Rogers, J. M. (1993). Sexual harassment at North Carolina State University. In G. L. Kreps (Ed.), *Sexual harassment: Communication implications* (pp. 170–194). Cresskill, NJ: Hampton.

Leong, G. B. (1993). De Clérambault syndrome (erotomania) in the criminal justice system: Another look at this recurring problem. *Journal of Forensic Sciences, 39*, 378–385.

Leong, G. B., & Silva, J. A. (1991, May). Lovesick: The erotomania syndrome. *VA Practitioner*, 39–43.

LePard, D. P. (2002). Managing stalkers: Coordinating treatment and supervision. In J. Boon & L. Sheridan (Eds.), *Stalking and psychosexual obsession: Psychological perspectives for prevention, policing and treatment* (pp. 141–164). West Sussex, England: John Wiley & Sons.

Lettieri, R. (1996). I love you to death: Intimacy, pathologic attachments and the evaluation of violence potential. *American Journal of Forensic Psychology, 14*, 5–23.

Levine, T. R., & McCornack, S. A. (1991). The dark side of trust: Conceptualizing and measuring types of communicative suspicion. *Communication Quarterly, 39*, 325–340.

Levitt, M. J., Silver, M. E., & Franco, N. (1996). Troublesome relationships: A part of human experience. *Journal of Social and Personal Relationships, 13*, 523–536.

Levy, M. B., & Davis, K. E. (1988). Love styles and attachment styles compared. *Journal of Social and Personal Relationships, 5*, 439–471.

Lewis, S. F., Fremouw, W. J., Del Ben, K., & Farr, C. (2001). An investigation of the psychological characteristics of stalkers: Empathy, problem-solving, attachment and borderline personality features. *Journal of Forensic Sciences, 46*, 80–84.

Lindsay, W. R., Olley, S., Jack, C., Morrison, F., & Smith, A. H. W. (1998). The treatment of two stalkers with intellectual disabilities using a cognitive approach. *Journal of Applied Research in Intellectual Disabilities, 11*, 333–344.

Lindsey, M. (1993). *The terror of batterer stalking: A guideline for intervention*. Littleton, CO: Gylantic.

Linell, P. (1998). *Approaching dialogue: Talk, interaction and contexts in dialogical perspectives*. Amsterdam: John Benjamins.

Lion, J. R., & Herschler, J. A. (1998). The stalking of clinicians by their patients. In J. R. Meloy (Ed.), *The psychology of stalking* (pp. 163–173). San Diego, CA: Academic Press.

Lipschultz, J. H., & Hilt, M. L. (2002). *Crime and local television news: Dramatic, breaking, and live from the scene*. Mahwah, NJ: Lawrence Erlbaum Associates.

Lipson, G. S., & Mills, M. J. (1998). Stalking, erotomania, and the Tarasoff cases. In J. R. Meloy (Ed.), *The psychology of stalking* (pp. 257–273). San Diego, CA: Academic Press.

Lloyd-Goldstein, R. (1998). De Clérambault on-line: A survey of erotomania and stalking from the old world to the world wide web. In J. R. Meloy (Ed.), *The psychology of stalking* (pp. 193–212). San Diego, CA: Academic Press.

Locke, E. A., & Latham, G. P. (1990). *A theory of goal setting and task performance.* Englewood Cliffs, NJ: Prentice Hall.

Logan, TK, Lambert, J., & Leukefield, C. (1998). *Stalking behavior and perceptions among male and female college students.* Unpublished manuscript, Center on Drug and Alcohol Research, University of Kentucky, Lexington, KY.

Logan, TK, Leukefeld, C., & Walker, B. (2000). Stalking as a variant of intimate violence: Implications from a young adult sample. *Violence and Victims, 15,* 91–111.

Logan, TK, Nigoff, A., Walker, R., & Jordan, C. (2002). Stalker profiles with and without protective orders: Reoffending or criminal justice processing. *Violence and Victims, 17,* 541–553.

Lowney, K. S., & Best, J. (1995). Stalking strangers and lovers: Changing media typifications of a new crime problem. In J. Best (Ed.), *Images of issues: Typifying contemporary social problems* (2nd ed., pp. 33–57). New York: Aldine de Gruyter.

Lowry, D. T., Nio, T. C. J., & Leitner, D. W. (2003). Setting the public fear agenda: A longitudinal analysis of network TV crime reporting, public perceptions of crime, and FBI statistics. *Journal of Communication, 53,* 61–73.

Lucks, B. D. (2001). Electronic crime, stalkers, and stalking: Relentless pursuit, harassment, and terror online in cyberspace. In J. A. Davis (Ed.), *Stalking crimes and victim protection: Prevention, intervention, threat assessment, and case management* (pp. 161–204). Boca Raton, FL: CRC Press.

Lyon, D. R. (1997). *The characteristics of stalkers in British Columbia: A statistical comparison of persons charged with criminal harassment and persons charged with other criminal code offences.* Unpublished master's thesis, Simon Fraser University, British Columbia, Canada.

MacDonald, J. M. (1968). *Homicidal threats.* Springfield, IL: Charles C. Thomas.

Maier, G. J. (1996). Managing threatening behavior: The role of talk down and talk up. *Journal of Psychosocial Nursing, 34,* 25–30.

Malsch, M. (2000, December). *Stalking in the Netherlands.* Paper presented to the Criminal Justice Responses Conference, Australian Institute of Criminology, Sydney, Australia.

Manitoba Law Reform Commission. (1997). *Stalking* (Report no. 98). Winnipeg, Manitoba, Canada: Manitoba Law Reform Commission.

Markman, R., & Labrecque, R. (1994). *Obsessed: The stalking of Theresa Saldana.* New York: William Morrow.

Marshall, J., & Castle, C. (1998, February). Restraining orders and stalking offences in 1995 and 1996. *Information Bulletin, 6,* 1–16.

Martin, L. L., & Tesser, A. (1989). Toward a motivational and structural theory of ruminative thought. In J. S. Uleman & J. A. Bargh (Eds.), *Unintended thought* (pp. 306–326). New York: Guilford.

Martin, L. L., & Tesser, A. (1996a). Clarifying our thoughts. In R. S. Wyer (Ed.), *Ruminative thoughts* (pp. 189–208). Mahwah, NJ: Lawrence Erlbaum Associates.

Martin, L. L., & Tesser, A. (1996b). Some ruminative thoughts. In R. S. Wyer (Ed.), *Ruminative thoughts* (pp. 1–47). Mahwah, NJ: Lawrence Erlbaum Associates.

Martinez-Diaz, J. A., & Edelstein, B. A. (1980). Heterosocial competence: Predictive and construct validity. *Behavior Modification, 4,* 115–129.

Maxey, W. (2001). Stalking the stalker: Law enforcement investigation and intervention. In J. A. Davis (Ed.), *Stalking crimes and victim protection: Prevention, intervention, threat assessment, and case management* (pp. 351–374). Boca Raton, FL: CRC Press.

Maxey, W. (2002). The San Diego Stalking Strike Force: A multi-disciplinary approach to assessing and managing stalking and threat cases. *Journal of Threat Assessment, 2,* 43–53.

Maxey, W. (2003). Storming the ivory towers: A look at violence and stalking on campus. *Psychosocial Nursing, 41* (4), 26–31.

McAdams, D. P. (1988). *Power, intimacy, and the life story.* New York: Guilford.

McAnaney, K. G., Gurliss, L., & Abeyta-Price, C. (1993). From imprudence to crime: Anti-stalking laws. *Notre Dame Law Review, 68,* 819–909.

McCabe, K. A. (2001, June). *Protective orders in South Carolina: An examination of variables for 1997–1999.* Columbia, SC: Office of Justice Programs, South Carolina. Retrieved December 9, 2002 from http://www.scdps.org/ojp/ statistical_analysis.html.

McCann, J. T. (1995). Obsessive attachment and the victimization of children: Can antistalking legislation provide protection? *Law and Psychology Review, 19,* 93–112.

McCann, J. T. (1998a). Risk of violence in stalking cases and legal case management. *Pennsylvania Bar Association Quarterly, 69,* 117–122.

McCann, J. T. (1998b). Subtypes of stalking (obsessional following) in adolescents. *Journal of Adolescence, 21,* 667–675.

McCann, J. T. (2000a). A descriptive study of child and adolescent obsessional followers. *Journal of Forensic Sciences, 45,* 195–199.

McCann, J. T. (2000b). *Stalking in children and adolescents: The primitive bond.* Washington, DC: American Psychological Association.

McCann, J. T. (2001). The relationship between threats and violence in juvenile stalking. *Journal of Threat Assessment, 1,* 81–90.

McCann, J. T. (2002). The phenomenon of stalking in children and adolescents. In J. Boon & L. Sheridan (Eds.), *Stalking and psychosexual obsession: Psychological perspectives for prevention, policing and treatment* (pp. 181–200). West Sussex, England: John Wiley & Sons.

McCormick, N. B., & Jones, A. J. (1989). Gender differences in nonverbal flirtation. *Journal of Sex Education & Therapy, 15,* 271–282.

McCreedy, K. R., & Dennis, B. G. (1996). Sex-related offenses and fear of crime on campus. *Journal of Contemporary Criminal Justice, 12,* 69–80.

McCutcheon, L. E., Lange, R., & Houran, J. (2002). Conceptualization and measurement of celebrity worship. *British Journal of Psychology, 93,* 67–87.

McFarlane, J., Campbell, J. C., Sharps, P., & Watson, K. (2002). Abuse during pregnancy and femicide: Urgent implications for women's health. *Obstetric Gynecology, 100,* 27–36.

McFarlane, J., Campbell, J. C., & Watson, K. (2002). Intimate partner stalking and femicide: Urgent implications for women's safety. *Behavioral Sciences and the Law, 20,* 51–68.

McFarlane, J., Campbell, J. C., Wilt, S., Sachs, C. J., Ulrich, Y., & Xu, X. (1999). Stalking and intimate partner femicide. *Homicide Studies, 3,* 300–316.

McFarlane, J., Willson, P., Lemmey, D., & Malecha, A. (2000). Women filing assault charges on an intimate partner. *Violence Against Women, 6,* 396–408.

McFarlane, J., Willson, P., Malecha, A., & Lemmey, D. (2000). Intimate partner violence: A gender comparison. *Journal of Interpersonal Violence, 15,* 158–169.

McGee, J. P., & DeBernardo, C. R. (1999). The classroom avenger. *Forensic Examiner, 8*(5–6), 1–16.

McGrath, M. G., & Casey, E. (2002). Forensic psychiatry and the internet: Practical perspectives on sexual harassers in cyberspace. *Journal of the American Academy of Psychiatry and the Law, 30,* 81–94.

McGruder-Johnson, A. K., Davidson, E. S., Gleaves, D. H., Stock, W., & Finch, J. F. (2000). Interpersonal violence and posttraumatic symptomology: The effects of ethnicity, gender, and exposure to violent events. *Journal of Interpersonal Violence, 15,* 205–221.

McGuire, B., & Wraith, A. (2000). Legal and psychological aspects of stalking: A review. *Journal of Forensic Psychiatry, 11,* 316–327.

McIntosh, W. D. (1996). When does goal nonattainment lead to negative emotional reactions, and when doesn't it?: The role of linking and rumination. In L. L. Martin & A. Tesser (Eds.), *Striving and feeling: Interactions among goals, affect, and self-regulation* (pp. 53–77). Mahwah, NJ: Lawrence Erlbaum Associates.

McIntosh, W. D., Harlow, T. F., & Martin, L. L. (1995). Linkers and nonlinkers: Goal beliefs as a moderator of the effects of everyday hassles on rumination, depression, and physical complaints. *Journal of Applied Social Psychology, 25*(14), 1231–1244.

McIntosh, W. D., & Martin, L. L. (1992). The cybernetics of happiness: The relation of goal attainment, rumination, and affect. In M. S. Clark (Ed.), *Emotion and social behavior* (pp. 222–246). Newbury Park, CA: Sage.

McKenna, K. Y. A., Green, A. S., & Gleason, M. E. J. (2002). Relationship formation on the internet: What's the big attraction. *Journal of Social Issues, 58*, 9–32.

McLennan, W. (1995/1996). *Crimes family violence act.* 1995/96 monitoring report. Victoria, Australia: Magistrates' and Children's Courts.

McLennan, W. (1996). *Women's safety, Australia, 1996.* Canberra, Commonwealth of Australia: Australian Bureau of Statistics.

McMillen, C., Zuravin, S., & Rideout, G. (1995). Perceived benefit from child sexual abuse. *Journal of Consulting and Clinical Psychology, 63*, 1037–1043.

McNamee, S., & Gergen, K. J. (Eds.). (1999). *Relational responsibility: Resources for sustainable dialogue.* Thousand Oaks, CA: Sage.

McReynolds, G. (1996, January–February). The enemy you know. *Sacramento Magazine, 22*(1), 39–42, 84.

Mechanic, M. B., Uhlmansiek, M. H., Weaver, T. L., & Resick, P. A. (2000). The impact of severe stalking experienced by acutely battered women: An examination of violence, psychological symptoms and strategic responding. *Violence and Victims, 15*, 443–458.

Mechanic, M. B., Weaver, T. L., & Resick, P. A. (2000). Intimate partner violence and stalking behavior: Exploration of patterns and correlates in a sample of acutely battered women. *Violence and Victims, 15*, 55–72.

Meloy, J. R. (1989). Unrequited love and the wish to kill: Diagnosis and treatment of borderline erotomania. *Bulletin of the Menninger Clinic, 53*, 477–492.

Meloy, J. R. (1992). *Violent attachments.* Northvale, NJ: Jason Aronson.

Meloy, J. R. (1996a). A clinical investigation of the obsessional follower: "She loves me, she loves me not … " In L. Schlesinger (Ed.), *Explorations in criminal psychopathology* (pp. 9–32) Springfield, IL: Charles C. Thomas.

Meloy, J. R. (1996b). Stalking (obsessional following): A review of some preliminary studies. *Aggression and Violent Behavior, 1*, 147–162.

Meloy, J. R. (1997a). The clinical risk management of stalking: "Someone is watching over me … " *American Journal of Psychotherapy, 51*, 174–184.

Meloy, J. R. (1997b). Predatory violence during mass murder. *Journal of Forensic Sciences, 42*, 326–329.

Meloy, J. R. (1997c). A Rorschach case study of stalking: "All I wanted was to love you … " In J. R. Meloy, M. W. Acklin, C. B. Gacono, J. F. Murray, & C. B. Peterson (Eds.), *Contemporary Rorschach interpretation* (pp. 177–189). Mahwah, NJ: Lawrence Erlbaum Associates.

Meloy, J. R. (1998). The psychology of stalking. In J. R. Meloy (Ed.), *The psychology of stalking* (pp. 2–24). San Diego, CA: Academic Press.

Meloy, J. R. (1999a). Erotomania, triangulation, and homicide. *Journal of Forensic Sciences, 44*, 421–424.

Meloy, J. R. (1999b). Stalking: An old behavior, a new crime. *Psychiatric Clinics of North America, 22*, 85–99.

Meloy, J. R. (2000). *Violence risk and threat assessment.* San Diego, CA: Specialized Training Services.

Meloy, J. R. (2001). Threats, stalking, and criminal harassment. In G. F. Pinard & L. Pagani (Eds.), *Clinical assessments of dangerousness: Empirical contributions* (pp. 238–257). Cambridge: Cambridge University Press.

Meloy, J. R. (2002). Stalking and violence. In J. Boon & L. Sheridan (Eds.), *Stalking and psychosexual obsession: Psychological perspectives for prevention, policing and treatment* (pp. 105–125). West Sussex, England: John Wiley & Sons.

Meloy, J. R. (in press). When stalkers become violent: The threat to public figures and private lives. *Psychiatric Annals.*

Meloy, J. R., & Boyd, C. (2003). Female stalkers and their victims. *Journal of the American Academy of Psychiatry and the Law, 31,* 211–219.

Meloy, J. R., Cowett, P. Y., Parker, S. B., Hofland, B., & Friedland, A. (1997). Domestic protection orders and the prediction of subsequent criminality and violence toward protectees. *Psychotherapy, 34,* 447–458.

Meloy, J. R., Davis, B., & Lovette, J. (2001). Risk factors for violence among stalkers. *Journal of Threat Assessment, 1,* 3–16.

Meloy, J. R., & Gothard, S. (1995). Demographic and clinical comparison of obsessional followers and offenders with mental disorders. *American Journal of Psychiatry, 152,* 258–263.

Meloy, J. R., Rivers, L., Siegel, L., Gothard, S., Naimark, D., & Nicolini, J. R. (2000). A replication study of obsessional followers and offenders with mental disorders. *Journal of Forensic Sciences, 45,* 147–152.

Melton, H. C. (2000). Stalking: A review of the literature and direction for the future. *Criminal Justice Review, 25,* 246–262.

Melton, H. C. (2001). *Stalking in the context of domestic violence.* Unpublished doctoral dissertation, Department of Sociology, University of Colorado, Boulder.

Menzies, R. P. D., Fedoroff, J. P., Green, C. M., & Isaacson, K. (1995). Prediction of dangerous behaviour in male erotomania. *British Journal of Psychiatry, 166,* 529–536.

Messman, S. J., Canary, D. J., & Hause, K. S. (2000). Motives to remain platonic, equity, and the use of maintenance strategies in opposite-sex friendships. *Journal of Social and Personal Relationships, 17,* 67–94.

Metts, S. (1992). The language of disengagement: A face-management perspective. In T. L. Orbuch (Ed.), *Close relationship loss: Theoretical approaches* (pp. 111–127). New York: Springer-Verlag.

Metts, S. (1994). Relational transgressions. In W. R. Cupach & B. H. Spitzberg (Eds.), *The dark side of interpersonal communication* (pp. 217–239). Hillsdale, NJ: Lawrence Erlbaum Associates.

Metts, S. (2000). Face and facework: Implications for the study of personal relationships. In K. Dindia & S. Duck (Eds.), *Communication and personal relationships* (pp. 77–93). New York: John Wiley & Sons.

Metts, S., & Cupach, W. R. (1995). Post divorce relations. In M. A. Fitzpatrick and A. Vangelisti (Eds.), *Explaining family interactions* (pp. 232–251). Newbury Park, CA: Sage.

Metts, S., Cupach, W. R., & Bejlovec, R. A. (1989). "I love you too much to ever start liking you": Redefining romantic relationships. *Journal of Social and Personal Relationships, 6,* 259–274.

Metts, S., Cupach, W. R., & Imahori, T. T. (1992). Perceptions of sexual compliance-resisting messages in three types of cross-sex relationships. *Western Journal of Speech Communication, 56,* 1–17.

Metts, S., & Spitzberg, B. H. (1996). Sexual communication in interpersonal contexts: A script-based approach. In B. R. Burleson (Ed.), *Communication yearbook 19* (pp. 49–91). Thousand Oaks, CA: Sage.

Meyer, C. B., & Taylor, S. E. (1986). Adjustment to rape. *Journal of Personality and Social Psychology, 50,* 1226–1234.

Meyers, J. (1998). Cultural factors in erotomania and obsessional following. In J. R. Meloy (Ed.), *The psychology of stalking* (pp. 213–224). San Diego, CA: Academic Press.

Meyers, M. (1997). *News coverage of violence against women: Engendering blame.* Thousand Oaks, CA: Sage.

Miceli, S. L., Santana, S. A., & Fisher, B. S. (2001). Cyberaggression: Safety and security issues for women worldwide. *Security Journal, 14*(2), 11–27.

Miell, D. (1987). Remembering relationship development: Constructing a context for interactions. In R. Burnett, P. McGhee, & D. Clarke (Eds.), *Accounting for relationships: Explanation, representation and knowledge* (pp. 60–73). London: Methuen.

Mikula, G. (1994). Perspective-related differences in interpretations of injustice by victims and victimizers: A test with close relationships. In M. J. Lerner & G. Mikula (Eds.), *Entitlement and the affectional bond: Justice in close relationships* (pp. 175–203). New York: Plenum Press.

Millar, K. U., Tesser, A., & Millar, M. (1988). The effects of a threatening life event on behavior sequences and intrusive thought: A self-disruption explanation. *Cognitive Therapy and Research, 12,* 441–457.

Miller, N. (1999). *Report of a national survey of law enforcement and prosecution initiatives against stalking.* Fourth Annual Report to Congress on Stalking and Domestic Violence. Washington, DC: U.S. Department of Justice.

Miller, N. (2001a). Stalking investigation, law, public policy, and criminal prosecution as problem solver. In J. A. Davis (Ed.), *Stalking crimes and victim protection: Prevention, intervention, threat assessment, and case management* (pp. 387–426). Boca Raton, FL: CRC Press.

Miller, N. (2001b). *Stalking laws and their implementation: What stalking investigators and prosecutors do—A problem solving perspective.* Final Report, available from Institute for Law and Justice, Alexandria, VA.

Miller, N., & Nugent, H. (2001, October). *Stalking laws and implementation: A national review for policymakers and practitioners.* Executive Summary, available from Institute for Law and Justice, Alexandria, VA.

Miller, R. D. (1985). The harassment of forensic psychiatrists outside of court. *Bulletin of the American Academy of Psychiatry and the Law, 13,* 337–343.

Miller, R. S. (1997). We always hurt the ones we love: Aversive interactions in close relationships. In R. M. Kowalski (Ed.), *Aversive interpersonal behaviors* (pp. 11–29). New York: Plenum Press.

Mitchell, K. J., Finkelhor, D., & Wolak, J. (2001). Risk factors for and impact of online sexual solicitation of youth. *Journal of the American Medical Association, 285,* 3011–3014.

Mohandie, K., Hatcher, C., & Raymond, D. (1998). False victimization syndromes in stalking. In J. R. Meloy (Ed.), *The psychology of stalking* (pp. 225–256). San Diego, CA: Academic Press.

Monaghan, P. (1998, March 6). Beyond the Hollywood myths: Researchers examine stalkers and their victims. *Chronicle of Higher Education,* pp. A17, A20.

Mongeau, P. A., Ramirez, A., & Vorell, M. (2003, February). *Friends with benefits: Initial explorations of sexual, non-romantic, relationships.* Paper presented at the Western States Communication Association Convention, Salt Lake City, UT.

Montero, M. S. (2003). *Personality characteristics of perpetrators of stalking-like behaviors.* Unpublished master's thesis, University of South Carolina, Columbia.

Moore, M. M. (1985). Nonverbal courtship patterns in women: Context and consequences. *Ethology and Sociobiology, 6,* 237–247.

Moore, M. M. (1995). Courtship signaling and adolescents: "Girls just wanna have fun"? *Journal of Sex Research, 32,* 319–328.

Moore, M. M., & Butler, D. L. (1989). Predictive aspects of nonverbal courtship behavior in women. *Semiotica, 3,* 205–215.

Moracco, K. E., Runyan, C. W., & Butts, J. D. (1998). Femicide in North Carolina, 1991–1993. *Homicide Studies, 2,* 422–446.

Morewitz, S. J. (2001a). *Age differences among stalkers.* Unpublished manuscript, Violence Prevention & Litigation Consultants, San Francisco, CA.

Morewitz, S. J. (2001b). Domestic violence and stalking during pregnancy. *Obstetrics & Gynecology, 97* (Supplement), 53S.

Morewitz, S. J. (2003). *Stalking and violence: New patterns of trauma and obsession.* New York: Kluwer Academic/Plenum.

Morgan, J. F., & Porter, S. (1999). Sexual harassment of psychiatric trainees: Experiences and attitudes. *Postgraduate Medical Journal, 75* (885), 417–413.

Morin, K. S. (1993). The phenomenon of stalking: Do existing state statutes provide adequate protection? *San Diego Justice Journal, 1,* 123–162.

Morris, W. (Ed.). (1979). The American heritage dictionary of the English language. Boston: Houghton Mifflin.

Morrison, K. A. (2001). Predicting violent behavior in stalkers: A preliminary investigation of Canadian cases in criminal harassment. *Journal of Forensic Sciences, 46,* 1403–1410.

Morton, K., Runyan, C. W., Moracco, K. E., & Butts, J. (1998). Partner homicide-suicide involving female homicide victims: A population-based study in North Carolina, 1988–1992. *Violence and Victims, 13,* 91–106.

Morton, T. L., Alexander, J. F., & Altman, I. (1976). Communication and relationship definition. In G. R. Miller (Ed.), *Explorations in interpersonal communication* (pp. 105–125). Beverly Hills, CA: Sage.

Morville, D. A. (1993). Stalking laws: Are they solutions for more problems? *Washington University Law Quarterly, 71,* 921–935.

Moses-Zirkes, S. (1992). Psychologists question anti-stalking laws' utility. *APA Monitor, 23*(10), 53.

Muehlenhard, C. L., Koralewski, M. A., Andrews, S. L., & Burdick, C. A. (1986). Verbal and nonverbal cues that convey interest in dating: Two studies. *Behavior Therapy, 17,* 404–419.

Muehlenhard, C. L., Sympson, S. C., Phelps, J. L., & Highby, B. J. (1994). Are rape statistics exaggerated? A response to criticism of contemporary rape research. *Journal of Sex Research, 31,* 144–145.

Mullen, P. E. (2000). Erotomanias (pathologies of love) and stalking. In F. Flach (Ed.), *The Hatherleigh guide to psychiatric disorders* (Part II, pp. 145–163). New York: Hatherleigh Press.

Mullen, P. E., & Martin, J. (1994). Jealousy: A community study. *British Journal of Psychiatry, 164,* 35–43.

Mullen, P. E., & Pathé, M. (1994a). The pathological extensions of love. *British Journal of Psychiatry, 165,* 614–623.

Mullen, P. E., & Pathé, M. (1994b). Stalking and the pathologies of love. *Australian and New Zealand Journal of Psychiatry, 28,* 469–477.

Mullen, P. E., Pathé, M., & Purcell, R. (2000a). *Stalkers and their victims.* Cambridge: Cambridge University Press.

Mullen, P. E., Pathé, M., & Purcell, R. (2000b). Stalking. *Psychologist, 13,* 454–459.

Mullen, P. E., Pathé, M., & Purcell, R. (2000c). Stalking: New constructions of human behaviour. *Australian and New Zealand Journal of Psychiatry, 35,* 9–16.

Mullen, P. E., Pathé, M., & Purcell, R. (2001). The management of stalkers. *Advances in Psychiatric Treatment, 7,* 335–342.

Mullen, P. E., Pathé, M., Purcell, R., & Stuart, G. W. (1999). Study of stalkers. *American Journal of Psychiatry, 156,* 1244–1249.

Murray, F. S. (1967). A preliminary investigation of anonymous nuisance telephone calls to females. *Psychological Record, 17,* 395–400.

Murray, F. S., & Beran, L. C. (1968). A survey of nuisance telephone calls received by males and females. *Psychological Record, 18,* 107–109.

Murray, S. L., Holmes, J. G., & Griffin, D. W. (1996). The benefits of positive illusions: Idealization and the construction of satisfaction in close relationships. *Journal of Personality and Social Psychology, 70,* 79–98.

Murstein, B. I. (Ed.). (1971). *Theories of attraction and love.* New York: Springer.

Murstein, B. I. (1974). *Love, sex, and marriage through the ages*. New York: Springer.

Mustaine, E. E., & Tewksbury, R. (1999). A routine activity theory explanation for women's stalking victimizations. *Violence Against Women, 5*, 43–62.

Nadkarni, R., & Grubin, D. (2000). Stalking: Why do people do it? *British Medical Journal, 320*, 1486–1487.

National Center on Addiction and Substance Abuse. (2000, August). *The United States Postal Service Commission on a safe and secure workplace*. New York: Columbia University.

National Institute of Justice. (1993). *Project to develop a model anti-stalking code for states*. Washington, DC: U.S. Department of Justice.

National Institute of Justice. (1996). *Domestic violence, stalking, and antistalking legislation* (Annual Report to Congress under the Violence Against Women Act, NCJ 160943). Washington, DC: U.S. Department of Justice.

Nelson, E. S., Hill-Barlow, D., & Benedict, J. O. (1994). Addiction versus intimacy as related to sexual involvement in a relationship. *Journal of Sex and Marital Therapy, 20*, 35–45.

Nestadt, G., Samuels, J. F., Romanoski, A. J., Folstein, M. F., & McHugh, P. R. (1994). Obsessions and compulsions in the community. *Acta Psychiatrica Scandinavica, 89*, 219–224.

New Jersey State Police. (1997). *Domestic violence: Offense report*. Trenton, NJ: New Jersey Department of Law & Public Safety.

Newcomb, T. M. (1956). The prediction of interpersonal attraction. *American Psychologist, 11*, 575–586.

Nicastro, A. M., Cousins, A. V., & Spitzberg, B. H. (2000). The tactical face of stalking. *Journal of Criminal Justice, 28*, 69–82.

Nishith, P., Griffin, M. G., & Poth, T. L. (2002). Stress-induced analgesia: Prediction of posttraumatic stress symptoms in battered versus nonbattered women. *Biological Psychiatry, 51*, 867–874.

Nixon, J. L. (1985). *The stalker*. New York: Random House.

Noone, J. A., & Cockhill, L. (1987). Erotomania: The delusion of being loved. *American Journal of Forensic Psychiatry, 8*, 23–31.

NOP. (1997, April 2). *One in four young adults knows a victim of stalking*. NOP Research Group. Retrieved February 8, 2001 from http://www.nop.co.uk/survey/archive/ public/public%5Fo2%5F04%5F97.htm.

Norris, F. H., & Kaniasty, K. (1994). Psychological distress following criminal victimization in the general population: Cross-sectional, longitudinal, and prospective analyses. *Journal of Consulting and Clinical Psychology, 62*, 111–123.

Oddie, J. (2000). *The prediction of violence in stalkers*. Unpublished doctoral dissertation, California School of Professional Psychology, Fresno.

Oettingen, G., & Gollwitzer, P. M. (2001). Goal setting and goal striving. In A. Tesser & N. Schwarz (Eds.), *Blackwell handbook of social psychology: Intraindividual processes* (pp. 329–347). Malden, MA: Blackwell.

Ogilvie, E. (2000, December). *The internet and cyberstalking*. Paper presented to the Criminal Justice Responses Conference, Australian Institute of Criminology, Sydney.

Ogilvie, E. (2001). Cyberstalking. *Crime & Justice International, 17* (50), 9–10, 26–29.

Oldham, J., Clarkin, J., Appelbaum, A., Carr, A., Kernberg, P., Lotterman, A., & Haas, G. (1985). A self-report instrument for borderline personality organization. In T. H. McGlashan (Ed.), *The borderline: Current empirical research* (pp. 3–18). Washington, DC: American Psychiatric Press.

Olsen, J. (1991). *Predator: Rape, madness, and injustice in Seattle*. New York: Delacorte Press.

Omata, K. (2002). Long-term psychological aftereffects of sexual victimization and influence of victim-assailant relationship upon them among Japanese female college students. *Japanese Journal of Criminal Psychology, 40*, 1–19.

Orion, D. (1997). *I know you really love me: A psychiatrist's journal of erotomania, stalking, and obsessional love*. New York: Macmillan.

Orth, S. (2002, June). *An examination of factors affecting post-relational persistence*. Unpublished manuscript, Brandon University, Manitoba, Canada.

O'Sullivan, L. F., & Gaines, M. E. (1998). Decision-making in college students' heterosexual dating relationships: Ambivalence about engaging in sexual activity. *Journal of Social and Personal Relationships, 15,* 347–363.

Oswell, D. (1999). The dark side of cyberspace: Internet content regulation and child protection. *Convergence: The Journal of Research Into New Media Technologies, 5,* 42–62.

Oxford University Press. (1971). *The compact edition of the Oxford English dictionary* (Vols. I–II). New York: Oxford University Press.

Palarea, R. E., Zona, M. A., Lane, J. C., & Langhinrichsen-Rohling, J. (1999). The dangerous nature of intimate relationship stalking: Threats, violence, and associated risk factors. *Behavioral Sciences and the Law, 17,* 269–283.

Pardun, C. J. (2002). Romancing the script: Identifying the romantic agenda in top-grossing movies. In J. D. Brown, J. R. Steele, & K. Walsh-Childers (Eds.), *Sexual teens, sexual media: Investigating media's influence on adolescent sexuality* (pp. 211–225). Mahwah, NJ: Lawrence Erlbaum Associates.

Parks, M. R., & Floyd, K. (1996). Making friends in cyberspace. *Journal of Communication, 46,* 80–97.

Parks, M. R., & Roberts, L. D. (1998). "Making MOOsic": The development of personal relationships on line and a comparison to their off-line counterparts. *Journal of Social and Personal Relationships, 15,* 517–537.

Parrott, H. J. (2000). Stalking: Evil, illness, or both? *International Journal of Clinical Practice, 54,* 239–242.

Pathé, M. (2002). *Surviving stalking*. Cambridge: Cambridge University Press.

Pathé, M., & Mullen, P. E. (1997). The impact of stalkers on their victims. *British Journal of Psychiatry, 170,* 12–17.

Pathé, M., & Mullen, P. (2002). The victim of stalking. In J. Boon & L. Sheridan (Eds.), *Stalking and psychosexual obsession: Psychological perspectives for prevention, policing and treatment* (pp. 1–22). West Sussex, England: John Wiley & Sons.

Pathé, M., Mullen, P. E., & Purcell, R. (1999). Stalking: False claims of victimisation. *British Journal of Psychiatry, 174,* 170–173.

Pathé, M., Mullen, P. E., & Purcell, R. (2000). Same-gender stalking. *Journal of the American Academy of Psychiatry and the Law, 28,* 191–197.

Pathé, M., Mullen, P. E., & Purcell, R. (2001). Management of victims of stalking. *Advances in Psychiatric Treatment, 7,* 399–406.

Pathé, M. T., Mullen, P. E., & Purcell, R. (2002). Patients who stalk doctors: Their motives and management. *Medical Journal of Australia, 176,* 335–338.

Patterson, J., & Kim, P. (1991). *The day America told the truth*. New York: Prentice-Hall.

Paul, E. L., & Hayes, K. A. (2002). The casualties of "casual" sex: A qualitative exploration of the phenomenology of college students' hookups. *Journal of Social and Personal Relationships, 19,* 639–661.

Paul, E. L., McManus, B., & Hayes, A. (2000). "Hookups": Characteristics and correlates of college students' spontaneous and anonymous sexual experiences. *Journal of Sex Research, 37,* 76–88.

Pearce, A., & Easteal, P. (1999). The "domestic" in stalking. *Alternative Law Journal, 24,* 165–170.

Pearce, W. B., & Pearce, K. A. (2000). Combining passions and abilities: Toward dialogic virtuosity. *Southern Communication Journal, 65,* 161–175.

Pedersen, D. M. (1999). Model for types of privacy by privacy functions. *Journal of Environmental Psychology, 19,* 397–405.

Peele, S. (1981). *Love and addiction*. New York: Signet Books.

Pepitone, A. (1964). *Attraction and hostility: An experimental analysis of interpersonal and self-evaluation*. New York: Atherton Press.

Perez, C. (1993). Stalking: When does obsession become a crime? *American Journal of Criminal Law, 20*, 263–280.

Perugini, M., & Bagozzi, R. P. (2001). The role of desires and anticipated emotions in goal-directed behaviours: Broadening and deepening the theory of planned behavior. *British Journal of Social Psychology, 40*, 79–98.

Petronio, S. (1991). Communication boundary management: A theoretical model of managing disclosure of private information between marital couples. *Communication Theory, 1*, 311–335.

Petronio, S. (1994). Privacy binds in family interactions: The case of parental privacy invasion. In W. R. Cupach & B. H. Spitzberg (Eds.), *The dark side of interpersonal communication* (pp. 241–257). Hillsdale, NJ: Lawrence Erlbaum Associates.

Petronio, S. (Ed.). (2000). *Balancing the secrets of private disclosures*. Mahwah, NJ: Lawrence Erlbaum Associates.

Petty, R. A., & Kosch, L. M. (2001). Workplace violence and unwanted pursuit: From an employer's perspective. In J. A. Davis (Ed.), *Stalking crimes and victim protection: Prevention, intervention, threat assessment, and case management* (pp. 459–486). Boca Raton, FL: CRC Press.

Pew Internet & American Life Project. (2001, June 20). *Teenage life online: The rise of the instant-message generation and the Internet's impact on friendships and family relationships*. Washington, DC: Author.

Pew Internet & American Life Project. (2002, September 15). *The Internet goes to college: How students are living in the future with today's technology*. Washington, DC: Author.

Pfeiffer, S. M., & Wong, P. T. (1989). Multidimensional jealousy. *Journal of Social and Personal Relationships, 6*, 181–196.

Phillips, L. M. (2000). *Flirting with danger: Young women's reflections on sexuality and domination*. New York: New York University Press.

Pillai, K., & Kraya, N. (2000). Psychostimulants, adult attention deficit hyperactivity disorder and morbid jealousy. *Australian and New Zealand Journal of Psychiatry, 34*, 160–163.

Pinto, R. P., & Hollandsworth, J. G., Jr. (1984). A measure of possessiveness in intimate relationships. *Journal of Social and Clinical Psychology, 2*, 273–279.

Piper, W. E., & Duncan, S. C. (1999). Object relations theory and short-term dynamic psychotherapy: Findings from the quality of object relations scale. *Clinical Psychology Review, 19*, 669–685.

Pistole, M. C. (1989). Attachment in adult romantic relationships: Style of conflict resolution and relationship satisfaction. *Journal of Social and Personal Relationships, 6*, 505–510.

Planalp, S. (1985). Relational schemata: A test of alternative forms of relational knowledge. *Human Communication Research, 12*, 3–29.

Planalp, S. (1987). Interplay between relational knowledge and events. In R. Burnett, P. McGhee, & D. Clarke (Eds.), *Accounting for relationships: Explanation, representation and knowledge* (pp. 175–191). London: Methuen.

Plutchik, R., & Conte, H. R. (Eds.). (1997). *Circumplex models of personality and emotions*. Washington, DC: American Psychological Association.

Pollina, L. K., & Snell, W. E., Jr. (1999). Coping in intimate relationships: Development of the multidimensional intimate coping questionnaire. *Journal of Social and Personal Relationships, 16*, 133–144.

Pomerantz, E. M., Saxon, J. L., & Oishi, S. (2000). The psychological trade-offs of goal investment. *Journal of Personality and Social Psychology, 79*, 617–630.

Popovich, P. M., Licata, B. J., Nokovich, D., Martelli, T., & Zoloty, S. (1986). Assessing the incidence and perceptions of sexual harassment behaviors among American undergraduates. *Journal of Psychology, 120*, 387–396.

Porter, J. F., & Critelli, J. W. (1992). Measurement of sexual aggression in college men: A methodological analysis. *Archives of Sexual Behavior, 21*, 525–542.

Pritchard, D., & Hughes, K. D. (1997). Patterns of deviance in crime news. *Journal of Communication, 47*(3), 49–67.

Proctor, M. (1995). Stalking: A behavioral overview with case management suggestions. *Journal of California Law Enforcement, 29*(3), 63–39.

Proctor, P. R., Hart, S. D., & Lyon, D. R. (2002). Risk assessment of stalkers: Some problems and possible solutions. *Criminal Justice and Behavior, 29*, 590–616.

Proulx, J., Koverola, C., Fedorowicz, A., & Kral, M. (1995). Coping strategies as predictors of distress in survivors of single and multiple sexual victimization and nonvictimized controls. *Journal of Applied Social Psychology, 25*, 1464–1483.

Pryor, J. B., & Merluzzi, T. V. (1985). The role of expertise in processing social interaction scripts. *Journal of Experimental Social Psychology, 21*, 362–379.

Puente, M. (1992, Tuesday, July 21). Legislators tackling the terror of stalking; But some experts say measures are vague. *USA Today*, p. 9A.

Purcell, R., Pathé, M., & Mullen, P. E. (2001). A study of women who stalk. *American Journal of Psychiatry, 153*(12), 2056–2060.

Purcell, R., Pathé, M., & Mullen, P. E. (2002). The prevalence and nature of stalking in the Australian community. *Australian and New Zealand Journal of Psychiatry, 36*, 114–120.

Purdon, C. (1999). Thought suppression and psychopathology. *Behaviour Research and Therapy, 37*, 1029–1054.

Purdon, C., & Clark, D. A. (1993). Obsessive intrusive thoughts in nonclinical subjects. Part I. Content and relation with depressive, anxious and obsessional symptoms. *Behaviour Research and Therapy, 31*, 713–720.

Pyszczynski, T., & Greenberg, J. (1987). Self-regulatory perseveration and the depressive self-focusing style: A self-awareness theory of reactive depression. *Psychological Bulletin, 102*, 122–138.

Rachman, S. (1997). A cognitive theory of obsessions. *Behaviour Research and Therapy, 35*, 793–802.

Rachman, S. (1998). A cognitive theory of obsessions: Elaborations. *Behaviour Research and Therapy, 36*, 385–401.

Radway, J. A. (1991). *Reading the romance: Women, patriarchy, and popular literature.* Chapel Hill: University of North Carolina Press.

Rainville, R. E., & Gallagher, J. G. (1990). Vulnerability and heterosexual attraction. *Sex Roles, 23*, 25–31.

Raskin, D. E., & Sullivan, K. E. (1974). Erotomania. *American Journal of Psychiatry, 131*, 1033–1035.

Rawlins, W. K. (1992). *Friendship matters: Communication, dialectics, and the life course.* Hawthorne, NY: Aldine de Gruyter.

Ray, E. B. (1993). When the links become chains: Considering dysfunctions of supportive communication in the workplace. *Communication Monographs, 60*, 106–111.

Regan, P. C., & Dreyer, C. S. (1999). Lust? Love? Status? Young adults' motives for engaging in casual sex. *Journal of Psychology & Human Sexuality, 11*, 1–24.

Ressler, R. K., Burgess, A. W., & Douglas, J. E. (1988). *Sexual homicide: Patterns and motives.* New York: Free Press.

Richardson, D. R., & Green, L. R. (1997). Circuitous harm: Determinants and consequences of nondirect aggression. In R. M. Kowalski (Ed.), *Aversive interpersonal behaviors* (pp. 171–188). New York: Plenum.

Rigakos, G. S. (1995). Constructing the symbolic complainant: Police subculture and the nonenforcement of protection orders for battered women. *Violence and Victims, 10*, 227–247.

Rigakos, G. S. (1997). Situational determinants of police responses to civil and criminal injunctions for battered women. *Violence Against Women, 3,* 204–216.

Riger, S., Raja, S., & Camacho, J. (2002). The radiating impact of intimate partner violence. *Journal of Interpersonal Violence, 17,* 184–205.

Roberts, A. R., & Dziegielewski, S. F. (1996). Assessment typology and intervention with the survivors of stalking. *Aggression and Violent Behavior, 1,* 359–368.

Roberts, K. A. (2002). Stalking following the breakup of romantic relationships: Characteristics of stalking former partners. *Journal of Forensic Sciences, 47,* 1070–1077.

Roehl, J., & Guertin, K. (1998). *Current use of dangerousness assessments in sentencing domestic violence offenders* (Report under State Justice Institute Grant SJI-97-181-078). Washington, DC: Justice Research Center.

Roloff, M. E., & Cloven, D. H. (1994). When partners transgress: Maintaining violated relationships. In D. J. Canary & L. Stafford (Eds.), *Communication and relational maintenance* (pp. 23–43). San Diego, CA: Academic Press.

Roloff, M. E., & Ifert, D. E. (2000). Conflict management through avoidance: Withholding complaints, suppressing arguments, and declaring topics taboo. In S. Petronio (Ed.), *Balancing the secrets of private disclosures* (pp. 151–163). Mahwah, NJ: Lawrence Erlbaum Associates.

Romans, J. S. C., Hays, J. R., & White, T. K. (1996). Stalking and related behaviors experienced by counseling center staff members from current or former clients. *Professional Psychology: Research and Practice, 27,* 595–599.

Romer, D., Jamieson, K. H., & Aday, S. (2003). Television news and the cultivation of fear of crime. *Journal of Communication, 53,* 88–104.

Rook, K. S., & Pietromonaco, P. (1987). Close relationships: Ties that heal or ties that bind? In W. H. Jones & D. Perlman (Eds.), *Advances in personal relationships* (Vol. 1, pp. 1–35). Greenwich, CT: JAI Press.

Roscoe, B., Kennedy, D., & Pope, T. (1987). Adolescents' views of intimacy: Distinguishing intimate from nonintimate relationships. *Adolescence, 22,* 511–516.

Roscoe, B., Strouse, J. S., & Goodwin, M. P. (1994). Sexual harassment: Early adolescent self-reports of experiences and acceptance. *Adolescence, 29,* 515–523.

Rose, S., & Frieze, I. H. (1993). Young singles' contemporary dating scripts. *Sex Roles, 28,* 499–509.

Rosenfeld, B. (2000). Assessment and treatment of obsessional harassment. *Aggression and Violent Behavior, 5,* 529–549.

Rosenfeld, B., & Harmon, R. (2002). Factors associated with violence in stalking and obsessional harassment cases. *Criminal Justice and Behavior, 29,* 671–691.

Ross, E. S. (1995). E-mail stalking: Is adequate legal protection available? *Journal of Computer and Information Law, 13,* 405–432.

Ross, R. R., & Allgeier, E. R. (1996). Behind the pencil/paper measurement of sexual coercion: Interview-based clarification of men's interpretations of sexual experiences survey items. *Journal of Applied Social Psychology, 26,* 1587–1616.

Rothman, E. K. (1984). *Hands and hearts: A history of courtship in America.* New York: Basic Books.

Roussel, R. (1986). *The conversation of the sexes: Seduction and equality in selected seventeenth- and eighteenth-century texts.* New York: Oxford University Press.

Rowatt, T. J., Cunningham, M. R., & O'Hara, B. (1999, June). *Let's just be friends: The communication of social rejection in unrequited love.* Paper presented at the International Network on Personal Relationships/International Society for the Study of Personal Relationships Joint Conference, Louisville, KY.

Ruch, L. O., Gartrell, J. W., Amedeo, S. R., & Coyne, B. J. (1991). The sexual assault symptom scale: Measuring self-reported sexual assault trauma in the emergency room. *Psychological Assessment, 3*, 3–8.

Rudden, M., Sweeney, J., & Frances, A. (1990). Diagnosis and clinical course of erotomanic and other delusional patients. *American Journal of Psychiatry, 147*, 625–628.

Rule, B. G., & Bisanz, G. L. (1987). Goals and strategies of persuasion: A cognitive schema for understanding social events. In M. P. Zanna, J. M. Olson, & C. P. Herman (Eds.), *The Ontario Symposium: Vol. 5. Social influence* (pp. 185–206). Hillsdale, NJ: Lawrence Erlbaum Associates.

Rule, B. G., Bisanz, G. L., & Kohn, M. (1985). Anatomy of a persuasion schema: Targets, goals, and strategies. *Journal of Personality and Social Psychology, 48*, 1127–1140.

Rumbough, T. (2001). The development and maintenance of interpersonal relationships through computer-mediated communication. *Communication Research Reports, 18*, 223–229.

Saal, F. E., Johnson, C. B., & Weber, N. (1989). Friendly or sexy? It may depend on whom you ask. *Psychology of Women Quarterly, 13*, 263–276.

Sabini, J., & Silver, M. (1982). *Moralities of everyday life*. Oxford: Oxford University Press.

Salame, L. (1993). A national survey of stalking laws: A legislative trend comes to the aid of domestic violence victims and others. *Suffolk University Law Review, 17*, 67–112.

Salkovskis, P. M., & Campbell, P. (1994). Thought suppression induces intrusion in naturally occurring negative intrusive thoughts. *Behaviour Research and Therapy, 32*, 1–8.

Samp, J. A., & Solomon, D. H. (1998). Communicative responses to problematic events in close relationships I: The variety and facets of goals. *Communication Research, 25*, 66–95.

Sandberg, D. A., McNiel, D. E., & Binder, R. L. (1998). Characteristics of psychiatric inpatients who stalk, threaten, or harass hospital staff after discharge. *American Journal of Psychiatry, 155*, 1102–1105.

Sandberg, D. A., McNiel, D. E., & Binder, R. L. (2002). Stalking, threatening, and harassing behavior by psychiatric patients toward clinicians. *Journal of the American Academy of Psychiatry and the Law, 30*, 221–229.

Sarwer, D. B., Kalichman, S. C., Johnson, J. R., Early, J., & Akram, S. (1993). Sexual aggression and love styles: An exploratory study. *Archives of Sexual Behavior, 22*, 265–275.

Saunders, R. (1998). The legal perspective on stalking. In J. R. Meloy (Ed.), *The psychology of stalking* (pp. 25–50). San Diego, CA: Academic Press.

Savitz, L. (1986). Obscene phone calls. In T. F. Hartnagel & R. A. Silverman (Eds.), *Critique and explanation: Essays in honor of Gwynne Nettler* (pp. 149–158). New Brunswick, NJ: Transaction.

Scharlott, B. W., & Christ, W. G. (1995). Overcoming relationship-initiation barriers: The impact of a computer-dating system on sex role, shyness, and appearance inhibitions. *Computers in Human Behavior, 11*, 191–204.

Schaum, M., & Parrish, K. (1995). *Stalked: Breaking the silence on the crime of stalking in America*. New York: Pocket Books.

Scheff, T. J. (1995). Self-defense against verbal assault: Shame, anger, and the social bond. *Family Process, 34*, 271–286.

Schell, B. H., & Lanteigne, N. M. (2000). *Stalking, harassment, and murder in the workplace*. Westport, CT: Quorum Books.

Schlesinger, L. B. (2002). Stalking, homicide, and catathymic process: A case study. *International Journal of Offender Therapy and Comparative Criminology, 46*, 64–74.

Schneider, B. E. (1991). Put up and shut up: Workplace sexual assaults. *Gender & Society, 5*, 533–548.

Schneider, C. S., & Kenny, D. A. (2000). Cross-sex friends who were once romantic partners: Are they platonic friends now? *Journal of Social and Personal Relationships, 17*, 451–466.

Schutz, W. C. (1966). *The interpersonal underworld*. Palo Alto, CA: Science & Behavior Books.

Schwartz, M. D., & Leggett, M. S. (1999). Bad dates or emotional trauma? The aftermath of campus assault. *Violence Against Women, 5,* 251–271.

Schwartz-Watts, D., & Morgan, D. W. (1998). Violent versus nonviolent stalkers. *Journal of the American Academy of Psychiatry and the Law, 26,* 241–245.

Schwartz-Watts, D., Morgan, D. W., & Barnes, C. J. (1997). Stalkers: The South Carolina experience. *Journal of the American Academy of Psychiatry and the Law, 25,* 541–545.

Scocas, E., O'Connell, J., Huenke, C., Nold, K., & Zoelker, E. (1996). *Domestic violence in Delaware 1994: An analysis of victim to offender relationships with special focus on stalking.* Dover, DE: Statistical Analysis Center.

Sczesny, S., & Stahlberg, D. (2000). Sexual harassment over the telephone: Occupational risk at call centres. *Work & Stress, 14,* 121–136.

Sebastiani, J. A., & Foy, J. L. (1965). Psychotic visitors to the White House. *American Journal of Psychiatry, 122,* 679–686.

Seeck, S. L. (1998). *Violence in the workplace: A study of violence by clients directed toward psychologists and social workers in Los Angeles.* Unpublished master's thesis, Department of Social Work, California State University, Long Beach.

Seeman, M. V. (1978). Delusional loving. *Archives of General Psychiatry, 35,* 1265–1267.

Segal, J. H. (1989). Erotomania revisited: From Kraepelin to DSM–III–R. *American Journal of Psychiatry, 146,* 1261–1266.

Senn, C. Y., & Dzina, K. (1996). Measuring fear of rape: A new scale. *Canadian Journal of Behavioural Science, 28,* 141–144.

Sharkey, W. F. (1997). Why would anyone want to intentionally embarrass me? In R. M. Kowalski (Ed.), *Aversive interpersonal behaviors* (pp. 57–90). New York: Plenum.

Sharps, P. W., Koziol-McLain, J., Campbell, J., McFarlane, J., Sachs, C., & Xu, X. (2001). Health care providers' missed opportunities for preventing femicide. *Preventative Medicine, 33,* 373–380.

Shaver, P. R., & Hazan, C. (1988). A biased overview of the study of love. *Journal of Social and Personal Relationships, 5,* 473–501.

Sheffield, C. J. (1989). The invisible intruder: Women's experiences of obscene phone calls. *Gender and Society, 3,* 483–488.

Sheils, M. (2000). Civil causes of action for stalking victims. *Victim Advocate, 2,* 13–16.

Sheridan, L. (2001). The course and nature of stalking: An in-depth victim survey. *Journal of Threat Assessment, 1,* 61–79.

Sheridan, L. P., Blaauw, E., & Davies, G. M. (2003). Stalking: Knowns and unknowns. *Trauma, Violence & Abuse, 4,* 148–162.

Sheridan, L., & Boon, J. (2002). Stalker typologies: Implications for law enforcement. In J. Boon & L. Sheridan (Eds.), *Stalking and psychosexual obsession: Psychological perspectives for prevention, policing and treatment* (pp. 63–82). West Sussex, England: John Wiley & Sons.

Sheridan, L., & Davies, G. M. (2001a). Stalking: The elusive crime. *Legal and Criminological Psychology, 6,* 133–147.

Sheridan, L., & Davies, G. M. (2001b). Violence and the prior victim–stalker relationship. *Criminal Behaviour and Mental Health, 11,* 102–116.

Sheridan, L., & Davies, G. M. (2001c). What is stalking? The match between legislation and public perception. *Legal and Criminological Psychology, 6,* 3–17.

Sheridan, L., Davies, G. M., & Boon, J. C. (2001a). The course and nature of stalking: A victim perspective. *Howard Journal of Criminal Justice, 40,* 215–234.

Sheridan, L., Davies, G. M., & Boon, J. C. (2001b). Stalking: Perceptions and prevalence. *Journal of Interpersonal Violence, 16,* 151–167.

Sheridan, L., Gillett, R., & Davies, G. M. (2000). "Stalking"—Seeking the victim's perspective. *Psychology, Crime & Law, 6,* 267–280

Sheridan, L., Gillett, R., & Davies, G. M. (2002). Perceptions and prevalence of stalking in a male sample. *Psychology, Crime & Law, 8*, 289–310.

Sheridan, L., Gillett, R., Davies, G. M., Blaauw, E., & Patel, D. (2003). "There's no smoke without fire": Are male ex-partners perceived as more "entitled" to stalk than acquaintance or stranger stalkers? *British Journal of Psychology, 94*, 87–98.

Sherman, L. W., & Berk, R. A. (1984). The specific deterrent effects of arrest for domestic assault. *American Sociological Review, 49*, 261–272.

Shipherd, J. C., & Beck, J. G. (1999). The effects of suppressing trauma-related thoughts on women with rape-related postraumatic stress disorder. *Behaviour Research and Therapy, 37*, 99–112.

Shore, D., Filson, C. R., Davis, T. S., Olivos, G., DeLisi, L., & Wyatt, R. J. (1985). White house cases: Psychiatric patients and the Secret Service. *American Journal of Psychiatry, 142*, 308–312.

Shore, D., Filson, C. R., Johnson, W. E., Rae, D. S., Muehrer, P., Kelley, D. J., Davis, T. S., Waldman, I. N., & Wyatt, R. J. (1989). Murder and assault arrests of white house cases: Clinical and demographic correlates of violence subsequent to civil commitment. *American Journal of Psychiatry, 146*, 645–651.

Shotland, R. L., & Craig, J. M. (1988). Can men and women differentiate between friendly and sexually interested behavior? *Social Psychology Quarterly, 51*, 66–73.

Shotland, R. L., & Goodstein, L. (1992). Sexual precedence reduces the perceived legitimacy of sexual refusal: An examination of attributions concerning date rape and consensual sex. *Personality and Social Psychology Bulletin, 18*, 756–764.

Signer, S. (1989). Homo-erotomania. *British Journal of Psychiatry, 154*, 729.

Signer, S. F., & Cummings, J. L. (1987). De Clérambault's syndrome in organic affective disorder: Two cases. *British Journal of Psychiatry, 151*, 404–407.

Silva, J. A., Derecho, D. V., Leong, G. B., & Ferrari, M. M. (2000). Stalking behavior in delusional jealousy. *Journal of Forensic Sciences, 45*, 77–82.

Simon, R. I. (1996). *Bad men do what good men dream*. Washington, DC: American Psychiatric Press.

Simpson, J. A. (1987). The dissolution of romantic relationships: Factors involved in relationship stability and emotional distress. *Journal of Personality and Social Psychology, 53*, 683–692.

Simpson, J. A. (1990). Influence of attachment styles on romantic relationships. *Journal of Personality and Social Psychology, 59*, 971–980.

Simpson, J. A., Rholes, W. S., & Phillips, D. (1996). Conflict in close relationships: An attachment perspective. *Journal of Personality and Social Psychology, 71*, 899–914.

Sinclair, H. C., & Frieze, I. H. (2000). Initial courtship behavior and stalking: How should we draw the line? *Violence and Victims, 15*, 23–40.

Singer, M. I., Hussey, D., & Strom, K. J. (1992). Grooming the victim: An analysis of a perpetrator's seduction letter. *Child Abuse and Neglect, 16*, 877–886.

Sinwelski, S. A., & Vinton, L. (2001). Stalking: The constant threat of violence. *AFFILIA, 16*, 46–65.

Skalias, L. V. (1994). *Stalked*. Fort Worth, TX: Summit Group.

Skoler, G. (1998). The archetypes and psychodynamics of stalking. In J. R. Meloy (Ed.), *The psychology of stalking* (pp. 85–112). San Diego, CA: Academic Press.

Smartt, U. (2001). The stalking phenomenon: Trends in European and international stalking and harassment legislation. *European Journal of Crime, Criminal Law and Criminal Justice, 9*, 209–232.

Smith, J. C. (1997, August). Assault (Commentary). *Criminal Law Review*, pp. 576–578.

Smith, M. D., & Morra, N. N. (1994). Obscene and threatening telephone calls to women: Data from a Canadian national survey. *Gender & Society, 8*, 584–596.

Snow, D. A., Robinson, C., & McCall, P. L. (1991). "Cooling out" men in singles bars and night-clubs: Observations on the interpersonal survival strategies of women in public places. *Journal of Contemporary Ethnography, 19,* 423–449.

Snow, R. L. (1998). *Stopping a stalker: A cop's guide to making the system work for you.* New York: Plenum Trade.

Sohn, E. F. (1994, May–June). Antistalking statutes: Do they actually protect victims? *Criminal Law Bulletin,* pp. 203–241.

Sommer, K. (2001). Coping with rejection: Ego-defensive strategies, self-esteem, and interpersonal relationships. In M. R. Leary (Ed.), *Interpersonal rejection* (pp. 167–188). New York: Oxford University Press.

Soyka, M., Naber, G., & Völcker, A. (1991). Prevalence of delusional jealousy in different psychiatric disorders: An analysis of 93 cases. *British Journal of Psychiatry, 158,* 549–553.

Spence-Diehl, E. (1999). *Stalking: A handbook for victims.* Holmes Beach, FL: Learning Publications.

Spence-Diehl, E., & Potocky-Tripodi, M. (2001). Victims of stalking: A study of service needs as perceived by victim services practitioners. *Journal of Interpersonal Violence, 16,* 86–94.

Spencer, A. C. (1998). *Stalking and the MMPI-2 in a forensic population.* Unpublished doctoral dissertation, University of Detroit Mercy, Detroit, MI.

Sperling, M. B., & Berman, W. H. (1991). An attachment classification of desperate love. *Journal of Personality Assessment, 56,* 45–55.

Speziale, B. A. (1994). Marital conflict versus sex and love addiction. *Families in Society: Journal of Contemporary Human Services, 75,* 509–512.

Spitzberg, B. H. (1987). Issues in the study of communicative competence. In B. Dervin & M. J. Voigt (Eds.), *Progress in communication sciences* (Vol. 8, pp. 1–46). Norwood, NJ: Ablex.

Spitzberg, B. H. (1989). Issues in the development of a theory of interpersonal competence in the intercultural context. *International Journal of Intercultural Relations, 13,* 241–268.

Spitzberg, B. H. (1993). The dialectics of (in)competence. *Journal of Social and Personal Relationships, 10,* 137–158.

Spitzberg, B. H. (1994). The dark side of (in)competence. In W. R. Cupach & B. H. Spitzberg (Eds.), *The dark side of interpersonal communication* (pp. 25–49). Hillsdale, NJ: Lawrence Erlbaum Associates.

Spitzberg, B. H. (1997). Intimate violence. In W. R. Cupach & D. J. Canary (Eds.), *Competence in interpersonal conflict* (pp. 174–201). New York: McGraw-Hill.

Spitzberg, B. H. (1998a). Sexual coercion. In B. H. Spitzberg & W. R. Cupach (Eds.), *The dark side of close relationships* (pp. 179–232). Mahwah, NJ: Lawrence Erlbaum Associates.

Spitzberg, B. H. (1998b, February). *Toward a propositional model of obsessive relational intrusion and stalking.* Paper presented to the Western States Communication Association Convention, Denver, CO.

Spitzberg, B. H. (1999). An analysis of empirical estimates of rape and sexual coercion. *Violence and Victims, 14,* 241–260.

Spitzberg, B. H. (2000a, November). *Forlorn love: Attachment styles, love styles, loneliness, and obsessional thinking as predictors of obsessive relational intrusion.* Paper presented at the National Communication Association Convention, Seattle, WA.

Spitzberg, B. H. (2000b). What is good communication? *Journal of the Association for Communication Administration, 29,* 103–119.

Spitzberg, B. H. (2002a). In the shadow of the stalker: The problem of policing unwanted pursuit. H. Giles (Ed.), *Law enforcement, communication, and the community* (pp. 173–200). Amsterdam: John Benjamins.

Spitzberg, B. H. (2002b). The tactical topography of stalking victimization and management. *Trauma, Violence, & Abuse, 3,* 261–288.

Spitzberg, B. H., & Cadiz, M. (2002). The media construction of stalking stereotypes. *Journal of Criminal Justice and Popular Culture, 9*(3), 128–149.

Spitzberg, B. H., Canary, D. J., & Cupach, W. R. (1994). A competence-based approach to the study of interpersonal conflict. In D. D. Cahn (Ed.), *Conflict in personal relationships* (pp. 183–202). Hillsdale, NJ: Lawrence Erlbaum Associates.

Spitzberg, B. H., & Cupach, W. R. (1984). *Interpersonal communication competence.* Beverly Hills, CA: Sage.

Spitzberg, B. H., & Cupach, W. R. (1989). *Handbook of interpersonal competence research.* New York: Springer-Verlag.

Spitzberg, B. H., & Cupach, W. R. (1998). Introduction: Dusk, detritus, and delusion—A prolegomenon to the dark side of close relationships. In B. H. Spitzberg & W. R. Cupach (Eds.), *The dark side of close relationships* (pp. xi–xxii). Mahwah, NJ: Lawrence Erlbaum Associates.

Spitzberg, B. H., & Cupach, W. R. (1999, June). *Jealousy, suspicion, possessiveness and obsession as predictors of obsessive relational intrusion.* Paper presented at the International Network on Personal Relationships and International Society for the Study of Personal Relationships Joint Conference, Louisville, KY.

Spitzberg, B. H., & Cupach, W. R. (2001a). Paradoxes of pursuit: Toward a relational model of stalking-related phenomena. In J. A. Davis (Ed.), *Stalking crimes and victim protection: Prevention, intervention, threat assessment, and case management* (pp. 97–136). Boca Raton, FL: CRC Press.

Spitzberg, B. H., & Cupach, W. R. (2001b, February). *Power, empathy, and sex role ideology as predictors of obsessive relational intrusion.* Top Four paper presented at the Western States Communication Association Convention, Coeur d'Alene, ID.

Spitzberg, B. H., & Cupach, W. R. (2002a). The inappropriateness of relational intrusion. In R. Goodwin & D. Cramer (Eds.), *Inappropriate relationships: The unconventional, the disapproved, and the forbidden* (pp. 191–219). Mahwah, NJ: Lawrence Erlbaum Associates.

Spitzberg, B. H., & Cupach, W. R. (2002b). Interpersonal skills. In M. L. Knapp & J. Daly (Eds.), *Handbook of interpersonal communication* (3rd ed., pp. 564–611). Newbury Park, CA: Sage.

Spitzberg, B. H., & Cupach, W. R. (2003). What mad pursuit? Obsessive relational intrusion and stalking related phenomena. *Aggression and Violent Behavior, 8*, 345–375.

Spitzberg, B. H., & Dillard, J. P. (2002). Meta-analysis, social skills, and interpersonal competence. In M. Allen, R. Preiss, K. Dindia, B. Gayle, & N. Burrell (Eds.), *Interpersonal communication: Advances through meta-analysis* (pp. 89–107). Mahwah, NJ: Lawrence Erlbaum Associates.

Spitzberg, B. H., & Hecht, M. L. (1984). A component model of relational competence. *Human Communication Research, 10*, 575–599.

Spitzberg, B. H., & Hoobler, G. D. (2002). Cyberstalking and the technologies of interpersonal terrorism. *New Media & Society, 4*, 71–92.

Spitzberg, B. H., Marshall, L., & Cupach, W. R. (2001). Obsessive relational intrusion, coping, and sexual coercion victimization. *Communication Reports, 14*, 19–30.

Spitzberg, B. H., Nicastro, A. M., & Cousins, A. V. (1998). Exploring the interactional phenomenon of stalking and obsessive relational intrusion. *Communication Reports, 11*, 33–48.

Spitzberg, B. H., & Rhea, J. (1999). Obsessive relational intrusion and sexual coercion victimization. *Journal of Interpersonal Violence, 14*, 3–20.

Sprecher, S. (1994). Two sides to the breakup of dating relationships. *Personal Relationships, 1*, 199–222.

Sprecher, S., Felmlee, D., Metts, S., Fehr, B., & Vanni, D. (1998). Factors associated with distress following the breakup of a close relationship. *Journal of Social and Personal Relationships, 15*, 791–809.

Stanko, E. (1985). *Intimate intrusions: Women's experience of male violence.* London: Routledge & Kegan Paul.

Stanko, E. (1990). *Everyday violence: How women and men experience sexual and physical danger.* San Francisco: Pandora/HarperCollins.

Stark, E. (1996). Mandatory arrest of batterers: A reply to its critics. In E. S. Buzawa & C. G. Buzawa (Eds.), *Do arrests and restraining orders work?* (pp. 115–149). Thousand Oaks, CA: Sage.

Stephen, T. D. (1984). Symbolic interdependence and post-break-up distress: A reformulation of the attachment construct. *Journal of Divorce, 8*(1), 1–16.

Stephens, B. J., & Sinden, P. G. (2000). Victims' voices: Domestic assault victims' perceptions of police demeanor. *Journal of Interpersonal Violence, 15*, 534–547.

Stets, J. E. (1990). Verbal and physical aggression in marriage. *Journal of Marriage and the Family, 52*, 501–514.

Stets, J. E. (1992). Interactive processes in dating aggression: A national study. *Journal of Marriage and the Family, 54*, 165–177.

Stith, S. B., Jester, S. B., & Bird, G. W. (1992). A typology of college students who use violence in their dating relationships. *Journal of College Student Development, 33*, 411–421.

Stocker, M., & Nielssen, O. (2000, December). *Apprehended violence orders and stalking.* Paper presented to the Criminal Justice Responses Conference, Australian Institute of Criminology, Sydney.

Straus, M. A. (1999). The controversy over domestic violence by women: A methodological, theoretical, and sociology of science analysis. In X. B. Arriaga & S. Oskamp (Eds.), *Violence in intimate relationships* (pp. 17–44). Thousand Oaks, CA: Sage.

Strikis, S. A. (1993). Stopping stalking. *Georgetown Law Journal, 81*, 2771–2813.

Stuckless, N., & Goranson, R. (1992). The vengeance scale: Development of a measure of attitudes toward revenge. *Journal of Social Behavior and Personality, 7*, 25–42.

Stuckless, N., & Goranson, R. (1994). A selected bibliography of literature on revenge. *Psychological Reports, 75*, 803–811.

Sugarman, D. B., Aldarondo, E., & Boney-McCoy, S. (1996). Risk marker analysis of husband-to-wife violence: A continuum of aggression. *Journal of Applied Social Psychology, 26*, 313–337.

Sugarman, J. E., & Hotaling, G. T. (1991). Dating violence: Prevalence, context, and risk markers. In M. A. Pirog-Good & J. E. Stets (Eds.), *Violence in dating relationships: Emerging social issues* (pp. 3–32). New York: Praeger.

Sunnafrank, M. (1991). Interpersonal attraction and attitude similarity: A communication-based assessment. In J. A. Anderson (Ed.), *Communication yearbook 14* (pp. 451–483). Newbury Park, CA: Sage.

Surrette, R. (1998). *Media, crime, and criminal justice: Images and realities* (2nd ed.). Belmont, CA: Wadsworth.

Suzuki, S. (1999). Victimization by stalkers among young females. *Reports of National Research Institute of Police Science, 40*, 53–66.

Swartz, M. S., Swanson, J. W., Hiday, V. A., Borum, R., Wagner, H. R., & Burns, B. J. (1998). Violence and severe mental illness: The effects of substance abuse and nonadherence to medication. *American Journal of Psychiatry, 155*, 226–231.

Symons, D., & Ellis, B. (1989). Human male–female differences in sexual desire. In A. E. Rasa, C. Vogel, & E. Voland (Eds.), *The sociobiology of sexual and reproductive strategies* (pp. 131–146). New York: Chapman & Hall.

Tamres, L. K., Janicki, D., & Helgeson, V. S. (2002). Sex differences in coping behavior: A meta-analytic review and an examination of relative coping. *Personality and Social Psychology Review, 6*, 2–30.

Taylor, P., Mahendra, B., & Gunn, J. (1983). Erotomania in males. *Psychological Medicine, 13*, 645–650.

Tedeschi, J. T., & Felson, R. B. (1994). *Violence, aggression, & coercive actions.* Washington, DC: American Psychological Association.

Tellefsen, L. J., & Johnson, M. B. (2000). False victimization in stalking: Clinical and legal aspects. *NYS Psychologist, 12*(1), 20–25.

Tennov, D. (1979). *Love and limerance.* New York: Stein and Day.

Tennov, D. (1998). Love madness. In V. C. de Munck (Ed.), *Romantic love and sexual behavior: Perspectives from the social sciences* (pp. 77–88). Westport, CT: Praeger.

Tesser, A. (1978). Self-generated attitude change. In L. Berkowitz (Ed.), *Advances in experimental social psychology* (Vol. 11, pp. 289–338). New York: Academic Press.

Tesser, A., & Conlee, M. C. (1975). Some effects of time and thought on attitude polarization. *Journal of Personality and Social Psychology, 31,* 262–270.

Thompson, M. P., Simon, T. R., Saltzman, L. E., & Mercy, J. A. (1999). Epidemiology of injuries among women after physical assaults: The role of self-protective behaviors. *American Journal of Epidemiology, 150,* 235–244.

Timmreck, T. C. (1990). Overcoming the loss of a love: Preventing love addiction and promoting positive emotional health. *Psychological Reports, 66,* 515–528.

Tjaden, P., & Thoennes, N. (1998a, November). *Prevalence, incidence, and consequences of violence against women: Findings from the national violence against women survey.* Washington, DC: U.S. Department of Justice, National Institute of Justice (NCJ 172837).

Tjaden, P., & Thoennes, N. (1998b). *Stalking in America: Findings from the National Violence Against Women Survey.* Washington, DC: National Institute of Justice and Centers for Disease Control and Prevention (NCJ 169592).

Tjaden, P., & Thoennes, N. (2000a). *Extent, nature, and consequences of intimate partner violence: Findings from the National Violence Against Women Survey.* Washington, DC: U.S. Department of Justice, Office of Justice Programs (NCJ 181867).

Tjaden, P., & Thoennes, N. (2000b). *Full report of the prevalence, incidence, and consequences of violence against women: Findings from the National Violence Against Women Survey.* Washington, DC: National Institute of Justice and Centers for Disease Control and Prevention (NCJ 183781).

Tjaden, P., & Thoennes, N. (2000c). Prevalence and consequences of male-to-female and female-to-male intimate partner violence as measured by the national violence against women survey. *Violence Against Women, 6,* 142–161.

Tjaden, P., & Thoennes, N. (2000d). The role of stalking in domestic violence crime reports generated by the Colorado Springs Police Department. *Violence and Victims, 15,* 427–441.

Tjaden, P. G., & Thoennes, N. (2001). Coworker violence and gender: Findings from the National Violence Against Women Survey. *American Journal of Preventative Medicine, 20,* 85–89.

Tjaden, P., Thoennes, N., & Allison, C. J. (2000). Comparing stalking victimization from legal and victim perspectives. *Violence and Victims, 15,* 7–22.

Tolhuizen, J. H. (1989). Communication strategies for intensifying dating relationships: Identification, use and structure. *Journal of Social and Personal Relationships, 6,* 413–434.

Topliffe, E. (1992). Why civil protection orders are effective remedies for domestic violence but mutual protective orders are not. *Indiana Law Journal, 67,* 1039–1065.

Trees, A. R., & Manusov, V. (1998). Managing face concerns in criticism: Integrating nonverbal behaviors as a dimension of politeness in female friendship dyads. *Human Communication Research, 24,* 564–583.

Trone, J. (n.d.). *Calculating intimate danger: MOSAIC® and the emerging practice of risk assessment.* New York: VERA Institute of Justice.

Trost, M. R., & Yoshimura, S. M. (1999, February). *The emotion profiles of strategies for expressing jealousy.* Paper presented at the Western States Communication Association, Vancouver, British Columbia, Canada.

Tryon, G. S. (1986). Abuse of therapists by patients: A national survey. *Professional Psychology: Research and Practice, 17,* 357–363.

Tucker, J. T. (1993). Stalking the problems with stalking laws. *Florida Law Review, 45,* 609–707.

Tucker, R. K., Martin, M. G., & Vivian, B. (1991). What constitutes a romantic act? An empirical study. *Psychological Reports, 69*, 651–654.

Turell, S. C. (2000). A descriptive analysis of same-sex relationship violence for a diverse sample. *Journal of Family Violence, 15*, 281–293.

Turner, J. H. (1990). The misuse and use of metatheory. *Sociological Forum, 5*, 37–53.

Ugolini, J. A., & Kelly, K. (2001). Case management strategies regarding stalkers and their victims: A practical approach from a private industry perspective. In J. A. Davis (Ed.), *Stalking crimes and victim protection: Prevention, intervention, threat assessment, and case management* (pp. 301–316). Boca Raton, FL: CRC Press.

U.S. Congress House Committee on the Judiciary. (1999). *Stalking prevention and victim protection act of 1999*. (106th Congress, Report 106–455).

U.S. Department of Justice. (1993). *Antistalking legislation*. Hearing before the Committee on the Judiciary, United States Senate (J-102-86). Washington, DC: U.S. Government Printing Office.

U.S. Department of Justice (1998). *Stalking and domestic violence*. Third Annual Report to Congress under the Violence Against Women Act. Washington, DC: Violence Against Women Grants Office, U.S. Department of Justice (NCJ 172204).

U.S. Department of Justice. (1999, August). *1999 Report on cyberstalking: A new challenge for law enforcement and industry*. Report from the Attorney General to the Vice President. Washington, DC: U.S. Department of Justice.

U.S. Department of Justice. (2001, May). *Stalking and domestic violence: Report to Congress*. Washington, DC: U.S. Department of Justice, Office of Justice Programs (NCJ 186157).

U.S. Department of Justice. (2002a, January). *Enforcement of protective orders* (Legal Series Bulletin no. 4, NCJ 189190). Washington, DC: U.S. Department of Justice, Office of Justice Programs, Office for Victims of Crime.

U.S. Department of Justice (2002b, January). *Strengthening antistalking statutes* (Legal Series Bulletin no. 1, NCJ 189192). Washington, DC: U.S. Department of Justice, Office of Justice Programs, Office for Victims of Crime.

Valentiner, D. P., Foa, E. B., Riggs, D. S., & Gershuny, B. S. (1996). Coping strategies and posttraumatic stress disoder in female victims of sexual and nonsexual assault. *Journal of Abnormal Psychology, 105*, 455–458.

VanderVelde, L. (1996). The legal ways of seduction. *Stanford Law Review, 48*, 817–901.

Vangelisti, A. L. (1994). Messages that hurt. In W. R. Cupach & B. H. Spitzberg (Eds.), *The dark side of interpersonal communication* (pp. 53–82). Hillsdale, NJ: Lawrence Erlbaum Associates.

Vangelisti, A. L., Daly, J. A., & Rudnick, J. R. (1991). Making people feel guilty in conversations: Techniques and correlates. *Human Communication Research, 18*, 3–39.

Vangelisti, A. L., & Young, S. L. (2000). When words hurt: The effects of perceived intentionality on interpersonal relationships. *Journal of Social and Personal Relationships, 17*, 393–424.

Vanwesenbeeck, I., Bekker, M., & van Lenning, A. (1998). Gender attitudes, sexual meanings, and interactional patterns in heterosexual encounters among college students in the Netherlands. *Journal of Sex Research, 35*, 317–327.

Vaughan, D. (1986). *Uncoupling: How relationships come apart*. New York: Vintage Books.

Voumvakis, S. E., & Ericson, R. V. (1984). *News accounts of attacks on women: A comparison of three Toronto newspapers*. Toronto: Centre of Criminology, University of Toronto.

Wachs, E. (1988). *Crime-victim stories: New York City's urban folklore*. Bloomington: Indiana University Press.

Wagner, J. (1980). Strategies of dismissal: Ways and means of avoiding personal abuse. *Human Relations, 33*, 603–622.

Wahl, O. F. (2000). Obsessive-compulsive disorder in popular magazines. *Community Mental Health Journal, 36*, 307–312.

Walker, L. E., & Meloy, J. R. (1998). Stalking and domestic violence. In J. R. Meloy (Ed.), *The psychology of stalking* (pp. 139–161). San Diego, CA: Academic Press.

Wall, D. S. (1998). Catching cybercriminals: Policing the Internet. *International Review of Law, Computers & Technology, 12*, 201–208.

Wallace, H. (1995). A prosecutor's guide to stalking. *Prosecutor, 29*(1), 26–30.

Wallace, H., & Kelty, K. (1995). Stalking and restraining orders: A legal and psychological perspective. *Journal of Crime and Justice, 18*, 99–111.

Wallace, H., & Silverman, J. (1996). Stalking and posttraumatic stress syndrome. *Police Journal, 69*, 203–206.

Wallis, M. (1996, December). Outlawing stalkers. *Policing Today, 2*, 25–29.

Wann, D. L. (1995). Preliminary validation of the sport fan motivation scale. *Journal of Sport & Social Issues, 19*, 377–396.

Waring, E. M., Tillman, M. P., Frelick, L., Russell, L., & Weisz, G. (1980). Concepts of intimacy in the general population. *Journal of Nervous and Mental Disease, 168*, 471–474.

Warner, P. K. (1988). Aural assault: Obscene telephone calls. *Qualitative Sociology, 11*, 302–318.

Way, R. C. (1994). The criminalization of stalking: An exercise in media manipulation and political opportunism. *McGill Law Journal, 39*, 379–400.

Weber, A. L. (1998). Losing, leaving, and letting go: Coping with nonmarital breakups. In B. H. Spitzberg & W. R. Cupach (Eds.), *The dark side of close relationships* (pp. 267–306). Mahwah, NJ: Lawrence Erlbaum Associates.

Wegner, D. M. (1992). You can't always think what you want: Problems in the suppression of unwanted thoughts. In M. Zanna (Ed.), *Advances in experimental social psychology* (Vol. 25, pp. 193–225). San Diego: Academic Press.

Wegner, D. M., & Erber, R. (1992). The hyperaccessibility of suppressed thoughts. *Journal of Personality and Social Psychology, 63*, 903–912.

Wegner, D. M., Lane, J. D., & Dimitri, S. (1994). The allure of secret relationships. *Journal of Personality and Social Psychology, 66*, 287–300.

Wegner, D. M., Schneider, D. J., Carter, S. R. III, & White, T. L. (1987). Paradoxical effects of thought suppression. *Journal of Personality and Social Psychology, 53*, 5–13.

Wegner, D. M., & Zanakos, S. (1994). Chronic thought suppression. *Journal of Personality, 62*, 615–640.

Weiss, R. S. (1991). The attachment bond in childhood and adulthood. In C. M. Parkes, J. Stevenson-Hinde, & P. Marris (Eds.), *Attachment across the life cycle* (pp. 66–76). London: Tavistock/Routledge.

Welch, J. M. (1995). Stalking and anti-stalking legislation: A guide to the literature of a new legal concept. *Reference Services Review, 23*, 53–58, 68.

Wells, K. (2001). Prosecuting those who stalk: A prosecutor's legal perspective and viewpoint. In J. A. Davis (Ed.), *Stalking crimes and victim protection: Prevention, intervention, threat assessment, and case management* (pp. 427–456). Boca Raton, FL: CRC Press.

Wells, K., & Maxey, W. (2001). Educating those who stalk the stalker: A training perspective. In J. A. Davis (Ed.), *Stalking crimes and victim protection: Prevention, intervention, threat assessment, and case management* (pp. 495–526). Boca Raton, FL: CRC Press.

Werner, C. M., & Haggard, L. M. (1992). Avoiding intrusions at the office: Privacy regulation on typical and high solitude days. *Basic and Applied Social Psychology, 13*, 181–193.

Weston, D., & Shedler, J. (1999a). Revising and assessing Axis II, Part I. Toward an empirically based and clinically useful classification of personality disorders. *American Journal of Psychiatry, 156,* 258–272.

Weston, D., & Shedler, J. (1999b). Revising and assessing Axis II, Part II. Toward an empirically based and clinically useful classification of personality disorders. *American Journal of Psychiatry, 156,* 273–285.

Westrup, D. (1998). Applying functional analysis to stalking behavior. In J. R. Meloy (Ed.), *The psychology of stalking* (pp. 275–294). San Diego, CA: Academic Press.

Westrup, D. (2000, December). *Stalking in the U.S.: Time to focus on treatment.* Paper presented to the Criminal Justice Responses Conference, Australian Institute of Criminology, Sydney.

Westrup, D., & Fremouw, W. J. (1998). Stalking behavior: A literature review and suggested functional analytic assessment technology. *Aggression and Violent Behavior: A Review Journal, 3,* 255–274.

Westrup, D., Fremouw, W. J., Thompson, R. N., & Lewis, S. F. (1999). The psychological impact of stalking on female undergraduates. *Journal of Forensic Sciences, 44,* 554–557.

White, J., Kowalski, R. M., Lyndon, A., & Valentine, S. (2000). An integrative contextual developmental model of male stalking. *Violence and Victims, 15,* 373–388.

White, S. G., & Cawood, J. S. (1998). Threat management of stalking cases. In J. R. Meloy (Ed.), *The psychology of stalking* (pp. 295–315). San Diego, CA: Academic Press.

Whitelaw, K. (1996). Fear and dread in cyberspace. *US News & World Report, 121*(18), 50.

Whitford, H., & Howells, K. (2000, December). *Stalking in domestic relationships: Preliminary analyses of the intrusiveness scale.* Paper presented to the Criminal Justice Responses Conference, Australian Institute of Criminology, Sydney.

Widiger, T. A., & Trull, T. J. (1994). Personality disorders and violence. In J. Monahan & H. J. Steadman (Eds.), *Violence and mental disorder* (pp. 203–226). Chicago: University of Chicago Press.

Wiener, D. (2000, December). *Stalking and the infliction of mental harm.* Paper presented to the Criminal Justice Responses Conference, Australian Institute of Criminology, Sydney.

Williams, D., & Schill, T. (1994). Adult attachment, love styles, and self-defeating personality characteristics. *Psychological Reports, 75,* 31–34.

Williams, K. D. (1997). Social ostracism. In R. M. Kowalski (Ed.), *Aversive interpersonal behaviors* (pp. 133–170). New York: Plenum.

Williams, W. L., Lane, J., & Zona, M. A. (1996, February). Stalking: Successful intervention strategies. *Police Chief,* 24–26.

Willson, P., McFarlane, J., Malecha, A., Watson, K., Lemmey, D., Schultz, P., Gist, J., & Fredland, N. (2000). Severity of violence against women by intimate partners and associated use of alcohol and/or illicit drugs by the perpetrator. *Journal of Interpersonal Violence, 15,* 996–1008.

Wilmot, W. W. (1994). Relationship rejuvenation. In D. J. Canary & L. Stafford (Eds.), *Communication and relational maintenance* (pp. 255–273). San Diego, CA: Academic Press.

Wilmot, W. W. (1995). *Relational communication.* New York: McGraw-Hill.

Wilmot, W. W., & Baxter, L. A. (1983). Reciprocal framing of relationship definitions and episodic interaction. *Western Journal of Speech Communication, 47,* 205–217.

Wilson, M., & Daly, M. (1993). Spousal homicide risk and estrangement. *Violence & Victims, 8,* 3–16.

Wilson, M., & Daly, M. (1998). Lethal and nonlethal violence against wives and the evolutionary psychology of male sexual proprietariness. In R. E. Dobash & R. P. Dobash (Eds.), *Rethinking violence against women* (pp. 199–230). Thousand Oaks, CA: Sage.

Wilson, S. R. (2002). *Seeking and resisting compliance: Why people say what they do when trying to influence others.* Thousand Oaks, CA: Sage.

Wilson, S. R., Whipple, E. E., & Grau, J. (1996). Reflection-enhancing regulative communication: How do parents vary across misbehavior types and child resistance? *Journal of Social and Personal Relationships, 13*, 553–569.

Wilt, G. M., Bannon, J. D., Breedlove, R. K., Kennish, J. W., Sandker, D. M., & Sawtell, R. K. (1977). *Domestic violence and the police: Studies in Detroit and Kansas City*. Washington, DC: Police Foundation.

Winfrey, O. (1993). *Inside the mind of the stalker* (Transcript of the Oprah Winfrey show for May 25, 1993). New York: Harpo Productions.

Winfrey, O. (1994). *Women in fear for their lives* (Transcript of the Oprah Winfrey show for January 21, 1994). New York: Harpo Productions.

Wisconsin Department of Justice. (1996, August). *Report of 1996 arrests for stalking/harassment in Wisconsin*. Madison: Wisconsin Department of Justice.

Wolf, M. E., Holt, V. L., Kernic, M. A., & Rivara, F. P. (2000). Who gets protection orders for intimate partner violence? *American Journal of Preventative Medicine, 19*, 286–291.

Wolfe, J., Sharkansky, E. J., Read, J. P., Dawson, R., Martin, J. A., & Ouimette, P. G. (1998). Sexual harassment and assault as predictors of PTSD symptomotology among U.S. female Persian Gulf war military personnel. *Journal of Interpersonal Violence, 13*, 40–57.

Wood, R. A., & Wood, N. L. (2002, December). Stalking the stalker: A profile of offenders. *FBI Law Enforcement Bulletin*, pp. 1–7.

Working to Halt Online Abuse. (2001, January 16). *Cyberstalking facts*. Retrieved from http://www.haltabuse.org/pr/011101.html

Wright, C. (2000). *Everything you need to know about dealing with a stalker*. New York: Rosen.

Wright, J. A., Burgess, A. G., Burgess, A. W., Laszlo, A. T., McCrary, G. O., & Douglas, J. E. (1996). A typology of interpersonal stalking. *Journal of Interpersonal Violence, 11*, 487–502.

Wright, J. A., Burgess, A. G., Burgess, A. W., McCrary, G. O., & Douglas, J. E. (1995). Investigating stalking crimes. *Journal of Psychosocial Nursing and Mental Health Services, 33*(9), 38–43.

Wright, R. A. (1996). Brehm's theory of motivation as a model of effort and cardiovascular response. In P. M. Gollwitzer & J. A. Bargh (Eds.), *The psychology of action: Linking cognition and motivation to behavior* (pp. 424–453). New York: Guilford.

Yokoi, Y. (1998). Investigative psychology and criminal personality profiling: A study of stalking crime. *Journal of Police Science, 51*, 146–155.

Yoshihama, M. (2002). Battered womens coping strategies and psychological distress: Differences by immigration status. *American Journal of Community Psychology, 30*, 429–452.

Zimmerman, N. (2000). Attempted stalking: An attempt-to-almost-attempt-to-act. *Northern Illinois University Law Review, 20*, 219–250.

Zoellner, L. A., Feeny, N. C., Alvarez, J., Watlington, C., O'Neill, M. L., Zager, R., & Foa, E. B. (2000). Factors associated with completion of the restraining order process in female victims of partner violence. *Journal of Interpersonal Violence, 15*, 1081–1099.

Zona, M. A., Palarea, R. E., & Lane, J. C. (1998). Psychiatric diagnosis and the offender-victim typology of stalking. In J. R. Meloy (Ed.), *The psychology of stalking* (pp. 69–84). San Diego, CA: Academic Press.

Zona, M. A., Sharma, K. K., & Lane, J. (1993). A comparative study of erotomanic and obsessional subjects in a forensic sample. *Journal of Forensic Sciences, 38*, 894–903.

Zorza, J. (2001). Some controversies concerning classifying and treating stalkers. *Domestic Violence Report, 7*, 3–5.

Zweig, J. M., Barber, B. L., & Eccles, J. S. (1997). Sexual coercion and well-being in young adulthood: Comparisons by gender and college status. *Journal of Interpersonal Violence, 12*, 291–308.

Author Index

Subject Index

It
Feels
Good
To
Forgive

Helen Kooiman Hosier

HARVEST HOUSE PUBLISHERS
Eugene, Oregon 97402

IT FEELS GOOD TO FORGIVE

Original edition Copyright © 1974 by Helen W. Kooiman under the title *Forgiveness in Action.*

Revised edition Copyright © 1980 by Helen Kooiman Hosier under the title *It Feels Good to Forgive.*

Revised edition published by Harvest House Publishers, Eugene, Oregon 97402.

Library of Congress Catalog Card Number 80-81474
ISBN 0-89081-251-9

Other Books by Helen Kooiman Hosier

Joyfully Expectant: Meditations Before Baby Comes
Cameos: Women Fashioned by God
Silhouettes: Women Behind Great Men
Suicide: A Cry for Help
The Other Side of Divorce
The Caring Jesus
Profiles: People Who Are Helping to Change the World
Kathryn Kuhlman: The Life She Led, The Legacy She Left
How To Know When God Speaks
Walter Knott: Keeper of the Flame
Coronary? Cancer? God's Answer: Prevent It! (Coauthored with
Dr. Brennan)
Struck By Lightning, Then By Love
(Coauthored with Wilma Stanchfield)
Better Than I Was (Coauthored with Frances Kelley)

iv

Acknowledgments

Contents

Preface

Author Joe Bayly once said to me, "You write with a sob in your throat, don't you?" Joe was right. We who write with sobs in our throats do so because we want to share the lessons we have been taught from God.

I often say, "He is such a good teacher!" I don't believe that God would have us waste any of these valuable lessons. When He entrusts certain experiences to us, it is so that we might help others.

The seed thoughts for this book were planted in my mind by a new Christian years ago. The idea lay in my thinking to be stirred up by something someone else said or did, by my own experiences and those of others, by books I read, by sermons I heard. I am deeply indebted to all who have in some way contributed to this book through conversations, or the writings of others. (Careful attention has been given to the giving of credit where credit is due.)

My new Christian friend, with tears in her eyes, said to me, "Helen, it makes me heartsick because I don't always see in action the things I expect from Christians. If I read my Bible correctly, we are not to judge others, to talk about people behind their backs, to indulge in gossip. We are to be loving and to show forgiveness in action, aren't we? I hate to say it, but I have seen more kindness and understanding in some of my friends from my old life than I have in some Christians."

It was an indictment that I could not dismiss lightly. She deserved an answer. I was one of her new Christian friends, and that day I pleaded with God to show me the areas in my life where I was guilty of the actions or omissions that this friend had described. I had to do some forgiving and to seek God's forgiveness!

When I was a little girl, I would beg my mother not

to bake until I got home from school. Not only was it a treat to lick the beater spoons and bowl, but Mama was always doing surprising things as she whipped up a batch of cookies, cake, or bread. I never ceased to be amazed when she baked banana bread. The recipe called for sour milk, which we never had. But Mama knew exactly what to do. I would watch in amazement as she mixed together some vinegar and soda and then stirred it into sweet milk. Instantly the milk curdled. Now Mama had her sour milk!

I don't know why that impressed me so much, but it did. Mama's secret became her daughter's secret. While writing this book I took time out one afternoon to bake banana bread. Sure enough, I didn't have sour milk, but the problem was remedied easily. And then I remembered a conversation from long ago: "Mama, will your lady friends like your banana bread when they come to quilt tonight?"

Mama assured me they'd enjoy her banana bread. I'm sure Mama didn't think her daughter's next comment was exactly necessary. All I remember her saying was, "Shame on you; that's not very nice!"

"Mama, your friends are like the milk—they look and act sweet and nice, but I think they're a bunch of sourpusses 'cuz they talk about people."

No, God doesn't allow us to waste our experiences, and that one was lodged in my memory only to germinate while this book was in process. Unforgiveness is the vinegar that sours our Christian sweetness. Unforgiveness curdles the spirit.

Helen Kooiman Hosier

1

Pandemonium In the Condominium

She was heartsick. No doubt about it—her face clearly registered the heartbreak she was feeling. Her eyes clouded over with tears as I asked, "Jan, what's the matter? Would you like a cup of coffee?" All she managed was an affirmative nod.

I barely knew the woman. We were neighbors, both new in the condominium complex. We had been casually introduced by the realtor's agent from whom we had purchased our homes, and we had met and conversed just a few times. Her husband was of medium build, had thinning brown hair combed across his forehead, wore thick glasses, dressed handsomely, and seemed very intelligent. They jokingly talked with the fellows in the condominium office about getting a water bed. Beyond that, and the fact that Jan was slim, tall, and shapely, I knew very little about my new neighbors.

Now we were walking past what I laughingly called our regurgitating stream—actually a running brook through the property—toward my place. Jan motioned to her house and said, "He's barricaded the door. He kicked me out last night after we got into an argument at a party. I left the party, and he followed me home. When we got here, he threw my clothes over the balcony into the alley and forced me to leave."

She had used her last six dollars to stay in an inexpensive motel and had come back hoping to get into her home. That's when I bumped into her as she sat heartsick and dispirited in the condominium's office.

My son and I were on our way to church, but I had stopped at the office first. I sensed that church would be home that day as I held Jan's arm and steered her toward our place.

She had no money left for breakfast, so we settled her at the table and gave her bacon and eggs and coffee. My son, sensing her mood as she sat tousel-haired and dejected, tried to liven her spirits with his funny antics.

She made one of numerous phone calls to her husband—calls that were to go on all day and on into the evening—only to be met with his slamming down the receiver each time.

"Jan, I don't want to hear the details of what's happened. That's between you and your husband. But I love you, and you are welcome to stay here until he sobers up and will allow you into the house." I suggested that she lie down. She was plainly exhausted, physically as well as emotionally.

I was facing a critical book deadline, and I concentrated my efforts at my desk. With each page I breathed a thankful sigh of relief; the end was in sight. The current project had been a grueling one. The manuscript, page upon page, lay on my desk—a stack that was growing as the day progressed.

After almost a year of a demanding schedule, which I meted out to myself with a discipline that I had fought hard to attain, I knew that I could soon say the book was finished. If anything happened to that precious manuscript, I was mumbling to myself as the thought

flashed through my thinking. Just as quickly I dismiss-
ed the thought: *Heaven forbid! What could happen to it?*

Jan was dialing the phone again. She looked at me,
tears streaming down her pretty face. "Did you
sleep?" I questioned.

"No," she responded, her face looking a little tense
and drawn, "but I'm rested."

"Good," I said. "Let's walk over to the clubhouse
and play some tennis. I need a change of pace and so
do you."

An hour or so later we returned home. Almost immediately there was a phone call. I indicated to Jan to
take the call. There was a brief exchange and a muffled
protest from her. Then she hung up.

"Mike's so drunk," she said. "Now he's cursing
you!"

My throat tightened. "Me?" *What had I let myself in
for!* But now, I wouldn't entertain fear. I'd only done
what any concerned individual would have done—offered a little breakfast and a place for her to rest and
make some phone calls. I still didn't know the actual
details of what had happened to precipitate the fight
between my neighbors. And I didn't care to know.

Earlier we had carried up her nurse's uniform and
shoes, which would need attention if she was to look
well. She hung the uniform in my closet and placed the
shoes on the floor by the bed, along with her purse and
keys. She would need the outfit for work the next day,
and the rumpled uniform had been thrown over the
balcony along with her other personal things.

"Jan, Kim next door has invited us for dinner," I
told her. "We're going to share our Thanksgiving

leftovers. I'm going over to help her." I left for Kim's with Jan reading the paper and looking wistfully at the phone, hopeful that he would call to say she could come home.

As I explained to Kim what had happened and related my increasing concern, Jan came bursting into Kim's house, frantically crying out, "Helen, he called, and now he's threatening *your* life. Oh, I'm so scared," and she shuddered.

We quieted her, and she told us between sobs about previous problems, of warnings from others that she should leave him because he could be violent when he'd been drinking too much. All her inner anguish gushed forth.

Kim urged her to call the police and provided the name and number of a reputable lawyer to seek counsel. She refused. I suggested that we call the condominium office and ask the realtor's agent to sober up her husband and try reasoning with him. This we did. The agent assured us that he would handle it. We relaxed a bit.

Then Jan remembered: "Oh, Helen, I left your front door wide open . . . ." Her hand flew to her mouth, and she gasped, "What . . . what if he's in there now?"

"Look, I'm not worried. I'll just run over and lock up the house. Relax. Wait here." I left, and Kim took charge of the trembling Jan.

As I stepped past the front door of my home, I was gripped by a strange feeling: *I'm not alone in this house. Why should all the lights be on?* I walked to the bedroom at the far end of the hall and knew immediately that Jan's husband had been there. The closet door was open, and Jan's uniform was gone.

Had he been there? I turned, and there, glaring at me, clutching his drink, was the crazed Mike. He lurched toward me, and I said calmly, surprising myself, "Mike, Jan's not here. Will you please leave my premises!"

He glared at me, retreated a few steps, and said, "Get my wife out of here or I'll get you . . . ." He reached down, picked up her shoes, purse, and keys, and staggered out.

I followed, locking the door after him as I leaned weakly against it. *Thank you, Lord.* All through the ordeal I was inwardly crying out, *God, protect me.*

After a few moments I climbed over the patio wall that separated my place from Kim's and entered her living room from the patio. When I told them what had happened, Kim once more begged Jan to call the police. Again she refused.

Later, after a dinner that we scarcely touched, we called the condominium office a second time. The agent, Frank, confirmed that he would straighten out Mike so that Jan could come home later.

"You gals, I must write a few more pages on that book tonight," I said.

Jan and I left. Back at my house once more, I settled myself at the desk, and Jan lay down on the couch. The doorbell rang. I looked through the peephole. It was the realtor's agent. I opened the door, and he came in, glass in hand. "I thought you were going to get my husband sober," Jan said in disgust.

"He's out there." The agent motioned to the front of the house. "He wants you to come home now. He's okay. I've talked to him."

"I'm scared," Jan said.

"Jan," I replied, "we've been waiting all day for him to say you could come home. I think you should leave now."

I felt ill-at-ease suggesting it, but what was I supposed to do? She had refused to call for police help. My life had been threatened. I had a son to consider. And the agent assured us it was safe.

Jan rose, walked fearfully to the door, looked out through the peephole, opened the door slightly, then slammed it shut, locking it, and screamed as she ran to the phone. "He's drunk as ever. I'm calling the police!"

As she dialed for help, I sat glued to my chair, stunned at what was taking place. Suddenly, Mike was outside shouting profanities and yelling at Jan to open up. After a moment I heard wood splintering, and from where I was sitting, I saw my front door being kicked in by a violent madman. I screamed, and the agent ran out the patio door, leaped the divider, and disappeared into the blackness of the night.

The door lock broke, and Mike pushed his way in, ran to Jan, who was still at the phone, and tried strangling her with the cord. She broke from his grasp, but he grabbed her and thrust her into the fireplace. Again she got away, but he lunged at her, grabbing the gold chain around her throat, and slammed her against the wall. The wall-lamp shade took the brunt of that.

The next thing I knew he was wrestling with her by the big yellow fireside chair, and he threw her against a table lamp. There was the awful sound of more splintering wood and breaking glass as lamp and table crashed to the floor. She broke away and cowered under my glass-topped dinette table.

All the while I'd been frozen to my desk chair. Now I decided to make a break for help. As I got up, Mike came at me and pushed me around. When I ducked away, eluding him, he grabbed up my precious manuscript and flung it into the air. Papers flew in every direction, landing in a flurry of white all over the living room. I was horrified as I ran out of the house.

Rushing to Kim's place, I banged on the locked door. "Let me in, let me in!" I pleaded.

There was no reply. What I did not know at the time was that Kim was on the phone calling the police while the realtor's agent was calming my son and her two sons. I was grateful that my son was safe inside Kim's house, but now I too wanted safety.

Suddenly I knew I was not alone on the steps, and I turned to see Mike stumbling toward me. I held out my arms full length and in a controlled voice that I didn't recognize as my own I said, "Don't touch me. Don't you dare lay a hand on me. All I've done is give your wife coffee, food, and shelter. I know nothing of what happened between the two of you. Now please move out of my way. I'm going to my home. I assure you Jan will be out of there immediately."

He backed off, shocked into submissive silence. The ranting, raving madman just stared at me as I walked past him. When I reached the house, Jan was standing in the front hall, a disheveled mess.

"Jan," I said, taking her in my arms, "the door won't close, and Mike broke the lock. I can't do anything more for you. You'll have to leave."

"I know," she answered, more composed than I would have been if I'd just taken such a beating. "I know. . . ." She moved to meet Mike, who was now back on my steps. I pushed her gently through the door, then shut it as best I could, quickly propping a chair against it.

I didn't watch as they left. Instead I wasted no time in running to the phone to call the police. Then I dialed a couple in the condominium, asking them to come to my assistance. After giving them the facts, I ran out the patio door, climbed over the divider, and banged on Kim's living room door. She let me in.

Within moments the police arrived. A thorough search of Mike and Jan's place and the immediate area turned up neither one. We did not know if she was dead or alive. One of three things could have happened, the police said: She might have broken away from Mike and was in hiding; he could have dragged her someplace and killed her; or they were together someplace.

I elected not to sign a warrant for Mike's arrest, which may have been unwise and was a very difficult decision to make at the time. However, in this instance I felt a restraining hand upon me. The police left after obtaining a report and assuring us that they would continue searching for Jan.

Meanwhile, the couple I'd phoned arrived. Kim, the realtor's agent, and my son stayed next door. My friends and I stood in my living room, which looked like it had been through a hurricane. I slowly began picking up the papers—the precious manuscript. *How will I ever assemble them back together in correct order?* I wondered. While trying to explain what had occurred, my mind was concerned about the manuscript and Jan's whereabouts. Over and over again I questioned, "What could have happened to them? Where is she?"

The phone rang. My friend Jan said, "Get the phone in the bedroom, Helen. I'll listen here."

I ran to the bedroom and heard, "Get my wife out of your house or I'll kill you!"

I screamed back, "Mike, Jan's not here. She left with you." He hung up.

I hurried back to the living room. Jim was already dialing the police again. Minutes later the phone rang a second time. Jim listened on the kitchen phone while I went into the bedroom. The same threat was made.

Shortly thereafter the police arrived. Just as they walked in, the phone rang a third time, and the officer took one phone while I took the other. As he heard the threat made upon my life, he interrupted and said, "This is Officer_____. Your wife is not here, and I must warn you . . . ." but the phone clicked before he could finish. Mike was off the line.

Other friends were called and arrived. The front door was barricaded, and the officers told us we could not spend the night in our home. My son and I left with our friends.

Later that night my friends and I went searching for Jan. More of her clothing had been thrown into the alley, but she was not to be found. The next morning, after I left for work, my friends found Jan running down the alley behind our homes with Mike in drunken pursuit. They threw open their car door and rescued her. They learned that the night before she had broken away from Mike and had hidden in the bathroom of a nearby empty condominium. When she came back and was picking up her clothes strewn in the alley below their balcony, Mike had come out and taken chase.

Jan did seek police help with the aid of my friends that day. Mike pulled the wires from her car, but my friends repaired the damage. The police made Mike release her keys, purse, and some money. Jan went to live with a work associate for a week, but later returned to her husband.

The day following this, as I walked into the condominium office, Mike appeared, brushed past me menacingly, and glared at me. It was frightening, I must admit. Still, I sensed an inner calm that assured me there was a reason for all of this.

On the second day following the episode I walked through the model office again, after picking up my mail, and Mike was seated by the desk. He was neatly and smartly dressed—and sober. Quite a contrast to what we'd been seeing!

It was totally unplanned. I walked over to him, extended my hand, and heard myself say, "Mike, how are you? You're looking better today. I think we should be friends."

He looked at me, disbelief registering on his features, gripped the arms of the chair, and struggled slowly to his feet.

I took his hands in mine, looked up at him, and said, "Mike, I'm sorry about everything. I love you, and I forgive you for what has happened."

Suddenly he withdrew his hands, took off his thick glasses, and the next thing I knew he was reaching for a handkerchief to wipe his eyes. "Thank you," he managed to say huskily.

2

Forgive As He Forgives

Forgive as He forgives. I'd read it all my life, heard it preached from pulpits, and quoted it dozens of times. I'd practiced it too, and many times had found it difficult.

As I looked at the downcast Mike, sitting by the desk in the condominium office when I walked through that day with my mail, I heard that still, small voice within me saying, *Forgive as He forgives*.

Forgive him? The objection flashed through my head as I paused, momentarily stunned at seeing this man who had so recently caused me such distress.

Yes!

That's all I heard. And then I crossed over to him. Was it difficult? No, as I retrace those steps now in my mind, I was carried forward, as it were, on wings of love. Does that sound too pat? Contrived? Simplistic? Nevertheless, it's true. My steps did not lag or falter.

I reached him and touched him. Instantly, I knew there was healing in that touch—healing for this man whose spirit was so wounded. How many times we read in the Gospel narrative of Jesus' touch, of His healing, and then of His words of loving forgiveness! At other times Jesus would say, ''Thy sins be forgiven thee,'' and would then follow with healing.

Our Lord always placed emphasis on the state of a person's soul, his inner being. Physical healing was important in the eyes of the loving Jesus, but the greater need was to assure a person of forgiveness, of his being in good standing with God.

Whenever Jesus' critics, especially the scribes and the Pharisees, heard Him speak of forgiveness, they were indignant. "Blasphemy!" they murmured to themselves and each other. "This man is saying He is God!" exclaimed the religious leaders.[1]

The criticism of the critics never deterred Jesus from His mission. It made no difference to Him what people said, thought, or did.

> Jesus knew what they were thinking and asked them, "Why are you thinking such evil thoughts? I, the Messiah, have the authority on earth to forgive sins. But talk is cheap—anybody could say that. So I'll prove it to you by healing this man." Then, turning to the paralyzed man, he commanded, "Pick up your stretcher and go on home, for you are healed."[2]

The Bible faithfully records, "And the boy jumped up and left."[3]

The reaction of the crowd standing nearby is interesting: "A chill of fear swept through the crowd as they saw this happen right before their eyes. How they praised God for giving such authority to a man!"[4] But not the religious leaders nor those who were unsympathetic to Jesus' teachings and the claims that He made about Himself. There were many people who simply did not understand, many who could not comprehend this man Jesus.

Now, as I stood before Mike, who just days earlier had so misunderstood me and my motives in helping his wife, I felt nothing but compassion and understanding toward him as I recognized the inner sickness that had caused him to act so terribly.

"How could you?" I was to hear that question over and over again from friends in the days that followed. "I just don't understand. Forgive him after what he put you through?"

The questions tumbled out. Word got around fast in succeeding days. "Forgive him after the way he wrecked your living room?"

"Forgive him? Look at your bruises!"

"Forgive him after the way he treated his wife?"

"Forgive him? Look what he did to your manuscript!"

Questions. Surprised reactions and more questions.

But if Mike was shocked that day, the realtor's agent was just as shocked. My disappointment at his running out leaving Jan and me that night in my living room with a drunken madman was pretty keen initially. Yet there was forgiveness for both. It was a forgiveness beyond me and my own capacity to forgive. But it was there, and it was real.

How do you explain the kind of forgiveness the Bible says we are to demonstrate? Words are so inadequate at times. Forgiveness in action does not usually come easy, nor is it readily comprehended by the receivers of such forgiveness or by those watching on the outside. It is especially hard to understand for persons who are unfamiliar with Jesus' life and teachings.

Jesus was the Master Forgiver, and He is our example. What did He say about forgiveness? And how did

He measure up to what He advocated?

"Father, forgive them, for they know not what they do."[5] He was hanging on a cross—that place of cruel death and ignominy, between two criminals. Inhuman abuse had been heaped upon Him. The fury and outrage of His persecutors was, the Bible says, "fierce." He had been wrongly charged with nothing deserving of death.[6] He was hurried to the cross by a noisy, unruly mob. Pilate, the Roman governor, tried unsuccessfully to have Jesus chastised and released, but the people, the chief priests, and the rulers would have none of it.

"Crucify Him, crucify Him!" they cried,[7] and a mighty roar rose from the crowd as the people with one voice shouted, "Kill Him, and release Barabbas to us!" Barabbas was in prison for starting an insurrection in Jerusalem against the government, and for murder.[8]

I knew the Bible story concerning this event and other events in Jesus' life. How did Jesus measure up to what He advocated about forgiving those who have wronged us? In the Gospels we see Him hanging on the cross between two thieves (as though He had been the worst of the three). He was reviled and reproached, treated with all the scorn and contempt imaginable.

As we view Jesus upon the cross, we hear Him praying for His enemies. "Father, forgive them." Often, especially at Easter, we hear sermons and read articles about Christ's last words. They are truly remarkable words.

One would think that Jesus should have prayed, "Father consume them." But no, He is making intercession for transgressors, for all those who spitefully use Him and speak evil against Him—even for those who hate Him without cause even today.

"Father, forgive them, for they know not what they do." The greatest thing Christ ever did was to suffer upon that cross and then die for us. He did it to procure for us the forgiveness of sins. This was forgiveness in action the likes of which the world had never seen, nor will ever see again.

But what did Jesus mean when He said, "They know not what they do"? Was He excusing them? No, He was saying that His crucifiers had been kept in ignorance by their rulers. They had prejudices against Jesus instilled into them; they actually thought they were doing God a service.[9] Such people are to be pitied and prayed for. Later, many of these same people were to hear the preaching of the gospel by Peter and they would then remember Jesus' prayer upon the cross and experience God's answer to the Son's prayer for forgiveness for themselves.

Jesus' example says to me that I must pray for my enemies—those who hate, persecute, or misuse me. Jesus' example reminds me that my neighbors are ignorant of His love and mercy, His forgiveness. If Jesus could pray for such enemies as would crucify Him—if He could forgive them—how can I withhold love and forgiveness from anyone? Yes, even my drunken neighbor who threatened my life.

3

Keep Short Accounts

"Keep short accounts." It was my friend Marj offering those words of wisdom. They were like an echo from the past—something my mother had frequently urged upon us as the better part of wisdom. "Always keep short accounts," Marj repeated herself, and then went on to explain.

"This was so vividly demonstrated a number of years ago, when my husband was desperately ill and we thought he was going to die. Word got around fast, and an old friend of my husband's heard about his illness. For years this fellow had maintained a coolness to us, and it hurt us very much.

"The most pitiful thing I ever saw was this man walking into our house when Warren was on what we thought was his deathbed. He came to apologize because he'd been carrying this grudge for years—ever since we'd gotten married—just because Warren hadn't asked him to be best man at our wedding. He drove many miles, came from a great distance, to ask Warren's forgiveness for something that should have been taken care of years ago."

How many people are like that—they carry unresolved grudges like heavy burdens, struggling with unsettled differences that may have happened long ago but still burden the memory like a gigantic weight that threatens to destroy.

What is gained by carrying a grudge? Ulcers. Insomnia. High blood pressure. Neurotic disorders. Slow suicide.

Carrying grudges can be devastating. S.I. McMillen, a Christian medical doctor who wrote the inspiring best-seller *None of These Diseases,* testified that health, happiness, and longer life can be achieved by following the teachings of the Bible. He states that the moment a person starts hating someone or carrying a grudge, he becomes that person's slave. Resentment produces stress hormones in our body and can have a tyrannical grasp on our mind. The price we pay for allowing our emotions to control us strikes to the very core of our being. Our reactions to life's problems determine how our body will react.

"Is it not a remarkable fact," the doctor asks, "that our reactions to stress determine whether stress is going to cure us or make us sick? Here is an important key to longer and happier living. We hold the key and can decide whether stress is going to work *for us* or *against us.* Our attitude decides whether stress makes us better or bitter."

And what does the Bible have to say on the subject of nursing a grudge and harboring hatred? Stop being mean, bad-tempered, and angry. Quarreling, harsh words, and dislike of others should have no place in your lives. Instead, be kind to each other, tenderhearted, forgiving one another, just as God has forgiven you because you belong to Christ.[1]

Paul is saying that with God there is forgiveness because of Jesus Christ. Who are we, therefore, to withhold that same spirit from those who may have wronged us in some way? Those who are forgiven by God should have a forgiving spirit toward others. God forgives speedily, sincerely, heartily, and forever.

In hatred everybody loses. The cost is exorbitant. A man or a woman can lose friends; a husband or a wife can lose each other; parents can be so alienated from their children that they are lost to each other forever; a store clerk can lose customers; a professional person can lose clients.

Resentment has been likened to a twelve-hour pill, a capsule with all the little grains inside. At regular intervals another is released, so that the effect keeps working hour after hour. Resentment within us releases these droplets of poison that circulate through our whole being, poisoning not only our minds but also our physical and spiritual well-being.

A well-known doctor of internal medicine at Mayo Clinic once said, "I tell my patients they cannot afford to carry grudges or maintain hate." Then he gave an illustration of how he saw a man kill himself inch by inch because of a quarrel with a sister over a family estate. The man became so embittered within himself that his breath was foul, the organs of his body stopped functioning properly, and in a matter of months he was physically dead. He literally killed himself a day at a time!

God has given us a timetable indicating how long we can harbor grudges or be angry. He knows what can happen when we allow grudges and grievances to simmer or when we brood over an injustice.

In Ephesians the Apostle Paul says, "If you are angry, don't sin by nursing your grudge. Don't let the sun go down with you still angry—get over it quickly; for when you are angry you give a mighty foothold to the devil."[2] God is not saying there aren't times when we will be angry; we will be. But He places a restriction upon our anger: "Be angry, *but sin not."*

We must be watchful about anger. It has been suggested that if we want to be angry without sinning, we must be angry at *nothing but sin.* We are to be more jealous for the glory of God than for any interest or reputation of our own. Strong words! We sin in our anger when we allow it to burn into full-blown wrath or allow it to fester within our systems. Paul says that the timetable of God ends at sundown.

What Paul is saying is *always keep short accounts!*

A woman relates that almost every night throughout the years of their tangled marriage relationship she pleaded with her husband, "Please tell me what you are upset about tonight. I'm truly sorry for whatever it is that I've said or done to cause you anger." She quoted Ephesians 4:26,27 to him repeatedly. Most of the time, she relates, her pleas were ignored, and her mate lived in what she referred to as a "constant state of mad." Today this couple—a Christian couple—are divorced.

There must be many thousands of husbands and wives who have allowed unresolved differences to rise up between them until the wall is impossible to scale or break down. Complete forgiveness, on-the-spot forgiveness, before-sundown forgiveness, is the only way to root out the cancer of anger, envy, resentment, and hate that can hurt and destroy the man or woman who harbors such feelings. These sometimes subtle but pervasive wounds are healed by the Great Healer when we act according to His directives.

There isn't a single individual who can escape from the truth covered in Paul's Ephesian letter, which was written while he was a prisoner in jail for serving the Lord. Here he was, imprisoned, with time on his hands—a good time for a man to do some reflective thinking. I'm thankful that Paul endured those prison hours and spent that time wisely, leaving us letters with advice for our own good.

Paul says, "Christ Himself is our way of peace."[3] Any feuds that may have existed in the past for which you have never granted forgiveness, or any grudges that may still exist between you and someone else, should end at the cross.[4]

The respected commentator Matthew Henry observes:

> If you have been provoked and have had your spirits greatly discomposed, and if you have bitterly resented any affront that has been offered, before night calms and quiets your spirits, be reconciled to the offender, and let all be well again: *Let not the sun go down upon your wrath.* If it burns into wrath and bitterness of spirit, see to it that you suppress it speedily. There is the utmost danger of anger becoming sinful if it is not carefully watched and speedily suppressed. And therefore, though anger may *come into* the bosom of a wise man, it *rests* only in the bosom of fools. *Neither give place to the devil.* Those who persevere in sinful anger and wrath let the devil into their hearts, and allow him to gain upon them till he brings them to malice and mischievous machinations. . . .

Has anger, nursing a grudge, or harboring resentment set up housekeeping in your heart and mind? There is only one way to rid yourself of it. Just as you go to the doctor when you have a rampaging infection in your body, so you must come to the Great Physician and allow Him to apply the treatment of 1 John 1:9. There we are told that if we confess our sins to Him, He will forgive us and cleanse us from every wrong.

4

Sad, Sad Words

Some of the saddest words are "If only . . . If only . . . " uttered when it's too late to say, "I'm sorry, forgive me," and a relative or friend lies cold and lifeless. I recall reading in my local newspaper about a tragic accident in which a teenager was killed. The mother's anguish was shown in her chilling words, "We hadn't talked for days. We'd had an argument."

In another incident involving the death of a child in a school bus accident, the mother screamed, "I didn't kiss him goodbye this morning! I was mad at him."

Then there is the individual who is found lifeless, hanging by a rope from the rafters in the garage, or slumped in the seat of a car with the engine running, or with a bullet in his head, with an overdose of pills, leaving behind a suicide note.

Suicide—that's the whispered word, you know. Some people reach the point where the problems of life loom so large that they prefer death. Suicide is considered the ultimate escape, but is it really? Actually, suicide doesn't end it all; it only changes a person's location.

To what extent do unforgiving attitudes enter into suicide? It is known that when unresolved conflicts and anxieties become unbearable, self-destruction seems more desirable for the depressed individual than trying to cope with the problems of life. Stormy personal relationships, broken romances, inability to make or keep friends—these are all determining causes in suicide:

> The most basic reason for the Christian's choice of life over death lies in the core of his faith. God, who forgives and accepts him, warts and all, created his life. Good stewardship of that life which God gave and Christ redeemed—that is, living instead of dying—becomes a form of worship, a means of glorifying God, an expression of gratitude for the promise of eternal life.[1]

The Apostle Paul says:

> I beg you . . . to live and act in a way worthy of those who have been called [by Christ]. Be humble and gentle. Be patient with each other, making allowance for each other's faults because of your love. Try always to be led along together by the Holy Spirit, and so be at peace with one another. We are all parts of one body, we have the same Spirit, and we have all been called to the same glorious future . . . lovingly follow the truth at all times—speaking truly, dealing truly, living truly—and so become more and more in every way like Christ, who is the Head of His body, the church. Under His direction the whole body is fitted together perfectly, and each part in its own special way helps the other parts, so that the whole body is healthy and growing and full of love.[2]

Unity and love, purity and holiness. Love is the law of Christ's kingdom, the lesson of His school. How do we attain to this high ideal which the Apostle Paul is setting before us? The means, he says, is through lowliness and meekness, humility and gentleness, and long-suffering, which implies a patient bearing of injuries, of hurts heaped upon us, of wrongs done to us either willfully or unknowingly—all of this without seeking revenge or carrying angry resentment or acting peevishly. A big order, you say—who is capable of obeying it?

Paul says that when we conscientiously practice this, we will build each other up, which means building up the body of Christ here on earth to a position of strength and maturity so that we are full-grown in the Lord, filled with Christ.[3]

Of course this is a big order, which we are incapable of responding to unless our lives are governed by the power of the Holy Spirit. And that means living constantly with the recognition that it is God's love, His strength, His power, His patience, His humility, and His gentleness that is the enabling force within us. In our own strength we fail. We keep bumping against impossible, unscalable walls. On our own we are incapable of forgiveness in action which enables us to live joyously and victoriously.

Jesus gave us a pattern to follow in regard to interpersonal relationships. It is found in Matthew 5, where Jesus gives His great discourse known as the Sermon on the Mount. In verses 21 through 25a we are told that if you are standing before the altar in the temple (or church), offering a sacrifice to God, and you suddenly remember that someone has something against you, leave your sacrifice there beside the altar and apologize and be reconciled to him, and then come and offer your sacrifice to God. Come to terms quickly with your enemy (or that individual with whom you have a disagreement or with whom you find it difficult to exercise forgiveness).

How radically different the life of the church would be if Christians actually exercised such a forgiving spirit! How different life would be among family members if what Jesus said were actually practiced! And what a difference it would make in all our relationships with friends, neighbors, and business associates if we actually lived this way!

The verses that precede this discourse speak of being angry with one's brother. "Under the law of Moses the rule was, 'If you kill, you must die.' " Jesus said, "But I have added to that rule, and tell you that if you are only *angry*, even in your own home, you are in danger of judgment!"[4]

Actually, God's laws are meant as a hedge of protection around our lives if we would only recognize them as such. What God has decreed, He has done for our own good. Christ is saying that rash anger is heart-murder. Anger is a natural passion, but it must be guarded and controlled. So often parents are angered at their children over things that are purely childish and cannot actually be helped—groundless circumstances, trivial reasons—when they should be exercising one of the great fruits of the spirit known as patience. How tragic for that parent to learn that her child has been killed in an accident after an unsettled argument in which no effort had been made to clear the air and offer forgiveness!

We hurt others and ourselves when we gratify our own brutish passions by venting our anger and refusing to forgive. This is a serious breach of the sixth commandment, Jesus says. For this Paul says we are *fools*. James says, *vain man*, Christ Himself says, *fools, and slow of heart*. The Psalmist says, *Bitter words are as arrows that wound suddenly, or as a sword in the bones*. The good name of that person against whom we have something is stabbed and murdered, as it were. The punishment for this, Jesus says, is severe.

We are to live at peace with others whenever a breach in a relationship occurs. God's Word to us is that we should waste no time in being reconciled—confessing our own failure and our own contribution to the disagreement, and humbling ourselves to make restitution. There are many reasons why we should quickly forgive and seek forgiveness. If we are Christians, we must recognize that performance of religious duties, even offering of daily prayers, is unacceptable to God if there is anything between us and someone else.

There are those who question why their prayers are not answered. They quote Mark 2, which says, "If you only have faith in God—this is the absolute truth—you can say to this Mount of Olives, 'Rise up and fall into the Mediterranean,' and your command will be obeyed. All that's required is that you really believe and have no doubt! Listen to me! You can pray for *anything*, and *if you believe, you have it; it's yours!*"⁵

There is a qualifying verse that follows, however, and that is seldom included when people talk about this matter of faith and believing prayer. Verse 25 says, "*But* when you are praying, first forgive anyone you are holding a grudge against, so that your Father in heaven will forgive you your sins too."

That little three-letter word "but" is freighted with meaning. But, you say, he wronged me. I'm in the clear. I'm absolutely innocent. Though you may protest loudly and though you may be correct—(someone actually has maligned your name, read something into your motives that doesn't exist, even scandalized your good name in some way), Jesus made it very clear that if you have been wronged by someone, regardless of whether that person realizes it or not, you are to go to that person and get it straightened out.

Not only are you to pray regarding this matter of forgiveness and say to God, "I do forgive my friend for slandering my name" (or whatever the grievance is), but you are to take one giant step further and go to that person and seek to make amends. How difficult this is! And how few people there are who really practice this way of life. How this would revolutionize Christianity in the world today if it were consistently practiced!

Love is so much better than all offerings and sacrifice. God would rather that we withhold our gifts, even our worship of Him and saying of prayers, if we are engaged in a quarrel or misunderstanding with someone. Just leave your gift, seek out the person who has wronged you, ask and grant forgiveness, and then return to worship and pray.

The Apostle Paul in writing to young Timothy, his son in the faith, gives wise instruction along this line. He tells Timothy that God wants men everywhere to pray with holy hands lifted up to God, free from sin and anger and resentment.[6]

There are men and women who refuse to go to church, or if they do go to church will not take Communion because they are at variance with a relative, family member, friend, or neighbor. But one sin does not justify a lack of piety, devotion, and loyalty to God. The difficulty can be remedied easily by tender, loving communications. Those who have wronged us we must forgive. To those we have wronged we must go and confess our fault.

Just as we are unfit to worship God or to seek His answers to our prayers if we are withholding forgiveness or not seeking forgiveness (even though we consider ourselves the innocent party), even so we are unfit to die in that condition. As the mother agonized over the untimely death of her son in a tragic accident, so death can come to us or someone we love in a similar sudden manner. We or our loved ones or friends can be snatched away at a time when our spiritual account with our Maker is not in good order. Oh, the senseless, needless tragedy we inflict upon ourselves! What folly to be so caught up in pride and stubbornness that we are insensitive to what we know God's Word says!

Agree quickly, the Bible says, while we are in the way—while we are alive, that is. So long as we are at enmity with another person, we are at enmity with God.

I recall hearing a young girl relate how easy it was for her to memorize Bible verses. She was given Matthew 5:22-24. Years earlier she had quarreled seriously with her brother, and there had been no communication between them for years. Now suddenly she was confronted with a Bible verse that told her to be reconciled to her brother. "What a difference between memorizing a verse and putting it to practice," she confessed!

The time to begin is *now*—today. Don't let another day go by without getting right with your fellowman or a family member, wherever he or she may be. Write a letter, make a phone call, pay a personal visit. Remember, it is actually God who is being sinned against, and you cannot stand in His presence with that on your record.

Yes, some of the saddest words in all the world are "If only . . . If only . . . ." uttered when it's too late to say, "I'm sorry, forgive me." Don't let this happen to you!

5

I Was Once Like Simon

Frequently when I see a young woman with beautiful long hair, I am reminded of the once-sinful woman who showed such great love for Jesus that she used her hair to dry His feet. Her story is told in each of the Gospel accounts, but no one treats it with more dignity and beauty than Luke.[1]

One of the Pharisees asked Jesus to come to his home for lunch, and Jesus accepted the invitation. As they sat down to eat, a prostitute heard that Jesus was there and brought an exquisite flask filled with expensive perfume. After she entered the house, she knelt behind Him at His feet, weeping, with her tears falling down upon His feet; and she wiped them off with her hair and kissed them and poured the perfume on them.[2]

What a picture this presents! The Oriental custom of reclining at the table while eating afforded this woman the opportunity to come behind Jesus and do this. It seems that she might have met Jesus on a previous occasion and repented of her sins, receiving from Him His word of forgiveness. Now, having heard that He was at Simon's house, she slipped in unbidden where Jesus was being entertained as a guest.

She came to anoint His feet, but as she beholds Him she is reminded of her sinful past, and in deep humiliation for sin she stands there weeping. Her hot tears of penitence fall upon the feet of Jesus. Quickly she unbinds her long hair, and, dropping to her knees, kisses those beautiful feet of the Savior. Her tears are tears of sorrow over sin and of joy because of Jesus' forgiveness; her kisses are of adoration as well as affection. Then she wipes those feet dry with her hair. There is so much love in that act! Hair is a woman's crowning glory, and for her to use her beautiful hair to wipe away the dust and grime from Jesus' feet, which had been washed by her tears, was indeed an expression of deepest devotion and love.

But she is not finished. She had come with the special purpose of pouring her expensive, fragrant oil upon the feet of the Lord. And now she does this. The fragrance filled the room, but even more beautiful than the sweet smell was the sweetness of her act. None of this went unnoticed by Jesus, His host Simon the Pharisee, and the other guests.

How do you confess guilt to Christ? How do you admit guilt and wrongdoing to someone whom you have offended? In this woman we learn how repentance acts. There is more to repentance than remorse. There is remorse plus love—a giving of one's self. Her tears represented repentant remorse, and the oil pictured her covering of love. No truer expression could have been given of her gratitude and passionate devotion.

Simon the Pharisee stared at her. But his stare missed so much. The self-righteous person has difficulty in seeing properly. We might say that the self-righteous Simons have a form of myopia—nearsightedness. That is, they can see most clearly that which concerns "me" or "my."

The Bible tells us that when Simon saw what was happening and who the woman was, he said to himself, "This proves that Jesus is no prophet, for if God had really sent Him, He would know what kind of woman this is!"

A Gentile, a sinner like this, a woman of such ill fame, with so notorious a reputation—these were Simon's thoughts. How dare she even enter my house! But if this Jesus were really what He claims to be, He would rise up with indignation. He wouldn't even allow her to come near Him, let alone do what she has done! If she had touched Simon, he would have backed off and said, "Stand by yourself, don't come near me, for I am holier than thou," and he thought Christ should have acted this way and reproved her, too.

The Book of Romans speaks much about being justified by faith,[3] and here we have a profound example of this very thing. It is God who justifies the ungodly.[4] Here we see Jesus speaking up, answering the thoughts of Simon, providing justification for this woman.

By His reply Jesus showed His ability to read even the secret thoughts of His host. Who else but the Son of God can do this? Jesus' words were a rebuke to Simon for his own impenitence and lack of faith. Jesus saw through this woman, all right; but what is far more important, He saw through Simon. And that's a pretty scary thought if you aren't willing to have your innermost thoughts exposed to the all-seeing eye of the Lord!

Jesus looked at the successful, pompous, self-righteous but pitiable Pharisee—this man who was so far from Him even though within arm's distance—and said, "Simon, I have something to say to you."[5]

In that look of Jesus there was nothing but love. Or should we say there was everything that denotes love and forgiveness? In sharp contrast to the way Jesus looked upon Simon, we see the way Simon looked upon this woman. One writer has suggested that when Simon looked at this woman he saw her as a sniper sees an enemy uniform. He saw her as a gull sees a floating minnow.[6] Simon saw her with the eyes of a vulture ready to pounce on its prey.

How proud and narrow we can be—like Simon. But Jesus has a lesson for us. He first gave it to Simon. It is the Spirit of God that is still offering reproof today. John's Gospel tells us that Jesus will reprove the world of sin[7] and unrighteousness. Paul tells Timothy that all Scripture—the whole Bible—was given to us by inspiration from God and is profitable for teaching, for reproof, for correction, for instruction in righteousness. It is useful to teach us what is true and to make us realize what is wrong in our lives; it straightens us out and helps us do what is right. It is God's way of making us well-prepared at every point, fully equipped to do good to everyone.[8]

"All right, Teacher," Simon replied, "go ahead." Simon is saying, "Say on, Teacher, say on."[9]

Then Jesus told him this story: "A man loaned money to two people—$5,000 to one and $500 to the other. But neither of them could pay him back, so he kindly forgave them both, letting them keep the money! Which do you suppose loved him most after that?"

"I suppose the one who had owed him the most," Simon answered.

"Correct," Jesus said.[10]

Jesus was about to show Simon that He was more than a prophet; *He is the one who has power on earth to forgive sins.* Because of this, He is worthy to receive what this sinful woman gave to Him—penitent tears, thankful tears, and the oil of loving gladness.

We who are obliged to forgive because of the plain teaching of the Bible and we who are forgiven can surely learn from this that we have an obligation both as debtor and as creditor. The Bible is severe in its warning that those who show no mercy shall have judgment without mercy.[11]

Here we have a picture of Jesus as our Creditor, and we are debtors to Him. Sin is a debt payable to God Almighty. For nonpayment of that debt we are liable to the penalty. The penalty for sin is death, and all of us are guilty of it. But God has made provision to pay for our debt. He has canceled it out and given us a blank check, as it were. All we need to do is place our names on it.

Simon was a debtor, though the lesser debtor if he thought of himself as other Pharisees did. Remember the parable Jesus gave of the two men who went up to the temple to pray: the one a Pharisee, the other a publican. The Pharisee stood and prayed, "Thank God, I am not a sinner like everyone else, especially like that tax collector over there! I don't commit adultery, I go without food twice a week, and I give to God a tenth of everything I earn."

In that parable, Jesus said that the corrupt tax collector stood at a distance and dared not even lift his eyes to heaven as he prayed, but beat upon his chest in sorrow, exclaiming, "God, be merciful to me, a sinner." Jesus said that this sinner, and not the Pharisee, returned home forgiven! The proud will be humbled, but the humble will be honored.[12]

If Simon that day had a typical reaction—typical, that is, of the usual pharisaical attitude—then he thought of that woman as being the greater debtor. Whether our debts are more or less than those of some other sinners, they are more than any of us are able to pay. No goodness of ours, no amount of money, no great sacrifice—nothing can satisfy that terrible debt we owe. But praise God! He is ready to forgive us even though our debt, like the notorious prostitute's, is ever so great. What an example that long-haired woman gave to us!

Let's listen to Jesus as He explains to Simon what He saw in her deed and actions:

> Look! See this woman kneeling here! When I entered your home, you didn't bother to offer me water to wash the dust from my feet, but she has washed them with her tears and wiped them with her hair. You refused me the customary kiss of greeting, but she has kissed my feet again and again from the time I first came in. You neglected the usual courtesy of olive oil to anoint my head, but she has covered my feet with rare perfume. Therefore her sins—and they are many—are forgiven, for she loved me much; but one who is forgiven little shows little love."[13]

Jesus showed how keenly He had felt the lack of love shown Him by His host, and He contrasted it with the affection shown by the woman. Jesus is not saying that He pardoned her because she showed Him so much love—there is no such condition with Christ. Her love resulted from the pardon He had given her on a previous occasion. She used this opportunity to show Him how much she loved Him; it was an expression of the debt she felt she owed Him, an effort to somehow give back to Him, by way of her love, that which she had received from Him. Her loving much was not the *cause* but the *effect* of her pardon by Christ.

Surely the woman noticed Simon's scorn. Contempt is not something one can conceal. Contempt is a betrayer to the discerning eye, especially to the individual (like this woman) who has experienced the love of Christ. Once you have been the recipient of Jesus' love and forgiveness, your sensitivities to the hearts and minds of others are that much greater.

Perhaps a hurt look crossed her face, a look of compassion for Simon the Pharisee. But also, womanlike, her emotions showed on her face. Sensing Simon's contempt, she looks puzzled and hurt. Jesus looks at her with His great understanding heart of love, and tenderly He assures her, "Your sins are forgiven."[14] He vindicates her in the eyes of Simon and the guests; He silences her fears as she looks at these condemning, critical men.

Sin is costly; be sure your sins will find you out, the Bible cautions. But also know that there is *forgiveness* with Christ. Jesus loves to speak peace and pardon to those who turn from sin and sinning. We see Him in action doing that very thing in this incident. While the men at the table said to themselves, "Who does this man think He is, going around forgiving sins?" She knew who He was.[15] Jesus said to her, "Your faith has saved you; go in peace."[16] If you have such faith, then Jesus' words are for you also.

Forgiveness Involves Forgetting

Actually, the marriage should never have taken place.

How many such marriages there are! In many cases of marriage failure the couples did not seek the Lord's guidance in the selection of a life partner to begin with; they were young, immature, and unwise. Others, however, may feel that they did seek God's will, but even these marriages sometimes go sour.

This particular marriage began in trouble and was characterized by distrust and lack of respect. The unhappiness was predictable. Eric's marriage disintegrated when, after 20 years of pretense, he could not resist the attractiveness and flirtations of a younger woman. After a time of clandestine meetings, they were discovered. He was brought to justice by his wife, and the dirty linen was aired before his business associates. Eric's wife insisted on revealing all the facts to the organization where her husband was employed. Reprimanded sharply, and cautioned against any such future behavior (because he was a valuable part of the organization), he was told that if he returned to his wife he would be forgiven and reinstated.

Forgiven? By whom? His wife? Members of his family? The members of the organization? All the friends whom the wife also felt must be told? She had been betrayed, she stated, and others had a right to know what she had suffered and be aware of her willingness to forgive.

From that moment onward his every movement was closely monitored. He had to account for each slot of his daily time schedule. He was a puppet on a string, manipulated by his wife and business associates. Made to feel like a person who could never be trusted and that he was indeed fortunate to be "accepted back into the fold," he felt less and less like a man and more and more in bondage.

His wife phoned to check on him periodically throughout the day. He would report to her when leaving the office at night so she could time his drive home. He was subjected to a third degree constantly. When they were invited out, she told him what he should and should not say. If he tried to be funny—and he possessed a natural sense of humor—she insulted him in the presence of others. When they dined out, she accused him of flirting with the waitresses. He was even accused of making advances to his daughter-in-law. Marriage became tyranny of the worst kind. Yet people marveled at his wife's beautiful demonstration of loving forgiveness.

Forgiveness? By whose definition?

This story is true, with much detail omitted, though it sounds like a poorly scripted melodrama. One wonders how many individuals—men and women—will identify with this gentleman.

Gentleman? Do you question the right for that respected term to be applied to such an individual? Of course the man sinned by wronging his wife and family. It was a sin which cannot be overlooked, but he compounded his own problem by continuing to live a lie. The marriage was nothing but a pretense and a farce on a grand scale—a grand "Christian" scale to save face and preserve a false image.

Eric was a handsome, virile man, and his frustrations and unhappiness sought release. He was also a very creative individual, but he felt trapped. A man needs employment, and he was engaged in the type of work for which he was best suited. And so the pretense went on for another 12 years of agony. Every night when he returned home from work it was like returning to his own vomit; his wife threw it up to him ceaselessly. She could not and would not forget.

Is forgetting involved in forgiveness? Can there be real forgiveness without forgetting? The memories of the pain of another's misdeed may still exist—it does take time to forget—but if there is a supreme desire to forget, God can take care of that.

Just as God's forgiveness depends not on our *feeling forgiven* but on God's *declaration of forgiveness* (which we accept on the basis of His Word), so the partners in a tangled marital situation like this who decide to stay together must declare forgiveness of each other and then accept forgiveness on the basis of each individual's word. But the person doing the forgiving needs to be willing to forget if true healing is to take place. Where there is unwillingness (or just a superficial effort mainly for appearance's sake), forgiveness is incomplete.

Regardless of how many times you may say to someone who has wronged you, "I forgive you," if you have not *forgotten,* then you have failed in forgiveness. If you find it necessary to remind that individual of his or her betrayal, unfaithfulness, or untrustworthiness, then you have not truly forgiven the other person.

God, in speaking through the Prophet Isaiah, gave us this pattern for forgiveness that also forgets: "I, yes, I alone am He who blots away your sins for My own sake and will never think of them again. Oh, remind me of this promise of forgiveness, for we must talk about your sins. Plead your case for My forgiving you."[1]

Speaking through the Prophet Jeremiah, the Lord declares, "For I will forgive your iniquity, and your sin I will remember no more."[2] And then, in the Book of Hebrews, the Holy Spirit bears witness to those who belong to Christ by saying, "Their sins and their lawless deeds I will remember no more."[3]

Forgiveness like that crosses out the past, buries it forever, and leaves it alone. It is to be buried in forgetfulness, just as God has shown that this is what He does. Throughout the Bible we find that God has set a precedent for us by His own actions and statements. His way of action should be the pattern for us. God wants us to be as lavish in our forgiveness of others as He is. In addition, He expects us to be just as lavish in our forgetfulness. Unlimited forgiveness is His criterion,[4] and so is unlimited forgetfulness.

What about forgiving and forgetting marital infidelity. Can this be done, or is this wishful thinking? Marital unfaithfulness is generally regarded as scriptural grounds for divorce, but, unfaithfulness need not *automatically* end a marriage.

Actually, many marriages have emerged from that kind of a messy situation better than they were in the beginning. Billy Graham has made the statement that to be successful, marriage requires two very good forgivers. In no marriage is this more true than one in which there has been unfaithfulness.

On the basis of conversations I have had with individuals involved in such situations, I am forced to conclude that unless there is a complete resurrender of both couples to each other and to God, it would be better for everyone concerned for that marriage to terminate. Jealousy, distrust, possessiveness, and unforgiving attitudes are fatal to a happy marriage.

Often the person considered the offender is forced by the mate to live with guilt. Does God make us live with a burden of guilt? The Psalmist said, "If thou, Lord, shouldest mark iniquities, Oh Lord, who shall stand? But there is forgiveness with thee . . . ."[5]

I believe we have to confront the question of "betrayal" and who is the "innocent party." It takes two to tango in a marriage. On this subject, Dr. Lars Granberg, eminent counselor and psychologist, says:

> A comment on the idea of "the innocent party" seems in order. Any experienced pastor knows that it is rare that such a term is more than relative. Married life is an intricate tapestry of interwoven actions and reactions. Both parties usually contribute to misunderstanding, each in his own way. Hence the pastor is well-advised to listen long and carefully and be slow to apportion blame. The more obvious offense is not necessarily the greater.[6]

Under normal circumstances, if a marriage relationship is what it should be at its inception, I do not believe that someone else can pose a threat or break up a marriage. Who has betrayed whom? Who is "the innocent party"?

If a man is receiving a banquet at home, why should he go elsewhere to get crumbs in a clandestine relationship? If a woman is being treated as she should by her spouse, why should she risk everything and search elsewhere for understanding, appreciation, and love? If either one is demeaning the other with a constant barrage of words, undermining self-confidence and a feeling of self-worth, is it any wonder that the aggrieved party seeks solace in the arms of another person who knows how to restore self-confidence and make him feel like a worthy man or woman?[7]

This is not to lightly excuse those who have been guilty of adultery, nor does this indicate a lack of sympathy on my part for the one considered the innocent party. But it is to honestly recognize that there is more to marital infidelity than appears on the surface. And we onlookers, who are supposed to be "kind to another tenderhearted, forgiving one another, even as God for Christ's sake has forgiven us,"[8] have no right to withhold such kindness, tenderheartedness, and forgiveness to *both* individuals in this kind of a situation.

Christianity Today magazine carried an enlightening article on rebuilding marital fidelity that has shed much light on my own thinking. The best solution, the writer believes, is to forgive the offender and rebuild the marriage.

> To begin the restoration, the hurt partner needs time to express his pain, bitterness, anger, hostility, or sorrow. Eventually, however, he must face the hard but necessary question, "What have I done that contributed to this situation?" Because the extramarital relationship

often supplies what the marriage lacks, the answer is frequently one or more sins of omission, such as taking the other for granted, neglect, failure to provide reassurance, negligence in expressing appreciation, or failure to be attractive, accessible, approachable . . . .

When the offended partner realizes his own shortcomings and their contribution to the breakdown, he can, with God's help, begin to forgive the offender and rebuild trust. Although man's forgiveness is—like all else that he does—imperfect, both partners need to be willing to forgive as totally as they can . . . . He must also learn to forgive himself, something that is often harder than forgiving the other person . . . .

Both partners will need to renew their spiritual commitment. They must cultivate their love for Christ. For the offended one, that love will salve the wounds and help cleanse away the anger. The offender needs it to cleanse away the sin and the guilt. Both must appropriate the Holy Spirit's power: one will need it to stay mind and tongue in forgetfulness; the other will need it to maintain faithfulness. Both need the fruit of His presence: love . . . .

. . . A minister's wise counsel, pointing them to God's example of love and forgiveness, may be the cornerstone of their new life together.[9]

If you find yourself in this kind of situation, the secret to rebuilding your marriage is to forgive and then to forget. It was said of Abraham Lincoln that his heart had no room for the memory of a wrong. I appreciate what writer David Augsburger says in this regard: "Now, let's be clear. Forgetful forgiveness is not a case of holy amnesia which erases the past. No, instead it is the experience of healing that draws the poison from the wound.''

Augsburger goes on to say that you may recall the hurt, but you will not relive it! No constant reviewing, no rehashing of the old hurt, no going back to sit on the old gravestones where past grievances lie buried.

True, the hornet of memory may fly again, but forgiveness has drawn its sting. The curse is gone. The memory is powerless to arouse or anger.

The past is the past. Nothing can alter the facts. What has happened has happened forever. But the *meaning* can be changed. That is forgiveness. Forgiveness restores the present, heals for the future, and releases us from the past.[10]

It helps to remember that with God it doesn't matter who is right or who is wrong. He is reading heart motives and sees through all excuses or attempts at rationalization. God isn't interested in excuses; His intent is to cancel out our sins! Jesus said with good reason, ''But if you forgive not men their trespasses, neither will your Father forgive your trespasses.''[11] Can you honestly say, ''Father, forgive my sins, just as I have forgiven those who have sinned against me?''

If, instead of reminding her husband of his affair, the wife had accepted the professional and wise counsel they were receiving and had worked with her husband to rebuild their relationship, the marriage that was mentioned at the outset of this chapter might have been saved. But in the end the wife's jealousy and possessiveness, and her failure to forgive with forgetfulness, destroyed the marriage. There was total, devastating disintegration, agonizing trauma, heartbreak, involvement of other innocent people, needless gossip and scandal, and finally divorce.

There was nothing left to salvage. Why? There was no forgetful forgiveness in action.

7

Hold Your Tongue

We've all experienced situations in which we have been wronged in one way or another. As long as we're alive we're going to bump into difficult and irritating circumstances, situations, and people. A friend says he finds it impossible to get through a single week without getting into a little dispute with someone—his wife, their children, someone at work, a policeman, a clerk, a waitress, or a friend.

Life is complex and explosive in our twentieth century. Sometimes we find ourselves the victom of someone's tongue, and word gets back to us about what has been said. Things get twisted and bent out of shape; what began as an innocent observation on your part may end up as vicious slander. Much hurt and heartache can result. The pain is very real, the anguish great. To forgive or not to forgive—that becomes the question. Our humanness cries out for revenge, retaliation. Get even, something inside us says!

Is that the answer? There is a saying that goes: Doing an injury puts you below your enemy; revenging an injury makes you even with him; forgiving an injury sets you above him!

We do need to exercise a spirit of forgiveness constantly, don't we? We need to show forgiveness toward our fellowman and forgiveness toward ourselves. Of greatest importance, we ourselves need the forgiveness of God.

Christians often go around eating each other up. Christian cannibals! With judgmental attitudes, slander, and defamation, we play right into the devil's hands and become his tool.

How can we fall into this trap when we are so aware of what the Bible has to say on the subject? Our trouble is that we haven't read James 3 or that we don't read it often enough—or else we mentally pitchfork its contents over onto someone else. Here is what James 3:1-13 says:

> Dear brothers, Don't be too eager to tell others their faults, for we all make many mistakes . . . . If anyone can control his tongue, it proves that he has perfect control over himself in every other way. We can make a large horse turn around and go wherever we want by means of a small bit in his mouth. And a tiny rudder makes a huge ship turn wherever the pilot wants it to go, even though the winds are strong. So also the tongue is a small thing, but what enormous damage it can do!
>
> A great forest can be set on fire by one tiny spark. And the tongue is a flame of fire. It is full of wickedness, and poisons every part of the body. And the tongue is set on fire by hell itself, and can turn our whole lives into a blazing flame of destruction and disaster.
>
> Men have trained, or can train, every kind of animal or bird that lives and every kind of reptile and fish, but no human being can tame the tongue. It is always ready to pour out its deadly

poison. Sometimes it praises our heavenly Father, and sometimes it breaks out into curses against men who are made like God. And so blessing and cursing come pouring out of the same mouth.

Dear brothers, surely this is not right. Does a spring of water bubble out first with fresh water and then with bitter water? Can you pick olives from a fig tree, or figs from a grape vine? No, and you can't draw fresh water from a salty pool. If you are wise, live a life of steady goodness, so that only good deeds will pour forth.[1]

Surely we need to heed what James is telling us in this passage! Hold your tongue, he is saying, for the Lord of the universe is listening! What He is hearing from His children must often break His heart.

The Apostle Paul talked about the fact that as Christians we are to be the body of Christ. Have you ever thought, when you are misusing your tongue in talking about someone, that while you are so busy tearing apart your fellow Christian, Christ sees His body being torn apart? Actually such cutting jabs are wounding the body of Christ, "Who bought our freedom with His blood and forgave us all our sins."[2]

The story is told of Stonewall Jackson, who saw his men fighting among themselves over strategy and the war. It is said that he jumped in and said, "Remember, gentlemen, the enemy is over there," and he pointed in the direction of the battle that was raging.

While Christians engage in verbal battle, cutting each other down with lingual mortar, Satan makes inroads to defeat the cause of Christ. How tragic! Yet we have the unmistakable warning from the Bible about this very thing: "Be sober, be vigilant, because your adversary the devil, is a roaring lion, seeking whom he may devour."[3]

How much better it would be if we were to act like those described in Isaiah 41:6: "Everyone helped his neighbor, and everyone said to his brother, 'Be of good courage.' "

How much more effective is a pat on the back than a kick in the pants! The pat encourages, but the kick knocks down. Self-centeredness recognizes no good in others, but Christ-likeness says "Take courage" and tries to refresh the heart of another person. Chronic mudslingers, gossips, and back-biters are basically unhappy, insecure individuals.

Who needs destructive criticism or sarcasm? What an uplift it is to be around a person who knows how to speak kindly and shows tenderheartedness and forgiveness, putting into action Ephesians 4:32.

Life is difficult enough without Christians going around making it more difficult for each other. If David needed to pray, "Help me, Lord, to keep my mouth shut and my lips sealed,"[4] how much more we need to pray that prayer today!

But David also prayed, "O Lord, open my lips, and my mouth shall show forth Thy praise."[5] This is the balance we need. In a world reeling from violence and hatred, fractured by people who have not learned how to forgive and who are being wounded by words, a great responsibility is thrust upon those of us who know better—whose mouths should by giving forth words of hope, love, encouragement, and forgiveness.

The song of the critic is sour. He seems to have an

underlying bitterness toward life in general and people in particular. Others may have insight into people and their problems, but they have developed a chronic pessimism. Cynicism is often insight gone sour. I think we've all been around such people. They have nothing good to say about anyone or anything.

There is a fine line between constructive criticism meant to help another person and destructive criticism which publicizes the weaknesses of others in order to call attention to one's own superiority and goodness. The Bible gives us a story that illustrates this.

After the flood that destroyed everyone except Noah and his sons and their families, Noah became a farmer and planted a vineyard, and he made wine. One day as he was drunk and lay naked in his tent, one of his sons, Ham (the father of Canaan), saw his father's nakedness, went outside, and told his two brothers. Then Shem and Japheth took a robe and held it over their shoulders. Walking backward into the tent, they let it fall across their father to cover his nakedness as they looked the other way.

First of all, an observation about Noah being found drunk. This is the only place that we read this about Noah. He was a good man chosen by God to be saved from the flood and was not given to drunkenness or lying exposed. It was said of him that he was perfect in his generations (not sinless perfection—only God is capable of that—but a man of sincerity, goodness, integrity, and other virtues pleasing to God).

But look at his son Ham. To have seen it accidentally and involuntarily would not have been a crime, but for him to have seen his father's nakedness and react the way he did was another thing. He seemed almost pleased by it as he reported it to his brothers, as if he were gloating over it.

Ham told his brothers in a scornful, deriding manner that their father was drunk and lying naked. He did it to paint his father in a vile way. The Bible clearly tells us that it is wrong to make a jest of sin.

We are not to publish the faults of others; we are not to expose them in any way. Ham should have immediately done what his two brothers, Shem and Japheth, did—that is, he should have covered his father and not spoken of it to anyone. There is a mantle of love that we are to throw over the faults of others.

There are many Bible references that bear this out. For example, "Continue to show deep love for each other, for love makes up for many of your faults."[6] There is a robe of reverence that we are to throw over the faults of parents and others in the body of Christ.

We are to understand and forgive as freely and as greatly as God through Christ has forgiven us. There is stark reality in this unchanging truth when we consider our own fallibility and proneness to fall into sin. A challenging thought for our ugly moments when we are tempted to get even with someone who has talked about or hurt us in some way, or damaged our good name, is to remember that God sees us mentally but forgives us anyway—a fact that should drive us to our knees in gratitude.

God doesn't expose us to the view of our family, friends, and neighbors! If others saw us as we really are, how many friends and family members would we have left?

How do you react when you know of another person's downfall? When someone whispers something to you about someone, do you expose it to someone else? Do you rejoice in it because it elevates you? What do you do with gossip and someone's unruly tongue? What do you do about your own tongue?

We need to recognize that seeing and remedying our own faults is far more rewarding than carping at others. In fact, it is vital to personal growth. Self-analysis and self-criticism can be a joyous and profitable undertaking that will yield far better dividends in the end than talking about others and exposing someone else's weaknesses and faults.

John Newton, profligate-turned-Christian, once said, "If my pocket were full of stones, I have no right to throw one at the greatest backslider upon earth. I have either done as bad or worse than he, or I certainly would have if the Lord had left me a little to myself; for I am made of just the same materials. If there be any difference, it is wholly of grace."

Paul, writing to the Philippians, reminded them to fix their thoughts on what is true and good and right. Think about things that are pure and lovely, and dwell on the fine, good things in others, he said.[7]

There are many things that we hear and even observe that are true, but are not necessarily of a good report. Paul says to keep quiet about it—don't dwell on it except to pray about it, and then only in the hearing of God. If something is not of a good report, if it looks wrong, Paul admonishes that we are not to pass it on to others. Only as we comply with this will the body of Christ come together and be edified and grow.

Yes, our fallibility as imperfect people frequently shows. There's a credibility gap between what we profess to be and what we say. We have become so proficient at carefully calculated innuendos! The subtle disparagements we make about others are inconsistent with the truth we profess to believe. Dr. Carl F. H. Henry, writing in *Christianity Today*, has said:

> If you are not satisfied with the way E. Stanley Jones, or Billy Graham, or this present lesser luminary holds out hope to this present generation, then for heaven's sake, for God's sake, and for the gospel's sake don't exhaust your energies in indexing their faults—which are many—but light a brighter light and live a life of great power.[8]

What is the remedy to this age-old evil of misusing our tongues? We need to see it for what it really is—a practice contrary to the very spirit of the gospel. We need to forgive it in others and admit it and forgive ourselves for it. From there we need to go on, determined with God's help not to succumb to the drag of Satan in this regard again. If we do fail, we must immediately confess it and seek God's forgiveness.

Several things are necessary if we are to escape this quagmire. First, we must have a love for people. We need to concentrate on agape-type love and to realize that our own virtues amount to an absolute nothing in God's sight if we are not practicing that kind of all-encompassing love. No wonder Henry Drummond, writing in the masterful book *The Greatest Thing in the World*, said, "What we *are* stretches past what we do, beyond what we possess."

This does not mean that we will gloss over the faults and weaknesses of others, but it means that we will exercise love, forgiveness, and understanding toward them. We will try to help them. We will recognize that there are some things that are better left unsaid. True love is more ready to sympathize with another person's weaknesses than to publicize them. We must try to help others, to bring about a healing in their own person. We must protect, restore, cover the sins and weaknesses of others, and always point them to Christ. One of the true tests of a Christlike character is seen in our attitude to another person's sins.

"If you know something that would hinder or hurt the life or reputation of another, bury it. Forget it. End it right there. It will rest in peace. So will you."[9]

If you love your neighbor, remember, "Love covers a multitude of sins."[10]

Love can even remove a beam of malice from a critical eye. Love heals. Love encourages. Love protects. Love looks for the best in others so that others may be their best.

"Vow never to pass on anything about anybody else that will hurt him in any way."[11]

The real remedy was given by Jesus. He said:

> Don't criticize, and then you won't be criticized. For others will treat you as you treat them. And why worry about a speck in the eye of a brother when you have a board in your own? Should you say, "Friend, let me help you get that speck out of your eye," when you can't even see because of the board in your own? Hypocrite! First get rid of the board. Then you can see to help your brother.[12]

Summarizing these words of Christ, William

Barclay suggests three reasons why no one should judge another person:

1. We never know the whole facts or the whole person.
2. It is almost impossible for any man to be strictly impartial in his judgment.
3. No man is good enough to judge any other man. Our own faults and our own inability to resolve them automatically disqualify us as fair critics.

The question may arise in your thinking, What of those times, however, when a person must make a judgment? What then? The Bible gives us the answer to that, too. Galatians 6:1 tells us, "Brethren, if a man be overtaken in a fault, you who are spiritual restore such a one in the spirit of meekness, considering yourself, lest you also be tempted."

John and Charles Wesley, founding fathers of the Wesleyan movement, drew up six points that they subscribed to in this regard. What a wonderful thing it would be if each of us would try to follow them!

1. We will not listen to, or willingly enquire after, any ill concerning each other.
2. If we do hear any ill of each other we will not be forward to believe it.
3. As soon as possible we will communicate what we hear, by speaking or writing to the person concerned.
4. Till we have done this, we will not write or speak a syllable of it to any person whatsoever.
5. Neither will we mention it, after we have done this, to any other person whatsoever.

6. We will not make any exception to these rules, unless we think ourselves absolutely obliged in conscience to do so.

The wise writer of still another era, Thomas a Kempis, wrote: "In judging others, a man labors to no purpose, commonly errs, and easily sins; but in examining himself, he is always wisely and usefully employed."

Then, to keep from being dragged down and caught in misuse of our tongues, we need a greater concept of God's sovereignty, the fact that He is still in control of man and this universe. We are bound to see organizations and individuals with fatal flaws in their makeup and personalities and organizational structure. They will have weaknesses. But we need not succumb to an attitude of hopelessness, as if God has been defeated.

God is still on the throne, Jesus is still interceding, and the Holy Spirit is still at work convicting men of their sins and their need of cleansing and the work of His power in their lives. If God can forgive and accept them, so can we. Man's corrupt sinful nature comes as no surprise to Almighty God!

Yes, we are to be discerning and we are to do all things in the spirit of love and forgiveness that Jesus demonstrated so beautifully in His life on earth.

Finally, we need to forgive ourselves for the gossiping, the slander, the abusiveness, that we have heaped upon others with our tongue. God is concerned about our tongues. He wants us to have good speech. He says, "A wholesome tongue is a tree of life."[13]

The human emotional makeup is very delicate. We are bruised so easily by careless words. Words are powerful, both for building someone up and for tearing him down. We must discipline our tongues lest we become a pawn in Satan's hand to wound others. If we know we have done this, we must quickly seek forgiveness from the one we have injured, and then we must quickly forgive ourselves.

The Second Greatest Commandment

You are to love yourself. Now wait a minute, you say. How vain can you be? Are we supposed to be self-centered, egotistical snobs? Before you back off from reading this chapter or throwing the book aside, give the Bible a chance—not me, but God's Word.

Jesus once told the self-righteous Pharisees who were trying to trip him up that their errors in thinking and acting were caused by their ignorance of the Scriptures and of God's power. These were strong words, especially to men who were supposed to be learned in the Scriptures, men who were thought to have the answers.

Actually, their talk and their actions were two different things. Their practice was in no way compatible with their preaching. Jesus said, "They say, but do not."[1]

The Bible tells us that the crowds of people who were gathered around Jesus were profoundly impressed by His answers to the questions of these learned men of the Jewish law. He surprised and baffled the Pharisees and routed the Sadducees with His replies. Dr. Shoemaker said:

> Religion can never be the answer to human problems. All of the religions of the world are inadequate. Christ alone is the answer. Christ alone understands. Christ alone forgives. Christ

alone eliminates your guilt. Christ alone saves
and then assures you that you are God's child
and the most wonderful person possible! Christ
alone fills the human heart with
love—joy—peace—self-confidence. No wonder a
genuine Christian really loves himself.[2]

Yes, you are to love yourself, and it's a completely
biblical statement! In fact, it's the second most important commandment. Listen to what Jesus said in
answer to the lawyer who asked him, "Which is the
most important command in the laws of Moses?"

Jesus replied, "Love the Lord your God with all
your heart, soul, and mind. This is the first and
greatest commandment. The second most important is
similar: Love your neighbor as much as you love
yourself. All the other commandments and all the
demands of the prophets stem from these two laws and
are fulfilled if you obey them. Keep only these and you
will find that you are obeying all the others."[3]

This puts loving yourself in the right perspective.
How can you possibly treat your neighbor right, how
can you possibly love your neighbor (including family
members, relatives and friends) unless you have a proper, healthy, balanced love of self? Hate yourself and
you'll hate others. All the law is fulfilled in one word,
and that is *love*—love for God, others, and self.

The Apostle Paul caught the implication of what
Jesus commanded. He said.:

Pay all your debts except the debt of love for
others—never finish paying that! For if you love
them, you will be obeying all of God's laws,
fulfilling all his requirements. If you love your

neighbor as much as you love yourself, you will not want to harm or cheat him, or kill him or steal from him. And you won't sin with his wife or want what is his, or do anything else the Ten Commandments say is wrong. All ten are wrapped up in this one, to love your neighbor as you love yourself. Love does no wrong to anyone. That's why it fully satisfies all of God's requirements. It is the only law you need.[4]

We are creatures cut out for love. God has made us that way—no use denying it. Love is a short and sweet word. It cannot be denied that there is a self-love that is corrupt and to be despised, but Christ taught a self-love that is both natural and right. You are to regard yourself with due dignity; you are to take care of yourself. This kind of self-love is another fruit of faith.

In more than a dozen places the Bible gives the command to love ourselves. Do nothing to demean your own character. Hold yourself in a healthy high regard just as Christ taught, but remember, don't hold yourself any higher than you hold your neighbor.

There are many people, however, who hate themselves. This can be proved in many cases of suicide and would-be suicide—people who cannot love and forgive themselves for misdeeds, real or imagined. And Satan is always watching for people like this and will pounce upon such individuals, using this weakness to ensnare and destroy them. To be aware of this is to be forewarned and ready to rout the attacker.

Are you beginning to understand why you are to cultivate a healthy self-love?

What is it that causes people to hate themselves or to have a low self-image? It is generally believed that depressing guilt, which is a condemning conscience, contributes more than anything else to feelings of fear, lonely emptiness, hostility toward self, and feelings of inadequacy and unworthiness. Guilty people are love-starved people, loving neither themselves nor others. And what does this do to their professed love of God? The guilt is compounded.

These are people who cannot forgive themselves. They suffer greatly for fear that they are not totally forgiven by God. What a vicious circle this is! No wonder God commands us to love ourselves. No wonder He said to forgive others as you wish to be forgiven. How important it is to take what the Bible says and live by it!

This is borne out in conversations I have had with pastors while researching for this book and in the "My Answer" column by Billy Graham. I have also frequently seen letters in the "Ann Landers" and "Dear Abby" columns that speak to this subject of guilt and the inability to forgive one's self.

Someone wrote to the "My Answer" column and asked:

> I got married at 16, had a child at 17, and ran away with a married man at 19. We each got a divorce, and married several years later. Now we've been together almost 40 years, but guilt has been my constant companion. Often I've thought of running away. Lately, though, I've felt an urgency to change our lives. Can we be forgiven and find happiness in these remaining years?

A sob caught in my throat as I read that. What a

needless waste—40 years of carrying a useless burden of guilt!

Billy Graham's answer read like this:

> Forgiveness and happiness are what the gospel is all about! What you report recently as a feeling of dissatisfaction with the past, and a longing for something better, could well be the impact of God's Spirit working in your life. This is His business—to show us our shortcomings and point to their remedy in Christ. That is your first and greatest need.
>
> Guilt is one of the most destructive forces in life. It can erode hope, smash dreams, and constantly give cause for anxiety. We can push it into our subconscious, but only God can push it aside forever.
>
> God's plan through faith in Christ His Son was that we be relieved of guilt. No wonder the hymn asserts: "He breaks the power of canceled sin—He sets the prisoner free." If we perpetuate the memory of our mistakes after God has forgiven and forgotten them, we do a great disservice to ourselves, not to mention God.
>
> Certainly no good purpose would be served by running away. Take your new life as it is now. Let the past be the past. Live each day with a conscious commitment to God—and to your husband. With this preoccupation, happiness will surely come.

A minister friend relates several very sad stories that show the great damage that we incur to our emotional and physical well-being when we harbor guilt and are unable to forgive ourselves. He tells of a vacationing family who were pulling a trailer behind their car. The wife asked the husband to stop at a trailer park—she was tired and so were the children— but the husband wanted to go just a little farther, and so they went on. Not too far down the road the axle on the trailer broke, and in the ensuing accident their four-year-old son was killed. To this day the father blames himself for his son's death. He cannot forgive himself for failing to heed his wife's request.

This same minister also told me—and this could be repeated with varying circumstances by thousands of ministers and counselors—of the happily married couple who discovered that the wife had a serious heart defect. Two things could be done: She could spend the rest of her life in a wheelchair, or she could submit to an operation that would restore her to full, normal health provided the surgery was successful.

The chances for surgical failure, it was felt, were very remote. The husband and wife prayed about it, and then the decision was left to the wife. She elected to have the operation, and her husband signed the consent agreement. But the unlikely happened, that slim possibility of failure occurred, and the woman died on the operating table. The husband lives with a haunting sense of guilt—he cannot forgive himself.

There are many people like the woman who unburdened her heart and said, "Fifteen years ago I disobeyed God's command and committed adultery. My husband has forgiven me, but I just can't seem to find peace of mind. I can't seem to think of anything else. What can I do?"

She had earnestly sought and received God's forgiveness, and her husband had forgiven her, but she had not forgiven herself.

Then there is the 24-year-old woman who wrote to a radio pastor saying she had been divorced and that in the year since the divorce was final she had been to bed with five different men. She too had confessed it to God and was seeking to live differently, but she could not forgive herself either.

David who sinned grievously and even had another man put into the line of battle, where he was killed (so David could have the man's wife, whom he had already taken), knew what it was to experience God's forgiveness. He could say that God removes our sins as far as the east is from the west. He forgives all my sins, said David, and He heals me.[5]

There's the key, the clue, the missing link—God forgives *and* heals. To free us from incriminating guilt, we need God's healing of our condemning conscience. Forgiveness of self follows as a natural result. Such forgiveness liberates our hearts from enslaving emotions and attitudes.

Dr. Harold J. Sala offers this suggestion in forgiving self:

> Picture your sins that have created separation from God and brought guilt to your soul as written on a sign, and nailed to the old rugged cross upon which Jesus was crucified. But picture those sins of yours covered, blotted out with the precious blood that flowed from the veins of God's only Son.

> This is the very picture that Paul used to show the Colossians that God's forgiveness is complete. He said that God has forgiven all our trespasses, "blotting out the handwriting of ordinances that was against us, which was contrary

to us, and took it out of the way, nailing it to his cross'' (Colossians 2:14).

Now here is the point: If a great God who loves justice is so merciful as to forgive you, *what right have you* to fail to forgive yourself? Ephesians 4:32 says we are to forgive each other because God has forgiven us. Can it help but follow: It is just as necessary to forgive yourself.[6]

In the Gospels we have the story of Jesus healing the man sick of the palsy; that is, he was a paralytic and had to be carried by four men.

Jesus said to the man, "Son, be of good cheer, your sins are forgiven."[7]

Jesus was saying, "Take heart, have courage." He instilled in the heart of that man a joy beyond description. To anyone reading this book who may be struggling with guilt and the inability to forgive yourself, Jesus offered the crippled man healing, forgiveness, and good cheer all in one package. That's an offer that's valid for you today! Forgiveness liberates, and Christ liberated this burdened man.

At the beginning of a political convention there is usually a keynote speech. Jesus keynoted His ministry of liberation when He stood up in the synagogue at the outset of His public work and read the Scriptures. The Book of Isaiah was handed to him, and he opened it to the place where it says:

> The Spirit of the Lord is upon me; he has appointed me to preach Good News to the poor; he has sent me to announce that captives shall be released and the blind shall see, that the downtrodden shall be freed from their oppressors, and that God is ready to give blessings to all who come to him.[8]

In the three brief years of His public ministry following that, Jesus showed what was meant by those words. He demonstrated what it means to be free from the guilt and power of sin. No one needs to carry around a burden of gnawing accusations that scream, You killed your son, You consented to the death of your wife, You are an adulterer. There is liberation through God's forgiveness and healing, and that healing takes place the moment you apply it to yourself and forgive yourself. Just that quickly the transaction is complete.

Notice the man who was a paralytic—no more will he have to be carried around by others, no more will he have to rely on crutches or lie upon a stretcher while others stare at him in his pathetic condition. I can almost see him. When Jesus said to him, "Be of good cheer," I can imagine that the look of fear was immediately erased from his face.

Christ wants us to exhibit a cheerful countenance also. Our faith and trust in Him should produce that look on our faces that lets others know we have been the recipient of something very special—God's love and forgiveness. The touch of Jesus heals!

God is willing to make the best of us, but we have to be willing to give the worst of us. That young paralytic man left praising and glorifying God. But what if he had held back? Would there have been such healing?

Forgiveness of self is like the surgeon's scalpel that can open and remove the pus from a wound. Forgiveness of self enables the ugly, hurting emotional wounds you have suffered to be freed of that which festers, poisons, and prevents healing. Give up your guilt to the Great Physician just as you would give up a gangrenous arm if it meant that the rest of you would be spared. Whatever it is that is placing you under a sentence of self-condemnation, give it up to Jesus. Name it for whatever it is then hand it over to Him.

He wants it. He is your burden-bearer. He came specifically to help people like you. He wants your guilt. See it as Jesus sees it—undesirable, damaging, and threatening. You represent the body of Christ; you are important to Him. He knows that you cannot represent Him well if you are unwilling to let Him cancel out your inability to forgive yourself without any mental reservations.

Do you like nursing your guilty conscience, licking your wounds, feeling sorry for yourself? In a very real sense this is what you are doing as long as you fail to forgive yourself.

Dr. Maxwell Maltz, famous plastic surgeon and author of many successful books (including his well-known *Psycho-Cybernetics)*, says this regarding the need to forgive one's self: "Not only do we incur emotional wounds from others, most of us inflict them upon ourselves."

We beat ourselves over the head with self-condemnation, remorse, and regret. We beat ourselves down with self-doubt. We cut ourselves up with excessive guilt!

Remorse and regret are attempts to live in the past emotionally. Excessive guilt is an attempt to make right *in the past* something we did wrong or thought of as wrong in the past.

Emotions are used correctly and appropriately when they help us to respond or react appropriately to some reality *in the present environment*. Since we cannot live in the past, we cannot appropriately react emotionally to the past. The past must be written off, closed, forgotten as far as our emotional reactions are concerned. We do not need to take an emotional position one way or the other regarding detours that might have taken us off course in the past. The important thing is our *present* direction and our *present* goal.

We need to recognize our own errors as mistakes. Otherwise we could not correct our course. Steering or guidance would be impossible. But it is futile and fatal to hate or condemn ourselves for our mistakes.[9]

Dr. Maltz goes on to say that in contemplating our own mistakes (or those of others) it is helpful and realistic to think of them in terms of what we *did or or did not do* rather than in terms of what the mistakes *made us*. Remember, he says, that "you" make mistakes, but mistakes don't make "you." To prevent or remove emotional hurts, we must be willing to live creatively, to be a little vulnerable. To trust, to love, to open ourselves to emotional communication with other people, he says, is to run the risk of being hurt.[10]

There is nothing more destructive than self-flagellation, which is what we are doing when we cannot forgive ourselves. We are all human and will make mistakes. At times we will do things that can leave us hating ourselves. But this is part of being a normal human being. Discover and accept your humanity and remember that God must have thought a lot about our humanness. After all, He Himself chose to come to earth in the form of humanity!

A wounded self-love will in the end destroy itself. "By contrast, a self-respecting person . . . recalls his accomplishments, relives the happy moments stored in his memory, and hopefully reflects on his optimistic future.[11] The result can be a strengthened, healthy self-love that is able to forgive one's self.

To be forgiven by God is to experience healing and deliverance. It triggers a wonderful liberation from a defeated past and signals the beginning of a fresh new start in life. The same can happen when you forgive yourself: You have nothing to lose and everything to gain. Forgiveness is not *a way;* it is *the way.* It is the *only way* for the Lord or for us to deal with a sinful, guilty past.

9

Once a Prodigal

Tom was angry! He'd had it with his parents. He had been accused of something that was absolutely not his fault, but his protestations of innocence were ignored. His parents simply would not believe him; they didn't trust him. Even when he had proved his innocence, they kept harping at him, nit-picking and making life miserable for him.

He couldn't forgive them for their treatment of him, so he decided to get his revenge by taking off. He split for California.

But the farther he got away from home, the heavier his backpack seemed to get. Yet he was lightening it every day—eating up the canned goods and food he had taken from his mother's well-stocked shelves.

Nights were the hardest. He felt lucky if he found a place to sleep. Sometimes he unrolled his sleeping bag and slept on the ground in a park or someplace where the police wouldn't find him and order him to move on.

One day he looked at himself in a gas station mirror—unshaven, with dirty hair, greasy jeans and soiled shirt. He knew he was a mess. He could hardly tolerate the odor of his own body. *You're a bummer*, he thought to himself.

He tried analyzing his feelings as he shuffled along a

lonely stretch of highway. Why had he left home? He tried answering that question as he grooved, rapped, and grassed his way to California. But deep down inside he knew the truth—he had made a mistake.

The terrible, gnawing feelings inside him grew. The consequences of running away from home were catching up with him. He was sick of it all—lonely, hurt, and depressed. That was the day he stopped beside a phone booth. *Should I call home and ask their forgiveness?* He pondered the thought. It didn't take him long to make up his mind. It was the end of a wayward journey!

It had been an angry, foolish, spur-of-the-moment act on Tom's part to leave home. It cost him agonizing, foot-weary, lonely hours of travel, sleepless nights, a hungry stomach much of the time, and no satisfaction whatever. It could have cost him his life.

But like the biblical prodigal, there is a time of coming to one's senses. How much better it is to spare oneself the misery and heartache by not doing rash, spur-of-the-moment things.

What is it that causes young people (as well as adults) to do things they only end up regretting later? In the case of hitchhiking young people, a California juvenile officer says that in almost every case the problem can be traced to lack of communication. Perhaps it would be more accurate to say *bad* communication. There may even be excessive vocalization—too many hasty, ill-considered words. Or there may be the silent treatment, which in many respects is noisier than a barrage of words. Again, there may be irritating action—slamming of doors, rattling of pans, kicking the pet cat, turning up the hi-fi, throwing down school books, or storming angrily out of the house. Bad communication may show itself in a flushed face, flashing eyes, or a rasping and abrasive tone of voice. If this is allowed to go unresolved, barriers build up. No one is willing to say, "I'm sorry, forgive me."

Tom is representative of thousands of young people who disregard adult advice and learn the hard way. Some never learn, but pay with their lives instead. You can read about them in newspapers and magazines, and hear about them on radio and TV news. They are playing a dangerous game of truth or consequences, but they soon learn it's not a fun game.

Even though some of us adults may never have tried running away from home and hitchhiking across the country, we can nevertheless look back on valuable lessons learned and try to spare our children the mistakes we made. In other ways even now, however, we may be playing an equally dangerous game of letting self-will take over. One writer, relating this to the subject of forgiveness (or lack of it), says we are often guilty of playing self-protective games of false forgiving. By whatever name you call it, or how you look upon it, it is phony forgiveness.

Rebellion against parental and adult hypocrisy accounts for much of the dissatisfaction and unhappiness so evident in many young people today. They see through our phony games. Tom looked beyond his present predicament to the end result. What he saw was not for him. He envisioned a life of emptiness. He may have been free from parental pressure, but what good was freedom when there was nothing to live for and no one with whom to share?

Consider the well-known biblical account of the prodigal son. Does a diet of corn husks stolen from a pigpen appeal to you? How about eating out of back-alley trash cans? It wasn't exactly what the prodigal had in mind when he left home to go his way! Contemporary prodigals are only repeating the sorry story.

The biblical story of the prodigal son shows the scope of God's mercy and forgiveness in a way in which the average individual can readily identify, for we have all been wayward prodigals to some degree, at one or more points in our life. The parable beautifully relates the forgiving fatherhood of God. The more we see and come to understand this readiness of God to forgive, the more anxious we should be to demonstrate such gracious forgiveness to others.

When the biblical prodigal decided to leave home, he did so with his father's knowledge, having first demanded of him his rightful share of the inheritance. "Give me my share of the estate now!" were his words. He might at least have had the courtesy to say, *"Please give me . . . ."*

But his yearning was for a phony liberty, as he soon learned. It became the greatest form of slavery he had ever known. He had been unappreciative of his father, distrustful, and dissatisfied with his lot in life. His desire for independence almost became his ruination—before his father showed willingness to forgive and take him back.

Our God is a giving Father—long-suffering, kind, and merciful. The prodigal's father exemplified our Lord's great love. What a compassionate heavenly Father He is! The nature and consequences of sin are clearly shown in the prodigal's actions. Self-will, shown here in such appalling color, always brings with it ultimate disillusionment, suffering, slavery, and despair. These are the inevitable consequences of indulging in action contrary to God's will.

The prodigal son packed all his belongings and took a trip to a distant land, leaving behind his father and an older brother. In his new environment he wasted all his money on parties and prostitutes. About the time the money was gone, a great famine swept over the land, and he began to starve. He persuaded a local farmer to hire him to feed his pigs, but he became so hungry that even the pods he was feeding the swine looked good to him. But no one gave him anything.[1]

What a commentary that is on human nature—no one gave him anything! No one took pity on him. No one offered to relieve him in his desperate plight. The same poeple who so gladly helped him spend all his money in riotous living were nowhere to be found. Willful waste brings woeful want!

The common misery of those who reject God's grace is that they throw away the favor of God, their interest in Christ and the admonitions of conscience. Not only was he hungry and longing for food, but there was no satisfaction for his soul. A sinful state is a state that cannot expect relief from any person. No mere man can feed and nourish someone who is starving for the sustenance that God alone can supply.

The prodigal finally came to his senses. His sin had not been mere folly; it had been madness and frenzy. But when the prodigal was brought to his last extremity and realized the extent of his desperate need, he did not give way to despair. He was saved from that.

I believe he had a praying father who was interceding on his behalf, a loving father who was pleading God's intervention and promising the heavenly Father that he, as an earthly father, would forgive his erring child. This father had never ceased to love his son; he prayed, hoped, and yearned for his eventual return. In fact, the Bible gives reason to believe he spent time looking for the prodigal's return.

Consideration of the sad state we are in is the first step toward conversion. The prodigal considered and turned. He compared his past and present circumstances. He had to see for himself his miserable state; just so, we must see ourselves for what we are if we are to be driven to our knees seeking the mercy and forgiving love of God the Father.

If you feel you have so violated God's will that there is no possible forgiveness for you, take heart! It makes no difference how much we have sinned—with God there is forgiveness.

There are two necessary conditions for receiving God's forgiveness and full pardon—confession and turning from sin. Notice the prodigal as he realizes that his offense has been not only against a loving earthly parent but also against God: "I have sinned against heaven"[2]

Yes, sin is an affront to the God of heaven. We forfeit the glories and joys of heaven when we refuse to admit this. The malignity of sin aims high; it is against heaven. The daring sinner has set his mouth against the heavens, according to the writer of Psalms. How we need to learn that what is shot against the heavens will return upon the head of him who shoots it. It literally boomerangs.[3]

The prodigal's admission of guilt is an acknowledgment that he knows he has forfeited all the privileges of sonship. God is pleased when we are willing to humble ourselves before Him like this. Genuine sorrow for sin reaches the heart of God. In this parable Jesus shows the matchless love of God to every repentant soul as we look at the prodigal's father and see forgiveness in action.

Did the father say, "Why didn't you stay with your prostitutes and pigs?" Was there condemnation? Rebuke? An I'll-give-him-just-what-he's-got-coming attitude? No. There was nothing but love and affection, for the father had been waiting for the return of this prodigal. The son returned slowly, under a burden of shame, guilt, and fear; but the tender father, who had been patiently and prayerfully watching, saw him coming even while he was a long distance away. The father was filled with loving pity; he ran and embraced and kissed his son. And because of Jesus, God is ready and willing to receive any person who is sorry for his sins and returns to Him.

The father's actions in embracing and kissing his son demonstrated forgiveness even before he spoke a word. There are times when actions speak louder than words. It was the son who uttered the first words, living up to what he had told himself when he first came to his senses: "Father, I have sinned . . . ." But he was interrupted by his parent, who began calling out directions to the servants: "Quick! Bring the finest robe in the house and put it on him. And a jeweled ring for his finger; and shoes! And kill the calf we have in the fattening pen. We must celebrate with a feast, for this son of mine was dead and has returned to life. He was lost and is found."[4]

The son would have been grateful if his father had just allowed him to go to work as one of his hired servants, but here was his father calling for beautiful clothes—not just to clothe him, but to adorn him. He was in rags and shoeless. No longer would he walk barefoot, looking and acting like a beggar. His father went even a step further in calling for a ring. The ring was a seal of power, a constant memorial of his father's kindness and forgiveness.

How rich this parable is in showing us God's forgiveness! No wonder Jesus used it to teach that God bestows blessings beyond our prayers. We may be fearful, lacking hope, aware of our shortcomings, and knowing that we deserve rejection, but our Father not only receives us but receives us with respect. It is a picture of complete restoration. It provides assurance that God takes us to Himself, into closest fellowship as sons and heirs. He gives us the righteousness of Christ as a robe, the garment of salvation.

There is something else here. The Apostle Paul tells us that the Christian's armor, which we put on spiritually, includes having feet shod with the preparation of the gospel of peace.[5] The father's action in calling for shoes for his son's feet signifies that when God receives us into His favor, He will use us for the convincing and converting of others. Sadly, there are those in the Christian world today who would strip restored prodigals not only of their robes of righteousness but also of their shoes!

David, when pardoned, taught transgressors the ways of God. And Peter, when he finally came to himself, not only strengthened his brothers and sisters in Christ but also went out and converted thousands through the power of the Holy Spirit that came upon him.

It is difficult enough to walk in the Way with shoes that are able to speed us on the way, but how difficult we make it for those whom we should be helping when we refuse forgiveness! We not only take away their shoes but throw broken glass and raw splinters in their way. May God have mercy on us who are more prodigal than *the* prodigal.

The prodigal came home ravenously hungry. His father not only fed him but feasted him. The fatted calf, which had been given special food and was reserved for some very special occasion, was brought out, killed, and prepared. Only the best would do for this child who was once dead to his father but was now alive again, who was once lost but was now found.

The return of prodigals ought to bring great rejoicing to God's people. We should take note of events that affect God in heaven and cause Him and His angels to rejoice. We are to rejoice in God's goodness. Just as the prodigal's father feasted him and welcomed him back into the family so we must not withhold forgiveness or the things that will nourish and strengthen those who may have offended us or in some way departed from what *we* feel is the acceptable way of doing things.

There is another side to this story that cannot remain without comment, and it involves the elder son—a hardworking fellow. When he returned home from the fields where he had labored for long hours, he heard music coming from the house. He asked one of the servants what was going on.

"Your brother is back," he was told, "and your father has killed the calf we were fattening and has prepared a great feast to celebrate his coming home again unharmed."[6]

One would think that this son would have broken into a run, shouting with joy, calling out his brother's name. But no, he was angry and wouldn't even go into the house! He begrudged his father's kindness, forgiveness, and love. He himself showed lovelessness and disgusting pride. He could not think in terms of what this meant to his father, nor how wonderful it was to have his brother back, restored to the family and reconciled to God. He was offended to the highest degree, and he betrayed his selfishness and self-righteousness as he boasted of his own virtue and obedience: "All these years I've worked hard for you and never once refused to do a single thing you told me to; and in all that time you never gave me even one young goat for a feast with my friends. Yet when this son of yours comes back after spending your money on prostitutes, you celebrate by killing the finest calf we have on the place."[7]

The elder brother showed a pharisaical attitude—surely not the spirit of Christ. He depicts souls out of fellowship with God just as much as the prodigal son before he came to himself. There is no real joy in God's service for such people. Their religion is merely a matter of unwilling obedience and loveless faithfulness to their own private interpretation of God's laws without regard to God's mercy. They do not know the meaning of true forgiveness because they hadn't experienced it for themselves. They may have a fairly clean slate, believing they have preserved their reputation, but they are sour ill-humored, harsh, and censorious.

The elder brother's forgiveness couldn't stretch far enough to include his once-fallen but now restored brother. The message of this parable comes through loud and clear: We are to receive those whom God has received; we are to admit them into favor, friendship, and fellowship. The elder brother was arrogant; he called his brother "your son" as he spoke of him to his father. "This son of yours," he said with contempt. He would not own him as his own brother.

The Bible tells us that God does not mark iniquities when they are confessed. The parable shows us up for what we are when *we* paint others with the blackest of colors, begrudging them the Father's kindness and forgiveness.

We should not forget that the Apostle Paul, before his conversion, had been a prodigal. Look at the havoc he was attempting to make of the early church. Then let us examine the other apostles who could rightly be considered his elder brothers. They had been faithfully serving Christ even while Paul, then called Saul, was persecuting them. Did they envy Paul's conversion experience, his visions, and the way God chose to use him? Certainly their attitude was the reverse of the prodigal's elder brother, showing us clearly the need to receive and help restore those who may have fallen away from the Lord, but who realize their mistakes and return to Him.

The father's answer to the elder son stands alone in beauty and truth. "Look, dear son," his father said to him, "you and I are very close, and everything I have is yours. But it is right to celebrate. For he is your brother; and he was dead and has come back to life! He was lost and is found!"[8]

The Scriptures do not tell us whether the elder brother yielded to his father's entreaty. All we can do is hope that he recovered his temper and came to his senses.

But Jesus was delivering a parable to the Pharisees. Did *they* catch all the rich meaning meant for their own good? Jesus was saying to them that He came to seek and save the lost, which included the hated Gentiles. He came to forgive men's sins, and He expected the same exercise of loving, forgiving grace from them. Would they continue to criticize and envy the repentant sinner? I believe that Jesus was saying to all of us, *Forgive as I forgive, and live together as the family of Christ. You are all my sons and my daughters.*

10

From Hater To Lover

You can't sit at a lunch counter in a restaurant or rub shoulders with your fellowman in various areas of life without coming away with the strong feeling that everyone is facing problems of one kind or another. No one is immune from situational difficulties or emotional disturbances. As I listen in on beauty parlor conversations, for instance, I see the need for everyone to possess the good grace that says, "Yes, I forgive you."

One day as I sat writing this book the doorbell rang. It was Larry, the termite inspector (we'd just sold our home). People are always curious about my occupation as a writer, a fact that cannot be denied when they encounter my desk.

When he learned the subject of this book—forgiveness—Larry sat down in a chair and said, "Now that's something I can tell you about. Have *I* ever had to do a lot of forgiving in *my* lifetime!

"Can you imagine spending four days in jail because you spanked your son when he ran out in the street and almost got run over?"

I glanced at the young father sitting opposite me. He was the personification of bright young fatherhood—dark-haired, slender in build, his ruddy features bright and animated. Earlier conversation had revealed his love of reading and the fact that he was very knowledgeable.

"You mean you were actually thrown into jail because you spanked your little boy after he ran out into the road and was almost run down by a passing motorist?" I rephrased the question, wanting to make sure I had heard him correctly.

"That's right," he replied. "My nosy neighbor, who didn't have anything better to do with her time than peer through her curtains looking for ways to devise trouble in the neighborhood, phoned the police after I paddled my son's behind, scolded him, and sent him into the house."

"And you ended up behind bars for four days?" I was incredulous.

"Yep! And lost my job to boot."

"You mean you were fired from your job because—"

"Because of all the newspaper publicity." He took the words out of my mouth.

"What did you say to the judge when you were being interrogated about this?" I questioned.

" 'Your Honor' "—he dramatized it grandly—" 'did your father ever spank you when you were little and did something wrong?' The judge said he'd been spanked plenty. 'Well, then, Your Honor, it shouldn't be too difficult for you to understand the situation I found myself in the other day. You see, my little son wandered out onto the busy street in front of our house when he'd been warned never to do this. I love my little boy and want to see him grow to manhood. I had to teach him a lesson he wouldn't soon forget, nor did I want him to repeat his mistake. Sir, I spanked my son in the proper place. And I spanked him so he'd remember it the next time he was tempted.

" 'Now, Your Honor, if you let me out of this jail, I'm going home to be a good father, same as I was before I got put into this place. And if one of my children does something wrong, something they've been told they must not do, I'm going to paddle them. If that's the wrong way to discipline children, then you'd just better lock me up again. The Good Book tells me to "train up a child in the way he should go, and when he's old he won't depart from it," and it also says, "Spare the rod and spoil the child." I know it tells me not to withhold correction from my children and even says something about using the rod. I used my hand and corrected him. I intend to keep on disciplining my children the way I believe is best. I'm doing it because I love them.' "

The outcome of that true story is that the judge was very impressed. Larry's son had not been harmed in any way, no bruises had been found on his little behind, and Larry was released.

"The judge asked me who was responsible for turning me in," Larry stated. "I had to point to my neighbor. The judge told her to stop meddling in other people's business and to get busy and involved in some worthwhile activity in the community."

"We were talking about forgiveness . . ." I reminded him with a smile.

"Ah, yes," he laughed. "Forgiveness. *Forgiveness in action,* you said. It took a lot of grace," he reminisced. "I was able to do it—I really did forgive her. I felt sorry for her. She got nothing but kindness from me. 'Vengeance is mine, saith the Lord, I will repay.' "

He knew his Bible and wasn't afraid to quote it. "I learned long ago that there's only one way to treat those who mistreat you—love 'em to death. They can't stand it; they can't figure out that kind of treatment. It really bugs them."

But that wasn't all. Larry had had another brush with the law that could have left him bitter. It seems that he had come home from work one evening to find a citation on the table. "My wife and kids were romping in the front yard with the dog. Guess they were really having a good time. This policeman came along and wrote out a citation because she didn't have the dog on a leash. Imagine that! In my own front yard! Ended up costing me 25 dollars.

"I couldn't take time off work to fight it. Would have ended up costing me more—lawyer, time off, et cetera. So we paid the money and I just say I don't like the system, the whole economics of the structure. But what's a man going to do? He shrugged his shoulders.

"Forgive?" I looked at him—a questioning look with raised eyebrows.

He laughed. "That's the answer." He nodded his head affirmatively. "Tell your readers it's *the only answer*. Sometimes you even have to forgive the law."

Yes, and then there are those times when we have to forgive and seek forgiveness from co-workers. Warren was caught in a dilemma at the aircraft plant where he worked in our community. He tells it like this.

"Two other Christians and myself got together at lunchtime for Bible study. We prayed that the Lord would open a door for us to have a growing Christian fellowship at work. One day in the plant newssheet we noticed a little footnote: 'Anyone interested in Bible study, please contact . . . .' So I called the name given. He was an enthusiastic, effervescent Christian. That began our Bible Fellowship, and we had a wonderful time for the first three months.

"Then my two friends and I got transferred to the main building, where the others in that fellowship were already located. I have a Bible school background, and so the fellows asked if I'd help teach. Well, the man who had put the notice in the newssheet was the teacher, and he took offense at that. I was really caught in the middle. But under pressure from the others I did do a lot of the teaching. It was a blessing, and the group grew.

"Eventually Nick dropped out of the fellowship, and I went to see him about it, feeling that according to the Bible this is what I must do. Actually, I have never seen such rancor, even in a nonbeliever. You talk about roots of bitterness—this was the best illustration I have ever seen of what can happen when a person is unforgiving.

"I spoke to him about the need for being reconciled according to Matthew 5:21-25. He called me names, said I was sneaky, subversive, and an egocentric maniac. It was a real blow. It took four years before he was willing to admit that he'd been nurturing this grudge. During all this time he'd been away from the Lord, he admitted. Ephesians 4:32 says to be kind one to another, tenderhearted, forgiving one another even as God for Christ's sake has forgiven you. But it prefaces that by stating, 'Let all bitterness, and wrath, and anger, and clamor, and evil speaking, be put away from you, with all malice.'

"I believe that the root of bitterness springs from

malice. Sometimes I think we are successful at putting away our anger about a given situation, but we overlook the necessity, as the Bible emphasizes, to be sure that any lingering malice is banished. Malice is evil intent, a desire to harm others. Believe me, I learned a lot from that experience.''

In Ephesians 4:20 we discover a clue as to why we, even as Christians, may fail in our relationships with others. The Apostle Paul says, ''You have not so learned Christ.'' The meaning is, ''This is not the way you have learned Christianity—the thing Christ taught and the rules of life prescribed by Him.''

The Amplified Bible says:

> Assuming that you have really heard Him and been taught by Him, as all Truth is in Jesus—embodied and personified in Him: Strip yourselves of your former nature—put off and discard your old renewed self—which characterized your previous manner of life . . . and be constantly renewed in the spirit of your mind—having a fresh mental and spiritual attitude; And put on the new nature [the regenerate self] created in God's image [Godlike] in true righteousness and holiness . . . .[1]

We are to learn Christ! Christ is not a book, a lesson, a way, a trade. He is a Life. In Jesus God expressed Himself. Until we come to Christ, we are ''alienated from the life of God.'' It is in Jesus' life that we see embodied the true standards of living that we should seek to imitate. Paul was writing to those who were once enthralled by pagan vices and vanities, but until we learn Christ and put on the virtues that belong to the new life of Christian holiness, we are no different from them.

There is a new-life concept that comes into focus when we accept Christ. The mind and the will must be brought into subjection while constantly changing for the better. Clothe yourself with this new nature, Paul says.[2] This new nature, this ideal humanity, that we learn from Christ's own life is to then express right conduct toward our fellowmen.

The precepts of the Apostle Paul are not out-of-date. He gives us a comprehensive list of non-Christian vices and Christian virtues, presenting a series of moral contrast. Falsehood is contrasted with truth, anger with forgiveness, theft with doing good, corrupt speech with edifying words, bitterness with love, uncleanness with purity, drunken folly with spiritual fervor.[3]

In this chapter we have been speaking of malice, which must have no place in the Christian's life. Every kind of ill will, malignity, rooted anger, and spite must go. The way to accomplish this is through the supreme Christian motive of love. We find our model and impelling motive in the forgiveness of God, "even as God also in Christ forgave you." This God who forgives like this that was Himself revealed in Christ.

Kindness and forgiveness are the spheres in which the example of God in Christ is to be followed. In Ephesians 5 Paul continues his argument, reasoning that the motive for living and walking in love can be best illustrated in the self-sacrificing pattern of Jesus. The whole course and conduct of our lives should reflect the fact that we are "imitators of God." Phillips translates it like this: "As children copy their fathers, you, as God's children, are to copy him. Live your lives in love—the same sort of love which Christ gives us and which he perfectly expressed when he gave himself up for us in sacrifice to God.''[4]

As parents we hope our children will imitate us in all things that are inherently good. The character we bear as God's children places us under a supreme obligation to resemble Him, especially in His love and goodness, in His mercy and readiness to forgive.

In the practical outworking of our lives, what does this do to and for us? It enables Larry, a termite inspector, to forgive his neighbor who had him thrown in jail for spanking his son and even makes it possible for him to forgive the law for imposing an unreasonable fine on him. It finally brings a man to his senses who had harbored malice for four years, and it makes Warren, the recipient of rooted anger, better able to relate to others and understand for himself the need to be forgiving. I think it can be safely said that the practice of loving forgiveness makes lovers out of haters.

11

Dealing
With Hostility

"When I get to heaven, the first thing I'm going to ask is what Jesus wrote in the dust on the ground!"

She sat on the couch in my living room, shaking her head with vehemence. Somehow her comment, uttered with such hostility, seemed out-of-place coming from this delicate creature. But I knew some of the background which prompted the outburst, and I could understand.

Penny was a victim of people forming judgments about her without any basis in facts. She suffered from a severe neurosis for which she was receiving specialized help. She herself was the first to admit that she had problems and needed help. Her very honesty and openness made her especially vulnerable. But there was a lack of sympathetic understanding of her situation on the part of Christian friends—people who made no attempt to accept her even though they could not understand her various behavior patterns. Penny's sensitivity made her aware that she was the subject of their uncontrolled tongues.

She was fortunate, however, to have a husband who was patient and long-suffering. He loved her and spared no effort to give her the help she needed. That night, sitting on the couch in my living room, after she had made her comment, Bob smiled as if to say, "I've heard this from her before."

Those of us who heard Penny's comment, did understand. We truly loved her and accepted her. We loved her for the past hurts which had caused her such pain, and we loved her now for the Herculean efforts she was making to regain her footing. It wasn't easy. The long-buried hostility would surface now and then and had to dealt with.

You may have said it yourself at one time or another, or surely you have heard it said by someone else—"When I get to heaven, I'm going to ask Jesus . . ." and then follows what often proves to be a revealing statement about an inner hurt.

But I believe that the many questions that plague us will be wiped out by the sheer beauty of His presence and the joys that await us there.

The Bible tells us, "Eye has not seen, nor ear heard, neither have entered into the heart of man, the things which God has prepared for those who love him."[1] We have no idea what a blessed prospect awaits us in heaven! Here on earth we put up with misery, heartache, unpleasantness, defeat, problems, hurts, humiliations, and misunderstandings, but the frustrations and sorrows of this life will vanish when we stand in the presence of God and our eyes drink in His glory and the greatness of His love.

There is a quality missing in the experience of many Christians. "They are so busy enduring their failure that they have no time to enjoy their faith. The one thing the world needs to see today is a quality of joy that cannot be obtained by human logic."[2]

Imagine writing a letter from prison and stating,

"Rejoice in the Lord always, and again I say, Rejoice."[3] Paul did it in the book that has been called the most joyous book in the Bible, his letter to the Philippians. He uses the words "joy" and "rejoice" 17 times in four short chapters!

Paul was no extra-special, privileged saint, but he had a confidence and courage that transcended the dismal experiences that were often his lot. "I know whom I have believed"[4] was his powerful testimony. The joy Paul experienced and wrote about is available for every believer today. God plays no favorites, and Paul was no exception.

Did Paul know something that you and I don't know that enabled him to speak with such confidence and certainty? Paul didn't have any private line to heaven that gave him additional insight that you and I can't possess. But Paul did have a truly adequate concept of God's forgiveness, and this so filled him that his every waking moment was lived in the consciousness of the greatness of God's generosity.

God's love was a power that had invaded Paul's life from the moment God first struck him down on his way to Damascus to persecute the Christians. In Acts 9 we read of Saul uttering threats and intentions of slaughter against the followers of Christ called Christians. God spoke to him even while he carried warrants to arrest every believer in Damascus. He was bent on persecuting and killing the Christians, yet this voice said to him, "Paul, Paul! Why are you persecuting me?"

When Paul asked who was speaking, the voice replied, "I am Jesus, the one you are persecuting."[5] God actually threw Paul, then called Saul, to the ground as he leveled the charge against him that he was persecuting Jesus. Before Saul could become a great saint, to be mightily used by God, he had to be made to see himself as a terrible transgressor rebelling and sinning against Christ.

Paul thought he was persecuting only a company of poor, weak, silly people who were an offense to the Pharisees and the Jewish religion. God set Paul straight and said in effect, *You are persecuting Me, the Lord of glory, the God of heaven and earth.*

A really humbling conviction of sin is necessary if we are to know a conscious reality of God's forgiveness. This is what Paul may have known to a greater degree than some of us, so that it was possible for him to say emphatically, "I know whom I have believed."

The recognition that he was actually persecuting Christ came quickly to him. He lay there convicted and condemned. He who had been a blasphemer of Christ's name now addressed Him as Lord. The experience on the Damascus road blinded him, but three days later he not only received his sight back but was filled with the Holy Spirit.

Paul had three days to reflect with terror about his past and to understand how close he had come to sinning even more against God if he had not been stopped in his tracks. God did not abandon him during those three days, but sent Ananias to care for him and to speak to him about what had happened.

Paul was to become a standard-bearer for Christ; he was destined to suffer great things for the One who bore the cross for him and suffered the agonies that would secure our forgiveness and access to heaven. Paul did have an extraordinary call, and for it he was given extraordinary qualifications. God revealed Himself to him in this dramatic way so that he would go out with great power. Paul was full of Christ, and the Spirit constrained him to preach, proving that Jesus was the Christ, the anointed of God, the one who forgives us and reconciles us to God.

God's love for us is the same as it was for Paul. He doesn't deal with us all in the same way—Paul's experience was unique—but *you* are unique to God also. Paul recognized that God's forgiveness and salvation began at the cross, and that His love stretched to the ultimate when it included him. That same recognition can be the experience of every child of God. Forgiveness is the access we have to the Father's heart. It is the access we have to heaven.

To you—whoever you are—and to myself, I point to the quality of faith Paul exhibited and to his joy, and I suggest that we examine closely the claims this man makes. He had earned the right to speak so boldly.

Paul once catalogued the catastrophes that happened to him. If ever anyone had reason to feel hostile or to question God when he got to heaven, it was Paul.

Paul knew what it meant to be mistreated by those who claimed to be brothers in Christ. But he submerged his hostility by saturating himself with thoughts of the forgiveness and love of Christ. It worked every time. Paul speaks from bitter experience. His word to us is that we too can have strength for all things in Christ, who empowers us—makes us ready for anything and equal to anything (and anyone) through Him who infuses inner strength into us. Paul says we can be self-sufficient in Christ's sufficiency.[6]

12

Understanding and Forgiveness

Jesus was *always* the perfect gentleman. I could weep thankful tears every time I read or hear Hebrews 4:15, which says, "We have not a high priest which cannot be touched with the feeling of our infirmities . . . ."

The Amplified Bible expresses it so tenderly: "We do not have a High Priest who is unable to understand and sympathize and have a fellow feeling with our weaknesses and infirmities and liability to the assaults of temptation, but One who has been tempted in every respect as we are, yet without sinning."

And Phillips says it like this: "For we have no superhuman High Priest to whom our weaknesses are unintelligible—he himself has shared fully in all our experience of temptation, except that he never sinned."

What comfort that gives to those of us who have weaknesses and who know what it is to be assaulted by temptation! We all stand soiled, accused before God, until we have accepted and experienced Christ's forgiveness. We are no worse and no better than the woman dragged before Jesus—this pitiful creature who had been caught in the act of adultery. You may not like being compared to her, since you may not be guilty of that particular sin, but we can never get away from the fact that our Lord said that impure thoughts are sinful as well as impure deeds.

The story can be found in John 8:1-11. Once again we encounter the self-righteous Pharisees. The way they tried to trap Jesus is a pitiful reflection on their character and motives.

They came dragging the woman caught in adultery. Their aim was to place Jesus in a dilemma, and they didn't care what means it took to do it.

We can imagine this woman's shame and embarrassment. She stood wretched and guilty before Jesus, the crowd, and her accusers. Charles L. Allen says that possibly she was standing there unclothed, since women were stoned while naked, and more than likely her garments had already been ripped off. The humiliation must have been very great. Her accusers had made up their minds to stone her to death, since according to the law of Moses this was what she deserved.[1]

Some people among the ranks of Christendom seem to enjoy another person's shame. But this was surely not true of Jesus. In no way would He add to her humiliation and agony. Jesus crouches down but does not look at her, and in that loving act He stands taller than any person in the crowd.

As Jesus bent down, His finger wrote out a message in the dirt. Much speculation has arisen over the content of Jesus' message. Whatever it was, it and the words He uttered—"Let him who is without sin among you be the first to throw a stone at her"[2]—had the desired effect.

Christ did not act contrary to either the ecclesiastical or the civil law of His time. He lifted the whole incident out of the sphere of mere legal technicalities into the realm of moral realities. It was a beautiful gesture. He and He alone is qualified to judge all men by this action and utterance. He silenced, convicted, and condemned His enemies and the woman's. It was as if He said, "Look, you self-appointed executor of divine justice, if you want to take the place of God, then make sure your lives are just as pure."

His penetrating gaze went right through those men. There wasn't one individual among them who was morally qualified to do what the group had set out to do. In another book I make the observation that these men did not dare take away with their hands a life that they had already tried to take away with their tongues.[3]

We have such limited knowledge, such limited understanding of the hearts and lives of other people. None of us can claim the right to point an accusing finger at another person.

There is a tendency in some Christian circles today to play Holy Spirit. We have become so good at pre-judging others. Labels are so easy to affix to another person, but, once they are stuck, they are terribly difficult to remove.

Our human understanding of what prompts someone to do or say something is limited. We simply do not possess all the facts to pass judgment. At this very moment, as I write this, a friend's wife is suing him for divorce. My heart cries out at the pain each partner is enduring. I cannot and I must not take sides. There is no way I or anyone else can fully understand what has brought their marriage to this sad state.

What I can and must do, however, is to extend understanding. I don't have to fully comprehend in order to do that.

Understanding is involved in forgiveness. It is

described by the Apostle Paul in his letter to the Colossians: "Accept life and be most patient and tolerant with one another, always ready to forgive if you have a difference with anyone. Forgive as freely as the Lord has forgiven you. And, above everything else, be truly loving, for love is the golden chain of all the virtues."[4]

This explains why Jesus did not condemn the woman caught in adultery. If she was standing there trembling and naked, as some commentators believe, then I would imagine that Jesus' first act was to cover her nakedness. He would, no doubt, have turned to the crowd and asked someone to drape something around her. The writer of Psalms expresses it so well when he says, "Blessed is he whose transgression is forgiven, whose sin is covered."[5] The idea is that forgiveness of our sins is something that needs to be continually exercised upon us. David, who wrote that, knew what it was to experience God's forgiveness.

"Forgiveness is the cloak for our naked, sinful souls."[6] He covers us with His love. He covered her with that love. As man, the perfect God-Man, He bore about Him like a beautiful golden chain this virtue of love, as the Apostle Paul described it.

The sin of the scribes and priests was that of self-righteousness and greed. Eugenia Price believes that the woman caught in this act did not run away (she could have after her accusers left) because she was seeking love, and in Jesus she recognized love personified. She waited, because as she stood before Him she saw not only the sin in her own life but the hope for forgiveness. And this is what forgiveness does for an individual—it opens the door of hope. "It has been said that the most redeemable person alive is the one who has sinned seeking love."[7]

Jesus sent this woman on her way uncondemned. He said to her, "I do not condemn you. Go on your way, and from now on sin no more."[8]

His favor to her and to all whom He forgives of sins that are past is a strong argument to do as He commands: "Go and sin no more." The Apostle Paul gives a lengthy treatise on this in Romans 6, and it would pay the reader to examine that passage closely.

Once again we have the lesson: "Judge not, that you be not judged. For with what judgment you judge, you shall be judged; and with what measure you mete, it shall be measured to you."[9]

Jesus did not mean that we should not condemn that which we know to be wrong, but if we are to communicate spiritual truth and show forth His love, we cannot engage in the spirit of faultfinding. If we are really interested in helping others overcome the environmental or internal factors that are tempting them and plunging them into sin, we will not drag them and their sinfulness into the gaze of the public eye. Rather, we will endeavor to help them overcome their besetting sin, their problems and defects in character.

It is God's prerogative to try the heart; we do wrong when we try to step into His throne. Jesus is saying that God will not show mercy in His judgment of us if we are showing no mercy to the reputation of others. The Bible says that the merciful shall find mercy. We show great reverence to the Word, as well as love of God and our fellowmen, when we consciously strive to refrain from rash judgment.

Why do you criticize and pass judgment on your brother? Or you, why do you look down upon or despise your brother? For we shall all stand before the judgment seat of God. For it is written, As I live, says the Lord, every knee shall bow to Me, and every tongue shall confess to God—that is, acknowledge Him to His honor and to His praise.

And so each of us shall give an account of himself—give an answer in reference to judgment—to God. Then let us no more criticize and blame and pass judgment on one another, but rather decide and endeavor never to put a stumbling block or an obstacle or a hindrance in the way of a brother.[10]

Paul is reminding us that the court of heaven is the only proper court for trial! Contentions and differences do exist among Christians, but Paul is here stating that Christ is to be the arbitrator at the great day of judgment; meanwhile, we need to keep *ourselves* in good account.

James has something to say on this also:

My brethren, do not speak evil about or accuse one another. He that maligns a brother or judges his brother is maligning and criticizing the Law and judging the Law. But if you judge the Law, you are not a practicer of the Law but a censor and judge of it.

One only is the Lawgiver and Judge—the One who has the absolute power of life and death—who is able to save and to destroy. But you, who are you that you presume to pass judgment on your neighbor?[11]

James, who wrote this, was called James the Just. It is believed that in this passage he was calling the people's attention to the Old Testament law of Moses that said, "Thou shalt not go up and down as a talebearer among thy people."[12]

Our lips must be governed by the law of kindness, as well as truth and justice, always holding out forgiveness and understanding.

13

The Devil Wears a Familiar Face

"I am deeply a part of the problem for which Christ died." That's the observation that Keith Miller made about himself. I greatly appreciate what he has done for the thinking Christian's life in jolting us into the necessity of being honest with ourselves. In his first book, *The Taste of New Wine*, he knocked the props out from under thousands of us by calling for a new kind of honesty that recognizes and faces squarely the nature and extent of our deceitfulness with God, with each other, and with ourselves.

Just whom do we think we are fooling, anyway? Certainly not God, for He sees us as we really are. When Samuel was sent by the Lord to find a king to take Saul's place, he was sent to the home of the sheepherder Jesse. We would be inclined to object, "Lord, what an unlikely place to find a king!" How much we need to learn what God so plainly taught Samuel, the prophet, that day!

As Samuel scanned Jesse's sons, he looked at one named Eliab and thought, "Surely the Lord's anointed is before Him." But the Lord said to Samuel, "Do not look at his appearance or at his height, because I have rejected him; for God sees not as man sees, for man looks at the outward appearance, but the Lord looks at the heart."[1]

We need to exercise our spiritual senses if we are to see ourselves as we really are. To do this requires honesty and courage. We must stop deluding ourselves. We must level with God. He wants us to. The Apostle Paul wrote, "Examine yourselves to see whether you are in the faith."[2] Paul is saying, "Take off your spiritual blinders and test yourself before you test others. If there is something counterfeit in you, acknowledge it to God." Paul's counsel is that God will not reject you when you put yourself on trial.

In this matter of judging others and failing to forgive others, as we look at ourselves we may find some long-buried matters that require straightening out.

The first recognition that we have not been practicing the kind of forgiveness the Bible speaks of, and to which this book is directed, may come with stunning impact. Our recollections of past unforgiving actions, attitudes, and words may make us very miserable.

At this point the devil may rear his familiar face with remembrance of misdeeds that others have done against us. He may remind us of the unkind word, the gossip, and the slander that others have said about us. The faces of family members and friends—those closest and dearest to us—may rise up to haunt and even taunt us. We may mentally draw up a long list of grievances and slam shut the door to future dealings with certain people.

The devil wears a familiar face. He may come disguised as a friend—one you considered to be a friend at one time, but no more, not after what he or she did to you and said about you. Unforgiveness! We practice it subtly, whether or not we consciously realize or admit it.

The devil wears a familiar face. He may come disguised as your husband or wife or ex-husband or ex-wife. The hurts and insults you took from him or her are a thing of the past, but now, as you look honestly at yourself, you find a host of unforgiven things.

The devil wears a familiar face. Does he look like an unforgiven son or daughter? An aunt, uncle, father, or mother? How about your neighbor or business acquaintance who cheated you ruthlessly? How about a brother, a sister, or an in-law? Something in you cries out, "Injustice has been done. They've lied about me. They stole from me. They've maligned my good name. They've kept me from getting that tremendous job . . . . " Yes, some of our scars are deep, and just looking at them again causes them to hurt once more.

You may be so disillusioned by what someone has done to you, particularly if he or she claims to be a Christian, that you've even stopped fellowshiping with that person and no longer attend church with any regularity, and possibly not at all. Have you said, "I've forgiven them, but I just don't want anything more to do with them"—or with Christianity or the church or whatever they represent?

That, my friend, is not forgiveness. And it is *you* who stands to be hurt and harmed the most. Unforgiveness is emotionally, physically, spiritually, and mentally destructive. It is keeping you from experiencing God's love and forgiveness, and it may keep you from heaven unless you come to this moment of truth before God and yourself by admitting that you've been harboring unforgiveness in your heart (which God sees) and are willing to make an honest confession.

Yes, the devil wears a familiar face. He may even look like you! And if you continue to give him a foothold in your life, refusing to do battle with him in this matter of forgiving others, then the reality of what I will talk about in the last chapter of this book applies to you. You may have a very respectable, righteous look about you, and you may attend church twice on Sunday and once on Wednesday night, but God knows that you're wearing a mask. He wants to relieve you of that false pretense once-and-for-all. He yearns for you to understand the truths of His Word relating to his need to forgive others and to treat others with justice and love.

There is hope and help. God knew that we would all fall short of His glory, but He did something about it: He sent His Son. You've read about Him in this book. You may even claim to know Him in a personal way. If you do, then you know that Jesus went all the way to the cross.

> Jesus Christ himself . . . suffered the scandalous, public death of a sinner in our stead. He was not ashamed to be crucified for us as an evildoer. It is nothing else but our fellowship with Jesus Christ that leads us to the ignominious dying that comes in confession, in order that we may in truth share in his Cross. The Cross of Jesus Christ destroys all pride.[3]

"Confession? Wait a minute." Are you saying something like that? Don't you like the implications of that word? "Okay, so I've been guilty of not forgiving certain people. If I confess it to Christ, does that get me off the hook? Does that make everything all right? Can I be sure of getting into heaven if I honestly admit to the Lord that I haven't forgiven those who've wronged me?''

David, the man after God's own heart, learned the hard way what it is to live with guilt and unconfessed sin. It was like a rotting of his bones, but let him tell you what happens when guilt like this has been forgiven.

> What happiness for those whose guilt has been forgiven! What joys when sins are covered over! What relief for those who have *confessed their sins and God has cleared their record.*
>
> There was a time when I wouldn't admit what a sinner I was. But my dishonesty made me miserable and filled my days with frustration. All day and all night your hand was heavy on me. My strength evaporated like water on a sunny day until I finally admitted all my sins to you and stopped trying to hide them. I said to myself, ''I will confess them to the Lord.'' And you forgave me! All my guilt is gone.
>
> Now I say that each believer should confess his sins to God when he is aware of them, while there is time to be forgiven. Judgment will not touch him if he does.[4]

Confession before God is therefore necessary. But there is also the possibility that you may need to make restitution and confession to those from whom you have been withholding forgiveness. This is where we back off, where we want to part company, where we want to say, "That's not for me."

"Where right relationships have been ruptured by sin, we sometimes need to show repentance through restitutions. To God we cannot make restitutions, we can only offer our worship. But for sins against men, restitution can and must be made." So writes John Stott in *Confess Your Sins*.[5]

Stott believes that we confess our sins in three ways. There is secret confession, made to God because they are secret sins. These are sins committed against God only. Then there are private confessions, made to individuals against whom we have sinned. Finally, there is public confession, because some sins are committed against a group or congregation and must be confessed publicly.

In the final analysis all sins are actually committed against God, and we are answerable for them before Him. But when our misdeeds and unforgiving attitudes are against man also, our spiritual development is impaired when confession is not made and forgiveness sought. It is true that to have a right relationship with God we must also have a right relationship with others. To what extent this means actively seeking out the offended ones and making confession is a matter that must be left with the reader.

The Book of James says, "Confess your sins to one another, and pray for one another."[6] The Amplified Bible enlarges on that idea: "Confess to one another therefore your faults—your slips, your false steps, your offenses, your sins; and pray (also) for one another, that you may be healed and restored—to a spiritual tone of mind and heart."

Dietrich Bonhoeffer says:

> Confession in the presence of a brother is the
> profoundest kind of humiliation. It hurts, it cuts
> a man down, it is a dreadful blow to pride. To
> stand before a brother as a sinner is an ignominy
> that is almost unbearable. In the confession of
> concrete sins the old man dies a painful,
> shameful death before the eyes of a
> brother . . . .[7]

Are there instances, however, when it is best not to
make open confession to someone else? If it will be
more redemptive and loving to the other person involved, the answer is yes. Do not seek healing for yourself
at the expense of another person's suffering which may
result.

How does this work, for instance, where a husband
or a wife has been unfaithful but the mate does not
know about it. Dr. Harold J. Sala writes:

> Of course, if a mate knows, you must face the
> matter and seek forgiveness, but if he or she does
> not know, and you are quite certain will never
> know, it is an entirely different matter. In some
> cases, I believe that confession to an innocent
> husband or wife who otherwise would never
> know of a mate's failure only brings greater per-
> sonal grief and distress. Why hurt an innocent
> person and destroy the confidence he or she
> feels?[8]

Dr. Sala recommends that after confession has been
made directly to God, confession to a trusted pastor is
in order, but he advises (and there are many trained
counselors, psychologists, and pastors who would agree
with this) that you spare your mate unless you can find
peace of mind no other way.

I believe a word of caution is in order about confessing to one's most intimate friends. Do not impose upon others your burden of guilt if it is not necessary to your own spiritual welfare. Remember, God is bigger than our problems and wants us to cast them upon Him, for He cares for us. God is our source of forgiveness and release from guilt.

David Augsburger believes that confession should only be as public as the commission of the act. Only those directly involved should be told in your confession. Confession should not be so intimate, so revealing, so painful that it will wound or scar the person to whom it is made. Careless, thoughtless confession to a close friend, a lover, or a spouse may bring you release, but it will transfer the painful burden to that person.[9]

Absolute honesty before God is the most crucial confession of all, and it leads to His forgiveness. Keith Miller was absolutely right when he said, "I am deeply a part of the problem for which Christ died."

14

A Man After God's Own Heart

Forgiveness, like love, kindness, and other virtues, is something one does, not just something one talks about. Actually, forgiveness is really the outworking of love, and to be true forgiveness it must spring from the heart. Jesus said, "A good man out of the good treasure of the heart brings forth good things, and an evil man out of the evil treasure brings forth evil things."[1]

The Amplified Bible makes it especially plain: "The good man from his inner good treasure flings forth good things, and the evil man out of his inner evil storehouse flings forth evil things." Preceding verses talk about one's words and speaking. Jesus always made His message to His listeners very easy to understand. He used common examples with which they were familiar. This time, in talking to the Pharisees, He used the illustration of a tree, reminding them that a tree is identified by its fruit. A tree from a select variety produces good fruit; poor varieties don't.[2] Then, in strong, startling words, Jesus said:

> You brood of snakes! How could evil men like
> you speak what is good and right? For a man's
> heart determines his speech. An evil-hearted

man is filled with venom, and his speech reveals
it. And I tell you this, that you must give account
on Judgment Day for every idle word you speak.
Your words now reflect your fate then: either you
will be justified by them or you will be condemned. [3]

The people looked upon the Pharisees as a generation of saints, but Jesus called them a generation of
vipers. Never forget that it was a snake that first
brought enmity between God and our original parents,
Adam and Eve. Jesus' words were heard by His
disciples that day—a warning to them (and us) to know
what kind of people we live among.

The heart is like a tree. Trees have roots. If it is a
good tree, its roots go down deep, and the tree produces good fruit. If there is a root of bitterness in our
lives springing from malice and unforgiving attitudes,
then it is impossible for us to speak and bring forth
words that will show we are men and women after
God's own heart.

The heart may also be likened to a fountain. Words
are the streams that issue from the fountain. Solomon,
considered by many to be the wisest man who ever lived, said:

> Like a muddied fountain and a polluted spring
> is a righteous man who yields, falls down and
> compromises his integrity before the
> wicked . . . The words of a whisperer or
> slanderer are as dainty morsels or words of sport
> (to some, but to others are as deadly wounds),
> and they go down into the innermost parts of the
> body (or of the victim's nature). Burning lips (ut-
> tering insincere words of love) and a wicked heart

are like an earthen vessel covered with the scum thrown off from molten silver (making it appear to be solid silver). He who hates, pretends with his lips, but stores up deceit within him.[4]

Elsewhere Jesus said, "Evil words come from an evil heart, and defile the man who says them. For from the heart come evil thoughts, murder, adultery, fornication, theft, lying, and slander. These are what defile . . . ."[5]

How we need to remember, even as Solomon said in Proverbs, that death and life are in the power of the tongue.[6] The Pharisees, to whom Jesus was speaking, were supposed to be familiar with Solomon's teachings. Jesus was only repeating what they supposedly already knew when he reminded them that by their words they would be justified and acquitted, and by their words they would be condemned and sentenced.[7]

When the heart is right, we do things right; but when the heart is wrong, there are so many things we do wrong. A heart that is right cannot withhold forgiveness.

> Forgiving is cooperating with God in the promotion of good will in His kingdom . . . . Forgiveness is one of the ways we can keep in tune with the Lord in His great redemptive program. Forgiveness is the great liberation God extends to all who commit their ways to Christ. Forgiving others liberates our own hearts from enslaving emotions and attitudes. Forgiving others is one of the good things we do for ourselves.[8]

What is it that makes a person a candidate to be

called a man after God's own heart? We have already seen what God thinks of a heart that is not producing good things. The logical place to look for what it is that God seeks in a man's heart is the man about whom it was said, "He was a man after God's own heart." That man is David, whose life we have already looked at to some degree in previous chapters.

The Apostle Paul, in reciting some of the history of the nation of Israel in the synagogue at Antioch, mentioned David by describing him as the man God chose to replace King Saul, whom God removed. Paul said God chose David, a man after His own heart, *because David would obey Him.* So we see that obedience is a requisite if a person is to know God's favor.

There are 62 chapters in the Bible devoted to David's life. His is the fullest biography in Scripture, and his was a spectacular rise from shepherd boy to the throne of Israel. Those quiet years in the home of his father in Bethlehem stand in vivid contrast to the years spent in the splendor of the palace; yet those years trained fhim for the high destiny to which God called him.

Solitude can teach us much if we are willing to be taught. While tending his flock of sheep, David was learning lessons of patience and courage. Here too on those quiet hills he could sing and play his harp, and many of his Psalms were probably composed while he was there tending sheep. It was not without reason that he was called the sweet singer of Israel.

David's father and Samuel the prophet were astounded that God should choose 16-year-old David rather than his more impressive older brothers. But God's choice only serves to emphasize even more the scriptural principle that God is more concerned with internal attributes than with physical appearance and appeal. From the moment that Samuel anointed David, the Bible tells us he was Spirit-filled.[9]

What would such an experience do to most young people? David remained unaffected by what occurred. His ego was not inflated. Rather, the anointing imparted a new purpose and sense of divine destiny to his young life; then, as in later life, David displayed amazing self-discipline. Often in his Psalms David speaks of "waiting patiently for the Lord." God had set him apart, and so David would not waste his time in impatient wondering or mistrusting God's plan and promise to him.

David knew what it was to meditate and pray. That is why through succeeding generations the Psalms have remained unexcelled for beauty in meditative purposes.

It was David's epic encounter with the giant Goliath that made him a national hero. The details of this famous combat are well-known; what is less generally known is that David's victory was essentially a triumph of *faith*. In what is considered the "roll call of faith" chapter in the Bible, Hebrews 11, David is mentioned. It was because these people, including David, trusted God that they won their battles.

David appeared before his adversary in a plain shepherd's coat. There was no breastplate of metal. In his hand he carried his sling and five smooth stones that he had picked up from the brook.[10] When Goliath saw David approaching, he sneered in contempt at this nice little red-cheeked boy.[11]

David depended upon God for success. David

shouted to Goliath, "You come to me with a sword and a spear, but I come to you in the name of the Lord of the armies of heaven and of Israel—the very God whom you have defied. Today the Lord will conquer you . . . . The whole world will know that there is a God in Israel! And Israel will learn that the Lord does not depend on weapons to fulfill His plans—He works without regard to human means![12] David was absolutely fearless because he was strong in his faith. He sought no honor for himself but devoted all the praise and glory to God. Is it any wonder that God, who sees the end from the beginning, would call David a man after His own heart?

But while David was now the idol of his nation, this episode made King Saul very jealous, and from that moment on David lived in constant danger, which ended only when Saul died. Four attempts on David's life were made by the king. When the tide of the king's displeasure ran against him, David conducted himself with great wisdom, and the Lord was continually with him.[13]

David's life was a kaleidoscope of experiences which touched the deep wells of human emotion at all points. It has been rightly said that no other Bible character experienced so many swift changes of fortune as David. He walked a rugged and lonely road for nine years while Saul pursued him. On two different occasions David could easily have killed Saul, but David demonstrated loyalty to the king. Even more important, he would not do anything that would frustrate God's purpose for himself and the nation he had been chosen to serve.

To live a life worthy of the potential with which God

has endowed us is difficult under any circumstances. For David it was even more difficult than for most people. David knew that God understands the language of the heart, so that often in the Psalms we read of him crying to the Lord with his voice, and we always read, "And the Lord heard me." Over and over again we also read, "And the Lord sustained me."

David's troubles always brought him to his knees. In spite of the circumstances surrounding his life (often most grievous and difficult), he could still say, "Thou has put gladness in my heart."[14] True joy like this is joy that God gives. It is solid and substantial. Jesus, when He knew He would be leaving His disciples, said, "I am leaving you with a gift—peace of mind and heart! And the peace I give isn't fragile like the peace the world gives. So don't be troubled or afraid."[15]

Though David did not live on this side of the cross, he experienced that peace and abiding joy. What was the secret of this secure feeling that David evidenced? It was in staying close to God, committing all his affairs to God, and contentedly leaving the issues with him. David kept himself in the love of God through obedience and seeking forgiveness when he knew he had strayed. This is what the man after God's own heart will always do.

David experienced the rejection of his favorite son, whom he had unwisely indulged and who later usurped his kingdom for a period of time. He knew what it was to be betrayed by his friends. His own nation rejected him and forced him into exile. He understood fatigue, hazards, and uncertainties. Through all of this, however, he practiced forgiveness of his enemies long before it was commanded by Christ.

All of this is not to say that David was a perfect man.

It is meant to show that it is possible to live a life that habitually and consciously practices forgiveness. David did have faults and did experience failure. David's life also vividly demonstrates that godly men and women may fail grievously. David was fully aware that God cannot tolerate sin, that it must be confessed and expiated. Psalm 5 is only one of many Psalms that reveal David's awareness that the Lord abhors and rejects deceitful men: "For You are not a God who has pleasure in wickedness, neither will evil man so much as dwell temporarily with You. Boasters can have no standing in Your sight. You abhor all evildoers. You will destroy those who speak lies."[16]

David's experience in yielding to the passions of the flesh and committing adultery with the beautiful Bathsheba, the wife of Uriah, was a dark stain on David's life. He paid for this sin with great guilt and grief: the child born to Bath-sheba died.

That sin left indelible marks on his home and family. There is no such thing as a simple sin; sin is always complicated. David lost the smile of God for a period of time. It has been said that the dove of peace flew from his heart. Even his throne lost its stability, and his testimony before his people and the surrounding countries was tarnished.

> The bright spot in the sordid affair was that the enormity of his sin was matched by the depth of his repentance. How men react *after* they have been sifted by Satan is a revelation of their true character. For a whole year, and maybe longer, David remained in stubborn unwillingness to confess his sin.[17]

It was the prophet Nathan whom God used to bring David to his senses (see 2 Samuel 12). When the prophet presented a hypothetical case that produced swift anger in David, we see David immediately confessing, "I have sinned against the Lord." David saw his sin in its true light. At that moment Psalm 51 had its birth:

O loving and kind God, have mercy. Have pity upon me and take away the awful stain of my transgressions. Oh, wash me, cleanse me from this guilt. Let me be pure again. For I admit my shameful deed—it haunts me day and night. It is against you and you alone I sinned, and did this terrible thing. You saw it all, and your sentence against me is just. But I was born a sinner, yes, from the moment my mother conceived me. You deserve honesty from the heart; yes, utter sincerity and truthfulness. Oh, give me this wisdom. Sprinkle me with the cleansing blood and I shall be clean again.

Wash me and I shall be whiter than snow. And after you have punished me, give me back my joy again. Don't keep looking at my sins—erase them from your sight. Create in me a new, clean heart, O God, filled with clean thoughts and right desires. Don't toss me aside, banished forever from your presence. Don't take your Holy Spirit from me. Restore to me again the joy of your salvation, and make me willing to obey you. Then I will teach your ways to other sinners, and they—guilty like me—will repent and return to you. Don't sentence me to death. O my God, you alone can rescue me. Then I will sing of your forgiveness, for my lips will be unsealed—oh, how I will praise you! [18]

Nathan assured David of God's forgiveness. "Yes, you have sinned against the Lord, but the Lord has forgiven you, and you won't die for this sin. But you have given great opportunity to the enemies of the Lord to despise and blaspheme him . . . . "[19] We see the results of disobeying God. The Apostle Paul warns of this when he says, "You dishonor God by breaking His laws. No wonder the Scriptures say that the world speaks evil of God because of you."[20] How we need to beware not to give occasion to those outside of Christ to point to us and say, "If that's Christianity, I don't want anything to do with it!" We must not furnish the enemies of God with anything that brings reproach and blasphemy.

The nature of God's forgiveness is that we do not come under condemnation. Contrary to what some people would teach, our sins do not have to mean our everlasting ruin when we confess and forsake them. Great sinners do not need to despair of finding mercy with God if they truly repent. We see this exemplified in the life of David.

David sinned another time in numbering the people in Israel.[21] There are those who say that David's greatest sin was not with Bath-sheba, but the occasion when 70,000 people lost their lives. God was displeased with David's political arithmetic. This was a sin of pride, not passion, and it involved the whole nation of Israel in God's judgment. God had said in a promise to Abraham that his seed would be as innumerable as the dust of the earth; yet here was David making calculations with no orders from God to do it, nor was there any occasion to warrant it. It smacked of distrust of God's promise and was an affront to Him.

David was guilty of proud conceit and proud confidence in numbers and the strength associated with numerical superiority. God does not need formidable numbers to overpower enemies, nor a multitude with force. It is wrong to trust in the arm of flesh when our reliance should be in God only. It took nine months and 20 days for this census to be taken. It involved a great deal of needless trouble and effort on the part of many people, and it was all so unnecessary. It was simply David's vanity that was being satisfied.

The sin of pride robs God of His glory. And when the sin of pride goes unconfessed and forsaken, it can be spiritually ruinous. Once again, however, David saw his mistake. The realization came right on the heels of the difficult assignment being completed. When his conscience was awakened, David felt great pain. The Bible says, "David's heart smote him after he had numbered the people." Notice how quickly his conscience bothered him as he said to the Lord, "What I did was very wrong. Please forgive this foolish wickedness of mine."[22]

Again, God did forgive. This time there was a just and necessary correction to be administered for this sin. Of the seven things that God hates, according to Proverbs 6:17, pride is the first. David referred himself and his people to God's mercy: "It is better to fall into the hands of the Lord, for His mercy is great, than into the hands of men."[23]

For this sin God sent a great pestilence to the land, and 70,000 men who had been in good health were sick and dead in a matter of a few hours. God can so easily bring down the proudest sinner! David was in great anguish and pleaded with God, "I have sinned. I have done wickedly, but these people, what have they done? Let your anger be only against me and my family.''

David is saying that we must be quick to seek God's forgiveness and then to accept whatever He gives as His mercy. Scripture tells us that Jesus was led as a lamb to the slaughter. He, our great Shepherd, was smitten for us, the sheep. I'm sure that David would say it is better to be severe with one's self now than to face God's judgment and condemnation later.

We wish that David's life had not included these episodes—and there were others—that seem to stand as an indictment against the man described as a man after God's own heart. I believe, however, that we would have to say that because he was so human—capable of great emotion, no stranger to tears, who knew what it was to hunger for human love, prone to make mistakes—we can more readily identify with him.

> He swung between extremes, but paradoxically evidenced an abiding stability. The oscillating needle always returned to its pole—God Himself. His ambitions were spiritual, not personal. His greatest concern was, in the main, the glory of God. Throughout his life there was a singular absence of carnal ambition, but a consuming desire to secure the glory of God. The key to David's life and achievements, marred though they were by failure, is found in *his inner attitude to God*. His defections were temporary, accidental rather than characteristic.[24]

If you would be called a man after God's own heart, it would pay you to become familiar with the life of

David. One important key to his nature is the strong element of gratitude that pervaded him. There was thankfulness for what God had accomplished in his life and for a God who forgives. The man after God's own heart must know what it is to receive God's forgiveness, and then he must be willing to hold out that same forgiveness to others.

15

God's Perfection
Calls for
Forgiveness

I did not know my father. He died five months before I was born. But I always knew he must have been a wonderful man. I knew because Mama spoke of him with such love. I especially liked to hear her tell of the time he was hit on the cheek by someone, and then he turned to that person and said, "The Bible says if someone strikes you on the cheek, you are to turn to him the other also." Often Mama would tell the tale when I was angry and would come in from play, all mad, hot, and bothered. It never failed to subdue me. I would reason to myself: *If Daddy could do that, so can I.*

Not only had my father on occasion willingly turned his cheek, but I saw my own mother turn hers. The blows she endured were strong. But she did endure them. Her faith was stronger, and in the end she was richer by far in other, more important ways. She did not strike back. Retaliation was not in her nature. She kept her little family together, supporting them with the loving work of her hands. (She was a professional seamstress). In addition, she kept a rooming house for young people from a nearby Christian academy.

Because she rented out every bedroom that could be spared, my sister and I shared Mother's bedroom. For years my sister slept in my father's bed, and I slept with my mother. I have vivid recollections of seeing Mother nightly on her knees by the side of the bed. She knew what it was to pray for forgiveness for ill will, which would understandably spring up in her heart when she considered her lot in life.

The Old Testament allowed a law of retaliation, "an eye for an eye, a tooth for a tooth, hand for hand, foot for foot, burning for burning, wound for wound, stripe for stripe."[1] If a neighbor killed one of your beasts, you could go out and kill one of his. If your neighbor in some way blemished you, you were entitled to blemish him.[2] They did not need to show pity; it was literally a life for a life.[3]

When Jesus came along, it was more than a little astonishing for those who were steeped in Jewish teaching and law to hear Him call for an entirely different way of life. The law of retaliation was to be abandoned and replaced by the law of love. We are not to take matters into our own hands but to leave everything in the hands of God. Jesus was calling for His followers to bear patiently the insults and injuries done to them by others. Listen to His words:

> The law of Moses says, "If a man gouges out another's eye, he must pay with his own eye. If a tooth gets knocked out, knock out the tooth of the one who did it." But I say: Don't resist violence! If you are slapped on one cheek, turn the other too. If you are ordered to court, and your shirt is taken from you, give your coat too. If the military demand that you carry their gear for a mile, carry it two. Give to those who ask, and don't turn away from those who want to borrow.
>
> There is a saying, "Love your friends and hate

your enemies.'' But I say: Love your *enemies!*
Pray for those who *persecute* you! In that way you
will be acting as true sons of your Father in
heaven. For he gives his sunlight to both the evil
and the good, and sends rain on the just and on
the unjust, too.

If you love only those who love you, what good
is that? Even scoundrels do that much. If you are
friendly only to your friends, how are you different from anyone else? Even the heathen do
that. But you are to be perfect, even as your
Father in heaven is perfect.[4]

Patiently endure. Conform to Christ's example. Do
not insist on your privileges and rights. Cheerfully accept whatever comes your way. We are to be
peacemakers. Kindness is to be the rule and law of our
life. We are to pray for others—pray that God will
forgive them for the wrongs they have committed
against us. Do not expect the reward of Christians if
you rise no higher in your virtue than that of heathens!

Some people cannot understand these words of
Christ urging us to be perfect. In fact, many throw up
their hands in despair and say, "I give up! I can't
possibly attain to that."

What we fail to realize is that God takes into account
our inner motives. God reads the intent of our heart.
My heart. Everyone's heart. We are to press toward
perfection as we consciously aim to put into practice the
teachings of the Bible. We may not always attain our
goals, for we are human, finite, and fallible. Only God
is infinite and infallible.

I don't mean to say I am perfect. I haven't
learned all I should even yet, but I keep working

toward that day when I will finally be all that Christ saved me for and wants me to be.

No, dear brothers, I am still not all I should be, but I am bringing all my energies to bear on this one thing: Forgetting the past and looking forward to what lies ahead, I strain to reach the end of the race and receive the prize for which God is calling us up to heaven because of what Christ Jesus did for us.

I hope all of you who are mature Christians will see eye-to-eye with me on these things . . . . [5]

Here is an "eye-to-eye" approach different from that to which the people of Paul's day were accustomed!

How does one attain to the perfection Jesus demanded? I believe it can be accomplished by looking at God's perfection and the perfect love of Christ, which sought the greatest and highest welfare of everyone by showing forgiveness in action. Christ was calling His followers to unclench their fists and learn the power of love.

It has been proved by the growth and survival of the early church that God blesses those who choose this perfect way of nonviolence and nonresistance as opposed to vicious persecution. How thankful we can be that those early Christians not only heard the Word and listened to the Apostles, but also responded with action.

Peter, who saw Christ insulted and struck by His enemies, remembered Jesus' reaction and faithfully recorded it. He shared it wherever he went preaching Christ and the crucifixion. It happened when Jesus was arraigned before those who had seized Him without cause. One of the officers struck Jesus with the palm of his hand.[6] Later, Peter said, "When he was insulted he offered no insult in return. When he suffered he made no threats of revenge. He simply committed his cause to the one who judges fairly."[7] Jesus did exactly what He advocated that His followers do.

I saw my mother overcome all the obstacles and hardships that came her way. I did not always understand or appreciate our situation in my growing-up years, but now I do understand. Mother was never overwhelmed by the events in our lives. We had plenty of problems, but Mother knew that there were no problems in heaven—only plans that included her and the three children God had entrusted to her. She could trust Him to see us safely through. She would train her children in the way they should go, just as the writer of Proverbs admonished. And she would trust God to supply our needs. Not always were our wants met, but our needs were. Though we lived sparingly, she poured out the riches of God's love and mercy as she read to us from the Bible.

In my mother I saw forgiveness in action. She was not perfect and never claimed to be, but she did seek God's forgiveness for herself and others, and she freely extended it to others also. In this and other ways she strove for perfection, and you and I can too.

16

It's So Good To Forgive

Writing this book was a learning experience. I needed to clarify my own understanding of the need to practice forgiveness. Daily living out the implications of the biblical teachings on forgiveness continues to challenge my best intentions. When I am insulted, not consulted, maligned, and hurt in daily living, the temptation exists to harbor a grudge, to cry on someone's shoulder and find a sympathetic ear. There is hardly a day goes by when, if I am to be honest, I wouldn't have to admit that in one way or another I am put to the test.

Regardless of how right we are, and how wrong someone else is, we are still confronted with the biblical mandate which makes no allowance for nursing a grudge. It takes a lot of strength to live in this way; I've known people who struggle with it constantly, never quite gaining the victory. Failure to forgive can result in toughened hides and hardened hearts.

But a bulldozer attitude is out of character for men and women with tender hearts who seek daily to practice forgiveness in action. You have revealed this to me in your letters, calls and conversations. You've shown me that a lot of us refuse to compromise our stand, are practicing forgiveness and, painful as it may be, will continue to do so. We know what forgiveness can do;

we also know what unforgiveness brings—more bitterness.

Purposeful living demands that we have fixed in our minds whose we are and whom we serve. We're not just earning a living, but are earning a reputation. We're not just contending with people but are doing battle with power—the spirit forces of wickedness. If the enemy of our souls can get us to act and talk like those who are in opposition to the model which God has given us in Christ, then we know nothing of Jesus' love which forgives and forgives and forgives.

If you are seeking to practice forgiveness, you will have more than an ordinary share of testings in your commitment to forgive as He forgives. I have found that I must habitually make it a practice to live with an attitude of forgiveness. The moment I hug my hurts to myself and indulge in a pity party, whether in matters large or small, I weaken a link in the chain of virtues, the fruit of the Holy Spirit, which sets the spiritual Christian apart from the carnal Christian, and especially from those outside of Christ altogether.

For good reason we have been told to be blameless and innocent, children of God, living above reproach in the midst of a crooked and perverse world. Can we do it on our own? We must have help. Jesus never weakened or gave up. He suffered reproach and physical pain beyond our imagining, but He forgave and He prayed for His enemies.

Prayer. Prayer is the key. What a difference it makes to start the day in prayer! Placing yourself in God's hands through prayer as a definite act of the will serves as a reminder as you go about your work that you are committed to something bigger than your own feelings or your own reputation. I like what Amy Carmichael says: If a sudden jar can cause me to speak an impatient, unloving word, then I know nothing of Calvary love. A cup brimful of sweet water cannot spill even one drop of bitter water, however suddenly jolted.[1] And the jolts do come, sometimes from the most unexpected sources!

How good it feels to forgive! I've said it before, but it bears repeating: I have to live with myself and so I want to be fit for myself to know. When I know I am harboring an unforgiven attitude, I feel miserable. I don't like living with myself when I know there is something unforgiven between me and someone else. I cannot bear to hold a grudge; it is a burden that crushes me. Unforgiveness is too heavy for my heart; it cannot stand that kind of strain.

I know of only one way to deal with the problems that arise as a result of interpersonal relationships that require forgiveness. Perhaps your child has disappointed you greatly; your expectations for that son or daughter were so high, but now they have been dashed to pieces. It seems there is nothing left to salvage. Oh, but there is! I know what it is to wait by the phone for the call that never comes, to look in the mailbox for the letter that never arrives, to grieve over that precious child, now a young adult, who seems to be throwing his life away. Such potential, we say; oh, dear God, how it is being wasted!

Then I can only do one thing—look up and trust God to correct the situation, and on my part, to forgive. Forgive as He forgives.

Perhaps someone has offended you beyond measure. How often *that* can happen! *Forgive*. Move on. Be tolerant toward this weakness in others. Help them to become what they could be if they weren't like that. Allow them to see in *your* response something worth emulating. Don't show super-piety, but disregard the offense and remind yourself that *they* have a problem. Then let God handle it. This kind of thing is too big to carry around. We don't have to do it; the Apostle Peter told us to cast all our care upon Him, for He cares for us.[2]

What does that mean in the practical outworking of forgiveness? First of all, it means to compose your mind. Recently I had occasion to practice this. Instead of replying back to the person who had attempted to cut me down, I excused myself and said I'd get back to him later. I went to my desk and asked God to release me from the pain, and to give me His composure. I closed my eyes and acted out the transference of the situation from my person to God. It was like handing over a heavy weight.

Next, it means to clear up the situation (if that is actually required) by a deliberate act of my will. In handing over the weight I asked God for clear direction as to how best to handle the matter. Sometimes this means saying, "Forgive me for upsetting you" (or whatever words are required). God will give you the right words to speak and you will have inner peace about it. Not always will there be a show of acceptance by the other party, but that's not important. If in your heart you are doing this out of a sincere desire to a be right before God and your fellowman, then you are not responsible for the other person's reaction. Your own spirit will be calmed, and your mind will no longer be distracted and hindered from functioning at its best.

God can be counted on to release us from these cares when we give the burden to Him.

Calvary was an infinite event; it was the ground upon which Christ secured our forgiveness. It cost Jesus His life. It was an enormous price to pay. There is no way I can withhold forgiveness to another person when I look at the forgiveness of God in Christ. It didn't feel good for Jesus to hang on that cross, but it feels good for me when I forgive. I feel right, cleansed, made new, recreated into a relationship that will honor Him. Joy is restored, and peace. "We have forgiveness through His blood," is the scarlet thread that runs through the Bible. If I am going to be fully identified with Christ, then it means that I will forever put into practice His forgiveness.

What was it that sent Jesus to the cross? *Love.* In the final analysis, if our forgiveness is not prompted by love, then even at its best it is phony forgiveness. Genuine forgiveness has *love* at its heart. I forgive you because I love you.

What a way to live! And what a way to die! It's the only way. Believe me, *believe Him,* try it. It feels so good to forgive!

Chapter Notes

Chapter 2

1. Matt. 9:3 TLB.
2. Matt. 9:4-6 TLB.
3. Matt. 9:7 TLB.
4. Matt. 9:8 TLB.
5. Luke 23:24.
6. Luke 23:22.
7. Luke 23:21.
8. Luke 23:17-19 TLB.
9. John 16:2.

Chapter 3

1. Eph. 4:31, 32 TLB.
2. Eph. 4:26, 27 TLB.
3. Eph. 3:14.
4. Eph. 3:16b.

Chapter 4

1. "Up from Suicide," editorial, *Christianity Today,* June 9, 1972.
2. Eph 4:1-4b, 15, 16 TLB.
3. Eph. 4:12, 13.
4. Matt. 5:21, 22a TLB.
5. Mark 11:22-24 TLB.
6. 1 Tim. 2:8 TLB.

Chapter 5

1. Luke 7:36-50.
2. Luke 7:36-38.
3. Rom. 5.
4. Rom. 4:5.
5. Luke 7:40.
6. *Eternity*, March 1972.
7. John 16:8.
8. 2 Tim. 3:16-18 TLB.
9. Luke 7:40 b TLB.
10. Luke 7:41-43 TLB.
11. Matt. 18:23-35.
12. Luke 18:10-14 TLB.
13. Luke 7:44-47 TLB.
14. Luke 7:48 TLB.
15. Luke 7:49 TLB.
16. Luke 7:50 TLB.

Chapter 6

1. Isa. 43:25, 26 TLB.
2. Jer. 31:34 NASB.
3. Heb. 10:17 NASB.
4. Matt. 18-21-35.
5. Psa. 130:3, 4a.
6. Lars Granberg, "Divorce and Remarriage," *Baker's Dictionary of Practical Theology*, ed. by Ralph G. Turnbull (Grand Rapids: Baker Book House, 1967).
7. See Helen Kooiman Hosier, *The Other Side of Divorce*.
8. Eph. 4:32.
9. Henry Wildeboer, "The Minister's Workshop: Rebuilding Marital Fidelity," *Christianity Today*, June 18, 1971.
10. David Augsburger, *70 x 7: The Freedom of Forgiveness* (Chicago: Moody Press, 1970).
11. Matt. 6:15.

Chapter 7

1. James 3:1-13 TLB.
2. Col. 1:14 TLB.
3. 1 Pet. 5:8.
4. Psa. 141:3 TLB.
5. Psa 51:15.
6. 1 Pet. 4:8 TLB.
7. Phil. 4:8 TLB.
8. Paul S. Rees, *Don't Sleep Through the Revolution* (Waco, Tex.: Word Books, 1969).
9. David Augsburger, *70 x 7: The Freedom of Forgiveness* (Chicago; Moody Press, 1970).
10. 1 Pet. 4:8 RSV.
11. A.W. Tozer.
12. Matt. 7:1-5 TLB.
13. Prov. 15:4.

Chapter 8

1. Matt. 22:3b.
2. Robert H. Schuller, *Self-Love: The Dynamic Force of Success* (New York: Hawthorn, 1969).
3. Matt. 22:36-40 TLB.
4. Rom. 13:8-10 TLB.
5. Psa. 103:3, 12.
6. Harold J. Sala, *Guidelines for Peace of Mind* (Redondo Beach, Calif.).
7. Matt. 9:2b.
8. Luke 4:18, 19 TLB.
9. Maxwell Maltz, *Psycho-Cybernetics* (Englewood Cliffs, N.J.: Prentice-Hall, 1969).
10. Ibid.
11. Schuller, *Self-love.*

Chapter 9

1. Luke 15:13-16 TLB.
2. Luke 15:18.
3. Psa. 7:16.
4. Luke 15:22-24 TLB.
5. Eph. 6:15.
6. Luke 15:26, 27 TLB.
7. Luke 15:29, 30 TLB.
8. Luke 15:31, 32 TLB.

Chapter 10

1. Eph. 4:21-24 *Amplified Bible*.
2. Eph. 4:24b TLB.
3. Eph. 4:25-32.
4. Eph. 5:1, 2 *Phillips*.

Chapter 11

1. 1 Cor. 2:9.
2. John Hunter, *Knowing God's Secrets* (Grand Rapids, Mich.: Zondervan, 1965).
3. Phil. 4:4.
4. 2 Tim. 1:12.
5. Acts 9:4, 5 TLB.
6. Phil. 4:13 *Amplified Bible*.

Chapter 12

1. Lev. 20:10; Deut. 22:22-24; John 8:5.
2. John 8:7b *Amplified Bible*.
3. Helen Kooiman Hosier, ,*The Other Side of Divorce*.

4. Col. 3:12-14 *Phillips*.
5. Psa. 32:1.
6. Charles L. Allen, *The Touch of the Master's Hand* (Old Tappan, N.J.: Fleming H. Revell, 1966).
7. Eugenia Price, *The Unique World of Women* (Grand Rapids: Zondervan, 1969).
8. John 8:11 *Amplified Bible*.
9. Matt. 7:1, 2.
10. Rom. 14:10-13 *Amplified Bible*.
11. James 4:11, 12 *Amplified Bible*.
12. Lev. 19:16.

Chapter 13

1. 1 Sam. 16:6, 7 NASB.
2. 2 Cor. 13:5.
3. Dietrich Bonhoeffer, *Life Together* (New York: Harper & Row, 1954).
4. Psa. 32:1-6 TLB.
5. John Scott, *Confess Your Sins* (Philadelphia: Westminster, 1973).
6. James 5:16 RSV.
7. Bonhoeffer, *Life Together*.
8. Harold J. Sala, *Guidelines for Peace of Mind* (Redondo Beach, Calif.: Guidelines, 1973).
9. David Augsburger, *70 x 7: The Freedom of Forgiveness* (Chicago: Moody Press, 1970).

Chapter 14

1. Matt. 12:35.
2. Matt. 12:33.
3. Matt. 12:33-37 TLB.
4. Prov. 25:26:22-24 *Amplified Bible*.

5. Matt. 15:18, 19, 20a TLB.
6. Prov. 18:21.
7. Matt. 12:37 *Amplified Bible*.
8. Ralph Bell, "Forgiveness: The Great Liberator," *Alliance Witness*, March 15, 1972.
9. 1 Sam. 16:13.
10. 1 Sam. 17:40-47.
11. 1 Sam. 17:42 TLB.
12. 1 Sam. 17:45-47 TLB.
13. 1 Sam. 18:14 TLB.
14. Psa. 4:7.
15. John 14:27 TLB.
16. Psa. 5:4-6 *Amplified Bible*.
17. J. Oswald Sanders, *Spiritual Manpower* (Chicago: Moody Press, 1965).
18. Psa. 51:1-15 TLB.
19. 2 Sam. 12:13b, 14 TLB.
20. Rom. 2:23, 24 TLB.
21. 2 Sam. 24:1-3.
22. 2 Sam. 24:10 TLB.
23. 2 Sam. 24:14 TLB.
24. Sanders, *Spiritual Manpower*.

Chapter 15

1. Exod. 21:24-25.
2. Lev. 24:17-22.
3. Deut. 19:21.
4. Matt. 5:38-48 TLB.
5. Phil. 3:12-15a TLB.
6. John 18:22.
7. 1 Pet. 2:23 *Phillips*.

Chapter 16

1. Amy Carmichael, *If* (Grand Rapids: Zondervan Publishers, 1973).
2. 1 Pet. 5:7.